Integrated Mathematics

COURSE II

Second Edition

AUTHORS

Edward P. Keenan

Isidore Dressler

REVISERS

Ann Xavier Gantert

Marilyn Occhiogrosso

AMSCO SCHOOL PUBLICATIONS, INC.
315 Hudson Street   New York, N.Y. 10013

Edward P. Keenan

Curriculum Associate, Mathematics
East Williston Union Free School District
East Williston, New York

Isidore Dressler

Former Chairman
Department of Mathematics
Bayside High School, New York City

Ann Xavier Gantert

Department of Mathematics
Nazareth Academy
Rochester, New York

Marilyn Occhiogrosso

Former Assistant Principal
Mathematics
Erasmus Hall High School, New York City

When ordering this book, please specify:
R 514 P *or* INTEGRATED MATHEMATICS: COURSE II, 2ND ED., PAPERBACK
   or
R 514 H *or* INTEGRATED MATHEMATICS: COURSE II, 2ND ED., HARDBOUND

ISBN 0-87720-271-0 (Softbound edition)
ISBN 0-87720-272-9 (Hardbound edition)

Copyright © 1990, 1981 by Amsco School Publications, Inc.

Preface

INTEGRATED MATHEMATICS: COURSE II, *Second Edition*, is a thorough revision of a textbook that has been a leader in presenting high school mathematics in a contemporary, integrated manner. Over the last decade, this integrated approach has undergone further changes and refinements. Amsco's Second Edition reflects these developments.

The Amsco book parallels the integrated approach to the teaching of high school mathematics that is being promoted by the National Council of Teachers of Mathematics (NCTM) in its STANDARDS FOR SCHOOL MATHEMATICS. Moreover, the Amsco book implements many of the suggestions set forth in the NCTM Standards, which are the acknowledged guidelines for achieving a higher level of excellence in the study of mathematics.

In this new edition, which fully satisfies the requirements of the revised New York State Syllabus:

● **Problem solving** has been expanded by (1) adding nonroutine problems for selected topics and to Chapter Reviews, and (2) providing, in the Teacher's Manual, Bonus questions for each chapter.

● **Integration** of Geometry, Logic, Algebra, and other branches of mathematics, for which the First Edition was well known, has been broadened by the inclusion of new topics and the earlier introduction of selected concepts.

● **Algebraic skills** from Course I have been maintained, strengthened, and expanded as a bridge to the requirements of Course III. Note that many of these skills, newly highlighted in the revised Syllabus, already appear in the First Edition of the AMSCO text.

● **Enrichment** has been extended by (1) increasing the number of challenging exercises, (2) introducing a variety of optional topics, and (3) adding to the Teacher's Manual more thought-provoking aspects of topics in the text, and supplementary material that reflects current thinking in mathematics education.

● **Hands-on activities** have been included in the Teacher's Manual to promote understanding through discovery.

The First Edition of the text had been written to provide effective teaching materials for a unified program appropriate for 10th-grade mathematics students, including topics not previously contained in a traditional Geometry course. These topics—Logic, Probability, Mathematical Systems, Transformation Geometry, and Quadratic-Linear Systems—are retained in the Second Edition. In addition, some have been expanded.

While Course I of this series is concerned with an *intuitive* approach to mathematics, the keystone of Course II is *proof*.

In this text, geometry is developed as a postulational system of reasoning, beginning with a review of definitions in Chapter 1. As the need for proof develops, Chapter 2 is devoted to a study of the laws of reasoning and logic proofs. A unique blending occurs in Chapter 3, wherein students are shown how proofs in logic are related to traditional deductive proofs in geometry, both direct and indirect. The integration of logic and geometry is seen throughout the text in the formulation of definitions and in many proofs, most notably those in Locus. Mathematical Systems, introduced in Chapter 14, provides the student with a completely different postulational system of reasoning, one based on arithmetic and algebra rather than on geometry, but leading to proof by the end of the chapter.

An intent of the authors was to make the original book of greatest service to average students. Since its publication, however, the text has been used successfully with students of varying ability levels. To maintain this broad spectrum of use, the basic elements of the original work have been preserved in the Second Edition. Once again:

- Concepts are carefully developed, using appropriate rigor and mathematical symbolism.

- Definitions, postulates, theorems, corollaries, principles, and procedures are stated precisely and explained by specific examples.

- The numerous model problems are solved through detailed step-by-step explanations.

- Varied and carefully graded exercises are provided in abundance.

This new edition is offered so that teachers may effectively continue to help students comprehend, master, and enjoy mathematics from an integrated point of view.

The Authors

a personal note

As the first edition of *Integrated Mathematics: Course II* was being written in 1980, Isidore Dressler became seriously ill. Before the book was completed that year, he died.

For many years, Isidore Dressler influenced teachers and students alike. Hundreds of thousands of students used his numerous books and were helped to learn mathematics by the style and clarity of his exposition and exercises. Portions of his *Geometry* have been used in both editions of *Integrated Mathematics: Course II*. For this, many people will be grateful.

It was a rare privilege for me to work as a coauthor with Isidore Dressler. As an educator and an author, Isidore Dressler cared about two mythical students he called "Average Joe" and "Average Jane." He taught and wrote with them always in mind. His books will live on, helping many more students learn mathematics. A warm, loving human being, he also cared deeply about his family, for whom the memory of a very special man will live on.

Faced with the task of organizing and writing portions of this book alone, I shall always be very grateful for the valuable criticisms and suggestions offered by Sister Ann Xavier Gantert of Nazareth Academy, Rochester, New York.

This book is dedicated to the memory of Isidore Dressler, and to Anna Keenan, whose perseverance, strength, and love influenced her son to pursue a higher education and higher goals than he once had. This author is forever indebted to both of these people.

Edward P. Keenan

Contents

CHAPTER 4   Triangle Congruence and Inequalities

CHAPTER 5   Perpendicular and Parallel Lines, Angle Sums, and More Congruences

CHAPTER 6   Quadrilaterals

CHAPTER 7   Similarity; Special Triangles

CHAPTER 8   Trigonometry of the Right Triangle

CHAPTER 9   Coordinate Geometry

CHAPTER 10   Quadratic Equations

CHAPTER 11   Locus With and Without Coordinate Geometry

CHAPTER 12   Transformation Geometry and Coordinates

CHAPTER 13   Probability

Chapter 1

Introducing Geometry

1-1 THE MEANING OF GEOMETRY

For thousands of years, civilized people have needed to know how to work with the size, shape, and position of things. Ancient Egyptians used geometry to solve many practical problems of landmarks, boundaries, and land areas. Eventually the Greeks became interested in organizing this branch of mathematics. In fact, the word *geometry* is derived from the Greek words *gē*, meaning *earth*, and *metron*, meaning *measure*. Today, we say that **geometry** is the study of the properties and relationships of points, lines, planes, and solids.

Beginning about 600 B.C., the Greeks sought explanations for the geometric facts that they had learned and scholars started to organize geometry into a *logical system*. In the same way, you have learned many facts about geometry in earlier courses. In Course I, you reached conclusions about some geometric facts based upon measurement with rulers and protractors, based upon observations, and based upon some algebraic manipulations. In this course, you will study geometry as a logical system. To do this, you will learn how to prove many known facts about geometry without the use of rulers and protractors. You will also discover many new geometric relationships.

Among the Greeks who contributed to geometry were Thales, Pythagoras, Plato, Aristotle, and Euclid. About 300 B.C., Euclid organized the geometry of his day into a single logical system. This system, known as **Euclidean geometry,** became the basis for the study of geometry for the next 2,000 years. While we will devote a large portion of this course to the study of Euclid's geometry, we will also study other logical systems in mathematics.

The work in this chapter contains a review of some of the geometry you learned in Course I, as well as some new terms in geometry that you have not yet seen. We will begin with a review of some properties of real numbers.

1

1-2 PROPERTIES OF THE REAL NUMBERS

Closure

The addition of real numbers is a binary operation, that is, the sum of two real numbers is a real number. The set of real numbers is closed under the operation addition.

For all real numbers a and b:
$a + b$ is a real number

The multiplication of real numbers is a binary operation, that is, the product of two real numbers is a real number. The set of real numbers is closed under the operation multiplication.

For all real numbers a and b:
ab is a real number

The Commutative Property

When we add two real numbers, we may change the order in which the numbers are added without changing the sum. This property is called the *Commutative Property of Addition.*

For all real numbers a and b:
$a + b = b + a$

When we multiply two real numbers, we may change the order in which the numbers are multiplied without changing the product. This property is called the *Commutative Property of Multiplication.*

For all real numbers a and b:
$ab = ba$

The Associative Property

When three real numbers are added, two are added first and their sum added to the third. The sum does not depend on which two numbers are added first. This property is called the *Associative Property of Addition.*

For all real numbers a, b, and c:
$a + (b + c) = (a + b) + c$

When three real numbers are multiplied, two are multiplied first and their product multiplied by the third. The product does not depend on which two numbers are multiplied first. This property is called the *Associative Property of Multiplication.*

For all real numbers a, b, and c:
$a(b \cdot c) = (a \cdot b)c$

The Identity Elements

When 0 is added to any real number a, the sum is a. The real number 0 is called the *additive identity*.

For every real number a:
$$a + 0 = 0 + a = a$$

When 1 is multiplied by any real number a, the product is a. The real number 1 is called the *multiplicative identity*.

For every real number a:
$$a \cdot 1 = 1 \cdot a = a$$

Inverses

Two real numbers are called *additive inverses* if their sum is the additive identity 0.

For every real number a:
$$a + (-a) = 0$$

Two real numbers are called *multiplicative inverses* if their product is the multiplicative identity 1.

For every real number $a \neq 0$:
$$a \left(\frac{1}{a} \right) = 1$$

The Distributive Property

The *distributive property* combines the operations of multiplication and addition. We say that multiplication distributes over addition.

For all real numbers a, b, and c:
$$a(b + c) = ab + ac$$

MODEL PROBLEM ───────────────────────────────

Name the property illustrated in each equality.

a. $2(5 \cdot 3) = (2 \cdot 5)3$ Associative property of multiplication

b. $\sqrt{5} + 2 = 2 + \sqrt{5}$ Commutative property of addition

c. $\frac{1}{3}(4 + \sqrt{6}) = \frac{1}{3}(4) + \frac{1}{3}(\sqrt{6})$ Distributive property of multiplication over addition

EXERCISES

1. Name the number that is the additive identity for the real numbers.
2. Name the number that is the multiplicative identity for the real numbers.
3. Name the real number that has no multiplicative inverse.

In 4–15: **a.** Give a replacement for the question mark that makes the statement true. **b.** Name the property illustrated in the equation formed when the replacement is made.

4. $8 + 12 = 12 + ?$ 5. $2(9) = ?(2)$ 6. $2(3 \cdot 5) = (? \cdot 3)5$

7. $1a = ?$ 8. $7 + ? = 7$ 9. $\frac{1}{2}(10) = 10(?)$

10. $8 + (?) = 0$ 11. $2 + (4 + x) = (? + 4) + x$

12. $5(4 + y) = 5(y + ?)$ 13. $4(3a) = (4 \cdot ?)a$

14. $5(a + 3) = 5a + ?$ 15. $5(?) = 1$

In 16–21, state whether the sentence is a correct application of the distributive property. If it is not, state the reason.

16. $3(a + 2) = 3a + 6$ 17. $5a + 7 = 5(a + 7)$
18. $2 + (4a) = (2 + 4)(2 + a)$ 19. $(x + 3)y = xy + 3y$
20. $3b(c - d) = 3bc - 3bd$ 21. $3 + 7a = (3 + 7)a$

In 22–26, find the value of x for which the real number represented by the expression has no multiplicative inverse.

22. x 23. $x - 5$ 24. $x + 3$ 25. $x - \sqrt{2}$ 26. $2x - 1$

27. If $a + b = a$, what is the value of ab?

1-3 UNDEFINED TERMS

We ordinarily define a term by using a simpler term or a previously defined term. The simpler term is then defined by using a still simpler term. But this process cannot go on endlessly. There comes a time when the definition must use a term whose meaning is assumed to be clear. Because its meaning is accepted without definition, such a term is called an *undefined term*.

The word *set*, which we used in the study of arithmetic and algebra, is one such undefined term. When a collection of distinct objects is so clearly described that we can always tell whether or not an object belongs to it, we call the collection a *set*. For example, the odd counting numbers less than 10 form a set. The numbers 1, 3, 5, 7, and 9 belong to this set but 6, 13, and −5 do not.

In geometry, we are concerned with such ideas as *point*, *line*, and *plane*.

Since we cannot give a satisfactory definition of these words using simpler defined words, we will consider them as undefined terms.

Although the words *point*, *line*, and *plane* are undefined terms, we still must make clear the properties and characteristics they possess.

A *point* may be represented as a dot on a piece of paper, and is usually named by a capital letter. The dot shown, for example, represents a point, which we call *point P*. A geometric point has no length, width, or thickness; it merely indicates a place or position.

A *line* is a set of points. A set of points may form a curved line or it may form a straight line as shown. We understand what a straight line is by considering the set of points that can be arranged along the edge of a ruler or along a stretched string.

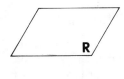

Unless it is otherwise stated, the term *line* will mean   straight line *straight line*.

While a ruler or a stretched string is limited in length, a line is an infinite set of points that extends endlessly in both directions. Arrowheads are sometimes used in a geometric drawing that represents a line to emphasize the fact that there are no endpoints.

To name a line, we usually use two capital letters that name two points on the line. The line shown may be named *line AB*, written as $\overleftrightarrow{AB}$. It may also be named *line AC* or *line BC*, written as $\overleftrightarrow{AC}$ or $\overleftrightarrow{BC}$. The line may also be named by a single lowercase letter; thus, we may call this *line k* or simply *k*.

A *plane* is a set of points that forms a completely flat surface extending indefinitely in all directions. The figure represents a plane, called *plane R*. Remember that this four-sided figure shows only part of the plane because a plane has no boundaries.

A plane may also be named by using letters that name three points in the plane, provided that they are not on the same line. The plane shown is named *plane ABC*.

1-4   DEFINITIONS INVOLVING LINES AND LINE SEGMENTS

A *definition* is a statement of the precise meaning of a term. We must define a word or a term so that it will be understood by all people in exactly the same way.

A good definition must be expressed in words that have already been defined or in words that have been accepted as undefined. It must state the class to which the defined word belongs and it must distinguish the defined word from other members of the class. It must be reversible.

Collinear Points

● **Definition.** A *collinear set of points* is a set of points all of which lie on the same straight line.

This definition has the properties of a good definition. That is:
(1) It is expressed in words that have already been defined or accepted as undefined.
    Set, *point*, and *line* are undefined terms.
(2) It states the class to which the defined term belongs.
    The class is a set of points.
(3) It distinguishes the defined term from other members of the class.
    The points must be on the same straight line.
(4) It is reversible.
    If the points are all on the same straight line, then the set of points is a collinear set.

A, B, and C are collinear points whereas D, E, and F are not collinear points. D, E, and F are called *noncollinear points*.

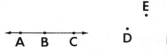

● **Definition.** A *noncollinear set of points* is a set of three or more points that do not all lie on the same straight line.

The Distance Between Two Points

In Course I, you learned that the set of real numbers can be associated with the set of points on a *number line.* To construct a number line, we select two points on the line. The first point corresponds to the number 0 and is called the *origin*; the second point corresponds to the number 1. Using the distance between these two points as the unit distance, we mark off points to the right and left of the origin. These points correspond to integers such as -3 and 2; other points correspond to rational numbers such as $\frac{1}{2}$, or to irrational numbers such as $\sqrt{3}$.

The number associated with a point on a number line is called the *coordinate* of the point. In the figure, the coordinate of A is $\frac{1}{2}$ and

the coordinate of B is 3. The point associated with a number on the line is called the *graph* of the number. In the figure, point C is the graph of $\sqrt{3}$ and point D is the graph of -3. We now assume that:

1. To every real number there corresponds exactly one point on the line.
2. To every point on the line there corresponds exactly one real number.

Thus, we say that there is a *one-to-one correspondence* between the set of points on a line and the set of real numbers. Such a correspondence is called a *coordinate system* on a line.

To find the distance between any two points on a number line, we find the difference between the coordinates assigned to these points. For example, the distance between G and C, written as GC, is 4 units, found by subtracting the coordinates of these points. Hence, $GC = 5 - 1 = 4$. However, the distance CG must equal the distance GC. We make use of **absolute value** in finding distance so that the difference of the coordinates will be independent of the order in which they are subtracted. Thus, we write:

$$GC = |5 - 1| = |4| = 4 \quad and \quad CG = |1 - 5| = |-4| = 4$$

Recall that:

1. The absolute value of a positive number p is p. Thus, $|6| = 6$.
2. The absolute value of a negative number n is $-n$. If $n = -5$, then $-n = -(-5) = 5$. Thus, $|-5| = 5$.
3. The absolute value of 0 is 0. Hence, $|0| = 0$.

We can now state the following definition:

● **Definition.** The **distance between any two points on the real number line** is the absolute value of the difference of the coordinates of the two points.

Hence, on the real number line, the distance between point A, whose coordinate is a, and point B, whose coordinate is b, can be represented by

$$AB = |a - b| \quad or \quad AB = |b - a|$$

Betweenness of Points on a Line

In the study of arithmetic and algebra, you saw that since 3 is less than 4, denoted by $3 < 4$, and 4 is less than 6, denoted by $4 < 6$, we wrote $3 < 4 < 6$, and we said that 4 is **between** 3 and 6. In general, if a, b, and c are real numbers such that $a < b$ and $b < c$, we write $a < b < c$, and we say that b is between a and c.

You can see that the position of point B with respect to points A and C is different from the position of point D with respect to points A and C.

These situations differ for the following reasons:

1. Points A, B, and C are collinear, whereas points A, D, and C are not collinear.
2. The sum of the distance between A and B and the distance between B and C is equal to the distance from A to C, denoted by $AB + BC = AC$. However, the sum of the distance between A and D and the distance between D and C is not equal to the distance between A and C, denoted by $AD + DC \neq AC$.

These considerations guide us in formulating the following definition:

● **Definition.** *B is between A and C* if A, B, and C are distinct collinear points and $AB + BC = AC$.

We can represent a line on which B is between A and C by the symbol $\overleftrightarrow{ABC}$.

It can be shown that if point B is between point A and point C, then b, the coordinate of point B, is between a, the coordinate of point A, and c, the coordinate of point C.

Line Segment

A line segment is a subset, or part of, a line. In the figure, A and B are two points on line m. Points A and B determine *line segment AB*, or *segment AB*, denoted in symbols as $\overline{AB}$.

$$\longleftrightarrow \underset{A \qquad\quad B}{\bullet\!\!-\!\!\!-\!\!\!-\!\!\!-\!\!\bullet} \longrightarrow m$$

● **Definition.** A *line segment,* or *segment,* is a set of points consisting of two points on a line, called endpoints, and all points on the line between the endpoints.

The segment AB is a set of points consisting of the union of points A and B and all points on the line AB between points A and B.

Note. Although a line may be named by any two of its points, a line segment is always named by its two endpoints.

To indicate that C is a point on $\overline{AB}$, but is not one of its endpoints, we write the symbol $\overline{ACB}$.

$$\underset{A \quad\ C \qquad B}{\bullet\!-\!\bullet\!-\!-\!\bullet}$$

Measuring a Line Segment

When we measure a line segment, we determine the distance between its endpoints.

● **Definition.** The *length or measure of a line segment* is the distance between its endpoints.

The length of every segment whose endpoints are distinct points is a unique positive number.

Note that: $\overleftrightarrow{AB}$ represents *line AB*,

$\overline{AB}$ represents *segment AB*,

AB represents *the measure of* $\overline{AB}$.

Congruence of Line Segments

The line segments shown have the same length or measure. We say that $\overline{AB}$ and $\overline{CD}$ are *congruent segments*.

● **Definition.** *Congruent segments* are segments that have the same measure.

To indicate that the segments AB and CD are congruent to each other, we write $\overline{AB} \cong \overline{CD}$, read *segment AB is congruent to segment CD*.

If $\overline{AB} \cong \overline{CD}$, then AB, the length of $\overline{AB}$, and CD, the length of $\overline{CD}$, are the same number. Hence, $\overline{AB} \cong \overline{CD}$ implies that $AB = CD$. We say that the congruence $\overline{AB} \cong \overline{CD}$ is equivalent to the equality $AB = CD$. We may use either notation at any time.

Correct Symbolism

$\overline{AB} \cong \overline{CD}$ The segments are congruent.

$AB = CD$ The measures or distances are the same number.

We would not write $\overline{AB} = \overline{CD}$ because this would indicate that $\overline{AB}$ and $\overline{CD}$ represent the same set of points.

If we were to move $\overline{AB}$ and $\overline{CD}$ by folding the paper on which they appear, we could fit one segment on top of the other. That is, we could make the segments *coincide*. Sometimes, congruent line segments are thought of as line segments that can be made to coincide.

When two or more segments are known to be congruent, or their lengths to be equal, we note this on the diagram by marking each segment with the same number of strokes.

To construct a line segment congruent (equal in length) to a given line segment.

See Chapter 16, Construction 1.

Midpoint of a Line Segment

● **Definition.** The *midpoint of a line segment* is the point of that line segment that divides the segment into two congruent segments.

If M is the midpoint of $\overline{AB}$, then $\overline{AM} \cong \overline{MB}$ or $AM = MB$.

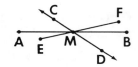

It is also true that $AM = \frac{1}{2} AB$, that $MB = \frac{1}{2} AB$, that $AB = 2AM$, and that $AB = 2MB$.

Bisector of a Line Segment

● **Definition.** The *bisector of a line segment* is any line or subset of a line that intersects the segment at its midpoint.

Segment AB is bisected at point M if M is the midpoint of $\overline{AB}$. This also means that $\overline{AM} \cong \overline{MB}$ or $AM = MB$.

Any line, such as $\overleftrightarrow{CD}$, or any segment, such as $\overline{EF}$, that is distinct from $\overline{AB}$ and that contains point M is a bisector of $\overline{AB}$ or *bisects* $\overline{AB}$ at M.

Note that, unlike a line segment, a line cannot be bisected since it extends indefinitely in two opposite directions and, therefore, does not have a midpoint.

To bisect a given line segment.

See Chapter 16, Construction 2.

Adding and Subtracting Line Segments

● **Definition.** A line segment RS is the *sum of two line segments $\overline{RP}$* and $\overline{PS}$ if point P is between points R and S. Thus, $\overline{RS} = \overline{RP} + \overline{PS}$. Remember that if P is between R and S, then P, R, and S are collinear.

Observe that point P divides $\overline{RS}$ into two segments, $\overline{RP}$ and $\overline{PS}$, such that the following relations are true for the lengths of the segments:

$$RS = RP + PS \qquad RP = RS - PS \qquad PS = RS - RP$$

Half-Line and Ray

● **Definition.** Two points, *A* and *B*, are *on one side of* point *P* if *A*, *B*, and *P* are collinear and *P* is not between *A* and *B*.

Every point on a line divides the line into two opposite sets of points called *half-lines*. A half-line consists of the set of all points on one side of the point of division. The point of division

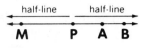

itself does not belong to the half-line. In the figure, point *P* divides $\overleftrightarrow{MB}$ into two half-lines.

● **Definition.** A *ray* is a part of a line that consists of a point on the line, called an endpoint, and all the points on one side of the endpoint.

Thus, a ray is a set of all the points in a half-line, *plus* the dividing point, which is called the endpoint of the ray.

A ray is named by placing an arrow pointing to the right over two capital letters. The first letter must be the letter that names the endpoint of the ray. The second letter may be the name of any other point on the ray. The figure shows ray *AB*, written $\overrightarrow{AB}$, which starts at the endpoint *A*, contains point *B*, and extends indefinitely in one direction.

Thus, a point on a line creates two *opposite rays,* each with the same endpoint. In the figure, $\overrightarrow{AB}$ and $\overrightarrow{AC}$ are opposite rays because points *A*,

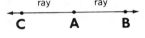

B, and *C* are collinear and points *B* and *C* are not on one side of point *A*, but are on opposite sides of point *A*.

● **Definition.** *Opposite rays* are two rays of the same line with a common endpoint and no other point in common.

Note that the ray whose endpoint is *O* may be named $\overrightarrow{OA}$ or $\overrightarrow{OB}$. However, it may not be named $\overrightarrow{AB}$, since the first capital letter in the name of a ray must represent its endpoint.

MODEL PROBLEMS

1. Find the distance between the points whose coordinates on the real number line are −4 and 3.

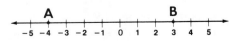

Solution

Let A be the point on the number line whose coordinate is -4.
Let B be the point on the number line whose coordinate is 3.
Let AB represent the distance between A and B.

Then, $AB = |a - b|$
$\quad\quad AB = |(-4) - 3|$
$\quad\quad AB = |-7|$
$\quad\quad AB = 7$

Answer: The distance is 7 units.

2. In the figure, A, B, and C are the vertices of a triangle, and D is a point on $\overline{AC}$.

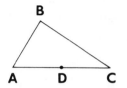

Answers

a. Name three collinear points.
b. Name three noncollinear points.

a. A, D, C
b. A, B, C; A, B, D; or D, B, C

c. Which point is between A and C?
d. If D is the midpoint of $\overline{AC}$, name two congruent segments in the figure.

c. D
d. $\overline{AD} \cong \overline{DC}$

EXERCISES

In 1–11, use the figure shown.

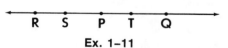

Ex. 1–11

1. Name two points on the same side of P.
2. Name two points on opposite sides of S.
3. Name all the points that are collinear.
4. Name a point between P and Q.
5. Name a point that is between R and T, and also between S and Q.
6. Name the segment determined by point R and point Q.
7. Name two segments that are subsets of the line.
8. Name two rays each of which has point T as an endpoint.
9. Name the opposite ray of $\overrightarrow{TQ}$.
10. Does $\overrightarrow{ST}$ represent the same ray as $\overrightarrow{TS}$? Why?
11. Is $\overrightarrow{ST}$ the opposite ray of $\overrightarrow{TS}$? Why?

12. a. Name all the line segments that appear in the figure.
  b. Use a ruler to measure all the line segments. Name the segments that seem to be congruent.

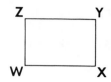

13. State the number of endpoints that there are for **(a)** a line segment **(b)** a ray **(c)** a line.

In 14–25, using the simplest numeral, represent the number without an absolute value symbol.

14. $|7|$ **15.** $|-2|$ **16.** $|0|$

17. $|3 + 7|$ **18.** $|(-2) + (-3)|$ **19.** $|3 + (-9)|$

20. $|0 - (3)|$ **21.** $|(-6) - 0|$ **22.** $|5 - 12|$

23. $|4 - (-2)|$ **24.** $|(-9) - 6|$ **25.** $|(-3) - (-1)|$

In 26–33, use the number line shown to find the distance between the two points.

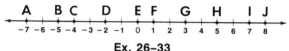

Ex. 26–33

26. E and H **27.** E and B **28.** E and A **29.** G and H

30. F and I **31.** D and C **32.** B and I **33.** J and D

In 31–41, find the distance on a number line between the two points that have the indicated coordinates.

34. 0 and 8 **35.** -7 and 0 **36.** 7 and 2 **37.** 2 and 10

38. 5 and -3 **39.** -8 and 4 **40.** -10 and -5 **41.** 15 and -5

In 42–45, find the required distance if A, B, and C are collinear points and point B is between points A and C.

42. $AB = 5$, $BC = 7$, $AC = ?$ **43.** $BC = 10$, $AB = 7$, $AC = ?$

44. $AB = 3$, $AC = 12$, $BC = ?$ **45.** $AC = 30$, $BC = 12$, $AB = ?$

46. Given that $AB = 8$ and $BC = 12$. Is it always true that $AC = 20$? Why?

47. Given that $AC = 35$ and $BC = 20$. Is it always true that $AB = 15$? Why?

48. If $AB = 12$, $BC = 7$, and $AC = 19$, what must be true of points A, B, and C?

49. If $AB = 6$, $BC = 9$, and $AC = 13$, what must be true of points A, B, and C?

50. Given that A, B, and C are collinear, $AB = 13$, and $BC = 7$. Is AC necessarily 20? Why?

51. Is the midpoint of a line segment always on the line segment?

52. Does a line have a midpoint? Why?

53. If X is the midpoint of $\overline{CD}$ in the diagram, can we say:
a. $\overline{CX} \cong \overline{XD}$? Why? **b.** $CX = XD$? Why?
c. $\overline{CX} = \overline{XD}$? Why?

54. If $\overleftrightarrow{XY}$ is the bisector of $\overline{RS}$, must $\overleftrightarrow{XY}$ contain the midpoint of $\overline{RS}$? Why?

55. If $\overline{XY}$ is the bisector of $\overline{RS}$, must $\overline{RS}$ be the bisector of $\overline{XY}$? Explain your answer with a diagram.

56. If $\overline{AM} \cong \overline{MB}$, does this necessarily mean that M is the midpoint of $\overline{AB}$? Explain your answer with a diagram.

57. Use the markings in the diagram to tell which of the following statements is incorrect.
(1) $\overline{AB} \cong \overline{CD}$ (2) $AB = CD$ (3) $\overline{AC} \cong \overline{BD}$ (4) $\overline{AC} \cong \overline{CD}$

In 58–61, state two conclusions that can be drawn from the given data for each figure, one conclusion using the symbol $\cong$, the other using the symbol $=$.

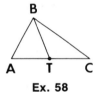
Ex. 58

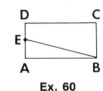
Ex. 59

Ex. 60

Ex. 61

58. T is the midpoint of $\overline{AC}$.   **59.** $\overline{MN}$ bisects $\overline{RQ}$.
60. E is the midpoint of $\overline{AD}$.   **61.** $\overline{XB}$ bisects $\overline{ZY}$.

62. Use the figure in Exercise 58 to complete the following statements:
a. $AT + TC = $ _____   **b.** $AC - AT = $ _____

1-5 DEFINITIONS INVOLVING ANGLES

● **Definition.** An *angle* is a set of points that is the union of two rays having the same endpoint.

$\overrightarrow{AB}$ and $\overrightarrow{AC}$, which form an angle, are called the *sides* of the angle. A, the endpoint of each ray, is called the *vertex* of the angle. The symbol for angle is $\angle$.

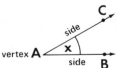

An angle, such as the one illustrated, may be named in any of the following ways:

1. By a capital letter that names its vertex. Example: $\angle A$
2. By a lowercase letter or by a number placed inside the angle. Example: $\angle x$
3. By three capital letters, the middle letter naming the vertex and each of the other letters naming a point on a different ray. Example: $\angle BAC$ or $\angle CAB$

Note. When several angles with the same vertex are in a figure, we avoid confusion by using three letters to name each of the angles. For example, in the figure, the smaller angles are $\angle RPS$ and $\angle SPT$; the large angle is $\angle RPT$.

● **Definition.** A *straight angle* is an angle that is the union of opposite rays.

$\overrightarrow{OA}$ and $\overrightarrow{OB}$ are opposite rays of $\overleftrightarrow{AB}$ because they have a common endpoint O, and no other points in common. Thus, $\angle AOB$ is a straight angle because it is the union of the opposite rays $\overrightarrow{OA}$ and $\overrightarrow{OB}$.

Note that the sides of a straight angle belong to the same straight line and that any point on the line may be considered the vertex of a straight angle.

Interior and Exterior Regions of an Angle That Is Not a Straight Angle

An angle divides the points of a plane that are not on the angle into two sets of points called *regions*. One region is called the *interior of the angle*; the other region is called the *exterior of the angle*. In the figure, if M is any point on one side of the angle and N is any point on the other side of the angle, neither M nor N being the vertex of the angle, then any point P on $\overline{MN}$ between points M and N belongs to the interior region of the angle. The region consisting of all points such as P is called the *interior of the angle*. All other points of the plane, except the points in the angle itself, form the region called the *exterior of the angle*.

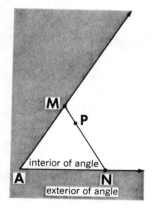

Measuring an Angle

In order to measure an angle, we must select a unit of measure and know how this unit is to be applied. In geometry, the unit used to measure an angle is usually a *degree*. The number of degrees in an angle is called its *degree measure*.

Since we assign to a straight angle the degree measure of 180, a ***degree*** is the measure of an angle that is $\frac{1}{180}$ of a straight angle. The *protractor* is an instrument that is used to measure angles. Study the model protractor shown.

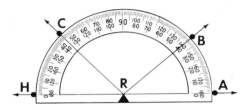

To measure an angle, place the center of the protractor on the vertex of the angle. Select one of the two scales on the protractor. Let the sides of the angle pass through the positive numbers on the same scale. The absolute value of the difference of these numbers tells us the degree measure of the angle.

$$\text{Upper Scale} \qquad \text{Lower Scale}$$
$$\text{m}\angle CRB = |140 - 45| = |40 - 135| = 95$$
$$\text{m}\angle HRC = |45 - 0| \ \ = |135 - 180| = 45$$

It is possible to use units of measure other than the degree to measure angles. However, in this book, the measure of an angle will always be given in degrees. When we write that m$\angle HRC = 45$, we mean that the measure of $\angle HRC$ is 45 degrees.

Classifying Angles According to Their Measures

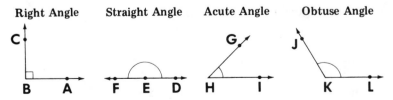

| Right Angle | Straight Angle | Acute Angle | Obtuse Angle |

● **Definition.** A ***right angle*** is an angle whose degree measure is 90.

$\angle ABC$ above is a right angle. Hence, we can say m$\angle ABC = 90$. Note that the symbol ⌐ at B is used to show that $\angle ABC$ is a right angle.

A *straight angle,* previously defined as the union of opposite rays, is an angle whose degree measure is 180.

∠*DEF*, in the figure above, is a straight angle. Hence, m∠*DEF* = 180. Note that $\overrightarrow{ED}$ and $\overrightarrow{EF}$, the sides of ∠*DEF*, are opposite rays and form a straight line.

● **Definition.** An *acute angle* is an angle whose degree measure is greater than 0 and less than 90. (See ∠*GHI.*)

● **Definition.** An *obtuse angle* is an angle whose degree measure is greater than 90 and less than 180. (See ∠*JKL.*)

Note. In this book, we will only use angles whose degree measures are positive numbers less than or equal to 180.

Congruent Angles

● **Definition.** *Congruent angles* are angles that have the same measure.

∠*ABC* and ∠*DEF* have the same measure, written as m∠*ABC* = m∠*DEF*. We may also say that these angles are congruent, symbolized by ∠*ABC* ≅ ∠*DEF*. We may use either notation at any time.

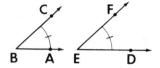

Correct Symbolism

∠*ABC* ≅ ∠*DEF*   The angles are congruent.
m∠*ABC* = m∠*DEF*   The measures of the angles are the same number.

We would not write ∠*ABC* = ∠*DEF* because this would indicate that ∠*ABC* and ∠*DEF* represent the same set of points.

If the representations of the congruent angles *ABC* and *DEF* were drawn on paper, we could move them about by folding the paper on which they appeared to fit one angle on top of the other; that is, we could make the congruent angles coincide.

When two angles are known to be congruent, we may mark each one with the same number of strokes, as shown in the figure, where each angle is marked with a single stroke.

To construct an angle congruent to a given angle.

See Chapter 16, Construction 3.

Bisector of an Angle

● **Definition.** A *bisector of an angle* is a ray whose endpoint is the vertex of the angle, and that divides the angle into two congruent angles.

For example, if $\overrightarrow{OC}$ is the bisector of $\angle AOB$, then $\angle AOC \cong \angle COB$ or $m\angle AOC = m\angle COB$.

Since the line OC contains the ray OC, and since the segment OC is part of the ray OC, then $\overrightarrow{OC}$, $\overleftrightarrow{OC}$, and $\overline{OC}$ all *bisect* $\angle AOB$.

Note. If $\overrightarrow{OC}$ bisects $\angle AOB$, we may say that $m\angle AOC = \frac{1}{2} m\angle AOB$, $m\angle COB = \frac{1}{2} m\angle AOB$, $m\angle AOB = 2m\angle AOC$, and $m\angle AOB = 2m\angle COB$.

To bisect a given angle.

See Chapter 16, Construction 4.

Adding and Subtracting Angles

● **Definition.** A nonstraight angle RST is the *sum of two angles* RSP and PST if point P is in the interior of angle RST. Thus, $\angle RST = \angle RSP + \angle PST$.

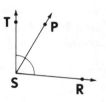

Observe that $\overrightarrow{SP}$ divides $\angle RST$ into two angles, $\angle RSP$ and $\angle PST$, such that the following relations are true for the measures of the angles:

$$m\angle RST = m\angle RSP + m\angle PST$$
$$m\angle RSP = m\angle RST - m\angle PST$$
$$m\angle PST = m\angle RST - m\angle RSP$$

Note that $\angle RST$ may be a straight angle with P any point not on $\angle RST$.

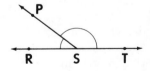

MODEL PROBLEM ───────────────────

In $\triangle ABC$, $\overline{CD}$ bisects $\angle ACB$.

a. Name $\angle 1$ in two other ways.
b. Write a conclusion that states the congruence of two angles.
c. Write a conclusion that states the equality of the measures of two angles.

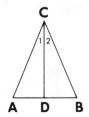

Answers: **a.** $\angle ACD$ and $\angle DCA$.
  b. $\angle ACD \cong \angle BCD$ or $\angle 1 \cong \angle 2$.
  c. $m\angle ACD = m\angle BCD$ or $m\angle 1 = m\angle 2$.

EXERCISES

1. For the figure shown:
   a. Name the vertex of the angle.
   b. Name the sides of the angle.
   c. Name the angle in four ways.

2. **a.** Name the vertex of $\angle BAD$ in the figure.
   b. Name the sides of $\angle BAD$.
   c. Name all the angles with A as vertex.
   d. Name the angle whose sides are $\overrightarrow{AB}$ and $\overrightarrow{AC}$.
   e. Name the ray that is a side of both $\angle BAD$ and $\angle BAC$.
   f. Name two angles in whose interior regions point R lies.
   g. Name the angle in whose exterior region point S lies.
   h. Are $\overrightarrow{AB}$ and $\overrightarrow{AC}$ opposite rays? Why?
   i. Is $\angle BAC$ a straight angle? Why?

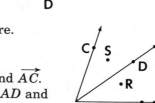

3. For the figure shown:
   a. Name $\angle 1$ in four other ways.
   b. Name $\angle 2$ in two other ways.
   c. Name $\angle 3$ in two other ways.
   d. Name the point of intersection of $\overline{AC}$ and $\overline{BD}$.
   e. Name two straight angles each of which has its vertex at E.
   f. Name two angles whose sum is $\angle ABC$.

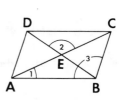

In 4–9, if an angle contains the given number of degrees, state whether the angle is an acute angle, a right angle, an obtuse angle, or a straight angle.

4. 18   **5.** 98   **6.** 110   **7.** 90   **8.** 64   **9.** 180

10. Find the measure of **(a)** $\frac{1}{2}$ of a right angle **(b)** $\frac{2}{3}$ of a right angle **(c)** $\frac{3}{5}$ of a straight angle.

In 11 and 12, use the information about the figure shown to **(a)** write a conclusion that states the congruence of two angles and **(b)** write a conclusion that states the equality of the measures of two angles.

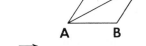

11. $\overline{CD}$ bisects $\angle ACB$.   **12.** $\overrightarrow{AC}$ is the bisector of $\angle DAB$.

13. If a straight angle is bisected, what type of angle is each of the resulting angles?

14. If an obtuse angle is bisected, what type of angle is each of the resulting angles?

15. Complete the following statements, which refer to the figure shown.
 a. m$\angle LMN$ = m$\angle LMP$ + m$\angle$ _____
 b. m$\angle LMP$ = m$\angle LMN$ − m$\angle$ _____
 c. m$\angle PMN$ = m$\angle$ _____ − m$\angle LMP$

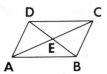

16. Use the figure shown to answer parts **a–d.**
 a. m$\angle ABE$ + m$\angle EBC$ = m$\angle$ _____
 b. m$\angle BEC$ + m$\angle CED$ = m$\angle$ _____
 c. m$\angle ADC$ − m$\angle CDE$ = m$\angle$ _____
 d. m$\angle AEC$ − m$\angle AEB$ = m$\angle$ _____

1-6 DEFINITIONS INVOLVING PAIRS OF ANGLES

● **Definition.** *Adjacent angles* are two angles in the same plane that have a common vertex and a common side but do not have any interior points in common.

As shown below, $\angle ABC$ and $\angle CBD$ are adjacent angles because they have B as their common vertex and $\overrightarrow{BC}$ as their common side, with no interior points in common. However, $\angle XWY$ and $\angle XWZ$ are not adjacent angles because, although they have W as their common vertex and $\overrightarrow{WX}$ as their common side, they do have interior points in common. For example, point P is in the interior of both $\angle XWY$ and $\angle XWZ$.

● **Definition.** *Vertical angles* are two angles in which the sides of one angle are opposite rays to the sides of the second angle.

∠ *a* and ∠ *b* are a pair of vertical angles; ∠ *x* and ∠ *y* are also a pair of vertical angles. Observe that in each pair of vertical angles, the opposite rays, which are the sides of the angles, form the straight lines $\overleftrightarrow{AB}$ and $\overleftrightarrow{CD}$.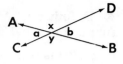

● **Definition.** *Complementary angles* are two angles the sum of whose degree measures is 90.

Each angle is called the *complement* of the other.

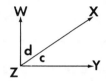 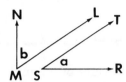

If m∠ *c* = 40 and m∠ *d* = 50, then ∠ *c* and ∠ *d* are complementary angles. If m∠ *a* = 35 and m∠ *b* = 55, then ∠ *a* and ∠ *b* are complementary angles. Complementary angles may be adjacent as in the case of ∠ *c* and ∠ *d*, or they may be nonadjacent as in the case of ∠ *a* and ∠ *b*.

Since m∠ *c* + m∠ *d* = 90, we say that ∠ *c* is the complement of ∠ *d*, and that ∠ *d* is the complement of ∠ *c*. We can represent the degree measure of the complement of an angle whose degree measure is *k* by (90 − *k*) because *k* + (90 − *k*) = 90.

● **Definition.** *Supplementary angles* are two angles the sum of whose degree measures is 180.

Each of the angles is called the *supplement* of the other.

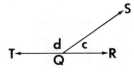 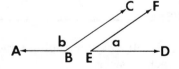

If m∠ *c* = 40 and m∠ *d* = 140, then ∠ *c* and ∠ *d* are supplementary angles. If m∠ *a* = 35 and m∠ *b* = 145, then ∠ *a* and ∠ *b* are supplementary angles. Supplementary angles may be adjacent as in the case of ∠ *c* and ∠ *d*, or they may be nonadjacent as in the case of ∠ *a* and ∠ *b*.

Since m∠ *c* + m∠ *d* = 180, we say that ∠ *c* is the supplement of ∠ *d* and that ∠ *d* is the supplement of ∠ *c*. We can represent the degree measure of the supplement of an angle whose degree measure is k by $(180 - k)$ because $k + (180 - k) = 180$.

● **Definition.** A *linear pair* of angles are two adjacent angles whose sum is a straight angle.

$\angle ABD$ is a straight angle and C is not on $\angle ABD$. Therefore, $\angle ABC + \angle CBD = \angle ABD$. Notice that $\angle ABC$ and $\angle CBD$ are adjacent angles whose common side is $\overrightarrow{BC}$ and whose remaining sides are opposite rays that together form the straight line, $\overleftrightarrow{AD}$. The term *linear* tells us that a *line* is part of the figure.

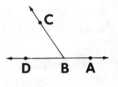

MODEL PROBLEM

Find the measure of an angle if its measure is 20 degrees more than the measure of its complement.

Solution: Let x = the measure of the complement of the angle.
    Then $x + 20$ = the measure of the angle.

The sum of the degree measures of an angle and its complement is 90.

Step 1. $x + x + 20 = 90$

Step 2. $2x + 20 = 90$

Step 3. $2x = 70$

Step 4. $x = 35, x + 20 = 55$

Answer: The measure of the angle is 55 degrees.

EXERCISES

1. In **a–d**, tell whether angles x and y are adjacent angles. Give a reason for each answer.

(a)   (b)   (c)   (d)

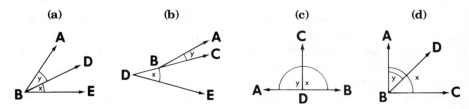

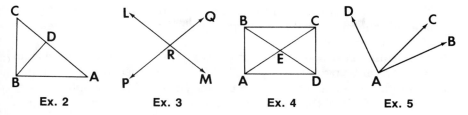

Ex. 2   Ex. 3   Ex. 4   Ex. 5

2. Name two pairs of adjacent angles in the figure shown.

3. In the figure, $\overleftrightarrow{LM}$ and $\overleftrightarrow{PQ}$ intersect at R. **a.** Name four pairs of adjacent angles. **b.** Name two pairs of vertical angles.

4. For the figure: **a.** Name the adjacent angles at B. **b.** Name two pairs of vertical angles. **c.** Name four pairs of supplementary angles.

5. If $\angle BAD$ is a right angle, name two complementary angles.

6. Find the degree measure of the complement of an angle whose degree measure is:
   a. 50   **b.** 27   **c.** 83   **d.** 19.5   **e.** 68
   f. x **g.** $2c$ **h.** $90 - k$ **i.** $x + 10$ **j.** $x - 30$

7. The measure of an angle is equal to the measure of its complement. Find the degree measure of the angle.

8. Two angles are complementary. The measure of the larger angle is five times the measure of the smaller angle. Find the degree measure of the larger angle.

9. Find the measure of an angle whose measure is 60 degrees more than the measure of its complement.

10. Two angles are complementary, and the degree measure of the smaller angle is 50 less than the degree measure of the larger. Find the degree measure of the larger angle.

11. The measures of two angles that are complementary are in the ratio 7:2. Find the degree measure of each angle.

12. The measure of the complement of an angle exceeds the measure of the angle by 24 degrees. Find the degree measure of the angle.

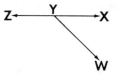

13. In the figure, $\angle XYZ$ is a straight angle. Name two supplementary angles.

14. Find the degree measure of the supplement of an angle whose degree measure is:
   a. 50   **b.** 27   **c.** 83   **d.** 78   **e.** 143.5
   f. x **g.** $2c$ **h.** $180 - n$ **i.** $x + 30$ **j.** $y - 80$

15. The degree measure of an angle and the degree measure of its supplement are equal. Find the degree measure of each angle.

16. Two angles are supplementary. The measure of the smaller angle is one-half the measure of the larger angle. Find the degree measure of the larger angle.

17. The measure of the supplement of an angle is 60 degrees more than twice the measure of the angle. Find the degree measure of the angle.

18. The difference between the degree measures of two supplementary angles is 80. Find the degree measure of the larger of the two angles.

In 19–22: **a.** Write a conclusion that can be drawn from the figure and the information given in the exercise. **b.** Name a linear pair of angles.

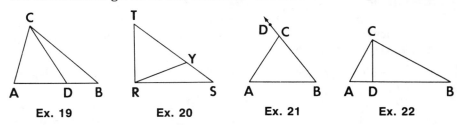

| Ex. 19 | Ex. 20 | Ex. 21 | Ex. 22 |

19. $\angle ADB$ is a straight angle.
20. $\angle SRT$ is a right angle.
21. $\angle BCA$ and $\angle ACD$ are supplementary.
22. $\angle ACD$ and $\angle BCD$ are complementary.

In 23–29, the statement will be true if the blank space is replaced by one of these three words: *always, sometimes,* or *never*. Select the word that will correctly complete the statement.

23. The complement of an angle is _____ an acute angle.
24. The supplement of an angle is _____ an obtuse angle.
25. The supplement of a right angle is _____ a right angle.
26. The complement of an angle is _____ an obtuse angle.
27. The supplement of an angle is _____ congruent to the complement of the angle.
28. If two angles have a common vertex, they are _____ adjacent angles.
29. If two angles are vertical, they are _____ adjacent angles.

In 30–35, write the *numeral* preceding the word or expression that best completes the statement.

30. The supplement of the complement of an acute angle is always
    (1) an acute angle   (2) an obtuse angle
    (3) a straight angle   (4) a right angle
31. Two angles that are both congruent and supplementary must be
    (1) adjacent angles   (2) acute angles
    (3) right angles   (4) complementary

32. If an acute angle varies so that its measure increases, the measure
of its supplement

(1) increases   (2) decreases   (3) remains the same

33. If an acute angle varies so that its measure decreases, the measure
of its complement

(1) increases   (2) decreases   (3) remains the same

34. The difference between the measure of the supplement and the
measure of the complement of an angle is the measure of

(1) an acute angle   (2) a right angle

(3) an obtuse angle   (4) a straight angle

35. If two adjacent angles have their noncommon sides in the same
straight line, they are always

(1) congruent   (2) complementary

(3) supplementary   (4) vertical

1-7 DEFINITIONS INVOLVING PERPENDICULAR LINES

$\overleftrightarrow{AB}$ and $\overleftrightarrow{PR}$ intersect at point S and form four
right angles: $\angle BSP$, $\angle PSA$, $\angle ASR$, and $\angle RSB$.
Therefore, $\overleftrightarrow{PR}$ is perpendicular to $\overleftrightarrow{AB}$, written in
symbols as $\overleftrightarrow{PR} \perp \overleftrightarrow{AB}$.

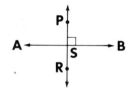

● **Definition.** *Perpendicular lines* are two lines that intersect to form
right angles.

Since rays and line segments are contained in perpendicular lines that
intersect to form right angles, these rays and line segments are also
perpendicular. For example, $\overrightarrow{SP} \perp \overleftrightarrow{AB}$ and $\overline{PR} \perp \overleftrightarrow{AB}$.

Also notice that when two lines are perpendicular, the adjacent angles
formed at the point of intersection must be congruent since all of these
angles are right angles.

● **Definition.** The *perpendicular bisector* of a line segment is a line,
a line segment, or a ray that is perpendicular to the line segment and
bisects the line segment.

If $\overleftrightarrow{EF}$ is the perpendicular bisector of $\overline{CD}$, then
$\overleftrightarrow{EF}$ is perpendicular to $\overline{CD}$, and M is the midpoint
of $\overline{CD}$. In symbols, $\overleftrightarrow{EF} \perp \overline{CD}$ and $\overline{CM} \cong \overline{MD}$.

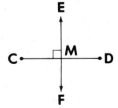

● **Definition.** The *distance from a point to a line* is the length of the perpendicular from the point to the line.

P is a point *not* on $\overleftrightarrow{AB}$, and $\overline{PR} \perp \overleftrightarrow{AB}$. The segment $\overline{PR}$ is called the perpendicular from *P* to $\overleftrightarrow{AB}$. The point *R* at which the perpendicular meets the line is called the *foot* of the perpendicular. The distance from *P* to $\overleftrightarrow{AB}$ is *PR* (the length of $\overline{PR}$).

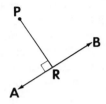

To construct a line perpendicular to a given line through a point on the line.

See Chapter 16, Construction 5.

To construct a line perpendicular to a given line through a point outside the line.

See Chapter 16, Construction 6.

EXERCISES

In 1–4, $\overleftrightarrow{PQ} \perp \overleftrightarrow{SR}$ at *T*, and $\overleftrightarrow{LTM}$ is a straight line.

1. Name four right angles.
2. Name two pairs of complementary angles.
3. Name two pairs of supplementary angles.
4. Tell whether the angle is acute, right, obtuse, or straight.
   a. ∠*PTR*   b. ∠*PTL*   c. ∠*LTQ*
   d. ∠*STR*   e. ∠*STM*   f. ∠*PTM*

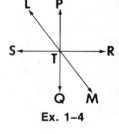

Ex. 1–4

In 5–7, ∠*ABC* is a straight angle and $\overrightarrow{BE} \perp \overrightarrow{BD}$.

5. If m∠*DBC* = 40, find m∠*ABE*.
6. If m∠*DBC* = *y*, represent the number of degrees in m∠*ABE* in terms of *y*.
7. If the measures of ∠*CBD* and ∠*ABE* are in the ratio of 1:2, find the degree measures of both angles.

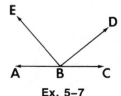

Ex. 5–7

8. In the diagram, $\overline{BD} \perp \overline{AC}$.

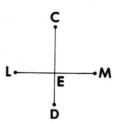

  a. Name two congruent adjacent angles.
  b. State the degree measure of $\angle BDA$.
  c. Name the point that is the foot of the perpendicular from B to $\overline{AC}$.
  d. Name the line segment whose length measures the distance from B to $\overline{AC}$.

9. In the diagram, $\overline{CD}$ is the perpendicular bisector of $\overline{LM}$.

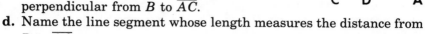

  a. Name two lines that are perpendicular to each other.
  b. Name four angles that are right angles.
  c. Name two line segments that are congruent.
  d. Must $\overline{LM}$ be the perpendicular bisector of $\overline{CD}$? Why?

In 10 and 11, write two conclusions that can be drawn from each piece of given information.

10. $\overline{CD}$ is the perpendicular bisector of $\overline{AB}$.

11. $\overline{DB}$ is the perpendicular bisector of $\overline{AC}$.

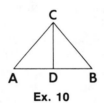

Ex. 10

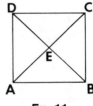

Ex. 11

1-8 DEFINITIONS INVOLVING TRIANGLES AND LINE SEGMENTS ASSOCIATED WITH TRIANGLES

● **Definition.** A *polygon* is a closed figure in a plane that is the union of line segments such that the segments intersect only at their endpoints and no segments sharing a common endpoint are collinear.

A polygon consists of three or more line segments, each of which is a side of the polygon. For example, a triangle has three sides, a quadrilateral has four sides, a pentagon has five sides, etc.

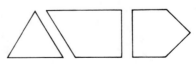

In the definition of a polygon, we will consider the word *closed* as an undefined term. We understand by the word *closed* the idea that if we start at any point on the figure and trace along the sides, we will at some time arrive back at the starting point. Here, you see a figure that is not a closed figure, and is, therefore, not a polygon.

The polygon at the right is named $ABCDE$.

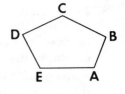

$\overline{AB}$, $\overline{BC}$, $\overline{CD}$, $\overline{DE}$, and $\overline{EA}$ are called the *sides* of the polygon. The endpoints of these line segments—points A, B, C, D, and E—are called the *vertices* (singular, *vertex*) of the polygon. These vertices are also the vertices of the *angles* of the polygon, namely $\angle A$, $\angle B$, $\angle C$, $\angle D$, and $\angle E$.

Examples of *consecutive angles* of this polygon are $\angle A$ and $\angle B$, $\angle B$ and $\angle C$, etc., named by *consecutive vertices* of the polygon.

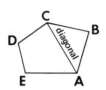

A *diagonal* of a polygon is a line segment that joins two nonconsecutive vertices. For example, $\overline{AC}$ is a diagonal of polygon $ABCDE$.

The *perimeter* of a polygon is the sum of the lengths of the sides. For example, if p represents the perimeter of $ABCDE$, then $p = AB + BC + CD + DE + EA$.

● **Definition.** A *triangle* is a polygon that has exactly three sides.

The polygon shown is triangle ABC, written $\triangle ABC$. In $\triangle ABC$, each of the points A, B, and C is a vertex of the triangle. $\overline{AB}$, $\overline{BC}$, and $\overline{CA}$ are the sides of the triangle. The length of a side of a triangle may be represented by a lowercase form of the letter naming the opposite vertex. For example, in $\triangle ABC$, $BC = a$, $CA = b$, and $AB = c$.

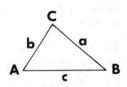

The three sides and the three angles ($\angle A$, $\angle B$, and $\angle C$) are called the six *parts* of the triangle.

Classifying Triangles According to Sides

Scalene Triangle	Isosceles Triangle	Equilateral Triangle
		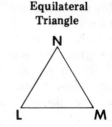

● **Definition.** A *scalene triangle* is a triangle that has no congruent sides.

● **Definition.** An *isosceles triangle* is a triangle that has two congruent sides.

● **Definition.** An *equilateral triangle* is a triangle that has three congruent sides.

Parts of an Isosceles Triangle

In isosceles triangle *RST*, the two congruent sides, $\overline{TR}$ and $\overline{TS}$, are called the *legs* of the triangle. The third side, $\overline{RS}$, is called the *base*.

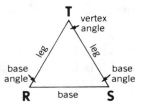

The angle formed by the two congruent sides of the triangle, ∠ *T*, which is the angle opposite the base, is called the *vertex angle* of the isosceles triangle.

The angles whose vertices are the endpoints of the base of the triangle, ∠ *R* and ∠ *S*, which are the angles opposite the congruent sides, are called the *base angles* of the isosceles triangle.

Classifying Triangles According to Angles

Acute Triangle

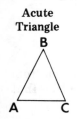

Equiangular Triangle

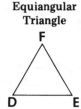

Right Triangle

Obtuse Triangle

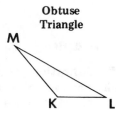

● **Definition.** An *acute triangle* is a triangle that has three acute angles.

● **Definition.** An *equiangular triangle* is a triangle that has three congruent angles.

● **Definition.** A *right triangle* is a triangle that has a right angle.

● **Definition.** An *obtuse triangle* is a triangle that has an obtuse angle.

Parts of a Right Triangle

In right triangle *GHI*, the two sides of the triangle that form the right angle, $\overline{GH}$ and $\overline{HI}$, are called the *legs* of the right triangle. The third side of the triangle, $\overline{GI}$, which is the side opposite the right angle, is called the *hypotenuse*.

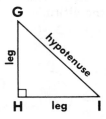

Included Sides and Included Angles in a Triangle

If a line segment is the side of a triangle, the endpoints of that segment are the vertices of two angles. For example, in $\triangle ABC$, the endpoints of $\overline{AB}$ are the vertices of $\angle A$ and $\angle B$. We say that the side, $\overline{AB}$, is *included* between the angles, $\angle A$ and $\angle B$. In $\triangle ABC$:

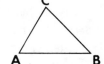

1. $\overline{AB}$ is included between $\angle A$ and $\angle B$.
2. $\overline{BC}$ is included between $\angle B$ and $\angle C$.
3. $\overline{CA}$ is included between $\angle C$ and $\angle A$.

In a similar way, two sides of a triangle are subsets of the rays of an angle, and we say that the angle is included between those sides. In $\triangle ABC$:

1. $\angle A$ is included between $\overline{AC}$ and $\overline{AB}$.
2. $\angle B$ is included between $\overline{BA}$ and $\overline{BC}$.
3. $\angle C$ is included between $\overline{CA}$ and $\overline{CB}$.

The Altitude of a Triangle

● **Definition.** An *altitude of a triangle* is a line segment drawn from any vertex of the triangle, perpendicular to and ending in the line that contains the opposite side.

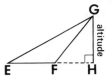

In $\triangle ABC$, the altitude from C to $\overline{AB}$ is $\overline{CD}$.
In $\triangle EFG$, the altitude from G to $\overline{EF}$ is $\overline{GH}$.
In $\triangle RST$, the altitude from R to $\overline{ST}$ is $\overline{RS}$.

In a right triangle, if one leg is the base, then the other leg must be the altitude.
Every triangle has three altitudes.

To construct an altitude of a given triangle.
See Chapter 16, Construction 7.

EXERCISES ────────────────────────────

1. Name the legs and the hypotenuse in each of the right triangles shown.
   a. $\triangle ABC$ **b.** $\triangle JKL$

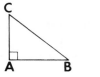

2. Name the legs, the base, the vertex angle, and the base angles in each of the isosceles triangles shown.
   a. $\triangle LMN$ **b.** $\triangle RST$

In 3–6, use rulers and protractors to draw each of the following:

3. An acute triangle that is isosceles.
4. An obtuse triangle that is isosceles.
5. A right triangle that is isosceles.
6. An obtuse triangle that is scalene.

In 7–9, write the *numeral* preceding the word or expression that best completes the sentence.

7. The vertex angle in an isosceles triangle is $\angle ABC$. The base angles of this triangle are
   (1) $\angle A$ and $\angle B$ (2) $\angle A$ and $\angle C$ (3) $\angle B$ and $\angle C$
8. In $\triangle DEF$, $\overline{DE}$ is included between
   (1) $\angle D$ and $\angle E$ (2) $\angle D$ and $\angle F$ (3) $\angle E$ and $\angle F$
9. In $\triangle RST$, $\angle S$ is included between
   (1) $\overline{RT}$ and $\overline{RS}$ (2) $\overline{TR}$ and $\overline{ST}$ (3) $\overline{ST}$ and $\overline{SR}$.

1-9   REVIEW EXERCISES

1. For *each* statement in **a** through **e**, write the *number* of the property of the real number system, *chosen from the list below*, that justifies that statement.

   a. $7 + (3 + 2) = (7 + 3) + 2$
   b. $(-5)(1) = -5$
   c. $3(x + 2) = 3x + 6$
   d. $4 + (-4) = 0$
   e. $7(8) = 8(7)$

   Properties
   (1) Additive inverse property
   (2) Multiplicative identity property
   (3) Commutative property of addition
   (4) Commutative property of multiplication
   (5) Associative property of addition
   (6) Associative property of multiplication
   (7) Distributive property of multiplication over addition

2. Which is *not* an undefined term?
   (1) point   (2) line   (3) segment   (4) plane

In 3–7, use the number line shown.

Ex. 3–7

3. Find the distance between points B and D.

4. Name the midpoint of $\overline{BE}$.

5. Which segment has a length of 5?
   (1) $\overline{AC}$ (2) $\overline{AD}$ (3) $\overline{BD}$ (4) $\overline{BE}$

6. Which segment is congruent to $\overline{AB}$?
   (1) $\overline{AC}$ (2) $\overline{BC}$ (3) $\overline{CE}$ (4) $\overline{DE}$

7. Since A, B, and C are collinear points and B is between A and C, which statement is true?   (1) $\overline{AB} \cong \overline{BC}$ (2) $AB + BC = AC$ (3) $AB = BC$ (4) B is the midpoint of $\overline{AC}$.

8. If R, S, and T are collinear points such that S is between R and T, and if $RS = 12$ and $RT = 15$, find ST.

In 9–14, use polygon $ABCD$, where diagonals $\overline{AC}$ and $\overline{BD}$ intersect at point E.

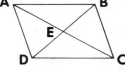

9. Name two straight angles, each having a vertex at E.

10. Name an angle that is adjacent to $\angle ABD$.

Ex. 9–14

11. Complete the statement:
   $m\angle ADE + m\angle EDC = $ _____.

12. Complete the statement: $\angle BEC$ and _____ are a pair of vertical angles.

13. Which two angles form a linear pair?
   (1) $\angle AEB$ and $\angle CED$ (2) $\angle AEB$ and $\angle EAB$
   (3) $\angle AEB$ and $\angle AED$ (4) $\angle AEB$ and $\angle ABE$

14. If $\overline{AC}$ is a bisector of $\overline{DB}$, what conclusion must be true?
   (1) $\overline{AE} \cong \overline{CE}$ (2) $\overline{DE} \cong \overline{BE}$ (3) $\overline{DC} \cong \overline{BC}$ (4) $\angle ACD \cong \angle ACB$

In 15–18, use $\triangle ABC$, where $\overline{AB} \perp \overline{BC}$, and $\overrightarrow{BD}$ bisects $\angle ABC$.

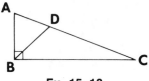

15. Name two congruent angles.

16. Name the altitude drawn to side $\overline{BC}$.

17. Name one pair of supplementary angles.

18. Name one pair of complementary angles.

Ex. 15–18

19. In $\triangle PQR$, which statement must be true?

(1) $\angle P$ is included between $\overline{QR}$ and $\overline{RP}$.

(2) $\overline{QR}$ is included between $\angle Q$ and $\angle P$.

(3) $\angle P$ is included between $\overline{QP}$ and $\overline{RP}$.

(4) $\overline{QP}$ is included between $\angle Q$ and $\angle R$.

20. In isosceles triangle ABC, if $AC = BC$, name the vertex angle.

21. The measures of two supplementary angles are in the ratio $4:5$. Find the degree measures of the angles.

22. The difference between the degree measures of two complementary angles is 20. Find the degree measure of the larger of the two angles.

23. Find $m\angle DBE$ if $\overleftrightarrow{AB} \perp \overleftrightarrow{CD}$ at B and $\overrightarrow{BE}$ bisects $\angle ABC$.

24. For each of the following, determine whether the figure can be traced without removing the pencil from the page or going over a segment twice.

(a) **(b)** **(c)** **(d)** **(e)** **(f)**

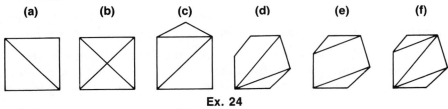

Ex. 24

25. How many triangles are there in the figure?

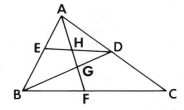

Chapter 2

Logic

2-1 THE NEED FOR LOGIC

Have you noticed that certain statements about lines, angles, and triangles were not listed in the first chapter as definitions? For example:

1. The sum of the degree measures of the angles of a triangle is 180.
2. In a right triangle, the square of the length of the hypotenuse is equal to the sum of the squares of the lengths of the legs ($c^2 = a^2 + b^2$).

These statements are *not* definitions. In Euclid's geometry, these are statements "to be proved." Euclid was able to prove these statements by first combining undefined terms, definitions, and certain statements accepted without proof and then using the *basic laws of reasoning.*

Before you continue your study of Euclidean geometry, you must first learn the basic laws of reasoning. These basic laws of reasoning are used to present a sequence of related statements that lead to a conclusion, whether you are studying Euclidean geometry or any other logical system of thinking.

The study of reasoning is called *logic.* Logic is the branch of mathematics that tells whether an argument is valid or invalid. Logic is the key that opens the door to sound thinking and correct proof.

Let us begin the study of logic by reviewing some concepts learned in Course I.

2-2 SENTENCES, STATEMENTS, AND TRUTH VALUES

A *mathematical sentence* is a sentence that states a fact or contains a complete idea. Some sentences have uncertain *truth values* since they are *true* for some people and *false* for others. Other mathematical

34

sentences, called **open sentences,** contain variables. We usually cannot assign a truth value to an open sentence until we choose replacements for the variable. Examples of such sentences follow.

1. Liver really tastes good.   Sentence with *uncertain* truth value.
2. $3x + 2 = 17$ *Open* sentence; the variable is x.
3. He is my friend.   *Open* sentence; the variable is *he*.

A sentence that can be judged to be either true or false is called a **statement,** or a **closed sentence.** A statement contains no variables. For example:

1. The degree measure of a right angle is 90.   *True* statement
2. $3(3) + 2 = 17$ *False* statement
3. $3(5) + 2 = 17$ *True* statement

2-3 CONNECTIVES IN LOGIC

In logic, we study the truth value of statements, that is, whether the statement is true or false.

In Course I, you learned that a letter can be used to represent a single complete thought, or a simple statement. For example, let p represent "a triangle is a polygon containing exactly three sides."

Connectives, such as *and, or, if . . . then,* and *if and only if,* are words or phrases that allow us to form compound statements that contain two or more thoughts. These new statements will be either true or false.

Negation

The **negation** of a statement is usually formed by placing the word **not** within the original, or given, statement. Notice that there are many ways of placing the word *not* into a statement to form its negation.

To show the negation of a simple statement in symbolic form, we place the symbol ~ before the letter that represents the original or given statement. In the following examples, truth values are listed to the right of the statements. The symbolic form is written first in every example.

1. p: There are seven days in every week.   (True)

   ~p: There are *not* seven days in every week.   (False)

   ~p: It is *not* the case that there are seven days
      in every week.   (False)

2. q: $8 + 9 = 10$ (False)

$\sim q$: $8 + 9 \neq 10$ (True)

● **A statement and its negation have opposite truth values.**

To study sentences in which different truth values can be assigned, we use a device called a truth table. A **truth table** is a compact way of listing symbols to show all possible truth values for a set of sentences. The letters T and F represent *True* and *False*.

p	$\sim p$
T	F
F	T

Truth Table for Negation

Conjunction

In logic, a **conjunction** is a compound sentence formed by using the word **and** to combine two simple sentences. The symbol for *and* is $\wedge$. Thus, when p and q represent simple sentences, the conjunction **p and q** is written symbolically as **$p \wedge q$.** For example:

p: Fred likes math.

q: Dorothy likes science.

$p \wedge q$: Fred likes math *and* Dorothy likes science.

● **The conjunction p and q is true only when both parts are true:** p must be true, and q must be true.

If p is false, or if q is false, or if both are false, then the conjunction p and q must be false.

Notice the order used to list truth values for the first two columns of the truth table. We will use this same order in every truth table of two elements.

p	q	$p \wedge q$
T	T	T
T	F	F
F	T	F
F	F	F

Truth Table for Conjunction

Disjunction

In logic, a **disjunction** is a compound sentence formed by using the word **or** to combine two simple sentences. The symbol for *or* is $\vee$. Thus, when p and q represent simple sentences, the disjunction **p or q** is written symbolically as **$p \vee q$.** For example:

p: The clock is fast.

q: The time is correct.

$p \vee q$: The clock is fast *or* the time is correct.

● **The disjunction *p or q* is true when any part of the compound sentence is true:** *p* is true, or *q* is true, or both *p* and *q* are true.

The disjunction *p or q* is false when both *p* and *q* are false.

In the example used above, "The clock is fast or the time is correct" would be false only when both parts are false.

p	*q*	*p* ∨ *q*
T	*T*	*T*
T	*F*	*T*
F	*T*	*T*
F	*F*	*F*

Truth Table for
Disjunction

The Conditional

In logic, a ***conditional*** is a compound sentence usually formed by using the words ***if . . . then*** to combine two simple sentences. When *p* and *q* represent simple sentences, the conditional ***if p then q*** is written in symbols as ***p → q.***

A conditional is sometimes called an ***implication.*** Thus, we may also read the symbols for the conditional *p → q* as ***p implies q.*** For example:

$$p: \overline{AB} \cong \overline{CD}$$
$$q: AB = CD$$
$$p \to q: \text{If } \overline{AB} \cong \overline{CD}, \text{ then } AB = CD.$$
$$p \to q: \overline{AB} \cong \overline{CD} \text{ implies that } AB = CD.$$

The parts of the conditional ***if p then q*** can be identified by name:

p is called the ***hypothesis*** or the ***antecedent.*** It is an assertion or a sentence that begins an argument. The antecedent usually follows the word *if.*

q is called the ***conclusion*** or the ***consequent.*** It is an ending or a sentence that closes an argument. The consequent usually follows the word *then.*

There are many ways to write the conditional *p → q* in words. Notice that the antecedent *p* follows the word *if* in both of the following examples.

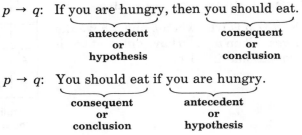

p → q: If you are hungry, then you should eat.

antecedent
or
hypothesis

consequent
or
conclusion

p → q: You should eat if you are hungry.

consequent
or
conclusion

antecedent
or
hypothesis

● The conditional *if p then q*, or *p implies q*, is false when a true hypothesis *p* leads to a false conclusion *q*.

In all other cases, the conditional *if p then q* will be true.

p	q	p → q
T	T	T
T	F	F
F	T	T
F	F	T

Truth Table for the Conditional

The Biconditional

A *biconditional* is a compound sentence formed by combining the two conditionals $p \rightarrow q$ and $q \rightarrow p$ under a conjunction *and*. Thus, the biconditional tells us that *p implies q and q implies p*, written symbolically as $(p \rightarrow q) \wedge (q \rightarrow p)$.

p	q	p → q	q → p	(p → q) ∧ (q → p)
T	T	T	T	T
T	F	F	T	F
F	T	T	F	F
F	F	T	T	T

Although the more common ways of reading $p \rightarrow q$ are *if p then q* and *p implies q*, other ways are also correct; for example, *p only if q* and *q if p*. Thus, the conjunction $(p \rightarrow q) \wedge (q \rightarrow p)$ can be read *p only if q and p if q*.

This is abbreviated in writing the *biconditional*:
in words: *p if and only if q*
in symbols: $p \leftrightarrow q$

● The biconditional *p if and only if q* is true when *p* and *q* are both true or both false.

In other words, $p \leftrightarrow q$ is true when *p* and *q* have the *same truth values*. When *p* and *q* have different truth values, the biconditional is false.

p	q	p ↔ q
T	T	T
T	F	F
F	T	F
F	F	T

Truth Table for the Biconditional

Compound Statements and Truth Values

A compound sentence can contain more than one connective. When the truth value of every simple sentence is certain within the compound being formed, we have a *compound statement*.

PROCEDURE. To find the truth value of a compound sentence:

1. Substitute the given truth values into the compound sentence.
2. Simplify the truth values within parentheses or other groupings, always working from the innermost group first.
3. Simplify negations.
4. Simplify other connectives, working from left to right.

EXAMPLE. Find the truth value of the compound sentence $(p \rightarrow \sim q) \wedge \sim r$ when p, q, and r are all true.

(1) First, substitute the truth values. $\qquad (T \rightarrow \sim T) \wedge \sim T$

(2) Within parentheses, simplify the negation. $\qquad (T \rightarrow \quad F) \wedge \sim T$

(3) Simplify parentheses. $\qquad\qquad\qquad\qquad F \quad \wedge \sim T$

(4) Simplify the negation. $\qquad\qquad\qquad\qquad F \quad \wedge \quad F$

(5) Simplify the conjunction. $\qquad\qquad\qquad\qquad\qquad F$

The compound sentence is false.

MODEL PROBLEMS ────────────────────────

In 1–6: Let s represent "There is school on Labor Day." (False)
$\qquad\qquad$ Let h represent "Labor Day is a holiday." (True)
$\qquad\qquad$ Let w represent "We work on Labor Day." (False)

For each given sentence: **a.** Write the sentence in symbolic form. **b.** Tell whether the statement is true or false, based upon the truth values listed above.

Answers

1. We work on Labor Day or Labor Day is a holiday.
a. $w \vee h$
b. $F \vee T$ = True

2. Labor Day is a holiday and we do not work on Labor Day.
a. $h \wedge \sim w$
b. $T \wedge \sim F = T \wedge T$ = True

3. If there is school on Labor Day, then we work on Labor Day.

   a. $s \to w$
   b. $F \to F$ = True

4. There is no school on Labor Day implies that we work on Labor Day.

   a. $\sim s \to w$
   b. $\sim F \to F = T \to F$ = False

5. We work on Labor Day if and only if there is school on Labor Day.

   a. $w \leftrightarrow s$
   b. $F \leftrightarrow F$ = True

6. If there is no school on Labor Day and Labor Day is a holiday, then we do not work on Labor Day.

   a. $(\sim s \wedge h) \to \sim w$
   b. $(\sim F \wedge T) \to \sim F$
     $= (T \wedge T) \to \sim F$
     $= T \to \sim F$
     $= T \to T$ = True

EXERCISES

In 1–10: **a.** Tell whether the sentence is true, false, or open. **b.** If the sentence is an open sentence, identify the variable.

1. Canada is a country in North America.
2. He went to Canada for a vacation.
3. A triangle is a four-sided polygon.
4. A ray has one endpoint and a segment has two endpoints.
5. A three-sided polygon is called a triangle or a quadrilateral.
6. Perpendicular lines do not meet to form right angles.
7. An angle is right if and only if the angle measures 90 degrees.
8. $x > 1$ and $x < 5$.
9. If $1 + 2 = 3$, then $2 + 3 = 4$.
10. $2^4 = 4^2$ if and only if $1^3 = 3^1$.

11. Use the domain of real numbers to find the truth set or solution set for each open sentence; that is, find the elements of the domain which, when used as replacements for x, make true sentences.

   a. $x + 7 = 16$ **b.** $x - 5 = 19$ **c.** $\dfrac{3x}{5} = 30$

   d. $2x - 3 = 57$ **e.** $x + 3x = 12$ **f.** $2x + 1 = 2$

   g. $.3x = 6$ **h.** $5x + 30 = 0$ **i.** $\dfrac{x}{6} = \dfrac{2}{3}$

   j. $x + \dfrac{1}{3} = 5$ **k.** $x + 7 = 3x$ **l.** $6 + .1x = 5$

12. Use the domain of whole numbers to find the truth set for each compound open sentence. If no replacements make true sentences, write { }.

a. $(x > 6) \wedge (x < 9)$ **b.** $(x > 3) \wedge (x \leq 5)$

c. $(x > 7) \wedge (x < 5)$ **d.** $(x < 3) \wedge (x < 4)$

e. $(x < 3) \vee (x < 4)$ **f.** $(x < 2) \vee (x \leq 5)$

g. $(3x \geq 2x + 3) \wedge (2x - 1 < 7)$ **h.** $(x + x = 10) \vee (3 + x < 5)$

In 13–18, choose the word "true" or the word "false" to replace the blank to make the resulting sentence true.

13. When p is true and q is false, then $p \wedge q$ is _____.

14. When p and q are both true, then $p \vee \sim q$ is _____.

15. When p and q have different truth values, then $p \leftrightarrow q$ is _____.

16. If both p and q are false, then $\sim p \wedge q$ is _____.

17. When the hypothesis p is false, then $p \rightarrow q$ is _____.

18. When the conclusion q is true, then $p \rightarrow q$ is _____.

In 19–24, select the *numeral* preceding the word or expression that best answers the question.

19. Let p represent "x is an even number" and q represent "x is divisible by 4." Which of the following is true when $x = 10$?
(1) $p \wedge q$ (2) $p \vee q$ (3) $\sim p$ (4) q

20. Let p represent "$2x + 5 = 17$" and let q represent "$2x + 3x = 20$." Which is true when $x = 6$?
(1) $p \wedge q$ (2) $p \rightarrow q$ (3) $p \leftrightarrow q$ (4) $p \vee q$

21. If p represents "the polygon has 4 sides" and q represents "all sides of the polygon are congruent," then which is true when the polygon is an isosceles triangle?
(1) $p \wedge q$ (2) $p \vee q$ (3) $p \rightarrow q$ (4) $\sim p \leftrightarrow q$

22. If the conjunction $p \wedge q$ is true, which statement must be false?
(1) $p \vee q$ (2) $p \rightarrow q$ (3) $\sim p$ (4) $p \leftrightarrow q$

23. If the conditional $p \rightarrow q$ is false, which statement must be true?
(1) q (2) $p \wedge q$ (3) $q \rightarrow p$ (4) $p \leftrightarrow q$

24. If the biconditional $p \leftrightarrow q$ is false, which statement must be true?
(1) $p \wedge q$ (2) $p \vee q$ (3) $\sim p \leftrightarrow \sim q$ (4) $\sim p \wedge \sim q$

In 25–34, for each given statement:
a. Write the statement in symbolic form, using the symbols given below.
b. Tell whether the statement is true or false.

Let *M* represent "May has 31 days."   (True)
Let *J* represent "June has 31 days."   (False)
Let *F* represent "June follows May."   (True)

25. May does not have 31 days.
26. May has 31 days and June has 31 days.
27. May or June has 31 days.
28. If June follows May, then May has 31 days.
29. If May has 31 days, then June has 31 days.
30. June follows May if and only if June has 31 days.
31. If June does not follow May, then June does not have 31 days.
32. June has 31 days if June follows May.
33. If May and June have 31 days, then June does not follow May.
34. June does not have 31 days implies that May has 31 days.

In 35–46, use the symbols assigned to represent the four true statements.

Let *m* represent "A segment is bisected at its midpoint."
Let *s* represent "Congruent segments are equal in length."
Let *b* represent "An angle bisector forms two congruent angles."
Let *a* represent "Congruent angles are equal in measure."

For the compound sentences in symbolic form:
a. Write a complete sentence in words to show what the symbols represent.
b. Tell whether the compound sentence is true or false.

35. $m \wedge s$ **36.** $a \wedge s$ **37.** $m \rightarrow s$
38. $\sim m \vee \sim s$ **39.** $s \leftrightarrow a$ **40.** $b \rightarrow \sim a$
41. $\sim a \rightarrow \sim s$ **42.** $(m \wedge b) \rightarrow (s \wedge a)$ **43.** $m \rightarrow \sim s$
44. $\sim b \vee m$ **45.** $\sim m \leftrightarrow \sim s$ **46.** $(b \vee \sim a) \rightarrow \sim s$

In 47–58, let *p* and *q* be *true* statements, and let *r* and *s* be *false* statements. Tell whether the compound sentence is true or false.

47. $p \rightarrow r$ **48.** $(p \wedge q) \wedge r$ **49.** $(q \vee r) \vee s$
50. $(p \vee r) \wedge s$ **51.** $q \leftrightarrow s$ **52.** $(p \wedge q) \rightarrow s$
53. $(q \vee s) \leftrightarrow p$ **54.** $p \wedge \sim r$ **55.** $\sim p \vee r$
56. $q \rightarrow (p \vee r)$ **57.** $(q \rightarrow p) \vee r$ **58.** $(\sim r \vee s) \rightarrow \sim s$

In 59–66, find the truth values for *m* and *k* that would make the statement *false*.

59. $m \vee k$ **60.** $m \rightarrow k$ **61.** $m \rightarrow \sim k$ **62.** $\sim m \rightarrow k$
63. $\sim m \rightarrow \sim k$ **64.** $m \vee \sim k$ **65.** $\sim(m \wedge k)$ **66.** $\sim m \vee \sim k$

2-4 TRUTH TABLES, TAUTOLOGIES, AND LOGICALLY EQUIVALENT STATEMENTS

When the simple sentences used to form a compound sentence can assume different truth values, we must consider cases where the sentences are true and where they are false. A truth table shows all possible truth values.

Tautologies

In logic, a **tautology** is a compound sentence that is *always true*, no matter what truth values are assigned to the simple sentences within the compound sentence. For example, let us study the truth value of $(p \wedge q) \to (p \vee q)$ by building a truth table.

p	q	$p \wedge q$	$p \vee q$	$(p \wedge q) \to (p \vee q)$
T	T	T	T	T
T	F	F	T	T
F	T	F	T	T
F	F	F	F	T

Tautology

Every entry in the last column is true. That is, $(p \wedge q) \to (p \vee q)$ is true for all possible truth values of p and of q. Therefore, we know that $(p \wedge q) \to (p \vee q)$ is a tautology, or a basic truth in logic.

Not every truth table is that of a tautology. For example, suppose we reverse the hypothesis and the conclusion in the conditional statement just made and look at the truth table of $(p \vee q) \to (p \wedge q)$.

p	q	$p \vee q$	$p \wedge q$	$(p \vee q) \to (p \wedge q)$
T	T	T	T	T
T	F	T	F	F
F	T	T	F	F
F	F	F	F	T

Not a Tautology

Notice that $(p \vee q) \to (p \wedge q)$ is *not* a tautology because *not* every element in the last column is true.

Remember that p and q can be any statements at all. Let p represent "Eric is handsome" and let q represent "Heidi is beautiful." The two preceding truth tables show us that:

1. A conjunctive statement will always imply a disjunctive statement since $(p \wedge q) \rightarrow (p \vee q)$ is a tautology. Thus, if "Eric is handsome *and* Heidi is beautiful," it follows that "Eric is handsome *or* Heidi is beautiful." This compound statement is true.

2. A disjunctive statement can*not* imply a conjunctive statement since $(p \vee q) \rightarrow (p \wedge q)$ is *not* a tautology. Thus, if "Eric is handsome *or* Heidi is beautiful," we can*not* conclude that "Eric is handsome *and* Heidi is beautiful."

Logically Equivalent Statements

When two statements always have the same truth values, we say that the statements are *logically equivalent.* To show that an *equivalence* exists between two statements, we use the biconditional *if and only if.* If the statements always have the same truth values, then the biconditional statement will be true in every case, resulting in a tautology.

Let p represent "I study."
Let q represent "I'll pass the test."

The two statements being tested for an equivalence follow:

$p \rightarrow q$: If I study, then I'll pass the test.
$\sim p \vee q$: I don't study or I'll pass the test.

Using the biconditional, we wish to test the truth of the statement:

$$(p \rightarrow q) \leftrightarrow (\sim p \vee q)$$

			Col. 4	Col. 5	Col. 6
p	**q**	**~p**	**~p ∨ q**	**p → q**	**(p → q) ↔ (~p ∨ q)**
T	T	F	T	T	T
T	F	F	F	F	T
F	T	T	T	T	T
F	F	T	T	T	T

Notice that the truth values of $\sim p \vee q$ in column 4 match exactly with the truth values of $p \rightarrow q$ in column 5. Thus $\sim p \vee q$ and $p \rightarrow q$ are logically equivalent statements. In fact, $\sim p \vee q$ is sometimes called the *conditional equivalence* because the statement $\sim p \lor q$ can be used to replace the conditional statement $p \to q$. This equivalence is verified by the tautology written as a biconditional statement in column 6.

MODEL PROBLEM

Let c represent "Simone takes chorus."
Let s represent "Simone takes Spanish."

a. Using c, s, and the proper logic connectives, express each of the following sentences in symbolic form.

If Simone takes chorus, then she cannot take Spanish.
If Simone takes Spanish, then she cannot take chorus.

b. Prove that the two statements are logically equivalent, or give a reason why they are not equivalent.

Solution

a. $c \to \sim s$ and $s \to \sim c$

b. To test for logical equivalence of these two statements, construct a truth table, using the following biconditional:

$$(c \to \sim s) \leftrightarrow (s \to \sim c)$$

				Col. 5	Col. 6	Col. 7
c	**s**	**~c**	**~s**	$c \to \sim s$	$s \to \sim c$	$(c \to \sim s) \leftrightarrow (s \to \sim c)$
T	T	F	F	F	F	T
T	F	F	T	T	T	T
F	T	T	F	T	T	T
F	F	T	T	T	T	T

The statements $c \to \sim s$ and $s \to \sim c$ are logically equivalent, as proved by their matching truth values in columns 5 and 6, or by the biconditional that is shown to be a tautology in column 7.

EXERCISES

In 1–8: **a.** Copy and complete the truth table for the given statement. (*Note.* In 2–8, prepare a complete truth table similar to the one shown in Exercise 1.) **b.** Indicate whether the statement is a tautology.

1.

p	q	$p \wedge q$	$(p \wedge q) \to p$
T	T		
T	F		
F	T		
F	F		

2.

p	q	$p \vee q$	$(p \vee q) \to p$

3.

p	q	$p \to q$	$p \vee (p \to q)$

4.

p	q	$q \to p$	$p \vee (q \to p)$

5.

p	q	$\sim q$	$p \to q$	$\sim q \to (p \to q)$

6.

p	q	$\sim p$	$p \vee \sim p$	$q \to (p \vee \sim p)$

7.

p	q	$p \wedge q$	$\sim(p \wedge q)$	$\sim(p \wedge q) \vee q$

8.

p	q	$q \to p$	$\sim(q \to p)$	$p \to q$	$(p \to q) \vee \sim(q \to p)$

In 9–12: **a.** Copy and complete the truth table for the given tautology. **b.** Tell which two statements within the compound statement are logically equivalent.

9.

p	q	$\sim q$	$p \to \sim q$	$p \wedge q$	$\sim(p \wedge q)$	$(p \to \sim q) \leftrightarrow \sim(p \wedge q)$

10.

p	q	$\sim p$	$\sim p \to q$	$p \vee q$	$(\sim p \to q) \leftrightarrow (p \vee q)$

11.

p	q	$\sim p$	$\sim q$	$\sim p \wedge \sim q$	$p \vee q$	$\sim(p \vee q)$	$(\sim p \wedge \sim q) \leftrightarrow \sim(p \vee q)$

12.

p	q	$\sim p$	$\sim p \vee q$	$p \wedge (\sim p \vee q)$	$p \wedge q$	$[p \wedge (\sim p \vee q)] \leftrightarrow (p \wedge q)$

In 13–18, prove that the two statements listed as (1) and (2) are logically equivalent or give a reason why they are not equivalent.

13. (1) $q \to p$ (2) $p \vee \sim q$ **14.** (1) $p \wedge \sim q$ (2) $\sim(\sim p \vee q)$

15. (1) $p \wedge \sim q$ (2) $\sim(p \to q)$ **16.** (1) $p \to q$ (2) $q \to p$

17. (1) $p \to q$ (2) $\sim p \to \sim q$ **18.** (1) $p \vee q$ (2) $p \vee (q \wedge \sim p)$

In 19–23: **a.** Using the letters given to represent sentences and the proper logic connectives, express each of the two compound sentences in symbolic form. **b.** Prove that the two compound sentences are logically equivalent or give a reason why they are not equivalent.

19. Let *f* represent "I eat the right foods."
Let *s* represent "I get sick."
Sentences: If I eat the right foods, then I don't get sick.
　　　　　I don't get sick or I don't eat the right foods.

20. Let *m* represent "Michael likes math."
Let *s* represent "Michael likes science."
Sentences: It is not true that Michael likes both math and science.
　　　　　Michael does not like math or Michael does not like science.

21. Let *t* represent "Ms. Wu is a teacher."
Let *e* represent "Ms. Wu is an engineer."
Sentences: If Ms. Wu is a teacher, then she is not an engineer.
　　　　　If Ms. Wu is not an engineer, then she is a teacher.

22. Let *s* represent "You succeed."
Let *t* represent "You try again."
Sentences: If you don't succeed, then you try again.
　　　　　You succeed or you try again.

23. Let *p* represent "Lines are perpendicular."
Let *r* represent "Right angles are formed by the lines."
Sentences: Right angles are formed by the lines if the lines are perpendicular.
　　　　　The lines are not perpendicular or right angles are formed by the lines.

2-5 THE LAW OF DETACHMENT

There are many laws of reasoning that allow us to present a convincing argument or a formal proof in logic. Before developing a formal proof in logic, let us first understand what is meant by a convincing argument.

An ***argument*** consists of a series of statements called ***premises*** and a final statement called the ***conclusion.*** We say that the premises lead to the conclusion, or that the conclusion follows from the premises. For example:

Premise:	If I play baseball, then I need a bat.
Premise:	I play baseball.
Conclusion:	I need a bat.

We have drawn a line to separate the premises from the conclusion. If we let p represent "I play baseball" and q represent "I need a bat," we can write this argument in symbolic form as:

Premise:	$p \rightarrow q$
Premise:	p
Conclusion:	q

A Test of Validity by Truth Values

An argument is called a *valid argument* if and only if (1) its premises are *true* and (2) by using the laws of reasoning, these premises force the conclusion to be *true*. We can test the validity of any argument by examining the possible truth values of the variables given in the premises.

(1) Since all premises must be true, we start by assigning T for true to the simplest premise in the argument. Here, we indicate that the premise p is true by writing T above the variable p.

$$p \rightarrow q$$
$$\overset{T}{p}$$
$$\overline{}$$
$$q$$

(2) Since p is true in the second premise, we must also label p as true in the first premise.

$$\overset{T}{p} \rightarrow q$$
$$\overset{T}{p}$$
$$\overline{}$$
$$q$$

(3) The conditional premise $p \rightarrow q$ must also be true. From the truth table for conditional, we know that T $\rightarrow$ F is a false statement. Therefore, we cannot label q as false because the premise $p \rightarrow q$ would then be false. Since T $\rightarrow$ T is a true statement, we label q as true to keep the premise $p \rightarrow q$ true.

$$\overset{T}{p} \rightarrow \overset{T}{q}$$
$$\overset{T}{p}$$
$$\overline{}$$
$$q$$

(4) Finally, since q is true in the first premise, we must also label q as true in the conclusion. In this way, we see that the set of true premises has led to a true conclusion. Therefore, we have a valid argument.

$$\overset{T}{p} \rightarrow \overset{T}{q}$$
$$\overset{T}{p}$$
$$\overline{}$$
$$\overset{T}{q}$$

A Test of Validity by Truth Tables

We can also test the validity of an argument by constructing a truth table. We treat the set of premises as a single hypothesis that will lead to the conclusion. Notice how we can connect the individual premises with the word *and* to form the single hypothesis. Let us state the preceding argument first in words and then in symbols:

If (*p* implies *q*) and *p*, then *q*.

$$[(p \rightarrow q) \wedge p] \rightarrow q$$

The truth table is then constructed for the statement $[(p \rightarrow q) \wedge p] \rightarrow q$.

p	q	p → q	(p → q) ∧ p	[(p → q) ∧ p] → q
T	T	T	T	T
T	F	F	F	T
F	T	T	F	T
F	F	T	F	T

We can use the truth table in either of two ways to conclude that the argument is valid.

Method 1: Find all rows of the truth table above in which the given premises are true. Here, *p* is true in rows 1 and 2, and $p \rightarrow q$ is true in rows 1, 3, and 4. Thus, it is *only in row 1* that all premises are true. We read the truth value of the conclusion *q* for row 1 *only* and find that the conclusion *q* is true.

Method 2: When the argument is a tautology, that is, the statement is always true, then the argument is valid. Since $[(p \rightarrow q) \wedge p] \rightarrow q$ is a tautology, the argument is valid.

The Law of Detachment

The argument that we have just tested, by assigning truth values to show its validity or by using a truth table, is called the ***Law of Detachment***. This law is the first of many *laws of reasoning*, or inference laws, that you will study. We call this a *law of inference* because, when the given premises are true, we can *infer* that the conclusion is true.

● The ***Law of Detachment*** states that when two given premises are true, one a conditional and the other the hypothesis of that conditional, it then follows that the conclusion of the conditional is true.

The Law of Detachment can also be identified by its Latin name, **Modus Ponens**. In this law of reasoning, and in other inference laws to follow, we use the symbol ∴ to mean the word *therefore*. We will use the symbol ∴ or the word *therefore* only when we reach a conclusion.

The Law of Detachment may be written symbolically in two ways:

$$p \rightarrow q$$
$$p$$
$$\overline{}$$
$$\therefore q$$

or $[(p \rightarrow q) \wedge p] \rightarrow q$

Note. In the example just given, q is called a valid conclusion. A **valid conclusion** is a true statement that is deduced from a set of true premises by using the laws of reasoning.

Hidden Conditionals

In an argument, a conditional statement is sometimes given in a form that does not use the words *if. . . then* or the word *implies*. Such a statement is called a **hidden conditional.** In cases like this, it is helpful to change the hidden conditional to a statement using the words *if. . . then*. Study the following examples:

1. Hidden Conditional: A polygon of three sides is called a triangle.
   If. . . then form: If a polygon has three sides, then the
                             polygon is called a triangle.

2. Hidden Conditional: What's good for Bill is good for me.
   If. . . then form: If it's good for Bill, then it's good for me.

3. Hidden Conditional: I'll get a job when I graduate.
   If. . . then form: If I graduate, then I'll get a job.

4. Hidden Conditional: Drink milk to stay healthy.
   If. . . then form: If you drink milk, then you will stay healthy.

MODEL PROBLEMS

1. Let r represent "It is raining."
   Let m represent "I have to mow the lawn."

   Given the following premises:
      If it is raining, then I don't have to mow the lawn.
      It is raining.

a. Using r, m, and the proper logic connectives, express the premises of this argument in symbolic form.

b. Write a conclusion in symbolic form.

c. Translate the conclusion into words.

Solution

a. $r \rightarrow \sim m$

r

b. Compare these premises to the general form used in the Law of Detachment to see that the conclusion must be $\sim m$.

$$
\begin{array}{cc}
p \rightarrow q & r \rightarrow \sim m \\
\underline{p} & \underline{r} \\
\therefore q & \therefore \sim m
\end{array}
$$

c. $\sim m$ represents "I don't have to mow the lawn."

Answer: **a.** $r \rightarrow \sim m$ **b.** $\sim m$

           r **c.** I don't have to mow the lawn.

2. Write a valid conclusion for the given premises or indicate that no conclusion is possible.

Premises: If adjacent angles are supplementary, then the angles form a linear pair.

           $\angle ABC$ and $\angle CBD$ are adjacent supplementary angles.

Solution

The diagram shows $\angle ABC$ and $\angle CBD$ to be adjacent and supplementary. To present the argument in symbolic form:

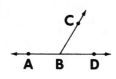

   Let a represent "Angles are adjacent."

   Let s represent "Angles are supplementary."

   Let p represent "Angles form a linear pair."

In the first premise, the hypothesis is written as a conjunction. Since two specific angles are named in the second premise, these angles are also named in the conclusion, which is reached by using the Law of Detachment.

$(a \wedge s) \rightarrow p$:   If angles are adjacent and supplementary, then the angles form a linear pair.

$(a \wedge s)$: $\angle ABC$ and $\angle CBD$ are adjacent and supplementary.

$\therefore p$: $\angle ABC$ and $\angle CBD$ form a linear pair. *Ans.*

3. Write a valid conclusion for the given premises or indicate that no conclusion is possible.

Premises: If adjacent angles are supplementary, then the angles form a linear pair.

∠*RST* and ∠*TSU* are adjacent angles.

Solution

The diagram shows ∠*RST* and ∠*TSU* to be adjacent. To study the premises in symbolic form:

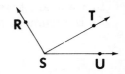

Let *a* represent "Angles are adjacent."
Let *s* represent "Angles are supplementary."
Let *p* represent "Angles form a linear pair."

Notice that, since ∠*RST* and ∠*TSU* are not supplementary, the second premise fails to meet all conditions stated in the hypothesis of the first premise. Thus, no conclusion can be drawn.

$(a \wedge s) \rightarrow p$: If angles are adjacent and supplementary, then the angles form a linear pair.

a: ∠*RST* and ∠*TSU* are adjacent.

∴ No conclusion is possible. *Ans.*

4. Write a valid conclusion for the given premises or indicate that no conclusion is possible.

Premises: Reading will give a person knowledge.

Mrs. Walker is an avid reader.

Solution

The first premise is a hidden conditional that can be restated in the *if . . . then* form. The premises are rewritten here, both in symbols and in words, as follows:

$p \rightarrow q$: If a person reads, then the reader gains knowledge.

p: Mrs. Walker reads.

By the Law of Detachment, we conclude q. We write this conclusion by including Mrs. Walker's name as the reader:

q: Mrs. Walker gains knowledge. *Ans.*

EXERCISES

In 1–4, use the Law of Detachment to state a correct conclusion from the given premises.

1. $p \rightarrow q$ **2.** $k \rightarrow \sim t$ **3.** $\sim a \rightarrow x$ **4.** $p \rightarrow (r \wedge s)$
   $\underline{p\hphantom{\;\;\;\;\;}}$ $\underline{k\hphantom{\;\;\;\;\;}}$ $\underline{\sim a\hphantom{\;\;\;\;}}$ $\underline{p\hphantom{\;\;\;\;\;\;\;\;}}$

In 5–7, identify the premises and the conclusion in each argument.

5. If n is an even number, then n is exactly divisible by 2.
   n is an even number.
   Therefore, n is exactly divisible by 2.
6. If an event is a certainty, then its probability is 1.
   The event that I am alive is a certainty.
   The probability that I am alive is 1.
7. Fredda watches TV if she has nothing better to do.
   Fredda has nothing better to do.
   Fredda watches TV.

In 8–12, express each hidden conditional in a sentence using the words *if . . . then.*

8. When points are on the same line, they are called collinear points.
9. I'll do my homework when I'm good and ready.
10. What Jack doesn't see, he doesn't believe exists.
11. The complement of an angle measuring x degrees is an angle measuring $(90 - x)$ degrees.
12. Flowers grow when given sun and water.

13. Given the premises $a \rightarrow b$ and a, which is a logical conclusion?
   (1) a (2) $\sim a$ (3) b (4) $\sim b$
14. Given the premises $p \rightarrow \sim q$ and p, which is a logical conclusion?
   (1) p (2) $\sim p$ (3) q (4) $\sim q$

In 15–18: Let r represent "It rains."
     Let s represent "It snows."
     Let v represent "Vegetables grow."

a. Using r, s, v, and the proper logic connectives, express the given premises of the argument in symbolic form.
b. Write the conclusion of the argument in symbolic form.
c. Translate the conclusion into words.

15. If it rains, then vegetables grow.
   It rains.

16. If it snows, then vegetables do not grow.
  It snows.
17. It does not snow if it rains.
  It rains.
18. If it rains and it does not snow, then vegetables grow.
  It rains and it does not snow.

In 19–24, write a valid conclusion for the given set of premises.

19. If you deserve a break today, then you should have lunch.
  Mr. Willig deserves a break today.
20. If two points are given, then a straight line can be drawn containing the points.
  Points *A* and *B* are given.
21. Tom will get an *A* if his essay is handed in on time.
  Tom's essay is handed in on time.
22. When *x* is an integer, then *x* is a real number.
  x is the integer 5.
23. The person who is late for supper will get into trouble.
  Matthew is late for supper.
24. Any friend of Jim Kavanagh is a friend of mine.
  Alex is a friend of Jim Kavanagh.

In 25–28, state whether or not the conclusion is *valid* based on the Law of Detachment.

25. When football season ends, we start baseball practice.
  Football season has ended.
  Conclusion: We have started baseball practice.

26. You can use the machine if you have exact change.
  You use the machine.
  Conclusion: You have exact change.

27. If I understand logic, then I can reason correctly.
  I understand logic.
  Conclusion: I can reason correctly.

28. A square is a rectangle.
  If a figure is a rectangle, then it has four right angles.
  Conclusion: A square has four right angles.

In 29–36, write a valid conclusion for the given set of premises or tell why no conclusion is possible.

29. If she is in love, then her head is in the clouds.
  Mary is in love.

30. You can buy a luxury car if you are rich.
    Mr. Lopez is rich.
31. If a point is a midpoint of a line segment, then that point divides
    the line segment into two congruent segments.
    M is the midpoint of $\overline{AB}$.
32. If two angles are both right angles, then the angles are congruent.
    $\angle A$ and $\angle B$ are congruent angles.
33. If two angles are congruent, then the angles have the same measure.
    $\angle C \cong \angle D$.
34. If I had the time and the energy, then I'd walk to work.
    I have the time.
35. When a polygon is regular, all sides of the polygon are congruent.
    A square is a regular polygon.
36. If a sentence has a truth value, then it is a statement.
    "3 + 8 = 11" is true.

2-6 THE LAW OF THE CONTRAPOSITIVE; PROOF IN LOGIC

The conditional *if p then q* is the connective most often used in reasoning. In Course I, you studied three related conditionals, each of which was formed by making some changes in the original conditional. These conditionals are called the *inverse*, the *converse*, and the *contrapositive*.

Let us examine these related conditionals both in symbolic form and in words. For an example, let *p* represent "It's −5°" and let *q* represent "It's cold."

Conditional ($p \rightarrow q$): If it's −5°, then it's cold. Certainly, we can agree that this statement is *true*.

Inverse ($\sim p \rightarrow \sim q$): If it's *not* −5°, then it's *not* cold. Here we are uncertain of the truth value of this statement. Perhaps it's 30° Celsius and the statement is true, or perhaps it's −10° and the statement is false. In any event, we know that this statement could *possibly be false*.

Converse ($q \rightarrow p$): If it's cold, then it's −5°. Again we are uncertain of the truth value of this statement. If it is cold, the temperature could be −5° or it could be some other low temperature. We know that this statement could *possibly be false*.

Contrapositive ($\sim q \rightarrow \sim p$): If it's *not* cold, then it's *not* −5°. Knowing that it is not cold does imply that the temperature cannot be −5°. Thus, we can agree that this statement is *true*.

To convince ourselves that the conditional statement and its contra-positive are *logically equivalent statements*, we can construct a truth table for the expression $(p \rightarrow q) \leftrightarrow (\sim q \rightarrow \sim p)$.

				Conditional	Contrapositive	Col. 7
p	*q*	~*q*	~*p*	*p* → *q*	~*q* → ~*p*	(*p* → *q*) ↔ (~*q* → ~*p*)
T	*T*	*F*	*F*	*T*	*T*	*T*
T	*F*	*T*	*F*	*F*	*F*	*T*
F	*T*	*F*	*T*	*T*	*T*	*T*
F	*F*	*T*	*T*	*T*	*T*	*T*

The truth values for the conditional in column 5 match the truth values for the contrapositive in column 6, resulting in a tautology in column 7.

The Law of the Contrapositive

The truth table we have just constructed verifies our second law of reasoning, or inference law, called the Law of the Contrapositive.

● The *Law of the Contrapositive* states that when a conditional prem-ise is true, it follows that the contrapositive of the premise is also true.

The Law of the Contrapositive may be written symbolically in two ways:

$$\frac{p \rightarrow q}{\therefore \sim q \rightarrow \sim p} \qquad or \qquad \boxed{(p \rightarrow q) \leftrightarrow (\sim q \rightarrow \sim p)}$$

Remember that a contrapositive is formed by taking any conditional statement, negating its hypothesis, negating its conclusion, and then reversing the roles of these negated statements. Therefore, in the contra-positive: (1) The hypothesis is the negated conclusion of the original conditional and (2) the conclusion is the negated hypothesis of the orig-inal conditional. Thus, we can see that:

1. The contrapositive of $a \rightarrow \sim b$ is $b \rightarrow \sim a$.
2. The contrapositive of $\sim c \rightarrow d$ is $\sim d \rightarrow c$.
3. The contrapositive of $\sim e \rightarrow \sim f$ is $f \rightarrow e$.

The Inverse and the Converse

It is possible to construct truth tables to show that:

1. A conditional $p \rightarrow q$ and its inverse $\sim p \rightarrow \sim q$ are *not* logically equivalent statements.
2. A conditional $p \rightarrow q$ and its converse $q \rightarrow p$ are *not* logically equivalent statements.
3. However, the inverse $\sim p \rightarrow \sim q$ and the converse $q \rightarrow p$ are logically equivalent statements. By examining the tautology, $(\sim p \rightarrow \sim q) \leftrightarrow (q \rightarrow p)$, we realize that this statement is merely another form of the Law of the Contrapositive.

A Proof in Logic

When we are given a series of premises that are true and we apply the laws of reasoning to reach a conclusion that is true, we say that we are proving an argument by means of a *formal proof.*

The most commonly used proof in logic involves two columns. The first column consists of *statements* and the second column consists of *reasons* that allow us to make the statements. Let us study an example.

Given the premises: If Joanna saves enough money, then she can buy a bike.

Joanna cannot buy a bike.

Prove the conclusion: Joanna did not save enough money.

To simplify this proof, let us assign variables to the statements and rewrite the premises and the conclusion in symbolic form.

Let m represent "Joanna saves enough money."
Let b represent "Joanna can buy a bike."

Given: $m \rightarrow b$
     $\sim b$

Prove: $\sim m$

Statements	*Reasons*
1. $m \rightarrow b$	1. Given.
2. $\sim b$	2. Given.
3. $\sim b \rightarrow \sim m$	3. Law of the Contrapositive (step 1).
4. $\sim m$	4. Law of Detachment (steps 2 and 3).

The proof just presented starts by listing the premises that are given and the conclusion that must be proved. In the statements that follow, we number the steps. Thus, steps 1 and 2 are the given premises. In step 3, we apply the Law of the Contrapositive to step 1, allowing us to say that when $m \to b$ is true, then $\sim b \to \sim m$ is also true. In step 4, we apply the Law of Detachment to steps 2 and 3. Thus, $\sim b \to \sim m$ and $\sim b$ lead to the conclusion $\sim m$, which must be true.

Note. Whenever we use a law of reasoning to make a statement in the first column, we must write in the second column *both* the name of the law of reasoning and the steps used to reach this new statement.

MODEL PROBLEMS

1. Which is logically equivalent to the statement "If I live in Brooklyn, then I live in New York"?
   (1) If I live in New York, then I live in Brooklyn.
   (2) If I do not live in New York, then I do not live in Brooklyn.
   (3) If I do not live in New York, then I live in Brooklyn.
   (4) If I do not live in Brooklyn, then I do not live in New York.

Solution

A conditional statement $B \to N$ is logically equivalent to its contrapositive $\sim N \to \sim B$. The contrapositive of the given statement is choice (2).

Answer: (2)

2. *Given the premises:*   If Al does not study, then he will fail.
   Al did not fail.

   Prove the conclusion: Al studied.

Solution

A formal proof is given here, after assigning variables to the statements and rewriting our premises and conclusion in symbolic form.

   Let s represent "Al studied."
   Let f represent "Al failed."

Given: $\sim s \to f$
         $\sim f$

Prove: s

Statements   *Reasons*

1. $\sim s \to f$ | 1. Given.

2. $\sim f$ | 2. Given.

3. $\sim f \to s$ | 3. Law of the Contrapositive (step 1).

4. s | 4. Law of Detachment (steps 2 and 3).

Therefore, we have proved s: Al studied.

EXERCISES

In 1–10, write the contrapositive of the given conditional statement.

1. $p \to q$ **2.** $k \to m$ **3.** $\sim r \to t$ **4.** $x \to \sim y$
5. If winter is here, then spring will soon follow.
6. If it is not raining, then Leah will not take her umbrella.
7. Rick feels good if he jogs.
8. If Ali is sick, then she will not go to school.
9. Linda is not happy if people are late to dinner.
10. Too many cooks implies that the broth is spoiled.

In 11–15, select the numeral preceding the statement or expression that best answers the question.

11. Which statement is logically equivalent to $\sim p \to r$?
   (1) $p \to r$ (2) $p \to \sim r$ (3) $\sim r \to p$ (4) $r \to p$

12. Which statement is logically equivalent to $p \to \sim q$?
   (1) $q \to \sim p$ (2) $\sim p \to q$ (3) $\sim q \to p$ (4) $q \to p$

13. Which is logically equivalent to the statement "If it's cold, then we go skiing"?
   (1) If we go skiing, then it's cold.
   (2) If we do not go skiing, then it's cold.
   (3) If it is not cold, then we do not go skiing.
   (4) If we do not go skiing, then it is not cold.

14. Which is logically equivalent to the statement "If I eat, then I live"?
   (1) If I do not eat, then I do not live.
   (2) If I do not live, then I do not eat.
   (3) If I live, then I eat.
   (4) If I eat, then I do not live.

15. Which is logically equivalent to the statement "You will get sick if you eat green apples"?
(1) If you get sick, then you have eaten green apples.
(2) If you don't get sick, then you have not eaten green apples.
(3) If you don't eat green apples, then you won't get sick.
(4) You've eaten green apples if you have gotten sick.

16. Construct a truth table to show that a conditional $p \rightarrow q$ and its inverse $\sim p \rightarrow \sim q$ are *not* logically equivalent statements.

17. Construct a truth table to show that a conditional $p \rightarrow q$ and its converse $q \rightarrow p$ are *not* logically equivalent statements.

In 18–30, tell whether the two given statements are logically equivalent or not equivalent.

18. $r \rightarrow t$
$\sim r \rightarrow \sim t$

19. $k \rightarrow m$
$m \rightarrow k$

20. $t \rightarrow \sim b$
$b \rightarrow \sim t$

21. $\sim d \rightarrow \sim h$
$h \rightarrow d$

22. $p \rightarrow \sim b$
$\sim b \rightarrow p$

23. $\sim n \rightarrow e$
$\sim e \rightarrow n$

24. $r \rightarrow \sim p$
$\sim r \rightarrow p$

25. $\sim p \rightarrow t$
$t \rightarrow \sim p$

26. If a triangle is isosceles, then it has exactly two congruent sides.
If a triangle does not have exactly two congruent sides, then it is not isosceles.

27. If $x + 2 = 5$, then $x \neq 4$.
If $x + 2 \neq 5$, then $x = 4$.

28. If $x + 2 = 5$, then $x = 3$.
If $x \neq 3$, then $x + 2 \neq 5$.

29. If two angles are vertical angles, then they are congruent.
If two angles are congruent, then they are vertical angles.

30. Dick will reach home plate if Doug hits a triple.
If Dick does not reach home plate, then Doug did not hit a triple.

In 31 and 32, copy the given proof on a separate paper and provide the reasons needed for each step.

31. *Given:* $a \rightarrow \sim b$
       b

Prove: $\sim a$

Statements	Reasons
1. $a \rightarrow \sim b$	1. ____
2. b	2. ____
3. $b \rightarrow \sim a$	3. ____
4. $\sim a$	4. ____

32. *Given:* $\sim p \rightarrow \sim t$
       t

Prove: p

Statements	Reasons
1. $\sim p \rightarrow \sim t$	1. ____
2. $t \rightarrow p$	2. ____
3. t	3. ____
4. p	4. ____

In 33–38, write a formal proof to show that the conclusion must follow from the given set of premises. (In 36–38, write all statements in symbolic form, using the given variables.)

33. *Given:* $p \rightarrow r$
      p

Prove: r

34. *Given:* $\sim k \rightarrow e$
      $\sim e$

Prove: k

35. *Given:* $q \rightarrow t$
      $\sim t$

Prove: $\sim q$

36. *Given:* If two lines intersect, the lines meet at only one point.
      Lines k and m do not meet at one point.

Prove: Lines k and m do not intersect.
(Let I represent "Two lines intersect.")
(Let P represent "Lines meet at one point.")

37. *Given:* Gabe went to medical school if he is a doctor.
      Gabe is a doctor.

Prove: Gabe went to medical school.
(Let M represent "Gabe went to medical school.")
(Let D represent "Gabe is a doctor.")

38. *Given:* Lights will go off if there is a power failure.
      The lights do not go off.

Prove: There is no power failure.
(Let O represent "Lights go off.")
(Let P represent "There is a power failure.")

2-7 THE LAW OF MODUS TOLLENS

In Ruritania, when Juliet is no longer the queen, then her son Prince Charles will take the throne as the new king. Let us use these facts to present a third law of reasoning. Let p represent "Charles is the prince" and let q represent "Juliet is the queen."

Premise $(p \rightarrow q)$:	If Charles is still the prince, then Juliet is still the queen.
Premise $(\sim q)$:	Juliet is no longer the queen.
Conclusion $(\sim p)$:	Charles is no longer the prince.

A Test of Validity by Truth Values

We can test the validity of this argument by assigning truth values to show us that true premises must lead to a true conclusion.

1. The simplest premise in this argument is $\sim q$. We show that $\sim q$ is true by writing T above the premise $\sim q$.

$$p \to q$$
$$\text{(T)}$$
$$\sim q$$
$$\overline{\sim p}$$

2. When $\sim q$ is true, q must be false. Since q is false in the second premise, we must label q as false in the first premise.

$$\text{(F)}$$
$$p \to q$$
$$\text{(T)}$$
$$\sim q$$
$$\sim p$$

3. The conditional premise $p \to q$ must also be true. From the truth table, we know that T $\to$ F is a false statement. Therefore, we cannot label p as true because the premise $p \to q$ would then be false. Since F $\to$ F is a *true* statement, we label p as false to keep the premise $p \to q$ true.

$$\text{(F)} \quad \text{(F)}$$
$$p \to q$$
$$\text{(T)}$$
$$\sim q$$
$$\overline{\sim p}$$

4. Finally, since p is false in the first premise, we know that $\sim p$ is true. This true conclusion tells us that we have a valid argument.

$$\text{(F)} \quad \text{(F)}$$
$$p \to q$$
$$\text{(T)}$$
$$\sim q$$
$$\overline{\quad}$$
$$\text{(T)}$$
$$\sim p$$

A Test of Validity by Truth Tables

We can also test the validity of this argument by constructing a truth table in which the given premises are treated as a single hypothesis leading to the conclusion $\sim p$.

If $(p \to q)$ and $\sim q$, then $\sim p$.

$$[(p \to q) \land \sim q] \to \sim p$$

p	q	$p \to q$	$\sim q$	$(p \to q) \land \sim q$	$\sim p$	$[(p \to q) \land \sim q] \to \sim p$
T	T	T	F	F	F	T
T	F	F	T	F	F	T
F	T	T	F	F	T	T
F	F	T	T	T	T	T

Recall that we can conclude that the argument is valid by either of two methods when using a truth table:

Method 1: The premise $p \rightarrow q$ is true in rows 1, 3, and 4. The premise $\sim q$ is true in rows 2 and 4. Thus, it is *only in row 4* that *both* premises are *true*. We read the truth value of the conclusion $\sim p$ for row 4 *only* and find that the conclusion $\sim p$ is true.

Method 2: Since the argument formed, $[(p \rightarrow q) \wedge \sim q] \rightarrow \sim p$, is a tautology, we conclude that the argument is valid.

The Law of Modus Tollens

The argument we have just tested is known by its Latin name, *Modus Tollens*. This is our third law of inference or law of reasoning.

● The *Law of Modus Tollens* states that when two given premises are true, one a conditional and the other the negation of the conclusion of that conditional, it then follows that the negation of the hypothesis of the conditional is true. This means that if a conditional is true and its conclusion is false, then its hypothesis is false.

The Law of Modus Tollens may be written symbolically in two ways:

$$\begin{array}{c} p \rightarrow q \\ \sim q \\ \hline \therefore \sim p \end{array} \quad or \quad [(p \rightarrow q) \wedge \sim q] \rightarrow \sim p$$

An Equivalence in Logic

Study the following two examples to discover an interesting equivalence in logic. In both cases, we start with the premises $p \rightarrow q$ and $\sim q$.

	Step 1 Contrapositive	Step 2 Detachment		Modus Tollens
$\begin{array}{c} p \rightarrow q \\ \sim q \\ \hline \end{array}$	$\begin{array}{c} \sim q \rightarrow \sim p \\ \sim q \\ \hline \end{array}$	$\begin{array}{c} \sim q \rightarrow \sim p \\ \sim q \\ \hline \therefore \sim p \end{array}$	*or*	$\begin{array}{c} p \rightarrow q \\ \sim q \\ \hline \therefore \sim p \end{array}$

● The Law of Modus Tollens is equivalent to applying both the Law of the Contrapositive and the Law of Detachment to a set of premises.

Thus, in a logic proof, Modus Tollens can be used as a single step to replace the two steps previously taken when applying *both* the Law of the Contrapositive and the Law of Detachment.

MODEL PROBLEM _____

Given the premises: If Al does not study, then he will fail.
Al did not fail.

Prove the conclusion: Al studied.

Solution

A formal proof is given here, after assigning variables to the statements and rewriting our premises and conclusion in symbolic form.

Let s represent "Al studied."
Let f represent "Al failed."

Given: $\sim s \rightarrow f$
$\sim f$

Prove: s

Statements	*Reasons*
1. $\sim s \rightarrow f$	1. Given.
2. $\sim f$	2. Given.
3. s	3. Law of Modus Tollens (steps 1 and 2).

Compare this example with Model Problem 2 in Section 2-6 to see that there are different ways to do the same proof. Thus, we have proved s: "Al studied."

EXERCISES _____

In 1–4, apply the Law of Modus Tollens to the given set of premises to reach a valid conclusion.

1. $a \rightarrow b$ **2.** $\sim p \rightarrow t$ **3.** $k \rightarrow \sim n$ **4.** $\sim r \rightarrow \sim q$
$\underline{\sim b\quad}$ $\underline{\sim t\quad}$ $\underline{n\quad}$ $\underline{q\quad}$

In 5–7, select the numeral preceding the statement or expression that best answers the question.

5. "If I am tired, then I sleep. I am not sleeping." Which is a valid conclusion from this given set of premises?
   (1) I am tired.   (2) I am sleeping.
   (3) I am not tired.   (4) I just woke up.

6. "If the temperature in my room is above 80°, the air conditioner will go on. The air conditioner is not on." Which best describes the temperature in my room?
(1) It is going up.   (2) It is going down.
(3) It is above 80°.   (4) It is not above 80°.

7. Given the premises: Perpendicular lines form right angles.
                            $\angle ABC$ is an obtuse angle.
Which of the following statements is a valid conclusion?
(1) $\overline{AB}$ is perpendicular to $\overline{CB}$.
(2) $\angle ABC$ is a right angle.
(3) $\overline{AB}$ is not perpendicular to $\overline{CB}$.
(4) There is no valid conclusion.

In 8–11, write a valid conclusion for the given set of premises.

8. If I am smart, then I like chemistry.
I do not like chemistry.

9. If both pairs of opposite sides of a quadrilateral are parallel, then the quadrilateral is a parallelogram.
Quadrilateral $ABCD$ is not a parallelogram.

10. Stacey will come to the party if her mother lets her.
Stacey does not come to the party.

11. If x is an even prime number, then $x = 2$.
$x = 3$.

In 12–16, write a valid conclusion for the given set of premises or indicate that no conclusion is possible.

12. If it doesn't rain, then Kristen will go swimming this weekend.
Kristen does not go swimming this weekend.

13. I'll be there when you call my name.
I'm not there.

14. If Bob wakes up early, then he will walk to school.
Bob did not wake up early.

15. If I fill up this notebook, then I must buy another notebook.
I must buy another notebook.

16. If today is Friday, then tomorrow is not a school day.
Today is Friday.

In 17–21, write a formal proof involving statements and reasons to show that the conclusion must follow from the given set of premises. (In 19–21, write all statements in symbolic form using the given variables.)

17. *Given:* $r \rightarrow t$
            $\sim t$

Prove: $\sim r$

18. *Given:* $\sim m \rightarrow e$
            $\sim e$

Prove: m

19. *Given:* If the tickets are sold out, then we'll wait for the next show. We do not wait for the next show.

Prove: The tickets were not sold out.
(Let *t* represent "The tickets are sold out.")
(Let *w* represent "We'll wait for the next show.")

20. *Given:* The scale is broken if Sal weighs less than 150 pounds. The scale is not broken.

Prove: Sal does not weigh less than 150 pounds.
(Let *b* represent "The scale is broken.")
(Let *w* represent "Sal weighs less than 150 pounds.")

21. *Given:* You can take driver's education if you're a senior. You can't take driver's education this year.

Prove: You are not a senior this year.
(Let *D* represent "You can take driver's education.")
(Let *S* represent "You are a senior.")

2-8 INVALID ARGUMENTS

At times, we may be confronted with an argument in which all of its premises are *true* but these premises do *not* always lead to a conclusion that is *true*. The conclusion could be *true* or *false*. Such an argument is called an ***invalid argument***.

We will study two examples of invalid arguments only to point out that these are *incorrect* forms of reasoning.

The First Invalid Argument

We start with the premises $p \rightarrow q$ and q, both of which must be true. Therefore, we label the second premise q as true and we must also label q as true in the first premise $p \rightarrow q$.

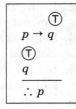

What truth value does p have? When p is true, then the premise $p \rightarrow q$ becomes T → T, which is true. However, when p is false, the premise $p \rightarrow q$ becomes F → T, which is also true. Thus, the premise $p \rightarrow q$ is true both when p is true and when p is false.

Since we cannot state that p is true nor can we state that it is false, this argument is invalid.

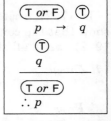

Invalid Argument

Let us consider an example of this *invalid* argument.

$p \rightarrow q$:   If I oversleep, then I'll be late for school.

q: I am late for school.

∴ p: I overslept.

While it is possible that I did oversleep, it is also possible that I did *not* oversleep. Perhaps the bus was late or I took too long to walk to school. In other words, we cannot conclude that "I overslept," is true.

We can also show that this argument is invalid by constructing a truth table for the following statement:

If $(p \rightarrow q)$ and q, then p.

$$[(p \rightarrow q) \wedge q] \rightarrow p$$

p	q	$p \rightarrow q$	$(p \rightarrow q) \wedge q$	$[(p \rightarrow q) \wedge q] \rightarrow p$
T	T	T	T	T
T	F	F	F	T
F	T	T	T	F
F	F	T	F	T

Notice that the statement $[(p \rightarrow q) \wedge q] \rightarrow p$ is *not* a tautology since not all values of the last column are true. Also notice that in the first and third rows, the premises $p \rightarrow q$ and q are both true, but the conclusion p, which we wish to reach, is *true* in the first row but *false* in the third row.

The Second Invalid Argument

We start with the premises $p \rightarrow q$ and $\sim p$, both of which must be true. Since $\sim p$ is true, it follows that p must be false. We label p as false in the first premise and $\sim p$ as true in the second premise.

What truth value does q have? Since F → T is true and F → F is true, we realize that the premise $p \rightarrow q$ will be true both when q is true and when q is false. If q can be true or false, then $\sim q$ can also be true or false.

Since we cannot state that $\sim q$ is true nor can we state that it is false, this argument is invalid.

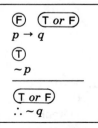

Invalid Argument

Let us consider an example of this invalid argument.

$p \rightarrow q$: "If $x = 10$, then x is greater than 5."

$\sim p$: "$x \neq 10$."

∴ $\sim q$: "x is not greater than 5."

The second premise tells us only that $x \neq 10$. If $x = 3$, it is *true* that 3 is not greater than 5. But if $x = 8$, it is *false* that 8 is not greater than 5. In other words, we cannot conclude that $\sim q$, which means x is not greater than 5, is true nor can we conclude that it is false.

We can also show that this argument is invalid by constructing a truth table for the following statement:

If $(p \rightarrow q)$ and $\sim p$, then $\sim q$.

$$[(p \rightarrow q) \wedge \sim p] \rightarrow \sim q$$

p	q	$p \rightarrow q$	$\sim p$	$(p \rightarrow q) \wedge \sim p$	$\sim q$	$[(p \rightarrow q) \wedge \sim p] \rightarrow \sim q$
T	T	T	F	F	F	T
T	F	F	F	F	T	T
F	T	T	T	T	F	F
F	F	T	T	T	T	T

Here, we see that the statement $[(p \rightarrow q) \wedge \sim p] \rightarrow \sim q$ is *not* a tautology since *not* all values of the last column are true. Also notice that in the third and fourth rows, the premises $p \rightarrow q$ and $\sim p$ are both true, but the conclusion $\sim q$, which we wish to reach, is *false* in the third row and *true* in the fourth row.

MODEL PROBLEMS _____

In 1–4, if the argument is valid, state the law of reasoning that tells why the conclusion is true. If the argument is invalid, write *Invalid*.

1. $p \rightarrow q$
  p
  ∴ q

2. $p \rightarrow q$
  $\sim p$
  ∴ $\sim q$

3. $p \rightarrow q$
  q
  ∴ p

4. $p \rightarrow q$
  $\sim q$
  ∴ $\sim p$

Solutions

1. Valid by the Law of Detachment

2. Invalid

3. Invalid

4. Valid by the Law of Modus Tollens

EXERCISES

In 1–12, if the argument is valid, state the law of reasoning that tells why the conclusion is true. If the argument is not valid, write *Invalid.*

1. $r \to t$
r
$\therefore t$

2. $k \to m$
$\sim k$
$\therefore \sim m$

3. $a \to b$
b
$\therefore a$

4. $p \to k$
$\sim k$
$\therefore \sim p$

5. $\sim p \to q$
$\sim p$
$\therefore q$

6. $\sim p \to q$
q
$\therefore \sim p$

7. $\sim p \to \sim q$
q
$\therefore p$

8. $\sim p \to \sim q$
$\sim q$
$\therefore \sim p$

9. $k \to t$
$\sim k$
$\therefore \sim t$

10. $k \to t$
$\sim t$
$\therefore \sim k$

11. $k \to \sim t$
t
$\therefore \sim k$

12. $k \to \sim t$
k
$\therefore \sim t$

In 13–17, select the numeral preceding the statement or expression that best answers the question.

13. Which of the following is an *invalid* argument?
(1) $[(a \to b) \land b] \to a$
(2) $[(c \to d) \land \sim d] \to \sim c$
(3) $[(e \to f) \land e] \to f$
(4) $[(g \to \sim h) \land h] \to \sim g$

14. Which of the following is an *invalid* argument?
(1) $[(p \to \sim t) \land p] \to \sim t$
(2) $[(p \to \sim t) \land \sim t] \to p$
(3) $[(p \to \sim t) \land t] \to \sim p$
(4) $[(\sim p \to t) \land \sim t] \to p$

15. Given the true statements: "If Fred catches fish today, then he will give me some" and "Fred will give me some fish." Which statement must be true?
(1) Fred will not give me some fish.
(2) Fred will not catch some fish today.
(3) Fred will catch some fish today.
(4) No conclusion is possible.

16. Assume that the statement "People who read well get good grades in school" is true. Which true statement leads to a valid conclusion?
(1) Kathy gets good grades in school. Therefore, Kathy reads well.
(2) Jeanne does not read well. Therefore, Jeanne does not get good grades in school.
(3) Debbie reads well. Therefore, Debbie gets good grades in school.
(4) If Jimmy gets good grades in school, then Jimmy reads well.

17. Assume that the statement "All geniuses have studied geometry" is true. Which true statement leads to a valid conclusion?
    (1) Karla has studied geometry; therefore, Karla is a genius.
    (2) Lou has not studied geometry; therefore, Lou is not a genius.
    (3) Jonathon is not a genius; therefore, Jonathon has not studied geometry.
    (4) If David studies geometry, then David is a genius.

In 18–24, state whether the argument is valid or invalid.

18. The winner of the Most Valuable Player award gets a trophy.
    Cathy Florio won a trophy.
    Conclusion: Cathy Florio won the Most Valuable Player award.
19. If x is an integer, then it is a real number.
    x is a real number.
    Conclusion: x is an integer.
20. If x is an integer, then it is a real number.
    x is not an integer.
    Conclusion: x is not a real number.
21. A shopper saves money if he uses coupons at the store.
    Tom Hunter uses coupons at the store.
    Conclusion: Tom Hunter saves money.
22. If the radio is loud, then you cannot hear the phone ring.
    The radio is not loud.
    Conclusion: You can hear the phone ring.
23. An acute angle has a degree measure between 0 and 90.
    m∠ABC = 130.
    Conclusion: ∠ABC is not an acute angle.
24. I take off my shoes when I get home.
    I am not home.
    Conclusion: I do not take off my shoes.

In 25–34, write a valid conclusion for the given set of premises. If no valid conclusion is possible, write *no conclusion.*

25. If you are honest, then you'll keep your word.
    You are not honest.
26. If David auditions, then he will get a role in the play.
    David auditions.
27. If Jennifer practices, then she will be a good musician.
    Jennifer is a good musician.
28. If Joe gets sick, then he will visit the doctor.
    Joe does not get sick.
29. Edna will gamble if she visits Atlantic City.
    Edna gambles.

30. If two angles are straight angles, then they are congruent.
 ∠ABC and ∠RST are not straight angles.
31. If two angles are straight angles, then they are congruent.
 ∠ABC is congruent to ∠RST.
32. If two angles are straight angles, then they are congruent.
 ∠ABC and ∠RST are both straight angles.
33. You can use a pencil if your pen runs out of ink.
 You use a pencil.
34. Thrifty people save money.
 Mrs. Melendy does not save money.

2-9 THE CHAIN RULE

A common form of reasoning is one that uses *many* conditional statements in an argument. Let us limit our premises to two conditional
statements in the following example. Let *p* represent "It's spring," let *q*
represent "Flowers blossom," and let *r* represent "I get allergies."

Premise (*p* → *q*):	If it's spring, then flowers blossom.
Premise (*q* → *r*):	If flowers blossom, then I get allergies.
Conclusion (*p* → *r*):	If it's spring, then I get allergies.

It is difficult to demonstrate the validity of this argument by assigning
truth values to the variables *p*, *q*, and *r* because there are many possible
arrangements. Instead, let us demonstrate the validity of this argument
by constructing a truth table. Here, it is necessary to construct a truth
table of eight lines to show all possible assignments
of truth values to *p*, *q*, and *r*.

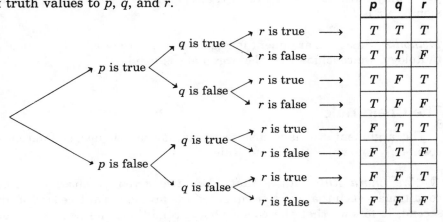

Tree Diagram

**Order of
Truth Table**

The **tree diagram** just displayed shows that there are eight possible "branches" for the truth values assigned to the variables p, q, and r. By following these "branches," you can see how to arrange the order of these truth values in a truth table. We will use this same order whenever we work with a truth table containing three variables. Let us now test the validity of the argument.

If $(p \rightarrow q)$ and $(q \rightarrow r)$, then $(p \rightarrow r)$.

$$[(p \rightarrow q) \wedge (q \rightarrow r)] \rightarrow (p \rightarrow r)$$

p	q	r	$p \rightarrow q$	$q \rightarrow r$	$(p \rightarrow q) \wedge (q \rightarrow r)$	$p \rightarrow r$	$[(p \rightarrow q) \wedge (q \rightarrow r)] \rightarrow (p \rightarrow r)$
T	T	T	T	T	T	T	T
T	T	F	T	F	F	F	T
T	F	T	F	T	F	T	T
T	F	F	F	T	F	F	T
F	T	T	T	T	T	T	T
F	T	F	T	F	F	T	T
F	F	T	T	T	T	T	T
F	F	F	T	T	T	T	T

Method 1: The premises $p \rightarrow q$ and $q \rightarrow r$ are *both* true *only in rows 1, 5, 7, and 8*. Therefore, we will read the truth values of the conclusion $p \rightarrow r$ only in those rows. In rows 1, 5, 7, and 8, we see that the conclusion $p \rightarrow r$ is *true*.

Method 2: Since the argument formed, $[(p \rightarrow q) \wedge (q \rightarrow r)] \rightarrow (p \rightarrow r)$, is a tautology, we conclude that the argument is valid.

The Chain Rule

The argument we have just tested is our fourth law of inference, commonly known as the Chain Rule.

● **The Chain Rule** states that when two given premises are true conditionals such that the consequent of the first is the antecedent of the second, it follows that the conclusion, a conditional formed using the antecedent of the first and the consequent of the second premise, is true.

The Chain Rule may be written symbolically in two ways:

$$\begin{array}{l} p \to q \\ q \to r \\ \hline \therefore p \to r \end{array}$$ *or* $$[(p \to q) \land (q \to r)] \to (p \to r)$$

The Chain Rule is sometimes referred to as the *Law of the Syllogism*.

Applications of the Chain Rule

The Chain Rule not only plays an important role in everyday thinking, but it is vital to every branch of mathematics.

In *algebra*, we use the Chain Rule to solve equations.

$p \to q$:   If $2x + 5 = 13$, then $2x = 8$.

$q \to r$:   If $2x = 8$, then $x = 4$.

$\therefore p \to r$:   If $2x + 5 = 13$, then $x = 4$.

We use the Chain Rule when doing any process involving multiple steps, such as this example in *statistics*.

$p \to q$:   If given 5, 8, and 14,
         then their sum is 27.

$q \to r$:   If the sum of three numbers is 27,
         then their mean average is 9.

$\therefore p \to r$:   If given 5, 8, and 14,
         then their mean average is 9.

We will use the Chain Rule in almost every *geometry* proof in chapters still to come.

For now, consider this one example.

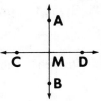

$p \to q$:   If $\overleftrightarrow{AB} \perp \overleftrightarrow{CD}$ at point M, then $\angle AMC$
       and $\angle AMD$ are right angles.

$q \to r$:   If $\angle AMC$ and $\angle AMD$ are right angles,
       then $\angle AMC \cong \angle AMD$.

$\therefore p \to r$:   If $\overleftrightarrow{AB} \perp \overleftrightarrow{CD}$ at point M, then
       $\angle AMC \cong \angle AMD$.

MODEL PROBLEMS

1. Given the premises: If I am invited, then I will go to the party.
If I do not buy a gift, then I will not go to the party.

Write *two* logical conclusions for the given set of premises.

Solution

Assign variables to represent the statements made.
    Let i represent "I am invited."
    Let p represent "I will go to the party."
    Let g represent "I buy a gift."

The premises written in symbolic form are:

$$i \to p$$
$$\sim g \to \sim p$$

In our first argument we change the second premise $\sim g \to \sim p$ to its contrapositive $p \to g$. Then, using the Chain Rule with the premises $i \to p$ and $p \to g$, we conclude $i \to g$.

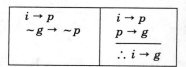

In our next argument, we change the first premise $i \to p$ to its contrapositive $\sim p \to \sim i$. Then, using the Chain Rule with the premises $\sim g \to \sim p$ and $\sim p \to \sim i$, we conclude $\sim g \to \sim i$.

$i \to p$		$\sim p \to \sim i$
$\sim g \to \sim p$		$\sim g \to \sim p$
		$\therefore \sim g \to \sim i$

Answer: $(i \to g)$ means "If I am invited, then I will buy a gift."

$(\sim g \to \sim i)$ means "If I do not buy a gift, then I am not invited."

Note that the conclusions are logically equivalent.

2. Given the premises: $a \to c$
$\sim a \to b$
$\sim c$

Prove the conclusion: b

Solution

There are many different ways to prove the conclusion b. Two different proofs are presented here. Can you find other proofs?

Statements	Reasons
1. $a \rightarrow c$	1. Given.
2. $\sim a \rightarrow b$	2. Given.
3. $\sim c$	3. Given.
4. $\sim c \rightarrow \sim a$	4. Law of the Contrapositive (1).
5. $\sim c \rightarrow b$	5. Chain Rule (4, 2).
6. b	6. Law of Detachment (5, 3).

Statements	Reasons
1. $a \rightarrow c$	1. Given.
2. $\sim a \rightarrow b$	2. Given.
3. $\sim c$	3. Given.
4. $\sim a$	4. Law of Modus Tollens (1, 3).
5. b	5. Law of Detachment (2, 4).

EXERCISES

In 1–10, apply the Chain Rule to the given set of premises to write a valid conclusion.

1. $a \rightarrow b$
$\underline{b \rightarrow c}$

2. $e \rightarrow f$
$\underline{f \rightarrow \sim g}$

3. $p \rightarrow q$
$\underline{t \rightarrow p}$

4. $\sim r \rightarrow m$
$\underline{p \rightarrow \sim r}$

5. If today is Monday, then I have school.
If I have school, then I have homework.

6. If I live in New York City, then I live in New York State.
If I live in New York State, then I live near the Atlantic Ocean.

7. If $9 - 2x > 3$, then $-2x > -6$.
If $-2x > -6$, then $x < 3$.

8. If Edgar is tired, then he sleeps.
If Edgar works hard, then he is tired.

9. My parents are happy when I get good grades.
I get out on weekends when my parents are happy.

10. If Phil is not on time, then he will be fired.
If Phil is fired, then Trude will get his job.

In 11–17, state whether the argument is valid or invalid.

11. $p \rightarrow \sim t$
$\underline{\sim t \rightarrow \sim q}$
$\therefore p \rightarrow \sim q$

12. $r \rightarrow k$
$\underline{k \rightarrow m}$
$\therefore m \rightarrow r$

13. $a \rightarrow \sim p$
$\underline{\sim b \rightarrow p}$
$\therefore a \rightarrow b$

14. $a \rightarrow x$
$\underline{b \rightarrow x}$
$\therefore a \rightarrow b$

15. If Carissa Sue is a child, then she will grow taller.
If Carissa Sue will grow taller, then she is not an adult.
Conclusion: If Carissa Sue is a child, then she is not an adult.

16. If Gary is tall, then regular clothes do not fit him.
     If regular clothes do not fit Gary, then he goes to a special clothing
       store.
     Conclusion: If Gary goes to a special clothing store, then he is tall.
17. If a plant blooms, it is well nourished.
     If a plant is not watered, it is not well nourished.
     Conclusion: If a plant blooms, it has been watered.

In 18–21, select the numeral preceding the statement or expression that best answers the question.

18. If $a \to b$ and $d \to \sim b$, then it logically follows that
     (1) $a \to d$ (2) $b \to a$ (3) $d \to a$ (4) $a \to \sim d$
19. Given $r \to t$ and $\sim s \to \sim t$. Which is a valid conclusion?
     (1) $r \to s$ (2) $\sim s \to r$ (3) $\sim t \to r$ (4) $r \to \sim s$
20. Which is logically concluded from the true statements "If I drive a
     smaller car, I will use less gas," and "If I use less gas, I will save
     money"?
     (1) If I use less gas, I will drive a smaller car.
     (2) If I drive a smaller car, I will save money.
     (3) If I save money, then I drive a smaller car.
     (4) If I do not drive a smaller car, I will not use less gas.
21. Which conclusion logically follows from the true statements "If we
     ruin our rivers, the fish will die" and "If we pollute, we ruin our
     rivers"?
     (1) If we do not pollute, the fish will not die.
     (2) If the fish die, then we pollute.
     (3) If we pollute, the fish will die.
     (4) If we do not pollute, we do not ruin our rivers.

In 22–27, write a valid conclusion for the given premises.

22. $r \to q$ **23.** $p \to t$ **24.** $\sim r \to s$ **25.** $k \to q$
     $\underline{q \to p}$ $\underline{\sim r \to \sim t}$ $\underline{m \to \sim s}$ $\underline{p \to \sim q}$

26. If I take math, then I will study logic.
     If I study logic, then I can think clearly.
27. If Mr. Beller is late, then he drives to work.
     If Mr. Beller is not late, then he walks to work.

In 28–34, for the given set of premises, write a valid conclusion in the form of a conditional statement, or write that no conclusion is possible.

28. $p \to q$ **29.** $p \to q$ **30.** $p \to q$ **31.** $\sim p \to r$
     $\underline{r \to p}$ $\underline{r \to q}$ $\underline{p \to r}$ $\underline{\sim r \to t}$

32. If it's period 3, then I have history.
   If I have English, then I don't have history.
33. I bleed if I get cut.
   If I get cut, then I need a bandage.
34. Ricardo buys a pumpkin if it's Halloween.
   If it's Election Day, Ricardo does not buy a pumpkin.

35. On a separate paper, copy the proof shown and provide the reasons needed for each step.

	Statements	*Reasons*
Given: $b \to c$	1. $b \to c$	1. _____
$\sim d \to \sim c$	2. $\sim d \to \sim c$	2. _____
$\sim d$	3. $\sim d$	3. _____
Prove: $\sim b$	4. $c \to d$	4. _____
	5. $b \to d$	5. _____
	6. $\sim b$	6. _____

In 36–38, write a formal proof to show that the conclusion must follow from the given set of premises. Include statements and reasons.

36. *Given:* $a \to m$ **37.** *Given:* $h \to w$ **38.** *Given:* $p \to q$
       $m \to t$ $x \to \sim w$ $r \to p$
       a x $q \to k$

Prove: t *Prove:* $\sim h$ *Prove:* $r \to k$

In 39–42, let w represent "I walk," let r represent "I run," let c represent "I collapse," and let b represent "I am out of breath."

a. Using w, r, c, b, and the proper logic connectives, express each of the given premises in symbolic form.
b. Using laws of inference, present a formal proof to show that the conclusion is true.

39. When I walk, I do not run.
   When I do not run, I do not get out of breath.
   Conclusion: When I walk, I do not get out of breath.
40. When I don't walk, I run.
   I get out of breath if I run.
   I am not out of breath.
   Conclusion: I am walking.
41. If I run, I collapse.
   If I am not out of breath, then I do not collapse.
   I run.
   Conclusion: I am out of breath.

42. If I walk, then I don't run.
I do not collapse if I don't run.
I collapse if I am out of breath.
Conclusion: If I walk, then I am not out of breath.

2-10   THE LAW OF DISJUNCTIVE INFERENCE

In the first four laws of inference presented, one or more of the premises was in the form of a conditional statement $p \rightarrow q$. In this next inference law, there are no conditional statements in the given premises.

As we watch a mystery show on television, we believe that the criminal is either the butler or the strange neighbor. We then discover a clue that rules out the neighbor. We can now infer that the butler did it! Let b represent "The butler is the criminal," and let n represent "The neighbor is the criminal." In words and in symbols, we say:

Premise $(b \lor n)$:	The butler is the criminal or the neighbor is the criminal.
Premise $(\sim n)$:	The neighbor is not the criminal.
Conclusion (b):	The butler is the criminal.

A Test of Validity by Truth Values

We start with the premises $b \lor n$ and $\sim n$, both of which must be true. Since $\sim n$ is true, it follows that n must be false. We label n as false in the first premise and $\sim n$ as true in the second premise.

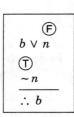

The first premise $b \lor n$ is a disjunction. We realize that b cannot be false since F $\lor$ F would give us a false premise. Since $b \lor n$ is true, we must label b true in the first premise. It follows that b is also true in our conclusion.

A Test of Validity by Truth Tables

We can also test the validity of this argument by constructing a truth table in which the given premises are treated as a single hypothesis leading to the conclusion b.

$$\text{If } (b \lor n) \text{ and } \sim n, \text{ then } b.$$
$$[(b \lor n) \land \sim n] \to b$$

b	n	b ∨ n	~n	(b ∨ n) ∧ ~n	[(b ∨ n) ∧ ~n] → b
T	T	T	F	F	T
T	F	T	T	T	T
F	T	T	F	F	T
F	F	F	T	F	T

Method 1: The premises $b \lor n$ and $\sim n$ are *both* true *only in row 2*. Therefore, we read the truth value of the conclusion b only in row 2 and discover that b is true.

Method 2: Since the argument formed, $[(b \lor n) \land \sim n] \to b$, is a tautology, we conclude that the argument is valid.

The Law of Disjunctive Inference

This fifth law of reasoning, or inference law, is called the Law of Disjunctive Inference because a disjunction is one of the premises.

● The **Law of Disjunctive Inference** states that when two given premises are true, one a disjunction and the other the negation of one of the disjuncts, it then follows that the other disjunct is true.

The Law of Disjunctive Inference is written symbolically as:

$p \lor q$	$p \lor q$
$\sim q$	$\sim p$
$\therefore p$	$\therefore q$

or

$$[(p \lor q) \land \sim q] \to p$$
$$[(p \lor q) \land \sim p] \to q$$

MODEL PROBLEMS _____

1. Write a valid conclusion for the given premises: $p \lor \sim q$
$$\sim p$$

Solution

Since $\sim p$ is true, we know that p is false. Apply the Law of Disjunctive Inference, using the premise $p \lor \sim q$, and conclude $\sim q$ is true.

Answer: $\sim q$

2. Given the following sentences:

(1) Either Peter joined the baseball team or he sings in the chorus.
(2) If he sings in the chorus, he will need a white shirt.
(3) If he needs a white shirt, then he cannot save his money.
(4) Peter saves his money.

Let *B* represent: "Peter joined the baseball team."
Let *C* represent: "He sings in the chorus."
Let *W* represent: "He needs a white shirt."
Let *M* represent: "He saves his money."

a. Using *B*, *C*, *W*, *M*, and the proper logic connectives, express each sentence in symbolic form.
b. Using laws of inference, show that Peter joined the baseball team.

Solution

a. (1) $B \lor C$ (2) $C \to W$ (3) $W \to \sim M$ (4) M

b. Many proofs are possible. One is presented here.

Statements	*Reasons*
1. $B \lor C$	1. Given.
2. $C \to W$	2. Given.
3. $W \to \sim M$	3. Given.
4. M	4. Given.
5. $C \to \sim M$	5. Chain Rule (2, 3).
6. $\sim C$	6. Modus Tollens (5, 4).
7. B	7. Law of Disjunctive Inference (1, 6).

Therefore, we have proved *B*: Peter joined the baseball team.

EXERCISES ─────────────────────────────────────

In 1–7, apply the Law of Disjunctive Inference to the given set of premises to write a valid conclusion.

1. $a \lor b$ **2.** $k \lor \sim m$ **3.** $k \lor \sim m$ **4.** $\sim p \lor q$
    $\underline{\sim a}$ $\underline{\sim k}$ $\underline{m \quad}$ $\underline{\sim q}$

5. We'll go to the movies or we'll go bowling.
We won't go to the movies.

6. Mrs. McGurn has coffee or tea at every meal.
Mrs. McGurn does not have coffee at dinner.

7. Grace studies or she does not pass her test.
Grace passes her test.

In 8–14, state whether the argument is valid or invalid.

8. $r \lor k$	**9.** $r \lor k$	**10.** $\sim p \lor t$	**11.** $\sim p \lor t$
$\sim r$	r	$\sim t$	p
$\therefore k$	$\therefore \sim k$	$\therefore p$	$\therefore t$

12. Either Abbie or Kate will win the award.
Abbie will not win the award.
Conclusion: Kate will win the award.

13. Ted hits a home run or his team does not win the game.
Ted's team does not win the game.
Conclusion: Ted did not hit a home run.

14. The stereo was defective or you were not careful in handling it.
The stereo was defective.
Conclusion: You were careful in handling the stereo.

In 15–18, write a valid conclusion for the given set of premises.

15. Either the key fits or we won't get in.
The key does not fit.
16. The shoes I buy hurt my feet or they don't look good.
I just bought shoes that look good.
17. Points are on the same line or they are noncollinear.
Points A, B, and C are not on the same line.
18. An integer is even or odd.
3 is not an even integer.

In 19–22, write a valid conclusion for the given set of premises or indicate that no conclusion is possible.

19. Paul is tall or Mort is short.
Paul is not tall.
20. Either it rains in April or flowers will not grow in May.
It did not rain in April.
21. Carl listens to the radio or he cannot do his homework.
Carl cannot do his homework.
22. In isosceles $\triangle ABC$, $AB = BC$ or $AB = AC$.
In isosceles $\triangle ABC$, $AB \neq AC$.

In 23–25, use laws of inference to prove that the conclusion is true. Include statements and reasons in your formal proof.

23. *Given:* $q \rightarrow r$
         $p \vee q$
         $\sim p$
  Prove: r

24. *Given:* $c \rightarrow b$
         $a \vee \sim b$
         c
  Prove: a

25. *Given:* $p \rightarrow (q \vee t)$
         p
         $\sim q$
  Prove: t

26. Four persons are standing on line. The following facts are true:
      Don is first or Nancy is second.
      If Nancy is second, then Chris is third.
      If Chris is third, then Pattie is fourth.
      Pattie is not fourth.

Let D represent "Don is first," let N represent "Nancy is second," let C represent "Chris is third," and let P represent "Pattie is fourth."
a. Using D, N, C, P, and proper logic connectives, express each of the four facts as sentences in symbolic form.
b. Using laws of inference, prove that Don is first.

27. Given the following statements:
      Ron diets or he spends money.
      If Ron diets, he loses weight.
      If Ron goes to restaurants, he does not lose weight.
      Ron goes to restaurants

Let D represent "Ron diets," let S represent "He spends money," let L represent "He loses weight," and let R represent "Ron goes to restaurants."
a. Using D, S, L, R, and proper connectives, express each of the statements in symbolic form.
b. Using laws of inference, prove that Ron spends money.

28. Given the following sentences:
      John will buy a stereo or a tape unit.
      If John buys a stereo, he will build a cabinet for it.
      John will quit his job if he builds a stereo cabinet.
      If John buys a tape unit, he will need cassettes.
      John does not quit his job.

Let S represent "John buys a stereo," let T represent "John buys a tape unit," let B represent "John builds a stereo cabinet," let J represent "John quits his job," and let C represent "John will need cassettes."
a. Using S, T, B, J, C, and proper connectives, express each of the sentences in symbolic form.
b. Using laws of inference, prove that John will need cassettes.

2-11   NEGATIONS AND DE MORGAN'S LAWS

In many of the arguments we have studied, we have made use of a law of inference without actually stating it by name. Compare the first form of each argument to the second (and much easier) form that we have been using.

1. By the Contrapositive, $\sim p \rightarrow q$ implies that $\sim q \rightarrow \sim(\sim p)$.
   We have been saying that $\sim p \rightarrow q$ implies that $\sim q \rightarrow p$.

2. By Modus Tollens, $[(\sim p \rightarrow q) \wedge \sim q]$ implies $\sim(\sim p)$.
   We have been saying that $[(\sim p \rightarrow q) \wedge \sim q]$ implies p.

In previous work, we have simply said that when $\sim p$ is false, it follows that p is true. We may also say that when $\sim p$ is false, then $\sim(\sim p)$ is true. These examples illustrate our sixth law of inference.

The Law of the Double Negation

● The *Law of the Double Negation* states that $\sim(\sim p)$ and p are logically equivalent statements.

Thus, given $\sim(\sim p)$ as a premise, we can conclude p. Or, given p as a premise, we can conclude $\sim(\sim p)$. Since $[\sim(\sim p) \rightarrow p]$ and $[p \rightarrow \sim(\sim p)]$, we can write the biconditional statement $\sim(\sim p) \leftrightarrow p$, which displays the logical equivalence.

The truth table below verifies that $\sim(\sim p)$ and p are logically equivalent by showing that $\sim(\sim p) \leftrightarrow p$ is a tautology.

p	$\sim p$	$\sim(\sim p)$	$\sim(\sim p) \leftrightarrow p$
T	F	T	T
F	T	F	T

In this book, the Law of Double Negation is not required as a reason in a proof. Simply follow the easier forms we have been using by writing p in place of $\sim(\sim p)$.

De Morgan's Laws

The next two laws of inference were discovered by an English mathematician named De Morgan and they bear his name. These inference rules tell how to negate a conjunction and how to negate a disjunction. Study the first example of a conjunction and its negation.

$(m \wedge s)$: Sy studies math *and* science.

$\sim(m \wedge s)$: It is *not* true that Sy studies math *and* science.

Is there a simpler form to express the second statement involving the negation? We know that Sy does not study both subjects. However, we cannot say that Sy does not study math *and* that he does not study science. It is possible that he does study one of these subjects. We can say only that Sy does not study math *or* he does not study science.

$\sim m \vee \sim s$: Sy does not study math *or* he does not study science.

Let us demonstrate that the statements $\sim(m \wedge s)$ and $\sim m \vee \sim s$ are logically equivalent by constructing a truth table.

			Col. 4			Col. 7	Col. 8
m	s	$m \wedge s$	$\sim(m \wedge s)$	$\sim m$	$\sim s$	$\sim m \vee \sim s$	$\sim(m \wedge s) \leftrightarrow [\sim m \vee \sim s]$
T	T	T	F	F	F	F	T
T	F	F	T	F	T	T	T
F	T	F	T	T	F	T	T
F	F	F	T	T	T	T	T

By examining the truth values for $\sim(m \wedge s)$ in column 4 and the truth values for $\sim m \vee \sim s$ in column 7, we see that the statements are logically equivalent. We also see that the biconditional statement $\sim(m \wedge s) \leftrightarrow [\sim m \vee \sim s]$ in column 8 is a tautology.

A similar equivalence can be found for the negation of a disjunction. Study the following example.

$(G \vee P)$: I will take Gloria *or* Patricia to the dance.

$\sim(G \vee P)$: It is *not* true that I will take Gloria *or* Patricia to the dance.

$\sim G \wedge \sim P$: I will *not* take Gloria to the dance *and* I will *not* take Patricia to the dance.

If I am not taking Gloria *or* Patricia to the dance, it follows that I am not taking Gloria *and* I am not taking Patricia. The statements $\sim(G \vee P)$ and $\sim G \wedge \sim P$ are logically equivalent. This can be verified by a truth table, which is left to the student as an exercise.

● *De Morgan's Laws* state that:

1. The negation of a conjunction of two statements is logically equivalent to the disjunction of the negation of each of the two statements.
2. The negation of a disjunction of two statements is logically equivalent to the conjunction of the negation of each of the two statements.

These laws of inference are more easily understood in symbolic form:

$$1.\ \sim(p \wedge q) \leftrightarrow (\sim p \vee \sim q)$$
$$2.\ \sim(p \vee q) \leftrightarrow (\sim p \wedge \sim q)$$

MODEL PROBLEMS

1. What is the negation of $\sim p \vee q$?

Solution

Indicate the negation of the compound sentence as: $\sim(\sim p \vee q)$. Apply De Morgan's Law by negating both $\sim p$ and q, and by changing the disjunction to a conjunction:

Answer: $p \wedge \sim q$

2. Given the statements: $(q \wedge r) \rightarrow p$
$$\sim p$$
$$r$$

Prove the conclusion: $\sim q$

Solution

Many proofs are possible. One proof is given here.

Statements	Reasons
1. $(q \wedge r) \rightarrow p$	1. Given.
2. $\sim p$	2. Given.
3. r	3. Given.
4. $\sim(q \wedge r)$	4. Modus Tollens (1, 2).
5. $\sim q \vee \sim r$	5. De Morgan's Law (4).
6. $\sim q$	6. Disjunctive Inference (5, 3).

EXERCISES

In 1–11, tell whether the two given statements are logically equivalent or not equivalent.

1. $\sim(\sim q)$
q

2. $\sim(\sim r)$
$\sim r$

3. $\sim(p \lor q)$
$\sim p \lor \sim q$

4. $\sim(p \land q)$
$\sim p \lor \sim q$

5. $\sim(\sim p \lor q)$
$p \land \sim q$

6. $\sim(p \land \sim q)$
$\sim p \land q$

7. $\sim p \lor \sim q$
$\sim(p \lor q)$

8. $\sim p \land \sim q$
$\sim(p \lor q)$

9. It is not true that Alice likes both vanilla and chocolate.
Alice does not like vanilla and Alice does not like chocolate.

10. It is not true that either $x = 5$ or $x > 5$.
$x \neq 5$ and x is not greater than 5.

11. I don't exercise and I am healthy.
It is false that either I exercise or I am not healthy.

12. Using a truth table, demonstrate De Morgan's Law for the negation of a disjunction:
$$\sim(p \lor q) \leftrightarrow (\sim p \land \sim q).$$

In 13 and 14, demonstrate that the given argument is invalid by constructing a truth table.

13. $\sim(p \land q) \leftrightarrow (\sim p \land \sim q)$

14. $\sim(p \lor q) \leftrightarrow (\sim p \lor \sim q)$

In 15–18, select the numeral preceding the statement or expression that best answers the question.

15. The statement $\sim(r \lor \sim t)$ is logically equivalent to
   (1) $\sim r \lor t$
   (2) $\sim r \land t$
   (3) $\sim r \lor \sim t$
   (4) $\sim r \land \sim t$

16. The negation of $\sim p \land k$ is
   (1) $p \lor \sim k$
   (2) $p \lor k$
   (3) $p \land \sim k$
   (4) $\sim p \lor \sim k$

17. The negation of $\sim k \lor \sim m$ is
   (1) $k \land m$
   (2) $k \lor m$
   (3) $\sim(k \lor m)$
   (4) $k \to m$

18. What is the negation of "Fred is old and Paul is not young"?
   (1) Fred is not old and Paul is young.
   (2) Fred is not old or Paul is not young.
   (3) Fred is old or Paul is young.
   (4) Fred is not old or Paul is young.

In 19–22, negate the given statement.

19. $p \wedge q$ **20.** $\sim p \vee q$ **21.** $\sim p \wedge \sim q$ **22.** $\sim (\sim p)$

In 23–26, write a valid conclusion for the given premises.

23. $\sim(\sim p \wedge t)$ **24.** $\sim(s \wedge \sim r)$ **25.** $\sim(\sim k \wedge \sim g)$

    $\underline{\sim p \qquad}$ $\underline{\sim r \qquad}$ $\underline{\sim g \qquad}$

26. It is not true that I chew gum and whistle at the same time. I am whistling.

In 27 and 28, write a formal proof to show that the conclusion must follow from the given premises.

27. *Given:* $(\sim a \wedge b) \rightarrow c$ **28.** *Given:* $t \rightarrow p$

              $\sim c$ $p \rightarrow \sim(q \wedge r)$

                b t

                                            q

    Prove: a *Prove:* $\sim r$

29. Given the following statements:

    If I had the talent and the energy, then I could be rich.

    I am not rich.

    I have the energy.

    Let T represent "I have the talent," let E represent "I have the energy," and let R represent "I am rich."

    a. Using T, E, R, and proper connectives, express each of the given statements in symbolic form.

    b. Using laws of inference, prove that "I do not have the talent."

30. Given the following statements:

    If Jay earns money and is not thrifty, then he will waste money.

    If Jay saves money, then he does not waste money.

    Jay earns money.

    Jay saves money.

    Let E represent "Jay earns money," let T represent "Jay is thrifty," let W represent "Jay wastes money," and let S represent "Jay saves money."

    a. Using E, T, W, S, and proper connectives, express each of the given statements in symbolic form.

    b. Use laws of inference to prove that "Jay is thrifty."

2-12   THE LAWS OF SIMPLIFICATION, CONJUNCTION, AND DISJUNCTIVE ADDITION

The three laws of reasoning that we will study in this section are relatively easy to understand. Tests of validity are left to the student.

The Law of Simplification

● The *Law of Simplification* states that when a single conjunctive premise is true, it follows that each of the individual conjuncts must be true.

The Law of Simplification is written symbolically as:

$$\frac{p \wedge q}{\therefore p} \qquad \frac{p \wedge q}{\therefore q} \qquad or \qquad \begin{array}{l} (p \wedge q) \rightarrow p \\ (p \wedge q) \rightarrow q \end{array}$$

For example, from the premise "Mel likes to read and to play basketball," we may conclude that "Mel likes to read." From this same premise, we may also conclude that "Mel likes to play basketball."

The Law of Conjunction

● The *Law of Conjunction* states that when two given premises are true, it follows that the conjunction of these premises is true.

The Law of Conjunction is written symbolically as:

$$\frac{\begin{array}{l} p \\ q \end{array}}{\therefore p \wedge q} \qquad or \qquad (p) \wedge (q) \rightarrow (p \wedge q)$$

For example, from the premises "$\overleftrightarrow{AB}$ is perpendicular to $\overline{CD}$" and "$\overleftrightarrow{AB}$ is a bisector of $\overline{CD}$," we may conclude that "$\overleftrightarrow{AB}$ is perpendicular to $\overline{CD}$ and $\overleftrightarrow{AB}$ is a bisector of $\overline{CD}$." In later chapters you will see that this conjunctive statement can be simplified to read "$\overleftrightarrow{AB}$ is the perpendicular bisector of $\overline{CD}$."

The Law of Disjunctive Addition

● The *Law of Disjunctive Addition* states that when a single premise is true, it follows that any disjunction that has this premise as one of its disjuncts must also be true.

The Law of Disjunctive Addition is written symbolically as:

$$\frac{p}{\therefore p \lor q} \quad or \quad \boxed{p \rightarrow (p \lor q)}$$

For example, we solve an equation and see that the premise $x = 5$ is true. We may conclude that the statement "$x = 5$ or $x > 5$" is also true. In fact, any statement may be added by a disjunction to the true statement "$x = 5$." Thus, "$x = 5$ *or* I have two left feet" is also true.

MODEL PROBLEMS _____

1. Given the statement r, which is a valid conclusion?

   (1) $r \land k$ (2) $r \lor k$ (3) $r \rightarrow k$ (4) $r \leftrightarrow k$

Solution

In all four cases, r is true but the truth value of k is not known. When k is true, all four choices are correct. However, when k is false, only choice (2) remains true. This demonstrates the Law of Disjunctive Addition, that is, we may "add" a statement k to a given statement r only by using disjunction.   *Answer:* (2) $r \lor k$

2. *Given:* $p \rightarrow t$
             $p \land q$

Prove: t

Solution

In the proof that follows, we must use the Law of Simplification to extract the single statement p from the conjunction $(p \land q)$. Then, having p by itself, we can use this premise with the conditional $(p \rightarrow t)$ to prove t.

Statements	*Reasons*
1. $p \rightarrow t$	1. Given.
2. $p \land q$	2. Given.
3. p	3. Law of Simplification (2).
4. $\therefore t$	4. Law of Detachment (1, 3).

EXERCISES

In 1–7, select the numeral preceding the statement or expression that best completes the sentence or answers the question.

1. Given "p" and "q," the Law of Conjunction leads to the conclusion
   (1) $p \vee q$ (2) $p \wedge q$ (3) $p \rightarrow q$ (4) $p \leftrightarrow q$
2. If $\sim m$ is the given premise, which is a valid conclusion?
   (1) $\sim m \wedge t$ (2) $\sim m \vee t$ (3) $\sim m \rightarrow t$ (4) m
3. Given $p \wedge r$, we can conclude
   (1) $\sim p$ (2) $\sim p \wedge r$ (3) r (4) $\sim r$
4. From the premise k, a valid conclusion is
   (1) $\sim k$ (2) $k \wedge b$ (3) $k \vee b$ (4) $\sim k \vee b$

5. Use the Law of Conjunction to write a valid conclusion for the premises "Carrie likes ice cream" and "Carrie likes cookies."
   (1) Carrie likes ice cream and cookies.
   (2) Carrie likes ice cream or cookies.
   (3) If Carrie likes ice cream, then she likes cookies.
   (4) Carrie likes ice cream if and only if she likes cookies.

6. Knowing that "13 is odd and prime," we can conclude
   (1) 13 is not odd.
   (2) If 13 is odd, it is not prime.
   (3) 13 is prime.
   (4) If 13 is prime, it is not odd.

7. Given that "Bob grows lettuce," a valid conclusion is
   (1) Bob grows lettuce or corn.
   (2) Bob grows lettuce and corn.
   (3) If Bob grows lettuce, then he grows corn.
   (4) If Bob grows lettuce, then he does not grow corn.

In 8–13, demonstrate that the argument is valid by constructing a truth table.

8. $(p \wedge q) \rightarrow p$ 9. $(p \wedge q) \rightarrow q$ 10. $p \rightarrow (p \vee q)$

11. $(r \wedge \sim t) \rightarrow r$ 12. $r \rightarrow (r \vee \sim t)$ 13. $(r \wedge \sim t) \rightarrow \sim t$

In 14–26, tell whether the argument is valid or invalid.

14. $p \rightarrow (p \wedge d)$ 15. $d \rightarrow (p \vee d)$ 16. $d \rightarrow (p \wedge d)$

17. $(\sim r \vee k) \rightarrow k$ 18. $(\sim r \wedge k) \rightarrow k$ 19. $(\sim r \wedge k) \rightarrow r$

20. $\sim (r \vee k) \rightarrow \sim k$ 21. $\sim (r \wedge k) \rightarrow \sim k$ 22. $\sim (r \vee k) \rightarrow r$

23. x is a rational number.
   Conclusion: The number x is rational or irrational.

24. Mrs. Burgdorf dresses well.
   Conclusion: Mrs. Burgdorf dresses well and wears jeans.
25. Mabel is famous for baking brownies or coffee cake.
   Conclusion: Mabel is famous for baking brownies.
26. Mr. Bancheri is a chemistry teacher.
   Conclusion: Mr. Bancheri teaches chemistry or homemaking.

In 27–29, use laws of inference to prove that the conclusion is true.

27. *Given:* $r \to t$
            $r \wedge m$
            $t \to k$

   Prove: k

28. *Given:* $b \to c$
            $c \to r$
            $p \wedge \sim r$

   Prove: $\sim b$

29. *Given:* $c \to p$
            $\sim c \to a$
            $\sim (p \vee t)$

   Prove: a

30. Given the statements:
   If Janet will go to college, then she will get a summer job.
   If Janet goes to the beach daily, she will not get a summer job.
   Janet will go to college and medical school.

   Let C represent "Janet will go to college," let S represent "She will get a summer job," let B represent "Janet goes to the beach daily," and let M represent "Janet will go to medical school."
   a. Using C, S, B, M, and proper logic connectives, express the given statements in symbolic form.
   b. Using laws of inference, prove that Janet does not go to the beach daily.

31. Given the statements:
   Jesse likes baseball or football.
   Jesse likes hockey and not baseball.

   Let B represent "Jesse likes baseball," let F represent "Jesse likes football," and let H represent "Jesse likes hockey."
   a. Using B, F, H, and proper logic connectives, express the given statements in symbolic form.
   b. Using laws of inference, prove that Jesse likes football.

2-13 PRACTICE WITH LOGIC PROOFS

The laws of reasoning that we have studied in this chapter are restated here as an aid. In an inference law, the hypothesis lets us "infer" the conclusion, as denoted by the symbol $\to$. However, when an inference law includes two statements that are normally treated as logical equivalents, we use the symbol $\leftrightarrow$ to denote that either of the two statements lets us infer the other.

Law of Inference	Symbolic Forms	
1. Law of Detachment (Modus Ponens)	$p \rightarrow q$ p $\overline{}$ $\therefore q$	$[(p \rightarrow q) \wedge p] \rightarrow q$
2. Law of the Contrapositive	$p \rightarrow q$ $\overline{}$ $\therefore \sim q \rightarrow \sim p$	$(p \rightarrow q) \leftrightarrow (\sim q \rightarrow \sim p)$
3. Law of Modus Tollens	$p \rightarrow q$ $\sim q$ $\overline{}$ $\therefore \sim p$	$[(p \rightarrow q) \wedge \sim q] \rightarrow \sim p$
4. Chain Rule (Law of the Syllogism)	$p \rightarrow q$ $q \rightarrow r$ $\overline{}$ $\therefore p \rightarrow r$	$[(p \rightarrow q) \wedge (q \rightarrow r)] \rightarrow (p \rightarrow r)$
5. Law of Disjunctive Inference	$p \vee q \quad\quad p \vee q$ $\sim p \quad\quad\quad \sim q$ $\overline{}$ $\therefore q \quad\quad\quad \therefore p$	$[(p \vee q) \wedge \sim p] \rightarrow q$ $[(p \vee q) \wedge \sim q] \rightarrow p$
6. Law of the Double Negation	$\sim(\sim p)$ $\overline{}$ $\therefore p$	$\sim(\sim p) \leftrightarrow p$
7. De Morgan's Laws	$\sim(p \wedge q) \quad\quad \sim(p \vee q)$ $\overline{}$ $\therefore \sim p \vee \sim q \quad \therefore \sim p \wedge \sim q$	$\sim(p \wedge q) \leftrightarrow (\sim p \vee \sim q)$ $\sim(p \vee q) \leftrightarrow (\sim p \wedge \sim q)$
8. Law of Simplification	$p \wedge q \quad\quad p \wedge q$ $\overline{}$ $\therefore p \quad\quad\quad \therefore q$	$(p \wedge q) \rightarrow p$ $(p \wedge q) \rightarrow q$
9. Law of Conjunction	p q $\overline{}$ $\therefore p \wedge q$	$(p) \wedge (q) \rightarrow (p \wedge q)$
10. Law of Disjunctive Addition	p $\overline{}$ $\therefore p \vee q$	$p \rightarrow (p \vee q)$

EXERCISES _____

In 1–4, assign truth values to the variables to make the premises true. Then, demonstrate that the arguments are valid by showing that true premises must lead to a true conclusion.

1. $p \rightarrow q$	**2.** $a \lor b$	**3.** $j \rightarrow i$	**4.** $d \land \sim h$
$q \rightarrow r$	$b \rightarrow \sim c$	$\sim j \rightarrow k$	$h \lor y$
p	c	$\sim k$	$y \rightarrow n$
$\therefore r$	$\therefore a$	$\therefore i$	$\therefore n$

In 5–8, let F represent "We save fuel," let E represent "There is an energy crisis," let L represent "Workers lose their jobs," and let S represent "Schools will close."

a. Using F, E, L, S, and proper connectives, express each of the given premises in symbolic form.
b. Using laws of inference, prove that the conclusion is true.

5. If we save fuel, then there is not an energy crisis.
   There is an energy crisis or workers do not lose their jobs.
   We save fuel.
   Conclusion: Workers do not lose their jobs.

6. If we do not save fuel, there is an energy crisis.
   If there is an energy crisis, schools will close.
   Schools will not close.
   Conclusion: We save fuel.

7. Workers will lose their jobs if there is an energy crisis.
   If workers lose their jobs, then we will save fuel.
   The schools will not close or there is an energy crisis.
   The schools will close.
   Conclusion: We save fuel.

8. If schools close, then workers will lose their jobs.
   If we save fuel, then workers will not lose their jobs.
   We save fuel or there is an energy crisis.
   Schools will close.
   Conclusion: There is an energy crisis.

9. Given the following sentences:
   If Karen takes wood shop, then she cannot take Spanish.
   Her parents will be upset if Karen cannot take Spanish.
   Karen takes auto shop or wood shop.
   Karen's parents are not upset.
   Let W represent "Karen takes wood shop," let S represent "Karen takes Spanish," let P represent "Karen's parents are upset," and let A represent "Karen takes auto shop."
   a. Using W, S, P, A, and proper logic connectives, express each sentence in symbolic form.
   b. Using laws of inference, prove that Karen takes auto shop.

10. Given the sentences:
    If Mr. Pappas washes his clothes, he will go to the laundromat.
    If he goes to the laundromat, he will need change.
    Mr. Pappas washes his clothes or brings them to the Dry Cleaners.
    If he brings his clothes to the Dry Cleaners, Mr. Pappas will get
        a receipt.
    Mr. Pappas does not get a receipt.

    Let W represent "Mr. Pappas washes his clothes," let L represent
    "He goes to the laundromat," let C represent "He will need change,"
    let D represent "He brings his clothes to the Dry Cleaners," and let
    R represent "Mr. Pappas will get a receipt."
    a. Using W, L, C, D, R, and proper logic connectives, express each
    sentence in symbolic form.
    b. Using laws of inference, prove that Mr. Pappas will need change.

11. Given the sentences:
    If Paul has the time, then he can iron his clothes.
    If the iron is cold, then he cannot iron his clothes.
    The iron is cold or Paul burns his finger.
    Paul has the time.

    Let T represent "Paul has the time," let I represent "He can iron
    his clothes," let C represent "The iron is cold," and let B represent
    "Paul burns his finger."
    a. Using T, I, C, B, and proper logic connectives, express each
    sentence in symbolic form.
    b. Using laws of inference, prove that Paul burns his finger.

In 12–23, present a formal proof in logic, using laws of inference to
reach the indicated conclusion.

12. $K \lor M$
     $K \to D$
     $\sim M$
     ——————
     $\therefore D$

13. $J \to T$
     $P \lor \sim T$
     $\sim P$
     ——————
     $\therefore \sim J$

14. $R \to Q$
     $S \to \sim Q$
     R
     ——————
     $\therefore \sim S$

15. $R \to K$
     $\sim(P \land K)$
     P
     ——————
     $\therefore \sim R$

16. $A \to B$
     $C \to \sim B$
     $C \lor N$
     A
     ——————
     $\therefore N$

17. $P \to Q$
     $Q \to \sim R$
     $\sim E \to R$
     P
     ——————
     $\therefore E$

18. $A \to C$
   $A \lor B$
   $\sim E \to \sim C$
   $\sim B$
   ∴ E

19. $\sim(\sim P \land T)$
   $P \to K$
   $K \to D$
   T
   ∴ D

20. $P \to A$
   $G \to \sim R$
   $A \to R$
   $G \lor H$
   P
   ∴ H

21. $A \to D$
   $D \to E$
   $A \lor B$
   $B \to C$
   $\sim C$
   ∴ E

22. $G \to M$
   $M \to \sim P$
   $\sim(\sim H \land \sim G)$
   $\sim L \to P$
   $\sim H$
   ∴ L

23. $D \to B$
   $\sim D \to P$
   $(A \land B) \to C$
   $\sim C$
   A
   ∴ P

In 24–27, present a formal proof in logic, using laws of inference to reach the indicated conclusion. Use the Law of Simplification in the proof.

24. $P \land Q$
   $Q \to R$
   $R \to F$
   ∴ F

25. $R \to P$
   $\sim R \to A$
   $\sim P \land Q$
   ∴ A

26. $A \land \sim B$
   $B \lor C$
   $C \to S$
   ∴ S

27. $P \to R$
   $\sim(\sim P \lor Q)$
   $R \to T$
   ∴ T

2-14 REVIEW EXERCISES

In 1–12, name the *inference law* that tells why the argument is valid, or state that the argument is *invalid*.

1. $p \to \sim r$
   p
   ∴ $\sim r$

2. $q \to \sim t$
   t
   ∴ $\sim q$

3. $b \to d$
   $\sim b$
   ∴ $\sim d$

4. $a \to b$
   $b \to h$
   ∴ $a \to h$

5. $m \to \sim p$
   $\sim p$
   ∴ m

6. $p \lor t$
   $\sim p$
   ∴ t

7. $\sim r \to k$
   $\sim k$
   ∴ $\sim r$

8. $\sim q \lor p$
   q
   ∴ p

9. $(r \to m) \leftrightarrow (\sim m \to \sim r)$

10. $\sim(p \lor \sim q) \leftrightarrow (\sim p \land q)$

11. $\sim(\sim p \land t) \leftrightarrow (p \land \sim t)$

12. $[(r \to d) \land \sim d] \to \sim r$

In 13–20, write a valid conclusion for the given set of premises, or indicate that no conclusion is possible.

13. If you live in the United States, then you do not live in Canada. Louise Arsena lives in the United States.

14. If you live in the United States, then you do not live in Canada.
    Pat McEntee lives in Canada.

15. If you live in the United States, then you do not live in Canada.
    Joe Fernandes does not live in Canada.

16. My mind wanders if I watch TV.
    I don't watch TV.

17. If Tyrone gets a good report card, then he can go out.
    If Tyrone fails science, then he cannot go out.

18. Mr. Cavallaro's favorite color is blue or brown.
    Mr. Cavallaro does not like the color blue.

19. If Johanna has a toothache, then she visits the dentist.
    Johanna does not have a toothache.

20. Lines that intersect at one point are not parallel lines.
    Lines k and m intersect at point P only.

In 21–28, write the numeral preceding the word or expression that best completes the statement or answers the question.

21. What is the negation of $\sim a \wedge b$?
    (1) $\sim a \vee b$ (2) $a \vee \sim b$ (3) $a \wedge \sim b$ (4) $a \wedge b$

22. What is the negation of "I run or I walk"?
    (1) I run and I walk.
    (2) I don't run or I don't walk.
    (3) I don't run and I walk.
    (4) I don't run and I don't walk.

23. If $P \to Q$ and $\sim R \to \sim Q$, which is a valid conclusion?
    (1) $P \to R$ (2) $P \to \sim R$ (3) $\sim P \to R$ (4) $\sim P \to \sim R$

24. If $a \to b$ and $g \to \sim b$, it can be shown that
    (1) $a \to g$ (2) $g \to a$ (3) $g \to \sim a$ (4) $a \to \sim b$

25. Which is logically equivalent to $\sim K \to M$?
    (1) $K \to \sim M$ (2) $M \to \sim K$ (3) $\sim M \to \sim K$ (4) $\sim M \to K$

26. Which statement is logically equivalent to "I run if I'm late"?
    (1) If I don't run, I'm not late.   (2) I'm late if I run.
    (3) If I'm not late, I don't run.   (4) If I run, I'm late.

27. Given the premises: Every line segment has a midpoint. $\overleftrightarrow{AB}$ does not have a midpoint. What conclusion can be inferred?
    (1) $\overleftrightarrow{AB}$ is not a line segment.
    (2) $\overleftrightarrow{AB}$ has a midpoint.
    (3) Some line segment has no midpoint.
    (4) There is no conclusion.

28. It is true that Brad likes eggs. It must be true that:
   (1) Brad likes bacon and eggs.
   (2) Brad likes bacon or eggs.
   (3) If Brad likes eggs, then he likes bacon.
   (4) If Brad likes eggs, then he does not like bacon.

   In 29 and 30, present a formal proof in logic, using laws of inference to reach the indicated conclusion.

29. $D \rightarrow B$
   $K \rightarrow D$
   $K \vee C$
   $\sim B$
   ∴ C

30. $(E \wedge \sim G) \rightarrow W$
   $S \rightarrow \sim W$
   E
   S
   ∴ G

31. Given the following sentences:
   I can do this proof or I cannot think clearly.
   If I know logic, then I can think clearly.
   If I don't know logic, then I need help.
   I don't need help.

   Let P represent "I can do this proof," let T represent "I can think clearly," let L represent "I know logic," and let H represent "I need help."
   a. Using P, T, L, H, and proper logic connectives, express each sentence in symbolic form.
   b. Using laws of inference, show that I can do this proof.

32. Mrs. Brown, Mrs. White, and Mrs. Gray are a teacher, a doctor, and a lawyer. Each has a horse. One horse is white, one is brown, and one is gray. From the clues, determine the occupation of each woman and the color of her horse.
   No one's name is the same as the color of her horse.
   The teacher owns a brown horse.
   Mrs. Gray is a doctor.

33. An engineer's brother married but the man who married had no brother. How is this possible?

Chapter **3**

Proving Statements in Geometry

The laws of reasoning that you studied in logic are used to reach conclusions and to prove statements. Let us return to the study of Euclidean geometry by examining the ways in which logic is used to prove statements in geometry.

3-1 INDUCTIVE REASONING

When you study science in school, you usually perform experiments in a laboratory. By doing the experiment once, twice, even many times, you hope to arrive at a conclusion that will be a true statement. This method of reasoning, in which a series of particular examples leads to a general truth, is called *inductive reasoning*.

In geometry, you can also perform experiments that may help you to discover properties of geometric figures and to determine geometric relationships. Most of these experiments involve measurements. Because all direct measurements are *approximate*, results can only be approximate. This is the first weakness in attempting to reach conclusions by inductive reasoning.

If you look at an isosceles triangle, △ABC, in which the vertex angle, ∠A, is acute, and $\overline{AB} \cong \overline{AC}$, you may observe that the base angles, ∠B and ∠C, appear to be congruent. To check your observation, measure ∠B and ∠C with a protractor. When you do, you will discover that ∠B and ∠C have the same degree measure. Therefore, ∠B ≅ ∠C.

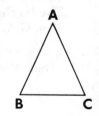

To convince yourself that this relationship is also true in other isosceles triangles, draw other isosceles triangles and measure their base angles. The figure shows isosceles △CDE in

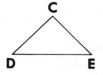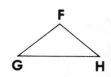

98

which the vertex angle, $\angle C$, is a right angle, and isosceles $\triangle FGH$ in which the vertex angle, $\angle F$, is obtuse. Using a protractor, you will again discover that the base angles have the same degree measure and are, therefore, congruent: $\angle D \cong \angle E$ and $\angle G \cong \angle H$.

Draw even more isosceles triangles by changing the number of degrees in the vertex angle. However, in each experiment you will find that the base angles have the same degree measure. From these experiments, you can arrive at the general conclusion that "The base angles of an isosceles triangle are congruent." This is an example of *inductive reasoning* in geometry.

Suppose a student, after examining several isosceles triangles, made the generalization that "all isosceles triangles are acute triangles." Here, a single *counterexample*, such as isosceles $\triangle CDE$ in which $\angle C$ is a right angle, is sufficient to show that the general conclusion just reached is false. When we use inductive reasoning, we must use extreme care because we are arriving at a general conclusion before we have examined every possible example. This is the second weakness in attempting to reach conclusions by inductive reasoning.

When a general conclusion is reached by inductive reasoning alone, it can at best be called probably true. Furthermore, although inductive reasoning may be a powerful aid in discovering new facts, it does not help in explaining or proving them.

EXERCISES

1. **a.** Draw three right triangles that have different sizes and shapes.
   b. In each right triangle, measure the two acute angles and find the sum of their measures.
   c. Using inductive reasoning based upon the experiments just made, write a general statement about the sum of the measures of the two acute angles of a right triangle that is probably true.

In 2–7, plan and perform a series of experiments to investigate whether each statement is *probably true* or *false*.

2. If two lines intersect, the vertical angles that are formed are congruent.
3. The sum of the degree measures of the interior angles of a triangle is 180.
4. If two parallel lines are cut by a transversal, the interior angles on the same side of the transversal are equal in measure.
5. The diagonals of a rectangle are congruent.
6. If a diagonal of a quadrilateral is drawn, it bisects the angles through whose vertices it passes.

7. The length of the line segment that joins the midpoints of two sides of a triangle is equal to one-half the length of the third side of the triangle.

8. Adam made the following statement: "For any counting number n, the expression $n^2 + n + 41$ will always be equal to some prime number." He reasoned:

   When $n = 1$, then $n^2 + n + 41 = 1 + 1 + 41 = 43$, a prime number.

   When $n = 2$, then $n^2 + n + 41 = 4 + 2 + 41 = 47$, a prime number.

   Use inductive reasoning by letting n be many different counting numbers to show that Adam's generalization is probably true, or find a counterexample to show that Adam's generalization is false.

In 9–12, state whether the conclusion drawn was justified.

9. One day, Ed drove home on Sunrise Highway and found traffic very heavy. He decided never again to drive on this highway on his way home.

10. Doris received an A on each of her first two math tests this term. She concluded that she would get A on every math test during the term.

11. From the angles shown, we conclude that if two adjacent angles are complementary, a side of one angle is probably perpendicular to a side of the other angle.

12. From the angles shown, we conclude that if two angles are adjacent, then they are probably complementary.

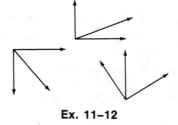

Ex. 11–12

3-2 DEFINITIONS AS BICONDITIONALS

Inductive reasoning that is based on the examination of individual cases may contain weaknesses. Before we discuss the type of reasoning normally used to prove statements in geometry, let us reexamine ways to write a definition in mathematics.

The first chapter of this book contained many definitions in geometry. For example, on page 28, the following definition was stated:

● **Definition.** A *triangle* is a polygon that has exactly three sides.

Using this definition of a triangle, we realize that:

1. The definition contains a hidden *conditional statement* and can be rewritten using the words "If . . . then" as follows:

   t: A polygon is a triangle.

   p: A polygon has exactly three sides.

   $t \rightarrow p$: If a polygon is a triangle, then it has exactly three sides.

2. In general, the converse of a true statement is not necessarily true. However, the *converse* of the conditional form of a *definition* is always true. For example, the following converse is a true statement:

   $p \rightarrow t$: If a polygon has exactly three sides, then it is a triangle.

3. When a conditional statement and its converse are both true, these statements can be combined under conjunction to write a biconditional statement. Thus, $(t \rightarrow p) \wedge (p \rightarrow t)$ is equivalent to the biconditional $(t \leftrightarrow p)$.

Therefore, since both the conditional statement and its converse are true, we can rewrite this definition as a *biconditional statement* using the words *if and only if* as follows:

● **Definition $(t \leftrightarrow p)$:** A polygon is a *triangle* if and only if it has exactly three sides.

Notice that the *if* tells what we must include, as in "exactly three sides," and the *only if* tells what we must exclude, as in "all cases that do not have exactly three sides."

This example shows us that:

● **A precise definition in mathematics is a biconditional statement.**

We have taken the time to reexamine definitions from a logical viewpoint because, as you will soon see, definitions play an important role in helping to prove statements in geometry.

We can conclude that:

1. **Every definition may be expressed as a biconditional statement $p \leftrightarrow q$.**

2. **Within every definition, there is a hidden conditional statement $p \rightarrow q$, which is true, and a converse of the conditional statement, $q \rightarrow p$, which is also true.**

MODEL PROBLEM

Given the *definition:* Supplementary angles are two angles the sum of whose degree measures is 180.

a. Write the definition in a conditional form.
b. Write the converse of the statement given as an answer in part **a.**
c. Write the biconditional form of the definition.

Solution

a. *Conditional:* If two angles are supplementary, then the sum of their degree measures is 180.

b. *Converse:* If the sum of the degree measures of two angles is 180, then the two angles are supplementary.

c. *Biconditional definition:* Two angles are supplementary *if and only if* the sum of their degree measures is 180.

EXERCISES

In 1–5: **a.** Write the given definition in a conditional form.
b. Write the converse of the statement given as an answer in part **a.**
c. Write the biconditional form of the definition.

1. An *isosceles triangle* is a triangle that has two congruent sides.
2. *Complementary angles* are two angles the sum of whose degree measures is 90.
3. An *obtuse angle* is an angle whose degree measure is greater than 90 and less than 180.
4. An *acute triangle* is a triangle that has three acute angles.
5. A *collinear set of points* is a set of points all of which lie on the same straight line.

In 6–10, write the biconditional form of the given definition.

6. A point *B* *is between A and C* if *A*, *B*, and *C* are distinct collinear points and $AB + BC = AC$.
7. *Congruent segments* are segments that have the same length.
8. The *midpoint of a line segment* is the point of that line segment that divides the segment into two congruent segments.
9. A *scalene triangle* is a triangle that has no congruent sides.
10. A *right angle* is an angle whose degree measure is 90.

3-3 DEDUCTIVE REASONING

Most proofs in geometry are very much like the proofs in logic. They are based on a series of statements that are assumed to be true, called the *premises* or the *hypotheses*.

When we use the laws of inference to link together the premises and any other true statements to arrive at a true conclusion, we are using *deductive reasoning*. Thus, proofs in logic are all examples of deductive reasoning. Note that the *conclusion* is sometimes called the *deduction* or the deduced statement.

Since definitions are true statements, we use definitions in a geometric proof. In the examples that follow, notice how the inference laws of logic are used in the proofs of geometric statements.

EXAMPLE 1.

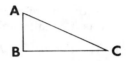

Given the premise: In $\triangle ABC$, $\overline{AB} \perp \overline{BC}$.

Prove the conclusion: $\angle ABC$ is a right angle.

In this proof, we will use the definition: Perpendicular lines are two lines that intersect to form right angles. This definition contains a hidden conditional and can be rewritten as: *If* two lines are perpendicular, *then* they intersect to form right angles.

Recall that this definition is true for perpendicular line segments as well as for perpendicular lines. Using the specific information cited above, let p represent "$\overline{AB} \perp \overline{BC}$" and let r represent "$\angle ABC$ is a right angle."

The proof is shown by the reasoning that follows:

	Statements		*Reasons*
1. p	$(\overline{AB} \perp \overline{BC}.)$		1. Given.
2. $p \rightarrow r$	(If $\overline{AB} \perp \overline{BC}$, then $\angle ABC$ is a right angle.)		2. Definition of perpendicular lines.
3. $\therefore r$	($\angle ABC$ is a right angle.)		3. Law of Detachment (1, 2).

In the logic proof above, we cited the Law of Detachment as a reason for reaching our conclusion. In a typical geometry proof, we use inference laws to deduce the conclusion but we do *not* list the inference laws among our reasons.

Let us restate this proof in the format used most often in geometry.

Given: In $\triangle ABC$, $\overline{AB} \perp \overline{BC}$.

Prove: $\angle ABC$ is a right angle.

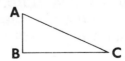

Statements	*Reasons*
1. $\overline{AB} \perp \overline{BC}$.	1. Given.
2. $\angle ABC$ is a right angle.	2. Definition of perpendicular lines.

Notice how the Law of Detachment was used in this geometry proof. By combining statement (1) with reason (2), we arrived at the conclusion written here as statement (2), just as p and $p \rightarrow r$ led us to conclude r.

EXAMPLE 2.

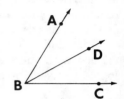

Given the premise: $\overrightarrow{BD}$ is the bisector of $\angle ABC$.

Prove the conclusion: m$\angle ABD$ = m$\angle CBD$.

In this proof, we will use two definitions. Each definition can be written as a conditional.

1. The *definition:* A bisector of an angle is a ray whose endpoint is the vertex of the angle and that divides the angle into two congruent angles.
   Conditional form: If a ray is the bisector of an angle, then the ray divides the angle into two congruent angles.

2. The *definition:* Congruent angles are angles that have the same measure.
   Conditional form: If angles are congruent, then the angles have the same measure.

Using specific information from the given problem, let P represent "$\overrightarrow{BD}$ is the bisector of $\angle ABC$," let Q represent "$\angle ABD \cong \angle CBD$," and let R represent "m$\angle ABD$ = m$\angle CBD$."

In logic, we would state this proof as follows:

Statements	*Reasons*
1. P ($\overrightarrow{BD}$ is the bisector of $\angle ABC$.)	1. Given.
2. $P \rightarrow Q$ (If $\overrightarrow{BD}$ is the bisector of $\angle ABC$, then $\angle ABD \cong \angle CBD$.)	2. Definition of angle bisector.
3. Q ($\angle ABD \cong \angle CBD$.)	3. Law of Detachment (1, 2).
4. $Q \rightarrow R$ (If $\angle ABD \cong \angle CBD$, then m$\angle ABD$ = m$\angle CBD$.)	4. Definition of congruent angles.
5. $\therefore R$ (m$\angle ABD$ = m$\angle CBD$.)	5. Law of Detachment (3, 4).

Here, we used the Law of Detachment twice: first with P and $P \rightarrow Q$ to infer Q, then again with Q and $Q \rightarrow R$ to infer R.

Let us restate this proof in the format used most often in geometry.

Given: $\overrightarrow{BD}$ is the bisector of $\angle ABC$.

Prove: $m\angle ABD = m\angle CBD$.

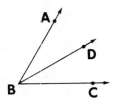

Statements	*Reasons*
1. $\overrightarrow{BD}$ is the bisector of $\angle ABC$.	1. Given.
2. $\angle ABD \cong \angle CBD$.	2. Definition of angle bisector.
3. $m\angle ABD = m\angle CBD$.	3. Definition of congruent angles.

Again, notice that the Law of Detachment was not cited in the reasons of this geometry proof. However, the diagram in the box below shows how this inference law was used.

Statement (n) —— and
Statement $(n + 1)$ ←——— Reason $(n + 1)$
                      infer

Thus, we see that:

From statement (1) and reason (2), we infer statement (2), just as from P and $(P \rightarrow Q)$, we infer Q.

From statement (2) and reason (3), we infer statement (3), just as from Q and $(Q \rightarrow R)$, we infer R.

Notice that the given premises and true statements used in this argument, namely P, $P \rightarrow Q$, and $Q \rightarrow R$, would allow us to use the Chain Rule in a logic proof by inferring the statement $P \rightarrow R$. A geometry proof is essentially a chain of reasoning in which we link the given premises and true statements to arrive at the conclusion.

These examples allow us to observe the following:

1. The laws of inference are *listed* as reasons in a **logic proof**.

2. The laws of inference are *not listed* as reasons in a **geometry proof**, but these inference laws are used to develop the proof.

MODEL PROBLEMS

1. *Given:* In $\triangle DEF$, $\overline{DE} \cong \overline{DF}$.

   a. State the given premise.

   b. After identifying a word or phrase from the given premise whose definition may be used in a proof, write the definition in a conditional form.

   c. From the given premise and the definition involved, draw a specific conclusion.

Solution

   a. The given premise states that two segments are congruent: $\overline{DE} \cong \overline{DF}$. *Ans.*

   b. The definition of congruent segments, in a conditional form, is: *If two segments are congruent, then they have the same length.* *Ans.*

   c. The given *premise* states: $\overline{DE} \cong \overline{DF}$.

     The *definition* can be rewritten to include the specific information in the statement: If $\overline{DE} \cong \overline{DF}$, then $DE = DF$.

     By the Law of Detachment, the specific conclusion is: $DE = DF$. *Ans.*

2. *Given:* M is the midpoint of $\overline{AB}$.
   Prove: $AM = MB$.

   Definition: The midpoint of a line segment is the point that divides the segment into two congruent segments.

   Definition: Congruent segments are segments that have the same length.

   a. Let M represent "M is the midpoint of $\overline{AB}$."
     Let C represent "$\overline{AM} \cong \overline{MB}$."
     Let E represent "$AM = MB$."
     Using M, C, E, conditional forms of the definitions, and laws of inference, write a logic proof to show that $AM = MB$.

   b. Using the given premise and definitions, write a geometry proof to show that $AM = MB$.

Solution

   a. The conditional form of the first definition is given as: If a point is a midpoint of a line segment, then the point divides the segment into two congruent segments. Using M as the midpoint of $\overline{AB}$, we can write the specific conditional:

$M \to C$: If M is the midpoint of $\overline{AB}$, then $\overline{AM} \cong \overline{MB}$.

The conditional form of the second definition is given as: If segments are congruent, then these segments have the same length. Using the segments $\overline{AM}$ and $\overline{MB}$ and their lengths, we can write:

$C \to E$: If $\overline{AM} \cong \overline{MB}$, then $AM = MB$.

The given premise is M. The conditional forms of the definitions are $M \to C$ and $C \to E$. The *logic proof* now follows:

	Statements	*Reasons*
1. M	(M is the midpoint of $\overline{AB}$.)	1. Given.
2. $M \to C$	(If M is the midpoint of $\overline{AB}$, then $\overline{AM} \cong \overline{MB}$.)	2. Definition of midpoint of a segment.
3. C	($\overline{AM} \cong \overline{MB}$.)	3. Law of Detachment (1, 2).
4. $C \to E$	(If $\overline{AM} \cong \overline{MB}$, then $AM = MB$.)	4. Definition of congruent segments.
5. $\therefore E$	($AM = MB$.)	5. Law of Detachment (3, 4).

b. The *geometry proof* can be stated as follows:

Statements	*Reasons*
1. M is the midpoint of $\overline{AB}$.	1. Given.
2. $\overline{AM} \cong \overline{MB}$.	2. Definition of midpoint of a segment.
3. $AM = MB$.	3. Definition of congruent segments.

Note. Compare the use of the Law of Detachment in this geometry proof with the logic proof presented in part **a**. In the geometry proof, we observe:

From statement (1) and reason (2), we infer statement (2), just as from M and $M \to C$, we infer C.

From statement (2) and reason (3), we infer statement (3), just as from C and $C \to E$, we infer E.

EXERCISES

In 1–10: **a.** State the given premise. **b.** After identifying a word or phrase from the given premise whose definition may be used in a proof, write the definition in a conditional form. **c.** From the premise and the definition involved, draw a specific conclusion.

1.

Given: ∠1 and ∠2 are
complementary angles.

2.

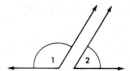

Given: ∠1 and ∠2 are
supplementary angles.

3.

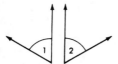

Given: ∠1 ≅ ∠2.

4.

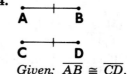

Given: $\overline{AB} \cong \overline{CD}$.

5.

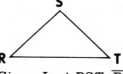

Given: In △*RST*, $\overline{RS} \perp \overline{ST}$.

6.

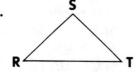

Given: In △*RST*, ∠*R* ≅ ∠*T*.

7.

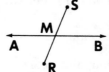

Given: ∠*ABC* is a right
angle.

8.

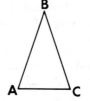

Given: $\overleftrightarrow{AB}$ bisects $\overline{RS}$
at point *M*.

9.

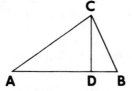

Given: In △*ABC*, $\overline{CD}$ is the
altitude to $\overline{AB}$.

10.

Given: $\overline{AB} \cong \overline{BC}$.

11. *Given:* In $\triangle ABC$, M is the midpoint of $\overline{AB}$.

Prove: $\overline{AM} \cong \overline{MB}$.

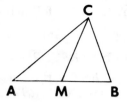

a. Let P represent "M is the midpoint of $\overline{AB}$."
Let Q represent "$\overline{AM} \cong \overline{MB}$."

On your paper, copy the following *logic proof*, filling in all missing statements in word form and all missing reasons.

Statements	Reasons
1. P (M is the midpoint of $\overline{AB}$.)	1. _____
2. $P \rightarrow Q$ (_____)	2. Definition of midpoint of a segment.
3. $\therefore Q$ (_____)	3. _____

b. Copy the following *geometry proof*, filling in the missing statement and the missing reason.

Statements	Reasons
1. M is the midpoint of $\overline{AB}$.	1. _____
2. _____	2. Definition of midpoint of a segment.

12. *Given:* $\triangle RST$.
$\overline{RS} \cong \overline{ST}$.

Prove: $\angle RST$ is the vertex angle of $\triangle RST$.

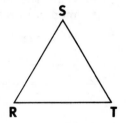

a. Let P represent "$\overline{RS} \cong \overline{ST}$."
Let Q represent "$\angle RST$ is the vertex angle of $\triangle RST$."

Copy the following *logic proof*, filling in all missing statements in word form and all missing reasons.

Statements	Reasons
1. P ($\overline{RS} \cong \overline{ST}$.)	1. _____
2. $P \rightarrow Q$ (_____)	2. Definition of vertex angle of an isosceles triangle.
3. $\therefore Q$ (_____)	3. _____

b. Copy the following *geometry proof*, filling in the missing reasons.

Statements	Reasons
1. In △RST, $\overline{RS} \cong \overline{ST}$.	1. _____
2. ∠RST is the vertex angle of isosceles △RST.	2. _____

13. *Given:* In △ABC, $\overrightarrow{CE}$ bisects ∠ACB.

Prove: m∠ACE = m∠BCE.

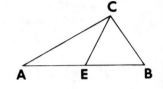

a. Let P represent "$\overrightarrow{CE}$ bisects ∠ACB."
Let Q represent "∠$ACE \cong$ ∠BCE."
Let R represent "m∠ACE = m∠BCE."

Copy the following *logic proof*, filling in all missing statements in word form and all missing reasons.

Statements		Reasons
1. P	($\overrightarrow{CE}$ bisects ∠ACB.)	1. _____
2. $P \rightarrow Q$	(_____)	2. Definition of angle bisector.
3. Q	(_____)	3. _____
4. $Q \rightarrow R$	(_____)	4. Definition of congruent angles.
5. ∴ R	(_____)	5. _____

b. Copy the following *geometry proof*, filling in all missing statements. In reasons 2 and 3, write the definitions as biconditionals.

Statements	Reasons
1. _____	1. Given.
2. _____	2. Definition of angle bisector.
3. _____	3. Definition of congruent angles.

14. *Given:* △ABC is an equilateral triangle.

Prove: $AB = BC = CA$.

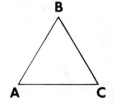

a. Let E represent "△ABC is equilateral."
Let S represent "$\overline{AB} \cong \overline{BC} \cong \overline{CA}$."
Let L represent "$AB = BC = CA$.

Copy the following *logic proof*, filling in all missing statements in word form and all missing reasons.

Statements	*Reasons*
1. *E* (△*ABC* is equilateral.)	1. _____
2. *E* → *S* (_____)	2. Definition of equilateral triangle.
3. *S* (_____)	3. _____
4. *S* → *L* (_____)	4. Definition of congruent segments.
5. ∴ *L* (_____)	5. _____

b. Using the given premise and definitions, write a *geometry proof* to show that *AB* = *BC* = *CA*.

15. *Given:* ∠*ADB* and ∠*BDC* are supplementary angles.

Prove: m∠*ADB* + m∠*BDC* = 180.

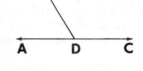

a. Let *S* represent "∠*ADB* and ∠*BDC* are supplementary angles."

Let *M* represent "m∠*ADB* + m∠*BDC* = 180."

Write a *logic proof* to show that m∠*ADB* + m∠*BDC* = 180.

b. Write a *geometry proof* to show that m∠*ADB* + m∠*BDC* = 180.

16. *Given:* In △*ABC*, $\overline{CD}$ is the altitude to $\overline{AB}$.

Prove: m∠*CDA* = 90.

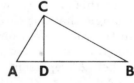

Definition: The altitude of a triangle is a line segment drawn from any vertex of the triangle, perpendicular to and ending in the opposite side.

Definition: Perpendicular segments are two segments that intersect to form right angles.

Definition: A right angle is an angle whose degree measure is 90.

a. Let *A* represent "$\overline{CD}$ is the altitude to $\overline{AB}$."
Let *P* represent "$\overline{CD}$ is perpendicular to $\overline{AB}$."
Let *R* represent "∠*CDA* is a right angle."
Let *M* represent "m∠*CDA* = 90."

Using *A*, *P*, *R*, *M*, conditional forms of the definitions, and laws of inference, write a *logic proof* to show that m∠*CDA* = 90.

b. Using the given premise and definitions, write a *geometry proof* to show that m∠*CDA* = 90.

3-4 DIRECT PROOF AND INDIRECT PROOF

There are basically two types of proof, called *direct proof* and *indirect proof*. In both types of proof, we use deductive reasoning to prove a valid conclusion based upon the given premises. Let us see how these two types of proof differ.

Direct Proof

All proofs seen in the previous section are examples of direct proofs. In a **direct proof**, we use laws of inference to link together true premises and statements that lead *directly* to a true conclusion.

The following is an example of a direct proof.

Given: △*ABC* is equiangular.

Prove: ∠*A* ≅ ∠*B* ≅ ∠*C*.

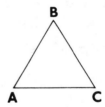

In this proof, we will use the definition: An equiangular triangle is a triangle that has three congruent angles. We can restate this definition in the conditional form: If a triangle is equiangular, then the triangle has three congruent angles.

Let **E** represent "△*ABC* is equiangular," and let **C** represent "∠*A* ≅ ∠*B* ≅ ∠*C*." Both the logic form and the geometric form of a direct proof follow.

Direct Proof in Logic

Statements		*Reasons*
1. **E**	(△*ABC* is equiangular.)	1. Given.
2. **E** → **C**	(If △*ABC* is equiangular, then ∠*A* ≅ ∠*B* ≅ ∠*C*.)	2. Definition of equiangular triangle.
3. ∴ **C**	(∠*A* ≅ ∠*B* ≅ ∠*C*.)	3. Law of Detachment (1, 2).

Direct Proof in Geometry

Statements	*Reasons*
1. $\triangle ABC$ is equiangular.	1. Given.
2. $\angle A \cong \angle B \cong \angle C.$	2. Definition of equiangular triangle.

Indirect Proof

When a statement is false, then the negation of this statement must be true. In an indirect proof, we use laws of inference to prove that a statement is false, leading us *indirectly* to the conclusion that the negation of the statement must be true.

In an **indirect proof**, the following steps are taken to show that the conclusion q is true:

1. Start with the true premise p.
2. Assume that the negation of the conclusion q is true, that is, assume that $\sim q$ is true.
3. Use p and $\sim q$ and the laws of inference to prove $\sim p$.
4. But, $\sim p$ is false.
5. From this contradiction, it follows that the assumption $\sim q$ is false, and we conclude that q is true.

Let us use the same premise and conclusion just stated for the direct proof. However, this time we will reach the conclusion by means of an indirect proof.

Given: $\triangle ABC$ is equiangular.

Prove: $\angle A \cong \angle B \cong \angle C.$

We again let E represent "$\triangle ABC$ is equiangular," and let C represent "$\angle A \cong \angle B \cong \angle C.$" In the proof, we must assume that the negation of the conclusion C is true, namely, that $\sim C$ is true.

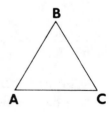

Indirect Proof in Logic

Statements		*Reasons*
1. E	($\triangle ABC$ is equiangular.)	1. Given.
2. $\sim C$	(It is *not* the case that $\angle A \cong \angle B \cong \angle C.$)	2. Assumed.
3. $E \rightarrow C$	(If $\triangle ABC$ is equiangular, then $\angle A \cong \angle B \cong \angle C.$)	3. Definition of equiangular triangle.
4. $\sim E$	($\triangle ABC$ is *not* equiangular.)	4. Modus Tollens (2, 3).

5. $E \wedge \sim E$ ($\triangle ABC$ is equiangular and $\triangle ABC$ is *not* equiangular.) | 5. Conjunction (1, 4).

6. $\therefore C$ (It is the case that $\angle A \cong \angle B \cong \angle C$.) | 6. Contradiction in (5), $\therefore$ assumption in (2) is false.

Indirect Proof in Geometry

Statements	*Reasons*
1. $\triangle ABC$ is equiangular.	1. Given.
2. It is *not* the case that $\angle A \cong \angle B \cong \angle C$.	2. Assumption.
3. $\triangle ABC$ is *not* equiangular.	3. If three angles of a triangle are not congruent, then the triangle is not equiangular. (Contrapositive of the conditional form of the definition of equiangular triangle)
4. $\angle A \cong \angle B \cong \angle C$.	4. Contradiction in (1) and (3). $\therefore$ assumption in (2) is false.

In both proofs, we assume that the conclusion C is false by writing $\sim C$ as an assumption. From this assumption that the three angles of the triangle are not congruent, we deduce that the triangle is not equiangular (a contradiction to the given premise). Thus, the assumption $\sim C$ must be false and its negation, which is the conclusion C, must be true.

Note. To learn how an indirect proof works, it will be necessary for you to prove some simple statements indirectly in this section. Thereafter, you should follow the general guidelines for proof, which are stated below.

KEEP IN MIND _____
1. Wherever possible, a statement in geometry should be proved by means of a direct proof.
2. An indirect proof should be used only when there is no clear way to prove the statement directly.

MODEL PROBLEMS _____

In 1 and 2, information is given regarding a proof. In each case:

a. Write the statement that is to be proved.
b. Write the assumption that must appear in an indirect proof of the statement.

1. *Given:* ∠1 ≅ ∠2.
  ∠2 ≅ ∠3.

  Prove: ∠1 ≅ ∠3.

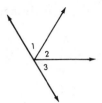

Solution

a. The conclusion to be proved is: ∠1 ≅ ∠3.

b. In an indirect proof, we must assume the negation of the conclusion, namely: ∠1 is ***not*** congruent to ∠3, or ∠1 ≇ ∠3.

2. *Given:* In △*ABC*, $\overline{AB}$ ≅ $\overline{BC}$ and $\overline{BD}$ is the altitude to $\overline{AC}$.

  Prove: $\overline{BD}$ ⊥ $\overline{AC}$ and *AD* = *DC*.

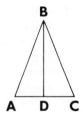

Solution

a. The conclusion to be proved consists of two statements: $\overline{BD}$ ⊥ $\overline{AC}$ and *AD* = *DC*.

b. In an indirect proof, we must assume the negation of the conclusion. Since there are two statements in the conclusion, think of the negation in terms of De Morgan's Law. We assume:

  ~(*P* ∧ *Q*): It is ***not*** the case that $\overline{BD}$ ⊥ $\overline{AC}$ ***and*** *AD* = *DC*, or

  ~*P* ∨ ~*Q*: $\overline{BD}$ is ***not*** ⊥ to $\overline{AC}$ ***or*** *AD* ≠ *DC*.

EXERCISES _____

In 1–8, information is given regarding a proof. In each case **(a)** write the statement that is to be proved and **(b)** write the assumption that must appear in an indirect proof of the statement.

1. *Given:* In △*RST*, ∠*R* ≅ ∠*T*.

  Prove: *RS* = *ST*.

2. *Given:* Points A, B, and C are collinear;
  B is between A and C.

Prove: $AB + BC = AC$.

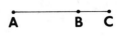

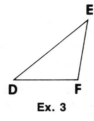

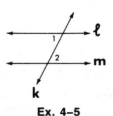

Ex. 3   Ex. 4–5

3. *Given:* $\triangle DEF$.
  Prove: $m\angle D + m\angle E + m\angle F = 180$.
4. *Given:* Parallel lines l and m are cut by transversal k.
  Prove: $\angle 1 \cong \angle 2$.
5. *Given:* Lines l and m are cut by transversal k; $\angle 1 \cong \angle 2$.
  Prove: $l \parallel m$.

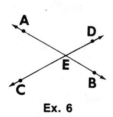

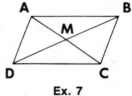

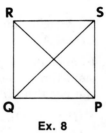

Ex. 6   Ex. 7   Ex. 8

6. *Given:* $\overleftrightarrow{AB}$ and $\overleftrightarrow{CD}$ intersect at E.
  Prove: $\angle AED \cong \angle BEC$ and $\angle AEC \cong \angle BED$.
7. *Given:* In parallelogram $ABCD$, diagonals $\overline{AC}$ and $\overline{BD}$ intersect
  at M.
  Prove: $AM = MC$ and $DM = MB$.
8. *Given:* Square $PQRS$ with diagonals $\overline{RP}$ and $\overline{QS}$.
  Prove: $\overline{RP} \cong \overline{QS}$ and $\overline{RP} \perp \overline{QS}$.

In 9–12, use the following information in the proof:

Given: $\triangle ABC$ where $\overrightarrow{BA} \perp \overrightarrow{BC}$.
Prove: $\angle ABC$ is a right angle.
Definition: Two rays with a common endpoint are
  perpendicular if and only if they form a right angle.

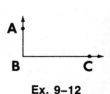

Ex. 9–12

In Exercises 9 and 11, let P represent "In $\angle ABC$, $\overrightarrow{BA} \perp \overrightarrow{BC}$," and let R represent "$\angle ABC$ is a right angle."

9. Given $\angle ABC$ where $\overrightarrow{BA} \perp \overrightarrow{BC}$, a *direct proof in logic* can be stated:

In $\angle ABC$, $\overrightarrow{BA} \perp \overrightarrow{BC}$.

If $\overrightarrow{BA} \perp \overrightarrow{BC}$, then $\angle ABC$ is a right angle.

Therefore, $\angle ABC$ is a right angle.

Write this direct proof in logic, listing statements in symbolic form and including reasons for the statements.

10. Given $\angle ABC$ where $\overrightarrow{BA} \perp \overrightarrow{BC}$, write a *direct proof in geometry* to show that $\angle ABC$ is a right angle. Include statements and reasons.

11. Given $\angle ABC$ where $\overrightarrow{BA} \perp \overrightarrow{BC}$, an *indirect proof in logic* can be stated:

Assume that $\angle ABC$ is *not* a right angle.

If $\overrightarrow{BA} \perp \overrightarrow{BC}$, then $\angle ABC$ is a right angle.

Thus, $\overrightarrow{BA}$ is not $\perp \overrightarrow{BC}$.

But in $\angle ABC$, $\overrightarrow{BA} \perp \overrightarrow{BC}$.

We see that $\overrightarrow{BA} \perp \overrightarrow{BC}$ and $\overrightarrow{BA}$ is not $\perp \overrightarrow{BC}$.

Therefore, we conclude $\angle ABC$ is a right angle.

Write this indirect proof in logic, listing statements in symbolic form and including reasons for the statements.

12. Given $\angle ABC$ where $\overrightarrow{BA} \perp \overrightarrow{BC}$, copy the following *indirect proof in geometry* and supply the missing reasons that tell why $\angle ABC$ is a right angle.

Statements	*Reasons*
1. In $\angle ABC$, $\overrightarrow{BA} \perp \overrightarrow{BC}$.	1. _____
2. Let $\angle ABC$ *not* be a right angle.	2. _____
3. Then $\overrightarrow{BA}$ is not $\perp \overrightarrow{BC}$.	3. _____
4. Therefore, $\angle ABC$ is a right angle.	4. _____

3-5 UNDERSTANDING THE NATURE OF A POSTULATIONAL SYSTEM

In reasoning, you saw that the premises of an argument must be taken as true statements in order to reach a conclusion that we are convinced is also true. In Chapter 1, we listed both undefined terms and definitions that we accept as being true.

At times, statements are made in geometry that are neither undefined terms nor definitions, and yet we know these are true statements. There are two such types of statements in geometry: one is called a *postulate* or an *axiom*, and the other is called a *theorem*.

A statement whose truth is assumed without any proof whatsoever is called a *postulate* or an *axiom*. Some mathematicians use the term *axiom* for a *general statement* whose truth is assumed without proof, and the term *postulate* for a *geometric statement* whose truth is assumed without proof. We will use the term *postulate* for both types of assumptions.

● **Definition.** A *postulate* is a statement whose truth is accepted without proof.

In a postulational system, the *undefined terms*, the *defined terms*, and the *postulates* are the seeds from which the tree of knowledge in the subject grows. They, together with the laws of reasoning, become the instruments with which we prove the truth of new statements, called *theorems*.

● **Definition.** A *theorem* is a statement that is proved by **deductive reasoning**.

Postulational thinking, which is the instrument used to make deductions in geometry, is a powerful technique for several reasons:

1. It makes it possible to arrive at a conclusion in situations where observation and measurement are not practical or possible.
2. Observation and measurement may help us to discover a fact, but they never explain the reason for the truth of the fact. Postulational thinking explains why the reasoning used in arriving at a conclusion is valid or invalid.
3. In a postulational system, the entire body of knowledge known as geometry can be discovered and explained by continually proving new theorems. These theorems are proved by applying the laws of reasoning to *undefined terms* and statements that are known to be true, namely, *definitions*, *postulates*, and *previously proven theorems*.

EXERCISES _____

In 1–4, answer *true* or *false*.

1. In a postulational system, all terms are defined.
2. A postulate is a true statement accepted without proof.
3. A theorem is a true statement that must be proved.
4. Every statement in geometry is a postulate or a definition.

5. Name the elements in a postulational system that are used to prove a new theorem.

3-6 THE FIRST POSTULATES USED IN PROVING CONCLUSIONS

You have seen that deductive reasoning is based upon the use of undefined terms, defined terms, and postulates. Now, you are going to examine some of these postulates and learn how to use them in deductive reasoning.

When we state the relation "a is equal to b," symbolized by "$a = b$," we mean that the symbol a and the symbol b are two different names for the same element of a set, usually a number. For example,

1. When we write $RS = LM$, we mean that the line segments, $\overline{RS}$ and $\overline{LM}$, have the same length.
2. When we write $m\angle A = m\angle B$, we mean that $\angle A$ and $\angle B$ contain the same number of degrees.

The following three *equality postulates* are also referred to as the *properties of equality*.

The Reflexive Property of Equality

$$a = a$$

This property is stated in words as follows:

● **POSTULATE 1. A quantity is equal to itself.**

EXAMPLES. In $\triangle ABC$, observe that:

1. The length of a segment is equal to itself:
    $$AB = AB \quad BC = BC \quad AC = AC$$
2. The measure of an angle is equal to itself:
    $$m\angle A = m\angle A \quad m\angle B = m\angle B \quad m\angle C = m\angle C$$

The Symmetric Property of Equality

If $a = b$, then $b = a$.

This property is stated in words as follows:

● **POSTULATE 2. An equality may be expressed in either order.**

EXAMPLES.

If $AB = CD$, then $CD = AB$.

If $m\angle R = m\angle S$, then $m\angle S = m\angle R$.

The Transitive Property of Equality

If $a = b$ and $b = c$, then $a = c$.

This property states that if a and b have the same value, and b and c have the same value, it follows that a and c have the same value. This property is stated in words as follows:

● **POSTULATE 3. If quantities are equal to the same quantity, they are equal to each other.**

Let us now see how these postulates of equality can be used in deductive reasoning.

Proofs With Postulates of Equality

From this point on, proofs will be presented in only one format. To arrange a geometry proof formally in two columns, we will:

1. state the premises or the hypothesis, which is also called the *given*, because the premises are the given facts.
2. state the conclusion, which is also called the *prove*, because the conclusion contains what is to be proved. (Note that the *drawing of a figure*, properly lettered, helps in stating the *given* premises and the conclusion that we are to *prove*.)
3. present the *proof*, the deductive reasoning, which is the series of logical arguments used in the demonstration. Each step in the proof should consist of a *statement* in one column and its *reason* in the other column. A reason may be the *given*, a *definition*, a *postulate*, or, as you will see later, a *previously proved theorem*.

EXAMPLE 1.

Given: $m\angle x = 40.$
$\qquad m\angle y = 40.$

Prove: $m\angle x = m\angle y.$

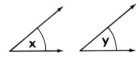

Statements	*Reasons*
1. $m\angle x = 40.$	1. Given.
2. $m\angle y = 40.$	2. Given.
3. $40 = m\angle y.$	3. The symmetric property of equality. (*Or:* An equality may be written in either order.)
4. $m\angle x = m\angle y.$	4. The transitive property of equality. (*Or:* If quantities are equal to the same quantity, they are equal to each other.)

Note. In the future, we will abbreviate the proof by eliminating step 3 and reason 3, the step that makes use of the symmetric property of equality. After presenting steps 1 and 2, we will immediately deduce the conclusion that $m\angle x = m\angle y$.

EXAMPLE 2.

Given: $AB = LM.$
$\quad\quad\quad CD = RS.$
$\quad\quad\quad LM = RS.$

A•————•B   L•————•M

C•————•D   R•————•S

Prove: $AB = CD.$

Statements	*Reasons*
1. $AB = LM.$	1. Given.
2. $LM = RS.$	2. Given.
3. $AB = RS.$	3. The transitive property of equality.
4. $CD = RS.$	4. Given.
5. $AB = CD.$	5. The transitive property of equality.

Notice that, in Example 2, we proved an illustration of the statement "If quantities are equal to equal quantities, they are equal to each other." In the future, we will feel free to use this statement, which is an expanded version of the transitive property of equality, as a reason in a proof.

EXERCISES _____

In 1–3, **(a)** state the postulate that can be used to show that the conclusion is valid and **(b)** write a formal proof.

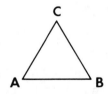

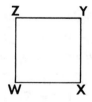

1. *Given:*
$\quad CD = 2$ inches.
$\quad XY = 2$ inches.

$\quad$ *Prove:*
$\quad\quad CD = XY.$

2. *Given:*
$\quad m\angle A = m\angle B.$
$\quad m\angle C = m\angle B.$

$\quad$ *Prove:*
$\quad\quad m\angle A = m\angle C.$

3. *Given:*
$\quad WZ = XY.$
$\quad ZY = WX.$
$\quad WZ = ZY.$

$\quad$ *Prove:*
$\quad\quad XY = WX.$

3-7 EQUIVALENCE RELATIONS

In the reflexive, symmetric, and transitive properties of equality, our examples indicated that the relation *is equal to* acted upon some set of numbers such as lengths of line segments or measures of angles. To discuss any relation R, we must clearly define a set S upon whose elements this relation will act. For example,

Let S = the set of real numbers (since these numbers are used to describe the lengths of line segments and the measures of angles).

Let R = the relation *is equal to* (symbolized by =).

Then, for the set of real numbers whose elements are represented as a, b, and c, and for the relation =, the following properties hold:

1. Reflexive property: $a = a$.
2. Symmetric property: If $a = b$, then $b = a$.
3. Transitive property: If $a = b$ and $b = c$, then $a = c$.

Because all three properties are true, we say that the relation = is an **equivalence relation** on the set of real numbers. To restate this, we say:

Equality of real numbers is an equivalence relation.

Using more general terms, we now define an equivalence relation:

● **Definition.** A relation R is an **equivalence relation** on some set S when the relation R is reflexive, symmetric, and transitive.

Let us investigate other relations to see if they form equivalence relations on sets in geometry.

Congruence of Line Segments

Let S = the set of all line segments and let R = the relation *is congruent to*, symbolized by $\cong$.

Since $\overline{AB} \cong \overline{CD}$ is equivalent to $AB = CD$, and $\overline{CD} \cong \overline{EF}$ is equivalent to $CD = EF$, it follows that the congruence of line segments has the same three properties as the equality of numbers:

1. Reflexive property: $\overline{AB} \cong \overline{AB}$.
2. Symmetric property: If $\overline{AB} \cong \overline{CD}$, then $\overline{CD} \cong \overline{AB}$.
3. Transitive property: If $\overline{AB} \cong \overline{CD}$, and $\overline{CD} \cong \overline{EF}$, then $\overline{AB} \cong \overline{EF}$.

Hence, congruence of line segments is an equivalence relation.

Congruence of Angles

Let S = the set of all angles and let R = the relation *is congruent to*, symbolized by $\cong$.

Since $\angle ABC \cong \angle DEF$ is equivalent to $m\angle ABC = \angle DEF$, and $\angle DEF \cong \angle XYZ$ is equivalent to $m\angle DEF = m\angle XYZ$, it follows that the congruence of angles has the same three properties as the equality of numbers:

1. Reflexive property: $\angle ABC \cong \angle ABC$.
2. Symmetric property: If $\angle ABC \cong \angle DEF$, then $\angle DEF \cong \angle ABC$.
3. Transitive property: If $\angle ABC \cong \angle DEF$, and $\angle DEF \cong \angle XYZ$, then $\angle ABC \cong \angle XYZ$.

Hence, congruence of angles is an equivalence relation.

Perpendicularity of Lines

Let S = the set of all lines and let R = the relation *is perpendicular to*, symbolized by $\perp$. Let a, b, and c represent any lines.

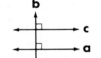

1. Reflexive property: $a \perp a$.   (False)
   In the figure, line a is *not* perpendicular to itself.

2. Symmetric property: If $a \perp b$, then $b \perp a$.   (True)
   The figure shows that this property holds.

3. Transitive property: If $a \perp b$ and $b \perp c$, then $a \perp c$.   (False)
   Although the hypothesis that $a \perp b$ and $b \perp c$ is true, the figure shows that a is *not* perpendicular to c.

Hence, perpendicularity of lines is *not* an equivalence relation.

At other points in this book, as we begin to work with a new relation, we will test to see if an equivalence relation exists.

EXERCISES _____

In 1–8, name the property that justifies the statement.

1. $\overline{AC} \cong \overline{AC}$.
2. If $\angle RST \cong \angle XYZ$, then $\angle XYZ \cong \angle RST$.
3. $\angle ABC \cong \angle ABC$.
4. If $\overline{LM} \cong \overline{XY}$, then $\overline{XY} \cong \overline{LM}$.
5. If $\overline{AB} \cong \overline{CD}$, and $\overline{CD} \cong \overline{ST}$, then $\overline{AB} \cong \overline{ST}$.
6. If $\angle XYZ \cong \angle RST$, and $\angle RST \cong \angle ABC$, then $\angle XYZ \cong \angle ABC$.

7. If $\overleftrightarrow{AB} \perp \overleftrightarrow{CD}$, then $\overleftrightarrow{CD} \perp \overleftrightarrow{AB}$.

8. If $AB = CD$ and $CD = EF$, then $AB = EF$.

In 9–15, tell which of the three properties of an equivalence relation are true for the given relation and the set given in parentheses.

9. is greater than (for natural numbers)
10. $\leq$ (for integers)
11. is a factor of (for natural numbers)
12. $\neq$ (for real numbers)
13. is the father of (for people)
14. is older than (for people)
15. lives in the same house as (for people)

16. Let the set S = a set of statements (namely, p, q, and r). Let the relation R = the relation *implies*, symbolized by $\rightarrow$. Notice that this relation is the one used to write conditional statements in logic.

    a. Is this relation reflexive, that is, will the statements $p \rightarrow p$, $q \rightarrow q$, and $r \rightarrow r$ always be true? Why?
    b. Is this relation symmetric, that is, if $p \rightarrow q$, does it follow that $q \rightarrow p$? Why?
    c. Is this relation transitive, that is, if $p \rightarrow q$ and $q \rightarrow r$, does it follow that $p \rightarrow r$? Why?
    d. Is this relation an equivalence relation? Why?

3-8 MORE POSTULATES AND PROOFS

The Substitution Postulate

● **POSTULATE 4. A quantity may be substituted for its equal in any expression.**

EXAMPLE 1.

Given: $AB = 2AD$.
       $AD = DB$.

Prove: $AB = 2DB$.

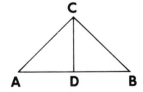

Statements	Reasons
1. $AB = 2AD$.	1. Given.
2. $AD = DB$.	2. Given.
3. $AB = 2DB$.	3. Substitution postulate. (*Or:* A quantity may be substituted for its equal in any expression.)

EXAMPLE 2.

Given: $m\angle a + m\angle b = 90$.
$m\angle a = m\angle c$.

Prove: $m\angle c + m\angle b = 90$.

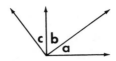

Statements	*Reasons*
1. $m\angle a + m\angle b = 90$.	1. Given.
2. $m\angle a = m\angle c$.	2. Given.
3. $m\angle c + m\angle b = 90$.	3. Substitution postulate.

EXERCISES _____

In 1–3, write a formal proof to show that the conclusion is valid.

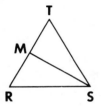

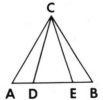

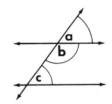

1. *Given:*
$MT = \frac{1}{2} RT$.
$RM = MT$.

Prove:
$RM = \frac{1}{2} RT$.

2. *Given:*
$AD + DE = AE$.
$AD = EB$.

Prove:
$EB + DE = AE$.

3. *Given:*
$m\angle a + m\angle b = 180$.
$m\angle a = m\angle c$.

Prove:
$m\angle c + m\angle b = 180$.

The Partition Postulate

● **POSTULATE 5. A whole is equal to the sum of all its parts.**

EXAMPLE 1.

$AD = AB + BC + CD$.
Also, $\overline{AD} = \overline{AB} + \overline{BC} + \overline{CD}$.

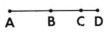

EXAMPLE 2.

$m\angle ABE = m\angle 1 + m\angle 2 + m\angle 3$.
Also, $\angle ABE = \angle 1 + \angle 2 + \angle 3$.

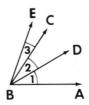

The Addition Postulate

● **POSTULATE 6.** If $a = b$, and $c = d$, then $a + c = b + d$.

This postulate can be restated as follows:

● **POSTULATE 6.** **If equal quantities are added to equal quantities, the sums are equal.**

EXAMPLE 1.

Given: $AB = DE$.
$\quad\quad\quad BC = EF$.

Prove: $AC = DF$.

Statements	*Reasons*
1. $\quad AB = DE$.	1. Given.
2. $\quad BC = EF$.	2. Given.
3. $AB + BC = DE + EF$.	3. Addition postulate. (*Or:* If equal quantities are added to equal quantities, the sums are equal.)
4. $AB + BC = AC$ and $\quad DE + EF = DF$.	4. Partition postulate. (*Or:* A whole is equal to the sum of all its parts.)
5. $\quad AC = DF$.	5. Substitution postulate.

Since $\overline{AB} \cong \overline{DE}$ is equivalent to $AB = DE$, and $\overline{BC} \cong \overline{EF}$ is equivalent to $BC = EF$, we will deal with the addition of congruent segments in the same way that we deal with the addition of segments whose lengths are equal. Thus, we will restate the Addition Postulate as follows:

● **POSTULATE 6A.** **If congruent segments are added to congruent segments, the sums are congruent.**

For similar reasons, when dealing with congruent angles, we will restate the Addition Postulate as follows:

● **POSTULATE 6B.** **If congruent angles are added to congruent angles, the sums are congruent.**

The following examples show how we use this postulate:

EXAMPLE 2.

Given: $\overline{AB} \cong \overline{DE}$.
$\quad\quad\quad \overline{BC} \cong \overline{EF}$.

Prove: $\overline{AC} \cong \overline{DF}$.

Statements	*Reasons*
1. $\overline{AB} \cong \overline{DE}$.	1. Given.
2. $\overline{BC} \cong \overline{EF}$.	2. Given.
3. $\overline{AB} + \overline{BC} \cong \overline{DE} + \overline{EF}$, or $\overline{AC} \cong \overline{DF}$.	3. Addition postulate. (*Or:* If congruent segments are added to congruent segments, the sums are congruent segments.)

Note. By the definition of the sum of two segments, $\overline{AC}$ is another name for $\overline{AB} + \overline{BC}$ only when A, B, and C are collinear; $\overline{DF}$ is another name for $\overline{DE} + \overline{EF}$ only when D, E, and F are collinear.

EXAMPLE 3.

Given: ∠*ABG* ≅ ∠*DEH*.
∠*GBC* ≅ ∠*HEF*.

Prove: ∠*ABC* ≅ ∠*DEF*.

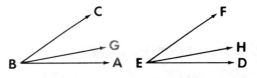

Statements	*Reasons*
1. ∠*ABG* ≅ ∠*DEH*.	1. Given.
2. ∠*GBC* ≅ ∠*HEF*.	2. Given.
3. ∠*ABG* + ∠*GBC* ≅ ∠*DEH* + ∠*HEF* or ∠*ABC* ≅ ∠*DEF*.	3. Addition postulate.

Note. By the definition of the sum of two angles, ∠*ABC* is another name for ∠*ABG* + ∠*GBC* only when G is an interior point of ∠*ABC*; similarly, ∠*DEF* is another name for ∠*DEH* + ∠*HEF*.

EXERCISES _____

In 1–6, write a formal proof to show that the conclusion is valid.

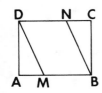

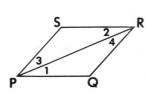

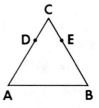

1. *Given:*
$AM = CN$.
$MB = ND$.

Prove:
$AB = CD$.

2. *Given:*
$m\angle 1 = m\angle 2$.
$m\angle 3 = m\angle 4$.

Prove:
$m\angle QPS = m\angle QRS$.

3. *Given:*
$\overline{CD} \cong \overline{CE}$.
$\overline{DA} \cong \overline{EB}$.

Prove:
$\overline{CA} \cong \overline{CB}$.

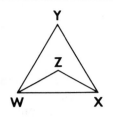

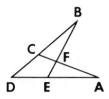

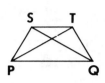

4. *Given:*
  $\angle XWZ \cong \angle WXZ.$
  $\angle ZWY \cong \angle ZXY.$

  Prove:
  $\angle XWY \cong \angle WXY.$

5. *Given:*
  $\overline{AF} \cong \overline{BF}.$
  $\overline{FC} \cong \overline{FE}.$

  Prove:
  $\overline{AC} \cong \overline{BE}.$

6. *Given:*
  $\angle QST \cong \angle PTS.$
  $\angle QSP \cong \angle PTQ.$

  Prove:
  $\angle PST \cong \angle QTS.$

The Subtraction Postulate

● **POSTULATE 7. If $a = b$, and $c = d$, then $a - c = b - d$.**

This postulate can be restated as follows:

● **POSTULATE 7. If equal quantities are subtracted from equal quantities, the differences are equal.**

EXAMPLE 1.

Given: $m\angle DAC = m\angle ECA.$
  $m\angle 1 = m\angle 2.$

Prove: $m\angle 3 = m\angle 4.$

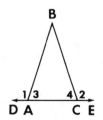

Statements	*Reasons*
1. $m\angle DAC = m\angle ECA.$	1. Given.
2. $m\angle 1 = m\angle 2.$	2. Given.
3. $m\angle DAC - m\angle 1 = m\angle ECA - m\angle 2.$ or $m\angle 3 = m\angle 4.$	3. Subtraction postulate.

In the same way that we dealt with addition of congruent angles and addition of congruent segments, so too will we deal with subtraction of congruent figures. This is illustrated in the following example:

EXAMPLE 2.

Given: $\overline{AB} \cong \overline{AC}$.
$\overline{DB} \cong \overline{EC}$.

Prove: $\overline{AD} \cong \overline{AE}$.

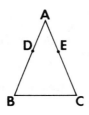

Statements	Reasons
1. $\overline{AB} \cong \overline{AC}$.	1. Given.
2. $\overline{DB} \cong \overline{EC}$.	2. Given.
3. $\overline{AB} - \overline{DB} \cong \overline{AC} - \overline{EC}$ or $\overline{AD} \cong \overline{AE}$.	3. Subtraction postulate.

EXERCISES

In 1–6, write a formal proof to show that the conclusion is valid.

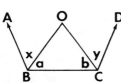

1. *Given:*
m∠ABC = m∠DCB.
m∠a = m∠b.

Prove:
m∠x = m∠y.

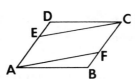

2. *Given:*
AD = BC.
AE = CF.

Prove:
DE = BF.

3. *Given:*
$\overline{DA} \cong \overline{CB}$.
$\overline{DE} \cong \overline{CF}$.

Prove:
$\overline{EA} \cong \overline{FB}$.

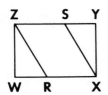

4. *Given:*
∠WZY ≅ ∠WXY.
∠RZY ≅ ∠RXS.

Prove:
∠WZR ≅ ∠YXS.

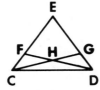

5. *Given:*
$\overline{FD} \cong \overline{GC}$.
$\overline{FH} \cong \overline{GH}$.

Prove:
$\overline{CH} \cong \overline{DH}$.

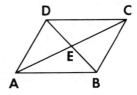

6. *Given:*
∠DEB ≅ ∠AEC.
∠DEA ≅ ∠BEC.

Prove:
∠AEB ≅ ∠DEC.

The Multiplication Postulate

● **POSTULATE 8.** If *a* = *b*, and *c* = *d*, then *ac* = *bd*.

This postulate can be restated as follows:

● **POSTULATE 8. If equal quantities are multiplied by equal quantities, the products are equal.**

When each of two equal quantities is multiplied by the number 2, we have a special case of this postulate, which is stated as follows:

● **Doubles of equal quantities are equal.**

EXAMPLE 1.

Given: $AB = CD$.
$RS = 2AB$.
$LM = 2CD$.

A•——•B R•————•S

C•——•D L•————•M

Prove: $RS = LM$.

Statements	*Reasons*
1. $AB = CD$.	1. Given.
2. $RS = 2AB$.	2. Given.
3. $LM = 2CD$.	3. Given.
4. $RS = LM$.	4. Multiplication postulate. (*Or:* Doubles of equal quantities are equal.)

We will deal with doubles of congruent segments and doubles of congruent angles in the same way that we deal with doubles of segments whose lengths are equal, and doubles of angles that have equal measures. See how this is illustrated in the following example:

EXAMPLE 2.

Given: $\angle r \cong \angle s$.
$m\angle BAD = 2m\angle r$.
$m\angle BCD = 2m\angle s$.

Prove: $\angle BAD \cong \angle BCD$.

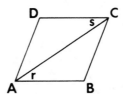

Statements	*Reasons*
1. $\angle r \cong \angle s$.	1. Given.
2. $m\angle BAD = 2m\angle r$.	2. Given.
3. $m\angle BCD = 2m\angle s$.	3. Given.
4. $\angle BAD \cong \angle BCD$.	4. Doubles of congruent angles are congruent.

EXERCISES

In 1–6, write a formal proof to show that the conclusion is valid.

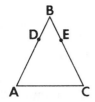

1. *Given:* $BD = BE$.
$\quad\quad\quad BA = 3BD$.
$\quad\quad\quad BC = 3BE$.

Prove: $BA = BC$.

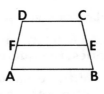

2. *Given:* $AF = BE$.
$\quad\quad\quad AD = 2AF$.
$\quad\quad\quad BC = 2BE$.

Prove: $AD = BC$.

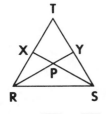

3. *Given:* $\overline{PX} \cong \overline{PY}$.
$\quad\quad\quad SP = 2PX$.
$\quad\quad\quad RP = 2PY$.

Prove: $\overline{SP} \cong \overline{RP}$.

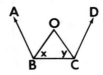

4. *Given:* $m\angle x = m\angle y$.
$\quad\quad\quad m\angle CBA = 2m\angle x$.
$\quad\quad\quad m\angle BCD = 2m\angle y$.

Prove: $m\angle CBA = m\angle BCD$.

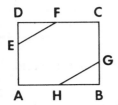

5. *Given:* $\overline{DF} \cong \overline{HB}$.
$\quad\quad\quad DC = 2DF$.
$\quad\quad\quad AB = 2HB$.

Prove: $\overline{DC} \cong \overline{AB}$.

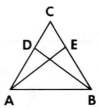

6. *Given:* $\angle EBD \cong \angle EAD$.
$\quad\quad\quad m\angle ABE = 2m\angle EBD$.
$\quad\quad\quad m\angle BAD = 2m\angle EAD$.

Prove: $\angle ABE \cong \angle BAD$.

The Division Postulate

● **POSTULATE 9.** If $a = b$, and $c = d$, then $\dfrac{a}{c} = \dfrac{b}{d}$.

(*c* is not 0 and *d* is not 0.)

This postulate can be restated as follows:

● **POSTULATE 9. If equal quantities are divided by nonzero equal quantities, the quotients are equal.**

When each of two equal quantities is divided by the number 2, we have a special case of this postulate, which is stated as follows:

● **Halves of equal quantities are equal.**

We will deal with halves of congruent segments and halves of congruent angles in the same way that we deal with halves of segments whose lengths are equal and halves of angles whose measures are equal. See how this is illustrated in the following example:

EXAMPLE.

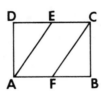

Given: $\overline{AB} \cong \overline{DC}$.
    $AF = \frac{1}{2}AB$.
    $EC = \frac{1}{2}DC$.

Prove: $\overline{AF} \cong \overline{EC}$.

Statements	*Reasons*
1. $\overline{AB} \cong \overline{DC}$.	1. Given.
2. $AF = \frac{1}{2}AB$.	2. Given.
3. $EC = \frac{1}{2}DC$.	3. Given.
4. $\overline{AF} \cong \overline{EC}$.	4. Division postulate. (*Or:* Halves of congruent segments are congruent segments.)

EXERCISES ──────────────────────────

In 1–4, write a formal proof to show that the conclusion is valid.

1. *Given:* $AD = AB$.
    $AE = \dfrac{AD}{3}$.
    $AF = \dfrac{AB}{3}$.

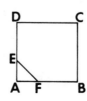

Prove: $AE = AF$.

2. *Given:* $m\angle DAB = m\angle DCB.$
$m\angle 2 = \frac{1}{2}m\angle DAB.$
$m\angle 1 = \frac{1}{2}m\angle DCB.$

Prove: $m\angle 1 = m\angle 2.$

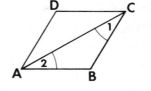

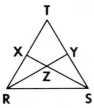

3. *Given:* $\angle SRX \cong \angle RSY.$
$m\angle SRY = \frac{1}{2}m\angle SRX.$
$m\angle RSX = \frac{1}{2}m\angle RSY.$

Prove: $\angle SRY \cong \angle RSX.$

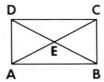

4. *Given:* $\overline{BD} \cong \overline{AC}.$
$BE = \frac{1}{2}BD.$
$AE = \frac{1}{2}AC.$

Prove: $\overline{BE} \cong \overline{AE}.$

Powers Postulate

● **POSTULATE 10.** **If** $a = b$, **then** $a^2 = b^2.$

This postulate can be restated as follows:

● **POSTULATE 10.** **The squares of equal quantities are equal.**

EXAMPLE. If $AB = 10$, then $(AB)^2 = (10)^2$, or $(AB)^2 = 100.$

Roots Postulate

● **POSTULATE 11.** **If** $a = b$, **then** $\sqrt{a} = \sqrt{b}.$

This postulate can be restated as follows:

● **POSTULATE 11.** **Positive square roots of equal quantities are equal.**

EXAMPLE. If $(AB)^2 = 25$, then $\sqrt{(AB)^2} = \sqrt{25}$, or $AB = 5.$

Motion Postulate

● **POSTULATE 12.** **A geometric figure may be moved without changing its size or shape. [A geometric figure may be copied.]**

Postulates Involving Lines, Line Segments, and Angles

● **POSTULATE 13.** **A line segment can be extended to any length in either direction.**

EXAMPLE. The line segment, $\overline{AB}$, can be extended indefinitely to the right and to the left. Remember, however, that the line, $\overleftrightarrow{AB}$, is *not* the original segment, $\overline{AB}$.

● **POSTULATE 14.** **Through two given points, one and only one line can be drawn. [Two points determine a line.]**

EXAMPLE. Through given points C and D, one and only one line can be drawn.

● **POSTULATE 15.** **Two lines cannot intersect in more than one point.**

EXAMPLE. If $\overleftrightarrow{AEB}$ and $\overleftrightarrow{CED}$ intersect, they cannot intersect in more than the one point E.

● **POSTULATE 16.** **One and only one circle can be drawn with any given point as a center and the length of any given line segment as a radius.**

EXAMPLE. Only one circle can be drawn that has point O as its center and a radius equal in length to segment r.

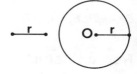

We make use of this postulate in constructions when we use compasses.

● **POSTULATE 17.** **At a given point on a given line, one and only one perpendicular can be drawn to the line.**

EXAMPLE. At point P on $\overleftrightarrow{APB}$, only one line, $\overleftrightarrow{PD}$, can be drawn perpendicular to $\overleftrightarrow{APB}$.

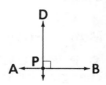

● **POSTULATE 18.** **From a given point not on a given line, one and only one perpendicular can be drawn to the line.**

EXAMPLE. From point P not on $\overleftrightarrow{CD}$, only one line, $\overleftrightarrow{PE}$, can be drawn perpendicular to $\overleftrightarrow{CD}$.

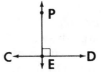

● **POSTULATE 19.** **For any two distinct points, there is only one positive real number that is called the *length* of the line segment joining the two points.**

EXAMPLE. For the distinct points A and B, there is one positive real number, represented by AB, which is the length of $\overline{AB}$.

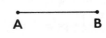

Since AB is also called the *distance* from A to B, we refer to this postulate as the ***distance postulate***.

● **POSTULATE 20.** **The shortest path between two points is the line segment joining these two points.**

EXAMPLE. The figure shows three paths that can be taken in going from A to B. The length of $\overline{AB}$ (the path through C, a point collinear with A and B) is less than the length of the path through D or the path through E. The measure of the shortest path from A to B is the distance, AB.

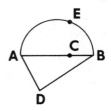

● **POSTULATE 21.** **A line segment has one and only one midpoint.**

EXAMPLE. $\overline{AB}$ has one and only one midpoint, point M.

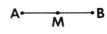

● **POSTULATE 22.** **An angle has one and only one bisector.**

EXAMPLE. $\angle ABC$ has one and only one bisector, namely, the ray, $\overrightarrow{BD}$.

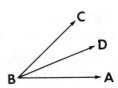

● **POSTULATE 23.** The sum of the degree measures of all the angles about a given point is 360.

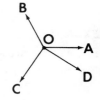

EXAMPLE. From point O, $\overrightarrow{OA}$, $\overrightarrow{OB}$, $\overrightarrow{OC}$, and $\overrightarrow{OD}$ are drawn. The sum of the degree measures of the consecutive angles formed is 360. Thus, $m\angle AOB + m\angle BOC + m\angle COD + m\angle DOA = 360$.

● **POSTULATE 24.** The sum of the degree measures of all the angles on one side of a given line, whose common vertex is a given point on the line, is 180.

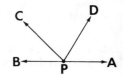

EXAMPLE. From point P on $\overleftrightarrow{AB}$, draw $\overrightarrow{PC}$ and $\overrightarrow{PD}$. Using the side of straight $\angle APB$ that contains $\overrightarrow{PC}$ and $\overrightarrow{PD}$, observe that the sum of the degree measures of the consecutive angles formed is 180. Thus, $m\angle APD + m\angle DPC + m\angle CPB = 180$.

Conditional Statements as They Relate to Proof

> *Given:* $\angle A \cong \angle B$.
> $\angle B \cong \angle C$.
>
> *Prove:* $\angle A \cong \angle C$.

At the left, you see the format normally used to present a proof. The "given" statements form the *hypothesis* that we assume to be true. From this hypothesis, we are asked to "prove" that another statement, called the *conclusion*, is true.

In logic, you learned that a conditional statement "If p, then q" contains the hypothesis p and the conclusion q. Thus, it is possible to state the "given" hypothesis and the conclusion that we are to "prove" in a conditional form. For example, we can write:

> If $\underbrace{\angle A \cong \angle B, \text{ and } \angle B \cong \angle C}_{\text{"given" hypothesis}}$, then $\underbrace{\angle A \cong \angle C.}_{\substack{\text{conclusion} \\ \text{"to prove"}}}$

When the information needed for a proof is presented in a conditional statement, remember that you are to:

1. assume the truth of the hypothesis, or the "given" statement.
2. prove the truth of the conclusion, or the "prove" statement.

Numerical and Algebraic Applications

In geometry, we are interested in proving that statements are true. You should also be aware that these true statements are used to help solve numerical and algebraic problems. When working with a numerical or algebraic application of some geometric fact, it might be helpful to remember that you:

1. are usually asked to find a missing quantity, such as the value of x, the length of a line segment, or the measure of an angle.

2. are *not* required to state a "Given" or "Prove" in numerical or algebraic examples. (See Model Problem 2 below.)

MODEL PROBLEMS ────────────────────────────────

1. Rewrite the conditional statement in the "Given" and "Prove" format:

   If $AB + BC = AC$ and $\overline{BC} \cong \overline{PR}$, then $AB + PR = AC$.

   Solution:

   > *Given:* $AB + BC = AC$.
   > $\overline{BC} \cong \overline{PR}$.
   >
   > *Prove:* $AB + PR = AC$.

2. **a.** If $\angle ABD \cong \angle DBE$, $m\angle ABD = 4x - 10$, and $m\angle DBE = 2x + 30$, find $m\angle ABD$ and $m\angle DBE$.

   b. If $\angle DBE$ and $\angle EBC$ are complementary, use an answer from part **a** to find $m\angle EBC$.

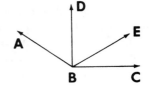

Solution

a. This is an *algebraic application* of a geometry situation.

  (1) Since congruent angles have equal measures: $m\angle ABD = m\angle DBE$

  (2) Substitute the given algebraic expressions: $4x - 10 = 2x + 30$

  (3) Solve for x: $2x = 40$
  $x = 20$

  (4) Let $x = 20$ in the given algebraic expressions to find the measures of the angles:
  $m\angle ABD = 4x - 10 = 4(20) - 10 = 80 - 10 = 70$ *Ans.*
  $m\angle DBE = 2x + 30 = 2(20) + 30 = 40 + 30 = 70$ *Ans.*

b. This is a *numerical application* of a geometric situation.

(1) The sum of the degree
measures of complementary
angles is 90. Thus: $m\angle DBE + m\angle EBC = 90$

(2) From part **a**, $m\angle DBE = 70$.
Thus: $70 + m\angle EBC = 90$

(3) By subtraction: $m\angle EBC = 90 - 70 = 20$ *Ans.*

Note. In both parts of this question, we are asked to *find* numerical quantities. We are *not* asked to prove geometric statements.

EXERCISES

In 1–14, **(a)** rewrite the conditional statement in the *Given* and *Prove* format, and **(b)** write a formal proof.

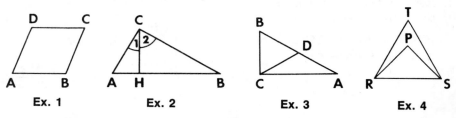

Ex. 1   Ex. 2   Ex. 3   Ex. 4

1. If $AB = AD$ and $DC = AD$, then $AB = DC$.
2. If $m\angle 1 + m\angle 2 = 90$ and $m\angle A = m\angle 2$, then $m\angle 1 + m\angle A = 90$.
3. If $\overline{AD} \cong \overline{CD}$ and $\overline{BD} \cong \overline{CD}$, then $\overline{AD} \cong \overline{BD}$.
4. If $\angle TRS \cong \angle TSR$ and $\angle PRT \cong \angle PST$, then $\angle PRS \cong \angle PSR$.

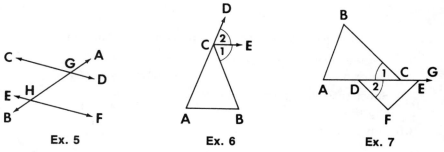

Ex. 5   Ex. 6   Ex. 7

5. If $m\angle AGH = 180$, $m\angle EHF = 180$, and $m\angle AGD = m\angle GHF$, then $m\angle DGH = m\angle GHE$.
6. If $m\angle A = m\angle B$, $m\angle 1 = m\angle B$, and $m\angle 2 = m\angle A$, then $m\angle 1 = m\angle 2$.
7. If $\angle ACG \cong \angle ADE$, and $\angle BCG \cong \angle ADF$, then $\angle 1 \cong \angle 2$.

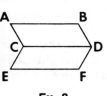

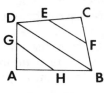

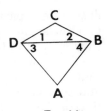

Ex. 8   **Ex. 9–10**   **Ex. 11**

8. If $\overline{AB} \cong \overline{CD}$, and $\overline{EF} \cong \overline{CD}$, then $\overline{AB} \cong \overline{EF}$.
9. If $EF = \frac{1}{2}DB$ and $GH = \frac{1}{2}DB$, then $EF = GH$.
10. If $CE = CF$, $CD = 2CE$, and $CB = 2CF$, then $CD = CB$.
11. If $\angle 1 \cong \angle 2$ and $\angle 3 \cong \angle 4$, then $\angle CDA \cong \angle CBA$.

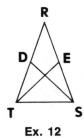

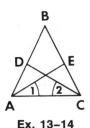

Ex. 12   **Ex. 13–14**

12. If $RT = RS$, $RD = \frac{1}{2}RT$, and $RE = \frac{1}{2}RS$, then $RD = RE$.
13. If $AD = CE$ and $DB = EB$, then $AB = CB$.
14. If $m\angle BAC = m\angle BCA$, $m\angle 1 = \frac{1}{2}m\angle BAC$, and $m\angle 2 = \frac{1}{2}m\angle BCA$, then $m\angle 1 = m\angle 2$.

In 15–17, $\overleftrightarrow{RST}$, $\overrightarrow{SQ}$, and $\overrightarrow{SP}$ are given.

15. If $\angle QSR \cong \angle PST$ and $m\angle QSP = 96$, find $m\angle QSR$.
16. If $m\angle QSR = 40$ and $\overrightarrow{SQ} \perp \overrightarrow{SP}$, find $m\angle PST$.
17. If $m\angle PSQ$ is twice $m\angle QSR$ and $\overrightarrow{SQ} \perp \overrightarrow{SP}$, find $m\angle PST$.

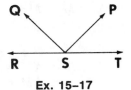

Ex. 15–17

3-9   USING POSTULATES AND DEFINITIONS IN PROOFS

Often, it is necessary to use a combination of definitions and postulates in order to prove a theorem. A carefully drawn figure can be very helpful in deciding upon the steps to use in the proof. However, you may not assume special relationships that appear to be true in the figure drawn for a particular problem. For example, you may not assume that two line segments in a figure are congruent or are perpendicular because they appear to be so in the figure.

On the other hand, unless otherwise stated, we will assume that lines that appear to be straight lines in a figure actually are straight lines and that points that appear to be on a given line actually are on that line in the order shown.

MODEL PROBLEMS

1. *Given:* $\overleftrightarrow{ABCD}$ with $\overline{AB} \cong \overline{CD}$.

Prove: $\overline{AC} \cong \overline{BD}$.

A•———•——•———•D
    B   C

Statements	*Reasons*
1. $\overline{AB} \cong \overline{CD}$.	1. Given.
2. $\overline{BC} \cong \overline{BC}$.	2. Reflexive property.
3. $\overline{AB} + \overline{BC} \cong \overline{CD} + \overline{BC}$ or $\overline{AC} \cong \overline{BD}$.	3. Addition postulate.

2. *Given:* M is the midpoint of $\overline{AB}$.

Prove: $AM = \frac{1}{2}AB$ and $MB = \frac{1}{2}AB$.

A•———•———•B
    M

Statements	*Reasons*
1. M is the midpoint of $\overline{AB}$.	1. Given.
2. $\overline{AM} \cong \overline{MB}$.	2. Definition of midpoint.
3. $AM = MB$.	3. Definition of congruent segments.
4. $AM + MB = AB$.	4. Partition postulate.
5. $AM + AM = AB$ or $2AM = AB$.	5. Substitution postulate.
6. $AM = \frac{1}{2}AB$.	6. Halves of equal quantities are equal.
7. Also, $MB + MB = AB$ or $2MB = AB$.	7. Substitution postulate.
8. $MB = \frac{1}{2}AB$.	8. Halves of equal quantities are equal.

EXERCISES

In 1–10, **(a)** rewrite the conditional statement in the *Given* and *Prove* format and **(b)** write a formal proof that demonstrates that the conclusion is valid.

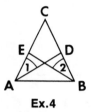

Ex. 1

Ex. 2

Ex. 3

1. If $\overline{AB} \cong \overline{CB}$, $\overline{FD}$ bisects $\overline{AB}$, and $\overline{FE}$ bisects $\overline{CB}$, then $\overline{AD} \cong \overline{CE}$.
2. If $\overline{CA}$ bisects both $\angle DCB$ and $\angle DAB$, and $\angle DCB \cong \angle DAB$, then $\angle r \cong \angle s$.
3. If $\overline{AD} \cong \overline{BE}$, then $\overline{AE} \cong \overline{BD}$.

Ex.4

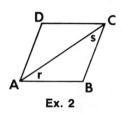

Ex. 5

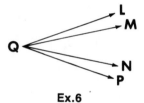

Ex.6

4. If $\overline{AD}$ bisects $\angle CAB$, $\overline{EB}$ bisects $\angle CBA$, and $\angle CAB \cong \angle CBA$, then $\angle 1 \cong \angle 2$.
5. If $\overline{DF} \cong \overline{BE}$, then $\overline{DE} \cong \overline{BF}$.
6. If $\angle LQM \cong \angle NQP$, then $\angle LQN \cong \angle MQP$.

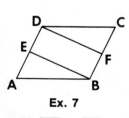

Ex. 7

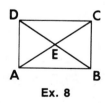

Ex. 8

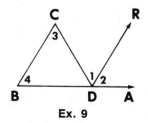

Ex. 9

7. If $\overline{AD} \cong \overline{BC}$, E is the midpoint of $\overline{AD}$, and F is the midpoint of $\overline{BC}$, then $\overline{AE} \cong \overline{FC}$.
8. If $\overline{AC} \cong \overline{DB}$ and $\overline{AC}$ and $\overline{DB}$ bisect each other, then $\overline{AE} \cong \overline{EB}$.
9. If $\overrightarrow{DR}$ bisects $\angle CDA$, $\angle 3 \cong \angle 1$, and $\angle 4 \cong \angle 2$, then $\angle 3 \cong \angle 4$.

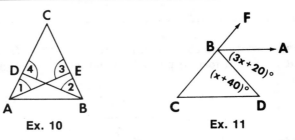

Ex. 10   Ex. 11

10. If $m\angle 1 + m\angle 3 + m\angle C = 180$, $m\angle 2 + m\angle 4 + m\angle C = 180$,   and $m\angle 3 = m\angle 4$, then $m\angle 1 = m\angle 2$.

11. If $\overrightarrow{BA}$ bisects $\angle FBD$ and $m\angle ABD = m\angle BDC$:
   a. Prove that $m\angle ABF = m\angle BDC$.
   b. Find the number of degrees in $\angle ABF$ when $m\angle ABD = 3x + 20$ and $m\angle BDC = x + 40$.

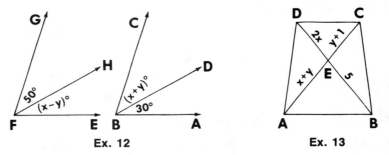

Ex. 12   Ex. 13

12. If $\angle EFG \cong \angle ABC$ and $\angle EFH \cong \angle ABD$:
   a. Prove that $\angle HFG \cong \angle DBC$.
   b. Solve for x and y when $m\angle EFH = (x - y)$, $m\angle HFG = 50$, $m\angle ABD = 30$, and $m\angle DBC = (x + y)$.

13. If $\overline{DB} \cong \overline{AC}$ and $\overline{AE} \cong \overline{EB}$:
   a. Prove that $\overline{DE} \cong \overline{EC}$.
   b. Find the lengths $DE, EC, DB,$ and AC when $AE = x + y$, $EB = 5$, $DE = 2x$, and $EC = y + 1$.

3-10   PROVING SIMPLE ANGLE THEOREMS

You already know that a theorem is a statement proved by deduction. Now, you will see how we can use undefined terms, defined terms, and postulates in proving some simple angle theorems. In Theorems 1–8 that follow, the proofs of Theorems 1, 3, and 8 are presented; the proofs of Theorems 2, 4, 5, 6, and 7 are left to the student.

● **THEOREM 1. If two angles are right angles, then they are congruent.**

Given: ∠*ABC* and ∠*DEF* are right angles.

Prove: ∠*ABC* ≅ ∠*DEF*.

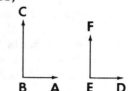

Statements	*Reasons*
1. ∠*ABC* and ∠*DEF* are right angles.	1. Given.
2. m∠*ABC* = 90, m∠*DEF* = 90.	2. Definition of right angle.
3. m∠*ABC* = m∠*DEF*.	3. Transitive postulate of equality.
4. ∠*ABC* ≅ ∠*DEF*.	4. Definition of congruent angles.

● **THEOREM 2. If two angles are straight angles, then they are congruent.**

The proof of this theorem is left to the student. However, here and in other theorems not proved in this book, clues are provided so that the student can understand the hypothesis and the conclusion.

Given ∠*ABC* and ∠*DEF*, which are both straight angles, prove that ∠*ABC* ≅ ∠*DEF*. The proof of this theorem is similar to the proof of Theorem 1.

● **THEOREM 3. If two angles are complements of the same angle, then they are congruent.**

Given: ∠1 is complementary to ∠2.
∠3 is complementary to ∠2.

Prove: ∠1 ≅ ∠3.

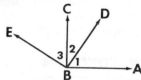

Statements	*Reasons*
1. ∠1 is complementary to ∠2.	1. Given.
2. m∠1 + m∠2 = 90.	2. Definition of complementary angles.
3. ∠3 is complementary to ∠2.	3. Given.
4. m∠3 + m∠2 = 90.	4. Definition of complementary angles.
5. m∠1 + m∠2 = m∠3 + m∠2.	5. Transitive postulate of equality.
6. m∠2 = m∠2.	6. Reflexive property of equality.
7. m∠1 = m∠3.	7. Subtraction postulate of equality.
8. ∠1 ≅ ∠3.	8. Definition of congruent angles.

This figure shows an algebraic explanation for the theorem just proved. Here, m∠*CBD* = *x*. Both ∠*ABD* and ∠*CBE* are complements to ∠*CBD*. Thus, m∠*ABD* = 90 − *x* and m∠*CBE* = 90 − *x*, and we conclude ∠*ABD* ≅ ∠*CBE*.

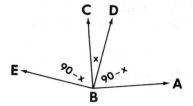

● **THEOREM 4. If two angles are congruent, their complements are congruent.**

If ∠*ABD* ≅ ∠*EFH*, ∠*CBD* is complementary to ∠*ABD*, and ∠*GFH* is complementary to ∠*EFH*, then ∠*CBD* ≅ ∠*GFH*. This proof is similar to the proof of Theorem 3 but requires the use of the substitution postulate.

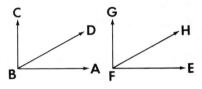

● **THEOREM 5. If two angles are supplements of the same angle, then they are congruent.**

If ∠*ABD* is supplementary to ∠*DBC*, and ∠*EBC* is supplementary to ∠*DBC*, then ∠*ABD* ≅ ∠*EBC*.

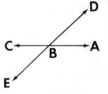

● **THEOREM 6. If two angles are congruent, then their supplements are congruent.**

If ∠*ABD* ≅ ∠*EFH*, ∠*CBD* is supplementary to ∠*ABD*, and ∠*GFH* is supplementary to ∠*EFH*, then ∠*CBD* ≅ ∠*GFH*.

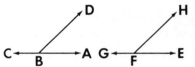

● **THEOREM 7. If two angles form a linear pair, they are supplementary.**

∠*ABC* and ∠*CBD* form a linear pair. They share a common side, $\overrightarrow{BC}$, and their remaining sides, $\overrightarrow{BA}$ and $\overrightarrow{BD}$, are opposite rays. Thus, ∠*ABC* and ∠*CBD* are supplementary.

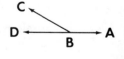

● **THEOREM 8. If two angles are vertical angles, then they are congruent.**

Given: ∠*BEC* and ∠*AED* are vertical angles.

Prove: ∠*BEC* ≅ ∠*AED*.

Statements	*Reasons*
1. ∠*BEC* and ∠*AED* are vertical angles.	1. Given.
2. $\overleftrightarrow{AEB}$ and $\overleftrightarrow{CED}$ intersect at *E*.	2. Definition of vertical angles.
3. ∠*BEC* is the supplement of ∠*AEC*; ∠*AED* is the supplement of ∠*AEC*.	3. If two angles form a linear pair, they are supplementary. (Theorem 7)
4. ∠*BEC* ≅ ∠*AED*.	4. If two angles are supplements of the same angle, they are congruent. (Theorem 5)

Notice how previously proven theorems can be used as reasons in deducing statements in a proof: See reasons 3 and 4 above.

How to Present a Formal Proof

In this chapter, you have seen the steps to be taken in presenting a formal proof in geometry using deductive reasoning:

1. As an aid, carefully draw a good *figure* which pictures the data of the theorem or the problem. Letter the figure.
2. State the *given*, which is the hypothesis of the theorem, in terms of the lettered figure.
3. State the *prove*, which is the conclusion of the theorem, in terms of the lettered figure.
4. Present the *proof*, which is a series of logical arguments used in the demonstration. Each step in the proof should consist of a *statement* and its *reason*. A reason may be the *given*, a *definition*, a *postulate*, or a *previously proven theorem*.

MODEL PROBLEM

Write a formal proof: If $\overleftrightarrow{CE}$ bisects ∠*ADB*, and $\overrightarrow{FDB}$ and $\overleftrightarrow{CDE}$ intersect, then ∠*ADE* ≅ ∠*FDC*.

Given: $\overleftrightarrow{CE}$ bisects ∠*ADB*.
  $\overrightarrow{FDB}$ and $\overleftrightarrow{CDE}$ intersect.

Prove: ∠*ADE* ≅ ∠*FDC*.

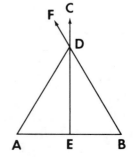

Statements	*Reasons*
1. $\overleftrightarrow{CE}$ bisects ∠ADB.	1. Given.
2. ∠ADE ≅ ∠BDE.	2. Definition of angle bisector.
3. $\overleftrightarrow{FDB}$ and $\overrightarrow{CDE}$ intersect.	3. Given.
4. ∠BDE and ∠FDC are vertical angles.	4. Definition of vertical angles.
5. ∠BDE ≅ ∠FDC.	5. If two angles are vertical angles, then they are congruent.
6. ∠ADE ≅ ∠FDC.	6. Transitive property.

EXERCISES ─────────────────────────────

In 1–9, write a formal proof, using the given, definitions, postulates, and theorems as the reasons for the statements used in the proof.

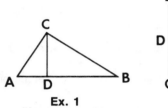
Ex. 1   Ex. 2

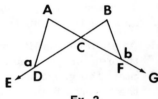
Ex. 3

1. If ABC is a triangle with ∠ACB a right angle and $\overline{CD} \perp \overline{AB}$, then ∠ACB ≅ ∠ADC.
2. If ∠1 ≅ ∠2, ∠B is complementary to ∠1, and ∠C is complementary to ∠2, then ∠B ≅ ∠C.
3. If $\overrightarrow{ACFG}$ and $\overrightarrow{BCDE}$ intersect and ∠a ≅ ∠b, then ∠ADC ≅ ∠BFC.

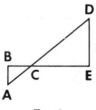

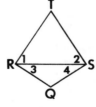

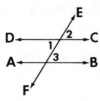

Ex. 4   Ex. 5   Ex. 6

4. If $\overline{BE}$ and $\overline{AD}$ intersect at C, ∠BAC is complementary to ∠ACB, and ∠EDC is complementary to ∠ECD, then ∠BAC ≅ ∠EDC.
5. If $\overline{TR} \perp \overline{RQ}$, $\overline{TS} \perp \overline{SQ}$, and ∠3 ≅ ∠4, then ∠1 ≅ ∠2.
6. If $\overleftrightarrow{EF}$ intersects $\overleftrightarrow{AB}$ and $\overleftrightarrow{DC}$, and ∠3 ≅ ∠2, then ∠1 ≅ ∠3.

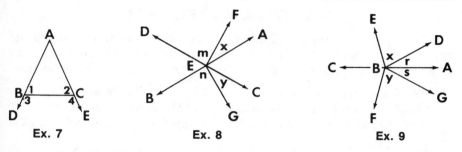

Ex. 7   Ex. 8   Ex. 9

7. If $\overrightarrow{ABD}$ and $\overrightarrow{ACE}$ intersect, and $\angle 1 \cong \angle 2$, then $\angle 3 \cong \angle 4$.

8. If $\overleftrightarrow{AEB}$ and $\overleftrightarrow{CED}$ intersect at E, and $\angle x \cong \angle y$, then $\angle m \cong \angle n$.

9. Given $\overleftrightarrow{ABC}$, $\angle r \cong \angle s$, $\overrightarrow{BE}$ bisects $\angle CBD$, and $\overrightarrow{BF}$ bisects $\angle CBG$, prove $\angle x \cong \angle y$.

Numerical and Algebraic Applications

In 10–13, $\overleftrightarrow{AEB}$ and $\overleftrightarrow{CED}$ intersect at E.

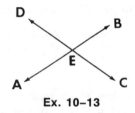

Ex. 10–13

10. If $m\angle BEC = 70$, find $m\angle AED$, $m\angle DEB$, and $m\angle AEC$.

11. If $m\angle DEB = 2x + 20$ and $m\angle AEC = 3x - 30$, find $m\angle DEB$, $m\angle AEC$, $m\angle AED$, and $m\angle CEB$.

12. If $m\angle BEC = 5x - 25$ and $m\angle DEA = 7x - 65$, find $m\angle BEC$, $m\angle DEA$, $m\angle DEB$, and $m\angle AEC$.

13. If $m\angle BEC = y$, $m\angle DEB = 3x$, and $m\angle DEA = 2x - y$, find $m\angle CEB$, $m\angle BED$, $m\angle DEA$, and $m\angle AEC$.

14. $\overleftrightarrow{RS}$ intersects $\overleftrightarrow{LM}$ at P, $m\angle RPL = x + y$, $m\angle LPS = 3x + 2y$, $m\angle MPS = 3x - 2y$.
    a. Solve for x and y.
    b. Find $m\angle RPL$, $m\angle LPS$, and $m\angle MPS$.

3-11 REVIEW EXERCISES

In 1–3: **a.** Write the given definition in a conditional form using the words "If . . . then." **b.** Write the converse of the statement given as an answer in part **a.** **c.** Write the biconditional form of the definition.

1. An *obtuse triangle* is a triangle that has one obtuse angle.
2. *Congruent angles* are angles that have the same measure.
3. *Perpendicular lines* are two lines that intersect to form right angles.

4. *Given:* $\overleftrightarrow{AB}$ bisects $\overline{CD}$ at M.
   Prove: $CM = MD$.

   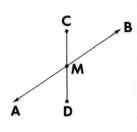

   a. Let P represent "$\overleftrightarrow{AB}$ bisects $\overline{CD}$ at M." Let Q represent "$\overline{CM} \cong \overline{MD}$." Let R represent "$CM = MD$." Write a *direct proof in logic*, listing statements in both symbols and words, and citing reasons, to show that $CM = MD$.
   b. Write a *direct geometry proof* to show that $CM = MD$.
   c. To prove that $CM = MD$ by *indirect methods*, what assumption must be made in the proof? (Do not write an indirect proof.)

5. Explain the difference between a postulate and a theorem.
6. Write the property that justifies the statement: If $AB = CD$, then $CD = AB$.

In 7–10, tell which properties of an equivalence relation are true for the given relation and the set given in parentheses.

7. $\cong$ (for angles)
8. is as tall as (for people)
9. $\neq$ (for integers)
10. is the sister of (for people)

In 11–17, write a formal proof to show that the conclusion is valid.

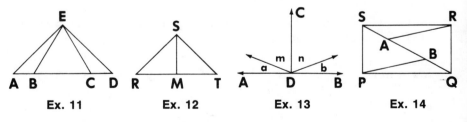

Ex. 11   Ex. 12   Ex. 13   Ex. 14

11. If $\overline{AC} \cong \overline{BD}$, then $\overline{AB} \cong \overline{CD}$.
12. If $\overline{RM} \cong \overline{MS}$ and $\overline{MS} \cong \overline{MT}$, then $\overline{RM} \cong \overline{MT}$.
13. If $\overleftrightarrow{CD} \perp \overleftrightarrow{AB}$ and $\angle m \cong \angle n$, then $\angle a \cong \angle b$.
14. If $SA = BQ$, then $SB = AQ$.

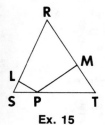

Ex. 15

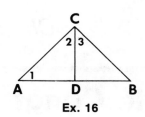

Ex. 16

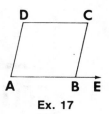

Ex. 17

15. If $\overline{PL} \perp \overline{RS}$ and $\overline{PM} \perp \overline{RT}$, then m∠$PLS$ = m∠PMT.

16. If ∠ACB is a right angle and ∠1 is complementary to ∠3, then ∠1 ≅ ∠2.

17. Given $\overleftrightarrow{ABE}$ and ∠CBE is supplementary to ∠ADC, then ∠ADC ≅ ∠ABC.

In 18–20, $\overleftrightarrow{AEB}$ and $\overleftrightarrow{CED}$ intersect at E.

Ex. 18–20

18. If m∠BEC = 125, find m∠BED and m∠AED.

19. If m∠BEC = $3x + 10$ and m∠AED = $4x - 30$, find m∠BEC.

20. If m∠BEC = $9x - 10$ and m∠CEA = $4x - 5$, find m∠BEC.

21. If ∠A and ∠B are complementary, and ∠A ≅ ∠B, find m∠A.

22. If $\overline{AB}$ ≅ $\overline{CD}$ and $\overline{CD}$ ≅ $\overline{EF}$, and if $AB = 2x + 3$ and $CD = 4x - 5$, find EF.

Chapter **4**

Triangle Congruence and Inequalities

4-1 CONGRUENT POLYGONS AND CORRESPONDING PARTS

When two polygons can be moved in such a way that the sides and angles of one polygon *fit exactly* upon the sides and angles of the second polygon, we call these figures *congruent polygons*. In simpler terms, we say that congruent polygons have the same shape and the same size.

As shown in the diagram, polygon *ABCD* is congruent to polygon *EFGH*. Notice that the congruent polygons were named in such a way that the order of their vertices indicates a *one-to-one correspondence* of points.

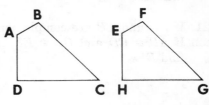

ABCD ≅ *EFGH* indicates that:
A corresponds to *E*; *E* corresponds to *A*.
B corresponds to *F*; *F* corresponds to *B*.
C corresponds to *G*; *G* corresponds to *C*.
D corresponds to *H*; *H* corresponds to *D*.

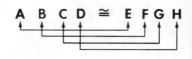

Congruent polygons should always be named so as to indicate the correspondences between the vertices of the polygons.

Corresponding Parts of Congruent Polygons

CORRESPONDING ANGLES. In the congruent polygons *ABCD* and *EFGH* shown, the vertex *A* corresponds to the vertex *E*. Angles *A* and *E* are called *corresponding angles* and ∠*A* ≅ ∠*E*.

In this example, there are four pairs of such corresponding angles:

$$∠A ≅ ∠E \quad ∠B ≅ ∠F \quad ∠C ≅ ∠G \quad ∠D ≅ ∠H$$

In congruent polygons, *corresponding angles are congruent.*

CORRESPONDING SIDES. Also, in congruent polygons $ABCD$ and $EFGH$, sides $\overline{AB}$ and $\overline{EF}$ are called *corresponding sides* and $\overline{AB} \cong \overline{EF}$. In this example, there are four pairs of such corresponding sides:

$$\overline{AB} \cong \overline{EF} \quad \overline{BC} \cong \overline{FG} \quad \overline{CD} \cong \overline{GH} \quad \overline{DA} \cong \overline{HE}$$

In congruent polygons, *corresponding sides are congruent.*

The pairs of congruent angles and the pairs of congruent sides are called the *corresponding parts of congruent polygons.* We can now present the formal definition for congruent polygons.

● **Definition.** *Two polygons are congruent* if and only if there is a one-to-one correspondence between their vertices such that:

1. Corresponding angles are congruent.
2. Corresponding sides are congruent.

Let us consider this definition in symbolic form, where
a represents "the angles of each pair of corresponding angles are congruent."
s represents "the sides of each pair of corresponding sides are congruent."
p represents "the two polygons are congruent."

Observe that the definition, which is stated in biconditional form, contains the conjunction $(a \wedge s)$. That is:

$(a \wedge s) \rightarrow p$: If the angles of each pair of corresponding angles are congruent and the sides of each pair of corresponding sides are congruent, then the two polygons are congruent, *and*

$p \rightarrow (a \wedge s)$: If two polygons are congruent, then the angles of each pair of corresponding angles are congruent and the sides of each pair of corresponding sides are congruent.

By the Law of Simplification, $(a \wedge s) \rightarrow a$
and $(a \wedge s) \rightarrow s$.

By the Chain Rule, from $p \rightarrow (a \wedge s)$ and $(a \wedge s) \rightarrow a$
we may conclude $p \rightarrow a$,
and from $p \rightarrow (a \wedge s)$ and $(a \wedge s) \rightarrow s$
we may conclude $p \rightarrow s$.

Thus, we may write:

$p \rightarrow a$: If two polygons are congruent, then the angles of each pair of corresponding angles are congruent.

$p \rightarrow s$: If two polygons are congruent, then the sides of each pair of corresponding sides are congruent.

These statements can be written more simply as:

● **Corresponding parts of congruent polygons are congruent.**

Congruent Triangles

The simplest possible polygon is the triangle, a polygon with exactly three sides. In the figure, $\triangle ABC$ and $\triangle DEF$ are congruent triangles.

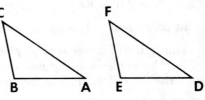

From the correspondence established, we can list six facts about these triangles: three facts about corresponding sides and three facts about corresponding angles. In the column at the left, the facts are stated as *congruences*; in the column at the right, the same facts are stated as *equalities*.

Congruences	Equalities
$\overline{AB} \cong \overline{DE}$.	$AB = DE$.
$\overline{BC} \cong \overline{EF}$.	$BC = EF$.
$\overline{AC} \cong \overline{DF}$.	$AC = DF$.
$\angle A \cong \angle D$.	$m\angle A = m\angle D$.
$\angle B \cong \angle E$.	$m\angle B = m\angle E$.
$\angle C \cong \angle F$.	$m\angle C = m\angle F$.

Since each congruence statement is equivalent to an equality statement, we will use whichever notation serves our purpose best in a particular situation.

For example, in one proof, we may prefer to write $\overline{AC} \cong \overline{DF}$, and in another proof, we may prefer to write $AC = DF$. In the same way, we might write $\angle C \cong \angle F$ or we might write $m\angle C = m\angle F$. From the definition, we may now say:

● **Corresponding parts of congruent triangles are equal in measure.**

In two congruent triangles, pairs of corresponding sides are always found opposite pairs of corresponding angles. The preceding figure, where $\triangle ABC \cong \triangle DEF$, shows that:

1. $\angle C$ and $\angle F$ are corresponding congruent angles.
2. $\overline{AB}$ is opposite $\angle C$, and $\overline{DE}$ is opposite $\angle F$.
3. $\overline{AB}$ and $\overline{DE}$ are corresponding congruent sides.

Equivalence Relation of Congruence

You have seen that the relation *is congruent to* is an equivalence relation for the set of angles, and again an equivalence relation for the set of line segments. Let us test this relation for the set of all triangles.

1. Reflexive property: $\triangle ABC \cong \triangle ABC$.
2. Symmetric property: If $\triangle ABC \cong \triangle DEF$, then $\triangle DEF \cong \triangle ABC$.
3. Transitive property: If $\triangle ABC \cong \triangle DEF$ and $\triangle DEF \cong \triangle RST$, then $\triangle ABC \cong \triangle RST$.

By referring to the congruence of corresponding angles and sides of triangles, we can prove that the congruence of triangles is an equivalence relation. In addition, these examples suggest that the congruence of geometric figures in general will be an equivalence relation. Therefore, we state these properties of congruence as the next three postulates.

● **POSTULATE 25. Any geometric figure is congruent to itself. (Reflexive property.)**

● **POSTULATE 26. A congruence may be expressed in either order. (Symmetric property.)**

● **POSTULATE 27. Two geometric figures congruent to the same geometric figure are congruent to each other. (Transitive property.)**

EXERCISES ━━━━━━━━━━━━━━━━━━━━━━━━━━━━━━━━━━━━━━

In 1–3, name three pairs of corresponding angles and three pairs of corresponding sides in the given congruent triangles. In each exercise, use the symbol $\cong$ to indicate that the angles named and also the sides named in your answers are congruent.

1. $\triangle ADC \cong \triangle BDC$ **2.** $\triangle AEC \cong \triangle BED$ **3.** $\triangle CDE \cong \triangle ABF$

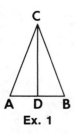

Ex. 1

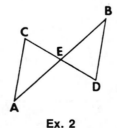

Ex. 2

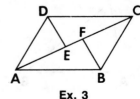

Ex. 3

4. Referring to the four triangles that follow: **a.** Name the figures that appear to be congruent, using the correct order of their vertices and the symbol ≅. **b.** Use the symbol = to indicate the corresponding parts whose measures are equal.

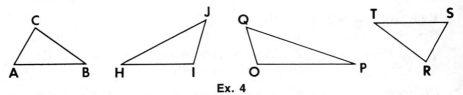

Ex. 4

In 5–10, *ABCD* is a square and diagonals $\overline{AC}$ and $\overline{BD}$ meet at *E*. Name the property that justifies the statement.

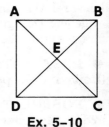

Ex. 5–10

5. △*CAD* ≅ △*CAD*.
6. If △*DBA* ≅ △*DBC*, then △*DBC* ≅ △*DBA*.
7. Square *ABCD* ≅ square *ABCD*.
8. If △*AED* ≅ △*CED* and △*CED* ≅ △*CEB*, then △*AED* ≅ △*CEB*.
9. If *DB* = *AC*, then *AC* = *DB*.
10. If △*CAD* ≅ △*CAB* and △*CAB* ≅ △*BDC*, then △*CAD* ≅ △*BDC*.

4-2 PROVING TRIANGLES CONGRUENT WHEN TWO PAIRS OF SIDES AND THE INCLUDED ANGLE ARE CONGRUENT

In Course I, you saw that it was possible to prove two triangles congruent by proving that fewer than three pairs of sides and three pairs of angles had to be congruent. For example, the diagram below and the explanation that follows show how to use a ruler and protractor to copy a triangle by drawing only two sides and the angle *included* between these sides.

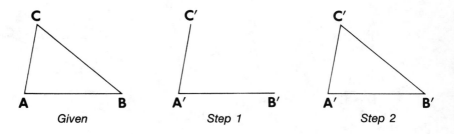

Given   Step 1   Step 2

Given $\triangle ABC$. In step 1, copy $\overline{AB}$ to form $\overline{A'B'}$, copy the included $\angle A$ to form the included $\angle A'$, and copy $\overline{AC}$ to form $\overline{A'C'}$. Although we have copied only two sides and their included angle, we see in step 2 that the only way we can complete the triangle is to connect B' and C'. The triangle $A'B'C'$ is formed where $\triangle A'B'C' \cong \triangle ABC$.

This experiment, repeated several times, leads to the following statement whose truth will be assumed without proof:

● **POSTULATE 28.   Two triangles are congruent if two sides and the included angle of one triangle are congruent respectively to two sides and the included angle of the other. [s.a.s. $\cong$ s.a.s.]**

Thus, in $\triangle ABC$ and $\triangle A'B'C'$ above, if $\overline{AB} \cong \overline{A'B'}$, $\angle A \cong \angle A'$ and $\overline{AC} \cong \overline{A'C'}$, it follows that $\triangle ABC \cong \triangle A'B'C'$.

Note. Although it has not been stated in the postulate, there has been established a correspondence between the vertices of the two triangles that are mentioned in the hypothesis. Here and in the future, although correspondences exist, we will not state the correspondences in postulates and theorems involving congruent triangles.

MODEL PROBLEM

In $\triangle ABC$, if $\overline{AC} \cong \overline{BC}$ and $\overline{CD}$ is the bisector of $\angle ACB$, prove that $\triangle ACD \cong \triangle BCD$.

Given: $\triangle ABC$ with $\overline{AC} \cong \overline{BC}$.
  $\overline{CD}$ bisects $\angle ACB$.

Prove: $\triangle ACD \cong \triangle BCD$.

Plan: Prove the triangles congruent by showing that s.a.s. $\cong$ s.a.s.

Statements	*Reasons*
1. In $\triangle ABC$, $\overline{AC} \cong \overline{BC}$. (s. $\cong$ s.)	1. Given.
2. $\overline{CD}$ bisects $\angle ACB$.	2. Given.
3. $\angle 1 \cong \angle 2$. (a. $\cong$ a.)	3. Definition of angle bisector.
4. $\overline{CD} \cong \overline{CD}$. (s. $\cong$ s.)	4. Reflexive property of congruence.
5. $\triangle ACD \cong \triangle BCD$.	5. s.a.s. $\cong$ s.a.s.

Note. In steps 1, 3, and 4, we wrote (s. ≅ s.) next to pairs of congruent sides and (a. ≅ a.) next to pairs of congruent angles to help identify the corresponding parts that prove the triangles are congruent.

As an additional aid, you may wish to mark corresponding parts in the diagram with the same number of strokes or arcs. For example, at the right:

∠1 and ∠2 are marked by single arcs to show ∠1 ≅ ∠2.

$\overline{AC}$ and $\overline{BC}$ are marked by single strokes to show $\overline{AC} ≅ \overline{BC}$.

$\overline{CD}$ is marked with an × to show $\overline{CD} ≅ \overline{CD}$.

EXERCISES

In 1–6: Pairs of line segments marked with the same number of strokes are congruent. Pairs of angles marked with the same number of arcs are congruent. A line segment or an angle marked with × is congruent to itself by the reflexive property of congruence.

Is the given information sufficient to prove congruent triangles?

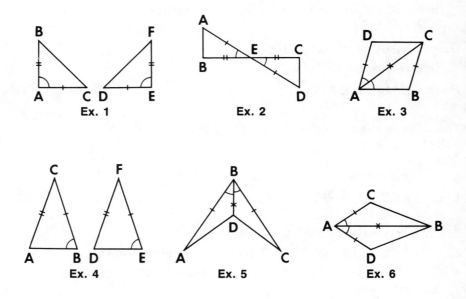

In 7–9, name the pair of corresponding sides or the pair of corresponding angles that would have to be proved congruent (in addition to those pairs marked congruent) in order to prove that the triangles are congruent by s.a.s. ≅ s.a.s.

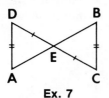

Ex. 7

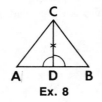

Ex. 8

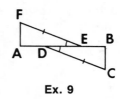

Ex. 9

10. *Given:* $\overline{DE} \cong \overline{AB}$, $\overline{EF} \cong \overline{BC}$,
    $\angle E$ and $\angle B$ are right angles.

    Prove: $\triangle DEF \cong \triangle ABC$.

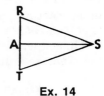

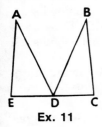

Ex. 11

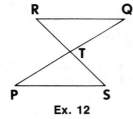

Ex. 12

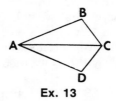

Ex. 13

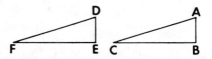

Ex. 14

11. *Given:* $\overline{AE} \cong \overline{BC}$, $\angle E \cong \angle C$, D is the midpoint of $\overline{EC}$.
    Prove: $\triangle ADE \cong \triangle BDC$.
12. *Given:* $\overline{RS}$ bisects $\overline{PQ}$ at T, $\overline{PQ}$ bisects $\overline{RS}$ at T.
    Prove: $\triangle PTS \cong \triangle QTR$.
13. *Given:* $\overline{AB} \cong \overline{AD}$, $\overline{AC}$ bisects $\angle BAD$.
    Prove: $\triangle ABC \cong \triangle ADC$.
14. *Given:* $\overline{AS} \perp \overline{RT}$, A is the midpoint of $\overline{RT}$.
    Prove: $\triangle RAS \cong \triangle TAS$.

15. If $\overline{AP} \cong \overline{CP}$, $\angle x \cong \angle y$, and $\overleftrightarrow{BPD}$,
    prove that $\triangle ABP \cong \triangle CBP$.

16. If $\overline{DB}$ and $\overline{AC}$ bisect each other
    at E, prove that $\triangle AEB \cong \triangle CED$.

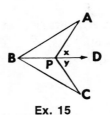

Ex. 15

Ex. 16

4-3 PROVING TRIANGLES CONGRUENT WHEN TWO PAIRS OF ANGLES AND THE INCLUDED SIDE ARE CONGRUENT

In Course I, you saw that we could copy a triangle using a ruler and protractor by drawing only two angles and the side *included* between these angles.

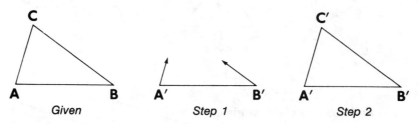

Given   *Step 1*   *Step 2*

Let us start with $\triangle ABC$. In step 1, copy $\angle A$ to form $\angle A'$, copy the included side $\overline{AB}$ to form the included side $\overline{A'B'}$, and copy $\angle B$ to form $\angle B'$. Although we have copied only two angles and their included side, we see in step 2 that, when we extend the rays at A' and B', these rays must meet at a point that we call C'. The triangle $A'B'C'$ is formed such that $\triangle A'B'C' \cong \triangle ABC$.

This experiment, repeated several times, leads to the following statement whose truth will be assumed without proof:

● **POSTULATE 29. Two triangles are congruent if two angles and the included side of one triangle are congruent respectively to two angles and the included side of the other. [a.s.a. ≅ a.s.a.]**

Thus, in $\triangle ABC$ and $\triangle A'B'C'$, if $\angle A \cong \angle A'$, $\overline{AB} \cong \overline{A'B'}$ and $\angle B \cong \angle B'$, it follows that $\triangle ABC \cong \triangle A'B'C'$. We will now use this postulate to prove two triangles congruent.

MODEL PROBLEM _____

Given: $\overleftrightarrow{CD}$ and $\overleftrightarrow{AB}$ intersect at E.
  $\overline{BA}$ bisects $\overline{CD}$. $\overline{AC} \perp \overline{CD}$,
  $\overline{BD} \perp \overline{CD}$.

Prove: $\triangle ACE \cong \triangle BDE$.

Plan: Prove the triangles congruent by showing that a.s.a. ≅ a.s.a. (Insert numbers for easy reference to angles.)

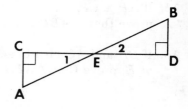

Statements	*Reasons*
1. $\overleftrightarrow{CD}$ and $\overleftrightarrow{AB}$ intersect E.	1. Given.
2. $\angle 1$ and $\angle 2$ are vertical angles.	2. Definition of vertical angles.
3. $\angle 1 \cong \angle 2$. (a. $\cong$ a.)	3. If two angles are vertical angles, they are congruent.
4. $\overline{BA}$ bisects $\overline{CD}$.	4. Given.
5. $\overline{CE} \cong \overline{ED}$. (s. $\cong$ s.)	5. Definition of bisector of a line segment.
6. $\overline{AC} \perp \overline{CD}, \overline{BD} \perp \overline{CD}$.	6. Given.
7. $\angle C$ and $\angle D$ are right angles.	7. Definition of perpendicular lines.
8. $\angle C \cong \angle D$. (a. $\cong$ a.)	8. If two angles are right angles, they are congruent.
9. $\triangle ACE \cong \triangle BDE$.	9. a.s.a. $\cong$ a.s.a.

EXERCISES

In 1–3, tell whether or not the triangles can be proved congruent by the a.s.a. $\cong$ a.s.a. postulate, using only the marked congruent parts in establishing the congruence.

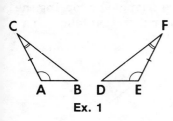

Ex. 1

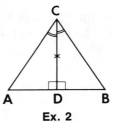

Ex. 2

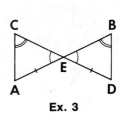

Ex. 3

In 4–6, name the pair of corresponding sides or the pair of corresponding angles that would have to be proved congruent (in addition to those pairs marked congruent) in order to prove that the triangles are congruent by a.s.a $\cong$ a.s.a.

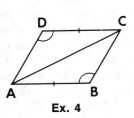

Ex. 4

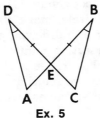

Ex. 5

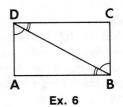

Ex. 6

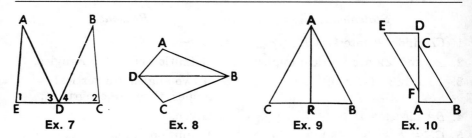

Ex. 7　　　　　Ex. 8　　　　　Ex. 9　　　　　Ex. 10

7. *Given:* ∠1 ≅ ∠2, *D* is the midpoint of $\overline{EC}$, ∠3 ≅ ∠4.
   Prove: △*AED* ≅ △*BCD*.
8. *Given:* $\overline{DB}$ bisects ∠*ADC*, $\overline{BD}$ bisects ∠*ABC*.
   Prove: △*ADB* ≅ △*CDB*.
9. *Given:* $\overline{AR}$ ⊥ $\overline{CB}$, $\overline{AR}$ bisects ∠*CAB*.
   Prove: △*ACR* ≅ △*ABR*.
10. *Given:* $\overline{DCFA}$, ∠*E* ≅ ∠*B*, $\overline{ED}$ ≅ $\overline{AB}$, $\overline{FD}$ ⊥ $\overline{DE}$, $\overline{CA}$ ⊥ $\overline{AB}$.
    Prove: △*DEF* ≅ △*ABC*.

4-4 PROVING TRIANGLES CONGRUENT WHEN THREE PAIRS OF SIDES ARE CONGRUENT

In Course I, you used compasses to construct a triangle by copying the three sides of the triangle. The diagram and explanation that follow show how to do this.

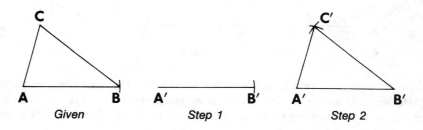

Given　　　　　Step 1　　　　　Step 2

Given △*ABC*. In step 1, copy side $\overline{AB}$ to form side $\overline{A'B'}$. In step 2, using *A'* as the center of a circle, mark off an arc whose radius is *AC*. Also, using *B'* as the center of a different circle, mark off an arc whose radius is *BC*. The arcs intersect at point *C'*, forming △*A'B'C'*. [You can measure the angles to see that ∠*A* ≅ ∠*A'*, ∠*B* ≅ ∠*B'*, and ∠*C* ≅ ∠*C'*.] Thus, using only three sides, we see that △*ABC* ≅ △*A'B'C'*. Repeated experiments lead to the next statement whose truth is assumed without proof:

● **POSTULATE 30. Two triangles are congruent if the three sides of one triangle are congruent respectively to the three sides of the other. [s.s.s. ≅ s.s.s.]**

Thus, in △ABC and △A'B'C', if $\overline{AB} \cong \overline{A'B'}$, $\overline{BC} \cong \overline{B'C'}$, and $\overline{CA} \cong \overline{C'A'}$, it follows that △ABC ≅ △A'B'C'. We will now use this postulate to prove two triangles congruent.

MODEL PROBLEM

Given: Isosceles triangle ABC with $\overline{CA} \cong \overline{CB}$.
    D is the midpoint of base $\overline{AB}$.

Prove: △ACD ≅ △BCD.

Plan: Prove the triangles congruent by showing that s.s.s. ≅ s.s.s.

Statements	*Reasons*
1. In isosceles triangle ABC, $\overline{CA} \cong \overline{CB}$. (s. ≅ s.)	1. Given.
2. D is the midpoint of base $\overline{AB}$.	2. Given.
3. $\overline{AD} \cong \overline{DB}$. (s. ≅ s.)	3. Definition of midpoint.
4. $\overline{CD} \cong \overline{CD}$. (s. ≅ s.)	4. Reflexive property of congruence.
5. △ACD ≅ △BCD.	5. s.s.s. ≅ s.s.s.

EXERCISES

In 1–3, tell whether or not the triangles can be proved congruent using only the marked congruent parts in establishing the congruence. Give the reason for your answer.

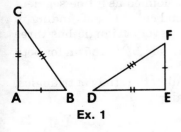

Ex. 1

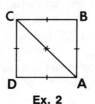

Ex. 2

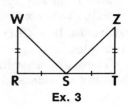

Ex. 3

In 4–6, name the pair of corresponding sides that would have to be proved congruent (in addition to those pairs marked congruent) in order to prove that the triangles are congruent by s.s.s. ≅ s.s.s.

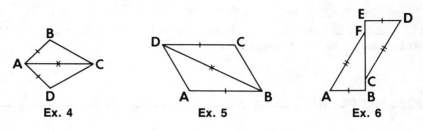

Ex. 4   Ex. 5   Ex. 6

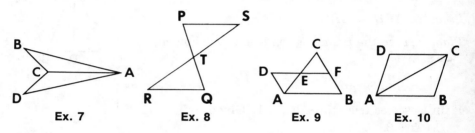

Ex. 7   Ex. 8   Ex. 9   Ex. 10

7. *Given:* $\overline{AB} \cong \overline{AD}$, $\overline{CB} \cong \overline{CD}$.
   Prove: $\triangle ABC \cong \triangle ADC$.
8. *Given:* T is the midpoint of $\overline{PQ}$, $\overline{PQ}$ bisects $\overline{RS}$, $\overline{RQ} \cong \overline{SP}$.
   Prove: $\triangle RTQ \cong \triangle STP$.
9. *Given:* $\overline{AC}$ and $\overline{DF}$ bisect each other at E, $\overline{AD} \cong \overline{CF}$.
   Prove: $\triangle DEA \cong \triangle FEC$.
10. If both pairs of opposite sides of quadrilateral $ABCD$ are congruent, prove that $\triangle ABC \cong \triangle CDA$.

4-5   MORE LINE SEGMENTS ASSOCIATED WITH TRIANGLES

In Chapter 1, an ***altitude of a triangle*** was defined as a line segment drawn from any vertex of the triangle, perpendicular to and ending in the line that contains the opposite side. Thus, every triangle has three altitudes. In $\triangle CED$ and $\triangle HEF$ below, the altitude $\overline{EF}$ is shown for both triangles.

There are other line segments that are useful in the study of triangles, namely *median* and *angle bisector* of a triangle.

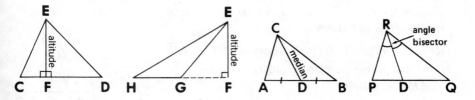

● **Definition.** A *median of a triangle* is a line segment that joins any vertex of the triangle to the midpoint of the opposite side.

In △*ABC* above, if *D* is the midpoint of $\overline{AB}$, then $\overline{CD}$ is the median drawn from vertex *C* to side $\overline{AB}$. We may also draw a median from vertex *A* to the midpoint of side $\overline{BC}$, and a median from vertex *B* to the midpoint of side $\overline{AC}$. Thus, every triangle has three medians.

To construct a median of a given triangle.

See Chapter 16, Construction 8.

● **Definition.** An *angle bisector of a triangle* is a line segment that bisects any angle of the triangle and terminates in the side opposite that angle.

In △*PQR* above, if ∠*PRD* ≅ ∠*QRD* and *D* is a point on side $\overline{PQ}$, then $\overline{RD}$ is the bisector of ∠*PRQ* in △*PQR*. An angle bisector may also be drawn from the vertex of ∠*P* to some point on $\overline{RQ}$; and an angle bisector may also be drawn from the vertex of ∠*Q* to some point on $\overline{PR}$. Thus, every triangle has three angle bisectors.

To construct the bisector of an angle of a given triangle.

See Chapter 16, Construction 9.

● In a scalene triangle, the *altitude*, the *median*, and the *angle bisector* drawn from any common vertex are three distinct line segments.

In △ABC, from the common vertex B, three line segments are drawn:

$\overline{BD}$ is the *altitude* from B because $\overline{BD} \perp \overline{AC}$;

$\overline{BE}$ is the *angle bisector* from B because
∠ABE ≅ ∠EBC;

$\overline{BF}$ is the *median* from B because F is the midpoint of $\overline{AC}$.

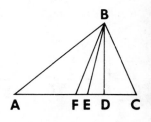

In some special triangles (such as the isosceles triangle and the equilateral triangle), some of these segments *coincide*, that is, fall on the same line. You will see these examples later.

EXERCISES

1. In each triangle below, name the type of line segment that $\overline{CD}$ is.

(a) **(b)** **(c)** **(d)**

 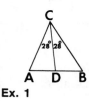

Ex. 1

2. Polygon ABC is a triangle. $\overline{CD}$ is an altitude. $\overline{CE}$ is an angle bisector. $\overline{CF}$ is a median.

a. Name two congruent angles, each of which has its vertex at C.

b. Name two line segments that are congruent.

c. Name two line segments that are perpendicular to each other.

d. Name two angles that are right angles.

4-6 MORE PRACTICE IN PROVING TRIANGLES CONGRUENT

Methods of Proving Triangles Congruent

To prove that two triangles are congruent, prove that any one of the following statements is true:

1. Two sides and the included angle of one triangle are congruent respectively to two sides and the included angle of the other. [s.a.s. ≅ s.a.s.]

2. Two angles and the included side of one triangle are congruent respectively to two angles and the included side of the other. [a.s.a. ≅ a.s.a.]
3. Three sides of one triangle are congruent respectively to the three sides of the other. [s.s.s. ≅ s.s.s.]

Analyzing a Congruence Problem

For the three given congruence postulates, a process of *analysis* can help to determine which postulate can be used to prove that two triangles are congruent. Let us see how to perform such an analysis for the following congruence problems.

MODEL PROBLEMS ───

1. *Given:* $\overleftrightarrow{ABE}$ bisects $\angle CAD$.
    $\angle CBE \cong \angle DBE$.

   Prove: $\triangle ACB \cong \triangle ADB$.

   Since $\overrightarrow{ABE}$ bisects $\angle CAD$, $\angle 1 \cong \angle 2$, giving us one pair of congruent angles. Also, $\overline{AB}$ is a common side in both triangles. Thus, $\overline{AB} \cong \overline{AB}$ by the reflexive property of congruence, giving us a pair of congruent sides. We will attempt to use either the a.s.a. postulate or the s.a.s. postulate.

   To use the s.a.s. postulate, we must prove that $\overline{AC} \cong \overline{AD}$. Having no information about these sides, we cannot use the s.a.s. postulate.

   To use the a.s.a. postulate, we must prove that $\angle 3 \cong \angle 4$.

   Since we know from the *given* that $\angle CBE \cong \angle DBE$ and that we have a straight line, $\overleftrightarrow{ABE}$, we can show that $\angle 3$ must be congruent to $\angle 4$ because two angles that are supplementary to congruent angles are congruent.

   Therefore, we prove $\triangle ACB \cong \triangle ADB$ by the a.s.a. postulate as follows:

Statements	*Reasons*
1. $\overleftrightarrow{ABE}$ bisects $\angle CAD$.	1. Given.
2. $\angle 1 \cong \angle 2$. (a. ≅ a.)	2. Definition of angle bisector.
3. $\overline{AB} \cong \overline{AB}$. (s. ≅ s.)	3. Reflexive property of congruence.
4. $\overleftrightarrow{ABE}$.	4. Given.
5. $\angle CBE \cong \angle DBE$.	5. Given.

Statements	Reasons
6. ∠3 is supplementary to ∠*CBE*. ∠4 is supplementary to ∠*DBE*.	6. If two angles form a linear pair, the angles are supplementary.
7. ∠3 ≅ ∠4. (a. ≅ a.)	7. If two angles are supplements of congruent angles, they are congruent.
8. △*ACB* ≅ △*ADB*.	8. a.s.a. ≅ a.s.a.

2. *Given:* $\overline{ABCD}$.

$\overline{AE} \cong \overline{DF}$.

∠*A* ≅ ∠*D*.

$\overline{AC} \cong \overline{DB}$.

Prove: △*AEB* ≅ △*DFC*.

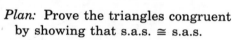

Plan: Prove the triangles congruent by showing that s.a.s. ≅ s.a.s.

To do this, it is necessary to prove that $\overline{AB} \cong \overline{DC}$.

Statements	*Reasons*
1. $\overline{AE} \cong \overline{DF}$. (s. ≅ s.)	1. Given.
2. ∠*A* ≅ ∠*D*. (a. ≅ a.)	2. Given.
3. $\overline{ABCD}$.	3. Given.
4. $\overline{AC} \cong \overline{DB}$.	4. Given.
5. $\overline{BC} \cong \overline{BC}$.	5. Reflexive property of congruence.
6. $\overline{AC} - \overline{BC} \cong \overline{DB} - \overline{BC}$, or $\overline{AB} \cong \overline{DC}$. (s. ≅ s.)	6. Subtraction postulate of congruent segments.
7. △*AEB* ≅ △*DFC*.	7. s.a.s. ≅ s.a.s.

EXERCISES

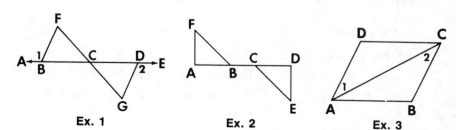

Ex. 1   Ex. 2   Ex. 3

1. *Given:* $\overleftrightarrow{ABCDE}$ and $\overrightarrow{FCG}$, C is the midpoint of $\overline{BD}$, $\angle 1 \cong \angle 2$.
   Prove: $\triangle BFC \cong \triangle DGC$.
2. *Given:* $\overline{ABCD}$, $\overline{FA} \perp \overline{AD}$, $\overline{ED} \perp \overline{AD}$, $\overline{AF} \cong \overline{DE}$, $\overline{AC} \cong \overline{DB}$.
   Prove: $\triangle ABF \cong \triangle DCE$.
3. *Given:* In quadrilateral $ABCD$, $\overline{AD} \cong \overline{CB}$ and $\angle 1 \cong \angle 2$.
   Prove: $\triangle ADC \cong \triangle CBA$.

Ex. 4

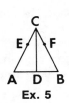
Ex. 5

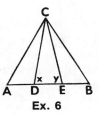
Ex. 6

4. *Given:* Isosceles $\triangle RST$ with $\overline{RT} \cong \overline{ST}$, $\overline{TP}$ is a median to base $\overline{RS}$.
   Prove: $\triangle RTP \cong \triangle STP$.
5. *Given:* In triangle ABC, $\overline{CD}$ is a median to $\overline{AB}$, $\overline{CE} \cong \overline{CF}$, $\overline{EA} \cong \overline{FB}$.
   Prove: $\triangle ACD \cong \triangle BCD$.
6. *Given:* Points D and E divide $\overline{AB}$ into three congruent parts,
   $\overline{CD} \cong \overline{CE}$, $\angle x \cong \angle y$.
   Prove: $\triangle ACD \cong \triangle BCE$.

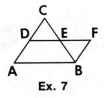
Ex. 7

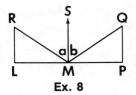
Ex. 8

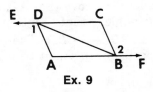
Ex. 9

7. *Given:* E is the midpoint of $\overline{BC}$, $\angle ACB \cong \angle FBC$, $\overline{AD} \cong \overline{CD}$,
   $\overline{FB} \cong \overline{AD}$.
   Prove: $\triangle CDE \cong \triangle BFE$.
8. *Given:* $\overrightarrow{MS}$ is the perpendicular bisector of $\overline{LP}$, $\overline{RM} \cong \overline{QM}$,
   $\angle a \cong \angle b$.
   Prove: $\triangle RLM \cong \triangle QPM$.
9. *Given:* $\overrightarrow{CDE}$ and $\overrightarrow{ABF}$, $\angle 1 \cong \angle 2$, $\angle EDB \cong \angle FBD$.
   Prove: $\triangle ADB \cong \triangle CBD$.

10. *Prove:* Two right triangles are congruent if the legs of one triangle
    are congruent to the legs of the other triangle.

4-7 USING CONGRUENT TRIANGLES TO PROVE LINE SEGMENTS CONGRUENT AND ANGLES CONGRUENT

Recall that when two triangles are congruent, their corresponding sides are congruent and their corresponding angles are congruent.

Thus, to prove that two line segments are congruent or two angles are congruent:

1. Choose two triangles that contain the segments or angles that are to be proved congruent.
2. Prove that the chosen triangles are congruent.
3. Show that the segments or angles that are to be proved congruent are corresponding parts of congruent triangles. Thus, these parts are congruent.

MODEL PROBLEM

In $\triangle ABC$, if $\overline{BD}$ bisects $\angle ABC$, and $\overline{BD} \perp \overline{AC}$, prove that $\overline{AD} \cong \overline{CD}$.

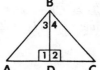

Given: In $\triangle ABC$, $\overline{BD}$ bisects $\angle ABC$.
$\overline{BD} \perp \overline{AC}$.

Prove: $\overline{AD} \cong \overline{CD}$.

Plan: To prove that $\overline{AD} \cong \overline{CD}$, show that the triangles that contain these segments are congruent, namely $\triangle ABD \cong \triangle CBD$. Then, $\overline{AD} \cong \overline{CD}$ because these are corresponding parts of congruent triangles.

Statements	*Reasons*
1. $\overline{BD}$ bisects $\angle ABC$.	1. Given.
2. $\angle 3 \cong \angle 4$. (a. $\cong$ a.)	2. Definition of angle bisector.
3. $\overline{BD} \perp \overline{AC}$.	3. Given.
4. $\angle 1$ and $\angle 2$ are right angles.	4. Definition of perpendicular lines.
5. $\angle 1 \cong \angle 2$. (a. $\cong$ a.)	5. If two angles are right angles, they are congruent.
6. $\overline{BD} \cong \overline{BD}$. (s. $\cong$ s.)	6. Reflexive property of congruence.
7. $\triangle ABD \cong \triangle CBD$.	7. a.s.a. $\cong$ a.s.a.
8. $\overline{AD} \cong \overline{CD}$.	8. Corresponding parts of congruent triangles are congruent.

EXERCISES

In 1–6, the figures have been marked to indicate pairs of congruent angles and pairs of congruent segments.
a. In each figure, name two triangles that are congruent.
b. State the reason why the triangles are congruent.
c. For each pair of triangles, name three additional pairs of parts that are congruent because they are corresponding parts of congruent triangles.

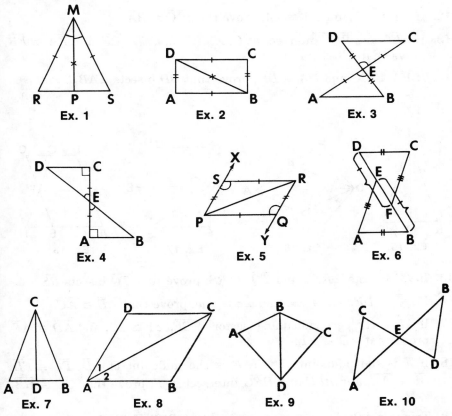

Ex. 1   Ex. 2   Ex. 3

Ex. 4   Ex. 5   Ex. 6

Ex. 7   Ex. 8   Ex. 9   Ex. 10

7. $\overline{CA} \cong \overline{CB}$ and $\overline{AD} \cong \overline{BD}$. **a.** Prove $\triangle ADC \cong \triangle BDC$. **b.** Find three pairs of congruent angles in $\triangle ADC$ and $\triangle BDC$.

8. $\overline{AD} \cong \overline{AB}$ and $\angle 1 \cong \angle 2$. **a.** Prove $\triangle ADC \cong \triangle ABC$. **b.** Find three more pairs of congruent parts in $\triangle ADC$ and $\triangle ABC$.

9. $\overline{BD}$ bisects $\angle ABC$, and $\overline{DB}$ bisects $\angle ADC$.
  a. Prove that $\triangle ABD \cong \triangle CBD$.
  b. Find three more pairs of congruent parts in $\triangle ABD$ and $\triangle CBD$.

10. If $\overline{AB}$ and $\overline{CD}$ bisect each other at E, prove that $\angle C \cong \angle D$.

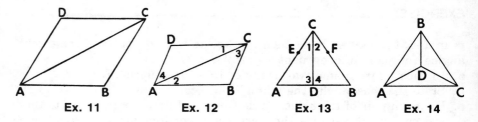

Ex. 11   Ex. 12   Ex. 13   Ex. 14

11. If $\overline{AB} \cong \overline{CD}$ and $\overline{BC} \cong \overline{DA}$, prove that $\angle B \cong \angle D$.

12. If $\angle 1 \cong \angle 2$ and $\angle 3 \cong \angle 4$, prove that $\overline{DC} \cong \overline{BA}$.

13. If $\overline{AEC}$ and $\overline{BFC}$ intersect at C, $\angle 1 \cong \angle 2$, $\overline{CE} \cong \overline{CF}$, and $\overline{EA} \cong \overline{FB}$, prove that $\angle 3 \cong \angle 4$.

14. If $\overline{BA} \cong \overline{BC}$ and $\overline{DA} \cong \overline{DC}$, prove that $\overline{BD}$ bisects $\angle ABC$.

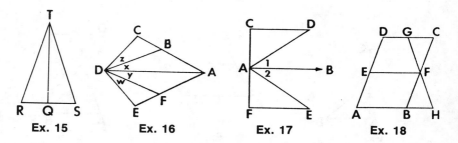

Ex. 15   Ex. 16   Ex. 17   Ex. 18

15. If $\overline{TQ}$ bisects $\angle RTS$ and $\overline{TQ} \perp \overline{RS}$, prove that $\overline{TQ}$ bisects $\overline{RS}$.

16. If $\overline{DC} \cong \overline{DE}$, $\angle x \cong \angle y$, and $\angle z \cong \angle w$, prove that $\overline{AE} \cong \overline{AC}$.

17. If $\overrightarrow{AB}$ is the perpendicular bisector of $\overline{CF}$, $\angle 1 \cong \angle 2$, and $\overline{AD} \cong \overline{AE}$, prove that $\angle D \cong \angle E$.

18. If F is the midpoint of $\overline{GH}$, E is the midpoint of $\overline{AD}$, $\overline{FC} \cong \overline{ED}$, $\overline{BF} \cong \overline{AE}$, and $\overline{BFC}$ and $\overline{HFG}$ intersect at F, prove that $\overline{GC} \cong \overline{HB}$.

19. Triangle ABC is congruent to triangle $A'B'C'$. If $m\angle C$ is represented by $2x - 10$ and $m\angle C'$ is represented by $x + 30$:
  a. Find x.
  b. Find $m\angle C$.
  c. Find $m\angle B$ if it is represented by $x - 25$.

20. Triangle DEF is congruent to triangle $D'E'F'$. If EF is represented by $3x + 2$, $E'F'$ is represented by $x + 10$, and ED is represented by $x + 2$, **(a)** find x, **(b)** find ED, and **(c)** find $E'D'$.

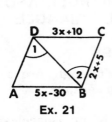

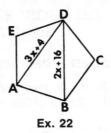

Ex. 21   Ex. 22

21. *Given:* $\overline{AD} \cong \overline{CB}$ and $\angle 1 \cong \angle 2$.

    a. *Prove:* $\triangle ADB \cong \triangle CBD$.　　**b.** *Prove:* $\overline{AB} \cong \overline{CD}$.

    c. If $AB = 5x - 30$, $CD = 3x + 10$, and $BC = 2x + 5$, write an equation to solve for x.

    d. Find the lengths of $\overline{AB}$, $\overline{CD}$ and $\overline{BC}$.

22. If all sides of polygon $ABCDE$ are congruent and $\angle E \cong \angle C$, find AD and BD.

23. Triangle ABC is congruent to triangle $A'B'C'$. If AB is represented by $2x + y$, $A'B' = 7$, $BC = 11$, and $B'C'$ is represented by $4x + y$, find x and y.

Miscellaneous Exercises

In 24–28, select the numeral preceding the word or expression that best completes the statement or answers the question.

24. If, in $\triangle ABC$, $\overline{BD}$ is the median to side $\overline{AC}$, and $\triangle ABD \cong \triangle CBD$, then $\triangle ABC$ must be
(1) scalene　(2) isosceles　(3) right　(4) equilateral

25. Two right triangles must be congruent if　(1) the hypotenuse of one triangle is congruent to the hypotenuse of the other　(2) an acute angle of one triangle is congruent to an acute angle of the other　(3) two legs of one triangle are congruent to two legs of the other　(4) each contains a right angle

26. Two isosceles triangles are congruent if　(1) the vertex angle of one triangle is congruent to the vertex angle of the other　(2) a base angle of one triangle is congruent to a base angle of the other　(3) a leg of one triangle is congruent to a leg of the other　(4) a leg and the vertex angle of one triangle are congruent to a leg and the vertex angle of the other

27. In $\triangle ABC$, D is a point on $\overline{BC}$ such that $\overline{AD}$ is both an angle bisector and an altitude in $\triangle ABC$. Which statement may be false?
(1) $BD = CD$　(2) $AB = AC$　(3) $AC = BC$　(4) $m\angle B = m\angle C$

28. In isosceles right triangle ABC, $\angle B$ is a right angle, $\overline{AB} \cong \overline{BC}$, and $\overline{BD}$ is a median. Which segment is not an altitude for $\triangle ABC$?
(1) $\overline{BD}$　(2) $\overline{AD}$　(3) $\overline{AB}$　(4) $\overline{BC}$

4-8   THE ISOSCELES TRIANGLE AND THE EQUILATERAL TRIANGLE

Properties of an Isosceles Triangle

● **THEOREM 9.** **If two sides of a triangle are congruent, the angles opposite these sides are congruent,** *or*

● **THEOREM 9.** **The base angles of an isosceles triangle are congruent.**

To begin, we draw an isosceles triangle and letter the vertices so that we can identify the congruent sides, namely, $\overline{CA} \cong \overline{CB}$. To prove this theorem it will be necessary to draw an additional line segment in the triangle. Then, we letter point D and identify $\angle 1$ and $\angle 2$ to help in writing the proof.

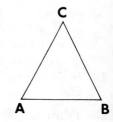

Given: $\triangle ACB$ with $\overline{CA} \cong \overline{CB}$.

Prove: $\angle A \cong \angle B$.

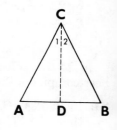

Plan: To prove that $\angle A \cong \angle B$, show that $\angle A$ and $\angle B$ are corresponding angles of two congruent triangles. If we draw the bisector of the vertex angle, we will separate $\triangle ABC$ into two triangles, $\triangle ACD$ and $\triangle BCD$, which can be proved congruent by s.a.s. $\cong$ s.a.s. From these congruent triangles, we can show that $\angle A \cong \angle B$.

Statements	*Reasons*
1. Let $\overline{CD}$ be the bisector of vertex $\angle ACB$, D being the point at which the bisector intersects $\overline{AB}$.	1. Every angle has one and only one bisector.
2. $\angle 1 \cong \angle 2$. (a. $\cong$ a.)	2. A bisector of an angle divides the angle into two congruent angles.
3. $\overline{CA} \cong \overline{CB}$. (s. $\cong$ s.)	3. Given.
4. $\overline{CD} \cong \overline{CD}$. (s. $\cong$ s.)	4. Reflexive property of congruence.
5. $\triangle ACD \cong \triangle BCD$.	5. s.a.s. $\cong$ s.a.s.
6. $\angle A \cong \angle B$.	6. Corresponding angles of congruent triangles are congruent.

● **Definition.** A *corollary* is a theorem that can easily be deduced from another theorem.

From Theorem 9, we can prove two other statements that are called corollaries of Theorem 9 because the statements are related to an isosceles triangle.

● **COROLLARY** *T9-1.* **The bisector of the vertex angle of an isosceles triangle bisects the base.**

From the preceding proof that $\triangle ACD \cong \triangle BCD$, we can also conclude $\overline{AD} \cong \overline{BD}$ since they, too, are corresponding parts of congruent triangles. Thus, $\overline{CD}$ bisects the base $\overline{AB}$.

● **COROLLARY** *T9-2.* **The bisector of the vertex angle of an isosceles triangle is perpendicular to the base.**

Again, from $\triangle ACD \cong \triangle BCD$, we can say that $\angle CDA \cong \angle CDB$ because they are corresponding parts of congruent triangles. Since the noncommon sides of these adjacent congruent angles form a line, $\angle CDA$ and $\angle CDB$ are both right angles, and $\overline{CD} \perp \overline{AB}$.

Properties of an Equilateral Triangle

Theorem 9 has shown that in an isosceles triangle where two sides are congruent, the angles opposite these sides are congruent. We may prove another corollary to this theorem for any equilateral triangle where three sides are congruent.

● **COROLLARY** *T9-3.* **Every equilateral triangle is equiangular.**

Given $\triangle ABC$ where $\overline{BC} \cong \overline{CA} \cong \overline{AB}$. It then follows that $\angle A \cong \angle B \cong \angle C$, or that $\triangle ABC$ is equiangular.

MODEL PROBLEM _____

Given: Isosceles $\triangle ABC$ with $\overline{CA} \cong \overline{CB}$, M is the midpoint of $\overline{AB}$, $\overline{AD} \cong \overline{BE}$.

Prove: $\overline{MD} \cong \overline{ME}$.

Plan: To prove $\overline{MD} \cong \overline{ME}$, prove $\triangle ADM \cong \triangle BEM$ since these two triangles have $\overline{MD}$ and $\overline{ME}$ as corresponding sides. Then, prove $\triangle ADM \cong \triangle BEM$ by s.a.s. $\cong$ s.a.s.

Statements	*Reasons*
1. $\overline{CA} \cong \overline{CB}$.	1. Given.
2. $\angle A \cong \angle B$. (a. $\cong$ a.)	2. If two sides of a triangle are congruent, the angles opposite these sides are congruent.
3. $\overline{AD} \cong \overline{BE}$. (s. $\cong$ s.)	3. Given.
4. M is the midpoint of $\overline{AB}$.	4. Given.
5. $\overline{AM} \cong \overline{BM}$. (s. $\cong$ s.)	5. A midpoint divides a line segment into two congruent parts.
6. $\triangle ADM \cong \triangle BEM$.	6. s.a.s. $\cong$ s.a.s.
7. $\overline{MD} \cong \overline{ME}$.	7. Corresponding parts of congruent triangles are congruent.

EXERCISES _____

Numerical and Algebraic Applications

1. In $\triangle ABC$, if $\overline{CA} \cong \overline{CB}$ and m$\angle A = 50$, find m$\angle B$.
2. In triangle ABC, $\overline{AB} \cong \overline{BC}$. If $AB = 5x$ and $BC = 2x + 18$, find AB and BC.
3. In isosceles $\triangle ABC$, $\overline{AB} \cong \overline{BC}$. If $AB = 5x + 10$, $BC = 3x + 40$, and $AC = 2x + 30$, find the length of each side of the triangle.
4. In triangle ABC, $\overline{AB} \cong \overline{BC}$. If m$\angle A = 7x$ and m$\angle C = 2x + 50$, find m$\angle A$ and m$\angle C$.
5. In triangle EFG, $\overline{EF} \cong \overline{FG}$. If m$\angle E = 4x + 50$, m$\angle F = 2x + 60$, and m$\angle G = 14x + 30$, find m$\angle E$, m$\angle F$, and m$\angle G$.

Proofs

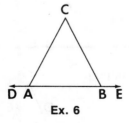

Ex. 6

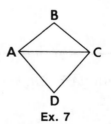

Ex. 7

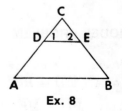

Ex. 8

6. *Given:* $\triangle ABC$ with $\overline{CA} \cong \overline{CB}$ and $\overleftrightarrow{DABE}$.
   Prove: $\angle CAD \cong \angle CBE$.
7. *Given:* Isosceles triangles ABC and ADC have the common base $\overline{AC}$.
   Prove: $\angle BAD \cong \angle BCD$.
8. If $\overline{CA} \cong \overline{CB}$, and $\overline{DA} \cong \overline{EB}$, prove that $\angle 1 \cong \angle 2$.

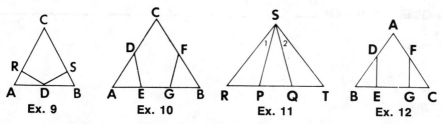

Ex. 9   Ex. 10   Ex. 11   Ex. 12

9. *Given:* In $\triangle ABC$, $\overline{CA} \cong \overline{CB}$, $\overline{AR} \cong \overline{BS}$, $\overline{DR} \perp \overline{AC}$, and $\overline{DS} \perp \overline{BC}$. *Prove:* $\overline{DR} \cong \overline{DS}$.

10. In isosceles triangle ABC, D and F are midpoints of the congruent legs. E and G are the trisection points of the base ($\overline{AE} \cong \overline{EG} \cong \overline{GB}$). Prove that $\overline{DE} \cong \overline{FG}$.

11. Given $\overline{RPQT}$, $\overline{SR} \cong \overline{ST}$, and $\angle 1 \cong \angle 2$, prove that $\triangle PSQ$ is an isosceles triangle.

12. In $\triangle ABC$, $\overline{AB} \cong \overline{AC}$, $\overline{DE} \perp \overline{BC}$, $\overline{FG} \perp \overline{BC}$, and $\overline{BG} \cong \overline{CE}$. Prove that $\overline{BD} \cong \overline{CF}$.

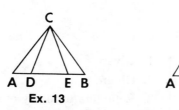

Ex. 13   Ex. 14

13. Given $\overline{AD} \cong \overline{BE}$, $\overline{CD} \cong \overline{CE}$, and $\overline{ADEB}$, prove that $\overline{AC} \cong \overline{BC}$.

14. If $\triangle ABC$ is an equilateral triangle and $\overline{CT} \cong \overline{AR} \cong \overline{BS}$, prove:
  a. $\overline{TA} \cong \overline{RB} \cong \overline{SC}$ **b.** $\triangle TAR \cong \triangle RBS \cong \triangle SCT$
  c. $\overline{TR} \cong \overline{RS} \cong \overline{ST}$ **d.** $\triangle TRS$ is an equilateral triangle.

15. *Prove:* The line segments joining the midpoint of the base of an isosceles triangle to the midpoints of the legs are congruent.

4-9 USING TWO PAIRS OF CONGRUENT TRIANGLES

Sometimes, it is impossible to use the *given* in order to prove immediately that a particular pair of triangles is congruent. In such cases, the *given* may contain enough information to first prove another pair of triangles congruent. Then, corresponding congruent parts in these congruent triangles may be used to prove the original pair of triangles congruent. See how this is done in the following example.

MODEL PROBLEM

Given: $\overline{AEB}$.
$\overline{AC} \cong \overline{AD}$.
$\overline{BC} \cong \overline{BD}$.

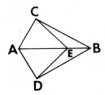

Prove: $\overline{CE} \cong \overline{DE}$.

From the *given* information, we can*not* prove immediately that $\triangle ACE \cong \triangle ADE$ nor can we prove that $\triangle CEB \cong \triangle DEB$.

However, we can prove that $\triangle CAB \cong \triangle DAB$. Using corresponding parts of these larger congruent triangles, we can then prove that either pair of the smaller triangles mentioned earlier are congruent. Thus, $\overline{CE} \cong \overline{DE}$ because they are corresponding parts of the smaller congruent triangles.

Plan: Prove $\triangle CAB \cong \triangle DAB$. Then, use corresponding parts of these congruent triangles to prove that $\triangle ACE \cong \triangle ADE$, resulting in $\overline{CE} \cong \overline{DE}$.

Statements	*Reasons*
1. $\overline{AC} \cong \overline{AD}$. (s. $\cong$ s.)	1. Given.
2. $\overline{BC} \cong \overline{BD}$. (s. $\cong$ s.)	2. Given.
3. $\overline{AB} \cong \overline{AB}$. (s. $\cong$ s.)	3. Reflexive property of congruence.
4. $\triangle CAB \cong \triangle DAB$.	4. s.s.s. $\cong$ s.s.s.
5. $\angle CAB \cong \angle DAB$, or $\angle CAE \cong \angle DAE$.	5. Corresponding parts of congruent triangles are congruent.
6. For $\triangle ACE$ and $\triangle ADE$, $\angle CAE \cong \angle DAE$. (a. $\cong$ a.)	6. Proved in step 5.
7. $\overline{AC} \cong \overline{AD}$. (s. $\cong$ s.)	7. Given.
8. $\overline{AE} \cong \overline{AE}$. (s. $\cong$ s.)	8. Reflexive property of congruence.
9. $\triangle ACE \cong \triangle ADE$.	9. s.a.s. $\cong$ s.a.s.
10. $\overline{CE} \cong \overline{DE}$.	10. Corresponding parts of congruent triangles are congruent.

Note that steps 6 and 7 repeat steps 5 and 1. Steps 6 and 7 could be omitted from the proof.

EXERCISES

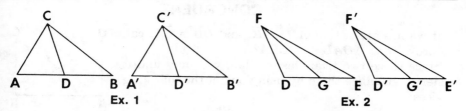

Ex. 1   Ex. 2

1. *Given:* $\triangle ABC \cong \triangle A'B'C'$, $\overline{CD}$ bisects $\angle C$, $\overline{C'D'}$ bisects $\angle C'$.
   Prove: $\overline{CD} \cong \overline{C'D'}$.
2. *Given:* $\triangle DEF \cong \triangle D'E'F'$, $\overline{FG}$ and $\overline{F'G'}$ are medians.
   Prove: $\overline{FG} \cong \overline{F'G'}$.

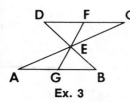

Ex. 3

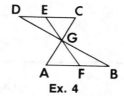

Ex. 4

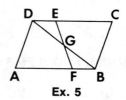

Ex. 5

3. *Given:* $\overline{AEC}$, $\overline{BED}$, and $\overline{GEF}$; $\overline{AE} \cong \overline{CE}$, $\overline{FE} \cong \overline{GE}$.
   Prove: **a.** $\triangle FEC \cong \triangle GEA$. **b.** $\angle C \cong \angle A$. **c.** $\triangle DEC \cong \triangle BEA$.
4. *Given:* $\overline{AC}$ and $\overline{BD}$ bisect each other at G; $\overline{EGF}$.
   Prove: **a.** $\triangle DGC \cong \triangle BGA$. **b.** $\angle D \cong \angle B$. **c.** $\overline{GE} \cong \overline{GF}$.
5. *Given:* $\overline{AD} \cong \overline{CB}$, $\overline{DC} \cong \overline{BA}$, $\overline{EF}$ bisects $\overline{BD}$ at G.
   Prove: **a.** $\triangle ADB \cong \triangle CBD$. **b.** $\angle ABD \cong \angle CDB$. **c.** $\overline{FG} \cong \overline{EG}$.

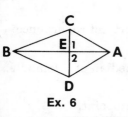

Ex. 6

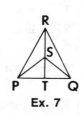

Ex. 7

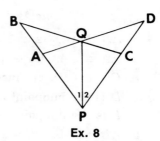

Ex. 8

6. *Given:* $\overline{AC} \cong \overline{AD}$, $\overline{BC} \cong \overline{BD}$, $\overline{AB}$ intersects $\overline{CD}$ at E.
   Prove: $\angle 1 \cong \angle 2$.
7. *Given:* $\overline{RP} \cong \overline{RQ}$, $\overline{SP} \cong \overline{SQ}$.
   Prove: $\overline{RT}$ bisects $\overline{PQ}$.
8. *Given:* $\overline{PQ}$, $\overline{PAB}$, $\overline{PCD}$, $\overline{AQD}$, and $\overline{CQB}$. $\angle 1 \cong \angle 2$ and $\overline{AP} \cong \overline{CP}$.
   Prove: $\overline{QB} \cong \overline{QD}$.

4-10   PROVING OVERLAPPING TRIANGLES CONGRUENT

If we are given that $\overline{AD} \cong \overline{BC}$ and $\overline{DB} \cong \overline{CA}$, can we prove that $\triangle DAB \cong \triangle CBA$?

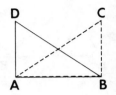

Since these two triangles overlap, you may find it easier to visualize them by using one of the following devices:

1. Outline one of the triangles with a solid line, and the other with a dotted line, as shown above, *or*

2. Separate the triangles, as shown at the right.

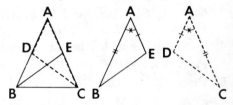

MODEL PROBLEMS ───────────────────────────────

1. *Given:* In $\triangle ABC$, $\overline{AB} \cong \overline{AC}$.
   $\overline{CD}$ and $\overline{BE}$ are medians.
   Prove: $\overline{BE} \cong \overline{CD}$.
   Plan: Prove $\triangle ABE \cong \triangle ACD$ by s.a.s. $\cong$ s.a.s. Then, $\overline{BE}$ and $\overline{CD}$ are corresponding parts of these congruent triangles.

Separate the Triangles

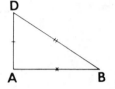

Statements	*Reasons*
1. $\overline{AB} \cong \overline{AC}$. (s. $\cong$ s.)	1. Given.
2. $\angle A \cong \angle A$. (a. $\cong$ a.)	2. Reflexive property of congruence.
3. $\overline{CD}$ and $\overline{BE}$ are medians.	3. Given.
4. D is the midpoint of $\overline{AB}$. E is the midpoint of $\overline{AC}$.	4. Definition of median of a triangle.
5. $AD = \frac{1}{2}AB$. $AE = \frac{1}{2}AC$.	5. Definition of midpoint.
6. $AD = AE$.	6. Halves of equal quantities are equal.
7. $\overline{AD} \cong \overline{AE}$. (s. $\cong$ s.)	7. Definition of congruent segments.
8. $\triangle ABE \cong \triangle ACD$.	8. s.a.s. $\cong$ s.a.s.
9. $\overline{BE} \cong \overline{CD}$.	9. Corresponding parts of congruent triangles are congruent.

2. Using the results of Model Problem 1, find the length of $\overline{BE}$ if $BE = 5x - 8$ and $CD = 3x + 12$.

Solution

(1) Since we proved the segments were congruent, they are equal in length:

$$BE = CD$$

(2) Substitute the given expressions:

$$5x - 8 = 3x + 12$$

(3) Solve for x:

$$2x = 20$$
$$x = 10$$

(4) Thus, $BE = 5x - 8 = 5(10) - 8 = 42$.

Answer: $BE = 42$

EXERCISES

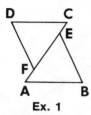

Ex. 1

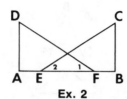

Ex. 2

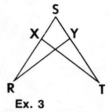

Ex. 3

1. *Given:* $\overline{AFEC}$, $\overline{DC} \cong \overline{BA}$, $\overline{DF} \cong \overline{BE}$, and $\overline{CE} \cong \overline{AF}$.
   Prove: $\triangle AEB \cong \triangle CFD$.

2. *Given:* $\overline{AEFB}$, $\overline{CE} \cong \overline{DF}$, $\angle 1 \cong \angle 2$, $\overline{AE} \cong \overline{BF}$.
   Prove: $\triangle AFD \cong \triangle BEC$.

3. *Given:* $\overline{SXR}$, $\overline{SYT}$, $\overline{SX} \cong \overline{SY}$, $\overline{XR} \cong \overline{YT}$.
   Prove: $\triangle RSY \cong \triangle TSX$.

Ex. 4

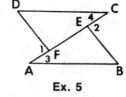

Ex. 5

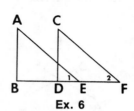

Ex. 6

4. *Given:* $\overline{DA} \cong \overline{CB}$, $\overline{DA} \perp \overline{AB}$, $\overline{CB} \perp \overline{AB}$.
   Prove: $\triangle DAB \cong \triangle CBA$.

5. *Given:* $\overline{AFEC}$, $\overline{AF} \cong \overline{EC}$, $\angle 3 \cong \angle 4$, $\angle 1 \cong \angle 2$.
   Prove: $\triangle ABE \cong \triangle CDF$.

6. *Given:* $\overline{AB} \perp \overline{BF}$, $\overline{CD} \perp \overline{BF}$, $\overline{BD} \cong \overline{FE}$, $\angle 1 \cong \angle 2$.
   Prove: $\triangle ABE \cong \triangle CDF$.

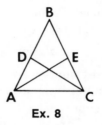

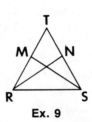

| Ex. 7 | Ex. 8 | Ex. 9 |

7. *Given:* $\overline{LP} \perp \overline{PN}$, $\overline{MN} \perp \overline{PN}$, $\overline{LP} \cong \overline{MN}$, $\overline{PR} \cong \overline{NS}$, and $\overline{PRSN}$.
   Prove: $\triangle LPS \cong \triangle MNR$.
8. *Given:* $\angle BAC \cong \angle BCA$, $\overline{CD}$ bisects $\angle BCA$, $\overline{AE}$ bisects $\angle BAC$.
   Prove: $\triangle ADC \cong \triangle CEA$.
9. *Given:* $\overline{TR} \cong \overline{TS}$, $\overline{MR} \cong \overline{NS}$.
   Prove: $\triangle RTN \cong \triangle STM$.

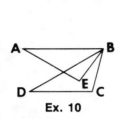

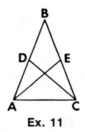

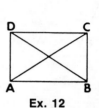

| Ex. 10 | Ex. 11 | Ex. 12 |

10. *Given:* $\overline{AB} \cong \overline{DB}$, $\angle A \cong \angle D$, $\angle DBA \cong \angle CBE$.
    Prove: $\triangle ABE \cong \triangle DBC$.
11. *Given:* $\overline{DA} \cong \overline{EC}$ and $\overline{DC} \cong \overline{EA}$.
    Prove: **a.** $\triangle CAD \cong \triangle ACE$. **b.** $\angle DCA \cong \angle EAC$.
12. *Given:* $\overline{DA} \perp \overline{AB}$, $\overline{CB} \perp \overline{AB}$, and $\overline{AD} \cong \overline{BC}$.
    Prove: **a.** $\triangle DAB \cong \triangle CBA$. **b.** $\overline{AC} \cong \overline{BD}$.

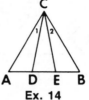

| Ex. 13 | Ex. 14 | Ex. 15 |

13. *Given:* $\overline{ADB}$, $\overline{BEC}$, $\overline{BD} \cong \overline{BE}$, and $\overline{DA} \cong \overline{EC}$.
    Prove: **a.** $\triangle DBC \cong \triangle EBA$. **b.** $\angle A \cong \angle C$.
14. *Given:* $\overline{ADEB}$, $\overline{AC} \cong \overline{BC}$, $\overline{CE} \cong \overline{CD}$, and $\overline{AE} \cong \overline{BD}$.
    Prove: **a.** $\triangle ACE \cong \triangle BCD$. **b.** $\angle 1 \cong \angle 2$.
15. If $\overline{RT} \cong \overline{ST}$ and median $\overline{RB} \cong$ median $\overline{SA}$, prove that $\angle RAS \cong \angle SBR$.

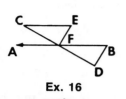

Ex. 16

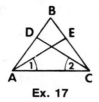

Ex. 17

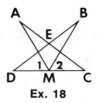

Ex. 18

16. Given $\overrightarrow{BFA}$, $\overline{CFD}$, $\angle ECF \cong \angle CFA$, $\overline{CF} \cong \overline{FD}$, and $\overline{CE} \cong \overline{FB}$, prove that $\overline{EF} \cong \overline{BD}$.

17. Given $\overline{ADB}$, $\overline{BEC}$, $\overline{BD} \cong \overline{BE}$, and $\overline{DA} \cong \overline{EC}$, prove that $\angle 1 \cong \angle 2$.

18. If $\overline{AC}$ and $\overline{BD}$ intersect at E, $\angle D \cong \angle C$, M is the midpoint of $\overline{DC}$, and $\angle 1 \cong \angle 2$, prove that $\overline{DB} \cong \overline{CA}$.

19. *Prove:* The medians to the legs of an isosceles triangle are congruent.

Miscellaneous Exercises

In 20–23, select the numeral preceding the expression that best completes the statement. Refer to the given figures.

20. It can be proved that $\angle YWX \cong \angle ZXW$
   if it is known that
   (1) $\overline{ZW} \cong \overline{YX}$ (2) $\overline{YW} \cong \overline{YX}$
   (3) $\overline{PW} \cong \overline{PX}$ (4) $\overline{PW} \cong \overline{YX}$

21. If $\triangle ZPW \cong \triangle YPX$, it can be proved that
   (1) $\triangle ZPW$ is isosceles   (2) $\triangle YPX$ is isosceles
   (3) $\triangle PWX$ is isosceles   (4) $\triangle YWX$ is isosceles

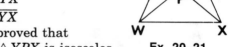

Ex. 20–21

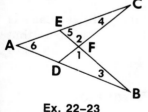

Ex. 22–23

22. If $\overline{AB} \cong \overline{AC}$, it can be proved that $\overline{CD} \cong \overline{BE}$
   if it is also known that
   (1) $\angle 1 \cong \angle 2$ (2) $\angle 3 \cong \angle 4$
   (3) $\angle 3 \cong \angle 5$ (4) $\angle 4 \cong \angle 6$

23. If $\angle 3 \cong \angle 4$, it can be proved that $\overline{EC} \cong \overline{DB}$
   if it is also known that
   (1) $\overline{CF} \cong \overline{BF}$ (2) $\overline{CD} \cong \overline{BE}$
   (3) $\overline{CA} \cong \overline{BA}$ (4) $\overline{EA} \cong \overline{DA}$

4-11 USING BASIC INEQUALITY POSTULATES

In an *equality*, the left-hand member of an equation is *equal* to the right-hand member of the equation.

In an *inequality*, the left-hand and right-hand members are not equal, usually indicated by one of two phrases: *is greater than* ($>$), or *is less than* ($<$). Examples of inequalities exist in geometry just as they exist in arithmetic and in algebra.

	Equality	*Inequalities*	
In arithmetic:	$3 + 5 = 8$	$3 + 5 > 2$	$3 + 5 < 10$
In algebra:	$x + x = 2x$	$x + 1 > x$	$x - 5 < x$
In geometry:	$AB = CD$	$AB > BC$	$AB < CE$
	$m\angle A = m\angle B$	$m\angle A > m\angle C$	$m\angle A < m\angle D$

Postulate Relating a Whole Quantity and Its Parts

The following postulate involving an inequality is related to the previously accepted postulate, *A whole is equal to the sum of all its parts.*

● **POSTULATE 31. A whole is greater than any of its parts.**

If a, b, and c represent positive numbers such that $a = b + c$, then $a > b$ and $a > c$.

Let us apply this concept to geometry. The lengths of line segments and the measures of angles are positive numbers.

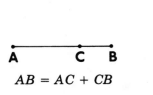

$$AB = AC + CB \qquad\qquad m\angle ABC = m\angle 1 + m\angle 2$$

$$AB > AC \;\text{ and }\; AB > CB \qquad m\angle ABC > m\angle 1 \;\text{ and }\; m\angle ABC > m\angle 2$$

Let us state some other postulates involving inequalities. Each of these postulates will be stated in two forms: (1) using symbols that represent real numbers and (2) using words.

Uniqueness of Order (The Trichotomy Postulate)

● **POSTULATE 32. If a and b are real numbers, then exactly one of the following relations is true: $a < b$, $a = b$, $a > b$.**

or: **Given any two quantities, exactly one of the following relations is true:**

1. **The first quantity is less than the second.**
2. **The first quantity is equal to the second.**
3. **The first quantity is greater than the second.**

Transitive Property of Inequality

● **POSTULATE 33.** If a, b, and c are real numbers such that $a > b$ and $b > c$, then $a > c$.

or: If the first of three quantities is greater than the second and the second is greater than the third, then the first is greater than the third.

EXAMPLE 1. If $10 > 8$ and $8 > 5$, then $10 > 5$.

EXAMPLE 2. If $BA > BD$
and $BD > BC$, then $BA > BC$.
Also, if $BC < BD$ and $BD < BA$,
then $BC < BA$.

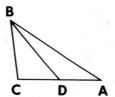

Substitution Postulate for Inequalities

● **POSTULATE 34.** If a, b, and c are real numbers such that $a > b$ and $c = b$, then $a > c$.

or: A quantity may be substituted for its equal in any inequality.

EXAMPLE 1. If $x > 7$ and $y = x$, then $y > 7$.

EXAMPLE 2.
   If $m\angle 3 > m\angle 1$,
 and $m\angle 2 = m\angle 1$,
then $m\angle 3 > m\angle 2$.

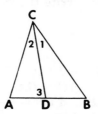

MODEL PROBLEMS

1. *Given:* In $\triangle ABC$,
    $m\angle ABC = m\angle 1 + m\angle 2$,
    $m\angle 2 > m\angle 3$.

   Prove: $m\angle ABC > m\angle 3$.

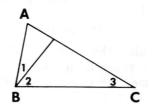

Statements	*Reasons*
1. m∠ABC = m∠1 + m∠2.	1. Given.
2. m∠ABC > m∠2.	2. A whole is greater than any of its parts.
3. m∠2 > m∠3.	3. Given.
4. m∠ABC > m∠3.	4. Transitive property of inequality.

2. *Given:* CB < CA.
        CD = CB.

   Prove: CD < CA.

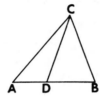

Statements	*Reasons*
1. CB < CA.	1. Given.
2. CD = CB.	2. Given.
3. CD < CA.	3. Substitution postulate for inequalities.

EXERCISES _____

In 1–5, which refer to the figure, write the inequality postulate that justifies each true statement.

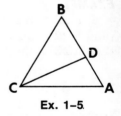

Ex. 1–5.

1. m∠ACB > m∠ACD.
2. AB > BD.
3. Given the premises: AC > CD and CD > DA.
   We deduce the true statement: AC > DA.
4. Given the premises: CD < CB and CB = CA.
   We deduce the true statement: CD < CA.
5. Given the premises:
   m∠BDC > m∠A and m∠A = m∠B.
   We deduce the true statement: m∠BDC > m∠B.

In 6–8, what inequality property justifies the conclusion?

6. If Mike is taller than Jeff, and Jeff and John are the same height, then Mike is taller than John.
7. If Joe is older than Carolyn, and Carolyn is older than Larry, then Joe is older than Larry.
8. If Alice earns more than Roberta, and Roberta earns more than Nancy, then Alice earns more than Nancy.

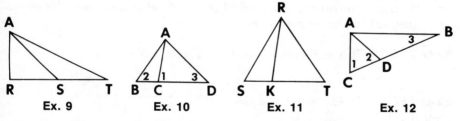

Ex. 9 Ex. 10 Ex. 11 Ex. 12

9. If $AT > AS$ and $AS > AR$, prove that $AT > AR$.
10. If m∠1 > m∠2 and m∠2 > m∠3, prove that m∠1 > m∠3.
11. If $SR > KR$ and $SR = TR$, prove that $TR > KR$.
12. If m∠3 < m∠2 and m∠2 = m∠1, prove that m∠3 < m∠1.

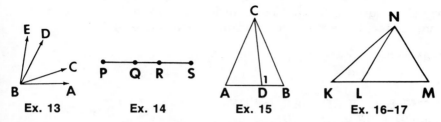

Ex. 13 Ex. 14 Ex. 15 Ex. 16–17

13. *Given:* m∠ABD = m∠ABC + m∠CBD; and m∠ABC = m∠DBE.
    Prove: **a.** m∠ABD > m∠ABC. **b.** m∠ABD > m∠DBE.
14. *Given:* $\overline{PQRS}$ where $PR = PQ + QR$ and $PQ = RS$.
    Prove: **a.** $PR > PQ$. **b.** $PR > RS$.
15. *Given:* $\triangle ABC$ is isosceles, $\overline{AC} \cong \overline{BC}$, and m∠1 > m∠A.
    Prove: m∠1 > m∠B.
16. Given $\overline{KLM}$ and $\overline{LM} \cong \overline{NM}$, prove that $KM > NM$.
17. If $KM > KN$, $KN > NM$, and $NM = NL$, prove that $KM > NL$.

18. Explain why the relation > is not an equivalence relation for the set of real numbers.

4-12 INEQUALITY POSTULATES INVOLVING OPERATIONS

In this section, you will study inequality postulates that involve the basic operations of addition, subtraction, multiplication, and division. You will see how these inequality postulates help to prove statements concerned with inequalities.

Inequality Postulates Involving Addition and Subtraction

● **POSTULATE 35.** **If a, b, c, and d are real numbers such that $a > b$ and $c = d$, then $a + c > b + d$.**

or: **If equal quantities are added to unequal quantities, the sums are unequal in the same order.**

EXAMPLE 1. If $5 < 8$ and $4 = 4$, then $5 + 4 < 8 + 4$, or
$$9 < 12.$$

EXAMPLE 2. If $AB > CD$ and $BE = DF$, then $AB + BE > CD + DF$, or $AE > CF$.

● **POSTULATE 36.** **If a, b, c, and d are real numbers such that $a > b$ and $c > d$, then $a + c > b + d$.**

or: **If unequal quantities are added to unequal quantities of the same order, the sums are unequal in the same order.**

EXAMPLE 1. If $6 > 4$ and $8 > 5$, then $6 + 8 > 4 + 5$, or
$$14 > 9.$$

EXAMPLE 2. If $CD < AB$ and $DF < BE$, then $CD + DF < AB + BE$, or $CF < AE$.

● **POSTULATE 37.** **If a, b, c, and d are real numbers such that $a > b$ and $c = d$, then $a - c > b - d$.**

or: **If equal quantities are subtracted from unequal quantities, the differences are unequal in the same order.**

EXAMPLE 1. If $15 > 12$ and $5 = 5$, then $15 - 5 > 12 - 5$, or
$$10 > 7.$$

EXAMPLE 2. If $AC < AB$ and $EC = DB$, then $AC - EC < AB - DB$, or $AE < AD$.

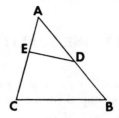

Note that it is not true that if unequal quantities are subtracted from unequal quantities, the differences are necessarily unequal in the same order. For example, if $5 > 4$ and $3 > 1$, it does not follow that $5 - 3 > 4 - 1$.

MODEL PROBLEM

Given: m∠ABG < m∠DEH.
   m∠GBC = m∠HEF.

Prove: m∠ABC < m∠DEF.

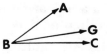
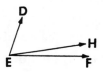

Statements	*Reasons*
1. m∠ABG < m∠DEH.	1. Given.
2. m∠GBC = m∠HEF.	2. Given.
3. m∠ABG + m∠GBC < m∠DEH + m∠HEF, or m∠ABC < m∠DEF.	3. If equal quantities are added to unequal quantities, the sums are unequal in the same order.

EXERCISES

In 1–8, use an inequality postulate to prove the conclusion.

1. If 10 > 7, then 18 > 15.   **2.** If 4 < 14, then 15 < 25.
3. If $x + 3 > 12$, then $x > 9$.   **4.** If $y - 5 < 5$, then $y < 10$.
5. If 8 > 6 and 5 > 3, then 13 > 9.   **6.** If 7 < 12, then 5 < 10.
7. If $y > 8$, then $y - 1 > 7$.   **8.** If $a = b$, then $180 - a > 90 - b$.

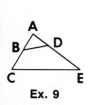

Ex. 9   Ex. 10   Ex. 11   Ex. 12

9. *Given:* $AB = AD$, and $BC < DE$.
   Prove: $AC < AE$.
10. *Given:* $AE > BD$, and $AF = BF$.
   Prove: $FE > FD$.
11. *Given:* m∠DAC > m∠DBC, and $\overline{AE} \cong \overline{EB}$.
   Prove: **a.** m∠EAB = m∠EBA.   **b.** m∠DAB > m∠CBA.
12. *Given:* m∠DCB < m∠DAB, and $\overline{AD} \cong \overline{DC}$.
   Prove: m∠ACB < m∠CAB.

Inequality Postulates Involving Multiplication and Division

● **POSTULATE 38.** If *a* and *b* are numbers such that $a > b$, and if *c* is a *positive* number, then $ac > bc$.

or: If unequal quantities are multiplied by equal *positive* quantities, the products are unequal in the same order. [A special case of this postulate is: Doubles of unequal quantities are unequal in the same order.]

EXAMPLE 1. If $9 > 7$ and $4 = 4$, then $9(4) > 7(4)$, or
$$36 > 28.$$

EXAMPLE 2. If $AB > DE$, $AC = 2AB$, and $DF = 2DE$, then $AC > DF$ because doubles of unequal quantities are unequal in the same order.

● **POSTULATE 39.** If *a* and *b* are numbers such that $a > b$, and if *c* is a *positive* number, then $\dfrac{a}{c} > \dfrac{b}{c}$.

or: If unequal quantities are divided by equal *positive* quantities, the quotients are unequal in the same order. [A special case of this postulate is: Halves of unequal quantities are unequal in the same order.]

EXAMPLE 1. If $12 > 8$ and $4 = 4$, then $\frac{12}{4} > \frac{8}{4}$, or
$$3 > 2.$$

EXAMPLE 2. If $AC < AB$, $AE = \frac{1}{2}AC$, and $AD = \frac{1}{2}AB$, then $AE < AD$ because halves of unequal quantities are unequal in the same order.

MODEL PROBLEMS

1. *Given:* $BA = 3BD$.
         $BC = 3BE$.
         $BE > BD$.

   Prove: $BC > BA$.

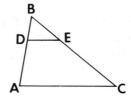

Statements	Reasons
1. $BE > BD$	1. Given.
2. $3BE > 3BD$	2. Unequal quantities multiplied by equal positive quantities are unequal in the same order.
3. $BC = 3BE$, $BA = 3BD$	3. Given.
4. $BC > BA$.	4. Substitution postulate for inequalities.

2. *Given:* m∠ABC > m∠DEF.
$\overrightarrow{BG}$ bisects ∠ABC.
$\overrightarrow{EH}$ bisects ∠DEF.

Prove: m∠ABG > m∠DEH.

Statements	Reasons
1. m∠ABC > m∠DEF.	1. Given.
2. $\frac{1}{2}$m∠ABC > $\frac{1}{2}$m∠DEF.	2. Halves of unequal quantities are unequal in the same order.
3. $\overrightarrow{BG}$ bisects ∠ABC, $\overrightarrow{EH}$ bisects ∠DEF.	3. Given.
4. m∠ABG = $\frac{1}{2}$m∠ABC, m∠DEH = $\frac{1}{2}$m∠DEF.	4. Definition of angle bisector.
5. m∠ABG > m∠DEH.	5. Substitution postulate for inequalities.

EXERCISES

In 1–6, use an inequality postulate to prove the conclusion.

1. If $8 > 6$, then $24 > 18$.　　　　**2.** If $30 < 35$, then $6 < 7$.
3. If $8 > 6$, then $4 > 3$.　　　　**4.** If $3x > 15$, then $x > 5$.
5. If $\dfrac{x}{2} > 6$, then $x > 12$.　　　**6.** If $\dfrac{y}{5} < 4$, then $y < 20$.

In 7–12: If a, b, and c are positive integers such that $a > b$, tell whether the relationship is true or false.

7. $ac > bc$　　　　**8.** $a + c > b + c$　　　　**9.** $c - a > c - b$
10. $a - c > b - c$　　　**11.** $\dfrac{c}{a} > \dfrac{c}{b}$　　　**12.** $\dfrac{a}{c} > \dfrac{b}{c}$

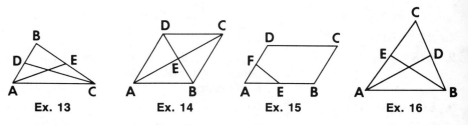

Ex. 13   Ex. 14   Ex. 15   Ex. 16

13. *Given:* $BD < BE$, D is the midpoint of $\overline{BA}$, E is the midpoint of $\overline{BC}$.
    Prove: $BA < BC$.
14. *Given:* $m\angle DBA > m\angle CAB$, $m\angle CBA = 2m\angle DBA$,
    $m\angle DAB = 2m\angle CAB$.
    Prove: $m\angle CBA > m\angle DAB$.
15. *Given:* $AB > AD$, $AE = \frac{1}{2} AB$, $AF = \frac{1}{2} AD$.
    Prove: $AE > AF$.
16. *Given:* $m\angle CAB < m\angle CBA$, $\overline{AD}$ bisects $\angle CAB$, $\overline{BE}$ bisects $\angle CBA$.
    Prove: $m\angle DAB < m\angle EBA$.

4-13   AN INEQUALITY INVOLVING THE LENGTHS OF THE SIDES OF A TRIANGLE

● **THEOREM 10. The sum of the lengths of two sides of a triangle is greater than the length of the third side.**

The proof of Theorem 10 is based upon an earlier postulate, which states that the shortest path between two points is the line segment joining the two points. Using $\triangle ABC$ and the lengths of its sides, we apply this theorem to state the following inequalities:

$$AC + CB > BA \qquad CB + BA > AC \qquad BA + AC > CB$$

MODEL PROBLEMS ————————————————————

1. Which of the following may be the lengths of the sides of a triangle?
   (1) 2, 3, 5   (2) 4, 4, 8   (3) 3, 4, 8   (4) 5, 6, 7

   Solution: Since each of the two shorter sides has a measure less than the third side, the length of each shorter side must be less than the sum of the other two lengths. Thus, we need only verify that the measure of the longest side is less than the sum of the other two lengths.

Therefore, add the two shorter lengths to see if their sum is greater than the third length.

(1) Is 2 + 3 > 5? No.   (3) Is 3 + 4 > 8? No.
(2) Is 4 + 4 > 8? No.   (4) Is 5 + 6 > 7? Yes.

Answer: Choice (4)

2. Two sides of a triangle have lengths 2 and 5. Find all possible lengths of the third side.

Solution:

(1) Let s = length of the third side of the triangle.
(2) Of the lengths 2, 5, and s, the longest side is either 5 or s.

(3) Assume the longest side of the triangle is 5.	(4) Assume the longest side of the triangle is s.
	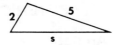

Then, 2 + s > 5 or
     s > 3.
	Then, 2 + 5 > s
	Add: 7 > s or
	     s < 7.

Answer: The length s is greater than 3 and less than 7.

Note that the solution $(s > 3) \wedge (s < 7)$ may be rewritten as $(3 < s) \wedge (s < 7)$, which becomes $(3 < s < 7)$.

EXERCISES ━━━━━━━━━━━━━━━━━━━━━━━━━━━━━

In 1–12, tell whether the given lengths may be the measures of the sides of a triangle.

1. 3, 4, 5   **2.** 5, 8, 13   **3.** 6, 7, 10   **4.** 3, 9, 15
5. 2, 2, 3   **6.** 1, 1, 2   **7.** 3, 4, 4   **8.** 5, 8, 11
9. 6, 2, 3   **10.** 5, 3, 7   **11.** 9, 4, 5   **12.** 4, 6, 3

In 13–16, which set of numbers can represent the lengths of the sides of a triangle?

13. (1) {2, 4, 6}   (2) {2, 4, 4}   (3) {4, 4, 8}   (4) {4, 6, 12}
14. (1) {3, 5, 7}   (2) {5, 8, 14}   (3) {5, 10, 15}   (4) {4, 4, 10}
15. (1) {1, 2, 4}   (2) {1, 2, $\sqrt{2}$}   (3) {2, 2, 4}   (4) {8, 4, 3}
16. (1) {2, 5, $\sqrt{50}$} (2) {1, 3, $\sqrt{20}$} (3) {2, 3, $\sqrt{20}$} (4) {1, 5, $\sqrt{40}$}

17. The lengths of two sides of a triangle are 6 and 3. The length of the
    third side may be: (1) 12   (2) 9   (3) 3   (4) 6
18. The lengths of two sides of a triangle are 10 and 14. The length of
    the third side may be: (1) 24   (2) 2   (3) 22   (4) 4
19. If the lengths of two sides of a triangle are 3 and 8, which best
    describes the length s of the third side of the triangle?
    (1) $3 < s < 8$ (2) $3 < s < 11$ (3) $5 < s < 8$ (4) $5 < s < 11$

In 20–23, using the two given lengths of the sides of a triangle, find
all possible lengths for the third side s.

20. 2 and 4   **21.** 4 and 7   **22.** 5 and 6   **23.** 3 and 9

4-14   AN INEQUALITY INVOLVING AN
EXTERIOR ANGLE OF A TRIANGLE

Exterior Angles

● **Definition.** An *exterior angle of a polygon* is an angle that forms
a linear pair with one of the angles of the polygon.

Recall that the angles in a linear pair are supplementary. Also notice
that the exterior angle lies outside the polygon.

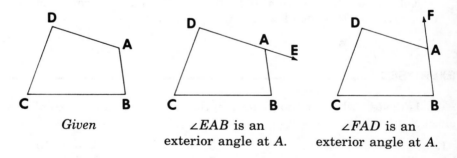

| *Given* | ∠*EAB* is an
exterior angle at *A*. | ∠*FAD* is an
exterior angle at *A*. |

The figure above gives polygon *ABCD*. We can form an exterior angle
at vertex *A* by using either one of two methods:

1. Draw $\overrightarrow{DA}$, of which $\overline{DA}$ is a subset, to some point *E* where *E* is not on
   $\overline{DA}$. Since ∠*EAB* forms a linear pair with ∠*DAB*, ∠*EAB* is an exterior angle at vertex *A*.
2. Draw $\overrightarrow{BA}$, of which $\overline{BA}$ is a subset, to some point *F* where *F* is not on
   $\overline{BA}$. Since ∠*FAD* forms a linear pair with ∠*DAB*, ∠*FAD* is an exterior angle at vertex *A*.

∠*EAB* and ∠*FAD* are each supplementary to ∠*DAB*. Since two angles that are supplementary to the same angle must be congruent, ∠*EAB* ≅ ∠*FAD*. Thus, we may use *either* ∠*EAB* or ∠*FAD* as the exterior angle at vertex *A*.

Exterior Angle of a Triangle

An exterior angle of a triangle is formed outside the triangle by extending a side of the triangle.

△*ABC* has three *interior* angles, namely ∠*a*, ∠*b*, and ∠*c*. By extending the sides of △*ABC*, three *exterior* angles are formed, namely ∠1, ∠2, and ∠3.

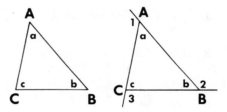

For each exterior angle, there is one **adjacent interior angle** and two **nonadjacent interior angles**. For △*ABC*, observe the following:

Exterior Angle	Adjacent Interior Angle	Nonadjacent Interior Angles
∠1	∠*a*	∠*b* and ∠*c*
∠2	∠*b*	∠*a* and ∠*c*
∠3	∠*c*	∠*a* and ∠*b*

With these facts in mind, we are now ready to prove another theorem about *inequalities* in geometry.

● **THEOREM 11. The measure of an exterior angle of a triangle is greater than the measure of either nonadjacent interior angle.**

Given: △*ABC* with exterior ∠*BCD* at vertex *C*; ∠1 and ∠2 are nonadjacent interior angles to ∠*BCD*.

Prove: m∠*BCD* > m∠1.
     m∠*BCD* > m∠2.

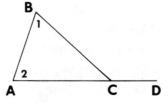

Plan: Since we must prove two inequalities, we present the proof in two parts. Each part requires drawing additional lines in the diagram. We use congruent triangles and substitution to show that ∠1 and ∠2 are each congruent to only a part of the whole exterior ∠*BCD*.

PART 1.

Prove that m∠BCD > m∠1.

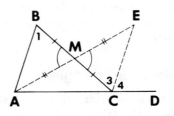

Statements	*Reasons*
1. Let *M* be the midpoint of $\overline{BC}$.	1. Every line segment has one and only one midpoint.
2. Draw $\overrightarrow{AM}$, extending the ray through *M* to point *E* so that $\overline{AM} \cong \overline{EM}$.	2. Two points determine a line, and a segment may be copied.
3. Draw $\overleftrightarrow{EC}$.	3. Through two given points, one and only one line can be drawn.
4. For exterior ∠BCD, let m∠BCD = m∠3 + m∠4.	4. A whole is equal to the sum of its parts.
5. $\overline{BM} \cong \overline{CM}$. (s. ≅ s.)	5. Definition of midpoint.
6. $\overline{AM} \cong \overline{EM}$. (s. ≅ s.)	6. By the construction in step 2.
7. ∠AMB ≅ ∠EMC. (a. ≅ a.)	7. Vertical angles are congruent.
8. △AMB ≅ △EMC.	8. s.a.s. ≅ s.a.s.
9. ∠1 ≅ ∠3.	9. Corresponding parts of congruent triangles are congruent.
10. m∠BCD > m∠3.	10. A whole is greater than any of its parts.
11. m∠BCD > m∠1.	11. Substitution postulate.

PART 2.

Prove that m∠BCD > m∠2.

Plan: Draw $\overline{BG}$ through midpoint *N* of $\overline{AC}$, such that *BN* = *GN*.
△ABN ≅ △CGN by s.a.s. ≅ s.a.s., and
∠2 ≅ ∠5. m∠ACF > m∠5, thus
m∠BCD > m∠5 and m∠BCD > m∠2
by substitution.

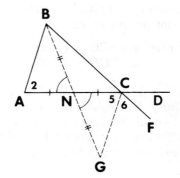

We have proved the theorem that the measure of an exterior angle of a triangle is greater than the measure of either nonadjacent interior angle. You are not expected to remember the steps in this proof because of its length, but you should have followed the reasoning.

Model Problem 6 that follows shows how you will use this theorem in a proof.

MODEL PROBLEMS

In 1–5, refer to the given triangle ABC where D is a point on $\overline{AB}$.

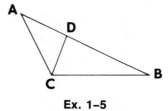

Ex. 1–5

Answers

1. Name the exterior angle of $\triangle DCB$ at vertex D.

2. Name the two nonadjacent interior angles of $\triangle DCB$ for the exterior angle given as an answer in 1.

3. Write the theorem that allows us to say:
$m\angle ADC > m\angle DCB$.

4. Write the postulate that allows us to say:
$m\angle ACB > m\angle DCB$.

5. Using the postulate stated as an answer in problem 4, give two illustrations of the postulate applied to lengths of line segments in the figure.

1. $\angle ADC$

2. $\angle DCB$
$\angle DBC$

3. The measure of an exterior angle of a triangle is greater than the measure of either nonadjacent interior angle.

4. A whole is greater than any of its parts.

5. $AB > AD$
$AB > DB$

6. *Given:* Right $\triangle ABC$, $m\angle C = 90$, and $\angle BAD$ an exterior angle at A.

Prove: $\angle BAD$ is obtuse.

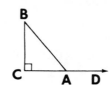

Plan: Use Theorem 11 to prove that m∠*BAD* > m∠*C* and therefore greater than 90. Then use the linear pair of angles at *A* to show that m∠*BAD* < 180.

Statements	*Reasons*
1. ∠*BAD* is an exterior angle.	1. Given.
2. m∠*BAD* > m∠*C*.	2. The measure of an exterior angle of a triangle is greater than the measure of either nonadjacent interior angle.
3. m∠*C* = 90.	3. Given.
4. m∠*BAD* > 90.	4. Substitution.
5. m∠*BAD* + m∠*BAC* = 180.	5. If two angles form a linear pair, they are supplementary.
6. 180 > m∠*BAD*.	6. The whole is greater than any of its parts.
7. 90 < m∠*BAD* < 180.	7. Steps 4 and 7.
8. ∠*BAD* is obtuse.	8. Definition of an obtuse angle.

EXERCISES _____

In 1–4: **a.** Name the given exterior angle of △*ABC*.   **b.** Name the two nonadjacent interior angles to that exterior angle.

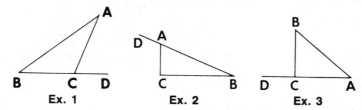

Ex. 1   Ex. 2   Ex. 3   Ex. 4

In 5–14, △*ABC* is scalene and $\overline{CM}$ is a median to side $\overline{AB}$.   **a.** Tell whether the given statement is *true* or *false*.   **b.** If the statement is true, indicate the postulate or theorem that justifies your answer.

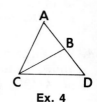

Ex. 5–14

5. *AM* = *MB*.
6. m∠*ACB* > m∠*ACM*.

7. m∠AMC > m∠ABC.
9. m∠CMB > m∠ACM.
11. BA > MB.
13. m∠BCA > m∠MCA.

8. AB > AM.
10. m∠CMB > m∠CAB.
12. m∠ACM = m∠BCM.
14. m∠BMC > m∠AMC.

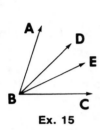

Ex. 15

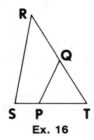

Ex. 16

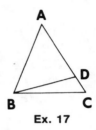

Ex. 17

15. $\overrightarrow{BD}$ and $\overrightarrow{BE}$ are interior rays of ∠ABC; $\overrightarrow{BD}$ is in the interior of ∠ABE and $\overrightarrow{BE}$ is in the interior of ∠DBC; ∠ABD ≅ ∠EBC. Prove that m∠ABE > m∠EBC.

16. In △RST, if Q is a point on $\overline{RT}$ and P is a point on $\overline{ST}$ such that $\overline{QT} ≅ \overline{PT}$, prove that m∠SPQ > m∠QPT.

17. In △ABC, D is a point on $\overline{AC}$. If $\overline{AD} ≅ \overline{BD}$, prove that m∠ABC > m∠A.

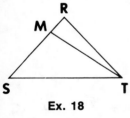

Ex. 18

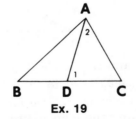

Ex. 19

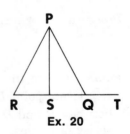

Ex. 20

18. If △RST is isosceles with $\overline{RS} ≅ \overline{RT}$ and M is a point on $\overline{RS}$, prove that m∠RMT > m∠STR.

19. In △ABC, $\overline{AD}$ is drawn to $\overline{BC}$ and ∠ABC ≅ ∠2. Prove that m∠1 > m∠2.

20. In isosceles △PQR, $\overline{PS}$ bisects vertex ∠RPQ and $\overline{RSQ}$ is extended through Q to T.
Prove: **a.** m∠PQT > m∠QPS.
  b. m∠PQT > m∠RPS.

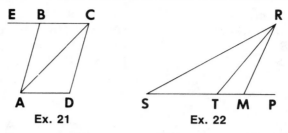

Ex. 21   Ex. 22

21. In quadrilateral $ABCD$, diagonal $\overline{AC}$ is drawn, and $\overline{CB}$ is extended through B to E. If $\overline{AB} \cong \overline{CD}$ and $\overline{BC} \cong \overline{DA}$, prove:
  a. $\triangle ABC \cong \triangle CDA$. **b.** $m\angle EBA > m\angle CAD$.
22. In $\triangle RSM$, T is on $\overline{SM}$, which is extended through M to P. Prove that $m\angle RMP > m\angle SRT$.

4-15 INEQUALITIES INVOLVING SIDES AND ANGLES IN A TRIANGLE

There are two other major inequality theorems involving the measures of the angles and sides of a triangle.

● **THEOREM 12. If the lengths of two sides of a triangle are unequal, the measures of the angles opposite these sides are unequal and the greater angle lies opposite the greater side.**

Given: $\triangle ABC$ with $AB > BC$.

Prove: $m\angle 1 > m\angle 2$.

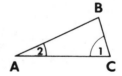

Plan: On the line containing the shorter side $\overline{BC}$, locate point D so that $BD = BA$, and C is between B and D. By drawing $\overline{AD}$, we form a series of angles. Applying the transitive property of inequality to the measures of these angles, we can show that $m\angle 1 > m\angle 2$.

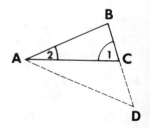

Statements	*Reasons*
1. $\triangle ABC$ with $AB > BC$.	1. Given.
2. Extend $\overline{BC}$ through C to point D so that $BD = BA$.	2. A line segment may be extended to a given length.

3. Draw $\overline{AD}$.	3. A line segment may be drawn joining two points.
4. For $\triangle ACD$, $m\angle 1 > m\angle BDA$.	4. The measure of an exterior angle of a triangle is greater than the measure of either nonadjacent interior angle.
5. For isosceles $\triangle ABD$, $m\angle BAD = m\angle BDA$.	5. Base angles of an isosceles triangle are equal in measure.
6. $m\angle 1 > m\angle BAD$.	6. Substitution postulate.
7. $m\angle BAD > m\angle 2$.	7. A whole is greater than any of its parts.
8. $m\angle 1 > m\angle 2$.	8. Transitive property of inequality.

Let us apply this theorem to $\triangle RST$, where $RT = 7$, $TS = 5$, and $SR = 4$.

Since $\overline{RT}$ has the greatest length and $\angle S$ is opposite $\overline{RT}$, then $\angle S$ is the angle with the greatest measure. Also, since $\overline{SR}$ has the smallest length and $\angle T$ is opposite $\overline{SR}$, then $\angle T$ is the angle with the smallest measure. In summary:

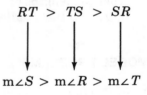

1. We can order the lengths of the three sides, from the largest to the smallest:

2. By looking at the angles opposite these three sides in the same given order, we can order the measures of the three angles from the largest to the smallest:

$$RT > TS > SR$$

$$\downarrow \qquad \downarrow \qquad \downarrow$$

$$m\angle S > m\angle R > m\angle T$$

The converse of this theorem, which now follows, is also true. Notice that the proof is presented using an indirect method.

● **THEOREM 13.   If the measures of two angles of a triangle are unequal, the lengths of the sides opposite these angles are unequal and the greater side lies opposite the greater angle.**

Given: $\triangle DEF$ with $m\angle D > m\angle E$.

Prove: $FE > FD$.

Plan: In an indirect proof, we must assume the negation of the conclusion and show that this assumption leads to a contradiction. Instead of listing all the steps in this proof, we will simply give a general plan for the proof.

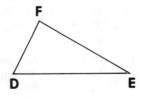

1. By the Trichotomy Postulate: $FE > FD$ or $FE = FD$ or $FE < FD$.
2. Assume the negation of the conclusion; that is, assume $FE \not> FD$. Therefore, we assume either $FE = FD$ or $FE < FD$.
3. If $FE = FD$, then $m\angle D = m\angle E$ because base angles of an isosceles triangle are equal in measure. This contradicts the given premise, $m\angle D > m\angle E$. Thus, $FE = FD$ is a false assumption.
4. If $FE < FD$, by our previous theorem, we must conclude that $m\angle D < m\angle E$. This also contradicts the given premise, that is, $m\angle D > m\angle E$. Thus, $FE < FD$ is also a false assumption.
5. Since $FE = FD$ and $FE < FD$ are both false, $FE > FD$ must be true.

If we apply this theorem to $\triangle ABC$, where $m\angle A = 40$, $m\angle B = 80$, and $m\angle C = 60$, then:

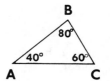

1. We can order the angle measures, from the largest to the smallest:

2. By looking at the sides opposite these angles in the same given order, we can order the lengths of the three sides from the largest to the smallest:

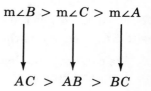

$$m\angle B > m\angle C > m\angle A$$

$$AC > AB > BC$$

MODEL PROBLEMS

1. In $\triangle ABD$, C is between A and D, and $\overline{BC}$ is drawn. If $m\angle D = 50$, $m\angle CBD = 55$, and $m\angle BCA = 105$, which is the longest side of $\triangle BCD$?

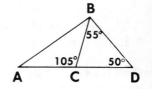

Solution

1. Since $\angle BCA$ and $\angle BCD$ are a linear pair, $m\angle BCD = 180 - 105 = 75$.
2. The longest side of a triangle is opposite the angle with the greatest measure. Therefore, the longest side of $\triangle BCD$ is $\overline{BD}$ because it is opposite $\angle BCD$, whose degree measure is 75.

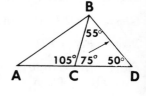

Answer: $\overline{BD}$ is the longest side of $\triangle BCD$.

2. *Given:* In $\triangle ACD$, $\overline{CB}$ is drawn to $\overline{ABD}$ so that $\overline{CB} \cong \overline{CA}$.

Prove: $CD > CA$.

Plan: To prove that $CD > CA$ in $\triangle ACD$, show that m$\angle 3$ (opposite $\overline{CD}$) is greater than m$\angle 1$ (opposite $\overline{CA}$).

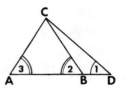

Statements	*Reasons*
1. In $\triangle CBD$, m$\angle 2 >$ m$\angle 1$.	1. The measure of an exterior angle of a triangle is greater than the measure of either nonadjacent interior angle.
2. $\overline{CB} \cong \overline{CA}$.	2. Given.
3. m$\angle 3 =$ m$\angle 2$.	3. Base angles of an isosceles triangle are equal in measure.
4. m$\angle 3 >$ m$\angle 1$.	4. A quantity may be substituted for its equal in any inequality.
5. $CD > CA$.	5. If the measures of two angles of a triangle are unequal, the lengths of the sides opposite these angles are unequal, and the greater side lies opposite the greater angle.

EXERCISES

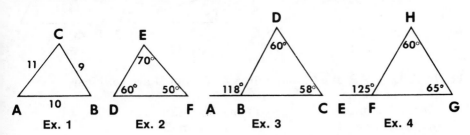

Ex. 1   Ex. 2   Ex. 3   Ex. 4

1. If $AB = 10$, $BC = 9$, and $CA = 11$, name the largest angle of $\triangle ABC$.
2. If m$\angle D = 60$, m$\angle E = 70$, and m$\angle F = 50$, name the shortest side of $\triangle DEF$.
3. Given: $\overleftrightarrow{ABC}$, m$\angle ABD = 118$, m$\angle D = 60$, and m$\angle C = 58$. Name the longest side of $\triangle BCD$.
4. Given: $\overleftrightarrow{EFG}$, m$\angle EFH = 125$, m$\angle G = 65$, and m$\angle H = 60$. Name the shortest side of $\triangle FGH$.

In 5 and 6, name the shortest side of △ABC, using the given information.

5. In △ABC, m∠C = 90, m∠B = 35, and m∠A = 55.
6. In △ABC, m∠A = 74, m∠B = 58, and m∠C = 48.

In 7 and 8, name the smallest angle of △ABC, using the given information.

7. In △ABC, AB = 7, BC = 9, and AC = 5.
8. In △ABC, AB = 5, BC = 12, and AC = 13.

9. In △RST, an exterior angle at R measures 80 degrees. If m∠S > m∠T, name the shortest side of the triangle.

In 10–13, select the numeral preceding the phrase that best completes the sentence.

10. In isosceles triangle ABC, $\overline{AC} \cong \overline{CB}$. If D is a point on base $\overline{AB}$ lying between A and B, and $\overline{CD}$ is drawn, then:
   (1) AC > CD   (2) CD > AC
   (3) m∠A > m∠ADC   (4) m∠B > m∠BDC

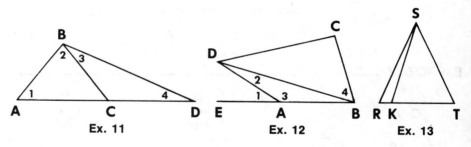

Ex. 11   Ex. 12   Ex. 13

11. In △ABD, $\overline{AB} \cong \overline{BC}$, and points A, C, and D are collinear. It is true that:
   (1) m∠1 > m∠2   (2) m∠1 > m∠4
   (3) m∠3 > m∠4   (4) m∠4 > m∠2
12. In quadrilateral ABCD, $\overline{BD}$ is a diagonal, and $\overleftrightarrow{BAE}$ is drawn. It is true that:
   (1) m∠1 > m∠2   (2) m∠1 > m∠3
   (3) m∠2 > m∠4   (4) m∠4 > m∠3
13. In isosceles △RST, $\overline{SR} \cong \overline{ST}$, and K is a point lying between R and T on base $\overline{RT}$. If $\overline{SK}$ is drawn, it is true that:
   (1) RS > SK   (2) SK > RS
   (3) m∠R > m∠RKS   (4) m∠T > m∠TKS

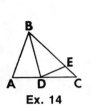

Ex. 14

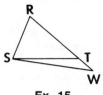

Ex. 15

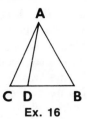

Ex. 16

14. *Given:* m∠*DEB* = m∠*DAB*. Points *B*, *E*, and *C* are collinear.
Prove: m∠*DAB* > m∠*BCD*.

15. *Given:* $\overline{RTW}$, m∠*RST* > m∠*RTS*.
Prove: m∠*RST* > m∠*RWS*.

16. *Given:* △*ABC*, $\overline{AB}$ ≅ $\overline{AC}$, *D* is a point between *B* and *C*.
Prove: *AB* > *AD*.

17. *Given:* △*ABC* ≅ △*CDA*, *AD* > *DC*.
Prove: **a.** m∠*ACD* > m∠*CAD*.
b. $\overline{AC}$ does not bisect ∠*A*.

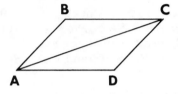

18. In isosceles △*ABC*, $\overline{CA}$ ≅ $\overline{CB}$. If *D* is a point on $\overline{AC}$ between *A* and *C*, prove that *DB* > *DA*.

4-16 REVIEW EXERCISES

In 1–6: **a.** Tell whether or not the triangles can be proved congruent by using only the marked congruent parts. **b.** If the triangles are congruent, give the reason for your answer.

Ex. 1

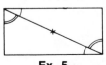

Ex. 2

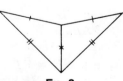

Ex. 3

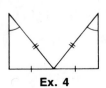

Ex. 4

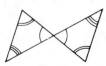

Ex. 5

Ex. 6

7. In △*RST*, $\overline{SA}$ is a median, $\overline{SB}$ is an angle bisector, and $\overline{SC}$ is an altitude.
   a. Name two perpendicular line segments.
   b. Name two congruent line segments.
   c. Name two right angles.
   d. Name two congruent angles, each with vertex at *S*.

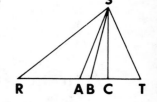

   e. If $\overline{SA}$, $\overline{SB}$, and $\overline{SC}$ should coincide, then △*RST* would have to be
   (1) right   (2) isosceles
   (3) scalene   (4) equilateral

In 8–13, △*PRS* is given, and *Q* is a point on $\overline{PR}$. State the inequality postulate or theorem that justifies each of the following true statements.

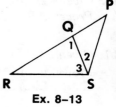

8. m∠*PSR* > m∠2   **9.** m∠1 > m∠2
10. *RS* + *SP* > *PR*   **11.** *PR* > *PQ*
12. m∠2 > m∠3, or m∠2 = m∠3, or m∠2 < m∠3
13. If *RP* > *PS* and *PS* > *SQ*, then *RP* > *SQ*.

Ex. 8–13

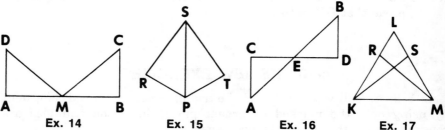

Ex. 14   Ex. 15   Ex. 16   Ex. 17

14. *Given:* $\overline{DA} \perp \overline{AB}$, $\overline{CB} \perp \overline{AB}$, $\overline{DA} \cong \overline{CB}$, and *M* is the midpoint of $\overline{AB}$.
    Prove: △*ADM* ≅ △*BCM*.

15. *Given:* $\overline{SR} \cong \overline{ST}$ and $\overline{RP} \cong \overline{TP}$.
    Prove: **a.** △*SRP* ≅ △*STP*.
              b. ∠*RSP* ≅ ∠*TSP*.

16. *Given:* $\overline{AB}$ and $\overline{CD}$ intersect at *E*, $\overline{BA}$ bisects $\overline{CD}$, $\overline{CA} \perp \overline{CD}$, and $\overline{BD} \perp \overline{CD}$.
    Prove: **a.** △*ACE* ≅ △*BDE*.
              b. $\overline{AE} \cong \overline{BE}$.

17. If $\overline{LR} \cong \overline{LS}$ and $\overline{RK} \cong \overline{SM}$, prove that △*RML* ≅ △*SKL*.

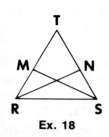

Ex. 18

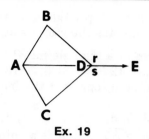

Ex. 19

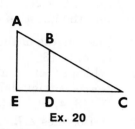

Ex. 20

18. If $\overline{TR} \cong \overline{TS}$, $\overrightarrow{RN}$ bisects $\angle R$, and $\overrightarrow{SM}$ bisects $\angle S$, prove that $\angle NRS \cong \angle MSR$.

19. Given $\overrightarrow{ADE}$, $\angle r \cong \angle s$, and $\overline{BD} \cong \overline{CD}$, prove that $\overline{AB} \cong \overline{AC}$.

20. *Given:* $\overline{ABC}$, $\overline{CDE}$, $AB > ED$, and $BC > DC$.
Prove: $AC > EC$.

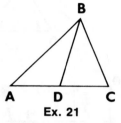

Ex. 21

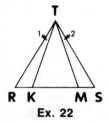

Ex. 22

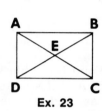

Ex. 23

21. *Given:* $\angle BDA$ is an exterior angle to $\triangle BCD$ at D, and $\overline{BD} \cong \overline{BC}$.
Prove: $m\angle BDA > m\angle BDC$.

22. If $\overline{RT} \cong \overline{ST}$ and $\angle 1 \cong \angle 2$, **(a)** prove $\overline{RK} \cong \overline{MS}$ and **(b)** prove $RM > MS$.

23. In quadrilateral $ABCD$, diagonals $\overline{AC}$ and $\overline{BD}$ bisect each other at E.
a. Prove that $\triangle AEB \cong \triangle CED$.
b. If $AB = 4x + 2$ and $CD = 7x - 19$, find AB.

24. In isosceles $\triangle ABC$, $\overline{AB} \cong \overline{BC}$, $m\angle A = x + 10$, and $m\angle C = 2x - 20$.
a. Find the value of x. **b.** Find $m\angle A$.

In 25–30, $\angle ACE$ is an exterior angle to $\triangle ABC$ at vertex C, D is a point on $\overline{BC}$, and $\overline{AD}$ is drawn. **a.** Tell whether the statement is always true or not necessarily true. **b.** If the statement is always true, indicate the postulate or theorem that justifies it.

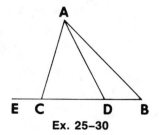

Ex. 25–30

25. $m\angle ACE > m\angle CAD$
26. $CB > CD$ **27.** $m\angle ACE > m\angle ABC$
28. $m\angle CAB > m\angle CAD$
29. $BC > CE$ **30.** $m\angle ACE > m\angle ACD$

In 31–34, select the numeral preceding the expression that best answers the question or completes the statement.

31. The lengths of the sides of a triangle may be:
(1) 4, 9, 13   (2) 5, 8, 12   (3) 5, 5, 13   (4) 5, 5, 10

32. Which set of numbers could represent the lengths of the sides of an isosceles triangle?
(1) {3, 4, 5}   (2) {3, 3, 8}   (3) {3, 8, 8}   (4) {3, 3, 6}

33. In isosceles $\triangle RST$, $\overline{SR} \cong \overline{ST}$, and K is a point between R and T on $\overline{RT}$. Which must be true?
(1) $SK > SR$ (2) $ST > SK$
(3) $m\angle R > m\angle SKR$ (4) $m\angle T > m\angle SKT$

34. In $\triangle ABC$, $\overline{BD}$ is drawn to $\overline{AC}$. Which must be true?
(1) $m\angle 1 > m\angle 3$ (2) $m\angle 2 > m\angle 4$
(3) $m\angle 2 > m\angle 3$ (4) $m\angle 3 > m\angle 4$

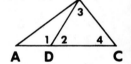

35. Point B is 4 blocks north and 3 blocks east of A. All streets run north and south or east and west except a street that slants from C to B. Of the three paths from A to B that are marked:
a. Which path is shortest?
b. Which path is longest?

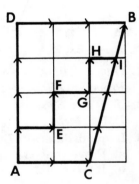

36. In order to keep a pasture gate from sagging, a board is nailed diagonally from one corner to the opposite corner of the four-sided gate. What theorem or postulate is illustrated?

Chapter 5

Perpendicular and Parallel Lines, Angle Sums, and More Congruences

5-1 PROVING LINES PERPENDICULAR

We have defined perpendicular lines as lines that intersect to form right angles. Since a definition is a biconditional, we may look at the figure shown in two ways:

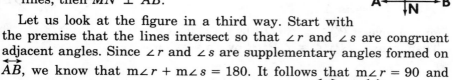

1. If $\overleftrightarrow{MN} \perp \overleftrightarrow{AB}$, then $\angle r$ and $\angle s$ are right angles. Or:

2. If $\angle r$ and $\angle s$ are right angles formed by intersecting lines, then $\overleftrightarrow{MN} \perp \overleftrightarrow{AB}$.

Let us look at the figure in a third way. Start with the premise that the lines intersect so that $\angle r$ and $\angle s$ are congruent adjacent angles. Since $\angle r$ and $\angle s$ are supplementary angles formed on $\overleftrightarrow{AB}$, we know that $m\angle r + m\angle s = 180$. It follows that $m\angle r = 90$ and $m\angle s = 90$, or $\angle r$ and $\angle s$ are right angles. Thus, $\overleftrightarrow{MN} \perp \overleftrightarrow{AB}$.

Prove the following theorem by using the steps suggested in this discussion.

● **THEOREM 14. If two intersecting lines form congruent adjacent angles, the lines are perpendicular.**

The Meaning of Equidistant

If $PX = PY$, we say that the distance from P to X is equal to the distance from P to Y, or, more simply, P is *equidistant* from X and Y.

If $MX = MY$, M is also equidistant from X and Y. Therefore, P and M are each equidistant from X and Y.

The diagram shows how to construct the **perpendicular bisector** $\overleftrightarrow{PM}$ of a line segment, $\overline{XY}$. Notice that $PX = PY$ and $MX = MY$. We say that $\overleftrightarrow{PM}$ is the perpendicular bisector of $\overline{XY}$ because $\overleftrightarrow{PM} \perp \overline{XY}$ and $\overleftrightarrow{PM}$ bisects $\overline{XY}$. From this information, we will state two more theorems.

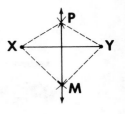

● **THEOREM 15.** **Any point on the perpendicular bisector of a line segment is equidistant from the endpoints of the line segment.**

Given: $\overleftrightarrow{CPD} \perp \overleftrightarrow{AB}$ and
  M is the midpoint of $\overline{AB}$.

Prove: $\overline{PA} \cong \overline{PB}$.

Plan: Prove $\triangle PMA \cong \triangle PMB$ by
  s.a.s $\cong$ s.a.s.

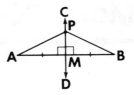

● **THEOREM 16.** **If two points are each equidistant from the endpoints of a line segment, the points determine the perpendicular bisector of the line segment.**

Given: $\overline{PA} \cong \overline{PB}$ and $\overline{QA} \cong \overline{QB}$.

Prove: $\overleftrightarrow{PQ} \perp \overleftrightarrow{AB}$ and
  $\overleftrightarrow{PQ}$ bisects $\overline{AB}$.

Plan: Prove $\triangle PQA \cong \triangle PQB$ by s.s.s. $\cong$ s.s.s.
  Then, prove $\triangle PMA \cong \triangle PMB$ by s.a.s. $\cong$ s.a.s.

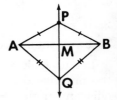

Methods of Proving Lines or Line Segments Perpendicular

To prove that two intersecting lines or line segments are perpendicular, prove that one of the following statements is true:

1. When the two lines or line segments intersect, they form right angles.
2. When the two lines or line segments intersect, they form congruent adjacent angles.
3. There are two points on one line or line segment, each of which is equidistant from the endpoints of the other line segment.

MODEL PROBLEM ───

Prove that the median to the base of an isosceles triangle is perpendicular to the base.

Given: $\triangle ABC$ with $\overline{CA} \cong \overline{CB}$.
$\overline{CM}$ is the median to base $\overline{AB}$.

Prove: $\overline{CM} \perp \overline{AB}$.

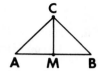

Plan: Prove that points C and M are each equidistant from the endpoints of $\overline{AB}$.

Statements	*Reasons*
1. $\overline{CA} \cong \overline{CB}$, or C is equidistant from A and B.	1. Given.
2. $\overline{CM}$ is a median.	2. Given.
3. M is the midpoint of $\overline{AB}$.	3. Definition of a median of a triangle.
4. $\overline{AM} \cong \overline{MB}$.	4. Definition of the midpoint of a line segment.
5. $\overline{CM} \perp \overline{AB}$.	5. If two points are each equidistant from the endpoints of a line segment, the points determine the perpendicular bisector of the line segment.

EXERCISES ───

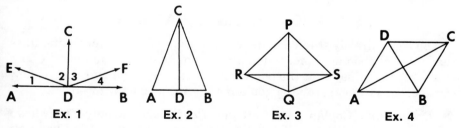

Ex. 1   Ex. 2   Ex. 3   Ex. 4

1. Given $\overleftrightarrow{ADB}$, $\angle 1 \cong \angle 4$, and $\angle 2 \cong \angle 3$, prove that $\overleftrightarrow{CD} \perp \overleftrightarrow{AB}$.
2. If $\overline{AC} \cong \overline{BC}$ and $\overline{CD}$ bisects $\angle ACB$, prove that $\overline{CD} \perp \overline{AB}$.
3. If $\overline{PR} \cong \overline{PS}$ and $\overline{QR} \cong \overline{QS}$, prove that $\overline{PQ} \perp \overline{RS}$.
4. If polygon $ABCD$ is equilateral ($AB = BC = CD = DA$), prove that $\overline{DB} \perp \overline{AC}$.

5. Given $\overline{CED}$, $\angle 1 \cong \angle 2$, and $\angle 3 \cong \angle 4$, prove that $\overline{CD}$ is the perpendicular bisector of $\overline{AB}$.

6. *Prove:* The bisector of the vertex angle of an isosceles triangle is perpendicular to the base of the triangle.

In 7–9, let D be a point on $\overleftrightarrow{AB}$ between A and B.

7. Given $m\angle ADC = 3x + 18$ and $m\angle CDB = 4x - 6$.
   a. Find the value of x.
   b. Show that $\overleftrightarrow{CD} \perp \overleftrightarrow{AB}$.

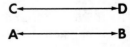

Ex. 7–9

8. If $\overleftrightarrow{CD} \perp \overleftrightarrow{AB}$, $m\angle ADC = 3x - y$, and $m\angle CDB = 2x + y$, find the value of x and the value of y.

9. If $\overleftrightarrow{CD} \perp \overleftrightarrow{AB}$, $m\angle CDA = 7x + y$, and $m\angle CDB = x + 4y$, find the value of x and the value of y.

10. $\overleftrightarrow{AB}$ intersects $\overleftrightarrow{CD}$ at E, $m\angle AEC = 3x$ and $m\angle AED = 5x - 60$.
    a. Find x. **b.** Show that $\overleftrightarrow{AB}$ is perpendicular to $\overleftrightarrow{CD}$.

11. In triangle ABC, a line drawn from vertex A intersects $\overline{BC}$ in D. If $m\angle ADB = 6x$ and $m\angle ADC = 9x - 45$, show that $\overline{AD} \perp \overline{BC}$.

12. In $\triangle RST$, a line drawn from vertex R intersects $\overline{ST}$ in B. If $m\angle SBR = \frac{3}{2}x + 30$ and $m\angle TBR = 4x - 70$, show that $\overline{RB}$ is an altitude in $\triangle RST$.

5-2 PROVING LINES PARALLEL

You have already studied many situations involving intersecting lines that lie in the same plane. When all the points or lines in a set lie in a single plane, we say that the points or the lines are *coplanar*. Let us now consider situations involving coplanar lines that do not intersect.

● **Definition.** Coplanar lines are **parallel lines** if and only if they have no points in common, or if the lines coincide and, therefore, have all points in common.

We indicate that $\overleftrightarrow{AB}$ is parallel to $\overleftrightarrow{CD}$ by writing $\overleftrightarrow{AB} \parallel \overleftrightarrow{CD}$. These parallel lines extended indefinitely will never intersect and, thus, have no points in common. However, using the concept of lines having all points in common, we may also say that a line is parallel to itself. Thus, $\overleftrightarrow{AB} \parallel \overleftrightarrow{AB}$, and $\overleftrightarrow{CD} \parallel \overleftrightarrow{CD}$.

The word *lines* in the definition means straight lines of unlimited extent. We say that segments and rays are parallel if the lines that contain them are parallel.

● **THEOREM 17. If coplanar lines are not parallel lines, then they are intersecting lines.**

The proof of this theorem uses the contrapositive of the definition of parallel lines: Coplanar lines are not parallel lines if and only if they have a point in common and do not have all points in common.

Given $\overleftrightarrow{AB}$ and $\overleftrightarrow{CD}$ as two coplanar lines, observe that one of the following situations may exist:

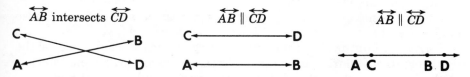

Equivalence Relation of Parallelism

Let us now consider whether the relation parallelism is an equivalence relation.

1. Reflexive property: $m \parallel m$, $p \parallel p$, and $t \parallel t$.
   (This property is true by reason of our definition.)
2. Symmetric property: If $m \parallel p$, then $p \parallel m$.
3. Transitive property: If $m \parallel p$ and $p \parallel t$, then $m \parallel t$.

From these examples, we sense that parallelism of lines is an equivalence relation because all three properties appear to be true. We will restate these properties of parallelism as follows:

● **POSTULATE 40. A line is parallel to itself.** (Reflexive property.)

● **POSTULATE 41. A parallelism of lines may be expressed in either order.** (Symmetric property.)

● **POSTULATE 42. Two lines each parallel to the same line are parallel to each other.** (Transitive property.)

Angles Formed by a Transversal

● **Definition.** A *transversal* is a line that intersects two other lines in two different points.

When two lines are cut by a transversal, two sets of angles, each containing four angles, are formed. In Course I, you learned names to identify special sets of these angles:

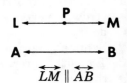

Interior angles: angles 3, 4, 5, 6
Exterior angles: angles 1, 2, 7, 8
Alternate interior angles are a pair of interior angles on opposite sides of the transversal, not sharing a common vertex: angles 3 and 6; also angles 4 and 5.

Alternate exterior angles are a pair of exterior angles on opposite sides of the transversal, not sharing a common vertex: angles 1 and 8; also angles 2 and 7.

Interior angles on the same side of the transversal: angles 3 and 5; also angles 4 and 6.

Corresponding angles are a pair of angles on the same side of the transversal, not sharing a common vertex, one exterior and one interior: angles 1 and 5; angles 2 and 6; angles 3 and 7; and angles 4 and 8.

In the diagram shown, the two lines cut by the transversal are not parallel lines. However, when two lines are parallel, many statements may be postulated or proved.

● **POSTULATE 43. Through a given point not on a given line, there exists one and only one line parallel to the given line.**

Given a line, $\overleftrightarrow{AB}$, and a point P, which is not on $\overleftrightarrow{AB}$. Through P, there exists one and only one line, $\overleftrightarrow{LM}$, which can be drawn parallel to $\overleftrightarrow{AB}$.

$$L \longleftarrow \overset{P}{\bullet} \longrightarrow M$$

$$A \longleftarrow \longrightarrow B$$

$$\overleftrightarrow{LM} \parallel \overleftrightarrow{AB}$$

For each of the next two theorems, we will use indirect proof, assuming the negation of the conclusion and showing that the assumption leads to a contradiction.

● **THEOREM 18. If a line intersects one of two parallel lines, it intersects the other.**

Given: $\overleftrightarrow{AB} \parallel \overleftrightarrow{CD}$, $\overleftrightarrow{EF}$ intersects $\overleftrightarrow{AB}$.

Prove: $\overleftrightarrow{EF}$ intersects $\overleftrightarrow{CD}$.

Plan: Use an indirect proof and the transitive property.

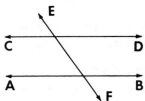

Proof: Assume $\overleftrightarrow{EF}$ does not intersect $\overleftrightarrow{CD}$. Then $\overleftrightarrow{EF} \parallel \overleftrightarrow{CD}$. By the transitive property, if $\overleftrightarrow{EF} \parallel \overleftrightarrow{CD}$ and $\overleftrightarrow{CD} \parallel \overleftrightarrow{AB}$, then $\overleftrightarrow{EF} \parallel \overleftrightarrow{AB}$. But, we are given that $\overleftrightarrow{EF}$ intersects $\overleftrightarrow{AB}$. Thus, we have a contradiction and our assumption must be false. Therefore, $\overleftrightarrow{EF}$ intersects $\overleftrightarrow{CD}$.

● **THEOREM 19. If two coplanar lines are cut by a transversal so that the alternate interior angles formed are congruent, then the two lines are parallel.**

Given: $\overleftrightarrow{AB}$ and $\overleftrightarrow{CD}$ are cut by transversal $\overleftrightarrow{EF}$ at points E and F, respectively; $\angle 1 \cong \angle 2$.

Prove: $\overleftrightarrow{AB} \parallel \overleftrightarrow{CD}$.

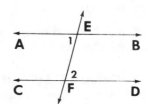

Plan: Use an ***indirect proof.*** Assume that the *negation* of the conclusion is true, namely, that $\overleftrightarrow{AB}$ is *not* parallel to $\overleftrightarrow{CD}$. Show that $\overleftrightarrow{AB} \parallel \overleftrightarrow{CD}$ implies that $\angle 1$ and $\angle 2$ are *not* congruent. Thus, the assumption is false and $\overleftrightarrow{AB} \parallel \overleftrightarrow{CD}$.

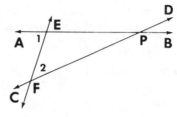

Statements	*Reasons*
1. $\overleftrightarrow{AB}$ and $\overleftrightarrow{CD}$ are cut by transversal $\overleftrightarrow{EF}$ at points E and F, respectively.	1. Given.
2. Let $\overleftrightarrow{AB}$ not be parallel to $\overleftrightarrow{CD}$.	2. Assumption.
3. $\overleftrightarrow{AB}$ and $\overleftrightarrow{CD}$ intersect at some point P, forming $\triangle EFP$.	3. If coplanar lines are not parallel, then they are intersecting lines.
4. $m\angle 1 > m\angle 2$.	4. The measure of an exterior angle of a triangle is greater than the measure of either nonadjacent interior angle.
5. But $\angle 1 \cong \angle 2$.	5. Given.
6. $m\angle 1 = m\angle 2$.	6. Congruent angles are equal in measure.
7. $\overleftrightarrow{AB} \parallel \overleftrightarrow{CD}$.	7. Contradiction in steps 4 and 6. Therefore, the assumption in step 2 is false.

Now that we have proved this theorem, we can use it in other theorems that also prove that two lines are parallel.

● **THEOREM 20. If two lines are cut by a transversal so that the corresponding angles are congruent, then the two lines are parallel.**

Given: $\overleftrightarrow{EF}$ intersects $\overleftrightarrow{AB}$ and $\overleftrightarrow{CD}$.
$\angle 1 \cong \angle 5$.

Prove: $\overleftrightarrow{AB} \parallel \overleftrightarrow{CD}$.

Plan: Show that $\angle 1 \cong \angle 3$ and $\angle 3 \cong \angle 5$.
Use Theorem 19.

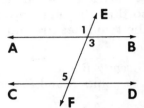

● **THEOREM 21. If two lines are cut by a transversal so that the interior angles on the same side of the transversal are supplementary, then the lines are parallel.**

Given: $\overleftrightarrow{EF}$ intersects $\overleftrightarrow{AB}$ and $\overleftrightarrow{CD}$.
$\angle 5$ is the supplement of $\angle 4$.

Prove: $\overleftrightarrow{AB} \parallel \overleftrightarrow{CD}$.

Plan: Show that $\angle 3$ is the
supplement of $\angle 4$. Since they
are supplements of the same
angle, $\angle 3 \cong \angle 5$. Then use Theorem 19.

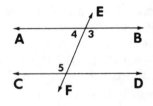

● **THEOREM 22. If two lines are perpendicular to the same line, then they are parallel.**

Given: $\overleftrightarrow{CD} \perp \overleftrightarrow{AB}$ and $\overleftrightarrow{EF} \perp \overleftrightarrow{AB}$.

Prove: $\overleftrightarrow{CD} \parallel \overleftrightarrow{EF}$.

Plan: Show that $\angle ADC \cong \angle DFE$.
Then use Theorem 20.

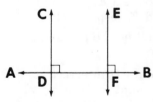

The proofs of these theorems are left to the student.

Methods of Proving Lines Parallel

To prove that two coplanar lines that are cut by a transversal are parallel, prove that any one of the following statements is true:

1. A pair of alternate interior angles are congruent.
2. A pair of corresponding angles are congruent.
3. A pair of interior angles on the same side of the transversal are supplementary.

Also, two coplanar lines may be proved parallel by proving:

4. Both lines are perpendicular to the same line.
5. Both lines are parallel to the same line.

To construct a line parallel to a given line through a given external point.

See Chapter 16, Construction 10.

MODEL PROBLEMS

1. If m∠A = 100 + 3x and m∠B = 80 − 3x, tell why $\overleftrightarrow{AD} \parallel \overleftrightarrow{BC}$.

Solution:
m∠A + m∠B = 100 + 3x + 80 − 3x = 180.
Thus, ∠A and ∠B are supplementary. Since $\overline{AD}$ and $\overline{BC}$ are cut by transversal $\overline{AB}$ to form supplementary interior angles on the same side of the transversal, then the segments are parallel, namely, $\overline{AD} \parallel \overline{BC}$.

2. If $\overline{BD}$ bisects ∠ABC, and $\overline{BC} \cong \overline{CD}$, prove $\overline{CD} \parallel \overrightarrow{BA}$.

Given: $\overline{BD}$ bisects ∠ABC and $\overline{BC} \cong \overline{CD}$.

Prove: $\overline{CD} \parallel \overrightarrow{BA}$.

Plan: Think of $\overline{CD}$ and $\overrightarrow{BA}$ as two lines cut by transversal $\overline{BD}$. If ∠2 ≅ ∠3, these congruent alternate interior angles make $\overline{CD} \parallel \overrightarrow{BA}$.

Statements	*Reasons*
1. $\overline{BC} \cong \overline{CD}$.	1. Given.
2. ∠3 ≅ ∠1.	2. If two sides of a triangle are congruent, the angles opposite these sides are congruent.
3. $\overline{BD}$ bisects ∠ABC.	3. Given.
4. ∠1 ≅ ∠2.	4. Definition of angle bisector.
5. ∠3 ≅ ∠2.	5. Transitive property of congruence.
6. $\overline{CD} \parallel \overrightarrow{BA}$.	6. If two lines are cut by a transversal forming a pair of congruent alternate interior angles, the two lines are parallel.

EXERCISES

1. Referring to the figure, show $\overleftrightarrow{AB} \parallel \overleftrightarrow{CD}$ if:
   a. m∠3 = 70 and m∠5 = 70.
   b. m∠2 = 140 and m∠6 = 140.
   c. m∠3 = 60 and m∠6 = 120.
   d. m∠2 = 150 and m∠5 = 30.
   e. m∠2 = 160 and m∠8 = 160.

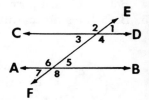

2. In quadrilateral $ABCD$, if m∠A = 120 + 5x and m∠B = 60 − 5x, show that $\overline{AD} \parallel \overline{BC}$.

3. In quadrilateral $ABCD$, $\overline{DC} \perp \overline{BC}$ and m∠ADC = 90. Prove $\overline{AD} \parallel \overline{BC}$.

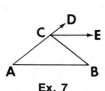
Ex. 4

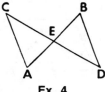
Ex. 5

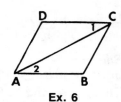
Ex. 6

4. If $\overline{AB}$ and $\overline{CD}$ bisect each other at point E, prove:
   a. $\triangle CEA \cong \triangle DEB$.   b. ∠$ECA \cong$ ∠EDB.   c. $\overleftrightarrow{CA} \parallel \overleftrightarrow{DB}$.

5. If $\overline{CD} \perp \overline{BC}$, $\overline{BA} \perp \overline{BC}$, $\overrightarrow{CE}$ bisects ∠BCD, and $\overrightarrow{BF}$ bisects ∠ABC, prove that $\overrightarrow{CE} \parallel \overrightarrow{BF}$.

6. If $\overline{AB} \cong \overline{CD}$ and ∠1 $\cong$ ∠2, prove:
   a. $\triangle CAB \cong \triangle ACD$.   b. $\overline{BC} \parallel \overline{DA}$.

Ex. 7

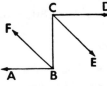
Ex. 8

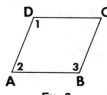
Ex. 9

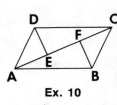
Ex. 10

7. Given $\overrightarrow{ACD}$, $\overline{CA} \cong \overline{CB}$, and ∠$ECB \cong$ ∠CAB, prove $\overrightarrow{CE} \parallel \overline{AB}$.

8. If ∠1 is supplementary to ∠2 and ∠3 $\cong$ ∠1, prove $\overline{AD} \parallel \overline{BC}$.

9. If $\overline{BA} \cong \overline{BC}$ and ∠$BDE \cong$ ∠BCA, prove $\overline{DE} \parallel \overline{AC}$.

10. If $\overline{DE} \perp \overline{AC}$, $\overline{BF} \perp \overline{AC}$, $\overline{AF} \cong \overline{CE}$, and $\overline{DE} \cong \overline{BF}$, prove:
    a. $\triangle ADE \cong \triangle CBF$.   b. $\overline{DA} \parallel \overline{BC}$.

11. *Prove:* If two lines are cut by a transversal forming a pair of alternate exterior angles that are congruent, then the two lines are parallel.

5-3 CONVERSE STATEMENTS; PROPERTIES
OF PARALLEL LINES

Logic has shown us that when a conditional statement $p \to q$ is true, the *converse* $q \to p$ may be true or it may be false. Each converse statement must be judged on its own merits before assigning a truth value.

In the previous section of this chapter, starting with given premises of angle relations, we were able to prove that lines were parallel. *Conversely*, starting with given premises that lines are parallel, we will now prove that certain angle relations exist.

● **THEOREM 23. If two parallel lines are cut by a transversal, then the alternate interior angles formed are congruent.**

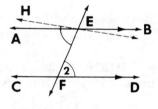

Given: $\overleftrightarrow{AB} \parallel \overleftrightarrow{CD}$; the lines are cut by transversal $\overleftrightarrow{EF}$ at points E and F, respectively. *Note.* As shown in the figure, arrowheads on the lines indicate that the lines are parallel.

Prove: $\angle 1 \cong \angle 2$.

Plan: Use an ***indirect proof.*** Assume $\angle 1 \not\cong \angle 2$. Construct $\overrightarrow{EH}$ so that $\angle HEF \cong \angle 2$. Since $\angle HEF$ and $\angle 2$ are congruent alternate interior angles, $\overleftrightarrow{HE} \parallel \overleftrightarrow{CD}$. But, $\overleftrightarrow{AB}$ is a line through E, and we were given $\overleftrightarrow{AB} \parallel \overleftrightarrow{CD}$. This contradicts Postulate 43 (through a point *not* on a given line, there is one and only one line parallel to the given line). Thus, the assumption is false and $\angle 1 \cong \angle 2$.

The proof is left as an exercise for the student.

Notice that Theorem 23 is the *converse* of Theorem 19.

Taking two lines, $\overleftrightarrow{AB}$ and $\overleftrightarrow{CD}$, cut by a transversal, $\overleftrightarrow{EF}$, we can compare the statements of the two theorems as follows:

Theorem 19 (Conditional $p \to q$): If $\angle 1 \cong \angle 2$, then $\overleftrightarrow{AB} \parallel \overleftrightarrow{CD}$.
Theorem 23 (Converse $\quad q \to p$): If $\overleftrightarrow{AB} \parallel \overleftrightarrow{CD}$, then $\angle 1 \cong \angle 2$.

Both theorems may be combined to form a single sentence:

If two parallel lines are cut by a transversal, then the alternate interior angles formed are congruent *and* conversely.

Each of the next two theorems is also a *converse* of a theorem stated in the preceding section of this chapter.

● **THEOREM 24.** **If two parallel lines are cut by a transversal, then the corresponding angles are congruent.** (This is the converse of Theorem 20.)

Given: $\overleftrightarrow{AB} \parallel \overleftrightarrow{CD}$.
$\quad\quad\quad$ $\overleftrightarrow{EF}$ intersects $\overleftrightarrow{AB}$ and $\overleftrightarrow{CD}$.

Prove: $\angle 1 \cong \angle 5$.

Plan: Show that $\angle 1 \cong \angle 3$ and $\angle 3 \cong \angle 5$. Then use the transitive property.

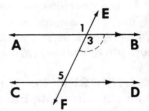

● **THEOREM 25.** **If two parallel lines are cut by a transversal, then two interior angles on the same side of the transversal are supplementary.** (This is the converse of Theorem 21.)

Given: $\overleftrightarrow{AB} \parallel \overleftrightarrow{CD}$.
$\quad\quad\quad$ $\overleftrightarrow{EF}$ intersects $\overleftrightarrow{AB}$ and $\overleftrightarrow{CD}$.

Prove: $\angle 4$ is the supplement of $\angle 5$.

Plan: Show that $\angle 4$ is the supplement of $\angle 3$, and $\angle 3 \cong \angle 5$. Then use substitution.

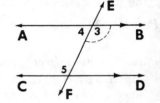

● **THEOREM 26.** **If a line is perpendicular to one of two parallel lines, it is perpendicular to the other.**

Given: $\overleftrightarrow{AB} \parallel \overleftrightarrow{CD}$ and $\overleftrightarrow{EF} \perp \overleftrightarrow{AB}$.

Prove: $\overleftrightarrow{EF} \perp \overleftrightarrow{CD}$.

Plan: Show that $\angle 6 \cong \angle 7$, and m$\angle 6 = 90$. Therefore, m$\angle 7 = 90$ or $\angle 7$ is a right angle. Use the definition of perpendicular lines.

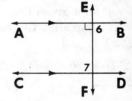

The proofs of these theorems are left to the student.

Summary of Properties of Parallel Lines

If two lines cut by a transversal are parallel:
1. Their alternate interior angles are congruent.
2. Their corresponding angles are congruent.
3. Two interior angles on the same side of the transversal are supplementary.

Also, if two lines are parallel:
4. A line perpendicular to one of them is also perpendicular to the other.
5. A line parallel to one of them is also parallel to the other.

MODEL PROBLEMS

1. Transversal $\overleftrightarrow{EF}$ intersects $\overleftrightarrow{AB}$ and $\overleftrightarrow{CD}$ at G and H, respectively. If $\overleftrightarrow{AB} \parallel \overleftrightarrow{CD}$, $m\angle BGH = 3x - 20$ and $m\angle GHC = 2x + 10$, (a) find the value of x and (b) find $m\angle DHF$.

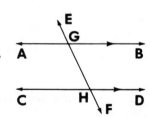

Solution:

a. Since $\overleftrightarrow{AB} \parallel \overleftrightarrow{CD}$ and these lines are cut by transversal $\overleftrightarrow{EF}$, the alternate interior angles are congruent. Thus,

$$m\angle BGH = m\angle GHC.$$
$$3x - 20 = 2x + 10$$
$$3x - 2x = 10 + 20$$
$$x = 30 \; Ans.$$

Note. A check can be made by substituting $x = 30$ in both given angle measures.

b. $\angle DHF$ is a corresponding angle to $\angle BGH$. Since parallel lines cut by a transversal form congruent corresponding angles, first find $m\angle BGH$.

$$m\angle BGH = 3x - 20 = 3(30) - 20 = 90 - 20 = 70$$
Then: $m\angle DHF = m\angle BGH = 70 \;\; Ans.$

2. *Given:* Quadrilateral $ABCD$; $\overline{BC} \cong \overline{DA}$; $\overline{BC} \parallel \overline{DA}$.

Prove: $\overline{AB} \parallel \overline{CD}$.

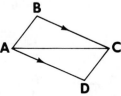

Plan: Show that alternate interior angles formed by transversal $\overline{AC}$ are congruent, namely, $\angle BAC \cong \angle DCA$. First prove that the triangles containing the angles are congruent. Use s.a.s. $\cong$ s.a.s.

Statements	*Reasons*
1. $\overline{BC} \cong \overline{DA}$. (s. $\cong$ s.)	1. Given.
2. $\overline{BC} \parallel \overline{DA}$.	2. Given.
3. $\angle BCA \cong \angle DAC$. (a. $\cong$ a.)	3. If two parallel lines are cut by a transversal, the alternate interior angles are congruent.
4. $\overline{AC} \cong \overline{AC}$. (s. $\cong$ s.)	4. Reflexive property of congruence.
5. $\triangle BAC \cong \triangle DCA$.	5. s.a.s. $\cong$ s.a.s.

6. ∠*BAC* ≅ ∠*DCA*.

6. Corresponding parts of congruent triangles are congruent.

7. $\overline{AB} \parallel \overline{CD}$.

7. If two lines cut by a transveral form alternate interior angles that are congruent, the lines are parallel.

EXERCISES

In 1–3: **a.** Write the converse of the given statement. **b.** State whether the converse is true or false.

1. If two lines are cut by a transversal forming a pair of alternate interior angles that are congruent, then the two lines are parallel.
2. If two lines are cut by a transversal forming a pair of corresponding angles that are congruent, then the two lines are parallel.
3. If two lines are cut by a transversal forming a pair of interior angles on the same side of the transversal that are supplementary, then the two lines are parallel.

4. In the figure, if $\overleftrightarrow{AB} \parallel \overleftrightarrow{CD}$, find:
   a. m∠5 when m∠3 = 80.
   b. m∠2 when m∠6 = 150.
   c. m∠4 when m∠5 = 60.
   d. m∠7 when m∠1 = 75.
   e. m∠8 when m∠3 = 65.

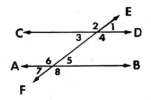

In 5–10, $\overleftrightarrow{AB} \parallel \overleftrightarrow{CD}$ and these lines are cut by transversal $\overleftrightarrow{EF}$ at *G* and *H*, respectively.

5. If m∠*BGH* = 3x and m∠*GHC* = 60, find x.
6. If m∠*EGA* is 2x and m∠*GHC* is 5x − 54, find the value of x.
7. If m∠*AGH* = x + 90 and m∠*DHG* = 3x − 10, find x.
8. If m∠*AGH* is twice the measure of ∠*GHC*, find m∠*GHC*.
9. If the ratio of the measures of ∠*BGH* to ∠*GHD* is 2:3, find **(a)** m∠*BGH* and **(b)** m∠*GHD*.
10. If m∠*AGH* = 3x − 40 and m∠*CHG* = x + 20, find:
    a. the value of x   **b.** m∠*AGH*
    c. m∠*CHG*   **d.** m∠*BGH*

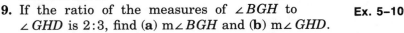

Ex. 5–10

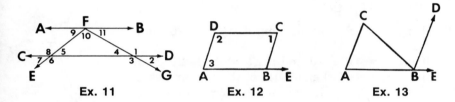

Ex. 11	Ex. 12	Ex. 13

11. If $\overleftrightarrow{AB} \parallel \overleftrightarrow{CD}$, m∠5 = 40, and m∠4 = 30, find the measures of the remaining angles in the figure.
12. If $\overrightarrow{AE} \parallel \overline{DC}$, $\overline{BC} \parallel \overline{AD}$, and m∠ *CBE* = 80, find m∠1, m∠2, and m∠3.
13. Given $\overleftrightarrow{ABE}$, $\overrightarrow{BD} \parallel \overline{AC}$, m∠*A* = 65, m∠*C* = 80, find m∠*CBE*.

Ex. 14	Ex. 15

14. If $\overline{AB} \parallel \overline{CD}$ and $\overline{BC} \parallel \overline{AD}$, find m∠1 and m∠2.
15. If $\overrightarrow{BA} \parallel \overrightarrow{DC}$, m∠*B* = 39, m∠*D* = 65, find m∠*DEB*.
    (*Hint.* Through *E*, draw $\overleftrightarrow{GEF} \parallel \overrightarrow{BA}$.)

16. Two parallel lines, $\overleftrightarrow{AB}$ and $\overleftrightarrow{CD}$, are cut at *E* and *F*, respectively, by transversal $\overleftrightarrow{GEFH}$. If ∠*AEG* and ∠*CFH* are exterior angles on the same side of $\overleftrightarrow{GH}$, and m∠*AEG* = 130, find m∠*CFH*.
17. Two parallel lines, $\overleftrightarrow{AB}$ and $\overleftrightarrow{CD}$, are cut by transversal $\overleftrightarrow{EF}$ where *E* is on $\overleftrightarrow{AB}$, and *F* is on $\overleftrightarrow{CD}$. The bisector of ∠*AEF* meets $\overleftrightarrow{CD}$ at point *P*. If m∠*AEF* = 64, find m∠*EPF*.
18. A transversal $\overleftrightarrow{GH}$ cuts two parallel lines, $\overleftrightarrow{AB}$ and $\overleftrightarrow{CD}$, at *E* and *F*, respectively. If ∠*AEG* is an exterior angle and ∠*DFE* is an interior angle found on opposite sides of $\overleftrightarrow{GH}$, and if m∠*AEG* = 35, find m∠*DFE*.
19. Two parallel lines are cut by a transversal. The degree measures of two interior angles on the same side of the transversal are represented by *x* and 4*x*. Find the measure of the smaller angle.
20. Two parallel lines are cut by a transversal. One of two interior angles on the same side of the transversal contains 15° more than the other. Find the degree measure of the smaller angle.

In 21–24, $\overleftrightarrow{AB} \parallel \overleftrightarrow{CD}$.

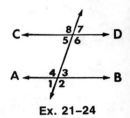

21. If $m\angle 3 = 2x + 40$ and $m\angle 7 = 3x + 20$, find $m\angle 3$.

22. If $m\angle 4 = 4x - 10$ and $m\angle 5 = 2x - 20$, find the measure of the smaller of the two angles.

23. If $m\angle 4 = 3x + 40$ and $m\angle 7 = 2x$, find $m\angle 7$.

24. If $m\angle 3 = 2y$, $m\angle 4 = x + y$, and $m\angle 5 = 2x - y$, find $m\angle 3$, $m\angle 4$, and $m\angle 5$.

Ex. 21–24

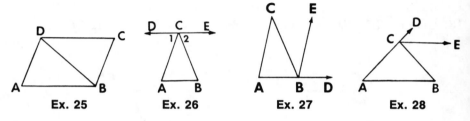

Ex. 25   Ex. 26   Ex. 27   Ex. 28

25. If $\overline{AB} \parallel \overline{DC}$ and $\overline{AB} \cong \overline{CD}$, prove that $\overline{AD} \cong \overline{CB}$ and $\overline{AD} \parallel \overline{BC}$.

26. If $\overleftrightarrow{DCE} \parallel \overleftrightarrow{AB}$ and $\angle 1 \cong \angle 2$, prove that $\angle A \cong \angle B$.

27. Given $\overleftrightarrow{ABD}$ and $\overrightarrow{BE} \parallel \overrightarrow{AC}$, prove that $m\angle CBD = m\angle A + m\angle C$.

28. If $\overleftrightarrow{CE}$ bisects $\angle DCB$ and $\overrightarrow{CE} \parallel \overline{AB}$, prove that $\angle A \cong \angle B$.

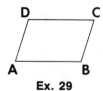   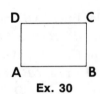

Ex. 29   Ex. 30

29. If $\overline{AB} \parallel \overline{DC}$ and $\overline{BC} \parallel \overline{AD}$, prove that $\angle B \cong \angle D$.

30. If $\overline{AB} \parallel \overline{DC}$, $\overline{BC} \parallel \overline{AD}$, and $\angle A$ is a right angle, prove that $\angle B$, $\angle C$, and $\angle D$ are also right angles.

31. *Prove:* If two lines cut by a transversal are parallel, the bisectors of a pair of alternate interior angles are parallel.

32. *Prove:* If both pairs of opposite sides of a quadrilateral are parallel, then both pairs of opposite sides are congruent. (*Hint.* Draw a diagonal.)

5-4 THE SUM OF THE MEASURES OF THE ANGLES OF A TRIANGLE

● **THEOREM 27.** The sum of the degree measures of the angles of a triangle is 180.

Given: $\triangle ABC$.

Prove: $m\angle A + m\angle B + m\angle C = 180$.

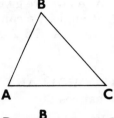

Plan: Draw $\overleftrightarrow{DE}$ through B so that $\overleftrightarrow{DE} \parallel \overleftrightarrow{AC}$. Since $\angle DBE$ is a straight angle, $m\angle DBE = 180$, or $m\angle 1 + m\angle B + m\angle 2 = 180$. Show that $m\angle 1 = m\angle A$, and $m\angle 2 = m\angle C$ so that $m\angle A + m\angle B + m\angle C = 180$.

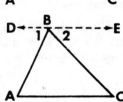

Statements	*Reasons*
1. Let $\overleftrightarrow{DE}$ be the line through B that is parallel to $\overleftrightarrow{AC}$.	1. Through a given point, not on a given line, there exists one and only one line parallel to the given line.
2. $m\angle DBE = 180$.	2. A straight angle is an angle whose degree measure is 180.
3. $m\angle 1 + m\angle B + m\angle 2 = 180$.	3. The whole is equal to the sum of all its parts.
4. $\angle A \cong \angle 1$; $\angle C \cong \angle 2$.	4. If two parallel lines are cut by a transversal, the alternate interior angles are congruent.
5. $m\angle A = m\angle 1$; $m\angle C = m\angle 2$.	5. Congruent angles are equal in measure.
6. $m\angle A + m\angle B + m\angle C = 180$.	6. Substitution postulate.

Many corollaries to this important theorem exist.

● **COROLLARY T27-1.** If two angles of one triangle are congruent, respectively, to two angles of another triangle, then the third angles are congruent.

In $\triangle ABC$ and $\triangle A'B'C'$, if $\angle A \cong \angle A'$ and $\angle B \cong \angle B'$, then we can prove $\angle C \cong \angle C'$. Use Theorem 27 and the subtraction property of equality.

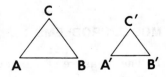

● **COROLLARY T27-2. The acute angles of a right triangle are complementary.**

When we are given right triangle ABC with $\angle C$ as the right angle, we can prove that $m\angle A + m\angle B = 90$, or that $\angle A$ and $\angle B$ are complementary.

● **COROLLARY T27-3. Each angle of an equilateral triangle measures 60°.**

Given equilateral $\triangle ABC$, we can prove that $m\angle A = 60$, $m\angle B = 60$, and $m\angle C = 60$. Use Theorem 27 with Corollary T9-3 (every equilateral triangle is equiangular).

To construct an angle of 60° at a given point, or to construct an equilateral triangle.

See Chapter 16, Construction 11.

● **COROLLARY T27-4. Each acute angle of an isosceles right triangle measures 45°.**

Triangle ABC is both right and isosceles. If $\angle C$ is a right angle and $\overline{AC} \cong \overline{BC}$, we can prove that $m\angle A = 45$ and $m\angle B = 45$. Use Theorem 27, the subtraction property of equality, and Theorem 9 (the base angles of an isosceles triangle are congruent).

● **COROLLARY T27-5. The sum of the degree measures of the angles of a quadrilateral is 360.**

Quadrilateral $ABCD$ is given. We can prove that $m\angle A + m\angle B + m\angle C + m\angle D = 360$. Draw a diagonal, $\overline{AC}$, forming two triangles. Then apply Theorem 27.

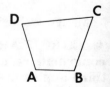

MODEL PROBLEMS _____

1. The measure of the vertex angle of an isosceles triangle exceeds the measure of each base angle by 30. Find the measure of each angle of the triangle.

Solution

Let x = the measure of each base angle.
Let $x + 30$ = the measure of the vertex angle.
The sum of the degree measures of the angles of a triangle is 180.

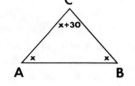

$$x + x + x + 30 = 180$$
$$3x + 30 = 180$$
$$3x = 150$$
$$x = 50, \text{ and } x + 30 = 80. \qquad Answer:\ 50, 50, 80$$

2. In $\triangle ABC$, the measures of the three angles are represented by $9x$, $3x - 6$, and $11x + 2$. Show that $\triangle ABC$ is a right triangle.

Solution

$\triangle ABC$ will be a right triangle if one of the angles is a right angle. Since the sum of the degree measures of the three angles of $\triangle ABC$ is 180:

$$9x + 3x - 6 + 11x + 2 = 180$$
$$23x - 4 = 180$$
$$23x = 184$$
$$x = 8$$

Substitute $x = 8$ in the representations of the angle measures.

$$9x = 9(8) = 72$$
$$3x - 6 = 3(8) - 6 = 24 - 6 = 18$$
$$11x + 2 = 11(8) + 2 = 88 + 2 = 90$$

Answer: $\triangle ABC$ is a right triangle because the degree measure of one of its angles is 90.

EXERCISES

1. Which of the following can represent the degree measures of the three angles of a triangle?
  a. 20, 100, 60   **b.** 55, 45, 90   **c.** 30, 110, 40   **d.** 35, 125, 10
2. Find the degree measure of the third angle of a triangle if the first two angles measure:
  a. 60, 40   **b.** 130, 20   **c.** 45, 55   **d.** 102, 34   **e.** 97, 59
3. In $\triangle ABC$, $\overline{AB} \cong \overline{BC}$ and $m\angle A = 40$. Find $m\angle B$.
4. In $\triangle DEF$, $\overline{DE} \perp \overline{EF}$ and $m\angle D = 30$. Find $m\angle F$.
5. In $\triangle PQR$, $\overline{PQ} \cong \overline{QR}$ and $\overline{PQ} \cong \overline{RP}$. Find $m\angle P$.
6. If the degree measures of the angles of a triangle are represented by $2x$, $x + 10$, and $3x - 10$, find **(a)** the value of x and **(b)** the degree measures of the three angles.

7. Find the degree measure of the vertex angle of an isosceles triangle if each base angle measures:
    a. 70   **b.** 35   **c.** 54   **d.** $37\frac{1}{2}$ **e.** 72.5

8. Find the degree measure of each base angle of an isosceles triangle if the vertex angle measures:
    a. 50   **b.** 70   **c.** 82   **d.** 100   **e.** 75

9. Each base angle of an isosceles triangle has a measure that is 20° more than 3 times the measure of the vertex angle. Find the measure of the vertex angle.

10. In $\triangle ABC$, $m\angle A = 40$ and $m\angle C = 30$. If $\overline{CD}$ is drawn so that $\overline{CD}$ is the bisector of $\angle C$ and D is a point on $\overline{AB}$, find:
    a. $m\angle B$ **b.** $m\angle ACD$ **c.** $m\angle ADC$ **d.** $m\angle BDC$

11. Find the degree measure of the *smallest* angle of a triangle if the ratio of the measures of the three angles is:
    a. 1:2:3   **b.** 1:3:5   **c.** 1:4:7   **d.** 1:2:6   **e.** 1:4:5

12. Find the degree measure of each angle of a triangle if the ratio of the measures of the three angles is:
    a. 4:3:2   **b.** 2:5:8   **c.** 2:5:2   **d.** 3:4:5   **e.** 3:5:7

13. In triangle RST, $m\angle T = 90$ and $m\angle R = 35$. If $\overline{TH}$ is drawn perpendicular to $\overline{RS}$, find **(a)** $m\angle S$ and **(b)** $m\angle HTS$.

14. In triangle RST, P is a point on $\overline{RT}$ such that $\overline{RS} \cong \overline{SP}$. If $m\angle RSP = 40$ and $m\angle STP = 50$, find **(a)** $m\angle R$, **(b)** $m\angle RPS$, **(c)** $m\angle TPS$, and **(d)** $m\angle PST$.

15. Each of the congruent angles of an isosceles triangle measures 9° less than four times the vertex angle. Find the measures of the angles of the triangle.

16. The degree measures of the angles of a triangle are represented by $2x + 10$, $x - 10$, and $2x - 20$. Show the triangle is a right triangle.

17. The degree measures of the angles of $\triangle ABC$ are represented by $x + 30$, $2x$, and $3x - 30$. Show that $\triangle ABC$ is equiangular.

18. Find the degree measure of the fourth angle of a quadrilateral if the first three angles measure:
    a. 60, 130, 90   **b.** 90, 90, 140   **c.** 120, 110, 60

19. Find the degree measure of each angle of a quadrilateral if the measures of its angles are represented by $3x + 20$, $2x + 40$, $4x - 50$, $x - 10$.

20. *Prove:* A triangle can contain no more than one right angle.

21. *Prove:* A triangle can contain no more than one obtuse angle.

22. *Prove:* If $\overline{CD}$ is the altitude drawn to hypotenuse $\overline{AB}$ of right triangle ABC, then angle BCD is congruent to angle A.

23. *Prove:* If the measure of one angle of a triangle is equal to the sum of the measures of the other two, the triangle is a right triangle.

5-5 PROVING TRIANGLES CONGRUENT WHEN TWO PAIRS OF ANGLES AND A PAIR OF OPPOSITE SIDES ARE CONGRUENT

● **THEOREM 28.** Two triangles are congruent if two angles and a side opposite one of the angles in one triangle are congruent to the corresponding two angles and side of the other. [a.a.s. ≅ a.a.s.]

Given: △ABC and △$A'B'C'$, ∠A ≅ ∠A',
    ∠C = ∠C'; and $\overline{AB}$ ≅ $\overline{A'B'}$.

Prove: △ABC ≅ △$A'B'C'$.

Plan: To prove that two triangles
are congruent by the statement
a.a.s. ≅ a.a.s., it will be necessary to show that the triangles can be
proved congruent by one of the accepted postulates. Here, we will show
△ABC ≅ △$A'B'C'$ by a.s.a. ≅ a.s.a.

Statements	*Reasons*
1. In △ABC and △$A'B'C'$, ∠C ≅ ∠C'.	1. Given.
2. ∠A ≅ ∠A'. (a. ≅ a.)	2. Given.
3. $\overline{AB}$ ≅ $\overline{A'B'}$. (s. ≅ s.)	3. Given.
4. ∠B ≅ ∠B' (a. ≅ a.)	4. If two angles of one triangle are congruent, respectively, to two angles of another triangle, then the third angles are congruent.
5. △ABC ≅ △$A'B'C'$.	5. a.s.a. ≅ a.s.a.

Therefore, from this point on, when two angles and a side opposite
one of these angles in one triangle are congruent to the corresponding
two angles and side of a second triangle (a.a.s. ≅ a.a.s.), we may say that
the triangles are congruent.

KEEP IN MIND ─────────────────────

You now have four ways to prove two triangles congruent:

s.s.s. ≅ s.s.s.   s.a.s. ≅ s.a.s.

a.s.a. ≅ a.s.a.   a.a.s. ≅ a.a.s.

Must Triangles Be Congruent When
a.a.a. ≅ a.a.a.   or   s.s.a. ≅ s.s.a.?

In addition to the four ways to prove two triangles congruent, let us consider two other cases.

CASE I. Must two triangles be congruent when three angles of one triangle are congruent, respectively, to three angles of the other triangle? In the figure, while a.a.a. ≅ a.a.a. in $\triangle ABC$ and $\triangle GHI$, the corresponding sides are not congruent. Thus, $\triangle ABC$ is *not* congruent to $\triangle GHI$.

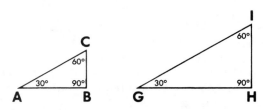

CASE II. Must two triangles be congruent when two sides and an angle opposite one of these sides of one triangle are congruent, respectively, to two sides and the corresponding angle of the other triangle?

Consider the following triangles. In $\triangle ABC$, imagine that compasses are placed at vertex C and an arc, BD, is swung. Thus, $\overline{CB} \cong \overline{CD}$ and $CB = CD$. Let m∠A = 30, AC = 20, and both CB = 15 and CD = 15.

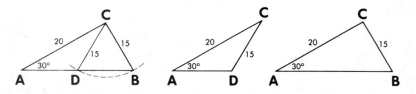

Here, while s.s.a. ≅ s.s.a. in $\triangle ACD$ and $\triangle ACB$, notice that one pair of corresponding sides is not congruent: $\overline{AD}$ is not congruent to $\overline{AB}$. Thus, $\triangle ACD$ is *not* congruent to $\triangle ACB$.

KEEP IN MIND ————————————————————————

Two triangles can*not* be proved to be congruent by

a.a.a. ≅ a.a.a.   or   s.s.a. ≅ s.s.a.

MODEL PROBLEM ―――――――――――――――――――――――――

Prove that the altitudes drawn to the legs of an isosceles triangle from the endpoints of the base are congruent.

Given: Isosceles $\triangle ABC$ with $\overline{BA} \cong \overline{BC}$.
$\overline{CD} \perp \overline{BA}$ and $\overline{AE} \perp \overline{BC}$.

Prove: $\overline{CD} \cong \overline{AE}$.

Plan: Prove $\triangle DAC \cong \triangle ECA$ by a.a.s. $\cong$ a.a.s.

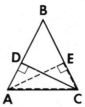

Statements	*Reasons*
1. In $\triangle ABC$, $\overline{BA} \cong \overline{BC}$.	1. Given.
2. $\angle BAC \cong \angle BCA$. (a. $\cong$ a.)	2. If two sides of a triangle are congruent, the angles opposite these sides are congruent.
3. $\overline{AE} \perp \overline{BC}$, $\overline{CD} \perp \overline{BA}$.	3. Given.
4. $\angle CDA$ and $\angle AEC$ are right angles.	4. Definition of perpendicular lines.
5. $\angle CDA \cong \angle AEC$. (a. $\cong$ a.)	5. All right angles are congruent.
6. $\overline{AC} \cong \overline{AC}$. (s. $\cong$ s.)	6. Reflexive property of congruence.
7. $\triangle DAC \cong \triangle ECA$.	7. a.a.s. $\cong$ a.a.s.
8. $\overline{CD} \cong \overline{AE}$.	8. Corresponding parts of congruent triangles are congruent.

EXERCISES ―――――――――――――――――――――――――――

In 1–6, the figures have been marked to indicate the *given* premises. Tell whether or not the triangles must always be congruent, and give your reason.

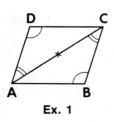

Ex. 1

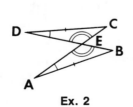

Ex. 2

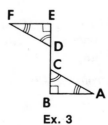

Ex. 3

Ex. 4

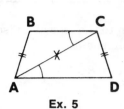

Ex. 5

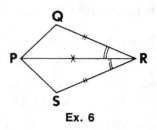

Ex. 6

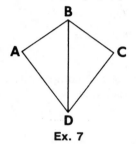

Ex. 7

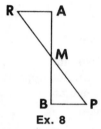

Ex. 8

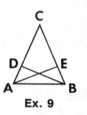

Ex. 9

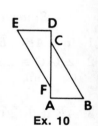

Ex. 10

7. *Given:* $\overline{BD}$ bisects $\angle B$ and $\angle A \cong \angle C$.
   Prove: $\triangle ADB \cong \triangle CDB$.

8. *Given:* $\overline{RMP}$ bisects $\overline{AMB}$ at M, and $\angle R \cong \angle P$.
   Prove: $\overline{RM} \cong \overline{PM}$.

9. *Given:* In $\triangle ACB$, $\overline{AC} \cong \overline{BC}$ and $\angle ADB \cong \angle BEA$.
   Prove: $\overline{AE} \cong \overline{BD}$.

10. *Given:* $\overline{AFCD}$, $\overline{ED} \perp \overline{DA}$, $\overline{BA} \perp \overline{DA}$, $\overline{DC} \cong \overline{AF}$, and $\angle E \cong \angle B$.
    Prove: $\overline{EF} \cong \overline{BC}$.

11. Prove the following corollary to Theorem 28.

● **COROLLARY T28-1. Two right triangles are congruent if the hypotenuse and an acute angle of right triangle are congruent to the hypotenuse and an acute angle of the other right triangle.**

Given: $\triangle ABC$ and $\triangle A'B'C'$ are right triangles with $\angle C$ and $\angle C'$ right angles; $\overline{AB} \cong \overline{A'B'}$; $\angle A \cong \angle A'$.

Prove: $\triangle ABC \cong \triangle A'B'C'$.

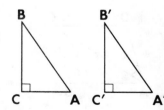

5-6 THE CONVERSE OF THE ISOSCELES TRIANGLE THEOREM

The Isosceles Triangle Theorem, proved in this book as Theorem 9 (see page 172), is restated here in its conditional form, $p \rightarrow q$.

● **THEOREM 9. If two sides of a triangle are congruent, then the angles opposite these sides are congruent.**

The *converse* of this theorem was once very difficult to prove. Now that two triangles can be proved congruent by a.a.s. ≅ a.a.s., this converse statement is relatively easy to prove. The converse of the Isosceles Triangle Theorem can be written as follows, in the form $q \rightarrow p$.

● **THEOREM 29. If two angles of a triangle are congruent, then the sides opposite these angles are congruent.**

Given: △ABC with ∠A ≅ ∠B.

Prove: $\overline{CA}$ ≅ $\overline{CB}$.

Plan: By drawing the bisector $\overline{CD}$ of the vertex ∠ACB, two triangles are formed. Prove △ACD ≅ △BCD and therefore, $\overline{CA}$ ≅ $\overline{CB}$.

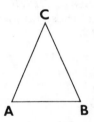 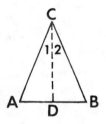

Statements	Reasons
1. Let $\overline{CD}$, the bisector of vertex ∠ACB, intersect $\overline{AB}$ at D.	1. Every angle has one and only one bisector.
2. ∠1 ≅ ∠2. (a. ≅ a.)	2. Definition of angle bisector.
3. $\overline{CD}$ ≅ $\overline{CD}$. (s. ≅ s.)	3. Reflexive property of congruence.
4. ∠A ≅ ∠B. (a. ≅ a.)	4. Given.
5. △ACD ≅ △BCD.	5. a.a.s. ≅ a.a.s.
6. $\overline{CA}$ ≅ $\overline{CB}$.	6. Corresponding sides of congruent triangles are congruent.

To prove that a triangle is isosceles, we may now prove that either of the following two statements is true:

1. Two sides of the triangle are congruent, or
2. Two angles of the triangle are congruent.

● **COROLLARY T29-1. If a triangle is equiangular, then it is equilateral.**

If we are given $\triangle ABC$ where $\angle A \cong \angle B \cong \angle C$, we can then prove that $\overline{BC} \cong \overline{CA} \cong \overline{AB}$ by using Theorem 29. Therefore, $\triangle ABC$ is equilateral.

MODEL PROBLEMS ———————————————————————————

1. In $\triangle PQR$, $\angle Q \cong \angle R$. If $PQ = 5x - 7$ and $PR = 2x + 11$, find:
   a. the value of x. **b.** PQ. **c.** PR.

   Solution

   a. Since two angles of $\triangle PQR$ are congruent, the sides opposite these angles are congruent. Thus, $PQ = PR$.

   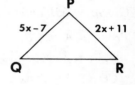

   $$5x - 7 = 2x + 11$$
   $$5x - 2x = 11 + 7$$
   $$3x = 18$$
   $$x = 6 \quad Ans.$$

   b. $PQ = 5x - 7 = 5(6) - 7 = 30 - 7 = 23 \quad Ans.$

   c. $PR = 2x + 11 = 2(6) + 11 = 12 + 11 = 23 \quad Ans.$

2. If the degree measures of the three angles of a triangle are represented by $x + 20$, $2x - 5$, and $3x + 15$, which of the following choices most completely describes the triangle?
   (1) scalene and right   (2) isosceles and acute
   (3) isosceles and right   (4) equiangular

   Solution

   The sum of the degree measures of the angles of a triangle is 180.

   $$x + 20 + 2x - 5 + 3x + 15 = 180$$
   $$6x + 30 = 180$$
   $$6x = 150$$
   $$x = 25$$

   Substitute $x = 25$ in the representations given for the three angle measures.
   $$x + 20 = 25 + 20 = 45$$
   $$2x - 5 = 2(25) - 5 = 50 - 5 = 45$$
   $$3x + 15 = 3(25) + 15 = 75 + 15 = 90$$

Since each of two angles measures 45°, the triangle is isosceles. Also, since one angle measures 90°, the triangle is right.

Answer: (3)

3. *Given:* In △*ABC*, $\overline{DHE}$, $\overline{FHG}$, $\overline{GH} \cong \overline{EH}$, and ∠1 ≅ ∠2.

Prove: △*ABC* is isosceles.

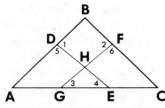

Plan: Prove that ∠*A* ≅ ∠*C* with △*ADE* and △*CFG*, which are separated and shown below.

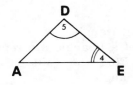 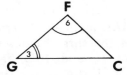

Statements	Reasons
1. $\overline{GH} \cong \overline{EH}$.	1. Given.
2. In △*GHE*, ∠3 ≅ ∠4. (a. ≅ a.)	2. If two sides of a triangle are congruent, the angles opposite these sides are congruent.
3. ∠1 ≅ ∠2.	3. Given.
4. ∠5 ≅ ∠6. (a. ≅ a.)	4. Supplements of congruent angles are congruent.
5. ∠*A* ≅ ∠*C*.	5. If two angles of one triangle are congruent, respectively, to two angles of another triangle, then the third angles are congruent.
6. △*ABC* is isosceles.	6. If two angles of a triangle are congruent, the sides opposite these angles are congruent and the triangle is isosceles.

EXERCISES

In 1–4, degree measures of two angles of a triangle are given.
a. Find the measure of the third angle of the triangle.
b. Tell whether the triangle is isosceles or not isosceles.

1. 70, 40   **2.** 30, 120   **3.** 35, 65   **4.** 100, 50

5. In triangle ABC, $\angle A \cong \angle C$, $AB = 5x + 6$, and $BC = 3x + 14$. Find x.
6. In triangle PQR, $\angle Q \cong \angle P$, $PR = 3x$, and $RQ = 2x + 7$. Find PR and RQ.
7. In $\triangle MNR$, $\angle M \cong \angle R$, $MN = 3x + 2$, $NR = x + 8$, and $MR = 2x$. Find: **a.** the value of x.   **b.** MN.   **c.** NR.   **d.** MR.
8. In triangle ABC, $m\angle A = 80$ and $m\angle B = 50$. If $AB = 4x - 4$ and $AC = 2x + 16$, find AB and AC.
9. The degree measures of the angles of triangle ABC are represented by $2x$, $x + 10$, and $2x - 30$.
   a. Express the sum of the measures of the angles in terms of x.
   b. Find the value of x.
   c. Show that triangle ABC is an isosceles triangle.
10. The degree measures of the angles of a triangle are represented by $x + 35$, $2x + 10$, and $3x - 15$.
    a. Find the value of x.
    b. Show that triangle ABC is an equilateral triangle.
11. The degree measures of the three angles of a triangle are represented by $3x + 18$, $4x + 9$, and $10x$. **a.** Find the value of x.
    b. Show that $\triangle ABC$ is an isosceles right triangle.

In 12–17, the given expressions represent the degree measures of the three angles of a triangle. Which of the following choices most completely describes the triangle?

(1) scalene and right   (2) isosceles and acute
(3) isosceles and right   (4) equiangular

12. x, $2x$, $3x$ 13. x, x, $2x$
14. $x + 30$, $4x + 30$, $10x - 30$ 15. $3x$, $4x - 20$, $2x + 20$
16. $x + 15$, $2x - 15$, $3x$ 17. x, $2x$, $3x - 36$

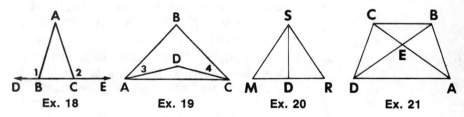

Ex. 18   Ex. 19   Ex. 20   Ex. 21

18. Given $\overleftrightarrow{DBCE}$ and $\angle 1 \cong \angle 2$, prove that $\triangle ABC$ is isosceles.
19. If $\overline{AB} \cong \overline{BC}$ and $\angle 3 \cong \angle 4$, prove that $\triangle ADC$ is isosceles.
20. If $\overline{SD} \perp \overline{MR}$, and $\overline{SD}$ bisects $\overline{MR}$, prove that $\triangle MRS$ is isosceles.
21. If $\overline{AB} \cong \overline{DC}$ and $\overline{AC} \cong \overline{DB}$, prove that **(a)** $\triangle ACD \cong \triangle DBA$, **(b)** $\angle CAD \cong \angle BDA$, and **(c)** $\triangle DEA$ is isosceles.

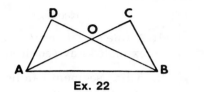

Ex. 22

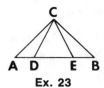

Ex. 23

22. If $\overline{DA} \cong \overline{CB}$ and $\angle DAB \cong \angle CBA$, prove that $\triangle AOB$ is isosceles.

23. *Given:* $\overleftrightarrow{ADEB}$, $\overline{AD} \cong \overline{BE}$, $\angle CDE \cong \angle CED$.
   Prove: $\triangle ACB$ is isosceles.

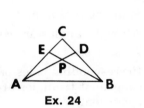

Ex. 24

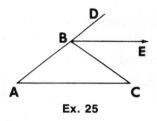

Ex. 25

24. *Given:* $\triangle ABC$, $\overline{CA} \cong \overline{CB}$, $\overline{APD}$, $\overline{BPE}$, $\angle PAB \cong \angle PBA$.
   Prove: $\overline{PE} \cong \overline{PD}$.

25. *Given:* $\triangle ABC$, $\overrightarrow{ABD}$, $\overrightarrow{BE}$ bisects $\angle DBC$, $\overrightarrow{BE} \parallel \overline{AC}$.
   Prove: $\overline{AB} \cong \overline{CB}$.

26. *Prove:* If a triangle is equiangular, it is equilateral.

5-7 PROVING RIGHT TRIANGLES CONGRUENT BY HYPOTENUSE AND LEG

● **THEOREM 30.** **Two right triangles are congruent if the hypotenuse and a leg of one triangle are congruent to the corresponding parts of the other. [hy. leg ≅ hy. leg]**

Given: Right $\triangle ABC$ with right $\angle B$;
   right $\triangle DEF$ with right $\angle E$;
   $\overline{AC} \cong \overline{DF}$; $\overline{BC} \cong \overline{EF}$.

Prove: Right $\triangle ABC \cong$ right $\triangle DEF$.

Plan: Construct a third triangle,
   $\triangle GEF$. Prove that each of the two given triangles is congruent to $\triangle GEF$ and, thus, to each other.

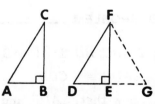

Statements	*Reasons*
1. Extend $\overline{DE}$ to G so that $\overline{EG} \cong \overline{AB}$. (s. $\cong$ s.)	1. A line segment may be extended any required length.
2. Draw $\overline{FG}$.	2. A line segment can be drawn joining two points.
3. $\overline{BC} \cong \overline{EF}$. (s. $\cong$ s.)	3. Given.
4. $\angle B$ and $\angle DEF$ are right angles.	4. Given.
5. $\overline{DG} \perp \overline{EF}$.	5. Definition of perpendicular lines.
6. $\angle GEF$ is a right angle.	6. Same as reason 5.
7. $\angle B \cong \angle GEF$. (a. $\cong$ a.)	7. All right angles are congruent.
8. $\triangle ABC \cong \triangle GEF$.	8. s.a.s. $\cong$ s.a.s.
9. $\overline{AC} \cong \overline{GF}$.	9. Corresponding sides of congruent triangles are congruent.
10. $\overline{AC} \cong \overline{DF}$.	10. Given.
11. $\overline{DF} \cong \overline{GF}$. (s. $\cong$ s.)	11. Transitive property of congruence.
12. $\angle D \cong \angle G$. (a. $\cong$ a.)	12. If two sides of a triangle are congruent, the angles opposite these sides are congruent.
13. $\angle DEF \cong \angle GEF$. (a. $\cong$ a.)	13. All right angles are congruent.
14. $\triangle DEF \cong \triangle GEF$.	14. a.a.s. $\cong$ a.a.s.
15. $\triangle ABC \cong \triangle DEF$.	15. Transitive property of congruence.

Therefore, from this point on, when two right triangles agree in the hypotenuse and a leg [hy. leg $\cong$ hy. leg], we may say that the triangles are congruent.

MODEL PROBLEM ⎯⎯⎯⎯⎯⎯⎯⎯⎯⎯⎯⎯⎯⎯⎯⎯⎯⎯⎯⎯⎯⎯⎯⎯

Given: $\triangle ABC, \overline{BD} \perp \overline{AC}, \overline{AB} \cong \overline{CB}$.

Prove: $\triangle ADB \cong \triangle CDB$.

Plan: Show that $\triangle ADB$ and $\triangle CDB$ are right triangles. Then use hy. leg $\cong$ hy. leg to prove them congruent.

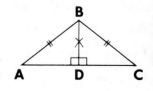

Statements	*Reasons*
1. $\overline{BD} \perp \overline{AC}$.	1. Given.
2. $\angle ADB$ and $\angle CDB$ are right angles.	2. Definition of perpendicular lines.
3. $\triangle ADB$ and $\triangle CDB$ are right triangles.	3. Definition of right triangle.
4. $\overline{AB} \cong \overline{CB}$. (hy. $\cong$ hy.)	4. Given.
5. $\overline{BD} \cong \overline{BD}$. (leg $\cong$ leg)	5. Reflexive property of congruence.
6. $\triangle ADB \cong \triangle CDB$.	6. Hy. leg $\cong$ hy. leg.

EXERCISES

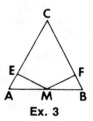

Ex. 1

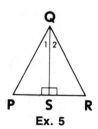

Ex. 2

1. *Given:* Right $\angle ABD$, right $\angle CDB$, and $\overline{AD} \cong \overline{CB}$.
   Prove: $\triangle ABD \cong \triangle CDB$.
2. *Given:* $\overrightarrow{PB} \perp \overrightarrow{AC}$, $\overrightarrow{PD} \perp \overrightarrow{AE}$, and $\overline{AB} \cong \overline{AD}$.
   Prove: $\triangle ABP \cong \triangle ADP$.

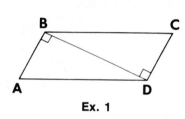

Ex. 3

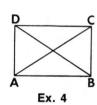

Ex. 4

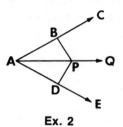

Ex. 5

3. If M is the midpoint of $\overline{AB}$, $\overline{ME} \perp \overline{AC}$, $\overline{MF} \perp \overline{CB}$, and $\overline{ME} \cong \overline{MF}$, prove that $\angle CAB \cong \angle CBA$.
4. If $\overline{DA} \perp \overline{AB}$, $\overline{CB} \perp \overline{AB}$, and $\overline{AC} \cong \overline{BD}$, prove that:
   a. $\triangle ACB \cong \triangle BDA$.   **b.** $\overline{AD} \cong \overline{BC}$.
5. In $\triangle PQR$, $\overline{QS} \perp \overline{PR}$, $\overline{PQ} \cong \overline{RQ}$, m$\angle 1 = 4x$, and m$\angle 2 = 2x + 18$.
   a. Prove $\triangle PQS \cong \triangle RQS$. **b.** Find the value of x. **c.** Find m$\angle 1$.

6. In quadrilateral *ABCD*, ∠*A* and ∠*C* are right angles, $\overline{AB} \cong \overline{CD}$.

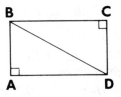

a. Prove △*ABD* ≅ △*CDB*.
b. If m∠*ABD* = 60, m∠*DBC* = 30, m∠*BDA* = *x* − *y*, and m∠*BDC* = *x* + *y*, find *x* and *y*.

5-8 EXTERIOR ANGLES OF A TRIANGLE

Let us now consider a theorem related to Theorem 11: The measure of an exterior angle of a triangle is greater than the measure of either nonadjacent interior angle.

● **THEOREM 31. The measure of an exterior angle of a triangle is equal to the sum of the measures of the two nonadjacent interior angles.**

Given: △*ABC* with exterior ∠*CBD* at vertex *B*, and two nonadjacent interior angles, ∠*A* and ∠*C*.

Prove: m∠*CBD* = m∠*A* + m∠*C*.

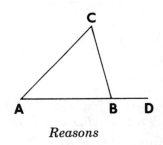

Statements	*Reasons*
1. In △*ABC*, ∠*CBD* is an exterior angle at vertex *B*.	1. Given.
2. ∠*CBD* and ∠*CBA* form a linear pair.	2. A linear pair of angles are two angles whose sum is a straight angle.
3. m∠*CBD* + m∠*CBA* = 180.	3. The degree measure of a straight angle is 180.
4. m∠*A* + m∠*CBA* + m∠*C* = 180.	4. The sum of the degree measures of the angles of a triangle is 180.
5. m∠*CBD* + m∠*CBA* = m∠*A* + m∠*CBA* + m∠*C*.	5. Transitive property of equality.
6. m∠*CBD* = m∠*A* + m∠*C*.	6. When equal quantities are subtracted from equal quantities, the results are equal.

MODEL PROBLEM

In $\triangle ABC$, $\overline{CD}$ is drawn so that $\overline{CD} \cong \overline{CA}$.
If m$\angle ACD = 70$, find:

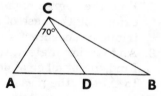

a. m$\angle CAD$ **b.** m$\angle CDB$

Solution:

a. Since $\overline{CD} \cong \overline{CA}$, $\triangle ACD$ is isosceles. Let the degree measure of each base angle equal x: m$\angle CAD = x$, and m$\angle CDA = x$. Then,

$$x + x + 70 = 180$$
$$2x + 70 = 180$$
$$2x = 110$$
$$x = 55$$

Answer: m$\angle CDA = 55$

b. Angle CDB is an exterior angle of $\triangle ACD$ at vertex D.
The measure of an exterior angle of a triangle equals the sum of the measures of the two nonadjacent interior angles.

$$\text{m}\angle CDB = \text{m}\angle DCA + \text{m}\angle CAD$$
$$= 70 + 55$$
$$= 125$$

Answer: m$\angle CDB = 125$

EXERCISES

In 1–5, find the number of degrees in the value of x.

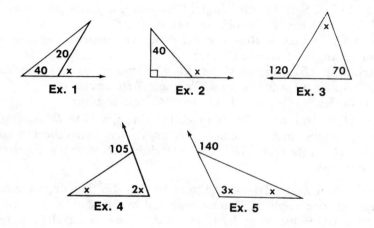

Ex. 1   Ex. 2   Ex. 3

Ex. 4   Ex. 5

6. In $\triangle RST$, if m$\angle S = 90$ and m$\angle T = 30$, find the degree measure of an exterior angle at R.

7. Find the degree measure of either of the exterior angles formed by extending the base of an isosceles triangle if the vertex angle of the triangle measures: **a.** 20   **b.** 40   **c.** 82   **d.** 120   **e.** 135

8. An exterior angle at the base of an isosceles triangle measures $140°$. Find the number of degrees in the vertex angle.

9. In $\triangle PQR$, the measure of $\angle P$ is twice the measure of $\angle Q$. If an exterior angle at vertex R has a degree measure of 120, find m$\angle Q$.

10. In $\triangle ABC$, m$\angle B$ is four times as large as m$\angle A$. An exterior angle at C measures 125. Find the degree measure of $\angle A$.

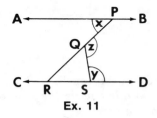

Ex. 11

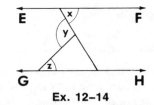

Ex. 12–14

11. In the figure, $\overleftrightarrow{AB} \parallel \overleftrightarrow{CD}$ and $\overleftrightarrow{PQR}$ and $\overline{QS}$ are drawn. If m$\angle x = 44$ and m$\angle y = 98$, find: **a.** m$\angle QRS$ **b.** m$\angle RQS$ **c.** m$\angle z$

12. If $\overleftrightarrow{EF} \parallel \overleftrightarrow{GH}$, m$\angle x = 68$, and m$\angle y = 117$, find m$\angle z$.

13. If $\overleftrightarrow{EF} \parallel \overleftrightarrow{GH}$, m$\angle x = 70$, and m$\angle z = 60$, find m$\angle y$.

14. If $\overleftrightarrow{EF} \parallel \overleftrightarrow{GH}$, m$\angle y = 123$, and m$\angle z = 58$, find m$\angle x$.

In 15–19, select the numeral preceding the best choice for the answer.

15. An exterior angle at the base of an isosceles triangle is always
(1) right (2) acute (3) obtuse (4) equal to the base angle

16. In $\triangle RST$, $\angle S$ is a right angle. The exterior angle at vertex S is
(1) right (2) acute (3) obtuse (4) straight

17. For $\triangle ABC$, m$\angle A = 40$ and m$\angle B = 60$. The degree measure of the exterior angle at vertex C is (1) 40 (2) 60 (3) 80 (4) 100

18. In triangle ABC, an exterior angle at C measures 100 degrees and angle B measures 20 degrees. Triangle ABC must be
(1) isosceles (2) right (3) obtuse (4) equiangular

19. Side $\overline{AC}$ of triangle ABC is extended through C to D. Angle BCD measures $108°$ and the measure of angle A is twice the measure of angle B. Triangle ABC is (1) right (2) obtuse (3) isosceles (4) scalene

20. In $\triangle DEF$, m$\angle D = 2x + 4$ and m$\angle E = 6x - 58$. The degree measure of an exterior angle at F is represented by $5x$.
a. Find the value of x. **b.** Show that $\triangle DEF$ is a right triangle.

21. *Prove:* If the two exterior angles formed by extending the line that contains one side of a triangle in both directions are congruent, the triangle is isosceles.

22. In $\triangle RST$, $\overline{RS} \cong \overline{ST}$. Prove that the bisector of an exterior angle at S is parallel to $\overline{RT}$.

5-9 INTERIOR ANGLES AND EXTERIOR ANGLES OF A POLYGON

You have learned that a polygon is a closed figure that is the union of line segments in a plane. The figure pictured is polygon *ABCDE*. You have already studied the properties of the triangle, the polygon that is the union of 3 sides. Other polygons that you will study are defined as follows:

● **Definition.**   A *quadrilateral* is a polygon that is the union of 4 sides.

● **Definition.**   A *pentagon* is a polygon that is the union of 5 sides.

● **Definition.**   A *hexagon* is a polygon that is the union of 6 sides.

● **Definition.**   An *octagon* is a polygon that is the union of 8 sides.

● **Definition.**   A *decagon* is a polygon that is the union of 10 sides.

● **Definition.**   A *convex polygon* is a polygon each of whose interior angles measures less than 180 degrees.

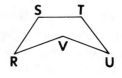

In the figure above, *ABCDE* is a convex polygon. When a polygon has at least one interior angle measuring more than 180°, as in *RSTUV* shown at the right, we call this a *concave polygon*. In this text, we will not deal with concave polygons.

● **Definition.**   A *regular polygon* is a polygon that is both equilateral and equiangular.

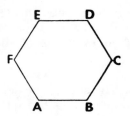

For regular hexagon *ABCDEF*:

$$\overline{AB} \cong \overline{BC} \cong \overline{CD} \cong \overline{DE} \cong \overline{EF} \cong \overline{FA}$$

and

$$\angle A \cong \angle B \cong \angle C \cong \angle D \cong \angle E \cong \angle F$$

For *regular polygons only*, the measures of interior and exterior angles have been indicated in the four simplest regular polygons as follows:

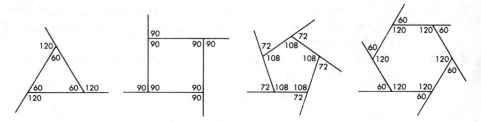

In these four examples, the following rules are true:

1. The sum of the degree measures of the interior angles of a polygon of n sides is $180(n - 2)$.
2. The sum of the degree measures of the exterior angles of a polygon is 360.

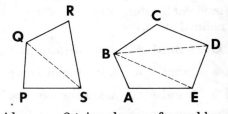

These rules are true for *any* polygon. In the figure, notice that diagonals are drawn from a single vertex so that in quadrilateral *PQRS*, two triangles are formed and $180 \cdot 2 = 360$. Also, in pentagon *ABCDE*, three triangles are formed and $180 \cdot 3 = 540$. In a polygon of n sides, $n - 2$ triangles are formed by drawing the diagonals from a single vertex. This can be used to prove the following theorem.

● **THEOREM 32. The sum of the degree measures of the interior angles of any polygon of n sides is $180\,(n - 2)$.**

Also, for any polygon, we may prove the following:

● **THEOREM 33. The sum of the degree measures of the exterior angles of any polygon of n sides, taking one exterior angle at each vertex, is 360.**

MODEL PROBLEMS

1. A *regular* polygon has 10 sides. **a.** Find the measure of one exterior angle. **b.** Find the measure of one interior angle. **c.** Find the sum of the measures of all interior angles of this polygon.

Solution

a. The sum of the degree measures of the exterior angles of any polygon is 360. Since this *regular* polygon contains 10 sides, it also has 10 congruent exterior angles. The measure of one exterior angle is $\frac{360}{10} = 36$ degrees. *Ans.*

b. An interior angle is supplementary to an exterior angle. Thus, the measure of one of the ten congruent interior angles is $180 - 36 = 144$ degrees. *Ans.*

c. The sum of the degree measures of the ten interior angles may be found by two methods.
First, ten angles of 144 degrees each $= 10(144) = 1,440$. *Ans.*
Or, using the rule $180(n - 2)$ where $n = 10$ sides, the sum of the degree measures of the interior angles is
$180(10 - 2) = 180(8) = 1,440$. *Ans.*

2. Find n, the number of sides of a *regular* polygon, if:
  a. each exterior angle contains $72°$.
  b. each interior angle contains $150°$.
  c. the sum of the degree measures of all the interior angles is 2,880.

Solution

a. The sum of the degree measures of the n exterior angles is 360.
$$\underbrace{72 + 72 + 72 + \ldots}_{n \text{ terms}} = 360$$
$$72n = 360$$
$$n = 5 \quad Ans.$$

b. For each interior angle of $150°$, there is a supplementary exterior angle of $180 - 150$ or $30°$. The sum of the degree measures of the n exterior angles is 360.
$$30n = 360$$
$$n = 12 \quad Ans.$$

c. The sum of the degree measures of the interior angles of any polygon of n sides is $180(n - 2)$.
$$180(n - 2) = 2,880$$
$$180n - 360 = 2,880$$
$$180n = 3,240$$
$$n = 18 \quad Ans.$$

EXERCISES

1. Find the sum of the degree measures of the interior angles of a polygon that has: **a.** 3 sides **b.** 7 sides **c.** 9 sides
2. Find the sum of the degree measures of the interior angles of:
  a. a hexagon **b.** an octagon **c.** a pentagon **d.** a quadrilateral
3. Find the sum of the measures of the exterior angles of a polygon that has: **a.** 4 sides **b.** 8 sides **c.** 10 sides **d.** 36 sides

In 4–11, for each *regular* polygon with the given number of sides, find the degree measure of **(a)** one exterior angle and **(b)** one interior angle.

4. 4 sides   **5.** 5 sides   **6.** 6 sides   **7.** 8 sides
8. 9 sides   **9.** 12 sides   **10.** 20 sides   **11.** 36 sides

12. Find the number of sides of a *regular* polygon each of whose exterior angles contains: **a.** 30° **b.** 45° **c.** 60° **d.** 120°

13. Find the number of sides of a *regular* polygon each of whose interior angles contains: **a.** 90° **b.** 120° **c.** 140° **d.** 160°

14. Find the number of sides a polygon has if the sum of the degree measures of its interior angles is: **a.** 180 **b.** 360 **c.** 540 **d.** 900 **e.** 1,440 **f.** 2,700 **g.** 1,800 **h.** 3,600

15. The measure of each exterior angle of a regular polygon is twice the measure of each interior angle. How many sides does the polygon have?

16. The angles of a quadrilateral are in the ratio 3:4:5:6. Find the number of degrees contained in the largest angle of the quadrilateral.

5-10   REVIEW EXERCISES

In 1–5, $\overleftrightarrow{AB} \parallel \overleftrightarrow{CD}$ and these lines are cut by transversal $\overleftrightarrow{GH}$ at points E and F, respectively.

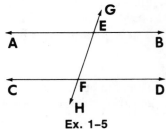

1. If $m\angle AEF = 5x$ and $m\angle DFE = 75$, find x.

2. If $m\angle CFE = 3y + 20$ and $m\angle AEG = 4y - 10$, find y.

3. If $m\angle BEF = 5x$ and $m\angle CFE = 7x - 48$, find x.

4. If $m\angle DFE = y$ and $m\angle BEF = 3y - 40$, find $m\angle DFE$.

Ex. 1–5

5. If $m\angle AEF = 4x$ and $m\angle EFD = 3x + 18$, find: **a.** the value of x **b.** $m\angle AEF$ **c.** $m\angle EFD$ **d.** $m\angle BEF$ **e.** $m\angle CFH$

6. The degree measure of the vertex angle of an isosceles triangle is 120. Find the measure of a base angle of the triangle.

7. In $\triangle ABC$, $\angle A \cong \angle C$. If $AB = 8x + 4$ and $CB = 3x + 34$, find x.

8. In an isosceles triangle, if the measure of the vertex angle is three times the measure of a base angle, find the degree measure of a base angle.

9. In a triangle, the degree measures of the three angles are represented by x, $x + 35$, and $x - 5$. Find the angle measures.

10. In $\triangle PQR$, if $m\angle P = 35$ and $m\angle Q = 85$, what is the degree measure of an exterior angle of the triangle at vertex R?

11. An exterior angle at the base of an isosceles triangle measures 130°. Find the measure of the vertex angle.

12. In △ABC, if $\overline{AB} \cong \overline{AC}$ and m∠A = 70, find m∠B.

13. In △DEF, if $\overline{DE} \cong \overline{DF}$ and m∠E = 70, find m∠D.

14. In △PQR, $\overrightarrow{PQ}$ is extended through Q to point T, forming exterior ∠RQT. If m∠RQT = 70 and m∠R = 10, find m∠P.

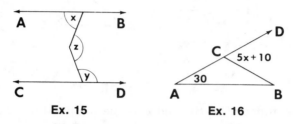

Ex. 15   Ex. 16

15. In the figure, $\overleftrightarrow{AB} \parallel \overleftrightarrow{CD}$, m∠x = 70, and m∠y = 102. Find m∠z.

16. In △ABC, $\overline{AC} \cong \overline{BC}$. The degree measure of an exterior angle at vertex C is represented by 5x + 10. If m∠A = 30, find x.

17. $\overleftrightarrow{AB}$ intersects $\overleftrightarrow{CD}$ at E; m∠AEC = 2x + 10; m∠AED = 3x − 30.
a. Find x. **b.** Show that $\overleftrightarrow{AB}$ is perpendicular to $\overleftrightarrow{CD}$.

In 18–24, select the numeral preceding the word or expression that best completes the statement or answers the question.

18. The measures of the angles of a triangle are in the ratio 2:3:5. The degree measure of the smallest angle of the triangle is
(1) 9 (2) 18 (3) 36 (4) 40

19. If the degree measures of the angles of a triangle are represented by x − 10, 2x + 20, and 3x − 10, the triangle must be
(1) isosceles (2) right (3) equilateral (4) scalene

20. If the degree measures of the angles of a triangle are represented by x, y, and x + y, the triangle must be (1) isosceles (2) right
(3) equilateral (4) scalene

21. If parallel lines are cut by a transversal so that the degree measures of two corresponding angles are represented by 2x + 50 and 3x + 20, then x equals (1) 22 (2) 30 (3) 94 (4) 110

22. If ∠1 and ∠2 are supplementary, which *must* be true?
(1) $k \perp p$ (2) $k \perp m$
(3) $k \parallel m$ (4) $p \parallel m$

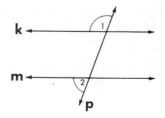

23. The measure of one exterior angle of a *regular* polygon is 60°. How many sides does the regular polygon contain?
(1) 8 (2) 6 (3) 3 (4) 4

24. What is the sum of the degree measures of the interior angles of a pentagon? (1) 360 (2) 540 (3) 900 (4) 1,260

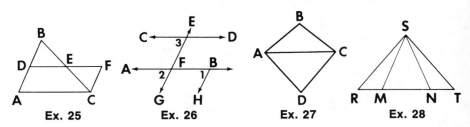

| Ex. 25 | Ex. 26 | Ex. 27 | Ex. 28 |

25. If E is the midpoint of $\overline{BC}$ and E is the midpoint of $\overline{DF}$, prove:
   a. $\triangle BED \cong \triangle CEF.$ **b.** $\angle DBE \cong \angle FCE.$ **c.** $\overline{AB} \parallel \overline{FC}.$

26. If $\angle 1 \cong \angle 3$ and $\angle 3 \cong \angle 2$, prove that $\overrightarrow{BH} \parallel \overleftrightarrow{EG}.$

27. If $\overline{BA} \cong \overline{BC}, \overline{DA} \perp \overline{AB},$ and $\overline{DC} \perp \overline{CB},$ prove that $\triangle ADC$ is an isosceles triangle.

28. If, in $\triangle RST,$ $\angle R \cong \angle T,$ $\overline{RM} \cong \overline{TN},$ and $\overleftrightarrow{RMNT},$ prove that $\triangle MSN$ is an isosceles triangle.

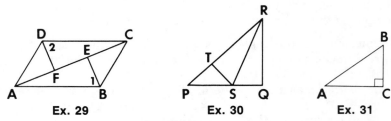

| Ex. 29 | Ex. 30 | Ex. 31 |

29. *Given:* $\overline{AFEC}, \overline{DF} \perp \overline{AC}, \overline{BE} \perp \overline{AC}, \angle 1 \cong \angle 2, \overline{AF} \cong \overline{CE}.$
   Prove: $\triangle ABE \cong \triangle CDF.$

30. *Given:* In $\triangle PQR,$ $\angle Q$ is a right angle, $\overline{ST} \perp \overline{PR}, \overline{RT} \cong \overline{RQ}.$
   Prove: $\triangle TRS \cong \triangle QRS.$

31. *Given:* Right $\triangle ABC$ with $\angle C$ the right angle.
   Prove: $AB > AC.$

32. In polygon $ABCD,$ $\overline{AD}$ is perpendicular to $\overline{AB}$ and to $\overline{CD};$ $\overline{BC}$ is perpendicular to $\overline{AB}$ and to $\overline{CD}.$ Separate $ABCD$ into 2 congruent polygons in 4 different ways.

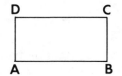

Chapter 6

Quadrilaterals

6-1 THE GENERAL QUADRILATERAL

A quadrilateral is a polygon with four sides. In this chapter you will study the various special quadrilaterals and the properties of each. Let us first name the general parts of any quadrilateral, using *PQRS* as an example.

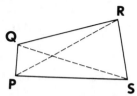

Consecutive vertices are vertices that are endpoints of the same side such as *P* and *Q*; *Q* and *R*; *R* and *S*; *S* and *P*.

Consecutive sides or *adjacent sides* are those sides that have a common endpoint, such as $\overline{PQ}$ and $\overline{QR}$; $\overline{QR}$ and $\overline{RS}$; $\overline{RS}$ and $\overline{SP}$; $\overline{SP}$ and $\overline{PQ}$.

Opposite sides of a quadrilateral are those sides that do not have a common endpoint, such as $\overline{PQ}$ and $\overline{RS}$; $\overline{PS}$ and $\overline{QR}$.

Consecutive angles of a quadrilateral are angles whose vertices are consecutive, such as $\angle P$ and $\angle Q$; $\angle Q$ and $\angle R$; $\angle R$ and $\angle S$; $\angle S$ and $\angle P$.

Opposite angles of a quadrilateral are those angles whose vertices are not consecutive, such as $\angle P$ and $\angle R$; $\angle Q$ and $\angle S$.

A *diagonal* of a quadrilateral is a line segment that joins two vertices that are not consecutive, such as $\overline{PR}$ and $\overline{QS}$.

6-2 THE PARALLELOGRAM

● **Definition.** A *parallelogram* is a quadrilateral with two pairs of opposite sides parallel.

Quadrilateral *ABCD* is a parallelogram because $\overline{AB} \parallel \overline{DC}$ and $\overline{AD} \parallel \overline{BC}$. The symbol for parallelogram *ABCD* is $\square ABCD$.

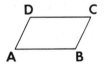

247

● **THEOREM 34. A diagonal divides a parallelogram into two congruent triangles.**

Given: Parallelogram $ABCD$ with diagonal $\overline{AC}$.

Prove: $\triangle ABC \cong \triangle CDA$.

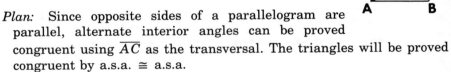

Plan: Since opposite sides of a parallelogram are parallel, alternate interior angles can be proved congruent using $\overline{AC}$ as the transversal. The triangles will be proved congruent by a.s.a. $\cong$ a.s.a.

Statements	*Reasons*
1. $ABCD$ is a parallelogram; $\overline{AC}$ is a diagonal.	1. Given.
2. $\overline{AD} \parallel \overline{CB}$ and $\overline{AB} \parallel \overline{CD}$.	2. A parallelogram is a quadrilateral with two pairs of opposite sides parallel.
3. $\angle BAC \cong \angle DCA$ and $\angle BCA \cong \angle DAC$.	3. If two parallel lines are cut by a transversal, alternate interior angles are congruent.
4. $\overline{AC} \cong \overline{AC}$.	4. Reflexive property of congruence.
5. $\triangle ABC \cong \triangle CDA$.	5. a.s.a. $\cong$ a.s.a.

Now that it is proved that a diagonal divides the parallelogram into two congruent triangles, many corollaries can be proved.

● **Corollary T34-1. Opposite sides of a parallelogram are congruent.**

In $\square ABCD$, $\overline{AB} \cong \overline{DC}$ and $\overline{BC} \cong \overline{AD}$.

● **Corollary T34-2. Opposite angles of a parallelogram are congruent.**

In $\square ABCD$, $\angle B \cong \angle D$ and $\angle A \cong \angle C$.

● **Corollary T34-3. Two consecutive angles of a parallelogram are supplementary.**

In $\square ABCD$, $\angle A$ is supplementary to $\angle B$, $\angle B$ is supplementary to $\angle C$, $\angle C$ is supplementary to $\angle D$, and $\angle D$ is supplementary to $\angle A$.

● **Corollary T34-4. The diagonals of a parallelogram bisect each other.**

In $\square ABCD$, $\overline{AC}$ bisects $\overline{BD}$ so that $\overline{BE} \cong \overline{DE}$; also, $\overline{BD}$ bisects $\overline{AC}$ so that $\overline{AE} \cong \overline{CE}$.

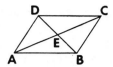

● **Definition.** The *distance between two parallel lines* is the perpendicular distance from any point on one line to the other line.

Given $\overleftrightarrow{AB} \parallel \overleftrightarrow{CD}$. The distance between these lines is LM or PQ or RS since each distance is determined by a segment perpendicular to the parallel lines.

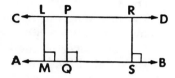

● **Corollary T34-5. Two distinct parallel lines are everywhere equidistant.**

If $\overleftrightarrow{AB} \parallel \overleftrightarrow{CD}$, $\overline{LM} \perp \overleftrightarrow{AB}$, $\overline{PQ} \perp \overleftrightarrow{AB}$, and $\overline{RS} \perp \overleftrightarrow{AB}$, we can prove that $LM = PQ = RS$ by using Corollary T34-1.

Properties of a Parallelogram

1. Opposite sides are parallel.
2. A diagonal divides it into two congruent triangles.
3. Opposite sides are congruent.
4. Opposite angles are congruent.
5. Consecutive angles are supplementary.
6. The diagonals bisect each other.

MODEL PROBLEM _____

In parallelogram $ABCD$, if $m\angle B$ exceeds $m\angle A$ by 50, find the degree measure of $\angle B$.

Solution: Let x = the degree measure of $\angle A$.
          Then $x + 50$ = the degree measure of $\angle B$.

Two consecutive angles of a parallelogram are supplementary.

$$m\angle A + m\angle B = 180$$
$$x + x + 50 = 180$$
$$2x + 50 = 180$$
$$2x = 130$$
$$x = 65$$
$$x + 50 = 115 \qquad \textit{Answer: } m\angle B = 115$$

EXERCISES

1. Find the degree measures of the other three angles of a parallelogram if one angle measures:
   a. 60   **b.** 68   **c.** 73   **d.** 110   **e.** 138   **f.** 160

2. In parallelogram $ABCD$, the degree measure of angle A is represented by $2x$ and the degree measure of angle B by $2x + 60$. Find the value of x.

3. In parallelogram $ABCD$, angle A measures x degrees and angle B measures $(2x - 30)$ degrees. Find the degree measure of angle A.

4. The measures of angles A and B of parallelogram $ABCD$ are in the ratio $2:7$. Find the degree measure of angle A.

5. In parallelogram $ABCD$, the measure of angle A exceeds the measure of angle B by $30°$. Find the degree measure of angle B.

6. The degree measures of two opposite angles of a parallelogram are represented by $3x + 40$ and $x + 70$. **a.** Find x. **b.** Find the degree measure of one of the angles.

7. In $\square ABCD$, $m\angle ABC = 3x - 12$ and $m\angle CDA = x + 40$. Find $m\angle ABC$, $m\angle CDA$, $m\angle BCD$, and $m\angle DAB$.

8. In $\square ABCD$, $AB = 7x - 4$ and $CD = 2x + 21$. Find AB and CD.

9. In parallelogram $ABCD$, $BC = 9y + 10$, $AD = 6y + 40$, and $AB = \frac{1}{2}y + 50$. Find BC, AD, AB, and DC.

Exercises 10–18 refer to parallelogram $ABCD$.

10. If $m\angle DAB = 4x - 60$ and $m\angle DCB = 30 - x$, find $m\angle DAB$, $m\angle DCB$, and $m\angle ABC$.

11. If $m\angle DCB = a + 12$ and $m\angle CDA = 4a + 18$, find the degree measures of the angles of the parallelogram.

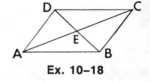

Ex. 10–18

12. If $AB = 4x + y$, $BC = y + 4$, $CD = 3x + 6$, $DA = 2x + y$, find the lengths of the sides of the parallelogram.

13. If $AE = 5x - 3$ and $EC = 15 - x$, find AC.

14. If $DE = 4y + 1$ and $EB = 5y - 1$, find DB.

In 15–18, select the numeral preceding the best answer.

15. In parallelogram $ABCD$, which is *always* true?
    (1) $AB = AD$ (2) $AB = DC$ (3) $\overline{AB} \parallel \overline{AD}$ (4) $\angle A \cong \angle B$

16. If the diagonals of parallelogram $ABCD$ are $\overline{AC}$ and $\overline{BD}$, which is *always* true?
    (1) $\overline{AC} \cong \overline{BD}$ (2) $\overline{AC} \perp \overline{BD}$
    (3) $\angle DAC \cong \angle BAC$ (4) $\triangle DAC \cong \triangle BCA$

17. In $\square ABCD$, diagonals $\overline{AC}$ and $\overline{BD}$ meet at E. Which is *always* true?
(1) $\overline{AE} \cong \overline{EC}$ (2) $\overline{AE} \cong \overline{DE}$ (3) $\overline{AE} \perp \overline{DE}$ (4) $\triangle AEB \cong \triangle AED$

18. In $\square ABCD$, diagonals $\overline{AC}$ and $\overline{BD}$ meet at E. Which is *always* true?
(1) $\triangle AED$ is an isosceles triangle.   (2) $\triangle ABD$ is a right triangle.
(3) $\triangle ABD \cong \triangle CDB$.   (4) $\triangle AEB$ is a right triangle.

Proving That a Quadrilateral Is a Parallelogram

If we wish to prove that a certain quadrilateral is a parallelogram, we can do so by proving its *opposite sides parallel*, thus satisfying the definition of a parallelogram. There are also other conditions that are sufficient to show that a quadrilateral is a parallelogram.

● **THEOREM 35. If both pairs of opposite sides of a quadrilateral are congruent, the quadrilateral is a parallelogram.**

Given: $\overline{AB} \cong \overline{CD}$ and $\overline{AD} \cong \overline{BC}$.

Prove: $ABCD$ is a parallelogram.

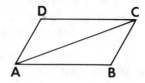

Plan: Draw $\overline{AC}$. Prove $\triangle ABC \cong \triangle CDA$ by s.s.s. $\cong$ s.s.s. Then, use congruent corresponding angles to prove that the opposite sides of $ABCD$ are parallel.

● **THEOREM 36. If one pair of opposite sides of a quadrilateral are both congruent and parallel, the quadrilateral is a parallelogram.**

Given: $\overline{AB} \parallel \overline{CD}$ and $\overline{AB} \cong \overline{CD}$.

Prove: $ABCD$ is a parallelogram.

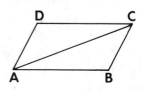

Plan: Draw $\overline{AC}$. Prove $\triangle ABC \cong \triangle CDA$ by s.a.s. $\cong$ s.a.s. Therefore, $\overline{BC} \cong \overline{DA}$. Then, use Theorem 35.

● **THEOREM 37. If both pairs of opposite angles of a quadrilateral are congruent, the quadrilateral is a parallelogram.**

Given: $\angle A \cong \angle C$ and $\angle B \cong \angle D$.

Prove: $ABCD$ is a parallelogram.

Plan:

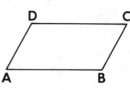

Show $m\angle A + m\angle B + m\angle C + m\angle D = 360$.
Use substitution and the division postulate
to show that $\angle A$ is the supplement of $\angle B$ and $\angle A$ is the supplement of $\angle D$. Then, use Theorem 21 (see page 214).

● **THEOREM 38.** **If the diagonals of a quadrilateral bisect each other, the quadrilateral is a parallelogram.**

Given: $\overline{AC}$ and $\overline{BD}$ intersect at E.
    $\overline{AE} \cong \overline{EC}$ and $\overline{BE} \cong \overline{ED}$.

Prove: $ABCD$ is a parallelogram.

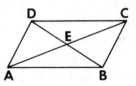

Plan:

Prove $\triangle AEB \cong \triangle CED$ by s.a.s. $\cong$ s.a.s. Therefore, $\overline{AB} \cong \overline{DC}$. Also, $\angle ABE \cong \angle CDE$ and, thus, $\overline{AB} \parallel \overline{DC}$. Then, use Theorem 36.

● **Summary.** To prove that a quadrilateral is a parallelogram, prove that any one of the following statements is true:

1. Both pairs of opposite sides are parallel.
2. Both pairs of opposite sides are congruent.
3. One pair of opposite sides are congruent and parallel.
4. The diagonals bisect each other.
5. Both pairs of opposite angles are congruent.

MODEL PROBLEM

Given: $ABCD$ is a $\square$, E is the midpoint of $\overline{AB}$, F is the midpoint of $\overline{DC}$.

Prove: $EBFD$ is a $\square$.

Plan: Show that one pair of opposite sides, $\overline{EB}$ and $\overline{DF}$, are both congruent and parallel.

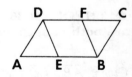

Statements	*Reasons*
1. $ABCD$ is a parallelogram.	1. Given.
2. $\overline{AB} \cong \overline{DC}$.	2. Opposite sides of a $\square$ are congruent.
3. E is the midpoint of $\overline{AB}$ and F is the midpoint of $\overline{DC}$.	3. Given.
4. $\overline{EB} \cong \overline{DF}$.	4. Halves of congruent segments are congruent.
5. $\overline{EB} \parallel \overline{DF}$.	5. A parallelogram is a quadrilateral with two pairs of opposite sides parallel.
6. $EBFD$ is a parallelogram.	6. If one pair of opposite sides of a quadrilateral are both congruent and parallel, the quadrilateral is a $\square$.

EXERCISES

1. In **(a)** to **(e)**, the *given* is marked on the figure. Tell why each quadrilateral *ABCD* is a parallelogram.

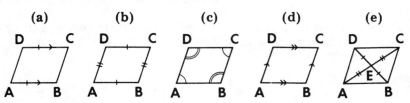

(a)   (b)   (c)   (d)   (e)

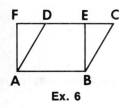 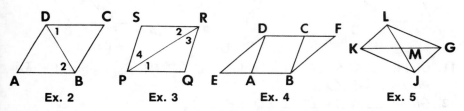

Ex. 2   Ex. 3   Ex. 4   Ex. 5

2. *Given:* *ABCD* is a quadrilateral, $\overline{AB} \cong \overline{CD}$, $\angle 1 \cong \angle 2$.
   Prove: *ABCD* is a parallelogram.
3. *Given:* *PQRS* is a quadrilateral, $\angle 1 \cong \angle 2$, $\angle 3 \cong \angle 4$.
   Prove: *PQRS* is a parallelogram.
4. *Given:* $\square ABCD$, $\overline{EAB}$, $\overline{DCF}$, $\overline{CF} \cong \overline{AE}$.
   Prove: *EBFD* is a $\square$.
5. *Given:* In $\triangle GKL$, $\overline{LM}$ is a median; $\overline{LM}$ is extended to *J* so that $\overline{LM} \cong \overline{MJ}$; $\overline{JK}$ and $\overline{JG}$ are drawn.
   Prove: *GJKL* is a parallelogram.

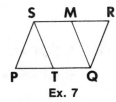 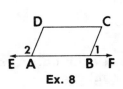

Ex. 6   Ex. 7   Ex. 8

6. *Given:* $\square ABCD$, $\overline{FDEC}$, $\overline{BE} \perp \overline{FC}$, $\overline{AF} \perp \overline{FC}$.
   Prove: *ABEF* is a $\square$.
7. *Given:* *PQRS* is a parallelogram, $\overline{PT} \cong \overline{RM}$.
   Prove: *TQMS* is a parallelogram.
8. *Given:* $\overleftrightarrow{EABF}$, $\angle 2$ is supplementary to $\angle 1$, $\angle C \cong \angle 1$.
   Prove: *ABCD* is a $\square$.

9. *Given:* $\square ABCD$ and $\square CDFE$.
   Prove: **a.** $ABEF$ is a $\square$.
   b. $\overline{FA} \cong \overline{EB}$ and $\overline{FA} \parallel \overline{EB}$.

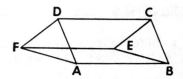

10. *Prove:* The line segment joining the midpoints of two opposite sides of a parallelogram is parallel to the other two sides.

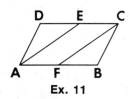

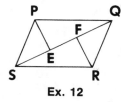

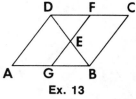

| Ex. 11 | Ex. 12 | Ex. 13 |

11. *Given:* $\square ABCD$, E is the midpoint of $\overline{DC}$, F is the midpoint of $\overline{AB}$.
    Prove: $\overline{AE} \cong \overline{CF}$.
12. *Given:* $\square PQRS$, $\overline{PE} \perp \overline{SQ}$, $\overline{RF} \perp \overline{SQ}$.
    Prove: $\overline{SE} \cong \overline{QF}$.
13. *Given:* $\square ABCD$, $\overline{FG}$ bisects $\overline{DB}$.
    Prove: $\overline{DB}$ bisects $\overline{FG}$.

14. *Given:* $\overline{AC}$ is a diagonal in $\square ABCD$,
    $\overline{AF} \cong \overline{CE}$.

    Prove: $\overline{DE} \parallel \overline{BF}$.

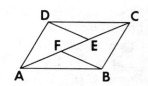

15. If $ABCD$ is a parallelogram with $AB > AD$, and $\overline{AC}$ is a diagonal, prove that $m\angle DAC > m\angle CAB$.

6-3 THE RECTANGLE

● **Definition.** A *rectangle* is a parallelogram one of whose angles is a right angle.

If one angle, $\angle A$, of parallelogram $ABCD$ is a right angle, then $\square ABCD$ is a rectangle.
Any side of a rectangle may be called the *base* of the rectangle. Thus, if side $\overline{AB}$ is taken as the base, then either consecutive side $\overline{AD}$ or $\overline{BC}$ is called the *altitude* of the rectangle.

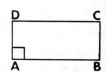

Since a rectangle is a special kind of parallelogram, a rectangle has *all the properties of a parallelogram.* In addition, we can prove two special properties for the rectangle.

● **THEOREM 39. All angles of a rectangle are right angles.**

Given: Rectangle *ABCD* with ∠*A* a right angle.

Prove: ∠*B*, ∠*C*, and ∠*D* are right angles.

Plan: Use Theorem 26 (see page 218) and the definition of perpendicular lines.

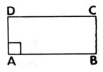

● **THEOREM 40. The diagonals of a rectangle are congruent.**

Given: *ABCD* is a rectangle.

Prove: $\overline{AC} \cong \overline{BD}$.

Plan: Prove △*DAB* ≅ △*CBA* by s.a.s ≅ s.a.s.

Properties of a Rectangle

1. A rectangle has all the properties of a parallelogram.
2. A rectangle contains four right angles and is therefore equiangular.
3. The diagonals of a rectangle are congruent.

Methods of Proving That a Quadrilateral Is a Rectangle

We prove that a quadrilateral is a rectangle by showing that it has the special properties of a rectangle. For example:

● **THEOREM 41. If the diagonals of a parallelogram are congruent, then the parallelogram is a rectangle.**

Given: Parallelogram *ABCD*.
   $\overline{AC} \cong \overline{BD}$.

Prove: *ABCD* is a rectangle.

Plan: Show that △*DAB* ≅ △*CBA* by s.s.s ≅ s.s.s. Therefore, ∠*DAB* ≅ ∠*CBA*. Then, use Corollary T34-3 (see page 248).

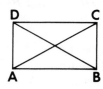

● **Summary.** To prove that a quadrilateral is a rectangle, prove that any one of the following statements is true:

1. The quadrilateral is a parallelogram with one right angle.
2. The quadrilateral is equiangular.
3. The quadrilateral is a parallelogram whose diagonals are congruent.

MODEL PROBLEM

Given: $ABCD$ is a $\square$.
      $\overline{DE} \perp \overline{AB}$.
      $\overline{CF} \perp \overline{AB}$.

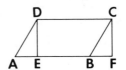

Prove: $DEFC$ is a rectangle.

Plan: Prove that $DEFC$ is a $\square$ that contains a right angle at E.

Statements	*Reasons*
1. $ABCD$ is a $\square$.	1. Given.
2. $\overline{DC} \parallel \overline{AB}$.	2. A parallelogram is a quadrilateral with two pairs of opposite sides parallel.
3. $\overline{DE} \perp \overline{AB}, \overline{CF} \perp \overline{AB}$.	3. Given.
4. $\overline{DE} \parallel \overline{CF}$.	4. Two lines perpendicular to the same line are parallel.
5. $DEFC$ is a $\square$.	5. Reason 2.
6. $\angle DEB$ is a right angle.	6. Definition of perpendicular lines.
7. $DEFC$ is a rectangle.	7. A rectangle is a parallelogram one of whose angles in a right angle.

EXERCISES

1. In rectangle $ABCD$, $CB = 6$, $AB = 8$, and $AC = 10$. Find the missing lengths:

   a. AD **b.** CD **c.** EC **d.** AE
   e. DE **f.** EB **g.** DB

   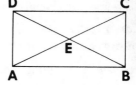

2. In rectangle $PQRS$, diagonals $\overline{PR}$ and $\overline{QS}$ meet at T. If $PT = 4$, find the length of: **a.** $\overline{TR}$ **b.** $\overline{TQ}$ **c.** $\overline{PR}$ **d.** $\overline{QS}$

3. In **(a)** and **(b)**, the *given* is marked on the figure. Tell why each parallelogram $ABCD$ is a rectangle.

   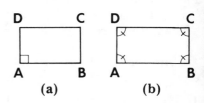

                                      (a)   **(b)**

4. In quadrilateral $DEFG$, diagonals $\overline{DF}$ and $\overline{EG}$ are drawn. Let $DE = 5$, $FG = 5$, $EF = 12$, $DG = 12$, $EG = 13$, and $DF = 13$. Prove that $DEFG$ is a rectangle.

5. a. In $\square ABCD$, $AE = 7x - 1$, and $EC = 5x + 5$.
    Find x.
  b. Find AC.
  c. If $DB = 10x + 10$, find DB.
  d. What kind of parallelogram is $ABCD$? Why?

6. In rectangle $ABCD$, the length of diagonal $\overline{AC}$ is represented by $6x - 2$ and the length of diagonal $\overline{BD}$ is represented by $4x + 2$.
  a. Find the value of x. **b.** Find AC and BD.

7. In rectangle $ABCD$, diagonals $\overline{AC}$ and $\overline{BD}$ intersect in E. If $AE = 3x + y$, $BE = 4x - 2y$, and $CE = 20$, find x and y.

In 8–11, tell if the argument is valid or invalid.

8. In a parallelogram, opposite sides are congruent.
    A rectangle is a parallelogram.
    Conclusion: In a rectangle, opposite sides are congruent.

9. In a parallelogram, the diagonals bisect each other.
    A rectangle is a parallelogram.
    Conclusion: In a rectangle, the diagonals bisect each other.

10. In a rectangle, the diagonals are congruent.
    A rectangle is a parallelogram.
    Conclusion: In a parallelogram, the diagonals are congruent.

11. All four angles of a rectangle are right angles.
    A rectangle is a parallelogram.
    Conclusion: All four angles of a parallelogram are right angles.

Ex. 12

Ex. 13

12. *Given:* $ABCD$ is a rectangle, M is the midpoint of $\overline{AB}$.
    Prove: $\overline{DM} \cong \overline{CM}$.

13. *Given:* $ABCD$ is a rectangle.
         Diagonals $\overline{AC}$ and $\overline{BD}$ intersect at E.
    Prove: $\triangle AEB$ is isosceles.

14. In rectangle $ABCD$, diagonals $\overline{BD}$ and $\overline{AC}$ are drawn. Prove that $\angle DBA \cong \angle CAB$.

15. *Given:* $\triangle ABC$ where $\angle ABC$ is a right angle and $\overline{BE}$ is the median drawn to $\overline{AC}$. Extend $\overline{BE}$ through E to point D so that $\overline{BE} \cong \overline{DE}$. Draw $\overline{AD}$ and $\overline{DC}$.
    Prove: $ABCD$ is a rectangle.

16. *Prove:* If the diagonals of a parallelogram are congruent, then the parallelogram is a rectangle.

17. Use an indirect method of proof to prove: If the diagonals of a parallelogram are not congruent, the parallelogram is not a rectangle.

6-4   THE RHOMBUS

● **Definition.** A *rhombus* is a parallelogram that has two congruent consecutive sides.

If the consecutive sides $\overline{AB}$ and $\overline{AD}$ of parallelogram $ABCD$ are congruent (that is, if $\overline{AB} \cong \overline{AD}$), then $\square ABCD$ is a rhombus.

Since a rhombus is a special kind of parallelogram, a rhombus has *all the properties of a parallelogram.* In addition, we can prove three special properties for the rhombus.

● **THEOREM 42. All sides of a rhombus are congruent.**

Given: $ABCD$ is a rhombus with $\overline{AB} \cong \overline{AD}$.

Prove: $\overline{AB} \cong \overline{BC} \cong \overline{CD} \cong \overline{DA}$.

Plan: Use Corollary T34-1 (see page 248) and the transitive property.

● **THEOREM 43. The diagonals of a rhombus are perpendicular to each other.**

Given: Rhombus $ABCD$.

Prove: $\overline{AC} \perp \overline{BD}$.

Plan: Use Theorem 42 above and Theorem 16 (see page 208).

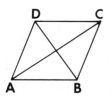

● **THEOREM 44: The diagonals of a rhombus bisect its angles.**

Given: Rhombus $ABCD$.

Prove: $\overline{AC}$ bisects $\angle DAB$ and $\angle DCB$.
        $\overline{DB}$ bisects $\angle CDA$ and $\angle CBA$.

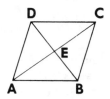

Plan: Show that $\triangle ABE \cong \triangle CBE \cong \triangle CDE \cong \triangle ADE$ by s.s.s $\cong$ s.s.s.

Properties of a Rhombus

1. A rhombus has all the properties of a parallelogram.
2. A rhombus is equilateral.
3. The diagonals of a rhombus are perpendicular to each other.
4. The diagonals of a rhombus bisect its angles.

Methods of Proving That a Quadrilateral Is a Rhombus

We prove that a quadrilateral is a rhombus by showing that it has the special properties of a rhombus. For example:

● **THEOREM 45. If a quadrilateral is equilateral, then it is a rhombus.**

Given: Quadrilateral $ABCD$.
     $\overline{AB} \cong \overline{BC} \cong \overline{CD} \cong \overline{DA}$.

Prove: $ABCD$ is a rhombus.

Plan: Use Theorem 35 (see page 251) to prove that $ABCD$ is a parallelogram.

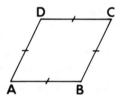

● **THEOREM 46. If the diagonals of a parallelogram are perpendicular to each other, then the parallelogram is a rhombus.**

Given: Parallelogram $ABCD$.
     $\overline{AC} \perp \overline{BD}$.

Prove: $ABCD$ is a rhombus.

Plan: Show that $\triangle AEB \cong \triangle AED$ by s.a.s. $\cong$ s.a.s.

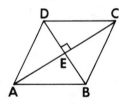

● **Summary.** To prove that a quadrilateral is a rhombus, prove that any one of the following statements is true:

1. The quadrilateral is a parallelogram with two congruent consecutive sides.
2. The quadrilateral is equilateral.
3. The quadrilateral is a parallelogram whose diagonals are perpendicular to each other.
4. The quadrilateral is a parallelogram, and a diagonal bisects the angles whose vertices it joins.

MODEL PROBLEMS

1. *PQRS* is a rhombus. The shorter diagonal $\overline{PR}$ measures 12 units and m∠*PQR* = 60. Find the length of a side of the rhombus.

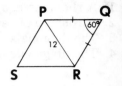

Solution

Since all sides of a rhombus are congruent, we know that $\overline{PQ} \cong \overline{RQ}$. Thus, $\triangle PQR$ is isosceles and its base angles are equal in measure.

Let m∠*PRQ* = m∠*RPQ* = *x*.

$$x + x + 60 = 180$$
$$2x + 60 = 180$$
$$2x = 120$$
$$x = 60$$

Therefore, m∠*PRQ* = 60, m∠*RPQ* = 60, and m∠*PQR* = 60. Since an equiangular triangle is also equilateral, if *PR* = 12, then *PQ* = 12 and *RQ* = 12.

Answer: The length of any side of rhombus *PQRS* is 12.

2. *Given:* *ABCD* is a parallelogram; *AB* = 2*x* + 1; *DC* = 3*x* − 11; *AD* = *x* + 13.

   Show: *ABCD* is a rhombus.

   Plan: Show two consecutive sides congruent $(\overline{AB} \cong \overline{AD})$.

Solution

Step 1. Since *ABCD* is a parallelogram, opposite sides are equal in length.

$$DC = AB$$
$$3x - 11 = 2x + 1$$
$$3x - 2x = 1 + 11$$
$$x = 12$$

Step 2. Substitute *x* = 12 to find the lengths of sides $\overline{AB}$ and $\overline{AD}$:

$$AB = 2x + 1 = 2(12) + 1 = 25$$
$$AD = x + 13 = (12) + 13 = 25$$

Thus, $\overline{AB} \cong \overline{AD}$. Since *ABCD* is a parallelogram having two consecutive sides congruent, *ABCD* is a rhombus.

EXERCISES ━━━━━━━━━━━━━━━━━━━━━━━━━━━━

In 1–5, refer to rhombus $ABCD$ where diagonals $\overline{AC}$ and $\overline{BD}$ intersect at E. For each exercise, tell which one of the four given statements is *false*.

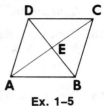

Ex. 1–5

1. (1) $\overline{AB} \cong \overline{DC}$ (2) $\overline{AB} \cong \overline{BC}$
   (3) $\overline{AB} \cong \overline{AC}$ (4) $\overline{AB} \cong \overline{AD}$

2. (1) $\overline{AC} \perp \overline{DB}$ (2) $\overline{AC} \cong \overline{DB}$
   (3) $\angle DAB \cong \angle DCB$ (4) $\angle ADB \cong \angle CDB$

3. (1) $AE = EC$ (2) $DE = EB$
   (3) $AE = DE$ (4) $\overline{AE} \perp \overline{DE}$

4. (1) $\angle DEA \cong \angle DEC$ (2) $m\angle DEA = 90$
   (3) $\angle DCA \cong \angle BAC$ (4) $m\angle DCA = 90$

5. (1) $\triangle ADC$ is isosceles.   (2) $\triangle ADE$ is a right triangle.
   (3) $\triangle ADB$ is a right triangle.   (4) $\triangle ADE \cong \triangle ABE$.

6. In parallelogram $PQRS$, $PQ = x + 4$ and
$SR = 3x - 36$.
  a. Find x.   **b.** Find PQ and SR.
  c. If $QR = 2x - 16$, show that $PQRS$ is a
    rhombus.

7. In parallelogram $PQRS$, $m\angle SQP = 4x - 2$ and
$m\angle QSR = 3x + 6$.
  a. Find x.   **b.** Find $m\angle SQP$ and $m\angle QSR$.
  c. If $m\angle QPT = 8x - 4$, show that $PQRS$ is a rhombus.

Ex. 6–7

8. If the length of the shorter diagonal $\overline{AC}$ of rhombus $ABCD$ is 7 and $m\angle ABC = 60$, find the length of a side of the rhombus.

9. In rhombus $ABCD$, $AB = 8$ and $m\angle ABC = 120$. Find the length of the shorter diagonal $\overline{BD}$.

In 10–13, tell if the argument is valid or invalid.

10. In a parallelogram, opposite sides are parallel.
A rhombus is a parallelogram.
Conclusion: In a rhombus, opposite sides are parallel.

11. In a rhombus, diagonals are perpendicular to each other.
A rhombus is a parallelogram.
Conclusion: In a parallelogram, diagonals are perpendicular to each other.

12. The diagonals of a rhombus bisect its angles.
A rhombus is a parallelogram.
Conclusion: The diagonals of a parallelogram bisect its angles.

13. Opposite angles of a parallelogram are congruent.
A rhombus is a parallelogram.
Conclusion: Opposite angles of a rhombus are congruent.

14. Prove that when the diagonals of a rhombus intersect, four congruent triangles are formed.

15. In rhombus $ABCD$, diagonal $\overline{BD} \cong$ side $\overline{AB}$.
a. Prove that $\triangle ADB$ is equilateral.
b. Find the measure of each angle of the rhombus.

16. *Prove:* If a quadrilateral is equilateral, it is a rhombus.

17. *Prove:* If the diagonals of a parallelogram are perpendicular to each other, the parallelogram is a rhombus.

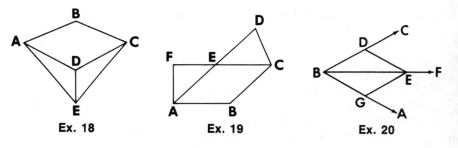

Ex. 18   Ex. 19   Ex. 20

18. *Given:* $ABCD$ is a rhombus, $\overline{AE} \cong \overline{CE}$.
Prove: $\angle ADE \cong \angle CDE$.

19. *Given:* $AECB$ is a rhombus, $\overline{AED}$, $\overline{FEC}$, $\angle FAB \cong \angle DCB$.
Prove: **a.** $\triangle FAE \cong \triangle DCE$.   **b.** $\overline{FE} \cong \overline{DE}$.

20. *Given:* $\overrightarrow{BF}$ bisects $\angle CBA$, $\overline{DE} \parallel \overrightarrow{BA}$, $\overline{GE} \parallel \overrightarrow{BC}$.
Prove: $GEDB$ is a rhombus.

21. Use an indirect method of proof to prove: If a diagonal of a parallelogram does not bisect the angles through whose vertices the diagonal is drawn, the parallelogram is not a rhombus.

22. If $ABCD$ is a rhombus and $m\angle B > m\angle A$, prove that $AC > BD$.
(*Hint:* Use one of the four congruent triangles formed by the diagonals.)

6-5 THE SQUARE

● **Definition.** A *square* is a rectangle that has two congruent consecutive sides.

If the consecutive sides $\overline{AB}$ and $\overline{AD}$ of rectangle $ABCD$ are congruent (that is, if $\overline{AB} \cong \overline{AD}$), then rectangle $ABCD$ is a square.

The following theorems are easily proved:

● **THEOREM 47. A square is an equilateral quadrilateral.**

Given: $ABCD$ is a square with $\overline{AB} \cong \overline{BC}$.

Prove: $\overline{AB} \cong \overline{BC} \cong \overline{CD} \cong \overline{DA}$.

Plan: Use Corollary T34-1 (see page 248) and the transitive property.

● **THEOREM 48. A square is a rhombus.**

Given: Square $ABCD$.

Prove: $ABCD$ is a rhombus.

Plan: Use Theorem 47 and then Theorem 45.

Properties of a Square

1. A square has all the properties of a rectangle.
2. A square has all the properties of a rhombus.

Methods of Proving That a Quadrilateral Is a Square

We prove that a quadrilateral is a square by showing that it has the special properties of a square. For example:

● **THEOREM 49. If one of the angles of a rhombus is a right angle, then the rhombus is a square.**

Given: $ABCD$ is a rhombus with $\angle A$ a right angle.

Prove: $ABCD$ is a square.

Plan: Show that $ABCD$ is a rectangle and that $\overline{AB} \cong \overline{BC}$.

● **Summary.** To prove that a quadrilateral is a square, prove either of the following statements:

1. The quadrilateral is a rectangle with two consecutive sides congruent.
2. The quadrilateral is a rhombus one of whose angles is a right angle.

MODEL PROBLEM ———————————————

Given: Quadrilateral *ABCD*; $\overline{AM} \cong \overline{MC}$; $\overline{DM} \cong \overline{MB}$; ∠*ABC* is a right angle; $\overline{AB} \cong \overline{AD}$.

Prove: *ABCD* is a square.

Plan: Show that *ABCD* is a rectangle and that $\overline{AB} \cong \overline{AD}$.

Statements	*Reasons*
1. $\overline{AM} \cong \overline{MC}$ and $\overline{DM} \cong \overline{MB}$.	1. Given.
2. *ABCD* is a parallelogram.	2. If the diagonals of a quadrilateral bisect each other, the quadrilateral is a parallelogram.
3. ∠*ABC* is a right angle.	3. Given.
4. *ABCD* is a rectangle.	4. A rectangle is a parallelogram one of whose angles is a right angle.
5. $\overline{AB} \cong \overline{AD}$.	5. Given.
6. *ABCD* is a square.	6. A square is a rectangle that has two congruent consecutive sides.

EXERCISES ———————————————

In 1–4, refer to square *ABCD* with diagonal $\overline{BD}$. For each exercise, tell which statement is *not* true.

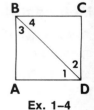

Ex. 1–4

1. (1) $\overline{AB} \cong \overline{BC}$ (2) $\overline{AB} \perp \overline{BC}$
   (3) $\overline{AB} \cong \overline{BD}$ (4) $\overline{AB} \cong \overline{CD}$

2. (1) ∠1 ≅ ∠2   (2) ∠2 ≅ ∠3
   (3) ∠1 ≅ ∠3   (4) ∠*A* ≅ ∠4

3. (1) $\overline{AB} \perp \overline{AD}$ (2) ∠*A* ≅ ∠*CBA*
   (3) $\overline{BC} \parallel \overline{AD}$ (4) $\overline{BD} \perp \overline{AD}$

4. (1) △*ABD* is isosceles.   (2) △*ABD* is equilateral.
   (3) △*ABD* is a right triangle.   (4) △*ABD* ≅ △*CDB*.

In 5–9, tell if the conclusion is valid or invalid.

5. In a rhombus, all sides are congruent.
A square is a rhombus.
Conclusion: In a square, all sides are congruent.

6. The diagonal of a parallelogram separates the parallelogram into two congruent triangles.
   A square is a parallelogram.
   Conclusion: The diagonal of a square separates the square into two congruent triangles.
7. In a square, all angles are right angles.
   A square is a rhombus.
   Conclusion: In a rhombus, all angles are right angles.
8. If a quadrilateral is a square, then it is a rhombus.
   If a quadrilateral is a rhombus, then it is a parallelogram.
   Conclusion: If a quadrilateral is a square, then it is a parallelogram.
9. A square is equilateral.
   A square is a rectangle.
   Conclusion: A rectangle is equilateral.
10. In square $ABCD$, diagonal $\overline{AC}$ is drawn. Find m$\angle ACB$ and m$\angle DCA$.
11. *Prove:* The diagonals of a square are perpendicular to each other.
12. *Prove:* The diagonals of a square divide the square into four congruent isosceles triangles.
13. *Prove:* If the midpoints of the sides of a square are joined in order, another square is formed.
14. *Given:* $PQRS$ is a rectangle; $\overline{QR} \cong \overline{RS}$.
    Prove: $PQRS$ is a square.
15. *Given:* $ABCD$ is a rhombus; $\overline{CD} \perp \overline{DA}$.
    Prove: $ABCD$ is a square.

16. *Given:* $\triangle ABC$ is an isosceles right triangle;
    $\angle ABC$ is a right angle; $\overline{BA} \cong \overline{BC}$;
    $\overline{BM}$, a median of $\triangle ABC$, is extended to D
    so that $\overline{BM} \cong \overline{DM}$; $\overline{DC}$ and $\overline{DA}$ are drawn.
    Prove: $ABCD$ is a square.

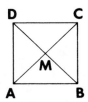

6-6 THE TRAPEZOID

● **Definition.** A *trapezoid* is a quadrilateral that has two and only two sides parallel.

If $\overline{AB} \parallel \overline{DC}$ and $\overline{AD}$ is not $\parallel \overline{BC}$, then quadrilateral $ABCD$ is a trapezoid. The parallel sides $\overline{AB}$ and $\overline{DC}$ are called the *bases* of the trapezoid; the nonparallel sides $\overline{AD}$ and $\overline{BC}$ are called the *legs* of the trapezoid.

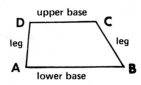

The Isosceles Trapezoid and Its Properties

● **Definition.** An *isosceles trapezoid* is a trapezoid in which the nonparallel sides are congruent.

If $\overline{QT} \cong \overline{RS}$, and $\overline{TS} \parallel \overline{QR}$, then $QRST$ is an isosceles trapezoid. The angles at the ends of a base are called *base angles*. Here, $\angle Q$ and $\angle R$ are one pair of base angles because they are at the ends of base $\overline{QR}$. Notice that $\angle T$ and $\angle S$ are

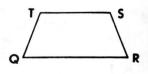

a second pair of base angles because they are at the ends of base $\overline{TS}$.

Methods of Proving That a Quadrilateral Is an Isosceles Trapezoid

We prove that a quadrilateral is an isosceles trapezoid by showing that it has the special properties of an isosceles trapezoid: Only two sides are parallel; the nonparallel sides are congruent.

We may also prove special theorems for an isosceles trapezoid.

● **THEOREM 50. If a trapezoid is isosceles, then the base angles are congruent, and conversely.**

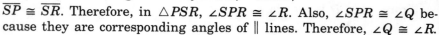

Conditional

Given: Isosceles trapezoid $QRST$ with $\overline{TQ} \cong \overline{SR}$.

Prove: $\angle Q \cong \angle R$.

Plan: Draw $\overline{SP} \parallel \overline{TQ}$ to form $\square SPQT$. Thus, $\overline{SP} \cong \overline{TQ}$. But, given $\overline{TQ} \cong \overline{SR}$; hence, $\overline{SP} \cong \overline{SR}$. Therefore, in $\triangle PSR$, $\angle SPR \cong \angle R$. Also, $\angle SPR \cong \angle Q$ because they are corresponding angles of $\parallel$ lines. Therefore, $\angle Q \cong \angle R$.

Converse

Given: Trapezoid $QRST$ with $\angle Q \cong \angle R$.

Prove: $\overline{QT} \cong \overline{RS}$.

Plan: Draw $\overline{TA} \perp \overline{QR}$ and $\overline{SB} \perp \overline{QR}$.

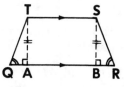

Prove $\triangle QTA \cong \triangle RSB$ by a.a.s. $\cong$ a.a.s. ($\overline{TA} \cong \overline{SB}$ since $\parallel$ lines are everywhere equidistant).

● **THEOREM 51. If a trapezoid is isosceles, then the diagonals are congruent, and conversely.**

Conditional

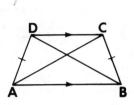

Given: Trapezoid $ABCD$ with $\overline{AD} \cong \overline{BC}$.

Prove: $\overline{AC} \cong \overline{BD}$.

Plan: Prove $\triangle DAB \cong \triangle CBA$ by s.a.s. $\cong$ s.a.s.

Converse

Given: Trapezoid $ABCD$ with $\overline{AC} \cong \overline{BD}$.

Prove: $\overline{AD} \cong \overline{BC}$.

Plan: Draw $\overline{DE}$, the altitude of $\triangle ADB$, and $\overline{CF}$, the altitude of $\triangle ACB$. Prove $\triangle ACF \cong \triangle BDE$ by hy. leg $\cong$ hy. leg. Therefore, $\angle CAB \cong \angle DBA$. Now, prove that $\triangle ACB \cong \triangle BDA$ by s.a.s. $\cong$ s.a.s.

MODEL PROBLEM _____

Given: Quadrilateral $ABCD$,
   $m\angle ABD = 30$, $m\angle BDC = 30$,
   $m\angle ADB = 40$, $m\angle BCD = 70$,
   $AD = x + 5$, and $BC = 3x - 21$.

   a. Show that $ABCD$ is an isosceles trapezoid.

   b. Find the lengths AD and BC.

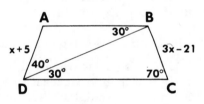

Solution:

a. *Step 1:* Since $m\angle ABD = 30$ and $m\angle BDC = 30$, we know that $\overline{AB}$ and $\overline{DC}$ are cut by transversal $\overline{DB}$ to form congruent alternate interior angles. Thus, $\overline{AB} \parallel \overline{DC}$.

   Step 2: The base angles of $ABCD$ are equal in measure because $m\angle ADC = m\angle ADB + m\angle BDC = 40 + 30 = 70$, and also $m\angle BCD = 70$.

   [*Note.* Since $\angle BCD$ and $\angle ADC$ are interior angles on the same side of transversal $\overline{DC}$ and they are *not* supplementary, we know $\overline{AD} \not\parallel \overline{BC}$.]

   Thus, $ABCD$ is an isosceles trapezoid.

b. The nonparallel sides are congruent in an isosceles trapezoid.

Thus: $AD = BC$ | Substitute $x = 13$ to find AD and BC:
$x + 5 = 3x - 21$ | $AD = x + 5 = (13) + 5 = 18$
$5 + 21 = 3x - x$ | $BC = 3x - 21 = 3(13) - 21 = 39 = 21 = 18$
$26 = 2x$
$13 = x$

Answer: $AD = 18$ and $BC = 18$.

EXERCISES ─────────

In 1–6, *ABCD* is an isosceles trapezoid, $\overline{AB} \parallel \overline{DC}$ and $\overline{AD} \cong \overline{BC}$.

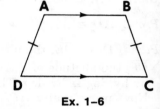
Ex. 1–6

1. If m∠*ADC* = 80, find **(a)** m∠*BCD* and **(b)** m∠*DAB*.
2. If $AD = 3x + 4$ and $BC = 22$, find the value of x.
3. If $AD = 2y - 7$ and $BC = y + 5$, find AD.
4. If m∠*ADC* = $4x - 5$ and m∠*BCD* = $3x + 15$, find the value of x.
5. If m∠*ADC* = $4x + 20$ and m∠*DAB* = $8x - 20$, find **(a)** the value of x, **(b)** m∠*ADC*, **(c)** m∠*DAB*, **(d)** m∠*BCD*, and **(e)** m∠*ABC*.
6. If $AD = 2x + y$, $BC = 7y - 2x$, and $x = 3$, find AD.

In 7–12, answer true or false.

7. In an isosceles trapezoid, nonparallel sides are congruent.
8. In a trapezoid, at least two sides must be congruent.
9. In a trapezoid, base angles are always congruent.
10. The diagonals of a trapezoid are congruent only if the nonparallel sides of the trapezoid are congruent.
11. A trapezoid is a special kind of parallelogram.
12. In a trapezoid, two consecutive angles that are not angles on the same base must be supplementary.

In 13–16, *ABCD* is a trapezoid with $\overline{AB} \parallel \overline{DC}$. When *ABCD* is isosceles, sides $\overline{AD}$ and $\overline{BC}$ are marked as congruent. Find the measures of the angles indicated by arcs in the diagrams.

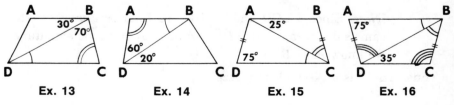

Ex. 13   Ex. 14   Ex. 15   Ex. 16

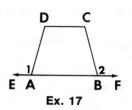

Ex. 17

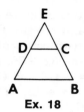

Ex. 18

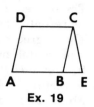

Ex. 19

17. *Given:* $ABCD$ is an isosceles trapezoid, $\overline{DC} \parallel \overline{AB}$, $\overleftrightarrow{EABF}$.
   Prove: $\angle 1 \cong \angle 2$.

18. *Given:* $\overline{ADE}$, $\overline{BCE}$, $\overline{AE} \cong \overline{BE}$, $\overline{DE} \cong \overline{CE}$, $\overline{DC} \parallel \overline{AB}$.
   Prove: $ABCD$ is an isosceles trapezoid.

19. *Given:* $ABCD$ is a parallelogram, $\overline{ABE}$, $\angle CBE \cong \angle CEB$.
   Prove: **a.** $\angle DAE \cong \angle CEA$. **b.** $AECD$ is an isosceles trapezoid.

20. Prove by an indirect method of proof: If a quadrilateral is a trapezoid, then its diagonals cannot bisect each other.

6-7   REVIEW EXERCISES

1. Copy the table that follows. In the spaces **a** through **g**, answer "yes" or "no" to the following questions for each of the five given quadrilaterals:
   a. Are opposite sides congruent and parallel?
   b. Are opposite angles congruent?
   c. Are the diagonals congruent?
   d. Do the diagonals bisect each other?
   e. Are the diagonals perpendicular to each other?
   f. Are all angles congruent?
   g. Are any two consecutive sides congruent?

	a	b	c	d	e	f	g
parallelogram							
rectangle							
rhombus							
square							
trapezoid							

2. In parallelogram $ABCD$, $m\angle A = 3x$ and $m\angle B = 2x + 60$. Find x.

3. In parallelogram $ABCD$, $AB = 3y - 7$ and $CD = y + 15$. Find y.

4. The degree measures of two opposite angles of a parallelogram are represented by $2n + 30$ and $n + 45$. Find n.

5. The degree measures of two consecutive angles of a rhombus are represented by $5x + 10$ and $3x + 50$. Find x.

6. In rhombus $PQSR$, $PQ = y + 8$ and $QS = 4y - 7$. Find PQ.

7. In rectangle $ABCD$, $AB = x + 15$, $BC = x - 8$, and $CD = 2x + 3$. Find: **a.** x **b.** AB **c.** BC

8. In rhombus $DEFG$, if m$\angle DEF = 60$ and the shorter diagonal $\overline{DF}$ has a length of 7, find the length of a side of the rhombus.

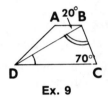
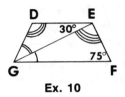

Ex. 9   **Ex. 10**

9. In trapezoid $ABCD$, $\overline{AB} \parallel \overline{DC}$ and diagonal $\overline{BD}$ is drawn. If m$\angle ABD = 20$ and m$\angle C = 70$, find: **a.** m$\angle BDC$ **b.** m$\angle DBC$

10. In isosceles trapezoid $DEFG$, $\overline{DE} \parallel \overline{GF}$ and $\overline{DG} \cong \overline{EF}$. Using the two given angle measures in the diagram, find all remaining angle measures.

In 11–18, select the *numeral* preceding the word or expression that best answers the question or completes the sentence.

11. In parallelogram $PQRS$, diagonals $\overline{PR}$ and $\overline{QS}$ intersect at M. Which is always true?
   (1) $\overline{PR} \perp \overline{QS}$ (2) $\overline{PM} \cong \overline{RM}$
   (3) $\overline{PQ} \cong \overline{QR}$ (4) $\triangle PMS \cong \triangle PMQ$

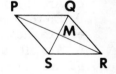

12. In rectangle $ABCD$, $\overline{AC}$ is a diagonal. Which is always true?
   (1) $\overline{AB} \cong \overline{AC}$ (2) $\overline{AB} \cong \overline{AD}$
   (3) m$\angle DAC = $ m$\angle BAC$
   (4) $\triangle DAC \cong \triangle BCA$

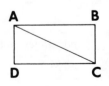

13. A quadrilateral whose diagonals are congruent but are not perpendicular to each other is: (1) a rectangle (2) a rhombus (3) a parallelogram (4) a square

14. A quadrilateral whose diagonals are perpendicular to each other is: (1) a rectangle (2) a rhombus (3) a parallelogram (4) a trapezoid

15. A quadrilateral that is equiangular but not equilateral is:
    (1) a rectangle (2) a rhombus (3) a square (4) a parallelogram
16. A quadrilateral that is not a parallelogram is:
    (1) a rectangle (2) a rhombus (3) a square (4) a trapezoid
17. Which of the following statements is false?
    (1) A square is a rhombus. (2) A rhombus is a square.
    (3) A square is a rectangle. (4) A rhombus is a parallelogram.
18. The diagonals of a rectangle are always: (1) congruent
    (2) perpendicular to each other (3) parallel (4) bisectors of the
    angles of the rectangle

In 19–22, tell if the argument is valid or invalid.

19. In a rectangle, diagonals are congruent.
    A square is a rectangle.
    Conclusion: In a square, diagonals are congruent.
20. The diagonals of a parallelogram bisect each other.
    A rhombus is a parallelogram.
    Conclusion: The diagonals of a rhombus bisect each other.
21. A rhombus is equilateral.
    A rhombus is a parallelogram.
    Conclusion: A parallelogram is equilateral.
22. Two consecutive angles of a parallelogram are supplementary.
    A rectangle is a parallelogram.
    Conclusion: Two consecutive angles of a rectangle are supplemen-
    tary.

In 23–27, write *true* if the statement is always true; write *false* if the
statement is not always true.

23. If one angle of a parallelogram is a right angle, all the other angles
    of the parallelogram are also right angles.
24. If a quadrilateral is equilateral, the quadrilateral is a square.
25. A trapezoid has at least one acute angle.
26. The diagonals of a parallelogram divide it into four congruent
    triangles.
27. If the diagonals of a quadrilateral are congruent, the quadrilateral
    is a rectangle.

28. *Given:* In quadrilateral *PQRS,*
    ∠1 ≅ ∠2 and ∠3 ≅ ∠4.
    Prove: PQRS is a parallelogram.

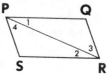

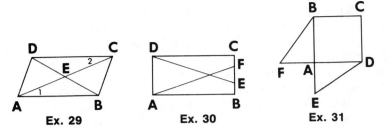

Ex. 29   Ex. 30   Ex. 31

29. *Given:* $\overline{DB}$ bisects $\overline{AC}$ at E, $\angle 1 \cong \angle 2$.
Prove: $ABCD$ is a parallelogram.

30. *Given:* $ABCD$ is a rectangle, $\overline{BE} \cong \overline{CF}$.
Prove: $\overline{DE} \cong \overline{AF}$.

31. *Given:* $ABCD$ is a square, $\overline{BAE}$, $\overline{DAF}$, $\overline{AE} \cong \overline{AF}$.
Prove: **a.** $\triangle BAF \cong \triangle DAE$.   **b.** $\angle CBF \cong \angle CDE$.

32. A set of four quadrilaterals consists of a parallelogram, a rectangle, a rhombus, and a square. One of the four quadrilaterals is selected at random. Find the *probability* that the quadrilateral:
   a. is both equiangular and equilateral.
   b. is equiangular.   **c.** is equilateral.
   d. has congruent diagonals.
   e. has diagonals that are congruent and perpendicular to each other.
   f. has diagonals that bisect each other.
   g. has only one pair of parallel lines.
   h. has a diagonal that divides the quadrilateral into two congruent triangles.

33. How many quadrilaterals are there in the figure?

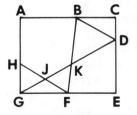

34. Prove that any line through the midpoint of a diagonal of a parallelogram separates the parallelogram into two congruent polygons. (To prove two polygons congruent, show that each pair of corresponding sides and angles are congruent.)

35. A dressmaker has a length of cloth. She knows that the cloth is woven with the selvage edges (woven edges on two opposite sides) parallel. By folding the cloth and cutting along the fold, then folding and cutting again, she can cut a square of cloth. How can this be done?

Chapter **7**

Similarity;
Special Triangles

Up to this point, you have studied the conditions under which polygons, particularly triangles, are congruent; that is, have the same size and the same shape.

Now you will study conditions under which polygons, particularly triangles, have the same shape but not necessarily the same size. For this study, it is necessary to have a clear understanding of *ratio* and *proportion*, particularly in relation to line segments.

We will begin by reviewing some material on square roots and radicals, which you will need to know for your work on proportions and for later work.

7-1 SQUARE ROOTS AND RADICALS

● A *square root* of a number a is one of the two equal factors whose product is a.

A square root of 25 is 5 because $(5)(5) = 25$. Another square root of 25 is -5 because $(-5)(-5) = 25$. Thus, the two square roots of 25 can be written as $+\sqrt{25}$ and $-\sqrt{25}$, or as $+5$ and -5.

If a number such as 3 is not a perfect square, its square root can be expressed as a radical. One square root of 3 is $\sqrt{3}$ because $(\sqrt{3})(\sqrt{3}) = 3$ and another square root of 3 is $-\sqrt{3}$ because $(-\sqrt{3})(-\sqrt{3}) = 3$. There are two square roots of 3, $+\sqrt{3}$ and $-\sqrt{3}$, or $\pm\sqrt{3}$. The numbers $+\sqrt{3}$ and $-\sqrt{3}$ are called *radicals* and 3 is called the *radicand*.

● The *principal square root* of a positive number is its positive square root.

Note that the radical sign $\sqrt{}$ designates the principal square root.

Thus, although both 5 and −5 are square roots of 25, the symbol $\sqrt{25}$ refers specifically to 5.

For real numbers that are not positive numbers, we observe:
1. The square root of 0 is 0, that is $\sqrt{0} = 0$. Zero has only one square root, which can be thought of as its principal square root.
2. The square root of a negative real number is not a real number. For example, $\sqrt{-4}$ is not a real number because there is no real number that, when squared, equals −4.

MODEL PROBLEMS

1. Find the square roots of 81.

   Solution: There are two square roots of 81, $\pm\sqrt{81}$. Since $(9)(9) = 81$ and $(-9)(-9) = 81$, $\pm\sqrt{81} = \pm 9$.

   Answer: +9 and −9, or ±9.

2. Find, if possible, the real number that is the principal square root of each of the following.
   a. 36   **b.** 20   **c.** $\frac{4}{9}$ **d.** −9

   Solution: The principal square root is the positive square root of a positive number. There is no real number that is the square root of a negative number.

   Answers: **a.** 6 **b.** $\sqrt{20}$ **c.** $\frac{2}{3}$ **d.** no real number

3. Solve for x: $3x^2 = 15$

   Solution: $3x^2 = 15$ Write the equation.
   $x^2 = 5$ Divide each side of the equation by 3.
   $x = \pm\sqrt{5}$ Write the square root of each side of the equation.

   Answer: $x = \pm\sqrt{5}$

Simplifying Square-Root Radicals

Since $\sqrt{4 \cdot 25} = \sqrt{100} = 10$ and $\sqrt{4} \cdot \sqrt{25} = 2 \cdot 5 = 10$, we can conclude that $\sqrt{4 \cdot 25} = \sqrt{4} \cdot \sqrt{25}$. This example illustrates the following property:

If a and b are positive real numbers:

$$\sqrt{a \cdot b} = \sqrt{a} \cdot \sqrt{b}$$

We can use this rule to write a radical as an equivalent radical. For example:

$$\sqrt{800} = \sqrt{16 \cdot 50} = \sqrt{16} \cdot \sqrt{50} = 4\sqrt{50}$$
$$\sqrt{800} = \sqrt{25 \cdot 32} = \sqrt{25} \cdot \sqrt{32} = 5\sqrt{32}$$
$$\sqrt{800} = \sqrt{100 \cdot 8} = \sqrt{100} \cdot \sqrt{8} = 10\sqrt{8}$$
$$\sqrt{800} = \sqrt{400 \cdot 2} = \sqrt{400} \cdot \sqrt{2} = 20\sqrt{2}$$

Each of the results, $4\sqrt{50}$, $5\sqrt{32}$, $10\sqrt{8}$, and $20\sqrt{2}$, are equivalent to $\sqrt{800}$. However, each of the radicands in $4\sqrt{50}$, $5\sqrt{32}$, and $10\sqrt{8}$ have factors that are perfect squares. Only the number $20\sqrt{2}$ is expressed in a form in which the radicand does not have a perfect square factor. We say that $20\sqrt{2}$ is the *simplest form* of $\sqrt{800}$.

● The *simplest form* of a square-root radical is a monomial of the form $k\sqrt{r}$ where k is a nonzero rational number and r is a positive integer having no perfect-square factor other than 1.

Simplifying Square-Root Radicals With Fractional Radicands

Since $\sqrt{\dfrac{4}{25}} = \dfrac{2}{5}$ and $\dfrac{\sqrt{4}}{\sqrt{25}} = \dfrac{2}{5}$, we can conclude that $\sqrt{\dfrac{4}{25}} = \dfrac{\sqrt{4}}{\sqrt{25}}$. This example illustrates the following property:

If a and b are positive real numbers:

$$\sqrt{\frac{a}{b}} = \frac{\sqrt{a}}{\sqrt{b}}$$

We can use this rule to write a radical with a fractional radicand in simplest form. For example:

$$\sqrt{\frac{3}{4}} = \frac{\sqrt{3}}{\sqrt{4}} = \frac{\sqrt{3}}{2} \text{ or } \frac{1}{2}\sqrt{3}$$

In this result, there is no radical in the denominator because the denominator of the given radical was a perfect square. If the denominator of the given radicand is not a perfect square, write the radicand as an equivalent fraction whose denominator is a perfect square.

$$\sqrt{\frac{3}{8}} = \sqrt{\frac{6}{16}} = \frac{\sqrt{6}}{\sqrt{16}} = \frac{\sqrt{6}}{4} \text{ or } \frac{1}{4}\sqrt{6}$$

$$\sqrt{\frac{1}{3}} = \sqrt{\frac{3}{9}} = \frac{\sqrt{3}}{\sqrt{9}} = \frac{\sqrt{3}}{3} \text{ or } \frac{1}{3}\sqrt{3}$$

In like manner, a decimal radicand can also be expressed in an equivalent form, so that no decimal appears in the simplified radicand.

$$\sqrt{.2} = \sqrt{.20} = \sqrt{.04 \cdot 5} = \sqrt{.04} \cdot \sqrt{5} = .2\sqrt{5}$$

MODEL PROBLEM

Simplify the radicals:

1. $\sqrt{98} = \sqrt{49 \cdot 2} = \sqrt{49} \cdot \sqrt{2} = 7\sqrt{2}$

2. $2\sqrt{24} = 2\sqrt{4 \cdot 6} = 2\sqrt{4} \cdot \sqrt{6} = 2 \cdot 2\sqrt{6} = 4\sqrt{6}$

3. $\sqrt{.03} = \sqrt{.01 \cdot 3} = \sqrt{.01} \cdot \sqrt{3} = .1\sqrt{3}$

4. $\sqrt{.5} = \sqrt{.50} = \sqrt{.25 \cdot 2} = \sqrt{.25} \cdot \sqrt{2} = .5\sqrt{2}$

5. $\sqrt{\dfrac{2}{5}} = \sqrt{\dfrac{10}{25}} = \dfrac{\sqrt{10}}{\sqrt{25}} = \dfrac{\sqrt{10}}{5}$ or $\dfrac{1}{5}\sqrt{10}$

6. $\sqrt{4x^3} = \sqrt{4x^2 \cdot x} = \sqrt{4x^2} \cdot \sqrt{x} = 2x\sqrt{x}$ when $x \geq 0$

7. $2\sqrt{\dfrac{3a^3}{50}} = 2\sqrt{\dfrac{6a^3}{100}} = \dfrac{2\sqrt{a^2} \cdot \sqrt{6a}}{10} = \dfrac{a\sqrt{6a}}{5}$ when $a \geq 0$

EXERCISES

In 1–6, how many real square roots does the given number have?

1. 9   **2.** 4   **3.** 12   **4.** 0   **5.** -1 **6.** 3

In 7–12, find the two square roots of the given number.

7. 100   **8.** 49   **9.** 121   **10.** 3   **11.** $\frac{1}{9}$ **12.** .09

In 13–24, find the principal square root of the given number.

13. 4   **14.** 0   **15.** 144   **16.** 2   **17.** 8   **18.** 7

19. $\frac{1}{4}$ **20.** $\frac{1}{25}$ **21.** $\frac{3}{4}$ **22.** .01   **23.** .16   **24.** .3

In 25–30, solve for the variable when the replacement set is the set of real numbers.

25. $x^2 = 9$ **26.** $2y^2 = 8$ **27.** $k^2 - 3 = 5$

28. $n^2 - 1 = 0$ **29.** $b^2 + 1 = 0$ **30.** $9c^2 - 1 = 0$

31. What two numbers are equal to their principal square roots?

In 32–47, simplify the radical expression.

32. $\sqrt{8}$ **33.** $\sqrt{45}$ **34.** $\sqrt{200}$ **35.** $\sqrt{12}$

36. $\sqrt{28}$ **37.** $\sqrt{128}$ **38.** $\sqrt{250}$ **39.** $\sqrt{54}$

40. $\sqrt{.32}$ **41.** $\sqrt{.75}$ **42.** $\sqrt{.48}$ **43.** $\sqrt{.2}$

44. $\sqrt{\frac{8}{9}}$ **45.** $\sqrt{\frac{3}{4}}$ **46.** $\sqrt{\frac{9}{2}}$ **47.** $\sqrt{\frac{4}{5}}$

In 48–59, write each radical expression in simplest form. All variables represent positive real numbers.

48. $3\sqrt{12}$ **49.** $5\sqrt{20}$ **50.** $2\sqrt{18a^2}$ **51.** $5\sqrt{300x^3}$

52. $3\sqrt{\frac{5}{36}}$ **53.** $12\sqrt{\frac{2}{3}}$ **54.** $10\sqrt{\frac{3}{5}}$ **55.** $4\sqrt{\frac{x^5}{12}}$

56. $4\sqrt{.12}$ **57.** $20\sqrt{.4}$ **58.** $3\sqrt{2.4}$ **59.** $10\sqrt{.008}$

In 60 and 61, select the radical that is in simplest form.

60. (1) $3\sqrt{.2}$ (2) $\sqrt{1.8}$ (3) $.3\sqrt{20}$ (4) $.6\sqrt{5}$

61. (1) $\sqrt{240}$ (2) $4\sqrt{15}$ (3) $2\sqrt{60}$ (4) $8\sqrt{3.75}$

7-2 RATIO AND PROPORTION

The Meaning of Ratio

These two triangles have the same shape but not the same size.

$\overline{AB}$ is 18 millimeters long and $\overline{DE}$ is 9 millimeters long. We can compare their lengths by means of a *ratio*: $\dfrac{AB}{DE} = \dfrac{18}{9}$.

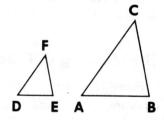

● **Definition.** *The ratio of two numbers a and b, where b is not zero, is the number* $\dfrac{a}{b}$.

The ratio $\dfrac{a}{b}$ can also be written as $a : b$.

In the example just given, the numbers 18 and 9 are called the *terms* of the ratio. The ratio $\frac{18}{9}$ can be read as "18 to 9" or "18 is to 9." This ratio, or comparison, of $\frac{18}{9}$ can be expressed in its simplest form as $\frac{2}{1}$, showing that $\overline{AB}$ is twice as long as $\overline{DE}$.

Keep in mind that we find the ratio of numbers, not objects. Here the numbers represent lengths. Such lengths must be expressed in terms of the *same unit of measure* for the ratio to be meaningful.

For example, in the preceding figure, if $\overline{EF}$ has a measure of 10 millimeters and $\overline{BC}$ has a measure of 2 centimeters, we can find the ratio of EF to BC only after converting the measures to the same units:

$$\frac{EF}{BC} = \frac{10 \text{ mm}}{2 \text{ cm}} = \frac{10 \text{ mm}}{20 \text{ mm}} = \frac{1}{2} \quad or \quad \frac{EF}{BC} = \frac{10 \text{ mm}}{2 \text{ cm}} = \frac{1 \text{ cm}}{2 \text{ cm}} = \frac{1}{2}$$

In the same way, we compare two angles by finding the ratio of the measures of the two angles. If $\angle R$ is a right angle (thus, $m\angle R = 90$) and $m\angle T$ is 30, we say $\dfrac{m\angle R}{m\angle T} = \dfrac{90}{30} = \dfrac{3}{1}$.

A ratio is expressed in simplest form by dividing the terms of the ratio by their greatest common factor. In the example above, the ratio of the given measures of the two angles is $3:1$ and the measures of the angles may be expressed as 3(30) and 1(30), where 30 is the greatest common factor.

When we do not know the actual value of two or more measures that are in a given ratio, we use a variable factor to express these measures. For example, if the measures of the three angles of a triangle are in the ratio $2:3:4$, we can let x be the greatest common factor of the measures of the angles. Then, the measures of the angles may be expressed as $2x$, $3x$, and $4x$. This allows us to write the equation $2x + 3x + 4x = 180$, which leads to the solution $x = 20$. Thus, we can state that the degree measures of these angles are 40, 60, and 80.

The Meaning of Proportion

Since the ratio $\frac{4}{12}$ is equal to the ratio $\frac{1}{3}$, we may write $\frac{4}{12} = \frac{1}{3}$. The equation $\frac{4}{12} = \frac{1}{3}$ is called a *proportion*. Another way of writing the proportion $\frac{4}{12} = \frac{1}{3}$ is $4:12 = 1:3$.

● **Definition.** A *proportion* is an equation that states that two ratios are equal.

The proportion $\dfrac{a}{b} = \dfrac{c}{d}$ can be written $a:b = c:d$.

The four numbers a, b, c, and d are the *terms* of the proportion. The first and fourth terms, a and d, are the *extremes* of the proportion. The second and third terms, b and c, are the *means* of the proportion.

$$a : b = c : d \qquad \frac{a}{b} = \frac{c}{d}$$

An extended proportion such as $\dfrac{a}{b} = \dfrac{c}{d} = \dfrac{e}{f} = \dfrac{g}{h}$ states that the four ratios represent the same number.

A Theorem Involving Proportions

● **THEOREM 52.** **In a proportion, the product of the means is equal to the product of the extremes, and conversely.**

Recall that a proportion is an equation. While we can demonstrate the statement of this theorem with a numerical example, it is necessary to prove the theorem using algebraic terms.

Numerical example: If $\frac{4}{8} = \frac{5}{10}$, then $8 \cdot 5 = 4 \cdot 10$, or $40 = 40$.

The conditional statement of Theorem 52 in algebraic terms:

$$\text{If } \frac{a}{b} = \frac{c}{d} \text{, then } bc = ad.$$

Given: $\dfrac{a}{b} = \dfrac{c}{d}$

Prove: $bc = ad$

Statements	*Reasons*
1. $\dfrac{a}{b} = \dfrac{c}{d}$.	1. Given.
2. $\dfrac{a}{b}(bd) = \dfrac{c}{d}(bd)$.	2. Multiplication postulate of equality.
3. $ad = bc$.	3. Simplification.

We use the conditional statement of Theorem 52 to solve for an unknown term of a proportion.

MODEL PROBLEM _____

Solve for y in the proportion $18:6 = y:9$.

Solution:

$18:6 = y:9$ or $\dfrac{18}{6} = \dfrac{y}{9}$

$\quad 6y = 18(9)$ In a proportion, the product of the means

$\quad 6y = 162$ is equal to the product of the extremes.

$\quad\;\; y = 27$

Check: $18:6 \stackrel{?}{=} 27:9$

$\qquad\quad 3:1 = 3:1$ by simplifying ratios.

Answer: $y = 27$

The converse statement of Theorem 52 in algebraic terms:

$$\text{If } bc = ad, \text{ then } \frac{a}{b} = \frac{c}{d}.$$

This converse allows us to form a proportion from two equal products. For example:

$$\text{Since } 8 \cdot 11 = 4 \cdot 22, \text{ then } \tfrac{4}{8} = \tfrac{11}{22}.$$

This converse also allows us to tell when two ratios do not form a proportion. For example, the ratios $\frac{2}{5}$ and $\frac{4}{28}$ cannot form a proportion since $5 \cdot 4 \neq 2 \cdot 28$.

● **COROLLARY T52-1.** **In a proportion, the means may be interchanged.**

Given that $a:b = c:d$, we can show that $a:c = b:d$ since for both proportions, $bc = ad$.

Since $d:b = c:a$ is another proportion for which $bc = ad$, we may state the following corollary.

● **COROLLARY T52-2.** **In a proportion, the extremes may be interchanged.**

Using these two corollaries, note that the proportion $\frac{4}{8} = \frac{11}{22}$ can be rewritten as $\frac{4}{11} = \frac{8}{22}$ or $\frac{22}{8} = \frac{11}{4}$.

The Mean Proportional

If the two means of a proportion are equal, either mean is called the *mean proportional* between the first and fourth terms of the proportion.

In the proportion $\frac{2}{8} = \frac{8}{32}$, the number 8 is the mean proportional between 2 and 32.

MODEL PROBLEMS ———————————————————————

1. Find the mean proportional between the lengths, 4 and 16.

   Solution: Let x = the mean proportional between 4 and 16.

   Then, $4:x = x:16$

   $\quad\quad x^2 = 64$

   $\quad\quad\quad x = \pm 8$ Find the square root.

   $\quad\quad\quad x = 8$ Restrict x to a positive value since it represents a length.

   Check: $4:8 \overset{?}{=} 8:16$

   $\quad\quad\quad 1:2 = 1:2$

   Answer: $x = 8$

2. Find the mean proportional between 8 and 12.

   Solution: Let x = the mean proportional.

   Then, $8:x = x:12$

   $\quad\quad x^2 = 8(12)$

   $\quad\quad x^2 = 96$

   $\quad\quad\; x = \pm\sqrt{96}$ Simplify the square root by factoring so that

   $\quad\quad\; x = \pm\sqrt{16}\cdot\sqrt{6}$ one factor is the largest perfect square.

   $\quad\quad\; x = \pm 4\sqrt{6}$

   Answer: $x = \pm 4\sqrt{6}$

EXERCISES ———————————————————————

1. In which of the following may the ratios form a proportion?
   a. $\frac{2}{3}, \frac{24}{26}$ **b.** $\frac{4}{5}, \frac{32}{40}$ **c.** $\frac{3}{4}, \frac{9}{16}$ **d.** $\frac{2}{9}, \frac{10}{54}$ **e.** $\frac{9}{12}, \frac{15}{20}$

2. Use each set of numbers to form two proportions.
   a. 40, 10, 1, 4   **b.** 4, 6, 18, 12   **c.** 2, 9, 6, 3   **d.** 28, 6, 24, 7

3. Determine which of the following is a true statement.
   (1) $5:10 = 10:20$ (2) $3:4 = 15:30$ (3) $12:18 = 36:72$

4. Find and check the value of x in each proportion.
   a. $\dfrac{x}{10} = \dfrac{3}{20}$ **b.** $\dfrac{20}{x} = \dfrac{10}{24}$ **c.** $\dfrac{4}{12} = \dfrac{x}{x+8}$
   d. $5:x = 8:24$ **e.** $x:10 = 65:5$

5. Given $XZ = 4$ and $ZY = 6$. State the numerical value of each ratio.
   a. $XZ:ZY$ **b.** $ZY:XZ$ **c.** $XZ:XY$ **d.** $XY:ZY$

6. B is a point on $\overline{AC}$ such that $\dfrac{AB}{BC} = \dfrac{1}{2}$.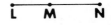
State each of the following ratios.
a. $BC:AB$ **b.** $AB:AC$ **c.** $BC:AC$

7. Find the mean proportional between:
   a. 4 and 9   **b.** 2 and 32   **c.** 4 and 25
   d. $\frac{1}{2}$ and $\frac{1}{8}$ **e.** .27 and .03   **f.** a and d

8. M is a point on $\overline{LN}$ such that $LM:MN = 3:4$.
   a. If $LM = 9$, find MN.
   b. If $MN = 20$, find LN.

9. A line segment 36 inches long is divided into two parts whose measures are in the ratio $1:8$. Find the measure of each part.

10. The measures of two supplementary angles are in the ratio $1:9$. Find the degree measure of each of the two angles.

11. Find and check the value of x in each proportion.

   a. $\dfrac{12 - x}{x} = \dfrac{16}{8}$ **b.** $\dfrac{20 - x}{x} = \dfrac{6}{4}$ **c.** $\dfrac{10 + x}{x} = \dfrac{6}{2}$ **d.** $\dfrac{x + 8}{x} = \dfrac{15}{5}$

12. In $\triangle ABC$, $\dfrac{AD}{DB} = \dfrac{AE}{EC}$.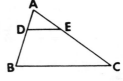
   a. If $AD = 5$, $DB = 15$, and $AE = 8$, find EC.
   b. If $AD = 2$, $AE = 6$, and $EC = 18$, find DB.
   c. If $DB = 6$, $AE = 12$, and $EC = 24$, find AD.
   d. If $AB = 25$, $AD = 10$, and $AE = 8$, find EC. (*Hint.* First find DB by $DB = AB - AD$.)
   e. If $AB = 10$, $DB = 2$, and $EC = 3$, find AE.

13. In $\triangle ABC$, $CD:DB = DB:DA$.
   a. If $CD = 4$ and $DB = 10$, find DA.
   b. If $CD = 2$ and $DB = 8$, find DA.
   c. If $CD = 3$ and $DA = 12$, find DB.
   d. If $CD = 3$ and $DA = 48$, find DB.

7-3 RATIO, PROPORTION, AND CONGRUENT LINE SEGMENTS

The midpoint of any line segment divides the segment into two congruent parts. In the figure, M is the midpoint of $\overline{AB}$. Thus, $\overline{AM} \cong \overline{MB}$ and the ratio of the lengths of these segments $\dfrac{AM}{MB}$ is $\dfrac{1}{1}$.

● **The lengths of two congruent line segments are in the ratio $\frac{1}{1}$.**

Let us examine a triangle in which two midpoints are given. In $\triangle ABC$, D is the midpoint of $\overline{AB}$ and E is the midpoint of $\overline{BC}$. Thus, $\overline{AD} \cong \overline{DB}$ and $\overline{CE} \cong \overline{EB}$. Therefore, the lengths of each pair of congruent segments are in the ratio of $\frac{1}{1}$:

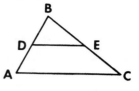

$$\frac{AD}{DB} = \frac{1}{1} \quad and \quad \frac{CE}{EB} = \frac{1}{1}$$

We may now say that $\overline{DE}$, the segment joining the midpoints, *divides the sides $\overline{AB}$ and $\overline{BC}$ proportionally* since $\dfrac{AD}{DB} = \dfrac{CE}{EB}$.

The segment, $\overline{DE}$, which joins two midpoints of a triangle, is a special segment, as you will see in the next theorem.

● **THEOREM 53. If a line segment joins the midpoints of two sides of a triangle, the segment is parallel to the third side and its length is one-half the length of the third side.**

Given: $\triangle ABC$, D is the midpoint of $\overline{AB}$, E is the midpoint of $\overline{BC}$.

Prove: $\overline{DE} \parallel \overline{AC}$ and $DE = \frac{1}{2} AC$.

Plan: Extend $\overline{DE}$ through E to point F so that $\overline{FE} \cong \overline{DE}$. Then, prove that $ACFD$ is a parallelogram. It will follow that $\overline{DE} \parallel \overline{AC}$ and $DE = \frac{1}{2} AC$.

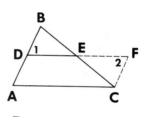

Statements	*Reasons*
1. $\triangle ABC$, D is the midpoint of $\overline{AB}$, E is the midpoint of $\overline{BC}$.	1. Given.
2. Extend $\overline{DE}$ through E to point F so that $\overline{EF} \cong \overline{DE}$.	2. A line segment may be extended to any length in either direction.
3. Draw $\overline{FC}$.	3. Through two points, one and only one line can be drawn.
4. $\overline{BE} \cong \overline{CE}$. (s. $\cong$ s.)	4. Definition of midpoint.
5. $\angle BED \cong \angle CEF$. (a. $\cong$ a.)	5. Vertical angles are congruent.
6. $\overline{DE} \cong \overline{FE}$. (s. $\cong$ s.)	6. Construction in step 2.

7. $\triangle BED \cong \triangle CEF$.	7. s.a.s. $\cong$ s.a.s.
8. $\angle 1 \cong \angle 2$.	8. Corresponding parts of congruent triangles are congruent.
9. $\overline{AB} \parallel \overline{CF}$ or $\overline{AD} \parallel \overline{CF}$.	9. If two lines are cut by a transversal to form congruent alternate interior angles, the two lines are parallel.
10. $\overline{BD} \cong \overline{CF}$.	10. Reason 8.
11. $\overline{BD} \cong \overline{AD}$.	11. Reason 4.
12. $\overline{AD} \cong \overline{CF}$.	12. Transitive property of congruence.
13. Quadrilateral $ACFD$ is a parallelogram.	13. If two opposite sides of a quadrilateral are both congruent and parallel, the quadrilateral is a parallelogram.
14. $\overline{DF} \parallel \overline{AC}$ or $\overline{DE} \parallel \overline{AC}$.	14. Opposite sides of a parallelogram are parallel.
15. $DE + EF = DF$.	15. The whole is equal to the sum of its parts.
16. $DE + EF = DE + DE = 2DE$.	16. Substitution postulate.
17. $2DE = DF$.	17. Transitive property.
18. $DE = \frac{1}{2}DF$.	18. Division postulate.
19. $\overline{DF} \cong \overline{AC}$.	19. Opposite sides of a parallelogram are congruent.
20. $DF = AC$.	20. Congruent segments have the same length.
21. $DE = \frac{1}{2}AC$.	21. Substitution postulate.

MODEL PROBLEM

In $\triangle ABC$, D is the midpoint of $\overline{AB}$ and E is the midpoint of $\overline{AC}$. If $BC = 7x + 1$, $DE = 4x - 2$, and m$\angle ADE = 75$, find: **(a)** the value of x, **(b)** DE and BC, and **(c)** m$\angle ABC$.

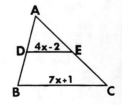

Solution

a. Since D and E are the midpoints of two sides of $\triangle ABC$, $DE = \frac{1}{2}BC$, or $2DE = BC$:

$$2DE = BC$$
$$2(4x - 2) = 7x + 1$$
$$8x - 4 = 7x + 1$$
$$x = 5 \ \ Ans.$$

b. Find DE and BC by substitution:

$$DE = 4x - 2 = 4(5) - 2 = 20 - 2 = 18 \ \ Ans.$$
$$BC = 7x + 1 = 7(5) + 1 = 35 + 1 = 36 \ \ Ans.$$

c. Since $\overline{DE}$ joins the midpoints of $\overline{AB}$ and $\overline{AC}$, then $\overline{DE} \parallel \overline{BC}$. When these two parallel lines are cut by transversal $\overline{AB}$, corresponding angles are congruent. Thus, $m\angle ABC = m\angle ADE = 75$.
Answer: $m\angle ABC = 75$

EXERCISES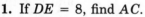

In 1–10, D is the midpoint of $\overline{AB}$ and E is the midpoint of $\overline{BC}$.

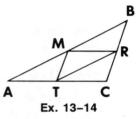
Ex. 1–10

1. If $DE = 8$, find AC.
2. If $DE = 6$, find AC.
3. If $AC = 20$, find DE.
4. If $AC = 17$, find DE.
5. If $BE = 4$, find EC.
6. If $AD = 7$, find DB.   7. If $DB = 5$, find AB.
8. If $BC = 9$, find EC.   9. If $m\angle BDE = 35$, find $m\angle BAC$.
10. If $m\angle BCA = 110$, find $m\angle DEB$.

11. In $\triangle ABC$, a segment joins D and E, the midpoints of $\overline{AB}$ and $\overline{CB}$, respectively. If $m\angle A = 40$, find $m\angle BDE$.
12. The segment joining the midpoints of two consecutive sides of a rectangle measures 20 units. How long is a diagonal of the rectangle?

In 13 and 14, M, R, and T are midpoints of $\overline{AB}$, $\overline{BC}$, and $\overline{CA}$, respectively, in $\triangle ABC$.

13. For each side of $\triangle ABC$, name a segment parallel to the side.
14. If $AB = 22$ cm, $BC = 12$ cm, and $AC = 20$ cm, **(a)** find the perimeter of $\triangle ABC$, **(b)** find the perimeter of $\triangle MRT$, and **(c)** write a conclusion based on your answers to parts **a** and **b**.

15. If the lengths of the sides of triangle ABC are represented by a, b, and c, represent the perimeter of the triangle whose vertices are the midpoints of the sides of triangle ABC.

In 16–18, D, E, and F are midpoints of $\overline{RT}$, $\overline{TS}$, and $\overline{SR}$, respectively, in $\triangle RTS$.

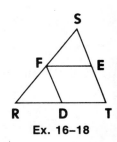

16. If $DF = 3y - 2$ and $TS = 4y + 4$, find:
  a. y **b.** DF **c.** TS
17. If $FE = x + 3$ and $RT = 4x - 7$, find:
  a. x **b.** FE **c.** RT
18. If $EFDT$ is a rhombus, $EF = 2x - 2$, and
  $FD = 4x - 9$, find:
  a. x **b.** EF **c.** FD **d.** ST **e.** RT

Ex. 16–18

19. In triangle RST, D is the midpoint of $\overline{RS}$, E is the midpoint of $\overline{ST}$, and F is the midpoint of $\overline{RT}$. If $\overline{DF}$ and $\overline{FE}$ are drawn, prove that $SDFE$ is a parallelogram.

20. In $\triangle ABC$, m$\angle A = 90$. The midpoints of sides $\overline{AB}$, $\overline{BC}$, and $\overline{CA}$ are, respectively, R, S, and T. Prove that $ARST$ is a rectangle.

21. *Given:* In $\triangle ABC$, $\overline{AB} \cong \overline{CB}$, D is the midpoint of $\overline{AB}$, and E is the midpoint of $\overline{BC}$.
  Prove: $ACED$ is an isosceles trapezoid.

22. *Given:* $\overleftrightarrow{AB} \parallel \overleftrightarrow{CD} \parallel \overleftrightarrow{EF}$,   transversals
  $\overleftrightarrow{ACE}$ and $\overleftrightarrow{BDF}$, $\overline{AC} \cong \overline{CE}$.

  Prove: $\overline{BD} \cong \overline{DF}$.

  [*Hint.* Draw $\overleftrightarrow{GH}$ through D so that
  $\overleftrightarrow{GH} \parallel \overleftrightarrow{AE}$, G is on $\overleftrightarrow{AB}$, and H is on
  $\overleftrightarrow{EF}$. Show that $AGDC$ and $CDHE$
  are parallelograms and prove that $\triangle GDB \cong \triangle HDF$.]

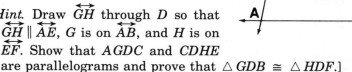

23. *Given:* In $\triangle ABC$, D is the
  midpoint of $\overline{AB}$, $\overline{DE} \parallel \overline{BC}$, and
  $\overline{DE}$ intersects $\overline{AC}$ at E.

  Prove: E is the midpoint of $\overline{AC}$.

  [*Hint.* See the diagram. Extend
  $\overline{DE}$ to F so that $\overline{DF} \cong \overline{BC}$.
  Draw $\overline{FC}$ to form $\square DFCB$. Prove $\triangle DEA \cong \triangle FEC$.]

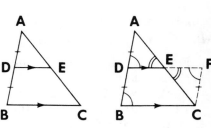

7-4 PROPORTIONS INVOLVING LINE SEGMENTS

● **Definition.** *Two line segments are divided proportionally* when the ratio of the lengths of the segments of one of them is equal to the ratio of the lengths of the segments of the other.

$\overline{DE}$ divides $\overline{AB}$ and $\overline{AC}$ proportionally if:

$$\frac{AD}{DB} = \frac{AE}{EC} \left[\frac{\text{length of upper segment}}{\text{length of lower segment}}\right]$$

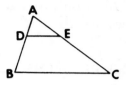

Here, D and E are *not* given as midpoints of $\overline{AB}$ and $\overline{AC}$, so the ratios $AD:DB$ and $AE:EC$ are *not* 1:1. Using positive numbers a and b, we say:

When $\dfrac{AD}{DB} = \dfrac{a}{b}$, it is also true that $\dfrac{AE}{EC} = \dfrac{a}{b}$. Thus, $\dfrac{AD}{DB} = \dfrac{AE}{EC}$.

The following postulate is based upon the theorem proved for midpoints and upon the definition just given. We will accept the truth of this statement:

● **POSTULATE 44. If a line is parallel to one side of a triangle and intersects the other two sides, the line divides those sides proportionally.**

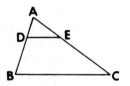

In $\triangle ABC$, when $\overline{DE} \parallel \overline{BC}$ and $\overline{DE}$ intersects $\overline{AB}$ and $\overline{AC}$, it follows that:

1. $\dfrac{AD}{DB} = \dfrac{AE}{EC} \left[\dfrac{\text{length of upper segment}}{\text{length of lower segment}} = \dfrac{\text{length of upper segment}}{\text{length of lower segment}}\right]$

2. $\dfrac{DB}{AD} = \dfrac{EC}{AE} \left[\dfrac{\text{length of lower segment}}{\text{length of upper segment}} = \dfrac{\text{length of lower segment}}{\text{length of upper segment}}\right]$

Other proportions may also be stated. For example:

3. $\dfrac{AD}{AE} = \dfrac{DB}{EC}$ or $\dfrac{AE}{AD} = \dfrac{EC}{DB} \left[\dfrac{\text{length of upper}}{\text{length of upper}} = \dfrac{\text{length of lower}}{\text{length of lower}}\right]$

4. $\dfrac{AB}{AD} = \dfrac{AC}{AE}$ or $\dfrac{AB}{DB} = \dfrac{AC}{EC} \left[\dfrac{\text{length of side}}{\text{length of part}} = \dfrac{\text{length of side}}{\text{length of part}}\right]$

5. $\dfrac{AD}{AE} = \dfrac{AB}{AC}$ or $\dfrac{DB}{EC} = \dfrac{AB}{AC} \left[\dfrac{\text{length of part}}{\text{length of part}} = \dfrac{\text{length of side}}{\text{length of side}}\right]$

We will also accept the truth of the *converse* statement:

● **POSTULATE 45. If a line divides two sides of a triangle proportionally, the line is parallel to the third side.**

Thus, in the previous figure, given that $\dfrac{AD}{DB} = \dfrac{AE}{EC}$, it follows that $\overline{DE} \parallel \overline{BC}$. Also, given any of the proportions stated after Postulate 44, it follows that $\overline{DE} \parallel \overline{BC}$.

MODEL PROBLEMS

1. In triangle RST, a line is drawn parallel to $\overline{ST}$ intersecting $\overline{RS}$ in K and $\overline{RT}$ in L. If $RK = 5$ in., $KS = 10$ in., and $RT = 18$ in., find RL.

Solution

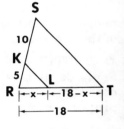

Method 1	*Method 2*

Method 1

Let $RL = x$ and $LT = 18 - x$.

If $\overline{KL} \parallel \overline{ST}$, then $\dfrac{RL}{LT} = \dfrac{RK}{KS}$.

By substitution:

$$\frac{x}{18-x} = \frac{5}{10}$$
$$10x = 90 - 5x$$
$$15x = 90$$
$$x = 6$$

Method 2

Let $x = RL$.

$$\frac{RL}{RT} = \frac{RK}{RS}$$

$$\frac{x}{18} = \frac{5}{15}$$
$$15x = 90$$
$$x = 6$$

Answer: $RL = 6$ in.

2. In $\triangle ABC$, $CD = 6$, $DA = 5$, $CE = 12$, and $EB = 10$. Is $\overline{DE}$ parallel to $\overline{AB}$?

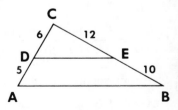

Solution

Since $\dfrac{CD}{DA} = \dfrac{6}{5}$, and $\dfrac{CE}{EB} = \dfrac{12}{10} = \dfrac{6}{5}$, then $\dfrac{CD}{DA} = \dfrac{CE}{EB}$. Therefore, in $\triangle ABC$, $\overline{DE}$ divides sides $\overline{CA}$ and $\overline{CB}$ proportionally, and $\overline{DE}$ must be parallel to the third side, $\overline{AB}$.

Answer: Yes.

EXERCISES

1. If $\overline{DE} \parallel \overline{AC}$, complete the following proportions:
   a. $BD:DA = BE:$_____.
   b. $BC:BE = $_____$:BD$.
   c. $AD:CE = AB:$_____.
   d. $BE:BD = BC:$_____.

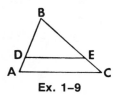

Ex. 1–9

2. If $\overline{DE} \parallel \overline{AC}$, which is a proportion?

   (1) $\dfrac{AB}{AD} = \dfrac{CE}{CB}$ (2) $\dfrac{CB}{EB} = \dfrac{AB}{DB}$ (3) $\dfrac{BD}{BA} = \dfrac{BC}{BE}$ (4) $\dfrac{BD}{EC} = \dfrac{BE}{DA}$

3. If $\overline{DE} \parallel \overline{AC}$, which is *not* a proportion?

   (1) $\dfrac{BD}{BE} = \dfrac{DA}{EC}$ (2) $\dfrac{BD}{DA} = \dfrac{BE}{EC}$ (3) $\dfrac{BC}{BA} = \dfrac{BE}{BD}$ (4) $\dfrac{BD}{DA} = \dfrac{CE}{EB}$

4. If $\overline{DE} \parallel \overline{AC}$ and $BD:DA = 3:1$, find the ratio $BE:EC$.
5. If $BD = 8$, $DA = 4$, $BE = 10$, and $EC = 5$, is $\overline{DE} \parallel \overline{AC}$?
6. If $AD = 6$, $BD = 9$, $EC = 4$, and $BE = 8$, is $\overline{DE} \parallel \overline{AC}$?
7. If $\overline{DE} \parallel \overline{AC}$, $BD = 6$, $DA = 2$, and $BE = 9$, find EC.
8. If $\overline{DE} \parallel \overline{AC}$, $BD:DA = 4:1$, and $BE = 40$, find EC.
9. If $\overline{DE} \parallel \overline{AC}$, $BE = 5$, $EC = 3$, and $BA = 16$, find BD.

In 10–14, use $\triangle RST$ where $\overline{DE} \parallel \overline{RT}$.

10. If $SD = 4$, $DR = 3$, and $ST = 21$, find SE.
11. If $SE = 4$, $ET = 2$, and $SR = 9$, find SD.
12. If $SD = 4$, $SR = 10$, and $ST = 5$, find SE.
13. If $SE = 6$, $ST = 15$, and $SR = 20$, what is the length of $\overline{SD}$?
14. If $ET = 3$, $DR = 4$, and $SR = 12$, what is the length of $\overline{SE}$?

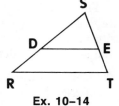

Ex. 10–14

15. In triangle ABC, D is a point on $\overline{AB}$, E is a point on $\overline{AC}$, and $\overline{DE}$ is drawn. If $AB = 8$, $AC = 12$, $DB = 3$, and $EC = 4$, is $\overline{DE} \parallel \overline{BC}$?

16. In triangle ABC, D is a point on $\overline{AB}$, E is a point on $\overline{AC}$, and $\overline{DE}$ is drawn. $AD = 6$ cm, $DB = 4$ cm, $AC = 15$ cm. In order for $\overline{DE}$ to be parallel to $\overline{BC}$, what must be the length of $\overline{EC}$?

17. Given triangle ABC with a line drawn parallel to $\overline{AC}$ intersecting $\overline{AB}$ at D and $\overline{CB}$ at E. If $AB = 8$, $BC = 12$, and $BD = 6$, find BE.

18. If $\angle BDE \cong \angle BAC$, prove that $BE:EC = BD:DA$.

19. If $\angle DEA \cong \angle CAE$, prove that $AB:BD = CB:BE$.

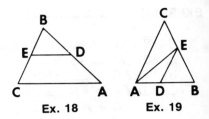

Ex. 18   **Ex. 19**

20. In $\triangle RST$, P is a point on $\overline{RT}$. Through P, a line is drawn parallel to $\overline{ST}$ that intersects $\overline{RS}$ in Y. Through P, a line is drawn parallel to $\overline{RS}$ that intersects $\overline{ST}$ in X. Prove $RY:YS = SX:XT$.

7-5 SIMILAR POLYGONS

The Meaning of Similar Polygons

Two polygons that have the same shape but not the same size are called *similar polygons*.

In symbols, polygon $ABCDE \sim$ polygon $A'B'C'D'E'$.

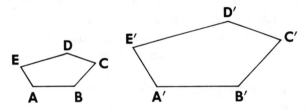

These polygons have the same shape because their corresponding angles are congruent and the ratios of the lengths of their corresponding sides are equal. Here the ratio $AB:A'B' = 1:2$, the ratio $BC:B'C' = 1:2$, and so on. This description will be used to state a formal definition.

● **Definition.** *Two polygons are similar* if there is a one-to-one correspondence between their vertices such that:

1. All pairs of corresponding angles are congruent.
2. The ratios of the lengths of all pairs of corresponding sides are equal.

Thus, in the figure above, polygon $ABCDE$ is similar to polygon $A'B'C'D'E'$ if:

1. $\angle A \cong \angle A'$, $\angle B \cong \angle B'$, $\angle C \cong \angle C'$, $\angle D \cong \angle D'$, $\angle E \cong \angle E'$

   and

2. $\dfrac{AB}{A'B'} = \dfrac{BC}{B'C'} = \dfrac{CD}{C'D'} = \dfrac{DE}{D'E'} = \dfrac{EA}{E'A'}$

Note. When the ratios of the lengths of the corresponding sides of two polygons are equal as just shown, we say that *the corresponding sides of the two polygons are in proportion.*

Notice that *both* conditions mentioned in the definition must be true for polygons to be similar.

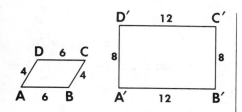

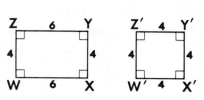

Why are *ABCD* and *A'B'C'D'* not similar?

The corresponding sides of the polygons are in proportion, but the corresponding angles are *not* congruent.

Why are *WXYZ* and *W'X'Y'Z'* not similar?

The corresponding angles are congruent, but the corresponding sides of the polygons are *not* in proportion.

Recall that a mathematical definition is reversible:

If two polygons are similar, *then* their corresponding angles are congruent and their corresponding sides are in proportion.

and

If two polygons have corresponding angles that are congruent and corresponding sides that are in proportion, *then* the polygons are similar.

Since triangles are polygons, the definition given for two similar polygons will also apply to two similar triangles.

● **Definition.** The *ratio of similitude* of two similar polygons is the ratio of the lengths of any two corresponding sides.

In the figure, $\triangle ABC \sim \triangle A'B'C'$.

$\angle A \cong \angle A'$, $\angle B \cong \angle B'$, and $\angle C \cong \angle C'$.

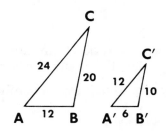

$$AB:A'B' = 12:6 = 2:1$$
$$BC:B'C' = 20:10 = 2:1$$
$$CA:C'A' = 24:12 = 2:1$$

The ratio of similitude is 2:1.

Equivalence Relation of Similarity

The relation *is similar to* is true for polygons when their corresponding angles are congruent and their corresponding sides are in proportion. Thus, for the set of triangles, we can test the following properties:

1. Reflexive property: $\triangle ABC \sim \triangle ABC$.
   (Here, the ratio of similitude = 1:1.)

2. Symmetric property: If $\triangle ABC \sim \triangle DEF$, then $\triangle DEF \sim \triangle ABC$.

3. Transitive property: If $\triangle ABC \sim \triangle DEF$, and $\triangle DEF \sim \triangle RST$, then $\triangle ABC \sim \triangle RST$.

These properties stated for *any similar geometric figures* are the next three postulates.

● **POSTULATE 46. Any geometric figure is similar to itself.** (Reflexive property.)

● **POSTULATE 47. A similarity may be expressed in either order.** (Symmetric property.)

● **POSTULATE 48. Two geometric figures similar to the same geometric figure are similar to each other.** (Transitive property.)

MODEL PROBLEM _____

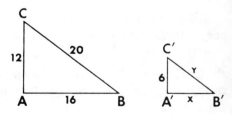

Triangle $ABC \sim$ triangle $A'B'C'$ and $A'C'$ corresponds to AC.

a. Find the ratio of similitude of the larger triangle to the smaller.

b. Find x and y.

Solution

a. The ratio of similitude of two similar polygons is the ratio of the lengths of any two corresponding sides.

Thus, ratio of similitude $= \dfrac{AC}{A'C'} = \dfrac{12}{6} = \dfrac{2}{1}$.

Answer: 2:1

b.

Method 1	*Method 2*
Since the ratio of similitude of $\triangle ABC$ to $\triangle A'B'C'$ is 2:1, each side of $\triangle A'B'C'$ is $\frac{1}{2}$ as long as its corresponding side in $\triangle ABC$. Therefore, $A'B' = \frac{1}{2} AB$, or $x = \frac{1}{2}(16) = 8$ $B'C' = \frac{1}{2} BC$, or $y = \frac{1}{2}(20) = 10$	Since the corresponding sides of similar polygons are in proportion, (1) $\dfrac{AC}{A'C'} = \dfrac{AB}{A'B'}$ and $\dfrac{AC}{A'C'} = \dfrac{BC}{B'C'}$ (2) $\dfrac{12}{6} = \dfrac{16}{x}$ $\qquad \dfrac{12}{6} = \dfrac{20}{y}$ (3) $12x = 96$ $\qquad\quad 12y = 120$ (4) $x = 8$ $\qquad\qquad y = 10$

Answer: $x = 8, y = 10$

EXERCISES

1. Are two congruent polygons always similar? Why?
2. What is the ratio of similitude of two congruent polygons?
3. Are all similar polygons congruent? Why?
4. What must be the ratio of similitude of two similar polygons in order for them to be congruent polygons?
5. Are all squares similar? Why?
6. Are all rectangles similar? Why?
7. The sides of a triangle measure 4, 8, and 10. If the smallest side of a similar triangle measures 12, find the measures of the remaining sides of this triangle.
8. The sides of a quadrilateral measure 12, 18, 20, and 16. The longest side of a similar quadrilateral measures 5. Find the measures of the remaining sides of this quadrilateral.
9. $\triangle ABC \sim \triangle A'B'C'$, and their ratio of similitude is 1:3. If the measures of the sides of $\triangle ABC$ are represented by a, b, and c, represent the measures of the sides of the larger $\triangle A'B'C'$.
10. Prove that any two equilateral triangles are similar.

Proving Triangles Similar

Since triangles are polygons, we can prove that two triangles are similar by showing that they satisfy the two conditions required in similar polygons.

In $\triangle ABC$ and $\triangle A'B'C'$, side lengths are given in exact linear measures and angle measures are given to the nearest degree.

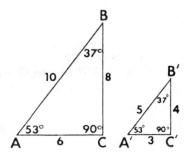

CONDITION 1. Corresponding angles are congruent:
$m\angle A = 53$ and $m\angle A' = 53$. Thus, $\angle A \cong \angle A'$.
$m\angle B = 37$ and $m\angle B' = 37$. Thus, $\angle B \cong \angle B'$.
$m\angle C = 90$ and $m\angle C' = 90$. Thus, $\angle C \cong \angle C'$.

CONDITION 2. Corresponding sides are in proportion:
$$\frac{AB}{A'B'} = \frac{10}{5} = \frac{2}{1}, \; \frac{BC}{B'C'} = \frac{8}{4} = \frac{2}{1}, \text{ and } \frac{CA}{C'A'} = \frac{6}{3} = \frac{2}{1}.$$

Thus, $\dfrac{AB}{A'B'} = \dfrac{BC}{B'C'} = \dfrac{CA}{C'A'}$.

Therefore, by the definition of similar polygons, $\triangle ABC \sim \triangle A'B'C'$.
However, there are shorter methods of proving triangles similar. These methods are indicated in the theorems and corollaries that follow. Be aware that a correspondence exists between vertices of the two triangles given in each hypothesis, just as in congruence theorems.

● **THEOREM 54. Two triangles are similar if two angles of one triangle are congruent to two corresponding angles of the other. [a.a. ≅ a.a.]**

Given: $\triangle ABC$ and $\triangle A'B'C'$ in which $\angle A \cong \angle A'$ and $\angle B \cong \angle B'$.

Prove: $\triangle ABC \sim \triangle A'B'C'$.

Plan: Prove that the remaining pair of angles are congruent. Also, prove that the corresponding sides of these triangles are in proportion.

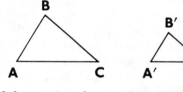

Statements	*Reasons*
1. In $\triangle ABC$ and $\triangle A'B'C'$, $\angle A \cong \angle A'$ and $\angle B \cong \angle B'$.	1. Given.
2. $\angle C \cong \angle C'$.	2. If two angles of one triangle are congruent, respectively, to two angles of a second triangle, the third angles are congruent.

For steps 3 to 12, construct $\triangle ADE \cong \triangle A'B'C'$ and show that D and E divide $\overline{AB}$ and $\overline{AC}$ proportionally.

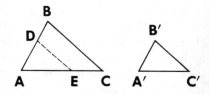

3. Let D be a point on $\overline{AB}$ so that $\overline{AD} \cong \overline{A'B'}$. (s. $\cong$ s.)

3. A line segment may be copied.

4. Let E be a point on $\overline{AC}$ so that $\overline{AE} \cong \overline{A'C'}$. (s. $\cong$ s.)

4. A line segment may be copied.

5. $\angle A \cong \angle A'$. (a. $\cong$ a.)

5. Given.

6. $\triangle ADE \cong \triangle A'B'C'$.

6. s.a.s. $\cong$ s.a.s.

7. $\angle ADE \cong \angle B'$.

7. Corresponding parts of congruent triangles are congruent.

8. $\angle B \cong \angle B'$.

8. Given.

9. $\therefore \angle ADE \cong \angle B$.

9. Transitive property of congruence.

10. $\overline{DE} \parallel \overline{BC}$.

10. If two lines are cut by a transversal making a pair of corresponding angles congruent, the lines are parallel.

11. $\dfrac{AB}{AD} = \dfrac{AC}{AE}$.

11. If a line is parallel to one side of a triangle and intersects the other two sides, the line divides those sides proportionally.

12. $\dfrac{AB}{A'B'} = \dfrac{AC}{A'C'}$.

12. Substitution postulate (from steps 3 and 4).

In step 13, construct $\triangle BFG \cong \triangle B'A'C'$.

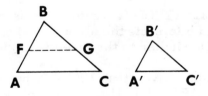

13. Similarly, by letting $\overline{BF} \cong \overline{B'A'}$ and $\overline{BG} \cong \overline{B'C'}$, we can prove that $\overline{FG} \parallel \overline{AC}$ and $\dfrac{BA}{BF} = \dfrac{BC}{BG}$, or $\dfrac{BA}{B'A'} = \dfrac{BC}{B'C'}$.

13. Similar proof, following steps 3 to 12.

14. Thus, $\dfrac{AB}{A'B'} = \dfrac{AC}{A'C'} = \dfrac{BC}{B'C'}$.

15. $\triangle ABC \sim \triangle A'B'C'$.

14. Transitive property of equality (from steps 12 and 13).

15. Two polygons are similar if their corresponding angles are congruent and their corresponding sides are in proportion.

To construct a triangle similar to a given triangle on a given line segment as a base.

See Chapter 16, Construction 12.

● **COROLLARY T54-1.** Two right triangles are similar if an acute angle of one triangle is congruent to an acute angle of the other.

In the figure, $\triangle ABC$ and $\triangle A'B'C'$ are right triangles with $\angle C$ and $\angle C'$ the right angles, and $\angle A \cong \angle A'$. Prove $\triangle ABC \sim \triangle A'B'C'$ by a.a. $\cong$ a.a.

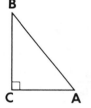

● **COROLLARY T54-2.** A line that is parallel to one side of a triangle and intersects the other two sides in different points cuts off a triangle similar to the given triangle.

In the figure, given that $\overleftrightarrow{DE} \parallel \overline{AC}$, prove that $\triangle DBE \sim \triangle ABC$. (*Hint.* Use corresponding angles formed by parallel lines and a transversal.)

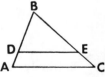

To divide a line segment into any number of congruent parts.

See Chapter 16, Construction 13.

MODEL PROBLEMS

1. *Given:* $\overline{AEC}$, $\overline{BED}$, and $\overline{AB} \parallel \overline{DC}$.

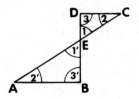

 a. Prove $\triangle ABE \sim \triangle CDE$.
 b. If $DE = 10$ cm, $BE = 15$ cm, and
  $CE = 20$ cm, find AE.

Solution

a. *Plan:* Prove that two angles in $\triangle ABE$ are congruent to two corresponding angles of $\triangle CDE$.

Statements	*Reasons*
1. $\overline{AEC}$ and $\overline{BED}$.	1. Given.
2. $\angle 1 \cong \angle 1'$. (a. $\cong$ a.)	2. Vertical angles are congruent.
3. $\overline{AB} \parallel \overline{CD}$.	3. Given.
4. $\angle 2 \cong \angle 2'$. (a. $\cong$ a.)	4. If parallel lines are cut by a transversal, the alternate interior angles are congruent.
5. $\triangle ABE \sim \triangle CDE$.	5. a.a. $\cong$ a.a.

b. (1) Corresponding sides of similar triangles are in proportion. By selecting pairs of sides opposite congruent angles, the proportion can be stated:

$$\frac{AE \text{ (opposite } \angle 3')}{CE \text{ (opposite } \angle 3)} = \frac{BE \text{ (opposite } \angle 2')}{DE \text{ (opposite } \angle 2)}$$

(2) Let $AE = x$. Substitute. $\dfrac{x}{20} = \dfrac{15}{10}$

(3) Solve for x.
$$10x = 20(15)$$
$$10x = 300$$
$$x = 30$$

Answer: $AE = 30$ cm

2. In $\triangle ABC$, D is a point on $\overline{AC}$ and
 E is a point on $\overline{BC}$ such that
 $\overline{DE} \parallel \overline{AB}$. If $DE = 8$ ft., $AB = 20$ ft.,
 $CD = 4$ ft., and $EB = 9$ ft., find:
 a. CA **b.** CE

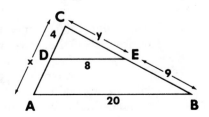

Solution

Since $\overline{DE} \parallel \overline{AB}$ and $\overline{DE}$ intersects sides $\overline{AC}$ and $\overline{BC}$, a triangle is formed that is similar to the given triangle: $\triangle DCE \sim \triangle ACB$.

a. Let $CA = x$.
Write a proportion.

$$\frac{DE}{AB} = \frac{CD}{CA}$$

$$\frac{8}{20} = \frac{4}{x}$$

$$8x = 20(4)$$

$$8x = 80$$

$$x = 10$$

Answer: $CA = 10$ ft.

b. Let $CE = y$.
Then, $CB = CE + EB = y + 9$.

$$\frac{CE}{DE} = \frac{CB}{AB}$$

$$\frac{y}{8} = \frac{y + 9}{20}$$

$$20y = 8(y + 9)$$

$$20y = 8y + 72$$

$$12y = 72$$

$$y = 6$$

Answer: $CE = 6$ ft.

3. In $\triangle ABC$, D is a point on $\overline{AB}$ and E is a point on $\overline{AC}$ such that $\overline{DE} \parallel \overline{BC}$. If $AD = 2$, $DB = x + 1$, $AE = x$, and $EC = x + 6$, write and solve an algebraic equation to find AE.

Solution

(1) Draw and label the figure.

$$AB = AD + DB$$
$$= 2 + (x + 1) = x + 3$$
$$AC = AE + EC$$
$$= x + (x + 6) = 2x + 6$$

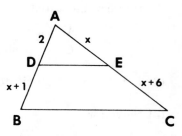

(2) Since $\triangle DAE \sim \triangle BAC$, their corresponding sides are in proportion.

$$\frac{AD}{AB} = \frac{AE}{AC}$$

(3) Substitute the given values.

$$\frac{2}{x + 3} = \frac{x}{2x + 6}$$

(4) The product of the means equals the product of the extremes.

$$x(x + 3) = 2(2x + 6)$$

$$x^2 + 3x = 4x + 12$$

(5) To solve a quadratic equation, write an equivalent equation with one side equal to zero. Then, factor.

$$x^2 + 3x - 4x - 12 = 0$$

$$x^2 - x - 12 = 0$$

$$(x - 4)(x + 3) = 0$$

(6) Set each factor equal to zero.

$x - 4 = 0$	$x + 3 = 0$
$x = 4$	$x = -3$
	Reject the negative value.

(7) *Check:* If $x = 4$, then $AB = 7$, $AE = 4$, and $AC = 14$. Thus,

$\dfrac{AD}{AB} = \dfrac{AE}{AC}$ becomes $\dfrac{2}{7} = \dfrac{4}{14}$ (true).

Answer: AE = 4 linear units

Note. Other proportions could have been used in the solution, such as $\dfrac{AD}{DB} = \dfrac{AE}{EC}$.

EXERCISES

1. In $\triangle ABC$, $m\angle A = 40$ and $m\angle B = 30$. In $\triangle EDF$, $m\angle D = 30$ and $m\angle E = 40$. Is $\triangle ABC$ similar to $\triangle EDF$? Why?
2. In $\triangle RST$, $m\angle R = 90$ and $m\angle S = 40$. In $\triangle ZXY$, $m\angle X = 40$ and $m\angle Y = 50$. Is $\triangle RST$ similar to $\triangle ZXY$? Why?

In 3–12, use $\triangle ABC$ where D is a point on $\overline{AC}$ and E is a point on $\overline{BC}$ such that $\overline{DE} \parallel \overline{AB}$.

3. If $CA = 8$, $AB = 12$, and $CD = 4$, find DE.
4. If $CE = 4$, $DE = 6$, and $CB = 10$, find AB.
5. If $AB = 12$, $DE = 8$, and $AC = 9$, find DC.
6. If $CD = 3$, $DE = 5$, and $AB = 10$, find CA.
7. If $CD = 4$, $DE = 4$, and $DA = 1$, find AB.
8. If $CD = 3$, $DA = 2$, and $AB = 10$, find DE.
9. If $CE = 4$, $EB = 2$, and $DE = 6$, find AB.
10. If $CD = 6$, $DE = 8$, and $AB = 12$, find DA.
11. If $DE = 4$, $DA = 1$, and $AB = 6$, find CD.
12. If $AB = 9$, $DE = 6$, and $EB = 2$, find CE.

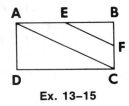

Ex. 3–12

In 13–15, $\overline{AC}$ is a diagonal of rectangle $ABCD$ and $\overline{EF}$ joins the midpoints of $\overline{AB}$ and $\overline{BC}$, respectively.

13. If $AC = 20$ mm, find the length of $\overline{EF}$.

14. If $EF = 13$ in., and $EB = 12$ in., find:
    a. AC b. AB

Ex. 13–15

15. Which one of the following four statements is true? (1) $\overline{EF} \perp \overline{BC}$ (2) $\triangle BEF \cong \triangle BAC$ (3) $\overline{BE} \cong \overline{BF}$ (4) $\triangle BEF \sim \triangle BAC$

In 16–19, tell whether the statement is *true* or *false*.

16. Equilateral triangles are similar.

17. Right triangles are similar.

18. Congruent triangles are similar.

19. Similar triangles are congruent.

20. If the vertex angles of two isosceles triangles are congruent, then the two triangles must be
(1) acute (2) right (3) congruent (4) similar

In 21–26, use $\triangle ABC$ with D a point on $\overline{AB}$ and E a point on $\overline{AC}$ such that $\overline{DE} \parallel \overline{BC}$. In each instance, write and solve an algebraic equation to find the indicated lengths.

Ex. 21–26

21. If $AD = 1$, $DB = x$, $AE = x$, and $EC = x + 2$, find DB.

22. If $AD = 2$, $DB = x - 1$, $AE = x$, and $EC = x + 2$, find AE.

23. If $AD = x$, $ED = 5$, $DB = 2$, and $BC = x + 2$, find AD.

24. If $AE = x$, $ED = 5$, $EC = 3$, and $CB = x + 7$, find AE.

25. If $ED = 3$, $CB = x$, $CE = x + 1$, and $EA = x + 4$, find CB.

26. If $ED = x$, $DA = 6$, $CB = 6$, and $BD = x - 1$, find ED.

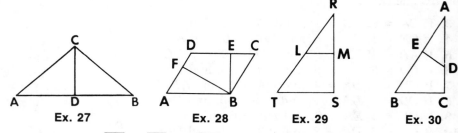

Ex. 27   Ex. 28   Ex. 29   Ex. 30

27. In $\triangle ABC$, $\overline{AC} \cong \overline{BC}$ and $\overline{CD}$ bisects $\angle C$. Prove $\triangle ACD \sim \triangle BCD$.

28. In $\square ABCD$, $\overline{BE} \perp \overline{DC}$ and $\overline{BF} \perp \overline{AD}$.
a. Prove $\triangle BAF \sim \triangle BCE$.
b. If $AB = 16$, $BC = 12$, and $FB = 14$, find EB.

29. In $\triangle RST$, $\overline{TS} \perp \overline{RS}$ and $\overline{LM} \perp \overline{RS}$.
a. Prove $\triangle LMR \sim \triangle TSR$.
b. If $LM = 6$, $TS = 9$, and $MS = 4$, find RM.

30. In $\triangle ABC$, $\overline{BC} \perp \overline{AC}$ and $\overline{DE} \perp \overline{AB}$.
a. Prove $\triangle ABC \sim \triangle ADE$.
b. If $DE = 5$, $AD = 6$, and $AB = 18$, find BC.

31. In acute $\triangle ABC$, altitudes $\overline{BD}$ and $\overline{CE}$ intersect at F. Prove that $\triangle BEF$ is similar to $\triangle CDF$.

7-6 USING SIMILAR TRIANGLES TO PROVE PROPORTIONS INVOLVING LINE SEGMENTS

To prove that the lengths of four line segments are in proportion, show that the line segments are corresponding sides in similar triangles.

MODEL PROBLEM ────────────────────────────────

In isosceles triangle ABC, $\overline{AB} \cong \overline{AC}$. $\overline{AF}$ is the altitude upon $\overline{BC}$. Through D, a point on $\overline{AB}$, a perpendicular to $\overline{AB}$ is drawn to meet $\overleftrightarrow{BC}$ at P. Prove $FC : DB = AC : PB$.

Given: $\triangle ABC$ with $\overline{AB} \cong \overline{AC}$.
$\overline{AF} \perp \overline{BC}$. $\overline{PD} \perp \overline{AB}$.

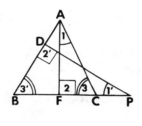

Prove:

$$\overset{\triangle FCA}{\overbrace{\dfrac{FC}{DB} = \dfrac{AC}{PB}}}_{\triangle DBP}$$

Plan: Prove $\triangle FCA \sim \triangle DBP$ by a.a. $\cong$ a.a.

Note. As shown in the figure, it is convenient to rename the corresponding angles 1, 2, 3 and 1', 2', 3'.

Statements	*Reasons*
1. $\overline{AB} \cong \overline{AC}$.	1. Given.
2. $\angle 3 \cong \angle 3'$. (a. $\cong$ a.)	2. If two sides of a triangle are congruent, the angles opposite these sides are congruent.
3. $\overline{AF} \perp \overline{BC}$, $\overline{PD} \perp \overline{AB}$.	3. Given.
4. $\angle 2$ and $\angle 2'$ are right angles.	4. Perpendicular lines intersect to form right angles.
5. $\angle 2 \cong \angle 2'$. (a. $\cong$ a.)	5. All right angles are congruent.
6. $\triangle FCA \sim \triangle DBP$.	6. a.a. $\cong$ a.a.
7. $\dfrac{FC \text{ (opp. } \angle 1)}{DB \text{ (opp. } \angle 1')} = \dfrac{AC \text{ (opp. } \angle 2)}{PB \text{ (opp. } \angle 2')}$.	7. Corresponding sides of similar triangles are in proportion.

EXERCISES

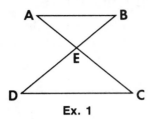
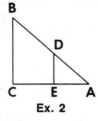
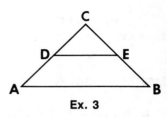

Ex. 1   Ex. 2   Ex. 3

1. $\overline{AB}$ is parallel to $\overline{DC}$. Prove: $\dfrac{AE}{CE} = \dfrac{BE}{DE}$.

2. In right $\triangle ABC$, m$\angle C$ = 90 and $\overline{DE} \perp \overline{CA}$. Prove: $\dfrac{AD}{AB} = \dfrac{DE}{BC}$.

3. In $\triangle ABC$, D is the midpoint of $\overline{AC}$ and E is the midpoint of $\overline{BC}$. Prove: $CD:CA = DE:AB$.

4. In right triangle ABC, m$\angle C$ = 90 and $\overline{CD} \perp \overline{AB}$. Prove that $AB:AC = AC:AD$.

5. In right triangle ABC, $\overline{CD}$ is the altitude to the hypotenuse $\overline{AB}$. Prove that BC is the mean proportional between AB and BD.

Ex. 4–5

6. In triangle ABC, D is a point on side $\overline{AB}$, E is a point on $\overline{AC}$, and $\overline{DE}$ is parallel to $\overline{BC}$. Prove that $AD:DE = AB:BC$. (First, prove $AD:AB = DE:BC$. Then interchange the means of the proportion.)

7. $ABCD$ is a parallelogram with side $\overline{BC}$ extended through C to any point E. $\overline{AE}$ is drawn intersecting $\overline{DC}$ in F. Prove:
   a. $CF:DF = CE:DA$.
   b. $CF:DF = CE:CB$.

8. In triangle ABC, altitudes $\overline{CE}$ and $\overline{BD}$ intersect at F. Prove that $AB:BD = AC:CE$.

9. In rectangle $WXYZ$, A is a point on $\overline{XY}$ such that $\overline{WY}$ intersects $\overline{ZA}$ at point P and $\overline{WY} \perp \overline{ZA}$.
   Prove: a. $\triangle WPZ \sim \triangle WZY$.
   b. $\triangle WPZ \sim \triangle YPA$.
   c. $AY:YP = YW:WZ$.

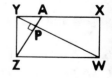

10. *Given:* Trapezoid $ABCD$ where $\overline{AB} \parallel \overline{DC}$ and diagonals $\overline{AC}$ and $\overline{BD}$ intersect at point E.
    Prove: $BE:AB = DE:DC$.

7-7 PROVING THAT PRODUCTS INVOLVING LINE SEGMENTS ARE EQUAL

To prove that the product of the lengths of two line segments is equal to the product of the lengths of two other line segments:

1. Form a proportion in which the lengths of the four line segments appear, based upon corresponding sides in similar triangles.
2. Apply the theorem: In a proportion, the product of the means is equal to the product of the extremes.

MODEL PROBLEM _____

Given: Isosceles $\triangle RST$ with $\overline{SR} \cong \overline{ST}$, $\angle TER$ and $\angle SDT$ are right angles.

Prove: $ER \times SD = TE \times DT$.

Plan: Prove $\triangle TER \sim \triangle SDT$ by a.a. $\cong$ a.a. Thus, $\dfrac{TE}{ER} = \dfrac{SD}{DT}$, and the product follows.

Statements	*Reasons*
1. In $\triangle RST$, $\overline{SR} \cong \overline{ST}$.	1. Given.
2. $\angle SRT \cong \angle STR$. (a. $\cong$ a.)	2. If two sides of a triangle are congruent, the angles opposite these sides are congruent.
3. $\angle TER$ and $\angle SDT$ are right angles.	3. Given.
4. $\angle TER \cong \angle SDT$. (a. $\cong$ a.)	4. All right angles are congruent.
5. $\triangle TER \sim \triangle SDT$.	5. a.a. $\cong$ a.a.
6. $\dfrac{TE}{ER} = \dfrac{SD}{DT}$.	6. Corresponding sides of similar triangles are in proportion.
7. $ER \times SD = TE \times DT$.	7. In a proportion, the product of the means is equal to the product of the extremes.

EXERCISES _____

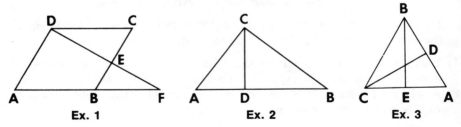

Ex. 1 Ex. 2 Ex. 3

1. If *ABCD* is a parallelogram, prove:
   a. $\triangle CED \sim \triangle BEF$. **b.** $\dfrac{CE}{DE} = \dfrac{BE}{FE}$. **c.** $DE \times BE = FE \times CE$.

2. In right triangle *ABC*, $\angle C$ is a right angle and $\overline{CD} \perp \overline{AB}$. Prove:
   a. $\triangle BCA \sim \triangle CDA$. **b.** $AD \times CB = DC \times AC$.

3. In isosceles triangle *ABC*, $\overline{AB} \cong \overline{BC}$. Altitudes $\overline{BE}$ and $\overline{CD}$ are drawn. Prove that $BC \times DA = CA \times EC$.

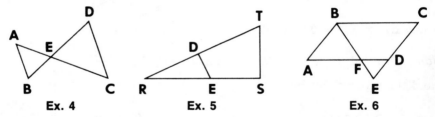

Ex. 4 Ex. 5 Ex. 6

4. If $\overline{AB} \parallel \overline{CD}$, and $\overline{AC}$ and $\overline{BD}$ intersect at *E*, prove that $DE \times AE = BE \times CE$.

5. In $\triangle RST$, angle *S* is a right angle and $\overline{ED} \perp \overline{RT}$. Prove that $DR \times TS = ED \times SR$.

6. *Given:* *ABCD* is a parallelogram, $\overline{BFE}$, $\overline{CDE}$, $\overline{AFD}$.
   Prove: $AF \times EF = DF \times BF$.

7. Given $\overline{ABE}$, $\overline{ADC}$, $\overline{BD}$ bisects $\angle ABC$, and $\overline{BD} \parallel \overline{EC}$, prove:
   a. $\triangle EBC$ is isosceles.
   b. $\triangle BAD \sim \triangle EAC$.
   c. $AD:AC = BA:EA$.
   d. $BA \times AC = EA \times AD$.

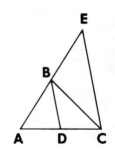

In 8–12, *PQRS* is a parallelogram. $\overline{QC}$ intersects diagonal $\overline{RP}$ at *B*, side $\overline{SP}$ at *A*, and the line containing side $\overline{RS}$ at *C*.

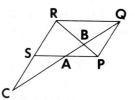

8. *Prove:* **a.** $\triangle ABP \sim \triangle QBR$.
  b. $AB \times BR = QB \times BP$.

9. *Prove:* **a.** $QBP \sim \triangle CBR$.
  b. $PQ \times CB = RC \times QB$.

10. *Prove:* **a.** $\triangle ACS \sim \triangle QCR$. **b.** $AS \times RC = SC \times QR$.

11. *Prove:* $QC \times QP = AQ \times CR$.

12. *Prove:* $QR \times RS = SP \times PQ$.

Ex. 8–12

7-8 USING PROPORTIONS INVOLVING CORRESPONDING LINE SEGMENTS IN SIMILAR TRIANGLES

You have seen that if two triangles are similar, then their corresponding sides are in proportion. Other corresponding segments in similar triangles are also in proportion. Note the following theorems.

● **THEOREM 55. If two triangles are similar, the lengths of corresponding altitudes have the same ratio as the lengths of any two corresponding sides.**

Given: $\triangle ABC \sim \triangle A'B'C'$,
  $BC = a, B'C' = a'$.
  $\overline{BD} \perp \overline{AC}$ and $BD = h$.
  $\overline{B'D'} \perp \overline{A'C'}$ and $B'D' = h'$.

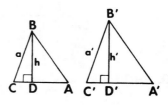

Prove: $\dfrac{h}{h'} = \dfrac{a}{a'}$

Plan: Prove $\triangle BCD \sim \triangle B'C'D'$ by a.a. $\cong$ a.a.

In Theorem 55, if the expression "corresponding altitudes" is replaced by "corresponding medians" or by "corresponding angle bisectors," the resulting theorems will also be true. Thus, the corollary follows:

● **COROLLARY T55-1. In two similar triangles, the lengths of any two corresponding line segments have the same ratio as the lengths of any pair of corresponding sides.**

● **THEOREM 56. The perimeters of two similar triangles have the same ratio as the lengths of any pair of corresponding sides.**

Given: $\triangle ABC \sim \triangle A'B'C'$.
   $BC = a, AC = b, AB = c$.
   $B'C' = a', A'C' = b', A'B' = c'$.
   Perimeter of $\triangle ABC = p$.
   Perimeter of $\triangle A'B'C' = p'$.

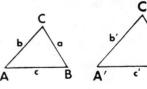

Prove: $\dfrac{p}{p'} = \dfrac{a}{a'}$

Plan: (1) Let $k:1$ be the ratio of similitude.

   (2) Corresponding sides have the same ratio, $k:1$.

$$\frac{a}{a'} = \frac{k}{1} \quad \frac{b}{b'} = \frac{k}{1} \quad \frac{c}{c'} = \frac{k}{1}$$

or

$$a = ka' \quad b = kb' \quad c = kc'$$

   (3) Express the perimeters.

$$p = a + b + c \ \ or \ \ p = ka' + kb' + kc'$$
$$p' = a' + b' + c'$$

   (4) The ratio of the perimeters is also $k:1$.

$$\frac{p}{p'} = \frac{ka' + kb' + kc'}{a' + b' + c'}$$

$$= \frac{k(a' + b' + c')}{a' + b' + c'} = \frac{k}{1}$$

MODEL PROBLEM _____

   Two triangles are similar. The sides of the smaller triangle have lengths of 4 cm, 6 cm, and 8 cm. The perimeter of the larger triangle is 27 cm. Find the length of the shortest side of the larger triangle.

Solution

(1) In the smaller triangle, find the
   perimeter p.

   $$p = 4 + 6 + 8 = 18$$

   The length of the shortest side is
   4 cm.

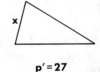

(2) In the larger triangle, the perimeter p' is 27 cm.
Let x = the length of the shortest side.

(3) Since the triangles are similar, use the following proportion.

$$\frac{\text{perimeter of smaller } \triangle}{\text{perimeter of larger } \triangle} = \frac{\text{length of shortest side in smaller } \triangle}{\text{length of shortest side in larger } \triangle}$$

$$\frac{18}{27} = \frac{4}{x}$$

(4) Solve for x.

$$18x = 27(4)$$
$$18x = 108$$
$$x = 6$$

Answer: The length of the shortest side of the larger triangle is 6 cm.

EXERCISES

1. The ratio of similitude in two similar triangles is 3:1. If a side in the larger triangle measures 30 cm, find the measure of the corresponding side in the smaller triangle.

2. If the lengths of the sides of two similar triangles are in the ratio 5:1, find the ratio of the lengths of a pair of corresponding altitudes, in the order given.

3. The lengths of two corresponding sides of two similar triangles are 8 in. and 12 in. If an altitude of the smaller triangle has a length of 6 in., find the length of the corresponding altitude of the larger triangle.

4. The ratio of similitude in two similar triangles is 4:3. If the length of a median in the larger triangle is 12 in., find the length of the corresponding median in the smaller triangle.

5. The ratio of the lengths of the corresponding sides of two similar triangles is 7:4. Find the ratio of the perimeters of the triangles.

6. Corresponding altitudes of two similar triangles have lengths of 9 mm and 6 mm. If the perimeter of the larger triangle is 24 mm, what is the perimeter of the smaller triangle?

7. In meters, the sides of a triangle measure 7, 9, and 11. Find the perimeter of a similar triangle in which the shortest side has a length of 21 meters.

8. In inches, the lengths of the sides of a triangle are 8, 10, and 12. If the length of the shortest side of a similar triangle is 6 inches, find the length of its longest side.

9. A vertical pole 10 ft. high casts a shadow 8 ft. long, and at the same time a nearby tree casts a shadow 40 ft. long. What is the height of the tree?

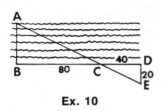

Ex. 10

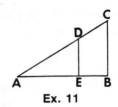

Ex. 11

10. AB represents the width of a river. $\overline{AE}$ and $\overline{BD}$ intersect at C, $\overline{AB} \perp \overline{BD}$, and $\overline{ED} \perp \overline{BD}$. If $BC = 80$ yd., $CD = 40$ yd., and $DE = 20$ yd., find AB.

11. In $\triangle ABC$, $\overline{DE} \perp \overline{AB}$ and $\overline{CB} \perp \overline{AB}$. If $CB = 40$ m, $DE = 30$ m, and $EB = 20$ m, find AE.

In 12–15, select the numeral preceding the expression that answers the question or completes the sentence.

12. Corresponding altitudes of two similar triangles measure 6 and 14. If the perimeter of the first triangle is 21, what is the perimeter of the second triangle?   (1) 9 (2) 27 (3) 49 (4) 64

13. In $\triangle RST$, $\overline{AB}$ joins points A and B on $\overline{RS}$ and $\overline{ST}$, respectively. If $\overline{AB} \parallel \overline{RT}$ and AB is one-third as long as RT, then the ratio of the perimeter of $\triangle ASB$ to the perimeter of $\triangle RST$ is:
(1) $\frac{1}{12}$ (2) $\frac{1}{9}$ (3) $\frac{1}{3}$ (4) $\frac{1}{6}$

14. The sides of a triangle have lengths 6, 8, and 10. What is the length of the *shortest* side of a similar triangle that has a perimeter of 12?
(1) 6 (2) 8 (3) 3 (4) 4

15. Two triangles are similar. The sides of the smaller triangle have lengths of 6, 7, and 12. The perimeter of the larger triangle is 75. The length of the *shortest* side of the larger triangle is:
(1) 18 (2) 2 (3) 36 (4) 4

16. Triangle DEF is similar to triangle $D'E'F'$. $\angle D$ corresponds to $\angle D'$ and $\angle E$ corresponds to $\angle E'$. If $DE = 2x + 2$, $DF = 5x - 7$, $D'E' = 2$, and $D'F' = 3$, find DE and DF.

17. In two similar triangles, the ratio of the lengths of two corresponding sides is 5:8. If the perimeter of the larger triangle is 10 feet less than twice the perimeter of the smaller triangle, find the perimeter of each triangle.

18. In triangle ABC, a line parallel to $\overline{AB}$ intersects $\overline{AC}$ at D and $\overline{CB}$ at E. If $CD = 6$, $DA = 12$, and AB is 8 less than 4 times DE, find DE and AB.

19. In yards, the sides of a triangle measure 10, 12, and 15. A segment whose length is 5 yards is parallel to the longest side of the triangle and has its endpoints on the other two sides of the triangle. Find the lengths of the two segments formed on the side of the triangle measuring 12 yards.

7-9 PROPORTIONS IN THE RIGHT TRIANGLE

Projection of a Point or of a Line Segment on a Line

Imagine that a bright light is on the ceiling of a room. Think of a line segment that might exist in the room (such as the edge of a book or a pencil) or a point that might exist in the room (such as the tip of the pencil) directly under the light. The *projection* of the line segment or the *projection* of the point will be suggested by the shadow formed on the floor of the room.

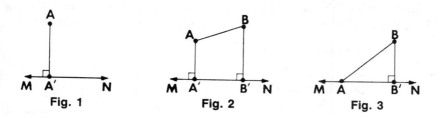

Fig. 1   Fig. 2   Fig. 3

● **Definition.** The *projection of a given point on a given line* is the foot of the perpendicular drawn from the given point to the given line.

In Fig. 1, point A' is the projection of point A on line $\overleftrightarrow{MN}$.

● **Definition.** The *projection of a segment on a given line,* when the segment is not perpendicular to the line, is the segment whose endpoints are the projections of the endpoints of the given line segment on the given line.

In Fig. 2, $\overline{A'B'}$ is the projection of $\overline{AB}$ on $\overleftrightarrow{MN}$.
In Fig. 3, $\overline{AB'}$ is the projection of $\overline{AB}$ on $\overleftrightarrow{MN}$.

Note. When the segment is perpendicular to the given line, the projection of the segment on the given line is a point.

Proportions in the Right Triangle

In the figure, $\triangle ABC$ is a right triangle with $\angle C$ as the right angle. Altitude $\overline{CD}$ is drawn to hypotenuse $\overline{AB}$ so that two smaller triangles are formed, $\triangle ACD$ and $\triangle CBD$.

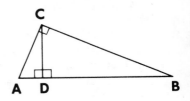

Notice that:

1. $\triangle ACD$ and $\triangle CBD$ are right triangles because $\overline{CD} \perp \overline{AB}$, and these segments intersect to form right angles, namely, $\angle CDA$ and $\angle CDB$.
2. $\overline{AD}$ is the *projection* of $\overline{AC}$ on the line, $\overleftrightarrow{AB}$. Also, $\overline{DB}$ is the *projection* of $\overline{CB}$ on the line, $\overleftrightarrow{AB}$.

● **THEOREM 57. If the altitude is drawn to the hypotenuse of a right triangle, then:**

a. The two triangles formed are similar to the given triangle and similar to each other.

b. The length of each leg of the given triangle is the mean proportional between the length of the whole hypotenuse and the length of the projection of that leg on the hypotenuse.

c. The length of the altitude is the mean proportional between the lengths of the projections of the legs on the hypotenuse.

Given: $\triangle ABC$ with right $\angle ACB$, $\overline{CD} \perp \overline{AB}$.

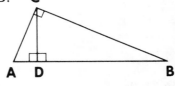

Prove: **a.** $\triangle ACD \sim \triangle ABC$.
$\triangle CBD \sim \triangle ABC$.
$\triangle ACD \sim \triangle CBD$.

b. $AB:AC = AC:AD$.
$AB:BC = BC:BD$.

c. $AD:CD = CD:BD$.

Plan: Using a.a. $\cong$ a.a., show that both $\triangle ACD$ and $\triangle CBD$ are similar to $\triangle ABC$ and, thus, to each other. The proportions follow.

Statements	*Reasons*
1. $\triangle ABC$ with right $\angle ACB$, $\overline{CD} \perp \overline{AB}$.	1. Given.
2. $\angle ADC$ and $\angle BDC$ are right angles.	2. Definition of perpendicular lines.
3. In $\triangle ACD$ and $\triangle ABC$: $\angle ADC \cong \angle ACB$ and $\angle A \cong \angle A$.	3. All right angles are congruent; reflexive property of congruence.

4. $\triangle ACD \sim \triangle ABC$.	4. a.a. $\cong$ a.a.
5. In $\triangle CBD$ and $\triangle ABC$: $\angle CDB \cong \angle ACB$ and $\angle B \cong \angle B$.	5. Reason 3.
6. $\triangle CBD \sim \triangle ABC$.	6. a.a. $\cong$ a.a.
7. $\triangle ACD \sim \triangle CBD$.	7. Transitive property of similarity.
8. $\triangle ABC \sim \triangle ACD \rightarrow AB{:}AC = AC{:}AD.$ $\triangle ABC \sim \triangle CBD \rightarrow AB{:}BC = BC{:}BD.$ $\triangle ACD \sim \triangle CBD \rightarrow AD{:}CD = CD{:}BD.$	8. Corresponding sides of similar triangles are in proportion.

MODEL PROBLEMS

1. In right triangle ABC, altitude $\overline{CD}$ is drawn on hypotenuse $\overline{AB}$. If $AD = 6$ cm and $DB = 24$ cm, find **(a)** CD and **(b)** AC.

Solution: Since $\overline{CD} \perp$ hypotenuse $\overline{AB}$ in right triangle ABC, then:

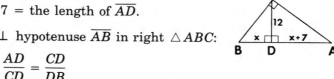

a. $\dfrac{AD}{CD} = \dfrac{CD}{DB}$

Let $x =$ length of $\overline{CD}$.

$\dfrac{6}{x} = \dfrac{x}{24}$

$x^2 = 144$

$x = 12$

Answer: $CD = 12$ cm

b. $\dfrac{AD}{AC} = \dfrac{AC}{AB}$

Let $y =$ length of $\overline{AC}$.

$\dfrac{6}{y} = \dfrac{y}{30}$

$y^2 = 180$

$y = \sqrt{180} = \sqrt{36} \cdot \sqrt{5} = 6\sqrt{5}$

Answer: $AC = 6\sqrt{5}$ cm

Note that since x and y represent the lengths of line segments, we use only the positive values of the square roots.

2. In right triangle ABC, altitude $\overline{CD}$ is drawn to hypotenuse $\overline{AB}$. If $CD = 12$ in. and AD exceeds DB by 7 in., find DB and AD.

Solution

(1) Let $x =$ the length of $\overline{DB}$.

Then, $x + 7 =$ the length of $\overline{AD}$.

(2) Since $\overline{CD} \perp$ hypotenuse $\overline{AB}$ in right $\triangle ABC$:

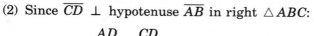

$$\dfrac{AD}{CD} = \dfrac{CD}{DB}$$

(3) Substitute.

$$\frac{x + 7}{12} = \frac{12}{x}$$

(4) Solve for x.

$$x(x + 7) = 12(12)$$
$$x^2 + 7x = 144$$
$$x^2 + 7x - 144 = 0$$
$$(x - 9)(x + 16) = 0$$

$$x - 9 = 0 \quad | \quad x + 16 = 0$$
$$x = 9 \quad | \quad \quad x = -16$$

| Reject the negative value.

(5) Then, $x + 7 = 9 + 7 = 16$.

Answer: $DB = 9$ in., and $AD = 16$ in.

EXERCISES

In 1–5, $\triangle ABC$ is a right triangle with the
right angle at C and altitude $\overline{CD} \perp \overline{AB}$ at point D.
Name the length that would replace the question
mark and make the sentence true.

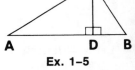

1. $\dfrac{AD}{DC} = \dfrac{?}{DB}$ 2. $\dfrac{AD}{AC} = \dfrac{?}{AB}$

Ex. 1–5

3. $\dfrac{?}{BC} = \dfrac{BC}{AB}$ 4. $DB:BC = BC:\underline{\ ?\ }$ 5. $AD:\underline{\ ?\ } = \underline{\ ?\ }:DB$

In 6–10, find the mean proportional for each pair of numbers.

6. 1, 16   **7.** 2, 18   **8.** 4, 36   **9.** 5, 10   **10.** $2\sqrt{5}, 10\sqrt{5}$

In 11–20, $\triangle ABC$ is a right triangle, $\angle C$ is a
right angle, and altitude $\overline{CD} \perp \overline{AB}$.

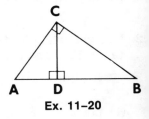

11. If $AD = 3$ and $CD = 6$, find DB.
12. If $AB = 8$ and $AC = 4$, find AD.
13. If $AC = 10$ and $AD = 5$, find AB.
14. If $AC = 6$ and $AB = 9$, find AD.
15. If $AD = 4$ and $DB = 9$, find CD.
16. If $DB = 4$ and $BC = 10$, find AB.
17. If $AD = 3$ and $DB = 27$, find CD.
18. If $AD = 2$ and $AB = 18$, find AC.
19. If $DB = 8$ and $AB = 18$, find BC.
20. If $AD = 3$ and $DB = 9$, find AC.

Ex. 11–20

In 21–23, the altitude to the hypotenuse of a right triangle divides the hypotenuse into two segments.

21. If the lengths of the segments are 5 inches and 20 inches, find the length of the altitude.

22. If the length of the altitude is 8 feet and the length of the shorter segment is 2 feet, find the length of the longer segment.

23. If the ratio of the lengths of the segments is 1:9 and the length of the altitude is 6 meters, find the lengths of the two segments.

In 24–26, select the numeral preceding the correct answer.

24. The altitude drawn to the hypotenuse of a right triangle divides the hypotenuse into two segments of lengths 4 and 5. What is the length of the altitude? (1) 20 (2) $\sqrt{20}$ (3) $4\sqrt{5}$ (4) $5\sqrt{2}$

25. If the altitude to the hypotenuse of a right triangle measures 8, the segments of the hypotenuse formed by the altitude may measure (1) 8 and 12 (2) 2 and 32 (3) 3 and 24 (4) 6 and 8

26. The altitude drawn to the hypotenuse of a right triangle divides the hypotenuse into segments of lengths 2 and 16. Then
(1) the altitude measures 4   (2) the altitude measures 6
(3) one leg measures 4   (4) one leg measures 6

27. In a right triangle whose hypotenuse measures 50 units, the shorter leg measures 30 units. Find the measure of the projection of the shorter leg on the hypotenuse.

28. In inches, the segments formed by the altitude on the hypotenuse of right $\triangle ABC$ measure 8 and 10. Find the length of the shorter leg of $\triangle ABC$.

29. In right $\triangle ABC$, $\overline{CD}$ is the altitude drawn to hypotenuse $\overline{AB}$. If $CD = 6$, $AD = 3$, and $DB = 5x - 3$, find x.

30. $\overline{CD}$ is the altitude on hypotenuse $\overline{AB}$ of right triangle ABC. $AC = 12$ and $AD = 6$. If BD is represented by x, write an equation that can be used to find x. Solve this equation for x.

31. ABC is a right triangle with $\overline{CD}$ the altitude on hypotenuse $\overline{AB}$. If $AC = 20$ and $AB = 25$, find: **a.** AD **b.** DB **c.** CD **d.** BC

32. In right $\triangle ABC$, $\overline{CD}$ is the altitude to hypotenuse $\overline{AB}$. The length of $\overline{DB}$ is 5 units longer than the length of $\overline{AD}$.
a. If $AD = x$, express the length of $\overline{DB}$ in terms of x.
b. If $CD = 6$, write an equation in terms of x to find AD.
c. Find AD by solving the equation written in part **b**.
d. Find AC. (Answer may be left in radical form.)

33. In right triangle ABC, $\overline{CD}$ is the altitude to hypotenuse $\overline{AB}$. If $CD = 3$ cm, and if DB exceeds AD by 8 cm, find AD and DB.

34. In right $\triangle RST$, $\overline{TP}$ is the altitude to hypotenuse $\overline{RS}$. If the length of $\overline{PS}$ is 9 units more than the length of $\overline{RP}$, and if $TP = 6$, find RP and PS.

35. In right triangle ABC, $\overline{CD}$ is the altitude to hypotenuse $\overline{AB}$, $AD = 21$ ft., and $CB = 10$ ft.
    a. Let $DB = x$. Write and solve an equation to find DB.
    b. Find the length of $\overline{CD}$, expressed in radical form.

36. In right triangle ABC, $\overline{BD}$ is the altitude to hypotenuse $\overline{AC}$, $BD = 4$ yd., and $AC = 10$ yd.
    a. If $CD = x$, what expression in terms of x represents AD?
    b. Write an equation that can be used to solve for x.
    c. Find the lengths of $\overline{CD}$ and $\overline{AD}$, formed on the hypotenuse.

7-10   THE PYTHAGOREAN THEOREM AND ITS APPLICATIONS

We are now prepared to prove the famous Pythagorean Theorem, which you have studied in earlier courses. Notice how the proof that follows is based upon concepts involving similar triangles.

● **THEOREM 58.   If a triangle is a right triangle, then the square of the length of the longest side (the hypotenuse) is equal to the sum of the squares of the lengths of the other two sides (the legs).**

Given: $\triangle ABC$ is a right triangle, $\angle ACB$ is a right angle, c = length of hypotenuse, a and b = lengths of the legs.

Prove: $c^2 = a^2 + b^2$.

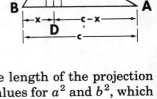

Plan: Draw $\overline{CD}$, the altitude to hypotenuse $\overline{AB}$. Since $\triangle ABC$ is a right triangle, the length of each leg is the mean proportional between the length of the hypotenuse and the length of the projection of that leg on the hypotenuse. This gives us values for a^2 and b^2, which are then added to show that $a^2 + b^2 = c^2$.

Statements	*Reasons*
1. $\triangle ABC$ is a right triangle. $\angle ACB$ is a right angle.	1. Given.
2. Draw $\overline{CD} \perp \overline{AB}$. Let $BD = x$ and $AD = c - x$.	2. From a point not on a given line, one and only one perpendicular can be drawn to the given line.

3. $\dfrac{c}{a} = \dfrac{a}{x}$ and $\dfrac{c}{b} = \dfrac{b}{c-x}$.

3. If the altitude is drawn to the hypotenuse of a right triangle, the length of each leg is the mean proportional between the lengths of the hypotenuse and the projection of that leg on the hypotenuse.

4. $cx = a^2$ and $c^2 - cx = b^2$.

4. In a proportion, the product of the means is equal to the product of the extremes.

5. $c^2 = a^2 + b^2$.

5. If equal quantities are added to equal quantities, the sums are equal quantities.

Pythagorean Triples

Let us find the length of the hypotenuse of a right triangle whose legs measure 3 and 4.

$$c^2 = a^2 + b^2$$
$$c^2 = (3)^2 + (4)^2$$
$$c^2 = 9 + 16$$
$$c^2 = 25$$
$$c = 5$$

The length of the hypotenuse is 5.

When three integers are so related that the sum of the squares of two of them is equal to the square of the third, the set of three integers is called a *Pythagorean triple*. For example, (3, 4, 5) is called a Pythagorean triple because the numbers 3, 4, and 5 satisfy the relation $a^2 + b^2 = c^2$.

In general, if we multiply each number of a Pythagorean triple by some positive number x, then the new triple created is also a Pythagorean triple because it will satisfy the relation $a^2 + b^2 = c^2$. For example:

If (3, 4, 5) is a Pythagorean triple, then $(3x, 4x, 5x)$ is also a Pythagorean triple for a similar triangle where the ratio of similitude of the second triangle to the first triangle is $x:1$.

Let $x = 2$. Then $(3x, 4x, 5x) = (6, 8, 10)$ and $6^2 + 8^2 = 10^2$.

Let $x = 3$. Then $(3x, 4x, 5x) = (9, 12, 15)$, and $9^2 + 12^2 = 15^2$.

Let $x = 10$. Then $(3x, 4x, 5x) = (30, 40, 50)$, and $30^2 + 40^2 = 50^2$.

Thus, if the lengths of the legs of the right triangle are 30 and 40, you might recognize quickly that these are multiples of the first two numbers of the (3, 4, 5) Pythagorean triple. Thus, $x = 10$ and the length of the hypotenuse $= 5 \cdot 10 = 50$.

Other examples of Pythagorean triples that occur frequently are:

(5, 12, 13) or, in general, ($5x$, $12x$, $13x$) where x is a positive integer.

(8, 15, 17) or, in general, ($8x$, $15x$, $17x$) where x is a positive integer.

With a knowledge of these Pythagorean triples, you can solve some right triangle problems without writing out a lengthy algebraic solution.

The Converse of the Pythagorean Theorem

Once we know the lengths of the three sides of a triangle, we can determine if the triangle is a right triangle or not by using the Pythagorean Theorem or its *converse*.

● **THEOREM 59. If the square of the length of one side of a triangle is equal to the sum of the squares of the lengths of the other two sides, then the triangle is a right triangle.**

Given: $\triangle ABC$ whose sides have lengths a, b, c, where $c^2 = a^2 + b^2$.

Prove: $\triangle ABC$ is a right triangle, $\angle C$ being the right angle.

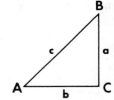

Plan: Draw right $\triangle RST$ where $\angle T$ is a right angle, $TS = a$, and $TR = b$. From the relation $c^2 = a^2 + b^2$, it follows that $RS = c$. Then, $\triangle ABC \cong \triangle RST$ by s.s.s. $\cong$ s.s.s., and corresponding $\angle C$ is a right angle. Therefore, $\triangle ABC$ is a right triangle.

Applications of this theorem are seen in the following problems:

1. In a triangle, the lengths of the sides are 8, 15, and 17. Is this a right triangle?
Let $c = 17$, the longest side.
Let $a = 8$ and $b = 15$.

$$c^2 \overset{?}{=} a^2 + b^2$$
$$17^2 \overset{?}{=} 8^2 + 15^2$$
$$289 \overset{?}{=} 64 + 225$$
$$289 = 289$$

Answer: Since $c^2 = a^2 + b^2$, this triangle is a right triangle.

2. In a triangle, the lengths of the sides are 7, 8, and 12. Is this a right triangle?
Let $c = 12$, the longest side.
Let $a = 7$ and $b = 8$.

$$c^2 \overset{?}{=} a^2 + b^2$$
$$12^2 \overset{?}{=} 7^2 + 8^2$$
$$144 \overset{?}{=} 49 + 64$$
$$144 \neq 113$$

Answer: Since $c^2 \neq a^2 + b^2$, this triangle is not a right triangle.

MODEL PROBLEMS

1. In a right triangle, the length of the hypotenuse is 20 cm and the length of one leg is 16 cm. Find the length of the other leg.

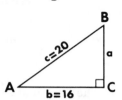

Solution:
$$a^2 + b^2 = c^2$$
$$a^2 + (16)^2 = (20)^2$$
$$a^2 + 256 = 400$$
$$a^2 = 144$$
$$a = 12$$

Answer: The length of the other leg is 12 cm.

Note. By recognizing that the length of the hypotenuse $20 = 5 \cdot 4$ and the length of the leg $16 = 4 \cdot 4$, we could have used the Pythagorean triple $(3x, 4x, 5x)$ to find the length of the other leg, namely, $3x = 3 \cdot 4 = 12$.

2. In an isosceles triangle, the length of each of the congruent sides is $3\sqrt{5}$ ft. and the length of the base is 12 ft. Find the length of the altitude drawn to the base.

Solution: In isosceles triangle ABC, altitude $\overline{BD} \perp \overline{AC}$ and $\overline{BD}$ bisects $\overline{AC}$. Therefore, $\triangle BDC$ is a right triangle with hypotenuse $\overline{BC}$; $BC = 3\sqrt{5}$ and $DC = 6$.

Let $x =$ the length of altitude $\overline{BD}$.

$$(x)^2 + (6)^2 = (3\sqrt{5})^2$$
$$x^2 + 36 = 45$$
$$x^2 = 9$$
$$x = 3$$

Note that $(3\sqrt{5})^2 = 3^2 (\sqrt{5})^2 = 9(5) = 45$.

Answer: The length of the altitude drawn to the base is 3 ft.

3. In inches, the lengths of the diagonals of a rhombus are 30 and 40. Find **(a)** the length of one side of the rhombus and **(b)** the perimeter of the rhombus.

Solution: Since the diagonals of a rhombus are perpendicular to each other and bisect each other, $\triangle AEB$ is a right triangle in which $EB = \frac{1}{2} (30)$, or 15, and $AE = \frac{1}{2} (40)$, or 20.

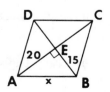

a. Let $x = AB$.

$$x^2 = (20)^2 + (15)^2$$
$$x^2 = 400 + 225$$
$$x^2 = 625$$
$$x = 25$$

b. Since the four sides of a rhombus are equal in length:

$$\text{perimeter} = 4(25)$$
$$= 100$$

Answer: **a.** The length of one side is 25 inches.
b. The perimeter is 100 inches.

4. The length of a rectangle is 7 meters more than its width. A diagonal of the rectangle measures 17 meters. Use algebraic methods to find the width and length of the rectangle.

   Solution: When a diagonal is drawn in a rectangle, two right triangles are formed. The diagonal is the hypotenuse of each of these right triangles.

   Let $x =$ the width of the rectangle.
   Let $x + 7 =$ the length of the rectangle.

   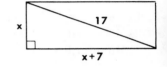

   By the Pythagorean Theorem:

$$a^2 + b^2 = c^2$$
$$(x)^2 + (x + 7)^2 = 17^2$$
$$x^2 + x^2 + 14x + 49 = 289$$
$$2x^2 + 14x + 49 = 289$$
$$2x^2 + 14x - 240 = 0$$
$$2(x^2 + 7x - 120) = 0$$
$$2(x + 15)(x - 8) = 0$$

$x + 15 = 0$	$x - 8 = 0$
$x = -15$	$x = 8$
Reject the negative value.	

Then, $x + 7 = 8 + 7 = 15$.

Check:

$$8^2 + 15^2 \overset{?}{=} 17^2$$
$$64 + 225 \overset{?}{=} 289$$
$$289 = 289 \quad \text{(true)}$$

Answer: The width $= 8$ meters and the length $= 15$ meters.

EXERCISES

Note. In all exercises, irrational answers may be left in radical form.

In 1–15, use the information marked on the figure to find the value of x.

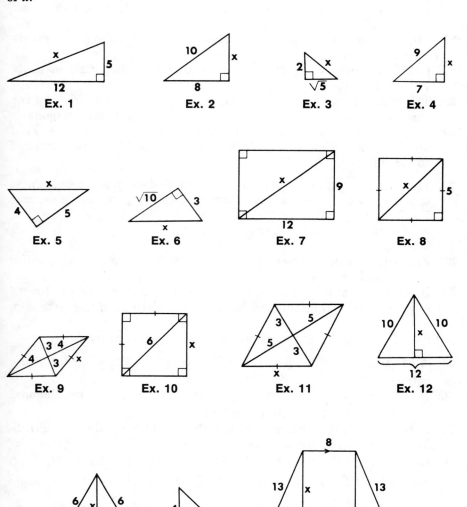

Ex. 1

Ex. 2

Ex. 3

Ex. 4

Ex. 5

Ex. 6

Ex. 7

Ex. 8

Ex. 9

Ex. 10

Ex. 11

Ex. 12

Ex. 13

Ex. 14

Ex. 15

In 16–27, the lengths of three sides of a triangle are given. Tell whether the triangle is or is not a right triangle.

16. 6, 8, 10   **17.** 7, 8, 12   **18.** 5, 7, 8
19. 10, 24, 26   **20.** 10, 15, 20   **21.** 7, 24, 25
22. 18, 24, 30   **23.** 20, 24, 31   **24.** 36, 48, 60
25. 4, $\sqrt{20}$, 6   **26.** 1, $\sqrt{3}$, 2   **27.** 4, 8, $4\sqrt{3}$

28. Find the length of the side of a rhombus whose diagonals measure 6 cm and 8 cm.
29. Find the length of a side of a rhombus whose diagonals measure 12 mm and 16 mm.
30. The length of each side of a rhombus is 13 feet. If the length of the shorter diagonal is 10 feet, find the length of the longer diagonal.
31. In yards, the diagonals of a rhombus measure 16 and 30. Find **(a)** the length of one side of the rhombus and **(b)** the perimeter of the rhombus.

32. The legs of a right triangle measure 3 cm and 4 cm. In another right triangle, one leg measures 4 cm and the hypotenuse measures 5 cm.
  a. Are the triangles congruent?
  b. Why?
33. Find the measure of the diagonal of a rectangle whose sides measure 14 mm and 48 mm.
34. If the length of the diagonal of a rectangle is 26 mm and the length of its base is 24 mm, find the length of the altitude of the rectangle.

In 35–38, write the numeral preceding the correct answer.

35. A square has a side of length 6. The length of the diagonal of the square is (1) 6 (2) $2\sqrt{6}$ (3) $6\sqrt{2}$ (4) 12
36. If the perimeter of a square is 20, then the length of its diagonal is (1) $5\sqrt{2}$ (2) $2\sqrt{5}$ (3) 10 (4) $10\sqrt{2}$
37. A rectangle has a diagonal of length 10 and one side of length 6. The perimeter of the rectangle is (1) 21 (2) 28 (3) 32 (4) 48
38. In right $\triangle ABC$, $\overline{CD}$ is the altitude on hypotenuse $\overline{AB}$. If $AC = 20$ and $CD = 12$, find AD. (1) 8 (2) 16 (3) 24 (4) $\sqrt{240}$

39. In rectangle $ABCD$, $\overline{EF}$ joins the midpoints of $\overline{AB}$ and $\overline{BC}$, respectively. If $BE = 8$ and $BF = 6$, find **(a)** EF, **(b)** AC, and **(c)** the perimeter of rectangle $ABCD$.

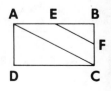

40. In an isosceles trapezoid, the lengths of the bases are 14 in. and 30 in. and the length of each of the nonparallel sides is 10 in. Find the length of the altitude of the trapezoid.

41. In right triangle ABD, the length of leg $\overline{AB}$ is 12 mm and the length of hypotenuse $\overline{AD}$ is 15 mm. C is a point on $\overline{DB}$. The length of $\overline{AC}$ is 13 mm. Find the length of $\overline{DC}$.

42. In feet, the lengths of two adjacent sides of a parallelogram are 21 and 28. If the length of a diagonal of the parallelogram is 35 feet, show that the parallelogram is a rectangle.

43. In right $\triangle ABC$, leg $\overline{CB}$ has a length of 8. The hypotenuse $\overline{AB}$ is 4 units longer than the leg $\overline{AC}$.
   a. Let $AC = x$. Then write an equation that can be used to find x.
   b. Find AC and AB.

44. In right triangle ABC, the length of hypotenuse $\overline{AB}$ is 2 units more than the length of leg $\overline{AC}$. If $BC = 10$, find the length of leg $\overline{AC}$.

45. In right $\triangle ABC$, $\angle C$ is a right angle. If AC is 3 cm more than BC, and AB is 6 cm more than BC, write and solve an algebraic equation to find the three lengths BC, AC, and AB.

46. In rectangle $ABCD$ with diagonal $\overline{AC}$, $AB = x$, $BC = x + 7$, and $AC = x + 8$. By means of an algebraic solution, find AC.

47. The length of a rectangle is 7 feet more than its width. The length of a diagonal of the rectangle is 9 feet more than the width. By algebraic methods, find the width of the rectangle.

48. The perimeter of a rectangle is 28 cm, and the length of a diagonal is 10 cm.
   a. If $x =$ the width of the rectangle, represent the length in terms of x.
   b. Use algebraic methods to find the number of centimeters in the width and length of the rectangle.

49. In $\square ABCD$, diagonals $\overline{AC}$ and $\overline{BD}$ intersect at E. $BC = 26$, $BE = 5x - 5$, $DE = 3x + 1$, $AE = 2y + 2$, and $CE = 4y - 20$.
   a. Find x and y.
   b. Show that $\square ABCD$ is a rhombus.

50. In isosceles trapezoid $ABCD$, the length of leg $\overline{DA}$ is 10 cm more than the length of shorter base $\overline{CD}$, and the length of longer base $\overline{AB}$ is 4 cm more than twice CD.
   a. If CD is represented by x, represent DA and AB in terms of x.
   b. If the perimeter of the trapezoid is 104 cm, find the value of x.
   c. Find the measure of the altitude of the trapezoid.
   d. Find the area of the trapezoid.

7-11 SPECIAL RIGHT TRIANGLES

The 30–60-Degree Right Triangle

In a special right triangle, called the 30–60-degree right triangle, we can find the lengths of all three sides when given the length of only one side. Let us develop the relationship of these sides by starting with an equilateral triangle.

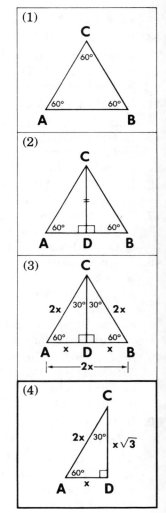

(1) In equilateral $\triangle ABC$, the measure of each angle is $60°$.

(2) Draw altitude $\overline{CD}$ to side $\overline{AB}$, forming two right angles at D. Since $\overline{AC} \cong \overline{BC}$, and $\overline{CD} \cong \overline{CD}$, it follows that $\triangle ADC \cong \triangle BDC$ by hy. leg $\cong$ hy. leg.

(3) Since $\triangle ADC \cong \triangle BDC$, their corresponding parts are congruent. Thus:
  a. $\angle ACD \cong \angle BCD$ and the measure of each of these angles is $30°$.
  b. $\overline{AD} \cong \overline{BD}$. Here, let $AD = x$, and $BD = x$. It follows that each side of equilateral triangle ABC has a length of $2x$.

(4) In right $\triangle ACD$, $\overline{AC}$ is the hypotenuse. Since $AD = x$ and $AC = 2x$, apply the Pythagorean Theorem to find the length of leg $\overline{CD}$:

$$(CD)^2 + (AD)^2 = (AC)^2$$
$$(CD)^2 + (x)^2 = (2x)^2$$
$$(CD)^2 + x^2 = 4x^2$$
$$(CD)^2 = 3x^2$$
$$CD = \sqrt{3x^2} = \sqrt{x^2} \cdot \sqrt{3}$$
$$CD = x\sqrt{3}$$

The final diagram shows the 30–60-degree right triangle and the following relationships:

1. If the side opposite the 30° angle has a length of x, then the side opposite the 60° angle has a length of $x\sqrt{3}$, and the side opposite the 90° angle has a length of $2x$.

2. The length of the hypotenuse is *twice* the length of the side opposite the 30° angle. Thus, the side opposite the 30° angle is *half* the length of the hypotenuse.

3. The length of the side opposite the 60° angle is equal to the length of the side opposite the 30° angle multiplied by $\sqrt{3}$.

MODEL PROBLEMS

1. Express in radical form the length of an altitude of an equilateral triangle whose side measures 12 cm.

Solution

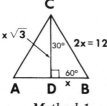

Method 1

Method 2

Draw altitude $\overline{CD}$, creating a 30–60-degree right triangle.	Draw altitude $\overline{CD}$, which bisects base $\overline{AB}$. Thus, $CB = 12$ and $DB = 6$. Let $h = $ length of altitude $\overline{CD}$.

Label the lengths of the sides as in the figure:

x (opposite 30° angle)
$2x$ (opposite 90° angle)
$x\sqrt{3}$ (opposite 60° angle)

Since $CB = 2x = 12$,
then $DB = x = 6$,
and $CD = x\sqrt{3} = 6\sqrt{3}$.

In right $\triangle CDB$, the Pythagorean Theorem states:

$$(h)^2 + (6)^2 = (12)^2$$
$$h^2 + 36 = 144$$
$$h^2 = 108$$
$$h = \sqrt{108} = \sqrt{36} \cdot \sqrt{3}$$
$$h = 6\sqrt{3}$$

Answer: The altitude measures $6\sqrt{3}$ cm.

2. In right $\triangle ABC$, m$\angle A = 30$, m$\angle B = 60$, and $AC = 6$ inches. Find BC to the *nearest tenth of an inch*.

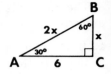

Solution

Method 1	*Method 2*

Method 1

Since the length of the hypotenuse is twice the length of the leg opposite the 30° angle:

Let x = the length of $\overline{BC}$.
Let $2x$ = the length of $\overline{AB}$.

$$(2x)^2 = (x)^2 + (6)^2$$
$$4x^2 = x^2 + 36$$
$$3x^2 = 36$$
$$x^2 = 12$$
$$x = \sqrt{12} = \sqrt{4} \cdot \sqrt{3}$$
$$x = 2\sqrt{3}$$

Method 2

Label the sides:

$BC = x$ (opposite 30° angle)
$AB = 2x$ (opposite 90° angle)
$AC = x\sqrt{3}$ (opposite 60° angle)

Since $AC = x\sqrt{3} = 6$:

$$\frac{x\sqrt{3}}{\sqrt{3}} = \frac{6}{\sqrt{3}}$$
$$x = \frac{6}{\sqrt{3}} \cdot \frac{\sqrt{3}}{\sqrt{3}}$$
$$x = \frac{6\sqrt{3}}{3} = 2\sqrt{3}$$

Since $\sqrt{3}$ is approximately 1.73:

$$x = 2(1.73) = 3.46$$
$$x = 3.5$$

Answer: $BC = 3.5$ inches, to the nearest tenth of an inch.

EXERCISES ───────────────────────────────

Note. In all exercises, irrational answers may be left in radical form unless otherwise indicated.

In 1–5, find the lengths of the segments marked x and y.

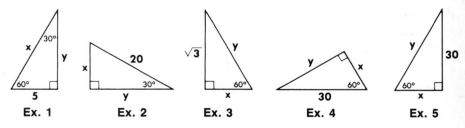

Ex. 1   Ex. 2   Ex. 3   Ex. 4   Ex. 5

6. Express in radical form the length of the altitude of an equilateral triangle whose side has a unit length of:
   a. 10   **b.** 16   **c.** 4   **d.** 7   **e.** 15   **f.** s

7. If one side of an equilateral triangle has a length of 6, the length of its altitude is (1) 6 (2) $3\sqrt{3}$ (3) 3 (4) $6\sqrt{3}$

8. If the altitude of an equilateral triangle measures $7\sqrt{3}$, then one side of the triangle measures (1) 7 (2) 14 (3) 21 (4) $14\sqrt{3}$

9. In inches, the lengths of two sides of a triangle are 10 and 14 and the angle included between these sides measures 30°. Find the length of the altitude on the side whose length is 14 inches.

10. In a right triangle, the measure of one acute angle is double the measure of the other acute angle. If the length of the shorter leg of the triangle is 3 cm, find the length of the hypotenuse.

11. If one angle of a right triangle measures 60° and the length of the hypotenuse is 8 cm, find the length of the side opposite the 60° angle, correct to the *nearest tenth of a centimeter*.

12. In an isosceles triangle ABC, the vertex angle C measures 120° and the length of $\overline{AC}$ is 8 inches. Find the length of the altitude on $\overline{AB}$. Find AB to the *nearest inch*.

13. In a rhombus that contains a 60° angle, the length of each side is 10 mm. Find the length of **(a)** the shorter diagonal and **(b)** the longer diagonal.

14. In $\triangle ABC$, $\angle B$ is a right angle, $\overline{DC} \cong \overline{DA}$, m$\angle CDB$ = 60, and DB = 5 yd.

Find the following measures:

   a. m$\angle DCB$ **b.** m$\angle CDA$
   c. m$\angle DCA$ **d.** m$\angle CAD$
   e. m$\angle ACB$ **f.** DC **g.** CB
   h. DA **i.** AC **j.** AB

In 15–19, $\triangle ABC$ is a right triangle with altitude $\overline{CD}$ drawn to hypotenuse $\overline{AB}$, m$\angle B$ = 60, and m$\angle A$ = 30.

15. If DB = 2 ft., find CB, AB, AD, CD, and AC.

16. If CB = 6 ft., find AB, DB, AD, CD, and AC.

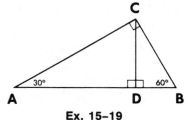

Ex. 15–19

17. If AB = 4, find CB, DB, AD, CD, and AC.

18. If AC = $8\sqrt{3}$, find CB, AB, DB, AD, and CD.

19. If CD = $6\sqrt{3}$, find DB, BC, AB, AD, and AC.

The Isosceles Right Triangle

In another special right triangle, called the 45–45-degree right triangle or the *isosceles right triangle*, we can find the lengths of all three sides when given the length of only one side. We can develop the relationships of these sides by starting with a square.

(1) In square *ABCD*, every angle has a measure of 90°, and all four sides are congruent.

(2) Draw diagonal $\overline{AC}$. Since $\angle ABC$ and $\angle ADC$ are right angles, $\overline{AB} \cong \overline{AD}$, and $\overline{AC} \cong \overline{AC}$, it follows that $\triangle ABC \cong \triangle ADC$ by hy. leg $\cong$ hy. leg.

(3) *a.* Since $\triangle ABC \cong \triangle ADC$, their corresponding angles are congruent. Thus, $\angle CAB \cong \angle CAD$, and $\angle ACB \cong \angle ACD$. Each of these angles measures 45°.
   b. Since all four sides of the square are congruent, let each side have a length *x*.

(4) In right $\triangle ABC$, $\overline{AC}$ is the hypotenuse. Since $AB = x$ and $BC = x$, apply the Pythagorean Theorem to find the length of hypotenuse $\overline{AC}$:

$$(AC)^2 = (AB)^2 + (BC)^2$$
$$(AC)^2 = x^2 + x^2$$
$$(AC)^2 = 2x^2$$
$$AC = \sqrt{2x^2} = \sqrt{x^2} \cdot \sqrt{2}$$
$$AC = x\sqrt{2}$$

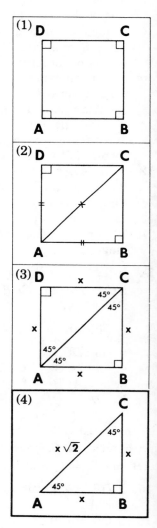

The final diagram shows the isosceles right triangle and the following relationships:

1. If each side opposite a 45° angle has a length of x, then the side opposite the 90° angle has a length of $x\sqrt{2}$.

2. In an isosceles right triangle, the length of the hypotenuse is equal to the length of a leg multiplied by $\sqrt{2}$.

MODEL PROBLEM

In square $ABCD$, the length of a side is 3 centimeters and $\overline{AC}$ is a diagonal. **a.** Find, in radical form, the number of centimeters in the length of $\overline{AC}$. **b.** Find AC, correct to the *nearest tenth of a centimeter.*

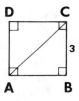

Solution

    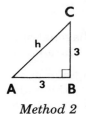

a.   *Method 1*   *Method 2*

In the isosceles right triangle formed by the diagonal of the square, label the length of each leg x and the length of the hypotenuse $x\sqrt{2}$.

Since $CB = AB = x = 3$:

$$AC = x\sqrt{2}$$
$$AC = 3\sqrt{2} \ \ Ans.$$

In square $ABCD$, $AB = 3$ and $BC = 3$. Let $h =$ the length of $\overline{AC}$. In right $\triangle ABC$, the Pythagorean Theorem states:

$$h^2 = (3)^2 + (3)^2$$
$$h^2 = 9 + 9$$
$$h^2 = 18$$
$$h = \sqrt{18} = \sqrt{9} \cdot \sqrt{2}$$
$$h = 3\sqrt{2} \ \ Ans.$$

b. Since $\sqrt{2}$ is approximately 1.41:

$$3\sqrt{2} = 3(1.41) = 4.23 = 4.2$$

Answer: $AC = 4.2$, to the nearest tenth of a centimeter.

EXERCISES

Note. In all exercises, irrational answers may be left in radical form unless otherwise indicated.

In 1–5, find the lengths of the segments marked x and y.

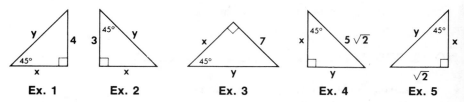

Ex. 1   **Ex. 2**   **Ex. 3**   **Ex. 4**   **Ex. 5**

6. What is the length of a side of a square whose diagonal has a measure of:
   a. $2\sqrt{2}$ **b.** $6\sqrt{2}$ **c.** $8\sqrt{2}$ **d.** $\sqrt{2}$ **e.** 4
7. What is the length of a diagonal of a square if the length of one of its sides is:
   a. 6   **b.** 2   **c.** 15   **d.** $3\sqrt{2}$ **e.** s
8. If the diagonal of a square has a length of $4\sqrt{2}$, then the perimeter of the square is (1) 8 (2) 16 (3) $16\sqrt{2}$ (4) 32

9. The length of a leg of an isosceles right triangle is 20 cm. Find the length of the hypotenuse **(a)** in radical form and **(b)** to the *nearest tenth of a centimeter.*
10. The lengths of the bases of an isosceles trapezoid are 7 in. and 15 in. Each leg makes an angle of 45° with the longer base. Find the length of the altitude of the trapezoid.
11. In square *PQRS*, diagonals $\overline{PR}$ and $\overline{QS}$ intersect at *M*. If *PM* = 3, find the length of **(a)** a diagonal of the square and **(b)** a side of the square.

Miscellaneous Problems With Both Special Right Triangles

In 12 and 13, $\triangle ABC$ is isosceles with base angles at *A* and *B*.

12. Find the length of side $\overline{AC}$ if altitude $\overline{CD}$ has a length of 6 and each base angle has a degree measure of:
    a. 30 **b.** 45 **c.** 60
13. Find the length of altitude $\overline{CD}$ if $AC = 18$ and each base angle has a degree measure of:
    a. 30 **b.** 45 **c.** 60

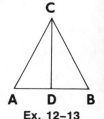

Ex. 12–13

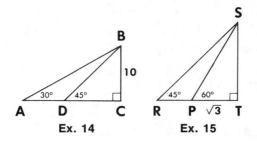

Ex. 14   Ex. 15

14. In △ABC, D is a point on $\overline{AC}$, m∠BDC = 45, m∠BAC = 30, and BC = 10. Find DC, DB, AB, and AC.

15. In △RST, P is a point on $\overline{RT}$, m∠SPT = 60, m∠SRT = 45, and PT = $\sqrt{3}$. Find PS, ST, RT, and RS.

7-12 REVIEW EXERCISES

1. B is a point on $\overline{AC}$ such that AB:BC = 2:3.
  a. Find the ratio BC:AB.
  b. Find the ratio AB:AC.
  c. If BC = 6, find AB.
  d. If AB = 6, find AC.

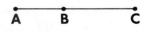

2. In △ABC, D is the midpoint of $\overline{AB}$, E is the midpoint of $\overline{BC}$, and $\overline{DE}$ is drawn.
  a. Answer true or false: $\overline{DE} \parallel \overline{AC}$
  b. If DE = 8, find AC.
  c. If m∠BDE = 70, find m∠BAC.
  d. What is the ratio of the perimeter of △DBE to the perimeter of △ABC?

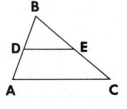

In 3–9, △ABC is given where D is a point on $\overline{AC}$, and E is a point on $\overline{CB}$ such that $\overline{DE} \parallel \overline{AB}$.

3. If CD = 8, DA = 4, and CE = 6, find EB.
4. If CE = 10, CB = 15, and CA = 12, find CD.
5. If CD = 6, DA = 3, and CB = 6, find CE.
6. If CE = 4, ED = 4, and BA = 6, find CB.
7. If CE = 6, ED = 6, and EB = 3, find BA.
8. If CD = 8, DA = 4, and AB = 15, find DE.
9. If CE = 6, EB = 3, and DE = 8, find AB.

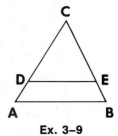

Ex. 3–9

10. In $\triangle RST$, A is a point on $\overline{RS}$, B is a point on $\overline{RT}$, and $\overline{AB}$ is drawn. $RA = 9$, $AS = 6$, and $RT = 10$. In order for $\overline{AB}$ to be parallel to $\overline{ST}$, what must be the length of $\overline{BT}$?

11. In rectangle $ABCD$, $\overline{EF}$ joins the midpoints of $\overline{AB}$ and $\overline{BC}$, respectively. If $BE = 5$ and $BF = 12$, find:
    a. EF
    b. AC
    c. the perimeter of rectangle $ABCD$

12. The sides of a triangle have lengths 4, 8, and 10. What is the length of the *shortest* side of a similar triangle that has a perimeter of 33?

In 13–16, $\triangle ABC$ is a right triangle and $\overline{CD}$ is the altitude drawn to hypotenuse $\overline{AB}$.

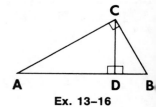

13. If $AD = 18$ and $DB = 2$, find CD.
14. If $DB = 4$ and $BC = 8$, find AB.
15. If $AC = 12$ and $AB = 18$, find AD.
16. If $AD = 20$ and $CD = 10$, find DB.

Ex. 13–16

17. The altitude to the hypotenuse of a right triangle divides the hypotenuse into two segments. If the length of the altitude is 6 and the length of the shorter segment is 4, **(a)** find the length of the longer segment and **(b)** find the length of the hypotenuse.

In 18–23, select the numeral preceding the expression that best completes the statement or answers the question.

18. The diagonals of a rhombus are 18 and 24. The length of a side of the rhombus is   (1) 15   (2) $15\sqrt{2}$ (3) $15\sqrt{3}$ (4) 30

19. The length of the altitude of an equilateral triangle whose side has a length of 10 is   (1) $5\sqrt{2}$ (2) $5\sqrt{3}$ (3) $10\sqrt{2}$ (4) $10\sqrt{3}$

20. The length of the diagonal of a square is $8\sqrt{2}$. The length of one side of the square is   (1) 16   (2) 8   (3) $16\sqrt{2}$ (4) 4

21. An acute angle of one right triangle is congruent to an acute angle of a second right triangle. The triangles are
    (1) congruent   (2) similar   (3) isosceles   (4) scalene

22. The lengths of the sides of a right triangle may be
    (1) 6, 7, 10   (2) 6, 8, 12   (3) 6, 8, 10   (4) 8, 12, 15

23. If the diagonal of a rectangle has a length of 25 and one of its sides has a length of 20, what is the perimeter of the rectangle?
    (1) 45   (2) 70   (3) 80   (4) 90

24. In rhombus *ABCD*, diagonals $\overline{AC}$ and $\overline{BD}$ intersect at *E*. The perimeter of the rhombus is 80 inches and ∠*ABC* measures 60°. Find the indicated measures.

    a. *AB*   **b.** m∠*AEB*   **c.** m∠*DAB*   **d.** m∠*DCA*

    e. *DE*   **f.** *DB*   **g.** m∠*ABD*   **h.** *AC*

    i. What kind of triangle is △*ADC*?

       (1) acute (2) right (3) obtuse (4) equilateral

25. *Solve by an algebraic equation:* In right triangle *ABC*, the length of hypotenuse $\overline{AC}$ is 5 ft. If *BC* exceeds *AB* by 1 ft., find the lengths of $\overline{AB}$ and $\overline{BC}$.

26. In a rectangle, the length is 7 cm more than the width. The diagonal of the rectangle is 8 cm more than the width. If *x* represents the width, write and solve an algebraic equation to find the width of the rectangle.

27. In right triangle *ABC*, altitude $\overline{CD}$ is drawn to hypotenuse $\overline{AB}$, *CD* = 6, and *BD* exceeds *AD* by 5.

    a. If *AD* = *x*, express *BD* in terms of *x*.

    b. Write and solve an equation to find *AD*.

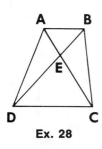

Ex. 28

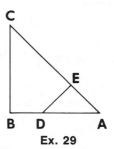

Ex. 29

28. In trapezoid *ABCD*, $\overline{AB} \parallel \overline{DC}$ and diagonals $\overline{AC}$ and $\overline{BD}$ meet at *E*.

    Prove: **a.** △*ABE* ~ △*CDE*.   **b.** $\dfrac{BE}{EA} = \dfrac{DE}{EC}$.

29. *Given:* $\overline{AB} \perp \overline{BC}, \overline{DE} \perp \overline{AC}$.

    Prove: **a.** △*ADE* ~ △*ACB*.   **b.** *AD* × *AB* = *AE* × *AC*.

30. In acute △*ABC*, $\overline{AD}$ and $\overline{BE}$ are altitudes.

    Prove: *AD* × *BC* = *BE* × *AC*.

Chapter 8

Trigonometry of the Right Triangle

In this chapter, you will study a branch of mathematics called *trigonometry.* The word *trigonometry*, Greek in origin, means *measurement of triangles.* Since right triangles and their measurements are an important part of trigonometry, you will see how this branch of mathematics relates to geometry.

8-1 DIRECT AND INDIRECT MEASURE

Many mathematical problems involve the measurement of line segments and angles. When we use a ruler to measure the length of a segment or we use a protractor to measure an angle, we are taking a *direct measurement* of the segment or the angle.

However, in many situations, it is inconvenient or impossible to directly measure an object. For example, it is difficult to answer the following questions by use of direct measure:

> What is the height of a tall tree?
> What is the width of a river?
> What is the distance to the sun?

We can answer these questions by using methods that involve *indirect measurement.* Starting with some known lengths of segments or angle measures, we make use of a formula or a mathematical relationship to *indirectly* find the measurement in question. In geometry, when we worked with similar triangles and the Pythagorean Theorem, we used indirect measurement.

In your study of trigonometry of the right triangle, you will discover ways in which the similarity of triangles will provide additional methods for measuring segments and angles indirectly. Engineers, surveyors, physicists, and astronomers frequently use these trigonometric methods in their work.

8-2   THE TANGENT RATIO

Naming Sides

In a right triangle, the *hypotenuse*, which is the longest side, is opposite the right angle. The remaining sides in a right triangle are called the legs. However, in trigonometry of the right triangle, we call these legs the *opposite* side and the *adjacent* side to describe the relationship of these sides to one of the acute angles in the triangle.

Notice that △ABC is the same right triangle in both figures below, but the position names we apply to the legs change with respect to the angles.

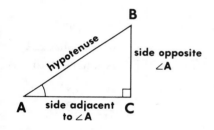

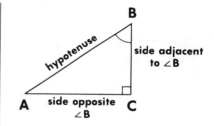

In △ABC: $\overline{BC}$ is *opposite* ∠A;
$\overline{AC}$ is *adjacent* to ∠A.

In △ABC: $\overline{AC}$ is *opposite* ∠B;
$\overline{BC}$ is *adjacent* to ∠B.

Similar Triangles

Three right triangles are drawn to coincide at vertex A. Since each triangle contains a right angle as well as ∠A, we know that all three triangles are *similar* by a.a. ≅ a.a.:

$$\triangle ABC \sim \triangle ADE \sim \triangle AFG$$

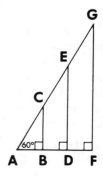

Also, since corresponding sides of similar triangles are in proportion, we can say:

$$\frac{CB}{BA} = \frac{ED}{DA} = \frac{GF}{FA}$$

Notice that the measure of $\angle A$ is $60°$. Thus, each of these similar triangles is a 30–60-degree right triangle. In the previous chapter, you learned that when the side opposite the $30°$ angle measures x, then the side opposite the $60°$ angle measures $x\sqrt{3}$. In the triangles shown here, the side opposite the $30°$ angle is the *adjacent* side to the $60°$ angle, or the *adjacent* side of $\angle A$.

The triangles seen in the preceding figure are now separated and two lengths are indicated for each triangle.

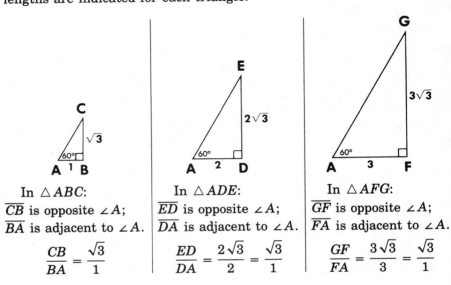

In $\triangle ABC$:

$\overline{CB}$ is opposite $\angle A$;
$\overline{BA}$ is adjacent to $\angle A$.

$$\frac{CB}{BA} = \frac{\sqrt{3}}{1}$$

In $\triangle ADE$:

$\overline{ED}$ is opposite $\angle A$;
$\overline{DA}$ is adjacent to $\angle A$.

$$\frac{ED}{DA} = \frac{2\sqrt{3}}{2} = \frac{\sqrt{3}}{1}$$

In $\triangle AFG$:

$\overline{GF}$ is opposite $\angle A$;
$\overline{FA}$ is adjacent to $\angle A$.

$$\frac{GF}{FA} = \frac{3\sqrt{3}}{3} = \frac{\sqrt{3}}{1}$$

In all three triangles, the angle referred to in naming the sides is a $60°$ angle. We see that the ratio of the lengths of the opposite and adjacent sides is $\dfrac{\sqrt{3}}{1}$, a constant value. Thus, the ratio is:

$$\frac{\text{length of the side } opposite \text{ the } 60° \text{ angle}}{\text{length of the side } adjacent \text{ to the } 60° \text{ angle}} = \frac{\sqrt{3}}{1} = \sqrt{3}$$

This ratio will be constant for a $60°$ angle in any right triangle, no matter how large or how small the sides of the triangles are.

What we have shown to be true for a $60°$ angle will also be true for any other acute angle in a right triangle. The ratio comparing the two lengths, *opposite* to *adjacent*, will always be a constant value for a specific acute angle—no matter what the size of the triangle. This ratio is called the *tangent of the angle.*

● **Definition.** The *tangent of an acute angle of a right triangle* is the ratio of the length of the side opposite the acute angle to the length of the side adjacent to the acute angle.

In right triangle ABC, with $m\angle C = 90$, the definition of the *tangent of angle A* is:

$$\text{tangent } A = \frac{\text{length of side opposite } \angle A}{\text{length of side adjacent to } \angle A} = \frac{BC}{AC} = \frac{a}{b}$$

Using *tan A* as an abbreviation for tangent A, and realizing that we are comparing lengths, we shorten the wording to say:

$$\tan A = \frac{\text{opposite}}{\text{adjacent}} = \frac{BC}{AC} = \frac{a}{b}$$

The Table of Tangents

As the measure of angle A changes, the tangent ratio for angle A also changes. The tangent ratio for angle A depends upon the measure of angle A, not upon the size of the right triangle that contains angle A. Mathematicians have found it useful to list the tangent ratios for acute angles. A table, which is called a table of trigonometric function values, is found on page 696. The tangent ratios are found in the fourth column.

To find tan 28° from this table, for example, first look in the column headed "Angle" for the angle 28°. Then, in the column headed "Tangent," on the same horizontal line as 28°, find the number .5317. Thus, tan 28° = .5317 to the *nearest ten-thousandth*.

Earlier we saw that in a 30–60-degree right triangle,

$$\tan 60° = \frac{\text{opposite}}{\text{adjacent}} = \frac{\sqrt{3}}{1}, \text{ or } \sqrt{3}.$$

Recall that $\sqrt{3}$ is an irrational number. An approximate rational value for $\sqrt{3}$ to the *nearest ten-thousandth* is 1.7321, or $\sqrt{3} \approx 1.7321$. In the table, notice that tan 60° = 1.7321.

Note. In our trigonometry work, we will use the symbol for equality, =, rather than the symbol for approximation, $\approx$. However, be aware that trigonometric ratios in the tables are, for the most part, approximations.

The table may also be used to find the measure of an angle when its tangent ratio is known. Thus, if tan A = 1.5399, we see from the table that angle A must contain 57°.

Sometimes the value of the tangent of an angle is not in the table. In such a case, we can estimate the measure of the angle to the *nearest degree*. For example, suppose we wish to find the measure of angle A when tan A = .5000. This value is not in the table of tangent ratios.

Step 1	*Step 2*	*Step 3*
Locate tangent values just larger and just smaller than .5000.	Since tan A = .5000, 26 < m∠A < 27.	Find the *differences* in the tangents.

Step 1

Angle	Tangent
26°	.4877
27°	.5095

Step 2

Angle	Tangent
26°	.4877
A	.5000
27°	.5095

Step 3

.5000 − .4877 = .0123

.5095 − .5000 = .0095

Step 4: Since .0095 is a smaller difference than .0123, then .5000 is closer to .5095, and m∠A is closer to 27 than it is to 26. We say that m∠A = 27 (to the *nearest degree*).

MODEL PROBLEM

In △ABC, ∠C is a right angle, BC = 3, AC = 4, and AB = 5. Find **(a)** tan A, **(b)** tan B, and **(c)** the measure of ∠B to the *nearest degree*.

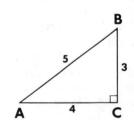

Solution

a. $\tan A = \dfrac{\text{length of side opposite } \angle A}{\text{length of side adjacent to } \angle A} = \dfrac{BC}{AC} = \dfrac{3}{4}$ *Ans.*

b. $\tan B = \dfrac{\text{length of side opposite } \angle B}{\text{length of side adjacent to } \angle B} = \dfrac{AC}{BC} = \dfrac{4}{3}$ *Ans.*

c. (1) Write the ratio for the tangent of angle B. $\tan B = \frac{4}{3}$

(2) Change the fraction to its decimal form, rounded off to the nearest ten-thousandth. $\tan B = 1.3333$

(3) In the table (page 696) under the "Tangent" column, 1.3333 is between 1.3270 and 1.3764. Since 1.3333 is closer to 1.3270, m∠B is closer to 53.   m∠B = 53

Answer: m∠B = 53, to the *nearest degree*.

EXERCISES

In 1–4, find **(a)** tan A and **(b)** tan B.

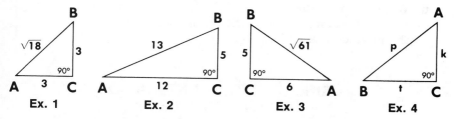

Ex. 1   **Ex. 2**   **Ex. 3**   **Ex. 4**

5. In triangle ABC, m∠C = 90, AC = 6, and AB = 10. Find tan A.
6. In triangle RST, m∠T = 90, RS = 13, and ST = 12. Find tan S.

In 7–14: Using the table on page 696, find each of the following:

7. tan 10°   **8.** tan 30°   **9.** tan 70°   **10.** tan 45°
11. tan 1°   **12.** tan 89°   **13.** tan 36°   **14.** tan 60°

In 15–20: Using the table, find the degree measure of angle A if:

15. tan A = .0875   **16.** tan A = .3640   **17.** tan A = .5543
18. tan A = 1.0000   **19.** tan A = 2.0503   **20.** tan A = 3.0777

In 21–26: Using the table on page 696, find the measure of angle A to the *nearest degree* if:

21. tan A = .3754   **22.** tan A = .7654   **23.** tan A = 1.8000
24. tan A = .3500   **25.** tan A = .1450   **26.** tan A = 2.9850

27. Does the tangent of an angle increase or decrease as the degree measure of the angle varies from 1 to 89?
28. a. Use the table to determine whether tan 40° is twice tan 20°.
   b. If the measure of an angle is doubled, is the tangent of the angle also doubled?
29. In triangle ABC, m∠C = 90, AC = 6, and BC = 6. **a.** Find tan A.
   b. Find the measure of angle A.
30. In △ABC, m∠C = 90, BC = 4, and AC = 9.
   a. Find tan A.   **b.** Find the measure of ∠A to the *nearest degree*.
   c. Find tan B.   **d.** Find the measure of ∠B to the *nearest degree*.

31. In △ABC, ∠C is a right angle, m∠A = 45, AC = 4, BC = 4, and AB = 4$\sqrt{2}$.
   a. Using the given lengths, write the ratio for tan A.
   b. Using the table on page 696, find tan 45°.

32. In $\triangle RST$, $\angle T$ is a right angle and r, s, and t are lengths of sides. Using these lengths:

a. Write the ratio for tan R.
b. Write the ratio for tan S.
c. Use parts **a** and **b** to find the numerical value of the product (tan R) (tan S).

8-3 USING THE TANGENT RATIO TO SOLVE PROBLEMS

There are many practical applications of trigonometry.

Angle of Elevation and Angle of Depression

When a telescope or some similar instrument is used to sight the top of a telephone pole, the instrument is *elevated* (tilted upward) from a horizontal position. Here, $\overleftrightarrow{OT}$ is the *line of sight* and $\overleftrightarrow{OA}$ is a horizontal line. The **angle of elevation** is the angle determined by the rays that are parts of the horizontal line and of the line of sight when looking upward. Here, $\angle TOA$ is the *angle of elevation*.

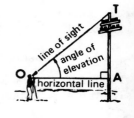

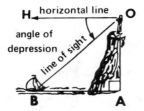

When an instrument is used to sight a boat from a cliff, the instrument is *depressed* (tilted downward) from a horizontal position. Here, $\overleftrightarrow{OB}$ is the *line of sight* and $\overleftrightarrow{OH}$ is the horizontal line. The **angle of depression** is the angle determined by the rays that are parts of the horizontal line and of the line of sight when looking downward. Here, $\angle HOB$ is the *angle of depression*.

Note that if $\overleftrightarrow{BA}$ is a horizontal line and $\overleftrightarrow{BO}$ is the line of sight from the boat to the top of the cliff, then $\angle ABO$ is called the angle of elevation from the boat to the top of the cliff. Since $\overleftrightarrow{HO} \parallel \overleftrightarrow{BA}$ and $\overleftrightarrow{OB}$ is a transversal, then alternate interior angles are congruent, namely, $\angle HOB \cong \angle ABO$. Thus, the angle of elevation measured from B to O is congruent to the angle of depression measured from O to B.

Using the Tangent Ratio to Solve Problems

To solve problems by use of the tangent ratio, proceed as follows:
1. Make a diagram for the problem so that somewhere a right triangle is included. Label the known measures of the sides and angles. Identify the unknown quantity by a variable.

2. If the right triangle has either (1) the lengths of two legs known or (2) the length of one leg and the measure of one acute angle known, then a formula may be written for the tangent of an acute angle.
3. Substitute known values in the formula and solve the resulting equation for the unknown value.

MODEL PROBLEMS

1. At a point on the ground 40 meters from the foot of a tree, the angle of elevation of the top of the tree contains 42°. Find the height of the tree to the *nearest meter*.

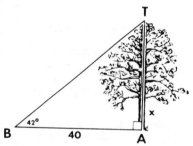

Solution: Draw $\triangle ABT$ where $\angle A$ is a right angle, $m\angle B = 42$, and $AB = 40$.
   Let $x = AT$ (height of tree).
   Since the problem involves $\angle B$, $\overline{AT}$ (its opposite side), and $\overline{AB}$ (its adjacent side), the tangent ratio is used.

$\tan B = \dfrac{AT}{BA}$ By definition, $\tan B = \dfrac{\text{opposite}}{\text{adjacent}}$.

$\tan 42° = \dfrac{x}{40}$ Substitute the given values.

$.9004 = \dfrac{x}{40}$ Substitute the value of $\tan 42°$ found in the table.

$x = 40(.9004)$ Solve the equation for x.

$x = 36.016$

Answer: The height of the tree is 36 meters, to the nearest meter.

2. From the top of a lighthouse 165 feet above sea level, the angle of depression of a boat at sea contains 35°. Find to the *nearest foot* the distance from the boat to the foot of the lighthouse.

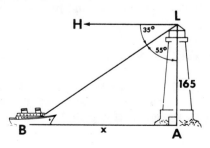

Solution: Draw right $\triangle ABL$. From $\overleftrightarrow{BA} \perp \overleftrightarrow{AL}$ and $\overleftrightarrow{HL} \parallel \overleftrightarrow{BA}$, it follows that $\overleftrightarrow{HL} \perp \overleftrightarrow{AL}$. Since $\angle HLB$ is the angle of depression, $m\angle HLB = 35$, $m\angle LBA = 35$, and $m\angle BLA = 90 - 35 = 55$.
   Let $x = BA$.

Method 1	*Method 2*
Using $\angle BLA$, $\overline{BA}$ is the opposite side and $\overline{LA}$ is the adjacent side. Form the tangent ratio.	Using $\angle LBA$, $\overline{LA}$ is the opposite side and $\overline{BA}$ is the adjacent side. Form the tangent ratio.

$$\tan \angle BLA = \frac{BA}{LA}$$

$$\tan 55° = \frac{x}{165}$$

$$1.4281 = \frac{x}{165}$$

$$x = 165(1.4281)$$

$$x = 235.6$$

$$\tan \angle LBA = \frac{LA}{BA}$$

$$\tan 35° = \frac{165}{x}$$

$$.7002 = \frac{165}{x}$$

$$.7002x = 165$$

$$x = \frac{165}{.7002} = 235.6$$

Answer: **236 feet, to the nearest foot.**

3. Find to the *nearest degree* the measure of the angle of elevation of the sun when a vertical pole 6 m high casts a shadow 8 m long.

Solution: The angle of elevation of the sun is the same as $\angle A$, the angle of elevation to the top of the pole from A. Since the segments mentioned in the problem are legs of a right triangle opposite and adjacent to $\angle A$, use the tangent ratio.

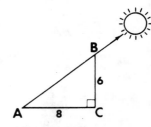

From the table:

(1) $\tan A = \dfrac{BC}{AC} = \dfrac{6}{8}$

(2) $\tan A = .7500$

(3) $m\angle A = 37$

$\tan 36° = .7265$ ⌐
                         → .0235
$\tan A = .7500$ ⌐
                         → .0036
$\tan 37° = .7536$ ⌐

Answer: **37°, to the nearest degree.**

EXERCISES

In 1–9, in the given triangle, find the length of the side marked x to the *nearest foot* or the number of degrees contained in the angle marked x to the *nearest degree*.

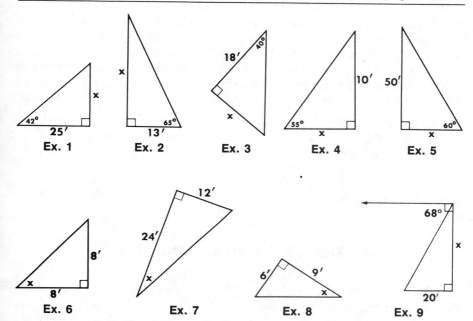

Ex. 1   Ex. 2   Ex. 3   Ex. 4   Ex. 5

Ex. 6   Ex. 7   Ex. 8   Ex. 9

10. At a point on the ground 50 meters from the foot of a tree, the angle of elevation of the top of the tree contains 48°. Find the height of the tree to the *nearest meter.*

11. A ladder is leaning against a wall. The foot of the ladder is 6.5 feet from the wall. The ladder makes an angle of 74° with the level ground. How high on the wall does the ladder reach? Round the answer to the *nearest tenth of a foot.*

12. A boy visiting New York City views the Empire State Building from a point on the ground, *A*, which is 940 feet from the foot, *C*, of the building. The angle of elevation of the top, *B*, of the building as seen by the boy contains 53°. Find the height of the building to the *nearest foot.*

13. Find to the *nearest meter* the height of a building if its shadow is 18 meters long when the angle of elevation of the sun contains 38°.

14. From the top of a lighthouse 50 meters high, the angle of depression of a boat out at sea is an angle of 15°. Find to the *nearest meter* the distance from the boat to the foot of the lighthouse, where the foot of the lighthouse is at sea level.

15. From the top of a school 60 feet high, the angle of depression to the road in front of the school contains 38°. Find to the *nearest foot* the distance from the road to the school.

16. Find to the *nearest degree* the measure of the angle of elevation of the sun when a student 170 cm tall casts a shadow 170 cm long.

17. Find to the *nearest degree* the measure of the angle of elevation of the sun when a woman 150 cm tall casts a shadow 40 cm long.

18. A ladder leans against a building. The top of the ladder reaches a point on the building that is 18 feet above the ground. The foot of the ladder is 7 feet from the building. Find to the *nearest degree* the measure of the angle that the ladder makes with the level ground.

19. In rhombus *ABCD*, diagonals $\overline{AC}$ and $\overline{BD}$ meet at *M*. If $BD = 14$ and $AC = 20$, find to the *nearest degree*:
    a. m∠*BCM*   b. m∠*MBC*
    c. m∠*ABC*   d. m∠*BCD*

8-4 THE SINE AND COSINE RATIOS

Since the tangent ratio involves the two legs of a right triangle, it is not directly useful in solving problems in which the hypotenuse is involved. In trigonometry of the right triangle, two ratios that involve the hypotenuse are called the *sine of an angle* and the *cosine of an angle*.

As in our discussion of the tangent ratio, we recognize that the figure shows three similar triangles because each triangle contains ∠*A* and a right angle (a.a. ≅ a.a.). Thus, $\triangle ABC \sim \triangle AB'C' \sim \triangle AB''C''$.

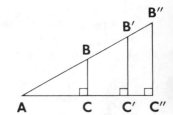

The Sine Ratio

From the figure, we see that $\dfrac{BC}{AB} = \dfrac{B'C'}{AB'} = \dfrac{B''C''}{AB''} = $ a constant value. This ratio is called the *sine of the angle A.*

● **Definition.** The **sine of an acute angle of a right triangle** is the ratio of the length of the side opposite the acute angle to the length of the hypotenuse.

In right $\triangle ABC$, with m∠ *C* = 90, the definition of the *sine of angle A* is:

$$\text{sine } A = \frac{\text{length of side opposite } \angle A}{\text{length of hypotenuse}} = \frac{BC}{AB} = \frac{a}{c}$$

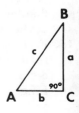

Using *sin A* as an abbreviation for sine A, and knowing that we are comparing lengths, we shorten the wording to say:

$$\sin A = \frac{\text{opposite}}{\text{hypotenuse}} = \frac{BC}{AB} = \frac{a}{c}$$

The Cosine Ratio

From the preceding figure that shows $\triangle ABC \sim \triangle AB'C' \sim \triangle AB''C''$, we see that $\dfrac{AC}{AB} = \dfrac{AC'}{AB'} = \dfrac{AC''}{AB''} = $ a constant. This ratio is called the *cosine of the angle A*.

● **Definition.** The *cosine of an acute angle of a right triangle* is the ratio of the length of the side adjacent to the acute angle to the length of the hypotenuse.

In right $\triangle ABC$, with $m\angle C = 90$, the definition of the *cosine of angle A* is:

$$\text{cosine } A = \frac{\text{length of side adjacent to } \angle A}{\text{length of hypotenuse}} = \frac{AC}{AB} = \frac{b}{c}$$

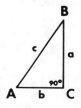

Using *cos A* as an abbreviation for cosine A, and knowing that we are comparing lengths, we shorten the wording to say:

$$\cos A = \frac{\text{adjacent}}{\text{hypotenuse}} = \frac{AC}{AB} = \frac{b}{c}$$

The Tables of Sines and Cosines

As the measure of angle A changes, both the sine ratio and the cosine ratio for angle A will change. Each ratio depends upon the measure of angle A, not upon the size of the right triangle that contains angle A. The sine ratios and cosine ratios for acute angles are given in the table of Values of the Trigonometric Functions found on page 696.

If we use this table as with the tangent ratio, we can obtain results such as the following:

Table of Sines	Table of Cosines
1. sin 25° = .4226	1. cos 55° = .5736
2. If sin A = .7660, then m∠A = 50.	2. If cos A = .9063, then m∠A = 25.
3. If sin A = .3500, then m∠A = 20 to the nearest degree (.3500 is closer to .3420 than it is to .3584).	3. If cos A = .3300, then m∠A = 71 to the nearest degree (.3300 is closer to .3256 than it is to .3420).

MODEL PROBLEM

In $\triangle ABC$, $\angle C$ is a right angle, $BC = 7$, $AC = 24$, and $AB = 25$. Find (a) sin A, (b) cos A, (c) sin B, (d) cos B, and (e) the measure of $\angle B$ to the *nearest degree*.

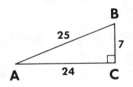

Solution

a. $\sin A = \dfrac{\text{length of side opposite } \angle A}{\text{length of hypotenuse}} = \dfrac{BC}{AB} = \dfrac{7}{25}$ *Ans.*

b. $\cos A = \dfrac{\text{length of side adjacent to } \angle A}{\text{length of hypotenuse}} = \dfrac{AC}{AB} = \dfrac{24}{25}$ *Ans.*

c. $\sin B = \dfrac{\text{length of side opposite } \angle B}{\text{length of hypotenuse}} = \dfrac{AC}{AB} = \dfrac{24}{25}$ *Ans.*

d. $\cos B = \dfrac{\text{length of side adjacent to } \angle B}{\text{length of hypotenuse}} = \dfrac{BC}{AB} = \dfrac{7}{25}$ *Ans.*

e. Start with the ratio in part **c** or part **d,** changing the fraction to a decimal form written to the *nearest ten-thousandth:*

	Method 1	*Method 2*

Method 1

$\sin B = \frac{24}{25}$

$\sin B = .9600$

Refer to the "Sine" column in the table: .9600 is closest to .9613, which is the sine of 74°.

Method 2

$\cos B = \frac{7}{25}$

$\cos B = .2800$

Refer to the "Cosine" column in the table: .2800 is closest to .2756, which is the cosine of 74°.

Answer: m∠B = 74, to the nearest degree.

EXERCISES

In 1–4, find (a) sin A, (b) cos A, (c) sin B, and (d) cos B.

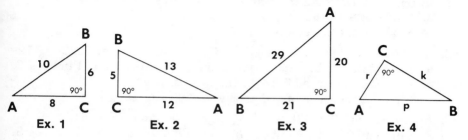

Ex. 1   Ex. 2   Ex. 3   Ex. 4

5. In triangle *ABC*, m∠C = 90, *AC* = 4, and *BC* = 3. Find sin A.
6. In triangle *RST*, m∠S = 90, *RS* = 5, and *ST* = 12. Find cos T.

In 7–18: Using the table on page 696, find each of the following:

7. sin 18°	**8.** sin 42°	**9.** sin 58°	**10.** sin 76°
11. sin 1°	**12.** sin 89°	**13.** cos 21°	**14.** cos 35°
15. cos 40°	**16.** cos 59°	**17.** cos 74°	**18.** cos 88°

In 19–27: Using the table on page 696, find the measure of ∠A if:

19. sin A = .1908	**20.** sin A = .8387	**21.** sin A = .3420
22. cos A = .9397	**23.** cos A = .0698	**24.** cos A = .8910
25. sin A = .8910	**26.** sin A = .9986	**27.** cos A = .9986

In 28–36: Using the table on page 696, find the measure of ∠A to the *nearest degree* if:

28. sin A = .1900	**29.** cos A = .9750	**30.** sin A = .8740
31. cos A = .8545	**32.** sin A = .5800	**33.** cos A = .5934
34. cos A = .2968	**35.** sin A = .1275	**36.** cos A = .8695

37. As an angle increases in measure from 1 to 89 degrees:
   a. Does the sine of the angle increase or decrease?
   b. Does the cosine of the angle increase or decrease?

38. a. Use the table on page 696 to see if sin 50° is twice sin 25°.
   b. If the measure of an angle is doubled, is the sine of the angle also doubled?

39. a. Use the table on page 696 to see if cos 80° is twice cos 40°.
   b. If the measure of an angle is doubled, is the cosine of the angle also doubled?

40. In triangle ABC, m∠ $C = 90$, $BC = 20$, and $BA = 40$.
   a. Find sin A to the *nearest ten-thousandth.*
   b. Find the measure of angle A.

41. In triangle ABC, m∠ $C = 90$, $AC = 40$, and $AB = 80$.
   a. Find cos A to the *nearest ten-thousandth.*
   b. Find the measure of angle A.

42. In △ ABC, ∠ C is a right angle, $AC = 8$, $BC = 15$, and $AB = 17$.
   a. Find sin A.   **b.** Find cos A.   **c.** Find sin B.   **d.** Find cos B.
   e. Find the measure of ∠ A to the *nearest degree.*
   f. Find the measure of ∠ B to the *nearest degree.*

43. In △ RST, m∠ $T = 90$, $ST = 11$, $RT = 60$, and $RS = 61$.
   a. Find sin R.   **b.** Find cos R.   **c.** Find sin S.   **d.** Find cos S.
   e. Find the measure of ∠ R to the *nearest degree.*
   f. Find m∠ S to the *nearest degree.*

44. In right △ ABC, ∠ C is a right angle, $BC = 1$,
   $AC = \sqrt{3}$, and $AB = 2$.
   a. Using the given lengths, write the ratios for
   sin A and cos A.
   b. Using the table on page 696, find sin 30° and
   cos 30°.
   c. What differences, if any, exist between the answers to **a** and **b**?

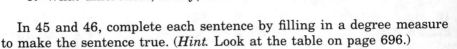

In 45 and 46, complete each sentence by filling in a degree measure to make the sentence true. (*Hint.* Look at the table on page 696.)

45. a. sin 70° = cos _____
   b. sin 23° = cos _____
   c. sin 38° = cos _____
   d. sin x° = cos _____

46. a. cos 50° = sin _____
   b. cos 17° = sin _____
   c. cos 82° = sin _____
   d. cos x° = sin _____

47. In △ ABC, where C is a right angle, show that sin A = cos B.

48. In △ ABC, if m∠ $C = 90$, and sin A = cos A, find m∠ A.

8-5   USING THE SINE RATIO AND THE COSINE RATIO TO SOLVE PROBLEMS

When a problem involves the hypotenuse, a leg, and one acute angle of a right triangle (with two of these measures known and one measure unknown), we can use either the sine ratio or the cosine ratio to find the unknown measure.

MODEL PROBLEMS ───────────────────

1. While flying a kite, Betty lets out 300 feet of string, which makes an angle of 38° with the ground. Assuming that the string is straight, how high above the ground is the kite?

Solution: Draw $\triangle BKG$ where $\angle G$ is a right angle, $m\angle B = 38$, and $BK = 300$.

Let $x = KG$ (height of the kite).

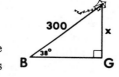

Since the problem involves $\angle B$, $\overline{KG}$ (its opposite side), and $\overline{BK}$ (the hypotenuse), the sine ratio is used.

$\sin B = \dfrac{KG}{KB}$ By definition, $\sin B = \dfrac{\text{opposite}}{\text{hypotenuse}}$.

$\sin 38° = \dfrac{x}{300}$ Substitute the given values.

$.6157 = \dfrac{x}{300}$ The value of $\sin 38°$ is found in the table.

$\qquad x = 300(.6157)$
$\qquad x = 184.71$

Answer: 185 feet, to the nearest foot.

2. A guy wire reaches from the top of a pole to a stake in the ground. The stake is 3.5 meters from the foot of the pole. The wire makes an angle of 65° with the ground. Find to the *nearest meter* the length of the wire.

Solution: In $\triangle BTS$, $\angle B$ is a right angle, $BS = 3.5$, and $m\angle S = 65$.

Let $x = ST$ (length of the wire).

Since the problem involves $\angle S$, $\overline{BS}$ (its adjacent side), and $\overline{ST}$ (the hypotenuse), the cosine ratio is used.

$$\cos S = \frac{BS}{ST}$$ By definition, $\cos S = \frac{\text{adjacent}}{\text{hypotenuse}}$.

$$\cos 65° = \frac{3.5}{x}$$

$$.4226 = \frac{3.5}{x}$$

$$.4226x = 3.5$$

$$x = \frac{3.5}{.4226}$$

$$x = 8.3$$

Answer: The wire is 8 meters long, to the nearest meter.

3. A ladder 25 feet long leans against a building and reaches a point 23.5 feet above the ground. Find to the *nearest degree* the angle that the ladder makes with the ground.

Solution: In right $\triangle ABC$, hypotenuse $\overline{AB}$ has a length of 25 and $BC = 23.5$. Since the problem involves $\angle A$, $\overline{BC}$ (its opposite side), and $\overline{AB}$ (the hypotenuse), the sine ratio is used.

$$\sin A = \frac{23.5}{25}$$ By definition, $\sin A = \frac{\text{opposite}}{\text{hypotenuse}}$.

$$\sin A = .9400$$
$$m\angle A = 70$$

Answer: 70°, to the nearest degree.

EXERCISES _____

In 1–8: In the given triangle, find to the *nearest centimeter* the length of the side marked x.

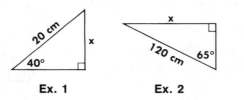

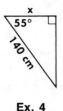

Ex. 1   **Ex. 2**   **Ex. 3**   **Ex. 4**

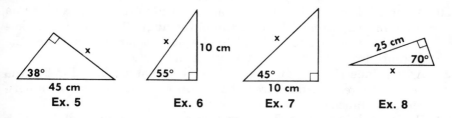

| Ex. 5 | Ex. 6 | Ex. 7 | Ex. 8 |

In 9–12: In the given triangle, find to the *nearest degree* the measure of the angle marked *x*.

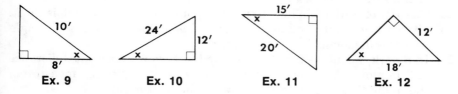

| Ex. 9 | Ex. 10 | Ex. 11 | Ex. 12 |

Exercises Involving the Sine Ratio

13. A wooden beam 6 meters long leans against a wall and makes an angle of 71° with the ground. Find to the *nearest tenth of a meter* how high up the wall the beam reaches.
14. A boy flying a kite lets out 400 feet of string, which makes an angle of 52° with the ground. Assuming that the string is stretched taut, find to the *nearest foot* how high the kite is above the ground.
15. A ladder that leans against a building makes an angle of 75° with the ground and reaches a point on the building 9.7 meters above the ground. Find to the *nearest meter* the length of the ladder.
16. From an airplane that is flying at an altitude of 3,000 feet, the angle of depression of an airport ground signal measures 27°. Find to the *nearest hundred feet* the distance between the airplane and the airport signal.
17. A 20-foot pole that is leaning against a wall reaches a point that is 18 feet above the ground. Find to the *nearest degree* the number of degrees contained in the angle that the pole makes with the ground.
18. To reach the top of a hill that is 1 kilometer high, one must travel 8 kilometers up a straight road that leads to the top. Find to the *nearest degree* the number of degrees contained in the angle that the road makes with the horizontal.

Exercises Involving the Cosine Ratio

19. A 20-foot ladder leans against a building and makes an angle of 72° with the ground. Find to the *nearest foot* the distance between the foot of the ladder and the building.

20. A wire, 2.4 meters in length, is attached from the top of a post to a stake in the ground. The measure of the angle that the wire makes with the ground is 35°. Find to the *nearest tenth* of a meter the distance from the stake to the foot of the post.

21. An airplane rises at an angle of 14° with the ground. Find to the *nearest ten feet* the distance it has flown when it has covered a horizontal distance of 1,500 feet.

22. Henry is flying a kite. The kite string makes an angle of 43° with the ground. If Henry is standing 100 meters from a point on the ground directly below the kite, find to the *nearest meter* the length of the kite string, which is stretched taut.

23. The top of a 40-ft. ladder touches a point on the wall that is 36 ft. above the ground. Find to the *nearest degree* the measure of the angle that the ladder makes with the wall.

24. In a park, a slide is 9 m long and is built over a horizontal distance of 6 m along the ground. Find to the *nearest degree* the measure of the angle that the slide makes with the horizontal.

8-6   USING ALL THREE TRIGONOMETRIC RATIOS

When solving a problem using trigonometry:
1. Draw a right triangle, identify all known measures, and assign a variable to represent the unknown measure.
2. Select the proper trigonometric ratio (which relates to the measures involved in the problem) to solve for the unknown measure.

KEEP IN MIND

$$\tan A = \frac{\text{length of side opposite } \angle A}{\text{length of side adjacent to } \angle A} = \frac{a}{b}$$

$$\sin A = \frac{\text{length of side opposite } \angle A}{\text{length of hypotenuse}} = \frac{a}{c}$$

$$\cos A = \frac{\text{length of side adjacent to } \angle A}{\text{length of hypotenuse}} = \frac{b}{c}$$

MODEL PROBLEM

Given: In isosceles triangle ABC, $AC = CB = 20$ and
  $m\angle A = m\angle B = 68$.
  $\overline{CD}$ is an altitude.

Find: **a.** Length of altitude $\overline{CD}$ to the *nearest tenth*.
      b. Length of $\overline{AB}$ to the *nearest tenth*.

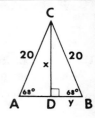

Solution

a. In rt. $\triangle BDC$, $\sin B = \dfrac{CD}{CB}$

Let $x = CD$.

$$\text{Sin } 68° = \frac{x}{20}$$

$$.9272 = \frac{x}{20}$$

$$x = 20(.9272)$$

$$x = 18.5440$$

$$x = 18.5$$

Answer: $CD = 18.5$, to the nearest tenth.

b. Since the altitude drawn to the base of an isosceles triangle bisects the base, $AB = 2DB$. Therefore, we will find DB in $\triangle BDC$ and double it to find AB.

In rt. $\triangle BDC$, $\cos B = \dfrac{DB}{CB}$

Let $y = DB$.

$$\text{Cos } 68° = \frac{y}{20}$$

$$.3746 = \frac{y}{20}$$

$$y = 20(.3746) = 7.4920$$

$$AB = 2y = 2(7.4920)$$

$$AB = 14.9840 = 15.0 \quad \textit{Ans.}$$

EXERCISES

In 1–8: In the given right triangle, find to the *nearest foot* the length of the side marked x; or find to the *nearest degree* the number of degrees in the angle marked x.

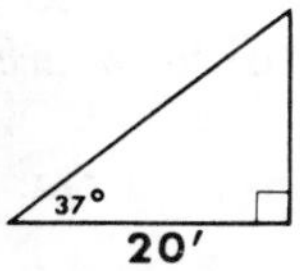

Ex. 1

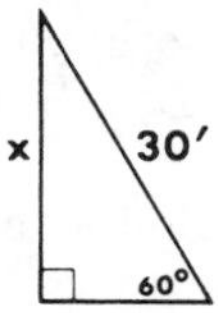

Ex. 2

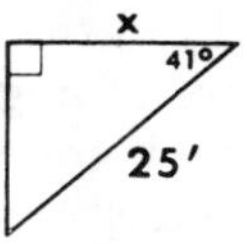

Ex. 3

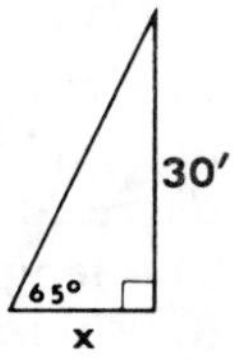

Ex. 4

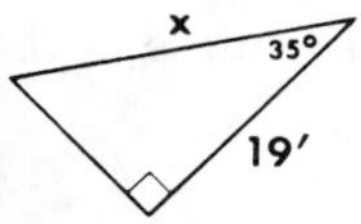

Ex. 5

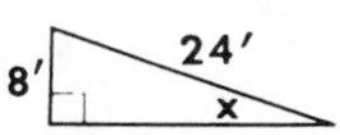

Ex. 6

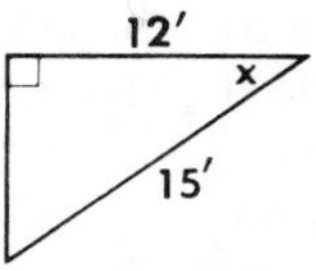

Ex. 7

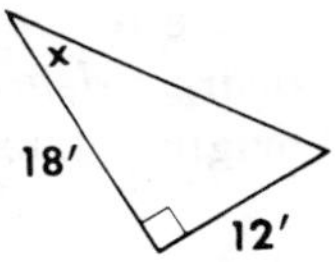

Ex. 8

9. In triangle ABC, m$\angle A$ = 42, AB = 14, and $\overline{BD}$ is the altitude to $\overline{AC}$. Find BD to the *nearest tenth*.

10. In triangle ABC, $\overline{AC} \cong \overline{BC}$, m$\angle A$ = 50, and AB = 30. Find to the *nearest tenth* the length of the altitude from vertex C.

11. The legs of a right triangle measure 3 and 4. Find to the *nearest degree* the measure of the smallest angle of this triangle.

12. The length of the hypotenuse $\overline{AB}$ of right triangle ABC is twice the length of leg $\overline{BC}$. Find the number of degrees in angle ABC.

13. The longer side of a rectangle measures 10 and a diagonal makes an angle of 27° with this side. Find to the *nearest integer* the length of the shorter side.

14. In rectangle $ABCD$, diagonal $\overline{AC}$ measures 11 cm and side $\overline{AB}$ measures 7 cm. Find to the *nearest degree* the measure of angle CAB.

15. Find to the *nearest meter* the height of a church spire that casts a shadow of 50 meters when the angle of elevation of the sun contains 68°.

16. From the top of a lighthouse 190 feet high, the angle of depression of a boat out at sea contains 34°. Find to the *nearest foot* the distance from the boat to the foot of the lighthouse.

17. A straight road to the top of a hill is 2,500 meters long and makes an angle of 12° with the horizontal. Find to the *nearest hundred meters* the height of the hill.

18. A wire attached to the top of a pole reaches a stake in the ground 20 ft. from the foot of the pole and makes an angle of 58° with the ground. Find to the *nearest foot* the length of the wire.

19. An airplane climbs at an angle of 11° with the ground. Find to the *nearest hundred feet* the distance it has traveled when it has attained an altitude of 400 feet.

20. Find to the *nearest degree* the measure of the angle of elevation of the sun if a child 90 cm high casts a shadow 180 cm long.

21. In right $\triangle ABC$, $\overline{CD}$ is the altitude to hypotenuse $\overline{AB}$. AB = 25 m and AC = 20 m. Find the lengths AD, DB, CD, and, to the *nearest degree*, the measure of angle B.

22. The lengths of the diagonals of a rhombus are 10 cm and 24 cm.
    a. Find the perimeter of the rhombus.
    b. Find to the *nearest degree* the measure of the angle that the longer diagonal makes with a side of the rhombus.

23. The altitude on the hypotenuse of a right triangle divides the hypotenuse into segments whose measures are 9 in. and 4 in. Find to the *nearest degree* the degree measure of the smaller acute angle of the original triangle.

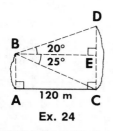

Ex. 24

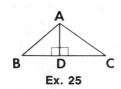

Ex. 25

Ex. 26

24. $\overline{AB}$ and $\overline{CD}$ represent cliffs on opposite sides of a river 120 meters wide. From B, the angle of elevation of D contains $20°$ and the angle of depression of C contains $25°$. Find to the *nearest meter* **(a)** the height of the cliff represented by $\overline{AB}$ and **(b)** the height of the cliff represented by $\overline{CD}$.

25. In triangle ABC, $AB = 30$ feet, $m\angle B = 42$, $m\angle C = 36$, and $\overline{AD}$ is an altitude. **a.** Find to the *nearest foot* the length of $\overline{AD}$. **b.** Using the result of part **a**, find to the *nearest foot* the length of $\overline{DC}$.

26. CD represents the height of a building. $AD = 85$ ft. and $m\angle D = 90$. At A, the angle of elevation of the top of the building, $\angle CAD$, contains $49°$. At B, the angle of elevation of the top of the building, $\angle CBD$, contains $26°$. **a.** Find the height of the building, CD, to the *nearest foot*. **b.** Find BD to the *nearest foot*.

27. Angle D in quadrilateral $ABCD$ is a right angle and diagonal $\overline{AC}$ is perpendicular to $\overline{BC}$. $BC = 20$, $m\angle B = 35$, and $m\angle DAC = 65$.
   a. Find AC to the *nearest integer*.
   b. Using the result of part **a**, find DC to the *nearest integer*.

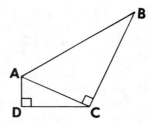

28. The diagonals of a rectangle each measure 22 and intersect at an angle whose measure is $110°$. Find to the *nearest integer* the length and width of the rectangle.

29. In rhombus $ABCD$, the measure of diagonal $\overline{AC}$ is 80 and $m\angle BAC = 42$.
   a. Find to the *nearest integer* the length of diagonal $\overline{BD}$.
   b. Find to the *nearest integer* the length of a side of the rhombus.

30. In right triangle ABC, the length of hypotenuse $\overline{AB}$ is 100 and $m\angle A = 18$.
   a. Find AC and BC to the *nearest integer*.
   b. Show that the results of part **a** are approximately correct by using the relationship $(AB)^2 = (AC)^2 + (BC)^2$.

8-7 REVIEW EXERCISES

In 1–6, refer to △ *RST* and give the value
of the ratio as a fraction.

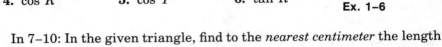

1. sin *R*   2. tan *T*   3. sin *T*
4. cos *R*   5. cos *T*   6. tan *R*

Ex. 1–6

In 7–10: In the given triangle, find to the *nearest centimeter* the length
of the side marked *x*.

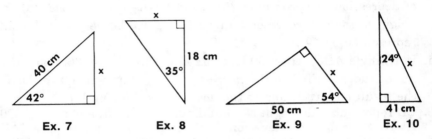

Ex. 7   Ex. 8   Ex. 9   Ex. 10

11. If cos *A* = sin 30°, angle *A* contains _____ degrees.
12. If, in right triangle *ACB*, m∠ *C* = 90, m∠ *A* = 66, and *AC* = 100,
    then *BC* to the *nearest integer* is _____.
13. In right triangle *ABC*, m∠ *B* = 90, m∠ *B* = 28, and *BC* = 30 ft. Find
    AB to the *nearest foot*.
14. In triangle *ABC*, m∠ *C* = 90, tan *A* = .7, and *AC* = 40. Find *BC*.
15. In triangle *ABC*, m∠ *C* = 90, *AB* = 30, and *BC* = 15. How many
    degrees are contained in angle *A*?
16. In triangle *ABC*, m∠ *C* = 90, *BC* = 5, and *AC* = 9. Find to the
    nearest degree the measure of angle *A*.
17. Find to the *nearest meter* the height of a building if its shadow is
    42 m long when the angle of elevation of the sun contains 42°.
18. A 5-foot wire attached to the top of a tent pole reaches a stake in
    the ground 3 feet from the foot of the pole. Find to the *nearest degree*
    the measure of the angle made by the wire with the ground.
19. While flying a kite, Doris let out 400 feet of string. Assuming that
    the string is stretched taut and it makes an angle of 48° with the
    ground, find to the *nearest foot* how high the kite is.
20. In rectangle *ABCD*, diagonal $\overline{AC}$ is drawn. If m∠ *BAC* = 62 and
    BC = 20, find to the *nearest integer* (a) the length of $\overline{AB}$ and (b) the
    length of $\overline{AC}$.

Chapter **9**

Coordinate Geometry

The geometry discussed so far in this book was developed more than 2,000 years ago by Greek mathematicians such as Euclid and Pythagoras. It was not until the seventeenth century that a French mathematician, René Descartes, saw how it was possible to apply algebraic principles and methods to geometric situations. This blending of algebra and geometry is known as *coordinate geometry* or *analytic geometry*.

In this chapter, we will continue the study of geometry by using the representation of the points of a plane as ordered pairs of real numbers in the Cartesian coordinate system.

9-1 THE COORDINATE PLANE

On the real number line, there exists a one-to-one correspondence between the set of points on the line and the set of real numbers. In other words, each point on the line corresponds to a unique real number, and each real number corresponds to a unique point on the line.

Let point A correspond to the number 0, point B correspond to the number 1, point C correspond to the number $\sqrt{5}$, and point D correspond to the number $-1\frac{1}{2}$. The number that corresponds to a point on a line is called the *coordinate* of the point; the point to which a number corresponds is called the *graph* of the number. For example, the number 1 is the coordinate of point B, and point B is the graph of the number 1.

To study geometric figures in a plane, we must extend this coordinate system by using two real number lines that intersect. Let us agree that the two number lines, called *coordinate axes,* are drawn so that:

1. The number lines are perpendicular to each other, *and*
2. The number lines use the same scale.

One of the coordinate axes is a horizontal line called the **x-axis**; the other is a vertical line called the **y-axis**. The point *O* at which the two axes intersect is called the **origin.** The axes divide the points of the plane (that are not on the axes) into four regions called **quadrants.** These quadrants are numbered in a counterclockwise direction starting from the upper right.

On the *x*-axis, coordinates to the right of *O* are positive, and coordinates to the left of *O* are negative. On the *y*-axis, coordinates above *O* are positive, and coordinates below *O* are negative.

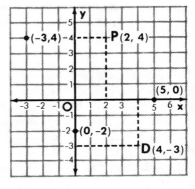

Let us use the two number lines to determine a pair of numbers that is associated with a point *P* in a plane. Through *P*, draw the line that is perpendicular to the *x*-axis. This line intersects the *x*-axis at 2. The number 2 is called the *x-coordinate*, or **abscissa,** of point *P*. Draw, through *P*, the line that is perpendicular to the *y*-axis. This line intersects the *y*-axis at 4. The number 4 is called the *y-coordinate*, or **ordinate,** of point *P*.

The *x*-coordinate, 2, and the *y*-coordinate, 4, are called the *coordinates* of point *P*, written (2, 4).

To designate the coordinates of any point, we agree to write the abscissa as the first element and the ordinate as the second element, forming an **ordered pair of numbers.** In general, the coordinates of a point are represented by (*x*, *y*).

Point *D* on the figure above is the graph of the ordered pair of numbers (4, −3) because the abscissa of the pair is 4 and the ordinate of the pair is −3. Note that the pair (4, −3) is not the same as the pair (−3, 4).

For every point on the *x*-axis, *y* = 0, and for every point on the *y*-axis, *x* = 0. The origin, called point *O*, represents the ordered pair of numbers (0, 0).

Thus, there is a one-to-one correspondence between the set of points in the plane and the set of ordered pairs of real numbers. In other words, every point in the plane represents a unique ordered pair of real numbers (*x*, *y*). Also, every ordered pair of numbers (*x*, *y*) corresponds to a unique point in the plane. This one-to-one correspondence is called a *coordinate system.*

This coordinate system is also called a *rectangular coordinate system* because the axes have been drawn perpendicular to each other, or the *Cartesian coordinate system* in honor of its originator, Descartes.

MODEL PROBLEM

Of the points *A*, *B*, *C*, and *D* shown, which point represents the graph of the ordered pair of real numbers ($\sqrt{5}$, 1)?

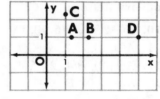

Solution: Since (*x*, *y*) = ($\sqrt{5}$, 1), the abscissa, or *x*-value, is $\sqrt{5}$, and the ordinate, or *y*-value, is 1. $\sqrt{5}$ is greater than $\sqrt{4}$ and less than $\sqrt{9}$, that is, $2 < \sqrt{5} < 3$. Only point *B* shows an abscissa between 2 and 3, and an ordinate of 1.

Answer: B

EXERCISES

In 1–5, refer to the graph shown.

1. Write as an ordered pair of numbers the coordinates of each point:
   A, *B*, *C*, *D*, *E*, *F*, *G*, *H*, and *O*.
2. Name the abscissa of each point:
   P, *R*, and *F*.
3. Name the ordinate of each point:
   Q, *T*, and *G*.
4. Which point represents the graph of (-2, $\sqrt{2}$)?
5. Which point represents the graph of ($\sqrt{2}$, -2)?

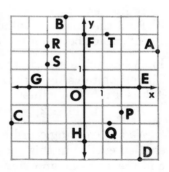

Ex. 1–5

6. On graph paper, draw and label a pair of coordinate axes. Then plot and label each point associated with the given ordered pair of real numbers.

A(4, 5)	*B*(-2, 5)	*C*(3, -4)	*D*(-3, -5)
E(6, 0)	*F*(-3, 0)	*G*(0, -4)	*H*(0, 4)
J(5, $-1\frac{1}{2}$)	*K*(-1, 2.5)	*L*($-\frac{3}{4}$, -6)	*M*(0, -2)
P(3, 0)	*Q*($\sqrt{3}$, 2)	*R*(-5, $\sqrt{5}$)	*S*(-4, $-\sqrt{2}$)

7. What are the coordinates of the origin?
8. If a point is on the *x*-axis, what is the value of its ordinate?
9. What is the value of the abscissa of every point on the *y*-axis?

In 10–13, graph the points A, B, C, D. Connect the points with line segments in the order given, and then connect D to A. What kind of quadrilateral is $ABCD$?

10. $A(-2, 3)$, $B(5, 3)$, $C(5, 1)$, $D(-2, 1)$
11. $A(0, 1)$, $B(1, 3)$, $C(4, 3)$, $D(3, 1)$
12. $A(1, 2)$, $B(4, 2)$, $C(4, -1)$, $D(1, -1)$
13. $A(-1, 0)$, $B(0, 4)$, $C(2, 4)$, $D(7, 0)$

9-2   THE DISTANCE BETWEEN TWO POINTS

When Two Points Have the Same Ordinate

The points $A(2, 1)$ and $B(6, 1)$ have the same ordinate, 1. The distance AB between points A and B is 4, found by one of two methods:

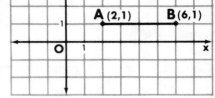

1. Count the number of units contained in $\overline{AB}$, or
2. Find the absolute value of the difference between the abscissas of points A and B.

In the example shown, the abscissa of B is 6 and the abscissa of A is 2. The absolute value of the difference of these abscissas gives the distance AB as a positive value:

$$|6 - 2| = |4| = 4 \quad and \quad |2 - 6| = |-4| = 4$$

We are treating coordinate geometry as an extension of the geometry studied earlier in this book. For this reason, we will number postulates and theorems as an extension of the earlier sequence. Thus, we state:

● **POSTULATE 49. The distance between two points having the same ordinate is the absolute value of the difference of their abscissas.**

In general terms, points A and B are shown to have the same ordinate, y_1, by letting $A = (x_1, y_1)$ and $B = (x_2, y_1)$. Thus, the distance d between A and B is the absolute value of the difference of their abscissas, namely:

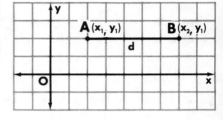

$$d = |x_2 - x_1| \quad or \quad d = |x_1 - x_2|$$

Note that the distance d may also be called AB to show the distance between points A and B. Therefore, $AB = |x_2 - x_1|$, or $AB = |x_1 - x_2|$.

When Two Points Have the Same Abscissa

The points $E(2, -1)$ and $F(2, 4)$ have the same abscissa, 2. The distance EF between the points is 5, found by one of two methods:

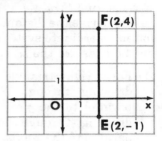

1. Count the number of units contained in $\overline{EF}$, or
2. Find the absolute value of the difference between the ordinates of points E and F.

In the example shown, the ordinate of E is -1 and the ordinate of F is 4. The absolute value of the difference of these ordinates gives the distance EF as a positive value:

$$|-1 - 4| = |-5| = 5 \quad and \quad |4 - (-1)| = |4 + 1| = |5| = 5$$

● **POSTULATE 50. The distance between two points having the same abscissa is the absolute value of the difference of their ordinates.**

In general terms, points E and F are shown to have the same abscissa, x_1, by letting $E = (x_1, y_1)$ and $F = (x_1, y_2)$. Thus, the distance d between E and F is the absolute value of the difference of their ordinates, namely:

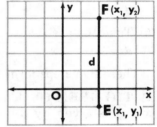

$$d = |y_2 - y_1| \quad or \quad d = |y_1 - y_2|$$

Finding the Distance Between Any Two Points

The methods previously discussed cannot be used to find the distance between the point $A(2, 3)$ and the point $B(5, 7)$ because these two points have different abscissas and different ordinates. However, if we form a right triangle, we can use the Pythagorean Theorem to find d, the length of $\overline{AB}$.

Here, $\angle ACB$ is a right angle, and the coordinates of C are $(5, 3)$. It follows that:

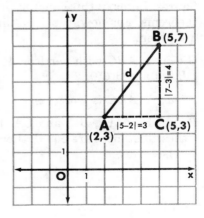

$$AC = |5 - 2| = |3| = 3$$
$$BC = |7 - 3| = |4| = 4$$

Therefore: $d^2 = 3^2 + 4^2$
$$d^2 = 9 + 16$$
$$d^2 = 25$$
$$d = 5$$

Let us now derive a formula for the distance d between any two points $R(x_1, y_1)$ and $S(x_2, y_2)$. It is possible for us to use the Pythagorean Theorem to derive the distance formula only because the axes we have chosen for our coordinate system are perpendicular to each other, and the scales on the axes are the same.

(1) Form right triangle RCS by drawing through S a line parallel to the y-axis and by drawing through R a line parallel to the x-axis, with the two lines intersecting at C.

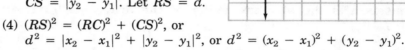

(2) The coordinates at C are (x_2, y_1).

(3) Therefore, $RC = |x_2 - x_1|$ and $CS = |y_2 - y_1|$. Let $RS = d$.

(4) $(RS)^2 = (RC)^2 + (CS)^2$, or
$d^2 = |x_2 - x_1|^2 + |y_2 - y_1|^2$, or $d^2 = (x_2 - x_1)^2 + (y_2 - y_1)^2$.

(5) Take the positive square root of each member of the equation:
$d = \sqrt{(x_2 - x_1)^2 + (y_2 - y_1)^2}$

These five steps form the proof of the following theorem.

● **THEOREM 60.　The distance d between two points (x_1, y_1) and (x_2, y_2) is given by the formula:**

$$d = \sqrt{(x_2 - x_1)^2 + (y_2 - y_1)^2}$$

Proofs Involving Specific Cases

By combining the distance formula with facts learned earlier in geometry, it is possible to determine specific relationships for given geometric figures. Later in this chapter, you will study coordinate proofs of general theorems. For now, consider this example in which specific coordinates are given.

Given: $\triangle ABC$ with vertices $A(-3, 0)$, $B(3, 0)$, and $C(0, 2)$.

Show: $\triangle ABC$ is isosceles.

Plan: Find AB, BC, and CA. If two of these distances are equal, then $\triangle ABC$ is isosceles.

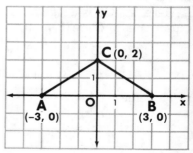

Solution:

(1) $AB = |x_2 - x_1| = |3 - (-3)| = |3 + 3| = |6| = 6$

(2) $BC = \sqrt{(x_2 - x_1)^2 + (y_2 - y_1)^2} = \sqrt{(3 - 0)^2 + (0 - 2)^2}$

$\qquad = \sqrt{(3)^2 + (-2)^2} = \sqrt{9 + 4} = \sqrt{13}$

(3) $CA = \sqrt{(x_2 - x_1)^2 + (y_2 - y_1)^2} = \sqrt{[0 - (-3)]^2 + [2 - 0]^2}$

$\qquad = \sqrt{(0 + 3)^2 + (2 - 0)^2}$

$\qquad = \sqrt{(3)^2 + (2)^2} = \sqrt{9 + 4} = \sqrt{13}$

(4) Since $BC = CA$, $\triangle ABC$ is isosceles.

Note. It is also possible to use the general distance formula in step (1) to find the distance AB. Here,

$$AB = \sqrt{(x_2 - x_1)^2 + (y_2 - y_1)^2} = \sqrt{[3 - (-3)]^2 + [0 - 0]^2}$$
$$= \sqrt{(3 + 3)^2 + (0)^2} = \sqrt{(6)^2 + (0)^2} = \sqrt{36 + 0} = \sqrt{36} = 6$$

Other proofs are shown in the model problems that follow.

MODEL PROBLEMS

1. Find the distance between the point $C(-3, -2)$ and the point $D(-3, 4)$.

   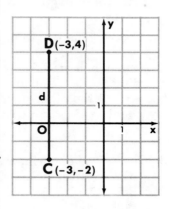

   Solution:

   Let $C = (x_1, y_1)$. Then $x_1 = -3$, $y_1 = -2$.

   Let $D = (x_2, y_2)$. Then $x_2 = -3$, $y_2 = 4$.

   ### *Method 1*

   Use the graph to count the number of units contained in $\overline{CD}$.

   ### *Method 2*

   Since points C and D have the same abscissa, -3, the distance is the absolute value of the difference of their ordinates. Thus:

   $$d = |y_2 - y_1|$$
   $$d = |4 - (-2)| = |4 + 2| = |6| = 6$$

Method 3

Use the general formula for the distance between two points:

$d = \sqrt{(x_2 - x_1)^2 + (y_2 - y_1)^2}$

$d = \sqrt{[-3 - (-3)]^2 + [4 - (-2)]^2} = \sqrt{(-3 + 3)^2 + (4 + 2)^2}$

$d = \sqrt{(0)^2 + (6)^2} = \sqrt{0 + 36} = \sqrt{36} = 6$

Answer: $CD = 6$

2. What is the length of the radius of a circle whose center is $C(-4, 2)$ and that passes through the point $D(-3, 5)$?
   [The answer may be left in radical form.]

Solution:

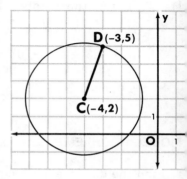

Let $C = (x_1, y_1)$. Then $x_1 = -4$, $y_1 = 2$.
Let $D = (x_2, y_2)$. Then $x_2 = -3$, $y_2 = 5$.

$CD = \sqrt{(x_2 - x_1)^2 + (y_2 - y_1)^2}$

$CD = \sqrt{[-3 - (-4)]^2 + [5 - 2]^2}$

$CD = \sqrt{(-3 + 4)^2 + (5 - 2)^2}$

$CD = \sqrt{(1)^2 + (3)^2} = \sqrt{1 + 9} = \sqrt{10}$

Answer: The length of the radius is $\sqrt{10}$ units.

Note. When we use the formula $d = \sqrt{(x_2 - x_1)^2 + (y_2 - y_1)^2}$ to find the distance between two points, either of the points may be named (x_1, y_1) and the other point (x_2, y_2), since the squares of the differences are equal: $(x_2 - x_1)^2 = (x_1 - x_2)^2$ and $(y_2 - y_1)^2 = (y_1 - y_2)^2$.

3. *Given:* The quadrilateral
   with vertices $A(2, 2)$,
   $B(5, -2)$, $C(9, 1)$, and
   $D(6, 5)$.

   Show: $ABCD$ is a rhombus.

   Plan: Show that $ABCD$ is
   a quadrilateral with four
   sides of equal length.

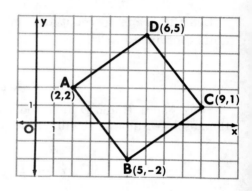

Solution:

(1) $d = \sqrt{(x_2 - x_1)^2 + (y_2 - y_1)^2}$

(2) $AB = \sqrt{(5 - 2)^2 + (-2 - 2)^2} = \sqrt{(3)^2 + (-4)^2}$
$= \sqrt{9 + 16} = \sqrt{25} = 5$

(3) $BC = \sqrt{[9 - 5]^2 + [1 - (-2)]^2} = \sqrt{(4)^2 + (1 + 2)^2}$
$= \sqrt{(4)^2 + (3)^2} = \sqrt{16 + 9} = \sqrt{25} = 5$

(4) $CD = \sqrt{(9 - 6)^2 + (1 - 5)^2} = \sqrt{(3)^2 + (-4)^2}$
$= \sqrt{9 + 16} = \sqrt{25} = 5$

(5) $DA = \sqrt{(6 - 2)^2 + (5 - 2)^2} = \sqrt{(4)^2 + (3)^2} = \sqrt{16 + 9}$
$= \sqrt{25} = 5$

(6) $AB = BC = CD = DA$.

(7) Since $ABCD$ is an equilateral quadrilateral, it is a rhombus.

4. *Given:* The triangle with vertices $A(4, -1)$, $B(5, 6)$, and $C(1, 3)$.

   Show: $\triangle ABC$ is an isosceles right triangle.

   Plan: To show that $\triangle ABC$ is isosceles, show that two sides are equal in length. To show that $\triangle ABC$ is a right triangle, test the Pythagorean Theorem.

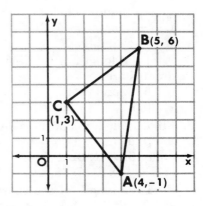

Solution:

(1) $d = \sqrt{(x_2 - x_1)^2 + (y_2 - y_1)^2}$

(2) $AB = \sqrt{[5 - 4]^2 + [6 - (-1)]^2} = \sqrt{(5 - 4)^2 + (6 + 1)^2}$
$= \sqrt{(1)^2 + (7)^2} = \sqrt{1 + 49} = \sqrt{50}$

(3) $BC = \sqrt{(5 - 1)^2 + (6 - 3)^2} = \sqrt{(4)^2 + (3)^2} = \sqrt{16 + 9}$
$= \sqrt{25} = 5$

(4) $CA = \sqrt{(4 - 1)^2 + (-1 - 3)^2} = \sqrt{(3)^2 + (-4)^2}$
$= \sqrt{9 + 16} = \sqrt{25} = 5$

(5) $BC = CA$. Therefore, $\triangle ABC$ is an isosceles triangle.

(6) The longest side of $\triangle ABC$ is $\overline{AB}$. Test the Pythagorean Theorem.

$$(AB)^2 \stackrel{?}{=} (BC)^2 + (CA)^2$$
$$(\sqrt{50})^2 \stackrel{?}{=} (5)^2 + (5)^2$$
$$50 \stackrel{?}{=} 25 + 25$$
$$50 = 50 \text{ (True)}$$

Therefore, $(AB)^2 = (BC)^2 + (CA)^2$, and $\triangle ABC$ is a right triangle.

(7) From steps (5) and (6), $\triangle ABC$ is an isosceles right triangle.

EXERCISES

Throughout this section, answers that are not whole numbers should be left in radical form.

1. Find the distance between each of the following pairs of points:
   a. (2, 7) and (12, 7)   b. (−3, 4) and (5, 4)
   c. (−1, −2) and (−1, 4)   d. (0, 0) and (4, 3)
   e. (−6, −8) and (0, 0)   f. (1, 4) and (4, 8)
   g. (4, 2) and (−2, 10)   h. (6, 4) and (3, 6)
   i. (−5, 0) and (−9, 6)   j. (0, 0) and (−2, 5)
   k. (0, c) and (b, 0)   l. (0, 0) and (a, b)

2. Find the length of the line segment joining the points whose coordinates are:
   a. (5, 2) and (8, 6)   b. (−5, 1) and (7, 6)
   c. (0, 5) and (−3, 3)   d. (−4, −5) and (1, −2)

3. Find the lengths of the sides of a triangle whose vertices are:
   a. (0, 0), (8, 0), (4, 3)   b. (1, 5), (5, 5), (5, 1)
   c. (3, 6), (−1, 3), (5, −5)   d. (6, −3), (0, 4), (8, −1)
   e. (−1, 7), (0, 0), (8, 4)   f. (−4, 2), (−1, 6), (5, 4)

4. Find the length of the shortest side of the triangle whose vertices are $R(-2, -1)$, $S(1, 3)$, and $T(1, 10)$.

5. Show that points A, B, and C are collinear; that is, they lie on the same straight line. [*Hint.* Show that $AB + BC = AC$.]
   a. $A(0, 0), B(5, 12), C(10, 24)$ b. $A(-1, -2), B(2, 2), C(8, 10)$
   c. $A(-2, -2), B(0, 2), C(1, 4)$ d. $A(-1, 2), B(2, -1), C(4, -3)$

6. Show that the triangles with the following vertices are isosceles.
   a. (2, 3), (5, 7), (1, 4)   b. (1, 0), (5, 0), (3, 4)
   c. (7, −1), (2, −2), (3, 3)   d. (4, −7), (−3, −4), (7, 0)

7. Show that the triangles that have the following vertices are right triangles:
   a. (1, 1), (4, 5), (4, 1)   b. (5, 6), (8, 5), (2, −3)
   c. (−1, 0), (6, 1), (2, 4)   d. (−4, −1), (0, −5), (1, 4)

8. Show that the line segments joining the points $(-1, 3)$, $(9, 3)$, and $(4, 8)$ form an isosceles right triangle.

9. The points $(1, 1)$, $(7, 1)$, $(7, 4)$, and $(1, 4)$ are the vertices of a rectangle. Show that the diagonals are equal in length.

10. Plot the following points:

$$A(5, 3), B(-5, 3), C(-5, -3), D(5, -3)$$

Connect these points in the order given. What kind of quadrilateral is $ABCD$? Prove your conclusion informally.

11. Draw the quadrilateral that has the following points as its vertices. What type of quadrilateral is formed? Prove your conclusion informally.
   a. $(1, 1)$, $(4, 1)$, $(4, -2)$, $(1, -2)$ **b.** $(2, 2)$, $(3, 4)$, $(6, 4)$, $(5, 2)$
   c. $(-1, -1)$, $(-1, -3)$, $(3, -3)$, $(3, -1)$
   d. $(6, 0)$, $(9, 4)$, $(6, 8)$, $(3, 4)$

12. Show that the quadrilaterals that have the following vertices are parallelograms.
   a. $(1, 2)$, $(2, 5)$, $(5, 7)$, $(4, 4)$ **b.** $(-1, 1)$, $(-3, 4)$, $(1, 5)$, $(3, 2)$

13. Show that the quadrilaterals that have the following vertices are rhombuses:
   a. $(1, 1)$, $(5, 3)$, $(7, 7)$, $(3, 5)$ **b.** $(-3, 2)$, $(-2, 6)$, $(2, 7)$, $(1, 3)$

14. **a.** Show that the quadrilateral whose vertices are $(1, 4)$, $(4, 9)$, $(-1, 12)$, $(-4, 7)$ is equilateral.
   b. Show that the diagonals of this quadrilateral are equal in length.
   c. What type of quadrilateral have you shown this to be?

15. The vertices of trapezoid $ABCD$ are $A(1, -4)$, $B(10, -4)$, $C(9, 2)$, and $D(2, 2)$.
   a. Show that $ABCD$ is an isosceles trapezoid.
   b. Show that the length of diagonal $\overline{AC}$ equals the length of diagonal $\overline{BD}$.

16. Plot the following points: $A(-2, 0)$, $B(0, -3)$, $C(2, 0)$. Connect the points in the order given. What kind of triangle is triangle ABC? Give an informal proof of your conclusion.

17. The vertices of $\triangle RST$ are $(1, 1)$, $(9, 4)$, and $(1, 7)$, respectively.
   a. Show that $\triangle RST$ is isosceles.
   b. Show that $\triangle RST$ is *not* a right triangle.

18. Find the length of a radius of a circle whose center is at $(0, 0)$ and that passes through the point $(12, 5)$.

19. The point $(2, 4)$ is on the circle whose center is $(6, 1)$. Find the length of a radius of the circle.

20. Find the length of a radius of a circle whose center is at the origin and that passes through the point $(-6, 8)$.

21. A circle whose center is at the point (5, 6) passes through the origin.
   a. Find the length of a radius.
   b. Show that (11, 11) lies on the circle.
   c. Show that (9, 12) does *not* lie on the circle.
22. A circle whose center is at (6, 8) passes through (12, 16).
   a. Find the length of a radius of the circle.
   b. On this circle, there is another point whose abscissa is 12. Find its ordinate.
23. $\triangle ABC$ has vertices $A(1, 1)$, $B(4, 1)$, and $C(4, 5)$. $\triangle DEF$ has vertices $D(3, -2)$, $E(6, -2)$ and $F(6, -6)$. Show $\triangle ABC \cong \triangle DEF$.

9-3 THE MIDPOINT OF A LINE SEGMENT

$A(1, 4)$ and $B(7, 4)$ determine a horizontal segment, $\overline{AB}$, whose midpoint M can be found by counting units. M has coordinates (4, 4), so that $AM = 3$ units and $MB = 3$ units.

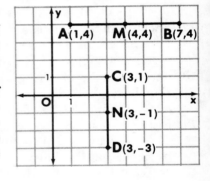

Notice how the binary operation of averaging can be used on the coordinates of A and B to determine the coordinates of the midpoint M. Here, the ordinate of point M is the same as the ordinate of points A and B.

Abscissa of M: $\dfrac{1 + 7}{2} = \dfrac{8}{2} = 4$.   Ordinate of M: $\dfrac{4 + 4}{2} = \dfrac{8}{2} = 4$.

Similarly, $C(3, 1)$ and $D(3, -3)$ determine a vertical segment, $\overline{CD}$, whose midpoint N can be found by counting units. N has coordinates $(3, -1)$, so that $CN = 2$ units and $ND = 2$ units. Again, notice how the binary operation of averaging can be used on the coordinates of C and D to determine the coordinates of the midpoint N. Here, the abscissa of point N is the same as the abscissa of points C and D.

Abscissa of N: $\dfrac{3 + 3}{2} = \dfrac{6}{2} = 3$.   Ordinate of N: $\dfrac{1 + (-3)}{2} = \dfrac{-2}{2} = -1$.

This concept of averaging is used to state our next theorem.

● **THEOREM 61. Each coordinate of the midpoint of a line segment is equal to the average of the corresponding coordinates of the endpoints of the line segment.**

Given: $\overline{AB}$ with coordinates $A(x_1, y_1)$ and $B(x_2, y_2)$. The midpoint of $\overline{AB}$ is point M.

Prove: The coordinates of midpoint M are $\left(\dfrac{x_1 + x_2}{2}, \dfrac{y_1 + y_2}{2}\right)$.

Plan: Draw right $\triangle ABC$ with hypotenuse $\overline{AB}$ and legs parallel to the x-axis and y-axis. Find the coordinates of the midpoint of each leg. From these coordinates, obtain the coordinates of midpoint M.

Proof:

Steps 1–2

1. Form $\triangle ABC$ by drawing through A a line parallel to the x-axis and by drawing through B a line parallel to the y-axis. Let C be the point at which the two lines intersect.

2. C has coordinates (x_2, y_1).

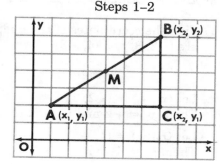

3. Let D be the midpoint of $\overline{BC}$. Then the coordinates of D are $\left(x_2, \dfrac{y_1 + y_2}{2}\right)$.

4. Let E be the midpoint of $\overline{AC}$. Then the coordinates of E are $\left(\dfrac{x_1 + x_2}{2}, y_1\right)$.

Steps 3–5

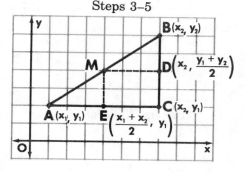

5. If a line joins the midpoints of two sides of a triangle, it is parallel to the third side (Theorem 53).

    $\overline{ME} \parallel \overline{BC} \parallel$ y-axis. M and E have the same x-coordinate.

    $\overline{MD} \parallel \overline{AC} \parallel$ x-axis. M and D have the same y-coordinate.

6. Therefore, the coordinates of M are $\left(\dfrac{x_1 + x_2}{2}, \dfrac{y_1 + y_2}{2}\right)$.

Step 6

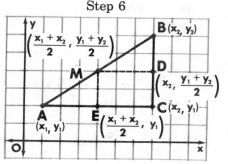

Using general coordinates, we now write the formula for the midpoint:

● **If the coordinates of the endpoints of $\overline{AB}$ are $A(x_1, y_1)$ and $B(x_2, y_2)$, and if $M(x_m, y_m)$ is the midpoint of $\overline{AB}$, then:**

$$x_m = \frac{x_1 + x_2}{2} \quad and \quad y_m = \frac{y_1 + y_2}{2}$$

MODEL PROBLEMS

1. Find the coordinates of the midpoint of the segment whose endpoints are $(-2, 3)$ and $(4, -3)$.

Solution

Let $(x_1, y_1) = (-2, 3)$.
Then, $x_1 = -2$ and $y_1 = 3$.

Let $(x_2, y_2) = (4, -3)$.
Then, $x_2 = 4$ and $y_2 = -3$.

$x_m = \dfrac{x_1 + x_2}{2} = \dfrac{-2 + 4}{2} = \dfrac{2}{2} = 1$

$y_m = \dfrac{y_1 + y_2}{2} = \dfrac{3 + (-3)}{2} = \dfrac{0}{2} = 0$

$(x_m, y_m) = (1, 0)$

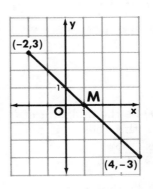

Answer: The coordinates of the midpoint are $(1, 0)$.

2. Midpoint M of $\overline{AB}$ has coordinates $(6, 5)$. If the coordinates of A are $(4, 1)$, what are the coordinates of B?

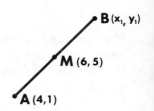

Solution

(1) Draw $\overline{AB}$ with midpoint M.
Label $A(4, 1)$ and $M(6, 5)$.

(2) The coordinates of B are unknown. Label $B(x_1, y_1)$.
Then, $A(4, 1)$ is (x_2, y_2). So, $x_2 = 4$ and $y_2 = 1$.
Also, $M(6, 5)$ is (x_m, y_m). So, $x_m = 6$ and $y_m = 5$.

(3) Write and solve two equations, one involving abscissas and one involving ordinates:

$$x_m = \frac{x_1 + x_2}{2} \qquad y_m = \frac{y_1 + y_2}{2}$$

$$6 = \frac{x_1 + 4}{2} \qquad 5 = \frac{y_1 + 1}{2}$$

$$12 = x_1 + 4 \qquad 10 = y_1 + 1$$

$$8 = x_1 \qquad 9 = y_1$$

Check: Is the midpoint of the segment with endpoints at (4, 1) and (8, 9) equal to (6, 5)?

$$\left(\frac{4 + 8}{2}, \frac{1 + 9}{2} \right) \stackrel{?}{=} (6, 5)$$

$$\left(\frac{12}{2}, \frac{10}{2} \right) \stackrel{?}{=} (6, 5)$$

(4) Therefore, $B(x_1, y_1) = (8, 9)$.

$$(6, 5) = (6, 5) \text{ (True)}$$

(5) *Check* the answer, as shown.

Answer: The coordinates of B are (8, 9).

---

3. Given the quadrilateral whose vertices are $A(-2, 2)$, $B(1, 4)$, $C(2, 8)$, and $D(-1, 6)$.

a. Find the coordinates of the midpoint of diagonal $\overline{AC}$.

b. Find the coordinates of the midpoint of diagonal $\overline{BD}$.

c. Show that $ABCD$ is a parallelogram.

Plan: Show that both diagonals have the same midpoint.

Solution:

a. (1) Let $A(-2, 2)$ be (x_1, y_1) and let $C(2, 8)$ be (x_2, y_2). Thus, $x_1 = -2$, $y_1 = 2$, $x_2 = 2$, $y_2 = 8$. Let the midpoint of $\overline{AC}$ be (x_m, y_m).

(2) By the midpoint formula:

$$(x_m, y_m) = \left(\frac{x_1 + x_2}{2}, \frac{y_1 + y_2}{2} \right)$$

$$(x_m, y_m) = \left(\frac{-2 + 2}{2}, \frac{2 + 8}{2} \right)$$

$$(x_m, y_m) = \left(\frac{0}{2}, \frac{10}{2} \right) = (0, 5)$$

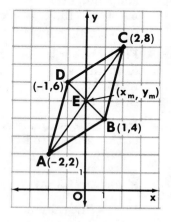

Answer: The midpoint of diagonal $\overline{AC}$ is (0, 5).

b. (1) Let $D(-1, 6)$ be (x_1, y_1) and let $B(1, 4)$ be (x_2, y_2). Thus, $x_1 = -1, y_1 = 6, x_2 = 1, y_2 = 4$. Let the midpoint of $\overline{BD}$ be (x_m, y_m).

(2) By the midpoint formula, $(x_m, y_m) = \left(\dfrac{x_1 + x_2}{2}, \dfrac{y_1 + y_2}{2}\right)$

$$(x_m, y_m) = \left(\dfrac{-1 + 1}{2}, \dfrac{6 + 4}{2}\right) = \left(\dfrac{0}{2}, \dfrac{10}{2}\right) = (0, 5)$$

Answer: The midpoint of diagonal $\overline{BD}$ is $(0, 5)$.

c. (1) Since the point $E(0, 5)$ is the midpoint of each diagonal, the diagonals bisect each other at point E.

(2) Since $ABCD$ is a quadrilateral whose diagonals bisect each other, it is a parallelogram.

EXERCISES

1. Find the coordinates of the midpoint of the line segment that joins each of the following pairs of points.
   a. $(6, 8), (4, 10)$ **b.** $(2, 6), (8, 4)$ **c.** $(2, 11), (7, 6)$
   d. $(5, -6), (-1, 9)$ **e.** $(-4, -8), (-6, -5)$ **f.** $(12, 11), (-1, -2)$
   g. $(2, 0), (5, 9)$ **h.** $(-2, 7), (0, -5)$ **i.** $(0, 0), (8, 10)$
   j. $(2, -7), (-2, 7)$ **k.** $(5c, 2c), (c, 8c)$ **l.** $(m, 0), (0, n)$

2. Find the abscissa of the midpoint of the line segment whose endpoints are:
   a. $(4, 8), (10, 12)$ **b.** $(6, -6), (12, -4)$ **c.** $(-7, -3), (-5, -7)$
   d. $(0, -5), (-7, 0)$ **e.** $(-4c, 2d), (8c, 6d)$ **f.** $(a, 0), (0, b)$

3. Find the ordinate of the midpoint of the line segment whose endpoints are:
   a. $(6, 10), (8, 6)$ **b.** $(8, -8), (14, -4)$ **c.** $(6, -4), (-9, 1)$
   d. $(-7, 6), (0, 0)$ **e.** $(a, 2b), (3a, 4b)$ **f.** $(c, 0), (0, d)$

4. In a circle, A and B are endpoints of a diameter, and P is the center of the circle. Find the coordinates of P, given the following coordinates for A and B.
   a. $(3, 4), (7, 8)$ **b.** $(-5, -2), (3, 7)$ **c.** $(0, 0), (10, 4)$
   d. $(8, 5), (-4, 5)$ **e.** $(1, 8), (1, -14)$ **f.** $(a, 0), (0, b)$

5. In $\triangle ABC$, the midpoints of sides $\overline{AB}$, $\overline{BC}$, and $\overline{CA}$ are points D, E, and F, respectively. Find the coordinates of D, E, and F, given the coordinates of the vertices.
   a. $A(2, 8), B(4, 12), C(6, 4)$ **b.** $A(-5, 2), B(7, 4), C(3, -6)$
   c. $A(8, 0), B(0, 5), C(4, 6)$ **d.** $A(-2, 0), B(0, -8), C(0, 0)$

6. Find the midpoints of the sides of a quadrilateral with vertices:
   a. $A(0, 0)$, $B(10, 0)$, $C(7, 5)$, $D(3, 5)$
   b. $P(-3, 3)$, $Q(11, 3)$, $R(7, 7)$, $S(1, 7)$

7. M is the midpoint of $\overline{CD}$. The coordinates of point C are $(8, 4)$ and of point $M(8, 10)$. Find the coordinates of point D.

8. M is the midpoint of $\overline{AB}$. Given the coordinates of points A and M, find the coordinates of point B.
   a. $A(4, 3)$, $M(4, 9)$ **b.** $A(4, 8)$, $M(6, 10)$ **c.** $A(2, 6)$, $M(0, 3)$
   d. $A(6, 10)$, $M(7, -2)$ **e.** $A(5, -1)$, $M(-1, 1)$ **f.** $A(a, 0)$, $M(2a, b)$

9. Given the points $A(-4, 6)$, $B(2, 7)$, and $C(r, s)$. If B is the midpoint of $\overline{AC}$, find the value of r and the value of s.

10. In parallelogram $ABCD$, the coordinates of A are $(6, 7)$, and the coordinates of C are $(12, 3)$. What are the coordinates of the point of intersection of the diagonals?

11. The points $A(2, 3)$, $B(7, 5)$, $C(8, 8)$, and $D(3, 6)$ are the vertices of a quadrilateral.
    a. Show that the diagonals of quadrilateral $ABCD$ bisect each other.
    b. Show that $ABCD$ is a parallelogram.

12. Show that the points $A(1, -3)$, $B(5, -2)$, $C(8, 2)$, and $D(4, 1)$ are the vertices of a parallelogram.

13. Show that the diagonals of the quadrilateral whose vertices are $A(3, 5)$, $B(6, 4)$, $C(7, 8)$, and $D(4, 12)$ do *not* bisect each other.

14. The points $A(4, 0)$, $B(14, 0)$, and $C(8, 6)$ are the vertices of triangle ABC. Show that the length of the line segment that joins the midpoints of $\overline{CA}$ and $\overline{CB}$ is equal to one-half of AB.

15. The points $A(2, 2)$, $B(6, -6)$, $C(8, 2)$, and $D(4, 4)$ are the vertices of polygon $ABCD$.
    a. Show that $\overline{LM}$, the line segment that joins the midpoints of $\overline{AD}$ and $\overline{DC}$, is congruent and parallel to $\overline{PN}$, the line segment that joins the midpoints of $\overline{BA}$ and $\overline{BC}$.
    b. If $\overline{MN}$ and $\overline{LP}$ are also drawn, what type of quadrilateral is $LMNP$?

In 16–23, answers that are not whole numbers should be left in radical form.

16. Given quadrilateral $ABCD$ whose vertices are $A(0, 0)$, $B(6, 8)$, $C(16, 8)$, and $D(10, 0)$.
    a. Using graph paper, draw quadrilateral $ABCD$.
    b. If R is the midpoint of $\overline{AB}$, S the midpoint of $\overline{BC}$, and T the midpoint of $\overline{AD}$: find: (1) RS, (2) ST, and (3) RT.
    c. Show that RST is a right triangle.

17. The vertices of quadrilateral $ABCD$ are $A(4, 0)$, $B(13, 3)$, $C(12, 6)$, and $D(3, 3)$.

    a. Find the coordinates of the midpoint of $\overline{AC}$.

    b. Find the coordinates of the midpoint of $\overline{BD}$.

    c. Show that $ABCD$ is a parallelogram.

    d. Find the lengths of diagonals $\overline{AC}$ and $\overline{BD}$.

    e. Show that $ABCD$ is a rectangle.

18. The vertices of a triangle are $R(7, 1)$, $S(2, 1)$, and $T(4, 7)$. Find the length of the median from R to $\overline{ST}$.

19. In $\triangle ABC$, the vertices are $A(4, 8)$, $B(-2, 6)$, and $C(0, -4)$. Find the lengths of the medians $\overline{AM}$, $\overline{BN}$, and $\overline{CP}$ in this triangle.

20. The vertices of $\triangle ABC$ are $A(0, 1)$, $B(6, 1)$, and $C(3, 5)$.

    a. Show that $\triangle ABC$ is isosceles.

    b. Find the length of the altitude from C to $\overline{AB}$.

21. The vertices of $\triangle RST$ are $R(11, -1)$, $S(13, 10)$, and $T(3, 5)$.

    a. Show that $\triangle RST$ is isosceles.

    b. Find the length of the altitude from S to $\overline{RT}$.

22. The vertices of $\triangle ABC$ are $A(3, 1)$, $B(9, 9)$ and $C(9, 1)$.

    a. Show that M, the midpoint of $\overline{AB}$, is equidistant from A, B, and C.

    b. Show that $\triangle ABC$ is a right triangle.

23. $P(2, 3)$ is the center of a circle.

    a. If $A(7, 3)$ and B are the endpoints of a diameter of this circle, find the coordinates of B.

    b. Find the length of a radius.

    c. Show that $C(-2, 0)$ is a point on the circle.

    d. Show that $\triangle ABC$ is a right triangle.

9-4   THE SLOPE OF A LINE

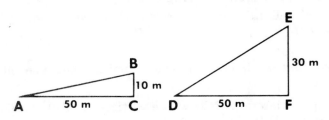

Of the two roads, $\overline{AB}$ and $\overline{DE}$, which is steeper? To answer this question, compare the slopes of the two roads. Recall that a *slope* is a ratio of the change in the vertical distance to the change in the horizontal distance. Therefore:

slope of road $\overline{AB}$ = $\dfrac{\text{change in the vertical distance, } CB}{\text{change in the horizontal distance, } AC}$ = $\dfrac{10 \text{ m}}{50 \text{ m}}$ = $\dfrac{1}{5}$

slope of road $\overline{DE}$ = $\dfrac{\text{change in the vertical distance, } FE}{\text{change in the horizontal distance, } DF}$ = $\dfrac{30 \text{ m}}{50 \text{ m}}$ = $\dfrac{3}{5}$

Since $\frac{3}{5} > \frac{1}{5}$, the slope $\overline{DE}$ is greater than the slope of $\overline{AB}$, and road $\overline{DE}$ is steeper than road $\overline{AB}$. Let us state a more precise definition of slope.

● **Definition.** The *slope, m, of a line,* $\overleftrightarrow{AB}$, where A has coordinates (x_1, y_1) and B has coordinates (x_2, y_2) and $x_1 \neq x_2$, is the ratio of the difference of the y-values to the difference of the corresponding x-values; that is, the slope is:

$$m = \frac{y_2 - y_1}{x_2 - x_1} \quad \text{or} \quad m = \frac{y_1 - y_2}{x_1 - x_2}$$

By letting $\Delta x = x_2 - x_1$, that is, delta x equals the difference in x-values, and $\Delta y = y_2 - y_1$, that is, delta y equals the difference in y-values, we may also represent the slope of a line by:

$$\text{slope} = m = \frac{\Delta y}{\Delta x}$$

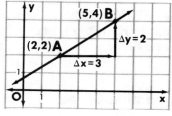

Replace the general terms with specific values given for coordinates of points on the line, $\overleftrightarrow{AB}$. Since $A(x_1, y_1) = (2, 2)$ and $B(x_2, y_2) = (5, 4)$, we can determine the slope by using the formulas noted above.

$$m = \frac{y_2 - y_1}{x_2 - x_1} = \frac{4 - 2}{5 - 2} = \frac{2}{3} \quad \text{or} \quad m = \frac{\Delta y}{\Delta x} = \frac{2}{3}$$

Also, $m = \dfrac{y_1 - y_2}{x_1 - x_2} = \dfrac{2 - 4}{2 - 5} = \dfrac{-2}{-3} = \dfrac{2}{3}.$

Either formula may be used to determine the slope of a line. Also, either of two points may be identified by the coordinates (x_1, y_1).

The definition of the slope of a line uses two points on the line. The following postulate assures us that two points exist.

● **POSTULATE 51. A line contains as least two points.**

Every line is classified as having either a positive slope, a negative slope, a zero slope, or no slope.

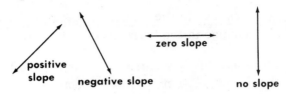

Positive Slope

In the figure, as we read from left to right, $\overleftrightarrow{CD}$ slants upward, or *rises*. What happens as a point moves from position C to position D? Let $C(x_1, y_1) = (3, 1)$, and $D(x_2, y_2) = (5, 4)$. Consider the slope m of $\overleftrightarrow{CD}$.

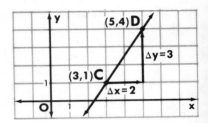

$$m = \frac{\Delta y}{\Delta x} = \frac{y_2 - y_1}{x_2 - x_1} = \frac{4 - 1}{5 - 3} = \frac{+3}{+2} = +\frac{3}{2}$$

Both Δy and Δx are positive, indicating that y increases as x increases. Thus, the ratio of two positive numbers is positive, illustrating:

● **PRINCIPLE 1. As a point moves from left to right along a line that is rising, y increases as x increases, and the slope of the line is positive.**

Negative Slope

In the figure, as we read from left to right, $\overleftrightarrow{EF}$ slants downward, or *falls*. What happens as a point moves from position E to position F? Let $E(x_1, y_1) = (2, 3)$, and $F(x_2, y_2) = (5, 1)$. Consider the slope m of $\overleftrightarrow{EF}$.

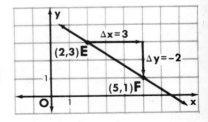

$$m = \frac{\Delta y}{\Delta x} = \frac{y_2 - y_1}{x_2 - x_1} = \frac{1 - 3}{5 - 2} = \frac{-2}{+3} = -\frac{2}{3}$$

Since Δy is negative and Δx is positive, y decreases as x increases. The ratio of a negative number to a positive number is negative, thus:

● **PRINCIPLE 2.   As a point moves from left to right along a line that is falling, y decreases as x increases, and the slope of the line is negative.**

Zero Slope

In the figure, $\overleftrightarrow{AB}$ is parallel to the x-axis. What happens as a point moves from position A to position B? Since the ordinates of points A and B must be equal, label $A(x_1,\ y_1)$ and $B(x_2,\ y_1)$ where $x_1 \neq x_2$. Using these general coordinates, we find the slope m of $\overleftrightarrow{AB}$.

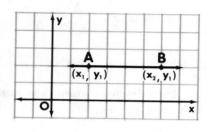

$$m = \frac{\Delta y}{\Delta x} = \frac{y_1 - y_1}{x_2 - x_1} = \frac{0}{x_2 - x_1} = 0$$

These steps form the basis of a proof for the following theorem:

● **THEOREM 62.   A line parallel to the x-axis has a slope of zero.**

Since a line is parallel to itself, the slope of the x-axis is zero.

No Slope

In the figure, $\overleftrightarrow{CD}$ is parallel to the y-axis. Since the abscissas of points C and D must be equal, label $C(x_1,\ y_1)$ and $D(x_1,\ y_2)$ where $y_1 \neq y_2$. Apply the definition of slope to find:

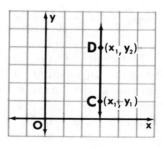

$$m = \frac{\Delta y}{\Delta x} = \frac{y_2 - y_1}{x_1 - x_1} = \frac{y_2 - y_1}{0} \text{ (undefined)}$$

Since division by zero is undefined, or meaningless, we have proved:

● **THEOREM 63.   A line parallel to the y-axis has no defined slope.**

Since a line is parallel to itself, the y-axis has no defined slope.

Slopes and Collinearity

The figure shows three *noncollinear* points: $A(2, 1)$, $B(4, 2)$, and $C(5, 5)$. Two distinct lines, $\overleftrightarrow{AB}$ and $\overleftrightarrow{BC}$, pass through the same point B.

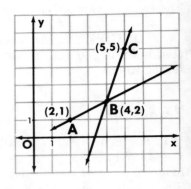

$$\text{Slope of } \overleftrightarrow{AB} = \frac{\Delta y}{\Delta x} = \frac{2 - 1}{4 - 2} = \frac{1}{2}.$$

$$\text{Slope of } \overleftrightarrow{BC} = \frac{\Delta y}{\Delta x} = \frac{5 - 2}{5 - 4} = \frac{3}{1}.$$

This example illustrates the fact that:

● **Two distinct lines that pass through the same point must have unequal slopes.**

The figure shows three *collinear* points: $D(2, 2)$, $E(4, 3)$, and $F(8, 5)$. Notice that the slope determined by any two distinct points on this line is always the same value.

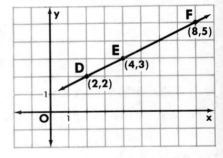

$$\text{Slope of } \overleftrightarrow{DE} = \frac{\Delta y}{\Delta x} = \frac{3 - 2}{4 - 2} = \frac{1}{2}.$$

$$\text{Slope of } \overleftrightarrow{EF} = \frac{\Delta y}{\Delta x} = \frac{5 - 3}{8 - 4} = \frac{2}{4} = \frac{1}{2}.$$

$$\text{Slope of } \overleftrightarrow{DF} = \frac{\Delta y}{\Delta x} = \frac{5 - 2}{8 - 2} = \frac{3}{6} = \frac{1}{2}.$$

In the figure, auxiliary lines have been drawn parallel to the x-axis or parallel to the y-axis. It can be shown that $\triangle EGD \sim \triangle FHE \sim \triangle FRD$. Therefore the lengths of corresponding segments are in proportion $\left(\dfrac{EG}{GD} = \dfrac{FH}{HE} = \dfrac{FR}{RD} \right)$, and thus the

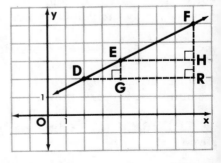

slope is a constant value. Similar reasoning can form the basis for the proof of the following statement:

● **THEOREM 64.** **Three points are collinear if the slope determined by the first point and the second point is equal to:**

(*a*) **The slope determined by the second point and the third point,**

or

(*b*) **The slope determined by the first point and the third point.**

MODEL PROBLEMS

1. Find the slope of the line that passes through the points $C(-2, 1)$ and $D(0, 4)$.

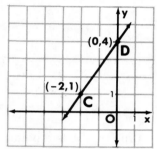

Solution

Let $C(-2, 1) = (x_1, y_1)$.
Then $x_1 = -2$, $y_1 = 1$.
Let $D(0, 4) = (x_2, y_2)$.
Then $x_2 = 0$, $y_2 = 4$.

Slope of $\overleftrightarrow{CD} = m = \dfrac{y_2 - y_1}{x_2 - x_1} = \dfrac{4 - 1}{0 - (-2)} = \dfrac{4 - 1}{0 + 2} = \dfrac{3}{2}$.

Answer: Slope of $\overleftrightarrow{CD} = \frac{3}{2}$.

2. Find the value of k so that the slope of the line passing through the points $(2, 3)$ and $(k, 4)$ will be $\frac{1}{3}$.

Solution

(1) Let $(x_1, y_1) = (2, 3)$. Let $(x_2, y_2) = (k, 4)$. The slope $m = \frac{1}{3}$. Then $x_1 = 2$, $y_1 = 3$, $x_2 = k$, and $y_2 = 4$.

(2) Write the slope formula: $\qquad m = \dfrac{y_2 - y_1}{x_2 - x_1}$

(3) Substitute the given values: $\qquad \dfrac{1}{3} = \dfrac{4 - 3}{k - 2}$

(4) Simplify and solve: $\qquad \dfrac{1}{3} = \dfrac{1}{k - 2}$

$$k - 2 = 3$$

$$k = 5$$

Check:
If $k = 5$, find the slope of the line passing through $(2, 3)$ and $(5, 4)$.

$$\frac{1}{3} \stackrel{?}{=} \frac{4 - 3}{5 - 2}$$

$\frac{1}{3} = \frac{1}{3}$ (True)

Answer: $k = 5$

3. Show that the points $A(1, 4)$, $B(3, 3)$, and $C(7, 1)$ are collinear.

   Plan: Show that the slope of $\overleftrightarrow{AB}$ is equal to the slope of $\overleftrightarrow{AC}$.

   Solution:

   (1) Let $A(1, 4) = (x_1, y_1)$.
   Let $B(3, 3) = (x_2, y_2)$.

   Slope of $\overleftrightarrow{AB} = \dfrac{y_2 - y_1}{x_2 - x_1}$

   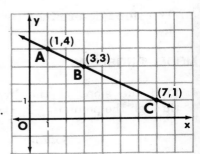

   $$= \frac{3 - 4}{3 - 1} = \frac{-1}{2} = -\frac{1}{2}.$$

   (2) Let $A(1, 4) = (x_1, y_1)$.
   Let $C(7, 1) = (x_2, y_2)$.

   Slope of $\overleftrightarrow{AC} = \dfrac{y_2 - y_1}{x_2 - x_1} = \dfrac{1 - 4}{7 - 1} = \dfrac{-3}{6} = \dfrac{-1}{2} = -\dfrac{1}{2}.$

   (3) Since A is a point on $\overleftrightarrow{AB}$ as well as $\overleftrightarrow{AC}$, and since the slope of $\overleftrightarrow{AB}$ is equal to the slope of $\overleftrightarrow{AC}$, points A, B, and C all lie on the same line, and are therefore collinear.

EXERCISES

1. For each of the lines in the diagram, $\overleftrightarrow{AB}$, $\overleftrightarrow{CD}$, $\overleftrightarrow{EF}$, $\overleftrightarrow{GH}$, $\overleftrightarrow{JK}$, $\overleftrightarrow{LM}$, $\overleftrightarrow{PQ}$, $\overleftrightarrow{RS}$, $\overleftrightarrow{TU}$, and $\overleftrightarrow{VW}$: **a.** Tell whether the line has a positive slope, a negative slope, a slope of zero, or no slope. **b.** If the line has a slope, find the slope of the line.

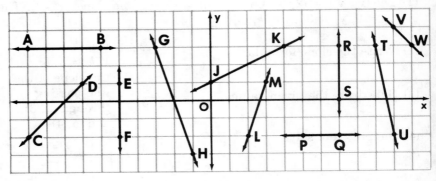

2. In each part, plot both points on graph paper, draw the line determined by these points, and find the slope of this line.
   a. $(0, 0)$ and $(9, 3)$ **b.** $(0, 0)$ and $(-2, 4)$ **c.** $(-2, -6)$ and $(0, 0)$

d. (0, 4) and (2, 8)   **e.** (−5, 6) and (−1, 0)   **f.** (0, −3) and (−6, 0)
g. (1, 5) and (3, 9)   **h.** (2, 3) and (4, 15)   **i.** (5, 8) and (4, 3)
j. (2, 7) and (6, 9)   **k.** (4, 6) and (−5, 9)   **l.** (5, −2) and (7, −8)

3. Find the slope of the line that passes through (3, 5) and (8, 5).
4. Find the value of k so that the slope of the line passing through the points (5, 3) and (k, 6) will be 1.
5. Find the value of t so that the slope of the line passing through the points (2, t) and (6, 10) will be $\frac{1}{2}$.
6. Find the value of y so that the slope of the line passing through the points (−8, −2) and (4, y) will be 0.
7. Find the value of x so that the line passing through the points (−4, 8) and (x, −2) will have no slope.
8. In each of the following, determine whether the points are collinear:
   a. (1, 2), (4, 5), (6, 7)   **b.** (−1, −4), (2, −2), (8, 2)
   c. (1, 1), (3, 4), (6, 5)   **d.** (−2, 6), (0, 2), (1, 0)
   e. (0, 0), (−8, −2), (4, 1)   **f.** (−3, 4), (−1, 1), (1, −3)
9. Given points A(1, 1), B(3, 2), and C(k, 4).
   a. Using the coordinates of A and B, find the slope of $\overleftrightarrow{AB}$.
   b. Using the coordinates of B and C, express the slope of $\overleftrightarrow{BC}$ in terms of k.
   c. If A, B, and C are collinear, write an equation that can be used to find the value of k.
   d. Find k.
10. Given points D(1, 3), E(5, 5), and F(7, d).
    a. Find the slope of $\overleftrightarrow{DE}$.
    b. Express the slope of $\overleftrightarrow{EF}$ in terms of d.
    c. If D, E, and F are collinear points, find the value of d.
11. $\overleftrightarrow{CD}$ passes through the points (−4, −2) and (8, 7).
    a. Find the slope of $\overleftrightarrow{CD}$.
    b. True or false: $\overleftrightarrow{CD}$ passes through the point (0, 1).
    c. True or false: $\overleftrightarrow{CD}$ passes through the point (11, 11).

In 12–17, draw a line with the given slope m through the given point.

12. (0, 3), $m = 1$ **13.** (1, 4), $m = 2$ **14.** (2, −1), $m = -1$
15. (4, 1), $m = \frac{1}{4}$ **16.** (−3, 5), $m = -\frac{1}{2}$ **17.** (0, −3), $m = \frac{2}{3}$

18. The points A(1, 0), B(3, 6), and C(9, 4) are the vertices of $\triangle ABC$.
    a. Find the slope of each side of $\triangle ABC$.
    b. If D, E, and F are the midpoints of $\overline{AB}$, $\overline{BC}$, and $\overline{CA}$, respectively, find the coordinates of D, E, and F.
    c. Find the slopes of the medians $\overline{AE}$, $\overline{BF}$, and $\overline{CD}$.

19. The points $R(1, 2)$, $S(5, 6)$, and $T(9, 4)$ are the vertices of $\triangle RST$.
   a. Find the slope of each side of $\triangle RST$.
   b. Find the slope of each of the three medians in $\triangle RST$, or indicate
   that a median has no slope.

9-5 PARALLEL LINES AND PERPENDICULAR LINES

We can use the slopes of lines to state conditions for parallelism or perpendicularity. For example, we already know that:

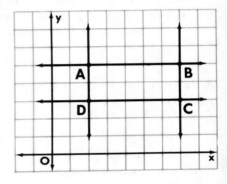

1. Two horizontal lines (lines that have a slope of 0) are parallel. Here, $\overleftrightarrow{AB} \parallel \overleftrightarrow{DC}$.

2. Two vertical lines (lines that have no defined slope) are parallel. Here, $\overleftrightarrow{AD} \parallel \overleftrightarrow{BC}$.

3. A vertical line (having no defined slope) and a horizontal line (having a slope of 0) are perpendicular to each other. Here, $\overleftrightarrow{AB} \perp \overleftrightarrow{AD}$, $\overleftrightarrow{AB} \perp \overleftrightarrow{BC}$, $\overleftrightarrow{AD} \perp \overleftrightarrow{DC}$, and $\overleftrightarrow{BC} \perp \overleftrightarrow{DC}$.

What relationships will be true for the slopes of parallel or perpendicular lines when the lines are neither horizontal nor vertical?

Parallel Lines

In the figure, $\overleftrightarrow{AB} \parallel \overleftrightarrow{CD}$. Use the coordinates given in the diagram:

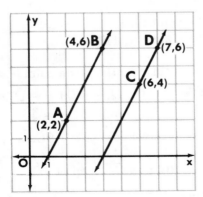

Slope of $\overleftrightarrow{AB} = \dfrac{y_2 - y_1}{x_2 - x_1}$

$$= \frac{6 - 2}{4 - 2} = \frac{4}{2} = \frac{2}{1}$$

Slope of $\overleftrightarrow{CD} = \dfrac{y_2 - y_1}{x_2 - x_1}$

$$= \frac{6 - 4}{7 - 6} = \frac{2}{1}$$

This example illustrates our next theorem, which will be proved without the use of specific coordinates.

● **THEOREM 65.** **If two nonvertical lines are parallel, then their slopes are equal.**

Given: $\overleftrightarrow{AB} \parallel \overleftrightarrow{CD}$.

Prove: The slope of $\overleftrightarrow{AB}$ is equal to the slope of $\overleftrightarrow{CD}$, that is, $\dfrac{BE}{AE} = \dfrac{DF}{CF}$.

Plan: (1) Draw $\overline{AE}$, $\overline{BE}$, $\overline{CF}$, and $\overline{DF}$, with $\overline{AE} \parallel x$-axis, $\overline{CF} \parallel x$-axis, $\overline{BE} \parallel y$-axis, and $\overline{DF} \parallel y$-axis.

(2) Thus, $\overline{BE} \perp \overline{AE}$ and $\overline{DF} \perp \overline{CF}$.

(3) $\angle BEA \cong \angle DFC$. (a. $\cong$ a.)

(4) $\angle A \cong \angle 1$, $\angle C \cong \angle 2$, and $\angle 1 \cong \angle 2$. Therefore, by substitution, $\angle A \cong \angle C$. (a. $\cong$ a.)

(5) $\triangle AEB \sim \triangle CFD$ (a.a. $\cong$ a.a.) and $\dfrac{BE}{AE} = \dfrac{DF}{CF}$.

In other words:

If $\overleftrightarrow{AB}$ is *parallel* to $\overleftrightarrow{CD}$, the slope of $\overleftrightarrow{AB} = m_1$, and the slope of $\overleftrightarrow{CD} = m_2$, then:

$$m_1 = m_2$$

The next theorem is the converse of Theorem 65, namely:

● **THEOREM 66.** **If two nonvertical lines have equal slopes, then the lines are parallel.**

Given: The slope of $\overleftrightarrow{AB}$ is equal to the slope of $\overleftrightarrow{CD}$.

Prove: $\overleftrightarrow{AB} \parallel \overleftrightarrow{CD}$.

Plan: Use an indirect proof.
Assume $\overleftrightarrow{AB} \not\parallel \overleftrightarrow{CD}$.
Draw $\overleftrightarrow{CG}$ parallel to $\overleftrightarrow{AB}$.
Use Theorems 64 and 65 to show that $\overleftrightarrow{CG}$ and $\overleftrightarrow{CD}$ must be the same line, or $\overleftrightarrow{AB} \parallel \overleftrightarrow{CD}$.

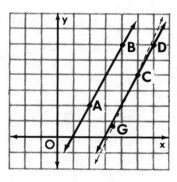

Perpendicular Lines

In the figure, $\overleftrightarrow{AB} \perp \overleftrightarrow{BC}$. Use the coordinates of A, B, and C to find:

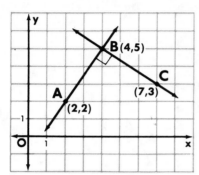

Slope of $\overleftrightarrow{AB} = \dfrac{y_2 - y_1}{x_2 - x_1}$

$$= \dfrac{5 - 2}{4 - 2} = \dfrac{3}{2}$$

Slope of $\overleftrightarrow{BC} = \dfrac{y_2 - y_1}{x_2 - x_1}$

$$= \dfrac{3 - 5}{7 - 4} = \dfrac{-2}{3} = -\dfrac{2}{3}$$

In this example, where $\overleftrightarrow{AB} \perp \overleftrightarrow{BC}$, the product of the slopes of the lines is -1, that is, $\left(\dfrac{3}{2}\right)\left(-\dfrac{2}{3}\right) = -1$.

● **Definition.** One number is the *negative reciprocal* of a second number if the product of the two numbers is -1.

In general terms, if $a \neq 0$ and $b \neq 0$, it can be said that $-\dfrac{b}{a}$ is the negative reciprocal of $\dfrac{a}{b}$ since $\left(\dfrac{a}{b}\right)\left(-\dfrac{b}{a}\right) = -1$.

Thus, to find the negative reciprocal of a fraction, we simply invert the fraction and change its sign.

● **THEOREM 67. If two nonvertical lines are perpendicular, then the slope of one line is the negative reciprocal of the slope of the other line.**

Given: $\overleftrightarrow{AB} \perp \overleftrightarrow{BC}$, slope of $\overleftrightarrow{AB} = m_1$, and slope of $\overleftrightarrow{BC} = m_2$.

Prove: $m_2 = -\dfrac{1}{m_1}$.

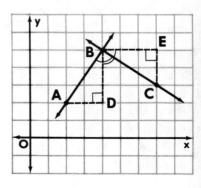

Plan: (1) Draw $\overline{AD}$, $\overline{BD}$, $\overline{BE}$, and $\overline{EC}$ so that $\overleftrightarrow{AD} \parallel x$-axis, $\overleftrightarrow{BE} \parallel x$-axis, $\overleftrightarrow{BD} \parallel y$-axis, and $\overleftrightarrow{EC} \parallel y$-axis. Thus, $\overleftrightarrow{BD} \perp \overleftrightarrow{AD}$, and $\overleftrightarrow{EC} \perp \overleftrightarrow{BE}$.

(2) $\angle BDA$ and $\angle BEC$ are both right angles, so $\angle BDA \cong \angle BEC$. (a. $\cong$ a.)

(3) Given $\overleftrightarrow{AB} \perp \overleftrightarrow{BC}$, $\angle ABC$ is a right angle. Then the complement of $\angle DBC$ is $\angle ABD$. Also, since $\overleftrightarrow{BE} \perp \overleftrightarrow{BD}$, $\angle DBE$ is a right angle. Then the complement of $\angle DBC$ is $\angle CBE$. Complements of the same angle are congruent, or $\angle ABD \cong \angle CBE$. (a. $\cong$ a.)

(4) $\triangle ABD \sim \triangle CBE$ by a.a. $\cong$ a.a. Since corresponding sides of similar triangles are in proportion, $\dfrac{BD}{AD} = \dfrac{BE}{CE}$.

(5) The slope of $\overleftrightarrow{AB} = m_1$. Therefore, $\dfrac{BD}{AD} = m_1$.

(6) From the proportion given in step (4), $\dfrac{BE}{EC} = m_1$, and therefore its reciprocal $\dfrac{EC}{BE} = \dfrac{1}{m_1}$.

(7) The slope of $\overleftrightarrow{BC} = m_2$. However, going from left to right, $\overleftrightarrow{BC}$ *falls*. Therefore, the slope of $\overleftrightarrow{BC}$ is a *negative* number, or the slope of $\overleftrightarrow{BC} = m_2 = -\left(\dfrac{EC}{BE}\right) = -\left(\dfrac{1}{m_1}\right)$.

In other words:

If $\overleftrightarrow{AB}$ is *perpendicular* to $\overleftrightarrow{CD}$, the slope of $\overleftrightarrow{AB} = m_1$, and the slope of $\overleftrightarrow{CD} = m_2$, then:

$$m_1 = -\frac{1}{m_2} \quad or \quad m_2 = -\frac{1}{m_1} \quad or \quad m_1 \cdot m_2 = -1$$

The converse of Theorem 67 may also be proved, namely:

● **THEOREM 68. If the slope of one line is the negative reciprocal of the slope of a second line, then the lines are perpendicular.**

Plan: Use the figure for Theorem 67. Using an indirect proof, assume that $\overleftrightarrow{AB}$ is *not* perpendicular to $\overleftrightarrow{BC}$. Through B, draw $\overleftrightarrow{BF}$ perpendicular to $\overleftrightarrow{AB}$. Use Theorems 67, 66, and 64 to show that $\overleftrightarrow{BF}$ and $\overleftrightarrow{BC}$ are parallel lines with a common point and, therefore, are the same line.

KEEP IN MIND ────────────────────────────────

When $\overleftrightarrow{AB}$ and $\overleftrightarrow{CD}$ are two nonvertical lines with the slope of $\overleftrightarrow{AB} = m_1$ and the slope of $\overleftrightarrow{CD} = m_2$:

(1) $\overleftrightarrow{AB} \parallel \overleftrightarrow{CD}$ if and only if $m_1 = m_2$.

(2) $\overleftrightarrow{AB} \perp \overleftrightarrow{CD}$ if and only if $m_1 = -\dfrac{1}{m_2}$, or $m_1 \cdot m_2 = -1$.

MODEL PROBLEMS ────────────────────────────

1. Quadrilateral $ABCD$ is a rectangle with vertices $A(2, 5)$, $B(2, -2)$, and $C(6, -2)$. What are the coordinates of point D?

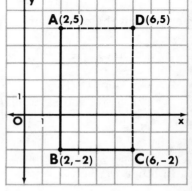

Solution:

(1) Plot points $A(2, 5)$, $B(2, -2)$, and $C(6, -2)$.

(2) Connect points A to B and B to C, forming two sides of the rectangle and right angle ABC.

(3) From A, draw a line parallel to $\overline{BC}$. Also, from C, draw a line parallel to $\overline{BA}$. These two lines meet at point D.

(4) The coordinates of D are $(6, 5)$. Notice that the abscissa, 6, is equal to the abscissa of point C. Also, the ordinate, 5, is equal to the ordinate of point A.

Answer: $(6, 5)$, or $x = 6$ and $y = 5$.

2. Show, by means of slopes, that the quadrilateral whose vertices are $A(1, 1)$, $B(3, -2)$, $C(4, 1)$, and $D(2, 4)$ is a parallelogram.

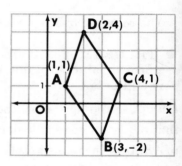

Plan: Show opposite sides parallel by demonstrating that their slopes are equal.

Solution:

(1) Let $A(1, 1) = (x_1, y_1)$. Let $B(3, -2) = (x_2, y_2)$.

Slope of $\overline{AB} = \dfrac{y_2 - y_1}{x_2 - x_1} = \dfrac{-2 - 1}{3 - 1} = \dfrac{-3}{2} = -\dfrac{3}{2}$

(2) Let $D(2, 4) = (x_1, y_1)$. Let $C(4, 1) = (x_2, y_2)$.

Slope of $\overline{DC} = \dfrac{y_2 - y_1}{x_2 - x_1} = \dfrac{1 - 4}{4 - 2} = \dfrac{-3}{2} = -\dfrac{3}{2}$

(3) Since slope of $\overline{AB}$ = slope of $\overline{DC} = -\dfrac{3}{2}$, $\overline{AB}$ is parallel to $\overline{DC}$.

(4) Let $B(3, -2) = (x_1, y_1)$. Let $C(4, 1) = (x_2, y_2)$.

Slope of $\overline{BC} = \dfrac{y_2 - y_1}{x_2 - x_1} = \dfrac{1 - (-2)}{4 - 3} = \dfrac{1 + 2}{4 - 3} = \dfrac{3}{1} = 3$

(5) Let $A(1, 1) = (x_1, y_1)$. Let $D(2, 4) = (x_2, y_2)$.

Slope of $\overline{AD} = \dfrac{y_2 - y_1}{x_2 - x_1} = \dfrac{4 - 1}{2 - 1} = \dfrac{3}{1} = 3$

(6) Since slope of $\overline{BC}$ = slope of $\overline{AD} = 3$, $\overline{BC}$ is parallel to $\overline{AD}$.

(7) Since the opposite sides of quadrilateral $ABCD$ are parallel, quadrilateral $ABCD$ is a parallelogram.

3. Show, by means of slopes, that the triangle whose vertices are $A(0, 2)$, $B(2, 3)$, and $C(1, 5)$ is a right triangle.

Plan: Show two sides perpendicular by demonstrating that their slopes are negative reciprocals.

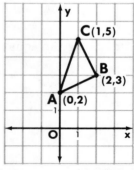

Solution:

(1) Let $A(0, 2) = (x_1, y_1)$. Let $B(2, 3) = (x_2, y_2)$.

Slope of $\overline{AB} = \dfrac{y_2 - y_1}{x_2 - x_1} = \dfrac{3 - 2}{2 - 0} = \dfrac{1}{2}$

(2) Let $B(2, 3) = (x_1, y_1)$. Let $C(1, 5) = (x_2, y_2)$.

Slope of $\overline{BC} = \dfrac{y_2 - y_1}{x_2 - x_1} = \dfrac{5 - 3}{1 - 2} = \dfrac{2}{-1} = -2$

(3) The slope of $\overline{AB}$ is the negative reciprocal of the slope of $\overline{BC}$ because $(\frac{1}{2})(-2) = -1$. Therefore, $\overline{AB}$ is perpendicular to $\overline{BC}$.

(4) $\triangle ABC$ is a right triangle because it contains right angle ABC.

4. In trapezoid $ABCD$, $\overline{AB} \parallel \overline{DC}$. The vertices are $A(1, 4)$, $B(3, 5)$, $C(k, 3)$, and $D(1, 1)$.
   a. Find the slope of $\overline{AB}$.
   b. Express the slope of $\overline{DC}$ in terms of k.
   c. Write an equation that can be used to solve for k.
   d. Find the value of k.

Solution:

a. Let $A(1, 4) = (x_1, y_1)$. Let $B(3, 5) = (x_2, y_2)$.

   Slope of $\overline{AB} = \dfrac{y_2 - y_1}{x_2 - x_1} = \dfrac{5 - 4}{3 - 1} = \dfrac{1}{2}$

b. Let $D(1, 1) = (x_1, y_1)$. Let $C(k, 3) = (x_2, y_2)$.

   Slope of $\overline{DC} = \dfrac{y_2 - y_1}{x_2 - x_1} = \dfrac{3 - 1}{k - 1} = \dfrac{2}{k - 1}$

c. Since $\overline{AB} \parallel \overline{DC}$, their slopes are equal. From parts **a** and **b**:

$$\frac{1}{2} = \frac{2}{k - 1}$$

d. Solve the equation: $k - 1 = 4$
$$k = 5$$

Check: If $k = 5$,

$$\frac{1}{2} \overset{?}{=} \frac{3 - 1}{5 - 1}$$

$$\frac{1}{2} \overset{?}{=} \frac{2}{4}$$

$$\frac{1}{2} = \frac{1}{2} \text{ (True)}$$

Answers: **a.** $\dfrac{1}{2}$ **b.** $\dfrac{2}{k - 1}$ **c.** $\dfrac{1}{2} = \dfrac{2}{k - 1}$ **d.** 5

EXERCISES

In 1–4, $ABCD$ is a rectangle, and coordinates are given for A, B, and C. Find the coordinates of point D.

1. $A(-1, 4)$, $B(3, 4)$, $C(3, 2)$
3. $A(-2, 0)$, $B(-2, -5)$, $C(-4, -5)$

2. $A(1, -1)$, $B(1, 6)$, $C(0, 6)$
4. $A(6, 1)$, $B(8, 3)$, $C(10, 1)$

5. In parallelogram *PQRS*, three of the four vertices are (0, 0), (4, 0), and (2, 3). Tell whether or not each of the following can be the coordinates of the fourth vertex of the parallelogram.
 a. (6, 3) **b.** (4, 3) **c.** (−2, 3) **d.** (3, −2) **e.** (2, −3)

6. In parallelogram *ABCD*, three of the four vertices are (1, 0), (0, 3), and (2, 3). Tell whether or not each of the following can be the coordinates of the fourth vertex of the parallelogram.
 a. (3, 0) **b.** (1, 6) **c.** (0, 0) **d.** (−1, 0) **e.** (0, −1)

7. The vertices of a parallelogram are (1, 3), (3, 5), (4, 1), and (*k*, 3). Find *k*.

8. Three vertices of a parallelogram are (0, 0), (2, 0), and (1, 3). Find *k* if the fourth vertex of the parallelogram is:
 a. (3, *k*) **b.** (−1, *k*) **c.** (1, *k*)

In 9–16, □*OABC* has vertices *O*(0, 0), *A*(4, 0), *B*(2, 2), and *C*(−2, 2). All other small parallelograms in the diagram are congruent to □*OABC*. Find the coordinates of the points named.

9. *D* **10.** *E* **11.** *F* **12.** *G*
13. *H* **14.** *J* **15.** *K* **16.** *L*

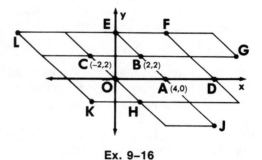

Ex. 9–16

17. Show that the line joining the points (1, 3) and (5, 6) is parallel to the line joining the points (5, 1) and (9, 4).

18. The vertices of quadrilateral *ABCD* are *A*(2, 3), *B*(8, 5), *C*(9, 9), and *D*(3, 7).
 a. Using graph paper, draw quadrilateral *ABCD*.
 b. Find the slope of each side of the quadrilateral.
 c. Show that *ABCD* is a parallelogram.

19. Using the formula for the slope of a line, show that the points (−2, 3), (2, 7), (8, 5), and (4, 1) are the vertices of a parallelogram.

20. a. Show, by using the formula for the slope of a line, that the points (3, 1), (6, 3), (10, 0), and (7, −2) are the vertices of a parallelogram.
 b. Show the same conclusion by showing that the diagonals of the quadrilateral bisect each other.

21. a. Show, by using the formula for the slope of a line, that the points (−4, 0), (−1, 3), (3, 1), and (0, −2) are the vertices of a parallelogram.
 b. Show the same conclusion by showing that both pairs of opposite sides of the quadrilateral are equal in length.

22. The coordinates of the vertices of quadrilateral $ABCD$ are $A(0, 5)$, $B(3, 4)$, $C(0, -5)$, and $D(-3, -4)$.
    a. Using graph paper, draw quadrilateral $ABCD$.
    b. Show that $ABCD$ is a parallelogram.
    c. Show that $ABCD$ is a rectangle.
23. Find the slope of a line perpendicular to a line whose slope is:
    a. $\frac{3}{4}$ b. $\frac{5}{9}$ c. $-\frac{2}{3}$ d. 4   e. -3 f. $1\frac{1}{4}$ g. .1
24. Find the slope of a line perpendicular to the line that passes through the points:
    a. $(5, 6)$ and $(8, 11)$ b. $(1, 4)$ and $(3, -7)$ c. $(-2, -3)$ and $(0, 3)$
25. Show that the line that passes through $(2, 3)$ and $(5, 1)$ is perpendicular to the line that passes through $(5, 4)$ and $(1, -2)$.

In 26 and 27, the given points A, B, and C are the vertices of a triangle. a. Find the slope of each side of the triangle. b. Find the slope of each altitude of the triangle.

26. $A(1, 1)$, $B(5, 2)$, $C(3, 4)$ 27. $A(-3, -2)$, $B(3, -1)$, $C(5, 4)$

28. Determine by means of slopes which of the following groups of points are the vertices of a right triangle. Check your answer by using the distance formula.
    a. $(2, 2)$, $(4, 1)$, $(4, 6)$ b. $(2, 5)$, $(-4, 3)$, $(-3, 0)$
    c. $(1, 1)$, $(4, 4)$, $(7, 2)$ d. $(1, 1)$, $(3, 0)$, $(0, -4)$
29. The vertices of a quadrilateral are $(3, 1)$, $(5, 6)$, $(7, 6)$, and $(10, 2)$. Show that the diagonals of the quadrilateral are perpendicular to each other.
30. The points $A(2, 1)$, $B(9, 4)$, $C(5, 8)$ are the vertices of $\triangle ABC$. Show that the median from A is perpendicular to $\overline{BC}$.

31. $\overleftrightarrow{AB} \parallel \overleftrightarrow{CD}$. The slope of $\overleftrightarrow{AB}$ is $\dfrac{3}{4}$. The slope of $\overleftrightarrow{CD}$ is $\dfrac{9}{x}$. Find x.

32. $\overleftrightarrow{EF} \parallel \overleftrightarrow{GH}$. The slope of $\overleftrightarrow{EF}$ is $\dfrac{2}{3}$. The slope of $\overleftrightarrow{GH}$ is $\dfrac{8}{x - 6}$. Find x.

33. $\overleftrightarrow{AB} \parallel \overleftrightarrow{CD}$. The slope of $\overleftrightarrow{AB}$ is $-\dfrac{3}{5}$. The slope of $\overleftrightarrow{CD}$ is $\dfrac{12}{x - 8}$. Find x.

34. $\overleftrightarrow{PQ} \perp \overleftrightarrow{RS}$. The slope of $\overleftrightarrow{PQ}$ is $\dfrac{x - 1}{4}$. The slope of $\overleftrightarrow{RS}$ is $\dfrac{4}{3}$. Find x.

35. The vertices of parallelogram $ABCD$ are $A(-2, 4)$, $B(2, 6)$, $C(7, 2)$, $D(x, 0)$.
    a. Find the slope of $\overline{AB}$.
    b. Express the slope of $\overline{DC}$ in terms of x.
    c. Using the results found in a and b, find the value of x.

36. Given the coordinates $A(2, -1)$, $B(5, 8)$, $C(-1, 1)$, and $D(3, k)$:

    a. Find the slope of $\overleftrightarrow{AB}$.

    b. Express the slope of $\overleftrightarrow{CD}$ in terms of k.

    c. If $\overleftrightarrow{AB} \parallel \overleftrightarrow{CD}$, find k.

37. The points $A(-1, 4)$, $B(-2, 1)$, $C(4, 3)$, and $D(t, 5)$ are the vertices of trapezoid $ABCD$ whose bases are $\overline{BC}$ and $\overline{AD}$.

    a. Find the slope of $\overline{BC}$.

    b. Express, in terms of t, the slope of $\overline{AD}$.

    c. Using the results found in **a** and **b**, find the value of t.

    d. Show that $ABCD$ is not an isosceles trapezoid.

38. Given trapezoid $ABCD$ with bases $\overline{AB}$ and $\overline{CD}$. The vertices are $A(1, 6)$, $B(7, 3k)$, $C(13, 2k)$, and $D(3, 1)$.

    a. Express the slope of $\overline{AB}$ in terms of k.

    b. Express the slope of $\overline{CD}$ in terms of k.

    c. Write an equation that can be used to solve for k.

    d. Find k.

9-6 GRAPHING LINEAR EQUATIONS

In Course I, you learned the following:

    The general form of a first-degree equation in two variables is $ax + by + c = 0$, where a and b are not both 0.

For example, $x + 2y = 6$ is a first-degree equation in two variables. The solution set of $x + 2y = 6$ consists of all ordered pairs of numbers (x, y) that replace the variables to form true statements. Therefore:

$(4, 1)$ is a solution of $x + 2y = 6$ because
$(4) + 2(1) = 6$ is a true statement.

$(6, 0)$ is a solution of $x + 2y = 6$ because
$(6) + 2(0) = 6$ is a true statement.

$(0, 3)$ is a solution of $x + 2y = 6$ because
$(0) + 2(3) = 6$ is true statement.

There are, of course, many more solutions that can be found for $x + 2y = 6$.

● **Definition.** The *graph of an equation* is the graph of all of the ordered pairs that are elements of the solution set of that equation.

The figure shows that the points (4, 1), (6, 0), and (0, 3), which are solutions of $x + 2y = 6$, lie on a straight line. The line consists of an infinite number of points, each of whose coordinates are also solutions of $x + 2y = 6$. For example, (2, 2) and $(5, \frac{1}{2})$ are also solutions of the equation $x + 2y = 6$.

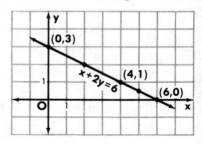

Note. The graph of $x + 2y = 6$ intersects the y-axis at (0, 3) and the x-axis at (6, 0). The *y-intercept* of a graph is the value of y at the point where the graph intersects the y-axis. Here, the y-intercept is 3. Also, the *x-intercept* of a graph is the value of x at the point where the graph intersects the x-axis. Here, the x-intercept is 6.

A first-degree equation in two variables is called a *linear equation* because its graph is a line. For example, $x - y = 10$ and $y = 3x + 5$ are linear equations. Also notice:

1. If $a = 0$, the graph of $ax + by + c = 0$ is a line parallel to the x-axis.

2. If $b = 0$, the graph of $ax + by + c = 0$ is a line parallel to the y-axis.

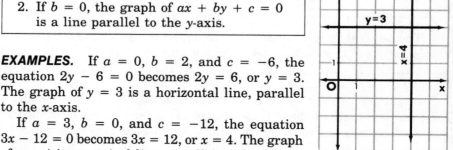

EXAMPLES. If $a = 0$, $b = 2$, and $c = -6$, the equation $2y - 6 = 0$ becomes $2y = 6$, or $y = 3$. The graph of $y = 3$ is a horizontal line, parallel to the x-axis.

If $a = 3$, $b = 0$, and $c = -12$, the equation $3x - 12 = 0$ becomes $3x = 12$, or $x = 4$. The graph of $x = 4$ is a vertical line, parallel to the y-axis.

Note that when the equation for a horizontal or vertical line is in simplest form, the equation shows the value of the intercept:

1. $y = b$ is the equation of a horizontal line whose y-intercept is b.

2. $x = a$ is the equation of a vertical line whose x-intercept is a.

MODEL PROBLEMS ────────────────────────────────

1. Draw the graph of $x - 2y = -2$.

Solution:

(1) Find three ordered pairs that satisfy the equation $x - 2y = -2$
    by: **(a)** selecting a value for either x or y, **(b)** substituting the value
    in the equation $x - 2y = -2$, and **(c)** solving for the remaining
    variable. (Although two points determine a line, the third point
    serves as a check of collinearity.)

$$x - 2y = -2$$

If $y = 0$, then $x - 2(0) = -2$, or $x = -2$.

If $y = 1$, then $x - 2(1) = -2$, or $x - 2 = -2$, or $x = 0$.

If $y = 2$, then $x - 2(2) = -2$, or $x - 4 = -2$, or $x = 2$.

x	y
-2	0
0	1
2	2

(2) Plot the points represented by
    the ordered pairs $(-2, 0)$, $(0, 1)$,
    and $(2, 2)$.

(3) Draw a line through the three
    points, and write the equation
    $x - 2y = -2$ to accompany the
    graph.

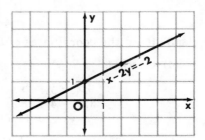

2. Find **(a)** the x-intercept and **(b)** the y-intercept of the graph of the
equation $3x - 2y = 12$.

Solution:

(a) The x-intercept is found on
the x-axis. On the x-axis,
$y = 0$ for all points. Let
$y = 0$ in $3x - 2y = 12$.

$$3x - 2(0) = 12$$
$$3x = 12$$
$$x = 4$$

Answer: **(a)** x-intercept $= 4$.

(b) The y-intercept is found on
the y-axis. On the y-axis,
$x = 0$ for all points. Let
$x = 0$ in $3x - 2y = 12$.

$$3(0) - 2y = 12$$
$$- 2y = 12$$
$$y = -6$$

Answer: **(b)** y-intercept $= -6$.

3. Solve graphically and check: $2x + y = 8$
$$y - x = 2$$

Solution:

(1) Graph $2x + y = 8$,
or $y = -2x + 8$.

x	-2x + 8	y
1	-2(1) + 8	6
3	-2(3) + 8	2
4	-2(4) + 8	0

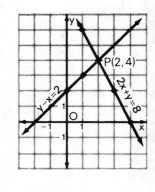

(2) Graph $y - x = 2$,
or $y = x + 2$.

x	x + 2	y
0	0 + 2	2
1	1 + 2	3
2	2 + 2	4

(3) Read the coordinates of the point of intersection $P(2, 4)$.

(4) *Check:* ($x = 2$, $y = 4$)

$$2x + y = 8 \qquad\qquad y - x = 2$$
$$2(2) + 4 \overset{?}{=} 8 \qquad\qquad 4 - 2 \overset{?}{=} 2$$
$$8 = 8 \quad \text{(True)} \qquad\qquad 2 = 2 \quad \text{(True)}$$

Answer: The common solution is (2, 4). The solution set is {(2, 4)}.

Note: When a pair of lines is graphed in the same coordinate plane on the same set of axes, one and only one of the following three possibilities can occur. The pair of lines will:

1. *intersect in one point* and have one ordered number pair in common. Such a system is called a *system of consistent equations.* The preceding model problem is an example.

2. be *parallel* and have no ordered number pairs in common. Such a system is called a *system of inconsistent equations.*

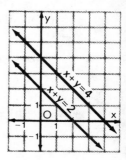

3. *coincide,* that is, be the same line with an infinite number of ordered number pairs in
common. Such a system is called a *system of
dependent equations.*

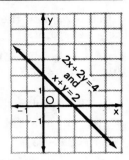

EXERCISES

1. Draw the graphs of the following equations:
   a. $y = 2x$ **b.** $y = -3x$ **c.** $x + y = 0$
   d. $x = 2y$ **e.** $x = 3y$ **f.** $y = \frac{1}{2}x$
   g. $y = x + 3$ **h.** $y = 3x - 1$ **i.** $x + y = 8$
   j. $x - y = 5$ **k.** $y - x = 6$ **l.** $y = -2x + 3$
   m. $x + 3y = 12$ **n.** $x - 2y = 6$ **o.** $2x + 3y = 6$
   p. $3x - 4y = 12$ **q.** $y - 2x = 4$ **r.** $5y - 2x = 10$
2. Find **(a)** the x-intercept and **(b)** the y-intercept of each equation in
   Exercise 1.
3. Which of the following ordered pairs are members of the solution set
   of the equation $2x - y = 6$?
   a. $(0, -6)$ **b.** $(4, -2)$ **c.** $(2, 2)$ **d.** $(4, 2)$
   e. $(3, 0)$ **f.** $(10, 14)$ **g.** $(1, 4)$ **h.** $(1, 8)$
4. For the equation $2x + 3y = 4$: **a.** What are the coordinates of
   the point at which the graph intersects the y-axis? **b.** Name the
   y-intercept.

In 5–10, state whether the given line passes through the given point.

5. $x + y = 7$, $(4, 3)$ **6.** $x - y = 5$, $(9, 4)$
7. $2y + x = 7$, $(1, 3)$ **8.** $3x - 2y = 8$, $(2, -1)$
9. $4x + y = 10$, $(2, -2)$ **10.** $2y = 3x - 5$, $(-1, -4)$

In 11–13, a point is to lie on a given line. Find the abscissa of the
point if its ordinate is 3.

11. $x + y = 12$ **12.** $3x + 2y = 24$ **13.** $x - 3y = 1$

In 14–16, a point is to lie on a given line. Find the ordinate of the
point if its abscissa is -2.

14. $x + 3y = 4$ **15.** $2x - y = 1$ **16.** $3x - 2y = -5$

In 17–20, find the value of k so that the given line will pass through the given point.

17. $x + y = k$, $(2, 5)$ **18.** $x - y = k$, $(5, -3)$
19. $x + ky = 7$, $(1, 3)$ **20.** $kx + 2y = 1$, $(-1, 2)$

In 21–23, solve the systems of equations graphically. Check.

21. $y = 2x$ **22.** $3x + y = 6$ **23.** $y = \frac{1}{3}x - 3$
     $y = 3x - 3$ $y = 3$ $2x - y = 8$

24. Determine which of the following systems is consistent.
     (1) $x + y = 1$ (2) $x + y = 5$ (3) $y = 2x + 1$
         $x + y = 3$ $2x + 2y = 10$ $y = 3x + 3$

25. a. Write a system of two first-degree equations involving the two variables x and y that represent the conditions stated in the following problem. **b.** Solve the system graphically.

The perimeter of a rectangle is 12 meters. Its length is twice its width. Find the dimensions of the rectangle.

9-7 WRITING AN EQUATION OF A LINE

Given certain information, such as points, slopes, and intercepts, it is possible to write equations of lines.

The Point-Slope Form

An equation of a line can be written by using the coordinates of one point on the line and the slope of the line. For example, in the figure:

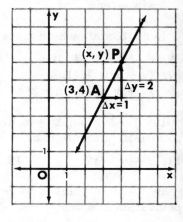

The coordinates of $A(3, 4) = (x_1, y_1)$.

The slope of the line $= m = \dfrac{\Delta y}{\Delta x} = \dfrac{2}{1}$.

Let $P(x, y)$ represent any point on the line, except point A. Thus, $x \neq x_1$.

Write the formula for slope: $m = \dfrac{y - y_1}{x - x_1}$

Substitute known values: $\dfrac{2}{1} = \dfrac{y - 4}{x - 3}$

Simplify: $y - 4 = 2(x - 3)$

The equation $y - y_1 = m(x - x_1)$ is called the ***point-slope form*** of an equation of a line. Remember that m and (x_1, y_1) are known values.

● **THEOREM 69.** **An equation of the line passing through the point (x_1, y_1) and having the slope m is $y - y_1 = m(x - x_1)$.**

Given: A line with a fixed point $P_1(x_1, y_1)$ and a slope m.

Prove: An equation of the line is $y - y_1 = m(x - x_1)$.

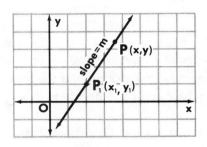

Statements	*Reasons*
1. A line exists with a fixed point $P_1(x_1, y_1)$ and a slope m.	1. Given.
2. Let $P(x, y)$ be any point on the line except $P_1(x_1, y_1)$, that is, $x \neq x_1$.	2. A line contains at least two points.
3. For the nonvertical line, $m = \dfrac{y - y_1}{x - x_1}.$	3. Definition of the slope of a line.
4. $y - y_1 = m(x - x_1)$	4. In a proportion, the product of the means is equal to the product of the extremes.

The Slope-Intercept Form

An equation of a line can also be written by knowing the slope of the line and the y-intercept of the line. Recall that in Course I, you learned how to graph lines by using equations of the form $y = mx + b$, where m represents the slope of the line and b represents the y-intercept.

● **THEOREM 70.** **An equation of a line whose slope is m and whose y-intercept is b is $y = mx + b$.**

Given: A line with a slope m, passing through the point $(0, b)$.

Prove: An equation of the line is $y = mx + b$.

Plan: Starting with the *point-slope form* of an equation of a line, let $(x_1, y_1) = (0, b)$ to obtain the *slope-intercept form* of the equation.

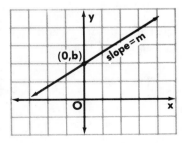

$$y - y_1 = m(x - x_1) \qquad \text{slope} = m, \ x_1 = 0, \ y_1 = b.$$
$$y - b = m(x - 0)$$
$$y - b = mx$$
$$y = mx + b$$

The equation $y = mx + b$ is called the **slope-intercept form** of an equation of a line. Remember that the slope m and the y-intercept b are known values. For example, if the slope of a line is $\frac{2}{3}$ and its y-intercept is 4, the equation of the line is $y = \frac{2}{3}x + 4$.

Using Two Given Points

If the coordinates of two points on a line are known, it is possible to find the slope of the line and write the point-slope form of an equation of the line. See Model Problem 2, which follows.

MODEL PROBLEMS

1. Write an equation of the line whose slope is 2 and that passes through the point (2, 3).

   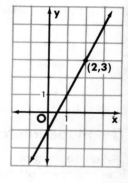

   Solution:

   (1) Let $(x_1, y_1) = (2, 3)$. Let $m = 2$.
   (2) Write the point-slope form of the equation of a line: $y - y_1 = m(x - x_1)$
   (3) Substitute: $y - 3 = 2(x - 2)$
   (4) Simplify: $y - 3 = 2x - 4$
   $$y = 2x - 1$$

   Answer: $y = 2x - 1$

2. Write an equation of the line that passes through the points $P_1(-1, -2)$ and $P_2(5, 1)$.

   Solution:

   (1) Use points P_1 and P_2 to find the slope of the line.

   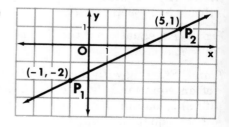

   $$\text{slope} = m = \frac{y_2 - y_1}{x_2 - x_1} = \frac{1 - (-2)}{5 - (-1)}$$

   $$m = \frac{1 + 2}{5 + 1} = \frac{3}{6} = \frac{1}{2}$$

(2) Using the slope of $\frac{1}{2}$, select either point P_1 or P_2, and apply the point-slope formula.

<table>
<tr><td align="center">Method 1</td><td align="center">Method 2</td></tr>
</table>

Use $P_1(-1, -2)$ and slope $m = \frac{1}{2}$:

$$y - y_1 = m(x - x_1)$$
$$y - (-2) = \frac{1}{2}[x - (-1)]$$
$$y + 2 = \frac{1}{2}(x + 1)$$
$$y + 2 = \frac{1}{2}x + \frac{1}{2}$$
$$y = \frac{1}{2}x - \frac{3}{2}$$

Use $P_2(5, 1)$ and slope $m = \frac{1}{2}$:

$$y - y_2 = m(x - x_2)$$
$$y - 1 = \frac{1}{2}(x - 5)$$
$$y - 1 = \frac{1}{2}x - \frac{5}{2}$$
$$y = \frac{1}{2}x - \frac{3}{2}$$

Note. Whether we are using point P_1 or P_2, the equation will be $y = \frac{1}{2}x - \frac{3}{2}$. To eliminate fractions, multiply both the left and right members of the equation by the greatest common denominator:

$$2(y) = 2(\tfrac{1}{2}x - \tfrac{3}{2}), \text{ or } 2y = x - 3$$

Answer: $y = \frac{1}{2}x - \frac{3}{2}$, or $2y = x - 3$

3. Write an equation of the line with slope $\frac{1}{3}$ and y-intercept -2.

Solution:

(1) Write the slope-intercept form of the equation: $y = mx + b$
(2) Substitute slope $m = \frac{1}{3}$, and y-intercept $b = -2$: $y = \frac{1}{3}x - 2$

Answer: $y = \frac{1}{3}x - 2$, or $3y = x - 6$

4. a. Name the slope and y-intercept of the line whose equation is $3y - 2x = -6$.
b. Graph $3y - 2x = -6$, using its slope and y-intercept.

Solution:

a. Transform the equation $3y - 2x = -6$ to the form $y = mx + b$.

(1) Write the equation: $3y - 2x = -6$
(2) Add $2x$: $3y = 2x - 6$
(3) Divide by 3: $y = \frac{2}{3}x - 2$

Answer: Slope $= \frac{2}{3}$ and y-intercept $= -2$

b. To graph by the slope-intercept method:

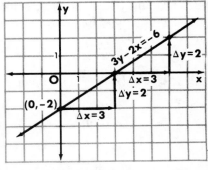

(1) Since the y-intercept is -2, the point $(0, -2)$ is on the graph. Plot $(0, -2)$.

(2) Since slope $= \dfrac{\Delta y}{\Delta x} = \dfrac{2}{3}$,

when x increases 3 units, y increases 2 units. Therefore, start at the point $(0, -2)$ and move 3 units to the right and 2 units up to plot a second point. Repeat these movements to plot a third point.

(3) Draw the line that passes through these three points.

5. Write an equation of the line that passes through the point $(1, 5)$ and is perpendicular to $y = \frac{1}{2}x - 3$.

Solution:

(1) Since the slope of the line whose equation is $y = \frac{1}{2}x - 3$ is $+\frac{1}{2}$, the slope of a line perpendicular to $y = \frac{1}{2}x - 3$ is its negative reciprocal, $-\frac{2}{1}$ or -2.

(2) Use the point-slope form. Substitute $m = -2$ and $(x_1, y_1) = (1, 5)$.

$$y - y_1 = m(x - x_1)$$
$$y - 5 = -2(x - 1)$$
$$y - 5 = -2x + 2$$
$$y = -2x + 7 \quad Ans.$$

EXERCISES

1. Write an equation of the line that has the given slope m and that passes through the given point.

    a. $m = 3, (1, 5)$ **b.** $m = 2, (-3, 5)$ **c.** $m = \frac{1}{2}, (-2, -3)$

    d. $m = \frac{2}{3}, (-1, 4)$ **e.** $m = -\frac{2}{5}, (0, 0)$ **f.** $m = 0, (-2, 8)$

2. Through the given point, draw the graph of a line with the given slope m.

    a. $(0, 0), m = 2$ **b.** $(1, 3), m = 3$ **c.** $(2, -5), m = -2$

    d. $(4, 6), m = \frac{2}{3}$ **e.** $(-4, 5), m = \frac{1}{2}$ **f.** $(-3, -4), m = -1$

    g. $(1, -5), m = -\frac{1}{2}$ **h.** $(2, 4), m = -\frac{3}{2}$ **i.** $(-2, 3), m = 0$

3. Write an equation of the line that passes through the given points.
   a. (1, 5) and (5, 13)
   b. (0, 3) and (2, 9)
   c. (−1, 3) and (1, −1)
   d. (0, 0) and (−2, −4)
   e. (−4, −1) and (−1, 11)
   f. (12, −5) and (−4, −1)
   g. (−2, 4) and (5, 4)
   h. (−2, 4) and (−2, 0)

4. Write an equation of the line whose slope and y-intercept are respectively:
   a. 4 and 5
   b. 2 and −5
   c. −3 and 2
   d. $\frac{3}{4}$ and 4
   e. $-\frac{2}{3}$ and −1
   f. 0 and 4
   g. −7 and 0
   h. 0 and 0

5. For each of the following, find the slope and the y-intercept.
   a. $y = 3x + 1$
   b. $y = x - 4$
   c. $y = -x$
   d. $y = \frac{1}{4}x + 5$
   e. $2x + y = 9$
   f. $4y - 2x = 16$

6. Determine the coordinates of the point at which the graph of each of the following equations intersects the y-axis.
   a. $y = x + 1$
   b. $y = x - 4$
   c. $x - y = 4$
   d. $x + 2y = 6$
   e. $x - 3y = 3$
   f. $3x - 2y + 12 = 0$

7. Graph each of the following lines, using its slope and y-intercept:
   a. $y = 2x + 5$
   b. $y = 3x - 1$
   c. $y = 4x$
   d. $y = \frac{2}{3}x + 1$
   e. $y = -\frac{4}{3}x + 2$
   f. $3x + y = 4$
   g. $y - 2x = 8$
   h. $3x + y = 4$
   i. $3x + 4y = 12$

8. In each part, state whether or not the two lines are parallel.
   a. $y = 3x + 2$; $y = 3x + 5$
   b. $y = -2x - 6$; $y = -3x - 6$
   c. $y - 2x = 8$; $2x - y = 4$
   d. $2x + 3y = 12$; $3x + 2y = 8$

9. Write an equation of the line whose slope is 4 and that passes through a point on the y-axis 2 units above the origin.

10. Write an equation of the line whose slope is 3 and that passes through a point on the y-axis 5 units below the origin.

11. Write an equation of the line that is:
    a. parallel to $y = 3x - 5$ and whose y-intercept is 7.
    b. parallel to $y - 2x = 4$ and whose y-intercept is −1.
    c. parallel to $2x + 3y = 6$ and that passes through the origin.
    d. parallel to $y = 5x + 1$ and passes through the point (3, 2).
    e. parallel to $y - 3x = 5$ and passes through the point (1, 6).
    f. parallel to $2y - 4x = 9$ and passes through the point (−2, 1).

12. Write an equation of the line that is parallel to $y = 3x + 5$ and has the same y-intercept as $y = 4x - 3$.

13. Write an equation of the line that is perpendicular to $y = \frac{2}{3}x$ and passes through the origin.

14. Write an equation of the line that is:
    a. perpendicular to $y = 4x - 3$ and whose y-intercept is 8.
    b. perpendicular to $2x + y = 3$ and whose y-intercept is 4.
    c. perpendicular to $y = -\frac{2}{3}x + 2$ and passes through $(2, 4)$.
    d. perpendicular to $y = \frac{3}{4}x + 7$ and passes through the origin.

In 15–26, select the numeral preceding the equation or the value that best answers the question.

15. Which is an equation for the line that is parallel to $4x - y = 8$ and passes through the point $(0, 2)$?
    (1) $y = x + 2$ (2) $y = 4x + 2$ (3) $y = -4x + 2$ (4) $y = 2x + 2$

16. Which is an equation of the line that passes through the point $(-4, 7)$ and is parallel to the x-axis?
    (1) $x = -4$ (2) $x = 7$ (3) $y = -4$ (4) $y = 7$

17. Which is an equation of a line whose slope is undefined?
    (1) $x = -4$ (2) $y = 7$ (3) $x = y$ (4) $x + y = 0$

18. What is the slope of a line parallel to $y - 3x = 6$?
    (1) $\frac{1}{3}$ (2) $-\frac{1}{3}$ (3) 3 (4) -3

19. Which is an equation of a line that has a y-intercept of 4 and a slope of -1?
    (1) $y = 4x - 1$ (2) $y = -4x + 1$
    (3) $y = -x + 4$ (4) $y = x - 4$

20. What is the slope of a line parallel to $3x + 4y = 12$?
    (1) $-\frac{3}{4}$ (2) $\frac{3}{4}$ (3) $-\frac{4}{3}$ (4) $\frac{4}{3}$

21. Which is an equation of the line that passes through the point $(2, 5)$ and has a slope of -3?
    (1) $y = \frac{2}{5}x - 3$ (2) $y = -3x + 11$
    (3) $y = -3x + 17$ (4) $y = -3x + 5$

22. Which of the following represents a line parallel to $x + y = 5$?
    (1) $y = x + 3$ (2) $y - x = 3$ (3) $x - y = 3$ (4) $y = -x + 3$

23. Which is an equation of a line perpendicular to $y = 2x + 5$?
    (1) $y = 2x + 7$ (2) $y = \frac{1}{2}x + 7$
    (3) $y = -\frac{1}{2}x + 7$ (4) $y = -2x + 7$

24. If r and s represent the slopes of two perpendicular lines, what is the value of the product rs?
    (1) 1 (2) -1 (3) 0 (4) undefined

25. Which is an equation of a line that has no y-intercept?
    (1) $y = 5$ (2) $x = 5$ (3) $y = x$ (4) $x + y = 0$

26. Which is *not* true for the line whose equation is $y = 2x$?
(1) The line passes through the origin.
(2) On the line, each abscissa is twice its corresponding ordinate.
(3) The line has a slope of 2.
(4) The line is parallel to a line passing through $(1, -3)$ and $(3, 1)$.

27. a. Using graph paper, draw the graphs of the following equations on the same set of coordinate axes.
  (1) $y = \frac{3}{2}x$ (2) $y = 3$ (3) $y = x + 3$
b. The points of intersection of the graphs in part **a** determine the vertices of a triangle. Write the coordinates of these vertices.

28. Given points $(-1, -2)$ and $(3, 4)$.
  a. Find the distance between the two points.
  b. Find the slope of the line containing these points.
  c. Find the coordinates of the midpoint of the segment determined by these points.
  d. Write an equation of the line containing the two given points.
  e. If the point $(2, k)$ lies on the line determined in part **d,** find the value of k.

29. Given points $A(3, 1)$, $B(0, -1)$, and $C(-3, -3)$.
  a. Write an equation of the line that passes through point A and is parallel to the y-axis.
  b. Write an equation of the line that passes through point B and has a slope of 1.
  c. Show that A, B, and C lie on the same line.
  d. Write an equation of the line that is parallel to $\overleftrightarrow{AB}$ and passes through the origin.

30. The vertices of quadrilateral $ABCD$ are $A(-6, -6)$, $B(14, 4)$, $C(3, 5)$, and $D(-5, 1)$.
  a. Show by means of slopes that $\overline{DC}$ is parallel to $\overline{AB}$.
  b. Write an equation of $\overleftrightarrow{BC}$.

31. The vertices of parallelogram $ABCD$ are $A(-2, 4)$, $B(2, 6)$, $C(7, 2)$, and $D(k, 0)$.
  a. Find the slope of $\overleftrightarrow{AB}$.
  b. Express the slope of $\overleftrightarrow{CD}$ in terms of k.
  c. Using the results found in the answers to **a** and **b,** find k.
  d. Write an equation of $\overleftrightarrow{BD}$.

32. Given the points $A(x, 4)$, $B(5, 6)$, $C(7, 5)$, and $D(11, 6)$.
  a. Find the slope of the line passing through points C and D.
  b. Write an expression that represents the slope of the line passing through points A and B.

   c. Find the value of x that will make the line through A and B parallel to the line through C and D.

   d. Write an equation of the line passing through the point B and perpendicular to the y-axis.

   e. Write an equation of the line passing through the origin and point D.

33. The points $A(-2, 0)$, $B(10, 3)$, $C(5, 7)$, and $D(2, k)$ are the vertices of a trapezoid whose bases are $\overline{AB}$ and $\overline{DC}$.

   a. Find the slope of $\overleftrightarrow{AB}$.

   b. Express the slope of $\overleftrightarrow{DC}$ in terms of k.

   c. Using the results of parts **a** and **b,** find the value of k.

   d. Show by slopes that $\overleftrightarrow{AB}$ does *not* pass through the origin.

   e. Write an equation of $\overleftrightarrow{AB}$.

34. Given the points $A(2, 4)$, $B(6, 12)$, and $C(x, y)$.

   a. Write an equation of the line through A and C if its slope is -1.

   b. Write an equation of the line through B and C if its slope is $\frac{1}{2}$.

   c. Find the coordinates of point C.

35. The vertices of parallelogram $ABCD$ are $A(1, 1)$, $B(4, 6)$, $C(x, y)$, and $D(2, 10)$.

   a. Express in terms of x and y the slopes of $\overleftrightarrow{BC}$ and $\overleftrightarrow{DC}$.

   b. Using the results obtained in part **a**, write two equations that can be used to find x and y.

   c. Find the coordinates of C.

9-8 MORE PROOFS USING COORDINATE GEOMETRY

In this section, we will expand on the proofs discussed earlier in this chapter and consider further proofs involving polygons.

There are two types of proofs in coordinate geometry:

1. *Proofs Involving Specific Cases.* Here, the coordinates of the vertices of a given polygon are stated as specific ordered pairs of numbers. Note that many of these cases can be proved by more than one method. (See Model Problem 1.)

2. *Proofs of General Theorems.* Here, the coordinates of the vertices of a polygon are stated in general terms by using variables. In such cases, it is often helpful to place the polygon so that one of its vertices is at the origin and one of its sides lies on the positive half-line of the x-axis. (See Model Problem 2.)

Summary of Techniques and Formulas	
1. To prove that line segments are congruent, show that the segments are equal in length by using the distance formula.	*Distance:* $$d = \sqrt{(x_2 - x_1)^2 + (y_2 - y_1)^2}$$
2. To prove that segments bisect each other, show that the same ordered pair represents the midpoint of each line segment.	*Midpoint:* $$(x_m, y_m) = \left(\frac{x_1 + x_2}{2}, \frac{y_1 + y_2}{2}\right)$$
3. To prove that lines intersect at a point, write an equation of each line and solve the system of equations.	*Line:* $$y = mx + b$$ $$m = \text{slope} = \frac{y_2 - y_1}{x_2 - x_1}$$ $b = y\text{-intercept}$
4. To prove that lines are parallel, show that the slopes of the lines are equal.	*Slopes:* $$m_1 = m_2$$
5. To prove that lines are perpendicular, show that their slopes are negative reciprocals, or that the product of the slopes is -1.	*Slopes:* $$m_1 = -\frac{1}{m_2} \text{ or } m_1 \cdot m_2 = -1$$

MODEL PROBLEMS

1. *Given: ABCD* with vertices $A(2, 2)$, $B(5, -2)$, $C(9, 1)$, and $D(6, 5)$.
  Show: ABCD is a rhombus.

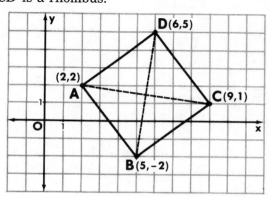

Solution: There are 3 ways to prove that *ABCD* is a rhombus.

Method 1. Show that $AB = BC = CD = DA$. Thus, $ABCD$ is an equilateral quadrilateral, or a rhombus. (See pages 362–363, Model Problem 3, for this proof.)

Method 2. Show that $ABCD$ is a parallelogram with two consecutive congruent sides.

(1) Let $A(2, 2) = (x_1, y_1)$. Let $B(5, -2) = (x_2, y_2)$.

   Slope of $\overline{AB} = \dfrac{y_2 - y_1}{x_2 - x_1} = \dfrac{-2 - 2}{5 - 2} = \dfrac{-4}{3}$

(2) Let $D(6, 5) = (x_1, y_1)$. Let $C(9, 1) = (x_2, y_2)$.

   Slope of $\overline{DC} = \dfrac{y_2 - y_1}{x_2 - x_1} = \dfrac{1 - 5}{9 - 6} = \dfrac{-4}{3}$

(3) Since the slope of $\overline{AB}$ = slope of $\overline{CD} = \frac{-4}{3}$, $\overline{AB}$ is parallel to $\overline{CD}$.

(4) Let $A(2, 2) = (x_1, y_1)$. Let $D(6, 5) = (x_2, y_2)$.

   Slope of $\overline{AD} = \dfrac{y_2 - y_1}{x_2 - x_1} = \dfrac{5 - 2}{6 - 2} = \dfrac{3}{4}$

(5) Let $B(5, -2) = (x_1, y_1)$. Let $C(9, 1) = (x_2, y_2)$.

   Slope of $\overline{BC} = \dfrac{y_2 - y_1}{x_2 - x_1} = \dfrac{1 - (-2)}{9 - 5} = \dfrac{1 + 2}{9 - 5} = \dfrac{3}{4}$

(6) Since the slope of $\overline{AD}$ = slope of $\overline{BC} = \frac{3}{4}$, $\overline{AD}$ is parallel to $\overline{BC}$.

(7) Since both pairs of opposite sides of the quadrilateral are parallel, $ABCD$ is a parallelogram.

(8) $AD = \sqrt{(x_2 - x_1)^2 + (y_2 - y_1)^2} = \sqrt{(6 - 2)^2 + (5 - 2)^2}$

   $= \sqrt{4^2 + 3^2} = \sqrt{16 + 9} = \sqrt{25} = 5$

(9) $DC = \sqrt{(x_2 - x_1)^2 + (y_2 - y_1)^2} = \sqrt{(9 - 6)^2 + (1 - 5)^2}$

   $= \sqrt{3^2 + (-4)^2} = \sqrt{9 + 16} = \sqrt{25} = 5$

(10) Since $AD = DC$, two consecutive sides of parallelogram $ABCD$ are equal in length (or congruent). Thus, $ABCD$ is a rhombus.

Method 3. Show that diagonals $\overline{AC}$ and $\overline{BD}$ bisect each other at right angles.

(1) Let $B(5, -2) = (x_1, y_1)$. Let $D(6, 5) = (x_2, y_2)$.

$$\text{Midpoint of } \overline{BD} = \left(\frac{x_1 + x_2}{2}, \frac{y_1 + y_2}{2}\right) = \left(\frac{5 + 6}{2}, \frac{-2 + 5}{2}\right)$$

$$= \left(\frac{11}{2}, \frac{3}{2}\right)$$

$$\text{Slope of } \overline{BD} = \frac{y_2 - y_1}{x_2 - x_1} = \frac{5 - (-2)}{6 - 5} = \frac{5 + 2}{6 - 5} = \frac{7}{1}$$

(2) Let $A(2, 2) = (x_1, y_1)$. Let $C(9, 1) = (x_2, y_2)$.

$$\text{Midpoint of } \overline{AC} = \left(\frac{x_1 + x_2}{2}, \frac{y_1 + y_2}{2}\right) = \left(\frac{2 + 9}{2}, \frac{2 + 1}{2}\right)$$

$$= \left(\frac{11}{2}, \frac{3}{2}\right)$$

$$\text{Slope of } \overline{AC} = \frac{y_2 - y_1}{x_2 - x_1} = \frac{1 - 2}{9 - 2} = \frac{-1}{7} = -\frac{1}{7}$$

(3) Since the midpoint of $\overline{BD}$ = the midpoint of $\overline{AC} = (\frac{11}{2}, \frac{3}{2})$, then $\overline{BD}$ and $\overline{AC}$ bisect each other.

(4) Since the slope of $\overline{BD} = \frac{7}{1}$ and the slope of $\overline{AC} = -\frac{1}{7}$, one slope is the negative reciprocal of the other. Thus, $\overline{BD}$ is perpendicular to $\overline{AC}$.

(5) In quadrilateral $ABCD$, the diagonals, $\overline{BD}$ and $\overline{AC}$, bisect each other at right angles. Therefore, $ABCD$ is a rhombus.

2. Using coordinate geometry, prove that the diagonals of a rectangle are congruent.

Solution: Place the rectangle so that one vertex, O, is at the origin, side $\overline{OA}$ is on the x-axis, and vertex B is in quadrant I. The coordinates of the vertices can be represented by $O(0, 0)$, $A(b, 0)$, $B(b, a)$, $C(0, a)$. Then write the proof as follows.

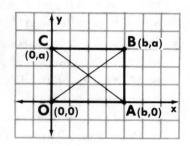

Given: Rectangle *OABC*.

Prove: $\overline{OB} \cong \overline{AC}$.

Plan: Use the distance formula to show that $OB = AC$.

Proof:

(1) Let $O(0, 0) = (x_1, y_1)$. Let $B(b, a) = (x_2, y_2)$.
$$OB = \sqrt{(x_2 - x_1)^2 + (y_2 - y_1)^2} = \sqrt{(b - 0)^2 + (a - 0)^2}$$
$$= \sqrt{b^2 + a^2}$$

(2) Let $C(0, a) = (x_1, y_1)$. Let $A(b, 0) = (x_2, y_2)$.
$$AC = \sqrt{(x_2 - x_1)^2 + (y_2 - y_1)^2} = \sqrt{(b - 0)^2 + (0 - a)^2}$$
$$= \sqrt{b^2 + a^2}$$

(3) Since $OB = AC = \sqrt{b^2 + a^2}$, it follows that $\overline{OB} \cong \overline{AC}$.

EXERCISES

Proofs Involving Specific Cases

1. Given points $A(0, 0)$, $B(4, 8)$, and $C(6, 2)$ are the vertices of $\triangle ABC$.
   a. Show that $\triangle ABC$ is an isosceles triangle.
   b. Find the coordinates of D, the midpoint of the base.
   c. Show that $\overline{CD}$ is perpendicular to $\overline{AB}$.

2. Given $\triangle RST$ with vertices $R(0, 6)$, $S(2, 0)$, and $T(8, 2)$.
   a. Show that $\triangle RST$ is a right triangle, and state a reason for your conclusion.
   b. If $\overline{SM}$ is a median to $\overline{RT}$, show that $SM = RM = TM$.

3. Given $\triangle PQR$ with vertices $P(2, 4)$, $Q(5, 8)$, and $R(9, 5)$. a. Show that $\triangle PQR$ is isosceles. b. Show that $\triangle PQR$ is a right triangle.

4. The vertices of $\triangle ABC$ are $A(1, 3)$, $B(7, 5)$, and $C(9, -3)$. If E is the midpoint of $\overline{AB}$ and F is the midpoint of $\overline{BC}$, show that:
   a. $\overline{EF}$ is parallel to $\overline{AC}$ b. $EF = \frac{1}{2}AC$

5. The vertices of isosceles $\triangle ABC$ are $A(3, -1)$, $B(7, 3)$, and $C(-1, 7)$.
   a. Write an equation of $\overleftrightarrow{AB}$.
   b. If $\overline{CD}$ is the altitude to $\overline{AB}$, and the slope of $\overline{CD}$ is -1, write an equation of $\overleftrightarrow{CD}$.
   c. Find the coordinates of D, the point of intersection of $\overleftrightarrow{AB}$ and $\overleftrightarrow{CD}$.
   d. Show that altitude $\overline{CD}$ intersects base $\overline{AB}$ at its midpoint.

6. The vertices of quadrilateral $PQRS$ are $P(0, 0)$, $Q(4, 3)$, $R(7, -1)$, and $S(3, -4)$. **a.** Show that $PQRS$ is a rhombus. **b.** Using the results of part **a**, show that rhombus $PQRS$ is a square.

7. The vertices of quadrilateral $ABCD$ are $A(1, 1)$, $B(3, 4)$, $C(9, 1)$, and $D(7, -2)$. Show that quadrilateral $ABCD$ is a parallelogram by each of the following methods: **(a)** both pairs of opposite sides are parallel, **(b)** both pairs of opposite sides are congruent, and **(c)** the diagonals bisect each other.

8. The vertices of quadrilateral $KLMN$ are $K(-1, 0)$, $L(0, -3)$, $M(2, 1)$, and $N(1, 4)$. Show that $KLMN$ is a parallelogram by demonstrating that two opposite sides are both parallel and congruent.

9. Quadrilateral $ABCD$ has vertices $A(4, 4)$, $B(2, 0)$, $C(-4, -2)$, and $D(-2, 2)$. Show that $ABCD$ is a parallelogram.

10. Quadrilateral $PQRS$ has vertices $P(0, 2)$, $Q(4, 8)$, $R(7, 6)$, and $S(3, 0)$. Show that $PQRS$ is a rectangle.

11. Quadrilateral $ABCD$ has vertices $A(-2, 5)$, $B(6, 9)$, $C(10, 1)$ and $D(0, -1)$. P, Q, R, and S are the midpoints of sides $\overline{AB}$, $\overline{BC}$, $\overline{CD}$, and $\overline{DA}$, respectively. Show that $PQRS$ is a parallelogram.

12. On graph paper, draw *any* quadrilateral $ABCD$.
    a. Find the coordinates of the midpoints E, F, G, and H of sides $\overline{AB}$, $\overline{BC}$, $\overline{CD}$, and $\overline{DA}$, respectively.
    b. Show that $EFGH$ is a parallelogram.

13. Quadrilateral $DEFG$ has vertices $D(-4, 0)$, $E(0, 1)$, $F(4, -1)$, and $G(-4, -3)$.
    a. Show that $DEFG$ is a trapezoid.
    b. Show that $DEFG$ is *not* an isosceles trapezoid.
    c. Show that diagonals $\overline{DF}$ and $\overline{EG}$ do *not* bisect each other.

14. $A(1, 3)$, $B(-1, 1)$, $C(-1, -2)$, and $D(4, 3)$ are the vertices of quadrilateral $ABCD$. Show that $ABCD$ is an isosceles trapezoid.

15. The vertices of $\triangle ABC$ are $A(0, 10)$, $B(5, 0)$, and $C(8, 4)$.
    a. Show that $\triangle ABC$ is a right triangle.
    b. Point $D(4, 2)$ lies on $\overline{AB}$. Show that $\overline{CD}$ is the altitude to $\overline{AB}$.
    c. Show that $\dfrac{BD}{DC} = \dfrac{DC}{DA}$, and state a reason for your conclusion.

16. $A(0, 2)$, $B(9, 14)$, and $C(12, 2)$ are the vertices of $\triangle ABC$. $D(6, 10)$ is a point on $\overline{AB}$, and $E(8, 2)$ is a point on $\overline{AC}$.
    a. Show that $\overline{DE}$ is parallel to $\overline{BC}$.
    b. Show that $\dfrac{AD}{AB} = \dfrac{AE}{AC}$, and state a reason for your conclusion.

Proofs With Variable Coordinates

17. The vertices of quadrilateral $RSTV$ are $R(0, 0)$, $S(a, 0)$, $T(a + b, c)$, and $V(b, c)$.
   a. Find the slopes of $\overline{RV}$ and $\overline{ST}$.
   b. Find the lengths of $\overline{RV}$ and $\overline{ST}$.
   c. Show that $RSTV$ is a parallelogram.

18. The vertices of triangle ABC are $A(0, 0)$, $B(4a, 0)$, and $C(2a, 2b)$.
   a. Find the coordinates of D, the midpoint of $\overline{AC}$.
   b. Find the coordinates of E, the midpoint of $\overline{BC}$.
   c. Show that $AB = 2DE$.

19. The vertices of quadrilateral $ABCD$ are $A(0, 0)$, $B(a, 0)$, $C(a, b)$, and $D(0, b)$.
   a. Show that $ABCD$ is a parallelogram.
   b. Show that diagonal $\overline{AC}$ is congruent to diagonal $\overline{BD}$.
   c. Show that quadrilateral $ABCD$ is a rectangle.

20. The vertices of quadrilateral $ABCD$ are $A(0, 0)$, $B(r, s)$, $C(r, s + t)$, and $D(0, t)$.
   a. Represent the slopes of $\overline{AB}$ and $\overline{CD}$.
   b. Represent the lengths of $\overline{AB}$ and $\overline{CD}$.
   c. Show that $ABCD$ is a parallelogram.

21. The vertices of $\triangle RST$ are $R(0, 0)$, $S(2a, 2b)$, and $T(4a, 0)$. The midpoints of $\overline{RS}$, $\overline{ST}$, and $\overline{TR}$ are L, M, and N, respectively.
   a. Express the coordinates of L, M, and N in terms of a and b.
   b. Prove $\overline{LM} \parallel \overline{RT}$.   **c.** Prove $\overline{SN} \perp \overline{RT}$.
   d. Prove that $\triangle RST$ is isosceles.

Proofs of General Theorems

In 22–26, use coordinate geometry.

22. Prove: The diagonals of a square are congruent.
   (*Hint.* Use $O(0, 0)$, $A(a, 0)$, $B(a, a)$, and $C(0, a)$.)

23. Prove: If a line bisects two sides of a triangle, then the line is parallel to the third side. (*Hint.* Use $A(0, 0)$, $B(2a, 0)$, and $C(2b, 2c)$. Let D and E bisect $\overline{AB}$ and $\overline{CB}$, respectively.)

24. Prove: The length of the line segment joining the midpoints of two sides of a triangle is one-half the length of the third side.

25. Prove: The diagonals of a rectangle bisect each other.

26. Prove: The median to the base of an isosceles triangle is perpendicular to the base of the triangle.

9-9 AREAS IN COORDINATE GEOMETRY

Area Formulas

In Course I, you learned rules to find the areas of certain polygons:

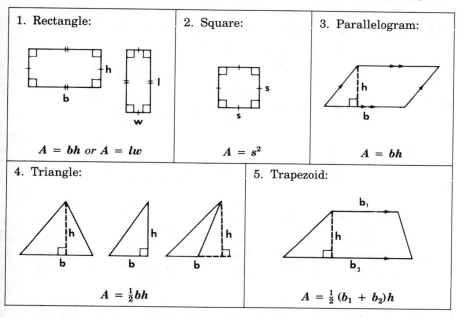

1. Rectangle:	2. Square:	3. Parallelogram:
$A = bh$ or $A = lw$	$A = s^2$	$A = bh$

4. Triangle:	5. Trapezoid:
$A = \frac{1}{2}bh$	$A = \frac{1}{2}(b_1 + b_2)h$

Since a rhombus is a parallelogram, it is possible to find the area of a rhombus by the rule: Area = base • height, or $A = bh$. Notice, however, that another area formula may be developed for the rhombus.

In rhombus $ABCD$, the length of diagonal $\overline{AC} = d_1$, and the length of diagonal $\overline{BD} = d_2$. The diagonals of a rhombus are perpendicular bisectors to each other. Therefore, the rhombus can be separated into two congruent triangles, $\triangle ACD$ and $\triangle ACB$, each with a base of d_1, and an

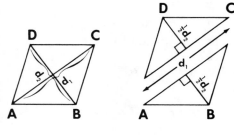

altitude of $\frac{1}{2}d_2$. Since the area of the rhombus is equal to the sum of the areas of the two triangles, we say:

Area of rhombus $ABCD$ = area of $\triangle ACD$ + area of $\triangle ACB$

$\qquad\qquad\qquad\quad = \frac{1}{2}$ base $\cdot$ height $+ \frac{1}{2}$ base $\cdot$ height

$\qquad\qquad\qquad\quad = \frac{1}{2}(d_1) \cdot (\frac{1}{2}d_2) + \frac{1}{2}(d_1) \cdot (\frac{1}{2}d_2)$

$\qquad\qquad\qquad\quad = \frac{2}{2}(d_1)(\frac{1}{2}d_2) = (d_1)(\frac{1}{2}d_2) = \frac{1}{2}d_1 d_2$

Therefore, we add to our list the formula for the area of a rhombus:

6. Rhombus:

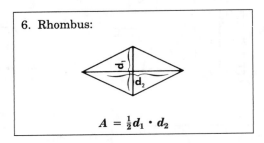

$$A = \tfrac{1}{2}d_1 \cdot d_2$$

Areas and Coordinates

To find areas of polygons in coordinate geometry, we use the area formulas previously developed. When a figure has one or more sides parallel to either of the axes, the process of finding its area usually is simpler.

EXAMPLE 1. Find the area of a triangle whose vertices are $A(3, 2)$, $B(7, 2)$, and $C(6, 5)$.

Plot and label the points.

Lengths can be found by counting units.

(1) In $\triangle ABC$, base $AB = 4$.
(2) Draw altitude $\overline{CD}$. Here, $CD = 3$.
(3) Area of $\triangle ABC$

$\qquad = \frac{1}{2}$ base $\times$ altitude

$\qquad = \frac{1}{2} AB \times CD$

$\qquad = \frac{1}{2} \times 4 \times 3$

Area of $\triangle ABC = 6$ square units

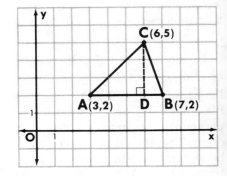

When a figure has no sides parallel to either axis, it is not possible to count units to find the lengths of its sides. However, the area of such a polygon can be found by a variety of other methods.

EXAMPLE 2. Find the area of a triangle whose vertices are $A(-2, 3)$, $B(1, 5)$, and $C(4, 2)$.

Method 1: Enclose the figure in a rectangle.

Through the uppermost and lowermost points, here B and C, draw lines parallel to the x-axis. Through the points farthest to the left and farthest to the right, here A and C, draw lines parallel to the y-axis. Thus, rectangle $CDEF$ is formed.

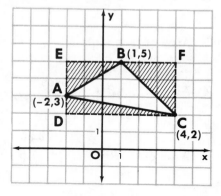

The area of $\triangle ABC$ is equal to the area of rectangle $CDEF$ minus the sum of the areas of right triangles $\triangle CDA$, $\triangle BEA$, and $\triangle BFC$.

Note that each of the sides of rectangle $CDEF$ and each of the legs of the right triangles is parallel to one of the axes. Thus, the lengths of these sides can be found by counting units.

(1) Area of rectangle $CDEF = DC \times DE = 6 \times 3 = 18$

(2) Area of rt. $\triangle CDA = \frac{1}{2}DC \times DA = \frac{1}{2}(6)(1) = 3$

(3) Area of rt. $\triangle BEA = \frac{1}{2}BE \times EA = \frac{1}{2}(3)(2) = 3$

(4) Area of rt. $\triangle BFC = \frac{1}{2}BF \times FC = \frac{1}{2}(3)(3) = 4.5$

(5) Area of $\triangle ABC = \begin{pmatrix} \text{area of} \\ \text{rect. } CDEF \end{pmatrix} - \begin{pmatrix} \text{area of} \\ \triangle CDA \end{pmatrix} + \begin{matrix} \text{area of} \\ \triangle BEA \end{matrix} + \begin{matrix} \text{area of} \\ \triangle BFC \end{matrix}\Big)$

$\qquad\qquad\quad = \qquad 18 \qquad - (\quad 3 \quad + \quad 3 \quad + \quad 4.5 \quad)$

$\qquad\qquad\quad = \qquad 18 \qquad - \qquad 10.5$

$\text{Area of } \triangle ABC = \qquad 7.5$

Method 2: Create trapezoids.

Draw a series of lines parallel to one of the axes. Here, $\overleftrightarrow{AD} \parallel \overleftrightarrow{BE} \parallel \overleftrightarrow{CF} \parallel$ the y-axis. Thus, $\overline{AD}, \overline{BE},$ and $\overline{CF}$ are bases in trapezoids $ADEB$, $BEFC$, and $DACF$.

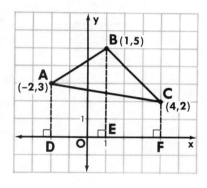

The area of $\triangle ABC$ is equal to the sum of the areas of trapezoids $ADEB$ and $BEFC$ minus the area of trapezoid $DACF$.

(1) Area of trap. $ADEB = \frac{1}{2}(DE)(DA + EB) = \frac{1}{2}(3)(3 + 5)$
$$= \frac{1}{2}(3)(8) = 12$$

(2) Area of trap. $BEFC = \frac{1}{2}(EF)(EB + FC) = \frac{1}{2}(3)(5 + 2)$
$$= \frac{1}{2}(3)(7) = 10.5$$

(3) Area of trap. $DACF = \frac{1}{2}(DF)(AD + FC) = \frac{1}{2}(6)(3 + 2)$
$$= \frac{1}{2}(6)(5) = 15$$

(4) Area of $\triangle ABC = \begin{pmatrix} \text{area of} \\ \text{trap. } ADEB \end{pmatrix} + \begin{pmatrix} \text{area of} \\ \text{trap. } BEFC \end{pmatrix} - \begin{pmatrix} \text{area of} \\ \text{trap. } DACF \end{pmatrix}$

$= ($ 12 $+$ 10.5 $) -$ 15

$=$ 22.5 $-$ 15

Area of $\triangle ABC =$ 7.5

MODEL PROBLEMS

1. Points $A(-4, -2)$, $B(2, -2)$, $C(4, 3)$, and $D(-2, 3)$ are the vertices of quadrilateral $ABCD$.
   a. Plot these points on graph paper and draw the quadrilateral.
   b. What kind of quadrilateral is $ABCD$?
   c. Find the area of quadrilateral $ABCD$.

Solution:

a. See graph.

b. (1) $\overline{AB}$ is parallel to $\overline{DC}$.
   (2) $AB = 6$, and $DC = 6$.
      Hence, $\overline{AB} \cong \overline{DC}$.
   (3) Since opposite sides $\overline{AB}$ and $\overline{DC}$ are both parallel and congruent, quadrilateral $ABCD$ is a parallelogram.

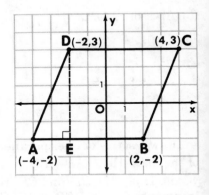

c. (1) In $\square ABCD$, draw altitude $\overline{DE}$ to side $\overline{AB}$. Here, $DE = 5$.
   (2) Area of $\square ABCD$ = base × altitude
   $$= AB \times DE = (6)(5) = 30$$

Answer: **a.** graph **b.** parallelogram **c.** 30 square units

2. *Given:* Quadrilateral *ABCD* with *A*(0, 2), *B*(2, 7), *C*(6, 10), and *D*(9, −2). Graph quadrilateral *ABCD* and find its area.

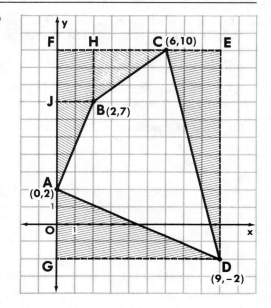

Solution:

Draw rectangle *DEFG* to enclose quadrilateral *ABCD*. From point *B*, draw $\overline{BH}$ ∥ the *y*-axis and $\overline{BJ}$ ∥ the *x*-axis, forming rectangle *BHFJ*.

The area of quadrilateral *ABCD* is equal to the area of rectangle *DEFG* minus the areas of the shaded region (four right triangles and the rectangle *BHFJ*).

(1) Area of rectangle $DEFG = GD \times DE = (9)(12) = 108$

(2) Find the area of the shaded region.

$$\text{Area of rt. } \triangle AGD = \tfrac{1}{2}AG \times GD = \tfrac{1}{2}(4)(9) = 18$$

$$\text{Area of rt. } \triangle DEC = \tfrac{1}{2}DE \times EC = \tfrac{1}{2}(12)(3) = 18$$

$$\text{Area of rt. } \triangle CHB = \tfrac{1}{2}CH \times HB = \tfrac{1}{2}(4)(3) = 6$$

$$\text{Area of rectangle } BHFJ = BH \times HF = (3)(2) = 6$$

$$\text{Area of rt. } \triangle BJA = \tfrac{1}{2}BJ \times JA = \tfrac{1}{2}(2)(5) = \underline{5}$$

Add these five areas to obtain the total: 53

(3) Area of quadrilateral $ABCD = \begin{pmatrix} \text{area of} \\ \text{rect. } DEFG \end{pmatrix} - \begin{pmatrix} \text{area of} \\ \text{shaded region} \end{pmatrix}$

$$= \quad 108 \quad - \quad 53$$

Area of quadrilateral $ABCD = \quad 55$

Answer: The area of quadrilateral *ABCD* is 55 square units.

3. The vertices of rhombus $ABCD$ are $A(1, 5)$, $B(-1, 2)$, $C(1, -1)$, and $D(3, 2)$. Graph rhombus $ABCD$ and find its area.

Solution:

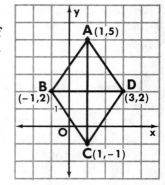

(1) Find the lengths of the diagonals of $ABCD$. $d_1 = AC = 6$, and $d_2 = BD = 4$.

(2) Area of rhombus $= \frac{1}{2}d_1d_2$

$\qquad\qquad\qquad\quad = \frac{1}{2} \cdot 6 \cdot 4$

$\qquad\qquad\qquad\quad = 12$

Answer: The area of rhombus $ABCD$ is 12 square units.

4. a. On the same set of axes, draw the graph of each of the following equations: (1) $x = 6$, (2) $y = x$, (3) $y = \frac{1}{2}x$.

b. The points of intersection of the graphs drawn in part **a** are the vertices of a triangle. Find the coordinates of these vertices.

c. Find the area of the triangle described in part **b**.

Solution:

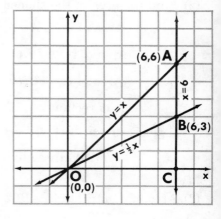

a. See graph.

b. Line $y = x$ intersects line $y = \frac{1}{2}x$ at $O(0, 0)$.
Line $y = x$ intersects line $x = 6$ at $A(6, 6)$.
Line $y = \frac{1}{2}x$ intersects line $x = 6$ at $B(6, 3)$.

c. There are many ways to find the area of $\triangle OAB$. Here, $\overline{AB}$ is the base and $\overline{OC}$ is the altitude. Note that the coordinates of point C are $(6, 0)$.

$\qquad$ Area of $\triangle OAB = \frac{1}{2}$ base $\times$ altitude $= \frac{1}{2} AB \times OC$

$\qquad$ Area of $\triangle OAB = \frac{1}{2}(3)(6) = 9$

Answer: **a.** graph　**b.** $O(0, 0)$, $A(6, 6)$, $B(6, 3)$　**c.** 9 square units

EXERCISES ━━━━━━━━━━━━━━━━━━━━━━━━━━━━━━━━━━

1. Find the area of a rectangle whose vertices are:
   a. (0, 0), (8, 0), (0, 5), (8, 5)   **b.** (−2, 3), (4, 3), (−2, 8), (4, 8)
2. Find the area of a parallelogram whose vertices are:
   a. (0, 0), (4, 0), (2, 3), (6, 3)   **b.** (−2, 8), (−3, 4), (5, 8), (4, 4)
3. Find the area of a triangle whose vertices are:
   a. (0, 0), (12, 0), (2, 8)   **b.** (0, 8), (0, −3), (4, 5)
   c. (2, −2), (8, −2), (4, −6)   **d.** (0, 0), (6, 0), (0, 5)
4. Find the area of a trapezoid whose vertices are:
   a. (0, 0), (12, 0), (2, 6), (7, 6)   **b.** (0, 4), (0, −8), (3, 1), (3, −4)
5. Points $Q(8, 2)$, $R(14, 6)$, $S(4, 6)$, $T(−2, 2)$ are the vertices of quadrilateral $QRST$.
   a. Plot these points on graph paper and draw the quadrilateral.
   b. What kind of quadrilateral is $QRST$?
   c. Find the area of quadrilateral $QRST$.
6. Points $C(1, −4)$, $D(9, −4)$, $E(9, 2)$, $F(1, 3)$ are the vertices of quadrilateral $CDEF$.
   a. Plot these points on graph paper and draw the quadrilateral.
   b. Find the lengths of $\overline{CD}$, $\overline{DE}$, and diagonal $\overline{CE}$.
   c. What kind of quadrilateral is $CDEF$?
   d. Find the area of the quadrilateral.
7. Find the area of a rhombus whose diagonals measure:
   a. 6 and 8   **b.** 4 and 5   **c.** 8 and 15   **d.** 13 and 17
8. Find the area of a rhombus whose vertices are:
   a. (2, 0), (0, 4), (−2, 0), (0, −4)   **b.** (1, 2), (5, 7), (9, 2), (5, −3)
   c. (1, 1), (4, 2), (1, 3), (−2, 2)   **d.** (1, 4), (−1, 2), (1, 0), (3, 2)
   e. (0, 5), (1.5, 0), (3, 5), (1.5, 10)
   f. (0, 0), (5, 10), (16, 12), (11, 2)
9. Find the area of a triangle whose vertices are the points:
   a. (2, 4), (8, 8), (16, 6)   **b.** (6, −2), (8, −10), (12, −6)
   c. (6, 4), (9, 2), (13, 6)   **d.** (−5, 4), (2, 1), (6, 5)
   e. (0, 6), (3, 0), (5, 2)   **f.** (2, 2), (7, 6), (4, −2)
10. Plot the points $A(2, 5)$, $B(11, 2)$, $C(9, 8)$, and $D(4, 8)$. Draw $\overline{AB}$, $\overline{BC}$, $\overline{CD}$, and $\overline{DA}$. Find the area of $ABCD$.
11. Find the area of a quadrilateral whose vertices are the points:
   a. (1, 7), (2, 4), (8, 6), (4, 10)   **b.** (−4, 2), (3, −4), (6, 2), (1, 4)
   c. (0, 3), (4, 0), (1, 4), (−3, 1)   **d.** (1, 2), (5, 4), (8, −2), (4, −4)
12. The coordinates of the vertices of triangle RST are $R(4, 5)$, $S(12, 5)$, and $T(8, 11)$. **a.** Find the length of the altitude of triangle RST drawn to side $\overline{RS}$. **b.** Find the area of triangle RST.

13. The coordinates of the vertices of triangle ABC are $A(-2, -5)$, $B(7, -2)$, and $C(-2, 1)$.
   a. Find the length of the altitude of triangle ABC drawn to side $\overline{AC}$.
   b. Find the area of triangle ABC.

14. The vertices of triangle RST are $R(4, 4)$, $S(12, 10)$, and $T(6, 13)$.
   a. Find the area of triangle RST.
   b. Find the length of side $\overline{RS}$.
   c. Using the results of parts **a** and **b**, find the length of the altitude drawn from T to $\overline{RS}$.

15. The coordinates of the vertices of $\triangle DEF$ are $D(1, 5)$, $E(5, 8)$, and $F(11, 0)$.
   a. Find the area of $\triangle DEF$.
   b. Show that $\triangle DEF$ is a right triangle.
   c. Find the lengths of sides $\overline{DE}$ and $\overline{EF}$.
   d. Show how the lengths found in part **c** can be used to find the area of $\triangle DEF$ by a second method.

16. The coordinates of the vertices of $\triangle ABC$ are $A(4, 4)$, $B(15, 2)$, and $C(12, 8)$.
   a. Draw $\triangle ABC$ on graph paper.
   b. Show that $\triangle ABC$ is a right triangle.
   c. Find the area of $\triangle ABC$.

17. Two of the vertices of $\triangle ABC$ are $B(-3, -2)$ and $C(5, 4)$. The midpoint of $\overline{AB}$ is $M(-3, 2)$. Find: **(a)** the coordinates of vertex A, **(b)** the area of $\triangle ABC$, **(c)** the coordinates of N, the midpoint of $\overline{AC}$, **(d)** the area of $\triangle AMN$, **(e)** the ratio of AM to AB, and **(f)** the ratio of the area of $\triangle AMN$ to the area of $\triangle ABC$.

18. a. Show that a quadrilateral whose vertices are $A(2, 1)$, $B(6, -2)$, $C(10, 1)$, and $D(6, 4)$ is a rhombus.
   b. Find the area of the rhombus.
   c. Find the length of an altitude of the rhombus.

19. a. Show that the quadrilateral whose vertices are $A(-7, 3)$, $B(-1, -5)$, $C(5, 3)$, and $D(-1, 11)$ is a rhombus.
   b. Find the area of the rhombus.
   c. Find the length of an altitude of the rhombus.

20. The vertices of $\triangle PQR$ are $P(1, 2)$, $Q(-3, -1)$, and $R(1, -4)$.
   a. Show that $\triangle PQR$ is not equilateral.
   b. Find the area of $\triangle PQR$.
   c. Find the coordinates of M, the midpoint of $\overline{QP}$.
   d. Find the coordinates of N, the midpoint of $\overline{QR}$.
   e. Find the area of $\triangle MQN$.
   f. What is the ratio of the area of $\triangle MQN$ to the area of $\triangle PQR$?

In 21–24: **a.** On the same set of axes, draw the graphs of the four given equations that intersect to form a quadrilateral. **b.** Find the area of the quadrilateral.

21. $x = 8$, $y = 4$, $x = -3$, $y = -5$
22. $x = 1$, $x = -3$, $y = 1$, $y = -5$
23. $x = 0$, $x = 3$, $y = x$, $y = x + 4$
24. $y = x$, $y = 0$, $y = -3$, $y = x - 5$

In 25–28: **a.** On the same set of axes, draw the graph of each of the three given equations. **b.** Find the coordinates of the points of intersection of the graphs, which are the vertices of a triangle. **c.** Find the area of the triangle.

25. $y = x$, $y = -\frac{1}{2}x$, $x = 4$ **26.** $y = x$, $y = 3x$, $y = 9$
27. $y = x$, $y = 2x$, $x = 5$ **28.** $y = x$, $y = 3x$, $y = -x + 8$

29. a. Starting with the formula $A = \frac{1}{2}d_1 d_2$ for the area of a rhombus with diagonals d_1 and d_2, show that the area of a square with diagonal d can be found by the formula $A = \frac{1}{2}d^2$.
    b. Find the area of a square whose diagonal measures:
      (1) 4   (2) 8   (3) 5   (4) $\sqrt{2}$ (5) $4\sqrt{2}$

30. In a square, s is the length of a side and d is the length of a diagonal.
    a. If $s = 3$, find d.   **b.** Using $A = s^2$, find the area of the square.
    c. Using $A = \frac{1}{2}d^2$, find the area of the square.

31. The vertices of square $ABCD$ are $A(1, 1)$, $B(-1, 3)$, $C(-3, 1)$, and $D(-1, -1)$.
    a. Find the length of $\overline{AB}$.
    b. Using AB, find the area of the square.
    c. Find the length of $\overline{AC}$.
    d. Using AC, find the area of the square.

9-10 REVIEW EXERCISES

In all exercises, answers that are irrational numbers should be left in radical form.

In 1–6, the diagram contains ten congruent rectangles, each measuring 2 by 4 units. Using $A(2, 0)$ and $B(0, 4)$, find the coordinates of the point named.

1. C **2.** D **3.** E
4. F **5.** G **6.** H

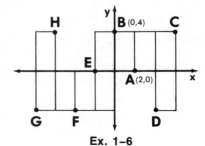

Ex. 1–6

In 7–12, find the length of the line segment that joins the two points whose coordinates are given.

7. (3, 9), (9, 9)   **8.** (−3, −1), (−3, 4)   **9.** (2, 0), (8, 8)
10. (−5, 1), (−1, −2)   **11.** (7, −2), (2, 1)   **12.** (−1, 3), (3, −3)

13. What is the length of a radius of a circle whose center is the origin and that passes through the point (5, −12)?

14. The vertices of right triangle ABC are $A(1, 2)$, $B(4, 2)$, and $C(4, 4)$. Find the length of the hypotenuse of $\triangle ABC$.

15. What is the midpoint of the segment whose endpoints are (−2, 7) and (−6, −11)?

16. The midpoint M of $\overline{AB}$ has coordinates (5, 4). If the coordinates of A are (2, 8), what are the coordinates of B?

17. The vertices of parallelogram $ABCD$ are $A(-3, -1)$, $B(3, -1)$, $C(7, 5)$, and $D(1, 5)$. Find the coordinates of the intersection of diagonals $\overline{AC}$ and $\overline{BD}$.

18. Three vertices of rectangle $ABCD$ are $A(-2, -2)$, $B(7, -2)$, and $C(7, 6)$. Find the coordinates of vertex D.

19. Find the value of k so that the slope of the line passing through (8, 4) and (k, 2) will be −1.

20. Find the slope of the line whose equation is $2x + 3y = 6$.

21. Write an equation of each line, given that the line:
   a. has a slope of 5 and a y-intercept of −3.
   b. passes through the point (4, 5) and is parallel to the y-axis.
   c. passes through the point (−2, 10) and has a zero slope.
   d. passes through the points (0, 5) and (2, 1).
   e. is parallel to $y = \frac{3}{4}x + 3$ and passes through the point (0, 7).
   f. is perpendicular to $y = \frac{3}{4}x + 3$ and passes through the origin.
   g. has a slope of 2 and passes through the point (4, 7).

In 22–28, select the numeral preceding the expression that best completes the statement or answers the question.

22. If the endpoints of $\overline{AB}$ are $A(2, -1)$ and $B(-3, 3)$, what is the length of $\overline{AB}$? (1) $\sqrt{5}$ (2) $\sqrt{17}$ (3) $\sqrt{29}$ (4) $\sqrt{41}$

23. If the vertices of a parallelogram are (3, 1), (8, 1), (6, 5), and (k, 5), a value of k may be (1) 1 (2) 2 (3) 0 (4) 10

24. In rhombus $ABCD$, the slope of diagonal $\overline{AC}$ is $\frac{1}{3}$. What is the slope of diagonal $\overline{BD}$? (1) $\frac{1}{3}$ (2) −3 (3) 3 (4) $-\frac{1}{3}$

25. Which of the following equations represents a line parallel to the line $y = 4x - 5$?
   (1) $y = 5 - 4x$ (2) $y + 4x = 8$ (3) $y - 4x = 6$ (4) $x = 4y - 5$

26. Which is an equation of a line whose slope is undefined?
   (1) $x = 7$ (2) $y = 7$ (3) $x + y = 7$ (4) $x + y = 0$

27. In right triangle RST, the slope of leg $\overline{RS}$ is b and the slope of leg $\overline{ST}$ is c. Which statement is true?

(1) $b = -c$ (2) $b = \dfrac{1}{c}$ (3) $bc = 1$ (4) $bc = -1$

28. If an equation of $\overleftrightarrow{AB}$ is $y = -\frac{1}{2}x + 4$, which statement is false?
(1) The x-intercept of $\overleftrightarrow{AB}$ is 8.   (2) The y-intercept of $\overleftrightarrow{AB}$ is 4.
(3) $\overleftrightarrow{AB}$ passes through the origin.   (4) The slope of $\overleftrightarrow{AB}$ is $-\frac{1}{2}$.

In 29–31, **(a)** draw the polygon on graph paper, and **(b)** find the area of the polygon.

29. $ABCD$ has vertices $A(2, 2)$, $B(2, -1)$, $C(-2, -3)$, and $D(-2, 0)$.

30. RST has vertices $R(0, 7)$, $S(4, 2)$, and $T(-2, -3)$.

31. $ABCD$ has vertices $A(8, 3)$, $B(6, -3)$, $C(0, -6)$, and $D(-2, -3)$.

32. The bases of trapezoid $ABCD$ are $\overline{AB}$ and $\overline{DC}$. The vertices are $A(1, 4)$, $B(7, 6)$, $C(11, 4)$, and $D(k, 1)$.   **a.** Find the slope of $\overline{AB}$.
b. Express the slope of $\overline{DC}$ in terms of k.   **c.** Find k.
d. Write an equation of the line that passes through B and D.

33. The vertices of $\triangle ABC$ are $A(-3, 6)$, $B(5, 2)$, and $C(1, -6)$.
a. Find the coordinates of D, the midpoint of $\overline{AB}$.
b. Find the coordinates of E, the midpoint of $\overline{AC}$.
c. Show $\overleftrightarrow{DE} \parallel \overleftrightarrow{BC}$.   **d.** Show $DE = \frac{1}{2} BC$.

34. The vertices of quadrilateral $ABCD$ are $A(0, 0)$, $B(2, 4)$, $C(8, 6)$, and $D(6, 2)$.
a. Graph the quadrilateral and draw diagonal $\overline{BD}$.
b. Show that $\triangle ABD$ is a right triangle.
c. Show that $ABCD$ is a parallelogram.

35. The vertices of quadrilateral $RSTV$ are $R(4, 4)$, $S(6, 1)$, $T(0, -3)$, and $V(-2, 0)$.
a. Prove that quadrilateral $RSTV$ is a rectangle.
b. Find the coordinates of A, the midpoint of $\overline{VR}$.
c. Find the coordinates of M, the midpoint of $\overline{TS}$.
d. If $\overline{MA}$ is drawn, prove that quadrilateral $MARS$ is a rhombus.

36. The vertices of $\triangle ABC$ are $A(8, 9)$, $B(10, 3)$, and $C(3, 4)$.
a. Prove that $\triangle ABC$ is isosceles.
b. Find the coordinates of M, the midpoint of $\overline{AB}$.
c. Prove that $\overline{CM} \perp \overline{AB}$.

37. Using coordinate geometry, prove that the diagonals of a square are perpendicular to each other.
[*Hint.* Use vertices $(0, 0)$, $(0, a)$, (a, a), and $(a, 0)$.]

Chapter **10**

Quadratic Equations

In previous chapters, we found that in order to solve some problems in geometry, it was necessary to solve quadratic equations. Incomplete quadratic equations of the form $x^2 = a$ were solved by taking the square root of each side of the equation. Other equations of the form $ax^2 + bx + c = 0$ were solved by factoring the left member of the equation. But not every quadratic equation can be solved by these methods.

In this chapter, we will review the techniques you already know for solving quadratic equations. Then we will present a method that will enable you to solve any quadratic equation whose solutions are real numbers.

We will begin with a review of the operations that can be performed on radicals, since you will need to know this material to do the new work.

10-1 OPERATIONS WITH SQUARE-ROOT RADICALS

Adding and Subtracting Radicals

PROCEDURE. To express the sum or difference of square-root radicals in simplest form:

1. Simplify each radical.

2. Combine like radicals by using the distributive property.

3. Indicate the sum or difference of unlike radicals.

MODEL PROBLEMS _____

1. Add: $2\sqrt{3} + \sqrt{27}$

   Solution: $2\sqrt{3} + \sqrt{27} = 2\sqrt{3} + \sqrt{9} \cdot \sqrt{3}$
   $$= 2\sqrt{3} + 3\sqrt{3}$$
   $$= (2 + 3)\sqrt{3}$$
   $$= 5\sqrt{3} \ Ans.$$

2. Subtract: $\sqrt{18a^5} - \sqrt{12a}$ when $a > 0$

   Solution: $\sqrt{18a^5} - \sqrt{12a} = \sqrt{9 \cdot 2 \cdot a^4 \cdot a} - \sqrt{4 \cdot 3 \cdot a}$
   $$= \sqrt{9a^4} \cdot \sqrt{2a} - \sqrt{4} \cdot \sqrt{3a}$$
   $$= 3a^2\sqrt{2a} - 2\sqrt{3a} \ Ans.$$

3. Combine: $\sqrt{48} - \sqrt{12} + \sqrt{98}$

   Solution: $\sqrt{48} - \sqrt{12} + \sqrt{98} = \sqrt{16} \cdot \sqrt{3} - \sqrt{4} \cdot \sqrt{3} + \sqrt{49} \cdot \sqrt{2}$
   $$= 4\sqrt{3} - 2\sqrt{3} + 7\sqrt{2}$$
   $$= (4 - 2)\sqrt{3} + 7\sqrt{2}$$
   $$= 2\sqrt{3} + 7\sqrt{2} \ Ans.$$

EXERCISES _____

In 1–26, express each sum or difference in simplest form. All variables represent positive real numbers.

1. $7\sqrt{5} + 3\sqrt{5}$
2. $3\sqrt{2} + 8\sqrt{2}$
3. $9\sqrt{7} - 5\sqrt{7}$
4. $6\sqrt{10} + \sqrt{10}$
5. $4\sqrt{3} - \sqrt{3}$
6. $12\sqrt{6} + \sqrt{6}$
7. $\sqrt{2} + \sqrt{8}$
8. $\sqrt{63} + \sqrt{7}$
9. $\sqrt{20} - 2\sqrt{5}$
10. $2\sqrt{6} + \sqrt{24}$
11. $\sqrt{75} + \sqrt{147}$
12. $4\sqrt{32} - 5\sqrt{20}$
13. $\sqrt{200a^2} - \sqrt{18a^2}$
14. $\sqrt{9x} + \sqrt{25x}$
15. $\sqrt{12y} + \sqrt{27y}$
16. $2\sqrt{18} - \sqrt{72}$
17. $3\sqrt{3b^2} - b\sqrt{75}$
18. $\sqrt{x^5} + x^2\sqrt{25x}$
19. $\sqrt{3} + \sqrt{27} - \sqrt{12}$
20. $\sqrt{5} - \sqrt{20} + \sqrt{125}$
21. $\sqrt{8} + \sqrt{24} + \sqrt{32}$
22. $\sqrt{200} + \sqrt{50} + \sqrt{175}$
23. $\sqrt{50a^2} + \sqrt{98a^2} - \sqrt{49a}$
24. $\sqrt{4x} + \sqrt{9x} - \sqrt{16y}$
25. $\sqrt{9s^3} - \sqrt{25s^3} + s\sqrt{16s}$
26. $\sqrt{25} + \sqrt{125} + \sqrt{80}$

In 27–30, express in simplest form the perimeter of a triangle if the measures of the sides in inches are:

27. $\sqrt{12}, \sqrt{48}, \sqrt{75}$

28. $\sqrt{200}, \sqrt{72}, \sqrt{128}$

29. $\sqrt{150}, \sqrt{150}, \sqrt{54}$

30. $10\sqrt{3}, 5\sqrt{12}, \sqrt{300}$

In 31–33, express in simplest form the perimeter of a rectangle if the measures of the length and width in meters are:

31. $\sqrt{20}, \sqrt{45}$

32. $\sqrt{27}, \sqrt{147}$

33. $5\sqrt{8}, 2\sqrt{18}$

34. The measures of two sides of a triangle are $3\sqrt{2}$ cm and $\sqrt{8}$ cm, and the measure of the perimeter is $\sqrt{98}$ cm. Find the measure of the third side.

Multiplying and Dividing Radicals

PROCEDURE. To express the product (or quotient) of square-root radicals in simplest form:

1. Multiply (or divide) the coefficients to find the coefficient of the product (or quotient).
2. Multiply (or divide) the radicands to find the radicand of the product (or quotient).
3. If possible, simplify the result.

MODEL PROBLEMS ———————————————————————————

1. Multiply: $6\sqrt{12}(8\sqrt{2})$

Solution: $6\sqrt{12}(8\sqrt{2}) = 6 \cdot 8(\sqrt{12} \cdot \sqrt{2}) = 48\sqrt{24}$
$$= 48\sqrt{4} \cdot \sqrt{6}$$
$$= 48 \cdot 2 \cdot \sqrt{6}$$
$$= 96\sqrt{6} \quad Ans.$$

2. Divide: $\dfrac{6\sqrt{12}}{4\sqrt{3}}$

Solution: $\dfrac{6\sqrt{12}}{4\sqrt{3}} = \dfrac{6}{4} \cdot \dfrac{\sqrt{12}}{\sqrt{3}} = \dfrac{3}{2} \cdot \sqrt{4}$
$$= \dfrac{3}{2} \cdot 2$$
$$= 3 \quad Ans.$$

3. Simplify: $\dfrac{9 + \sqrt{18}}{3}$

Solution: $\dfrac{9 + \sqrt{18}}{3} = \dfrac{9}{3} + \dfrac{\sqrt{18}}{3}$

$$= 3 + \dfrac{\sqrt{9} \cdot \sqrt{2}}{3}$$

$$= 3 + \dfrac{3 \cdot \sqrt{2}}{3}$$

$$= 3 + \sqrt{2} \quad Ans.$$

EXERCISES _____

In 1–24, multiply, and express the product in simplest form.

1. $\sqrt{5} \cdot \sqrt{20}$ **2.** $\sqrt{10} \cdot \sqrt{5}$ **3.** $\sqrt{7} \cdot \sqrt{7}$

4. $4\sqrt{3} \cdot 5\sqrt{3}$ **5.** $6\sqrt{2} \cdot 5\sqrt{8}$ **6.** $5\sqrt{12} \cdot 2\sqrt{3}$

7. $9\sqrt{10} \cdot \sqrt{30}$ **8.** $\sqrt{.4}(10\sqrt{.9})$ **9.** $2\sqrt{2}.4(3\sqrt{.6})$

10. $\frac{1}{2}\sqrt{8}(\frac{1}{2}\sqrt{2})$ **11.** $\frac{1}{5}\sqrt{20}(\frac{1}{2}\sqrt{10})$ **12.** $\frac{3}{4}\sqrt{24}(2\sqrt{2})$

13. $12\sqrt{.2}(5\sqrt{.2})$ **14.** $3\sqrt{2.5}(4\sqrt{.1})$ **15.** $8\sqrt{6}(3\sqrt{.12})$

16. $\frac{2}{3}\sqrt{3}(\frac{1}{2}\sqrt{27})$ **17.** $\frac{1}{5}\sqrt{15}(\frac{5}{3}\sqrt{5})$ **18.** $\frac{1}{8}\sqrt{12}(\frac{4}{5}\sqrt{3})$

19. $5(3 + \sqrt{3})$ **20.** $3(2\sqrt{3} + 7)$

21. $2\sqrt{5}(3 + 2\sqrt{5})$ **22.** $4\sqrt{6}(3 - 2\sqrt{2})$

23. $7\sqrt{2}(\sqrt{8} + \sqrt{20})$ **24.** $5\sqrt{10}(\sqrt{5} + \sqrt{2})$

In 25–39, divide, and express the quotient in simplest form.

25. $\sqrt{80} \div \sqrt{5}$ **26.** $\sqrt{150} \div \sqrt{3}$ **27.** $\sqrt{200} \div \sqrt{8}$

28. $\dfrac{\sqrt{40}}{\sqrt{5}}$ **29.** $\dfrac{8\sqrt{20}}{2\sqrt{10}}$ **30.** $\dfrac{12\sqrt{35}}{3\sqrt{5}}$

31. $\dfrac{48\sqrt{8}}{2\sqrt{2}}$ **32.** $\dfrac{30\sqrt{75}}{15\sqrt{15}}$ **33.** $\dfrac{20\sqrt{5}}{4\sqrt{5}}$

34. $\dfrac{12 + 4\sqrt{2}}{4}$ **35.** $\dfrac{36 + 18\sqrt{3}}{3}$ **36.** $\dfrac{24 + 8\sqrt{6}}{8}$

37. $\dfrac{12 + \sqrt{80}}{2}$ **38.** $\dfrac{15 + \sqrt{75}}{5}$ **39.** $\dfrac{18 + \sqrt{72}}{3}$

In 40–42, express in simplest form the area of a rectangle whose length and width in centimeters have the given measures.

40. $5\sqrt{2}, 8\sqrt{2}$ **41.** $3 + \sqrt{3}, \sqrt{3}$ **42.** $12\sqrt{6}, 9\sqrt{3}$

43. a. If the perimeter of a square is $\sqrt{160}$ meters, what is the length of one side?
   b. What is the area of the square?

44. The measure of the length of a rectangle is 24 inches, and the measure of the area is $(10 + \sqrt{300})$ square feet. Find the measure of the width.

10-2 SOLVING QUADRATIC EQUATIONS BY FACTORING

The equation $x^2 + 3x - 10 = 0$ is a *second-degree equation in one variable* because:

1. There is only *one variable* in the equation, namely, x.
2. The greatest exponent of this variable is 2. Therefore, the equation is of degree two, or the *second degree*.

An equation of the second degree in one variable is also known as a *quadratic equation*. The equation $x^2 + 3x - 10 = 0$ is in *standard form* when all terms of the equation are collected in descending order and set equal to zero; that is, one member of the equation contains the terms $x^2 + 3x - 10$, and the other member of the equation is 0.

● In general, the standard form of a quadratic equation is:

$$ax^2 + bx + c = 0$$

where a, b, and c are real numbers, and $a \neq 0$.

Factoring an Expression

An expression of the form $ax^2 + bx + c$, where $a \neq 0$ and the terms have no common factor, is not necessarily factorable. If the expression can be factored, we follow this process:

Factor the trinomial $ax^2 + bx + c$ into two binomial expressions such that:

1. The product of the first terms of the binomials equals ax^2.
2. The product of the last terms of the binomials equals c.
3. When the first term of each binomial is multiplied by the last term of the other binomial, the sum of these two products is bx.

Some polynomials may contain a *common monomial factor*, that is, a monomial term that exactly divides each of the terms of the polynomial expression. If so, we first factor out the greatest such common monomial factor.

EXAMPLE 1. Factor: $x^2 - 3x$

The greatest common monomial factor is x: $x^2 - 3x = x(x - 3)$. *Ans.*

EXAMPLE 2. Factor: $x^2 - 2x - 3$

(1) There is no common monomial factor other than 1. Factor the trinomial into binomials.

(2) Since the product of the first terms of the binomials is x^2, each first term is x. Therefore, $x^2 - 2x - 3 = (x\quad)(x\quad)$.

(3) Since the product of the last terms of the binomials is -3, the last terms will be either $(+3)$ and (-1), or (-3) and $(+1)$.

(4) Test the factors chosen in step (3) by multiplying the first term of each binomial by the last term of the other. The sum of these products must be $-2x$.

$$+3x$$
$$(x + 3)(x - 1)$$
$$-1x$$

$$-3x$$
$$(x - 3)(x + 1)$$
$$+1x$$

Here, $+3x - 1x = +2x$.
(Incorrect)

Here, $-3x + 1x = -2x$.
(Correct)

Answer: $x^2 - 2x - 3 = (x - 3)(x + 1)$

Note. It is convenient to refer to the products in step (4) as the *inner* and *outer* products. In the correct solution shown above, $-3x$ is the inner product and $+1x$ is the outer product.

EXAMPLE 3. Factor completely: $4x^2 - 8x - 12$

(1) The greatest common monomial factor is 4.

$$4x^2 - 8x - 12 = 4(x^2 - 2x - 3)$$

(2) Factor the trinomial into two binomials, as seen in Example 2 above.

$$= 4(x - 3)(x + 1)\ \textit{Ans.}$$

Solving a Quadratic Equation by Factoring

Recall that in the set of real numbers, if the product of two quantities is 0, then at least one of the quantities is 0, and conversely. In other words:

$$pq = 0 \text{ if and only if } p = 0 \text{ or } q = 0$$

This principle is used when a quadratic equation is solved by factoring.

PROCEDURE.   To solve a quadratic equation by factoring:

1. If necessary, transform the equation into standard form.
2. Factor the collected terms.
3. Set each factor containing the variable equal to zero.
4. Solve each of the resulting equations.
5. Check each value obtained in the original equation.

MODEL PROBLEMS ─────────────────────────────

1. Solve and check: $3x^2 = 2x$

How to Proceed	*Solution*
Given the equation:	$3x^2 = 2x$
(1) Transform into standard form.	$3x^2 - 2x = 0$
(2) Factor.	$x(3x - 2) = 0$
(3) Let each factor = 0.	$x = 0 \quad \mid \quad 3x - 2 = 0$
(4) Solve each equation.	$3x = 2$
	$x = \dfrac{2}{3}$

The check is left to the student.

Answer: $x = 0$ or $x = \dfrac{2}{3}$ *or*   the solution set $= \{0, \dfrac{2}{3}\}$.

Note. Never divide both members of the equation by an expression involving the variable. If we had divided both members of the equation $3x^2 = 2x$ by x, we would have obtained the equation $3x = 2$, whose solution is $x = \frac{2}{3}$. We would have lost the second root $x = 0$ because, in dividing by x, we would have been dividing by 0. Division by 0 is not defined.

2. In a rectangle whose area is 10 cm², the length is 3 cm more than the width. Write and solve an equation to find the dimensions of the rectangle.

x+3

x

How to Proceed	*Solution*
(1) Identify the variables.	Let x = width in centimeters. Let $x + 3$ = length in centimeters.
(2) Write the formula.	Area = width • length
(3) Substitute.	$10 = x(x + 3)$
(4) Simplify.	$10 = x^2 + 3x$
(5) Transform into standard form.	$0 = x^2 + 3x - 10$
(6) Factor.	$0 = (x + 5)(x - 2)$
(7) Let each factor = 0, and solve each equation.	$x + 5 = 0$ $x - 2 = 0$ $x = -5$ $x = 2$ (Reject this root because a segment cannot have a negative length.)

(8) Since $x = 2$, then $x + 3 = 5$.

Check: (2 cm) • (5 cm) = 10 cm², the given area.

Answer: The width measures 2 cm; the length measures 5 cm.

3. Write an equation of the form $ax^2 + bx + c = 0$ for which the solution set is {3, −7}.

Given a quadratic equation, you learned a process to find its roots. Now, given the roots, work backward to find the equation. As a last step, check the equation.

How to Proceed	*Solution*
(1) Write an equation for each root.	$x = 3$ $x = -7$
(2) Transform each equation so that its right member is 0.	$x - 3 = 0$ $x + 7 = 0$
(3) Since each binomial equals 0, their product equals 0.	$(x - 3)(x + 7) = 0$
(4) Multiply the binomial factors.	$x^2 + 4x - 21 = 0$
(5) Check this equation for {3, −7}.	

Check the solution 3.

$$x^2 + 4x - 21 = 0$$
$$(3)^2 + 4(3) - 21 \stackrel{?}{=} 0$$
$$9 + 12 - 21 \stackrel{?}{=} 0$$
$$0 = 0 \quad \text{(True)}$$

Check the solution −7.

$$x^2 + 4x - 21 = 0$$
$$(-7)^2 + 4(-7) - 21 \stackrel{?}{=} 0$$
$$49 - 28 - 21 \stackrel{?}{=} 0$$
$$0 = 0 \quad \text{(True)}$$

Answer: $x^2 + 4x - 21 = 0$

4. If -4 is a root of the equation $x^2 - 2x + k = 0$:
   a. Find the value of k.
   b. Find the second root of the equation.

Solution

a. Since -4 is a root of the equation, substitute $x = -4$ in the given equation. Then solve for k.

$$x^2 - 2x + k = 0$$
$$(-4)^2 - 2(-4) + k = 0$$
$$16 + 8 + k = 0$$
$$24 + k = 0$$
$$k = -24$$

b. Substitute $k = -24$ in the given equation. Then solve for x.

$$x^2 - 2x + k = 0$$
$$x^2 - 2x - 24 = 0$$
$$(x + 4)(x - 6) = 0$$

$$x + 4 = 0 \quad | \quad x - 6 = 0$$
$$x = -4 \quad | \quad x = 6$$

The second root is 6.

Answer: **a.** $k = -24$ **b.** 6.

EXERCISES

In 1–24, solve the equation and check.

1. $x^2 - 4x + 3 = 0$
2. $x^2 - 7x + 6 = 0$
3. $x^2 - 6x + 8 = 0$
4. $x^2 - 8x + 15 = 0$
5. $x^2 + 5x + 4 = 0$
6. $x^2 + 5x + 6 = 0$
7. $x^2 + 5x - 6 = 0$
8. $x^2 + 5x - 24 = 0$
9. $x^2 + 7x + 6 = 0$
10. $x^2 + x - 12 = 0$
11. $x^2 - 11x - 12 = 0$
12. $x^2 + 6x + 9 = 0$
13. $x^2 - 10x + 25 = 0$
14. $x^2 - 10x = 0$
15. $x^2 = 11x - 30$
16. $3x^2 = x$
17. $x^2 = 3x$
18. $3x^2 + 5x = x^2$
19. $x^2 + 5x = 40 - x$
20. $x(x - 4) = 5$
21. $x^2 = 2(x + 12)$
22. $\dfrac{x}{2} = \dfrac{3}{x + 1}$
23. $\dfrac{x}{5} = \dfrac{x + 6}{x - 2}$
24. $\dfrac{3x}{2} = \dfrac{x^2}{4}$

In 25–32, write an equation of the form $ax^2 + bx + c = 0$ for which the solution set is given.

25. $\{-1, -9\}$
26. $\{-6, -7\}$
27. $\{8, -2\}$
28. $\{-12, 3\}$
29. $\{5, 8\}$
30. $\{6, -6\}$
31. $\{0, -15\}$
32. $\{18, 0\}$

33. In a rectangle whose area is 12 cm^2, the measure of the width is 4 cm more than the measure of the length. Write and solve an equation to find the dimensions of the rectangle.

34. In a rectangle, the measure of the height is 5 less than the measure of the base, and the area is 14. Write and solve an equation to find the dimensions of the rectangle.

35. The area of a rectangle is 20, and its perimeter is 18.
  a. If x represents the measure of the base of the rectangle, explain why $9 - x$ represents the measure of its height.
  b. Write and solve an equation to find the dimensions of the rectangle.

36. If 6 is a root of the equation $x^2 - 8x + k = 0$, find the value of k.

37. If -8 is a root of the equation $x^2 + 11x + k = 0$, find k.

38. If one root of the equation $x^2 - 10x + k = 0$ is 12, **(a)** find the value of k and **(b)** find the other root of the equation.

39. One root of $x^2 - 3x = k$ is -6.
  a. Find k. **b.** Find the second root of the quadratic equation.

40. Find the positive root of $x^2 + 3x = 28$.

In 41–43, select the numeral preceding the expression that best completes the sentence or answers the question.

41. Which quadratic equation has roots of -3 and 9?
  (1) $x^2 + 6x - 27 = 0$ (2) $x^2 - 6x - 27 = 0$
  (3) $x^2 + 6x + 27 = 0$ (4) $-x^2 - 6x + 27 = 0$

42. If one root of $4x^2 = 5x$ is $\frac{5}{4}$, the other root is
  (1) 1   (2) $-\frac{5}{4}$ (3) -1 (4) 0

43. If 2 is a root of the equation $x^2 + 13x + k = 0$, the second root of the quadratic equation is (1) 30 (2) -30 (3) 15 (4) -15

10-3 QUADRATIC EQUATIONS WITH SPECIAL FACTORS

The Pure Quadratic Equation

Any equation of the form $ax^2 + c = 0$, where a and c are real numbers and $a \neq 0$, is called an *incomplete quadratic equation* or a *pure quadratic equation*. Notice that the first-degree term is missing in all such equations.

EXAMPLE 1. Solve: $x^2 - 25 = 0$

If c is a *nonpositive number* in the pure quadratic equation, $ax^2 + c = 0$, there are two methods by which the equation can be solved.

Method 1

Standard factoring is used. Notice that the factors are binomials; one, the *sum of two terms* and the other, *the difference of the same two terms.*

$$x^2 - 25 = 0$$
$$(x - 5)(x + 5) = 0$$

$x - 5 = 0$	$x + 5 = 0$
$x = 5$	$x = -5$

Method 2

After transforming the equation, use the principle that every positive real number has *two real square roots*, one of which is the opposite of the other.

$$x^2 - 25 = 0$$
$$x^2 = 25$$
$$x = \sqrt{25} \quad \text{or} \quad x = -\sqrt{25}$$
$$x = 5 \quad \text{or} \quad x = -5$$

Answer: $x = 5$ or $x = -5$ (sometimes written $x = \pm 5$) *or* the solution set $= \{5, -5\}$.

EXAMPLE 2. Solve for all real roots: $x^2 + 4 = 0$

If c is a *positive number* in the pure quadratic equation $ax^2 + c = 0$, then there are *no real roots*. For example:

(1) Using method 1, we cannot factor the expression $x^2 + 4$.
(2) Using method 2, we see that $x^2 + 4 = 0$ becomes $x^2 = -4$. However, there is no real number that, when squared, is -4.

Answer: $x^2 + 4 = 0$ has no real roots.

Quadratics With Perfect Square Trinomials

Each side of a given square has a length of $x + 3$. By separating the square into four regions, we can multiply monomial terms to find the area of each of these regions: $x \cdot x = x^2$, $x \cdot 3 = 3x$, $3 \cdot x = 3x$, and $3 \cdot 3 = 9$. The sum of the areas of these four regions is the area of the square. Thus, using $A = s^2$, observe that the area of the square is $(x + 3)^2$:

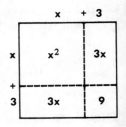

$$(x + 3)(x + 3) = x^2 + 3x + 3x + 9 = x^2 + 6x + 9$$

The expression $x^2 + 6x + 9$ is called a **perfect square trinomial** because:

1. The expression equals the *square of a binomial*, here $(x + 3)^2$, and
2. A polynomial consisting of *three terms* is a trinomial.

● **When a quadratic equation consists of a perfect square trinomial equal to zero, the two roots of the quadratic equation will be equal.**

EXAMPLE.   Solve and check:

	Check

$$x^2 - 16x + 64 = 0$$
$$(x - 8)(x - 8) = 0$$
$$x - 8 = 0 \mid x - 8 = 0$$
$$x = 8 \mid \quad x = 8$$

$$x^2 - 16x + 64 = 0$$
$$(8)^2 - 16(8) + 64 \stackrel{?}{=} 0$$
$$64 - 128 + 64 \stackrel{?}{=} 0$$
$$0 = 0 \quad (\text{True})$$

Answer: $x = 8$ *or* the solution set $= \{8\}$.

Leading Coefficients Other Than 1

In $ax^2 + bx + c$, the **leading coefficient** is a, the coefficient of the term containing the highest exponent of x. If $a \neq 1$ in the trinomial $ax^2 + bx + c$, it may be necessary to test several pairs of factors as the first terms in the resulting binomial factors of $ax^2 + bx + c$.

EXAMPLE.   Factor $4x^2 - 4x - 3$.

(1) Since the product of the first terms of the binomials is $4x^2$, the first terms of the binomials will be either $(2x)$ and $(2x)$, or $(4x)$ and (x).

$$4x^2 - 4x - 3 = (2x \quad)(2x \quad) \quad or \quad 4x^2 - 4x - 3 = (4x \quad)(x \quad)$$

(2) Since the product of the last terms of the binomials is -3, the last terms of the binomials will be either $(+3)$ and (-1) or (-3) and $(+1)$.

(3) Test all possible arrangements of first and last terms:

$$(2x + 3)(2x - 1) \quad (4x + 3)(x - 1) \quad (4x - 1)(x + 3)$$
$$(2x - 3)(2x + 1) \quad (4x - 3)(x + 1) \quad (4x + 1)(x - 3)$$

Only one set of factors will result in a middle term of $-4x$, namely:

$$4x^2 - 4x - 3 = (2x - 3)(2x + 1)$$

Answer: $(2x - 3)(2x + 1)$

MODEL PROBLEMS

1. Solve and check: $4x^2 - 4x - 3 = 0$

How to Proceed	*Solution*

Given the equation: $4x^2 - 4x - 3 = 0$

(1) Factor the trinomial. $(2x - 3)(2x + 1) = 0$

(2) Let each factor $= 0$. $2x - 3 = 0 \mid 2x + 1 = 0$

(3) Solve each equation. $2x = 3 \mid \quad 2x = -1$

$$x = \tfrac{3}{2} \mid \quad x = -\tfrac{1}{2}$$

(4) Check both values in the original equation.

<table>
<tr><td align="center">*Check* $x = \frac{3}{2}$</td><td align="center">*Check* $x = -\frac{1}{2}$</td></tr>
<tr><td align="center">$4x^2 - 4x - 3 = 0$</td><td align="center">$4x^2 - 4x - 3 = 0$</td></tr>
<tr><td align="center">$4(\frac{3}{2})^2 - 4(\frac{3}{2}) - 3 \overset{?}{=} 0$</td><td align="center">$4(-\frac{1}{2})^2 - 4(-\frac{1}{2}) - 3 \overset{?}{=} 0$</td></tr>
<tr><td align="center">$4(\frac{9}{4}) - 4(\frac{3}{2}) - 3 \overset{?}{=} 0$</td><td align="center">$4(\frac{1}{4}) - 4(-\frac{1}{2}) - 3 \overset{?}{=} 0$</td></tr>
<tr><td align="center">$9 - 6 - 3 \overset{?}{=} 0$</td><td align="center">$1 + 2 - 3 \overset{?}{=} 0$</td></tr>
<tr><td align="center">$0 = 0$ (True)</td><td align="center">$0 = 0$ (True)</td></tr>
</table>

Answer: $x = \frac{3}{2}$ or $x = -\frac{1}{2}$ *or*   the solution set $= \{\frac{3}{2}, -\frac{1}{2}\}$.

2. In a rectangle, the measures of the base and altitude are in a ratio of $4:1$. If the rectangle is equal in area to a square whose side has a length of 8 centimeters, find the dimensions of the rectangle.

Solution: Let $x =$ the measure of the altitude in centimeters.
         Let $4x =$ the measure of the base in centimeters.

(1) Area of rectangle $= bh$	(2) Area of square $= s^2$
$\qquad A = 4x \cdot x$	$\qquad A' = (8)^2$
$\qquad A = 4x^2$	$\qquad A' = 64$

(3) Since the area of the rectangle is equal to the area of the square, or $A = A'$, solve the equation:

$$4x^2 = 64$$
$$4x^2 - 64 = 0$$
$$4(x^2 - 16) = 0$$
$$4(x - 4)(x + 4) = 0$$
$$x - 4 = 0 \mid x + 4 = 0$$
$$x = 4 \qquad x = -4$$
Then $4x = 16$ | (Reject.)

Check

$A = A'$
$bh = s^2$
$16(4) \overset{?}{=} (8)^2$
$64 = 64$ (True)

Answer: The altitude measures 4 cm and the base measures 16 cm.

EXERCISES

In 1–24, solve the equation and check.

1. $x^2 - 9 = 0$
2. $x^2 - 400 = 0$
3. $25x^2 = 100$
4. $x^2 - 100 = 21$
5. $x^2 - 25 = 200$
6. $16x^2 = 64$
7. $(x + 3)(x + 3) = 0$
8. $(2x - 5)^2 = 0$
9. $x^2 - 8x + 16 = 0$
10. $x^2 + 100 = 20x$
11. $x^2 + 1 = 2x$
12. $4x^2 + 4x + 1 = 0$
13. $9x^2 - 6x + 1 = 0$
14. $4x^2 - 12x + 9 = 0$

15. $4x^2 + 8x - 5 = 0$

16. $4x^2 + 19x - 5 = 0$

17. $6x^2 - x - 2 = 0$

18. $6x^2 - 4x - 2 = 0$

19. $6x^2 + 11x - 2 = 0$

20. $6x^2 - 11x + 4 = 0$

21. $4x^2 - 8x + 4 = 0$

22. $\dfrac{x}{6} = \dfrac{24}{x}$

23. $\dfrac{x + 3}{2} = \dfrac{8}{x - 3}$

24. $x + 6 = \dfrac{13}{x - 6}$

25. Find the positive root of $2x^2 + 7x - 4 = 0$.

26. Find the positive root of $3x^2 - 13x - 10 = 0$.

27. The area of a rectangle is 56. If the measure of its base is represented by $x + 5$ and the measure of its height by $x - 5$, find its dimensions.

28. In a rectangle, the measures of the base and the altitude are in a ratio of 1:4. If the rectangle is equal in area to a square whose side measures 10 cm, find the dimensions of the rectangle.

29. In a rectangle, the measures of the base and altitude are in a ratio of 1:9. If the rectangle is equal in area to a square whose perimeter is 60 feet, find the dimensions of the rectangle.

30. **a.** If the length of a side of a square is represented by $x + 2$, express its area in terms of x.

b. If the dimensions of a rectangle are represented by x and $2x + 1$, express its area in terms of x.

c. If the area of the square equals the area of the rectangle, find the dimensions of each quadrilateral.

In 31–37, select the numeral preceding the expression that best completes the sentence or answers the question.

31. The solution set of $(3x - 6)(x + 5) = 0$ is
(1) $\{-6, 5\}$ (2) $\{6, -5\}$ (3) $\{-2, 5\}$ (4) $\{2, -5\}$

32. Which quadratic equation has roots of ± 4?   (1) $x^2 - 4 = 0$
(2) $x^2 + 4 = 0$ (3) $x^2 - 16 = 0$ (4) $x^2 - 8x + 16 = 0$

33. Which quadratic equation has no real roots?   (1) $x^2 + 16x = 0$
(2) $x^2 + 16 = 0$ (3) $x^2 - 16 = 0$ (4) $x^2 = 16x$

34. If one root of $x^2 + k = 0$ is 7, then k equals
(1) 7 (2) -7 (3) 49 (4) -49

35. If one root of $x^2 + k = 0$ is 14, then the second root of the quadratic equation is (1) 14 (2) -14 (3) 196 (4) -196

36. One root of the equation $4x^2 - 7x + 3 = 0$ is 1. What is the other root? (1) $\frac{3}{4}$ (2) $\frac{4}{3}$ (3) $\frac{7}{4}$ (4) $\frac{7}{3}$

37. One root of the equation $6x^2 + 13x - 15 = 0$ is -3. What is the other root? (1) $\frac{5}{3}$ (2) $\frac{5}{6}$ (3) $\frac{5}{2}$ (4) $\frac{3}{5}$

10-4 SOLVING QUADRATIC EQUATIONS BY COMPLETING THE SQUARE

Some quadratic equations can be solved by factoring, while others cannot.

To find the roots of $x^2 - 6x + 7 = 0$, for example, we need new techniques. One such method of solution, called *completing the square*, is based upon building a perfect square trinomial for one member of the equation, and then taking the square root of both members of the equation. Let us first study this method with an equation whose roots can be found by factoring. For example, you can verify that the roots of $x^2 - 2x - 3 = 0$ are $x = 3$ and $x = -1$.

EXAMPLE 1. Solve $x^2 - 2x - 3 = 0$ by completing the square.

How to Proceed	*Solution*
Given the equation:	$x^2 - 2x - 3 = 0$
(1) Transform the equation so that only terms containing variables are kept in the left member of the equation.	$x^2 - 2x = 3$
(2) Form a perfect square trinomial in the left member by adding 1. To maintain the equation, add 1 to the right member.	$x^2 - 2x + 1 = 3 + 1$
(3) Express the left member as the square of a binomial and simplify the right member.	$(x - 1)^2 = 4$
(4) Take the square root of both members of the equation. Show that every positive real number has two real square roots by writing $\pm$ before the right member.	$(x - 1) = \pm\sqrt{4}$ $x - 1 = \pm 2$
(5) Add 1 to both members.	$x = 1 \pm 2$
(6) Read the two roots from the expression.	$x = 1 + 2 \mid x = 1 - 2$ $x = 3 \mid x = -1$

Answer: $x = 3$ or $x = -1$ *or* the solution set $= \{3, -1\}$.

Let us now apply this technique to solving a quadratic equation that cannot be solved by factoring.

EXAMPLE 2. Solve $x^2 - 6x + 7 = 0$ by completing the square.

How to Proceed	*Solution*
Given the equation:	$x^2 - 6x + 7 = 0$
(1) Transform the equation, keeping variable terms only on the left.	$x^2 - 6x = -7$

(2) Form a perfect square trinomial on the left
by adding 9. Also, add 9 to the right
member.

$$x^2 - 6x + 9 = -7 + 9$$

(3) Show the square of a binomial on the left;
simplify the right member.

$$(x - 3)^2 = 2$$

(4) Take the square root of both members,
showing two roots at the right by using $\pm$.
(Note that $\sqrt{2}$ is irrational.)

$$(x - 3) = \pm\sqrt{2}$$
$$x - 3 = \pm\sqrt{2}$$

(5) Add 3 to both members to find the roots.

$$x = 3 \pm \sqrt{2}$$

Answer: $x = 3 + \sqrt{2}$ or $x = 3 - \sqrt{2}$, which may be written $x = 3 \pm \sqrt{2}$.

Hints for Completing the Square

To find a general method for completing the square, let us examine
the pattern in Example 2 above. The trinomial $x^2 - 6x + 9$ in step (2) is
the square of the binomial $x - 3$, that is, $x^2 - 6x + 9 = (x - 3)^2$.

1. Observe that the first term of the trinomial, x^2, is the square of the
first term of the binomial, x.
2. The last term of the trinomial, 9, is the square of the last term of the
binomial, -3.
3. The middle term is the key to completing the square. The middle term
of the trinomial, $-6x$, is twice the product of the two terms of the
binomial, $2(x)(-3)$.

In Example 1 that follows, the first term is a perfect square. In Example 2, the expression must be transformed so that the first term is a
perfect square.

EXAMPLE 1.   Complete the square and factor: $4x^2 + 20x$

(1) Write the known terms.

$$4x^2 + 20x + \underline{\quad} = (\underline{\quad} + \underline{\quad})^2$$

(2) The first term of the trinomial is the square of the first term of the
binomial.

$$4x^2 = (2x)^2$$
$$4x^2 + 20x + \underline{\quad} = (2x + \underline{\quad})^2$$

(3) The middle term of the trinomial is twice the product of the two terms
of the binomial. Find the missing factor by inspection.

$$20x = 2(2x)(\underline{\quad}) = 2(2x)(5)$$

The missing factor, 5, is the last term of the binomial.

$$4x^2 + 20x + \underline{\quad} = (2x + 5)^2$$

(4) The last term of the trinomial is the square of the last term of the
binomial.

$$5^2 = 25$$
$$4x^2 + 20x + 25 = (2x + 5)^2$$

EXAMPLE 2.   Complete the square and factor: $2x^2 + 3x$

(1) Write the known terms. $2x^2 + 3x +$ ____ $= ($ ____ $+$ ____ $)^2$

(2) Transform the expression so that the first term is a perfect square. Here, multiply by 8.

$8(2x^2 + 3x)$ $16x^2 + 24x +$ ____ $= ($ ____ $+$ ____ $)^2$

(3) The first term of the trinomial is the square of the first term of the binomial.

$16x^2 = (4x)^2$ $16x^2 + 24x +$ ____ $= (4x +$ ____ $)^2$

(4) The middle term of the trinomial is twice the product of the two terms of the binomial.

$24x = 2(4x)($____$) = 2(4x)(3)$

The missing factor, 3, is the last term of the binomial.

$16x^2 + 24x +$ ____ $= (4x + 3)^2$

(5) The last term of the trinomial is the square of the last term of the binomial.

$3^2 = 9$ $16x^2 + 24x + 9 = (4x + 3)^2$

Note. If we multiplied the given expression $2x^2 + 3x$ by 2, the result would be $4x^2 + 6x + \frac{9}{4} = (2x + \frac{3}{2})^2$. The choice of the multiplier 8 allows us to factor over the set of integers.

Remember that the process of completing the square is applied when we are solving equations. Thus, whatever operations are performed to make the left member of the equation a perfect square are balanced by performing the same operations on the right.

MODEL PROBLEM

Solve $x^2 - 3x + 1 = 0$ by completing the square.

Method 1:   *How to Proceed*   *Solution*

Given the equation: $x^2 - 3x + 1 = 0$

(1) Transform the equation, keeping only variable terms on the left. $x^2 - 3x = -1$

(2) Form a perfect square trinomial on the left by adding $\left(\frac{-3}{2}\right)^2$. Add the same value on the right and simplify.

$x^2 - 3x + \left(\frac{-3}{2}\right)^2 = -1 + \left(\frac{-3}{2}\right)^2$

$x^2 - 3x + \frac{9}{4} = -1 + \frac{9}{4}$

(3) Show the square of a binomial on the left; simplify the right.

$$\left(x - \frac{3}{2}\right)^2 = \frac{5}{4}$$

(4) Take the square root of both members. Show two roots at the right. Note that

$$\pm\sqrt{\frac{5}{4}} = \pm\frac{\sqrt{5}}{\sqrt{4}} = \pm\frac{\sqrt{5}}{2}.$$

$$\left(x - \frac{3}{2}\right) = \pm\sqrt{\frac{5}{4}}$$

$$x - \frac{3}{2} = \pm\frac{\sqrt{5}}{2}$$

(5) Add $\frac{3}{2}$ to both members.

$$x = \frac{3}{2} \pm \frac{\sqrt{5}}{2}$$

Method 2: Form an equivalent equation. By selecting the proper coefficient, we can avoid fractions until the last step.

How to Proceed	*Solution*
Given the equation:	$x^2 - 3x + 1 = 0$
(1) Multiply by 4.	$4x^2 - 12x + 4 = 0$
(2) Transform the equation.	$4x^2 - 12x = -4$
(3) Form a perfect square. Add 9 to both members.	$4x^2 - 12x + 9 = -4 + 9$
(4) Show the square of a binomial on the left; simplify the right.	$(2x - 3)^2 = 5$
(5) Take the square root of both members. Show two roots at the right.	$2x - 3 = \pm\sqrt{5}$
(6) Add 3 to both members.	$2x = 3 \pm \sqrt{5}$
(7) Divide both members by 2.	$x = \dfrac{3 \pm \sqrt{5}}{2}$

Answer: $x = \dfrac{3 \pm \sqrt{5}}{2}$

EXERCISES

In 1–6, find a value of k so that the given trinomial is a perfect square.

1. $x^2 + 12x + k$ **2.** $x^2 - x + k$ **3.** $x^2 + 5x + k$

4. $25x^2 - 10x + k$ **5.** $9x^2 - 12x + k$ **6.** $16x^2 - 40x + k$

In 7–12, solve the quadratic equation (a) by factoring and (b) by completing the square.

7. $x^2 - 10x + 9 = 0$ **8.** $x^2 - 4x - 5 = 0$
9. $x^2 - 10x + 21 = 0$ **10.** $x^2 - 3x - 18 = 0$
11. $x^2 - x - 12 = 0$ **12.** $4x^2 - 20x + 9 = 0$

In 13–27, solve the quadratic equation by completing the square, and express each root in simplest radical form.

13. $x^2 - 2x = 2$ **14.** $x^2 - 6x = 1$
15. $x^2 + 4x = 7$ **16.** $x^2 - 10x + 23 = 0$
17. $x^2 - 8x + 13 = 0$ **18.** $x^2 + 6x + 7 = 0$
19. $x^2 + 14x + 44 = 0$ **20.** $x^2 - 4x - 8 = 0$
21. $x^2 + 8x - 4 = 0$ **22.** $x^2 + 2x - 7 = 0$
23. $4x^2 - 4x - 5 = 0$ **24.** $4x^2 - 12x + 7 = 0$
25. $2x^2 - 2x - 1 = 0$ **26.** $x^2 + x - 1 = 0$
27. $3x^2 - 2x - 2 = 0$

10-5 THE DERIVATION AND USE OF THE QUADRATIC FORMULA

In the preceding section, we solved many quadratic equations by completing the square. Let us apply this technique to solving the general equation $ax^2 + bx + c = 0$ where $a \neq 0$. As we shall soon see, our result be a general formula that may be used to solve quadratic equations.

We will show two ways to derive the quadratic formula. Each derivation involves completing the square to solve for the variable x.

Derivation 1: How to Proceed   *Solution*

Given the general quadratic equation:

$$ax^2 + bx + c = 0 \quad (a \neq 0)$$

(1) Divide by a to obtain a leading coefficient of 1.

$$x^2 + \frac{bx}{a} + \frac{c}{a} = 0$$

(2) Transform the equation, keeping only variable terms on the left.

$$x^2 + \frac{bx}{a} = -\frac{c}{a}$$

(3) Form a perfect square trinomial on the left by adding $\left(\dfrac{b}{2a}\right)^2$ or $\dfrac{b^2}{4a^2}$; add the same on the right.

$$x^2 + \frac{bx}{a} + \left(\frac{b}{2a}\right)^2 = \left(\frac{b}{2a}\right)^2 - \frac{c}{a}$$

$$x^2 + \frac{bx}{a} + \frac{b^2}{4a^2} = \frac{b^2}{4a^2} - \frac{c}{a}$$

(4) Show the square of a binomial on the left; simplify the right.

$$\left(x + \frac{b}{2a}\right)^2 = \frac{b^2}{4a^2} - \frac{4ac}{4a^2}$$

Since $\dfrac{-c}{a} = \dfrac{-c}{a}\left(\dfrac{4a}{4a}\right) = \dfrac{-4ac}{4a^2}$, we can add fractions with like denominators.

$$\left(x + \frac{b}{2a}\right)^2 = \frac{b^2 - 4ac}{4a^2}$$

(5) Take the square root of both members. Show two roots for the right member by writing $\pm$. Note that the denominator on the right is a perfect square.

$$\left(x + \frac{b}{2a}\right) = \pm\sqrt{\frac{b^2 - 4ac}{4a^2}}$$

$$x + \frac{b}{2a} = \frac{\pm\sqrt{b^2 - 4ac}}{2a}$$

(6) Add $\dfrac{-b}{2a}$ to both members.

$$x = \frac{-b}{2a} \pm \frac{\sqrt{b^2 - 4ac}}{2a}$$

(7) Combine terms on the right to obtain the **quadratic formula**.

$$x = \frac{-b \pm \sqrt{b^2 - 4ac}}{2a}$$

Derivation 2: To use fractions only in the last step, we form an equation equivalent to $ax^2 + bx + c = 0$ by multiplying by $4a$. Note that $4a(ax^2) = 4a^2x^2$, a perfect square.

How to Proceed	*Solution*

Given the general quadratic equation:

$$ax^2 + bx + c = 0 \quad (a \neq 0)$$

(1) Multiply by $4a$.

$$4a^2x^2 + 4abx + 4ac = 0$$

(2) Transform the equation.

$$4a^2x^2 + 4abx = -4ac$$

(3) To form a perfect square, add b^2 to both members.

$$4a^2x^2 + 4abx + b^2 = b^2 - 4ac$$

(4) Show the square of a binomial on the left.

$$(2ax + b)^2 = b^2 - 4ac$$

(5) Take the square root of both members. Show two roots at the right by writing $\pm$ before the radical.

$$2ax + b = \pm\sqrt{b^2 - 4ac}$$

(6) Add $-b$ to both members.

$$2ax = -b \pm \sqrt{b^2 - 4ac}$$

(7) Divide both members by $2a$ to obtain the **quadratic formula**.

$$x = \frac{-b \pm \sqrt{b^2 - 4ac}}{2a}$$

The Roots of a Quadratic Equation

By the quadratic formula, the two roots of the equation are:

$$x_1 = \frac{-b + \sqrt{b^2 - 4ac}}{2a} \quad and \quad x_2 = \frac{-b - \sqrt{b^2 - 4ac}}{2a}$$

In this formula, $b^2 - 4ac$ (the expression under the radical sign) is called the **discriminant**. As you shall see in the model problems that follow, the nature of the roots of a quadratic equation with rational coefficients can be determined by knowing the value of the discriminant.

1. If $b^2 - 4ac$ is positive and a perfect square, the roots are rational and unequal.

2. If $b^2 - 4ac$ is positive but not a perfect square, the roots are irrational and unequal.

3. If $b^2 - 4ac = 0$, the roots are rational and equal.

4. If $b^2 - 4ac$ is negative, there are no real roots.

KEEP IN MIND _____

Given any quadratic equation of the form $ax^2 + bx + c = 0$, where a, b, and c are real numbers and $a \neq 0$, we can find the roots of the equation by the quadratic formula:

$$x = \frac{-b \pm \sqrt{b^2 - 4ac}}{2a}$$

MODEL PROBLEMS _____

1. Solve by the quadratic formula: $x^2 - 3x = 10$

How to Proceed	*Solutions*
(1) Write the equation in standard form.	$x^2 - 3x - 10 = 0$
(2) Compare the equation to $ax^2 + bx + c = 0$ to find the values of a, b, and c.	$a = 1$, $b = -3$, $c = -10$
(3) Write the quadratic formula.	$x = \dfrac{-b \pm \sqrt{b^2 - 4ac}}{2a}$

(4) Substitute known values.

$$x = \frac{-(-3) \pm \sqrt{(-3)^2 - 4(1)(-10)}}{2(1)}$$

(5) Simplify.

$$x = \frac{+3 \pm \sqrt{9 + 40}}{2}$$

$$x = \frac{3 \pm \sqrt{49}}{2} = \frac{3 \pm 7}{2}$$

(6) Determine the two roots. (The check is left to the student.)

$$x = \frac{3 + 7}{2} = \frac{10}{2} \qquad \bigg| \qquad x = \frac{3 - 7}{2} = \frac{-4}{2}$$

$$x = 5 \qquad \bigg| \qquad x = -2$$

Answer: $x = 5$ or $x = -2$ *or* the solution set $= \{5, -2\}$.

Note. Here, the discriminant $b^2 - 4ac = 49$, a number that is positive and a perfect square. The roots 5 and -2 are rational and unequal.

2. Find the roots and check: $x^2 + 2x - 1 = 0$

How to Proceed	*Solution*

(1) $x^2 + 2x - 1 = 0$ is in standard form.

$a = 1, b = 2, c = -1$

(2) Write the quadratic formula.

$$x = \frac{-b \pm \sqrt{b^2 - 4ac}}{2a}$$

(3) Substitute known values.

$$x = \frac{-(2) \pm \sqrt{(2)^2 - 4(1)(-1)}}{2(1)}$$

(4) Simplify.

$$x = \frac{-2 \pm \sqrt{4 + 4}}{2}$$

$\sqrt{8} = \sqrt{4}\,\sqrt{2} = 2\sqrt{2}$

$$x = \frac{-2 \pm \sqrt{8}}{2}$$

$$x = \frac{-2 \pm 2\sqrt{2}}{2}$$

$$x = -1 \pm 1\sqrt{2}$$

$$x = -1 \pm \sqrt{2}$$

Check for $x = -1 + \sqrt{2}$

$$x^2 + 2x - 1 = 0$$
$$(-1 + \sqrt{2})(-1 + \sqrt{2}) + 2(-1 + \sqrt{2}) - 1 \stackrel{?}{=} 0$$
$$+1 - 2\sqrt{2} + 2 - 2 + 2\sqrt{2} - 1 \stackrel{?}{=} 0$$
$$0 = 0$$

Check for $x = -1 - \sqrt{2}$

$$x^2 + 2x - 1 = 0$$
$$(-1 - \sqrt{2})(-1 - \sqrt{2}) + 2(-1 - \sqrt{2}) - 1 \stackrel{?}{=} 0$$
$$+1 + 2\sqrt{2} + 2 - 2 - 2\sqrt{2} - 1 \stackrel{?}{=} 0$$
$$0 = 0$$

Answer: $x = -1 + \sqrt{2}$ or $x = -1 - \sqrt{2}$,
which may be written $x = -1 \pm \sqrt{2}$.

Note. Here, the discriminant $b^2 - 4ac = 8$, a number that is positive but not a perfect square. The roots $-1 + \sqrt{2}$ and $-1 - \sqrt{2}$ are irrational and unequal.

3. Solve by the quadratic formula: $9x^2 - 6x + 1 = 0$

Solution:

(1) $9x^2 - 6x + 1 = 0$ is in standard form. $a = 9, b = -6, c = 1$

(2) Write the quadratic formula. $x = \dfrac{-b \pm \sqrt{b^2 - 4ac}}{2a}$

(3) Substitute known values and simplify. (The check is left to the student.)

$$x = \frac{-(-6) \pm \sqrt{(-6)^2 - 4(9)(1)}}{2(9)}$$

$$= \frac{+6 \pm \sqrt{36 - 36}}{18} = \frac{6 \pm \sqrt{0}}{18}$$

$$= \frac{6 \pm 0}{18} = \frac{6}{18} = \frac{1}{3}$$

Answer: $x = \dfrac{1}{3}$

Note. Here, the discriminant $b^2 - 4ac = 0$. The roots $\dfrac{6 + 0}{18}$ and $\dfrac{6 - 0}{18}$ can each be simplified to $\dfrac{1}{3}$. The roots are rational and equal.

EXERCISES

In 1–9: **a.** Determine the value of the discriminant, $b^2 - 4ac$.
b. Using the discriminant, describe the roots as one of the following:
(1) rational and unequal (2) irrational and unequal
(3) rational and equal   (4) there are no real roots.

1. $x^2 - 5x - 4 = 0$ **2.** $x^2 - 8x - 20 = 0$ **3.** $x^2 + 3x + 6 = 0$
4. $2x^2 + 7x - 4 = 0$ **5.** $4x^2 + 12x + 9 = 0$ **6.** $2x^2 - 6x + 3 = 0$
7. $2x^2 = 6x - 5$ **8.** $3x^2 - 5x = 0$ **9.** $6x^2 - 5 = 2x$

In 10–33, solve the given equation by using the quadratic formula. Answers that are irrational should be left in simplest radical form.

10. $x^2 - 7x - 8 = 0$ **11.** $x^2 + 3x - 28 = 0$
12. $x^2 - 14x + 49 = 0$ **13.** $x^2 - 9x + 10 = 0$
14. $x^2 + 3x - 7 = 0$ **15.** $x^2 - x - 1 = 0$
16. $3x^2 - 2x - 5 = 0$ **17.** $25x^2 + 10x + 1 = 0$
18. $5x^2 - 3x - 2 = 0$ **19.** $x^2 - 2x - 4 = 0$
20. $x^2 + 10x + 22 = 0$ **21.** $x^2 + 14 = 8x$

22. $x^2 = 4x + 3$ **23.** $4x^2 - 3x = 0$ **24.** $4x^2 - 3 = 0$
25. $x^2 + 2x = 10$ **26.** $x^2 = 6x + 4$ '   **27.** $x^2 + 4 = 8x$
28. $x^2 = 6x + 9$ **29.** $x^2 = 2x + 19$ **30.** $4x^2 = 4x + 1$
31. $4x^2 = 8x + 1$ **32.** $9x^2 + 6x = 2$ **33.** $2x^2 + 3 = 6x$

In 34–39, select the numeral preceding the expression that best completes the sentence or answers the question.

34. The roots of $3x^2 - 5x - 1 = 0$ are

(1) $\dfrac{5 \pm \sqrt{13}}{6}$ (2) $\dfrac{-5 \pm \sqrt{13}}{6}$ (3) $\dfrac{5 \pm \sqrt{37}}{6}$ (4) $\dfrac{-5 \pm \sqrt{37}}{6}$

35. The solutions to the quadratic equation $x^2 + 6x + 4 = 0$ are
(1) $-3 \pm \sqrt{20}$ (2) $-3 \pm \sqrt{10}$ (3) $-3 \pm \sqrt{5}$ (4) $-6 \pm \sqrt{10}$

36. What is the value of x in the equation $2x^2 + 7x + 4 = 0$?

(1) $\dfrac{7 \pm \sqrt{17}}{2}$ (2) $\dfrac{7 \pm \sqrt{17}}{4}$ (3) $\dfrac{-7 \pm \sqrt{17}}{2}$ (4) $\dfrac{-7 \pm \sqrt{17}}{4}$

37. Which equation has $x = \dfrac{-3 \pm \sqrt{5}}{2}$ as its solution?

(1) $x^2 + 3x - 1 = 0$ (2) $x^2 + 3x + 1 = 0$
(3) $x^2 - 3x - 1 = 0$ (4) $x^2 - 3x + 1 = 0$

38. For which equation are the roots $1 + \sqrt{6}$ and $1 - \sqrt{6}$?
(1) $x^2 + 2x + 5 = 0$ (2) $x^2 + 2x - 5 = 0$
(3) $x^2 - 2x - 5 = 0$ (4) $x^2 - 2x + 5 = 0$

39. For which equation are the roots irrational?
(1) $2x^2 - 7x + 3 = 0$ (2) $2x^2 - 6x + 3 = 0$
(3) $2x^2 - 5x - 3 = 0$ (4) $2x^2 - x - 3 = 0$

40. For any quadratic equation $ax^2 + bx + c = 0$ where $a \neq 0$, the roots
are $x_1 = \dfrac{-b + \sqrt{b^2 - 4ac}}{2a}$ and $x_2 = \dfrac{-b - \sqrt{b^2 - 4ac}}{2a}$.

    a. Demonstrate algebraically that the sum of the roots is $\dfrac{-b}{a}$.

    b. Demonstrate algebraically that the product of the roots is $\dfrac{c}{a}$.

10-6 GEOMETRIC APPLICATIONS OF QUADRATICS

Throughout this book, we have solved many problems in geometry by means of algebraic equations. In this section, we will review some of these geometry problems, each of which involves a quadratic equation.

KEEP IN MIND ━━━━━━━━━━━━━━━━━━━━━━━━━━━━━━━━━━━━━

1. A length is a positive number. Therefore, reject all roots leading to lengths that are zero or negative numbers.

2. Lengths may be irrational as well as rational. For example, if the length of a side of a square is 1 (rational), then the length of its diagonal is $\sqrt{2}$ (irrational).

MODEL PROBLEMS ━━━━━━━━━━━━━━━━━━━━━━━━━━━━━━━━━

1. In $\triangle ABC$, D is a point on $\overline{AB}$ and E is a point on $\overline{AC}$ such that $\overline{DE} \parallel \overline{BC}$. If $AE = 3$, $EC = x$, $ED = x + 1$, and $CB = x + 5$, find EC.

Solution:

(1) Draw $\triangle ABC$ and $\overline{DE}$; label the segments.

(2) Since $\overline{DE} \parallel \overline{BC}$, then $\triangle AED \sim \triangle ACB$. The lengths of corresponding sides of similar triangles are in proportion.

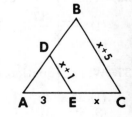

$$\frac{AE}{ED} = \frac{AC}{CB}$$

(3) Substitute known values.
(Note that $AC = AE + EC$.
Therefore, $AC = 3 + x$, or $x + 3$.)

$$\frac{3}{x + 1} = \frac{x + 3}{x + 5}$$

(4) The product of the means equals
the product of the extremes.

$$(x + 1)(x + 3) = 3(x + 5)$$
$$x^2 + 4x + 3 = 3x + 15$$

(5) Solve the resulting quadratic
equation.

$$x^2 + x - 12 = 0$$
$$(x + 4)(x - 3) = 0$$

(Reject the negative root.)

| $x + 4 = 0$ | $x - 3 = 0$ |
| $x = -4$ | $x = 3$ |

(6) *Check:* If $x = 3$, then $EC = 3$, $ED = 4$, $CB = 8$, and $AC = 6$.

Therefore, $\dfrac{AE}{ED} = \dfrac{AC}{CB}$ becomes $\dfrac{3}{4} = \dfrac{6}{8}$.   (True)

Answer: EC = 3

---

2. In right $\triangle ABC$, altitude $\overline{CD}$ is drawn to hypotenuse $\overline{AB}$. If $AD = 4$
and AC exceeds DB by 1, find DB.

Solution:

(1) Draw $\triangle ABC$ and altitude $\overline{CD}$; label
the segments.

     Let $x =$ the length of $\overline{DB}$.
     Then $x + 1 =$ the length of $\overline{AC}$.

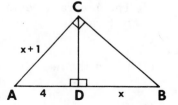

(2) Since $\overline{CD}$ is the altitude to hypotenuse $\overline{AB}$ in right $\triangle ABC$, the
length of leg $\overline{AC}$ is the mean proportional between the length of
hypotenuse $\overline{AB}$ and the length of the projection of the leg on the
hypotenuse, that is, AD.

     Therefore, we write:

$$\frac{AD}{AC} = \frac{AC}{AB}$$

(3) Substitute known values.
(Note that $AB = AD + DB$.
Therefore, $AB = 4 + x$, or $x + 4$.)

$$\frac{4}{x + 1} = \frac{x + 1}{x + 4}$$

(4) The product of the means equals
the product of the extremes.

$$(x + 1)(x + 1) = 4(x + 4)$$
$$x^2 + 2x + 1 = 4x + 16$$

(5) Solve the quadratic
equation.

$$x^2 - 2x - 15 = 0$$
$$(x + 3)(x - 5) = 0$$

$$
\begin{array}{c|c}
x + 3 = 0 & x - 5 = 0 \\
\end{array}
$$

(Reject the negative root.) $x = -3$ $|$ $x = 5$

(6) *Check:* If $x = 5$, then $DB = 5$, $AC = 6$, and $AB = 9$.

Therefore, $\dfrac{AD}{AC} = \dfrac{AC}{AB}$ becomes $\dfrac{4}{6} = \dfrac{6}{9}$, or $\dfrac{2}{3} = \dfrac{2}{3}$. (True)

Answer: DB = 5

---

3. In a rectangle, the length is twice the width and the area of the rectangle is 6. Find the dimensions of the rectangle.

Solution:

(1) Identify the variables, and form an equation.

Let x = the width of the rectangle.
Then $2x$ = the length of the rectangle.

$$lw = A$$
$$2x(x) = 6$$
$$2x^2 = 6$$

(2) The quadratic equation is not
factorable.

$$2x^2 = 6$$
$$x^2 = 3$$
$$x = \pm\sqrt{3}$$

(3) Reject the negative root.

$$x = \sqrt{3}$$
$$2x = 2\sqrt{3}.$$

(4) *Check:* Use $lw = A$.

$$(2\sqrt{3})(\sqrt{3}) \overset{?}{=} 6$$
$$2 \cdot 3 \overset{?}{=} 6$$
$$6 = 6 \quad \text{(True)}$$

Answer: The width is $\sqrt{3}$ and the length is $2\sqrt{3}$.

---

4. The perimeter of a rectangle is 16 cm, and the length of a diagonal is 6 cm. **a.** If x represents the width of the rectangle, represent the length in terms of x. **b.** Write and solve an equation to find the dimensions of the rectangle.

Solution:
a. Use the known perimeter, 16, to write an expression for the length l in terms of the width w.

$$p = 2l + 2w$$
$$16 = 2l + 2w$$
$$8 = l + w$$
$$8 - w = l$$

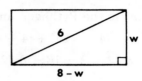

b. A diagonal separates a rectangle into two right triangles such that the diagonal is the hypotenuse of each triangle. Apply the Pythagorean Theorem:

$$a^2 + b^2 = c^2$$
$$(w)^2 + (8 - w)^2 = 6^2$$
$$w^2 + 64 - 16w + w^2 = 36$$
$$2w^2 - 16w + 64 = 36$$
$$2w^2 - 16w + 28 = 0$$
$$2(w^2 - 8w + 14) = 0$$
$$w^2 - 8w + 14 = 0$$

Since $w^2 - 8w + 14$ is not factorable, use the quadratic formula where $a = 1$, $b = -8$, and $c = 14$.

$$w = \frac{-b \pm \sqrt{b^2 - 4ac}}{2a} = \frac{-(-8) \pm \sqrt{(-8)^2 - 4(1)(14)}}{2(1)}$$

$$= \frac{8 \pm \sqrt{64 - 56}}{2} = \frac{8 \pm \sqrt{8}}{2} = \frac{8 \pm \sqrt{4}\sqrt{2}}{2}$$

$$= \frac{8 \pm 2\sqrt{2}}{2} = 4 \pm \sqrt{2}$$

Note. If width $w = 4 + \sqrt{2}$, then
length $(8 - w) = 8 - (4 + \sqrt{2}) = 8 - 4 - \sqrt{2} = 4 - \sqrt{2}$.

If width $w = 4 - \sqrt{2}$, then
length $(8 - w) = 8 - (4 - \sqrt{2}) = 8 - 4 + \sqrt{2} = 4 + \sqrt{2}$.

Either way, the dimensions of the rectangle are $4 + \sqrt{2}$ by $4 - \sqrt{2}$.

Check: Is the perimeter equal to 16?
$$(4 + \sqrt{2}) + (4 - \sqrt{2}) + (4 + \sqrt{2}) + (4 - \sqrt{2}) \overset{?}{=} 16$$
$$4 + \sqrt{2} + 4 - \sqrt{2} + 4 + \sqrt{2} + 4 - \sqrt{2} \overset{?}{=} 16$$
$$16 = 16 \quad \text{(True)}$$

Check: Is the Pythagorean relationship true?

$$(4 + \sqrt{2})^2 + (4 - \sqrt{2})^2 \overset{?}{=} 6^2$$

$$16 + 8\sqrt{2} + 2 + 16 - 8\sqrt{2} + 2 \overset{?}{=} 36$$

$$36 = 36 \quad \text{(True)}$$

Answer: **a.** $8 - w$ **b.** The dimensions are $4 + \sqrt{2}$ by $4 - \sqrt{2}$.

For reference as you work with the following exercises, you may wish to look back at other model problems involving quadratic equations with geometric applications.

On pages 298–299: Model Problem 3
(similar triangles and proportions).

On pages 311–312: Model Problems 1 and 2 (proportions with similar triangles in the right triangle).

On pages 317–318: Model Problems 1, 2, 3, and 4
(Pythagorean Theorem).

On page 427: Model Problem 2 (area of a rectangle).

On page 432: Model Problem 2 (two polygons, equal in area).

EXERCISES

In each of the following exercises, write and solve an algebraic equation to answer the question. Notice that, in some of the exercises, it is necessary to use the quadratic formula to find the solution.

1. In a rectangle whose area is 24 cm^2, the length is 5 cm more than the width. Find the dimensions of the rectangle.
2. The length of a rectangle is 5 times its width, and the area of the rectangle is 20 square feet. Find the dimensions.
3. The length of a rectangle is 4 times its width. If the area of the rectangle is 20 m^2, find its length and width.
4. If the length of a rectangle is 4 more than its width, and the area of the rectangle is 6 in.^{2}, find its length and its width.
5. The ratio of the measures of the base and altitude of a triangle is 3:4. If the area of the triangle is 600 cm^2, find the measures of its base and its altitude.
6. In a parallelogram, the measure of an altitude is 6 feet less than the measure of its base. If the area of the parallelogram is 41 square feet, find the measure of the base.

7. a. The length of a square is represented by $x + 2$. Express the area of the square in terms of x.
   b. The dimensions of a rectangle are represented by x and $2x + 4$. Express its area in terms of x.
   c. If the area of the square in part **a** is equal to the area of the rectangle in part **b**, find the value of x and the dimensions of each quadrilateral.

In 8–12, let b and h represent the measures of the base and height of a rectangle, and let s represent the length of a side of a square. If the area of the rectangle is equal to the area of the square, find (a) the value of x, (b) the measures of b and h, and (c) the length s.

8. *Rectangle:* $b = x - 1$, $h = 2x$. *Square:* $s = x$.
9. *Rectangle:* $b = 2x + 3$, $h = 2x - 3$. *Square:* $s = x$.
10. *Rectangle:* $b = x - 3$, $h = 2x + 8$. *Square:* $s = x + 4$.
11. *Rectangle:* $b = x$, $h = 12x + 20$. *Square:* $s = 3x + 5$.
12. *Rectangle:* $b = x$, $h = 2x - 2$. *Square:* $s = x + 2$.

13. (a) The measures of the bases of a trapezoid are $x + 6$ and $3x + 4$. If the measure of its altitude is $2x$, represent the area of the trapezoid in terms of x. **(b)** If a side of a square has a measure of $x + 4$, represent its area in terms of x. **(c)** If the area of the trapezoid equals the area of the square, find x and the various dimensions of the quadrilaterals.

14. The area of a rhombus is 5 yd.^{2}, and the lengths of its diagonals d_1 and d_2 are in a ratio of 1:2. Using the area formula $A = \frac{1}{2} d_1 d_2$, find the length of each diagonal.

In 15–21, $\triangle ABC$ is given in which D is a point on $\overline{AC}$, E is a point on $\overline{BC}$, and $\overline{DE} \parallel \overline{AB}$. Write and solve an equation to find the indicated length.

Ex. 15–21

15. If $CE = 3$, $EB = x + 2$, $CD = x$, and $DA = x + 4$, find CD.
16. If $CD = 2$, $DA = x + 2$, $CE = x$, and $EB = x + 1$, find CE.
17. If $CE = x$, $EB = 4$, $ED = x + 2$, and $BA = 2x$, find CE.
18. If $CD = 4$, $DE = x + 4$, $DA = x$, and $AB = 2x + 5$, find DA.
19. If $CE = 3$, $EB = x$, $DE = 2x + 1$, and $AB = 2x + 3$, find EB.
20. If $CD = 8$, $DA = 2x$, $CE = x$, and $EB = x + 2$, find CE.
21. a. If $CE = 5$, $EB = x$, $DE = 2x + 1$, and $AB = 4x - 1$, find two possible lengths for $\overline{EB}$.
   b. For each of the values of EB found in part **a**, find the lengths of all indicated segments, and write a numerical proportion.

In 22–28, $\triangle ABC$ is a right triangle, $\angle C$ is a right angle, and $\overline{CD}$ is the altitude to the hypotenuse $\overline{AB}$. Write and solve an equation to find the indicated length.

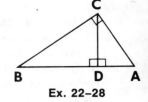

Ex. 22–28

22. If $AD = 1$, $CD = x$, and $BD = x + 12$, find CD.

23. If $DB = 9$, $BC = x + 5$, and $DA = x$, find DA.

24. If $BD = x + 2$, $DA = x - 2$, and $AC = x + 4$, find DA.

25. If $AD = x$, $DB = 2x + 3$, and $CD = 3$, find AD.

26. If $AC = 6$ and the ratio of $AD:DB = 1:3$, find AD.

27. If $AC = 6$ and the ratio of $AD:DB = 1:2$, find AD.

28. a. If $AD = 1$, $CD = x$, and $BD = 4x - 3$, find two possible lengths for $\overline{CD}$.

    b. For each value of CD found in part **a**, find the lengths of all indicated segments, and write a numerical proportion.

29. In right triangle ABC, the hypotenuse is $\overline{AB}$. If BC is 1 in. less than AC, and AB is 1 in. more than AC, find the lengths of all three sides of $\triangle ABC$.

30. In a rectangle, the altitude is 2 cm longer than the base. If a diagonal of the rectangle measures 4 cm, find the measures of the base and the altitude.

31. The length of a rectangle is 4 m more than its width. If a diagonal of the rectangle measures 8 m more than the width, find the width.

32. A baseball diamond has the shape of a square 90 feet on each side. The pitcher's mound is 60.5 feet from home plate on the line joining home plate and second base. Find the distance from the pitcher's mound to second base, to the nearest tenth of a foot.

33. In rhombus $ABCD$, diagonals $\overline{AC}$ and $\overline{BD}$ intersect at E. If $AE = x$, $BE = x + 7$, and $AB = x + 8$, find the lengths of the diagonals $\overline{AC}$ and $\overline{BD}$.

34. In isosceles $\triangle ABC$, $\overline{AB} \cong \overline{BC}$, and $\overline{BD}$ is the altitude to base $\overline{AC}$. If $DC = x$, $BD = 2x - 1$, and $BC = 2x + 1$, find the lengths of all three sides of the triangle.

35. The perimeter of a rectangle is 20 cm and the length of a diagonal is 8 cm.

    a. If x represents the width of the rectangle, represent the length in terms of x.

    b. Write and solve an equation to find the dimensions of the rectangle.

36. The perimeter of a right triangle is 30 in. and the length of its hypotenuse is 13 in.

    a. If x represents the length of one leg, represent the length of the other leg in terms of x.

    b. Write and solve an equation to find the lengths of the legs of the right triangle.

10-7 GRAPHING A QUADRATIC EQUATION IN TWO VARIABLES: $y = ax^2 + bx + c$

You have learned that the graph of every first-degree equation in two variables is a straight line. For example, the graph of $x + y = 4$ is a straight line. Now you will learn how to graph a quadratic equation of the form $y = ax^2 + bx + c$.

EXAMPLE 1.   Graph the quadratic equation $y = x^2 - 4x$, using integral values from $x = -1$ to $x = 5$ inclusive, that is, $-1 \leq x \leq 5$.

Solution

(1) Develop the following table of values:

x	$x^2 - 4x$	y
-1	$(-1)^2 - 4(-1)$	5
0	$(0)^2 - 4(0)$	0
1	$(1)^2 - 4(1)$	-3
2	$(2)^2 - 4(2)$	-4
3	$(3)^2 - 4(3)$	-3
4	$(4)^2 - 4(4)$	0
5	$(5)^2 - 4(5)$	5

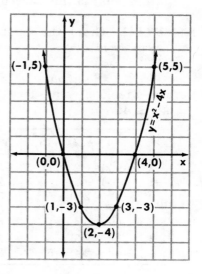

(2) Plot the points associated with each ordered pair (x, y): $(-1, 5)$, $(0, 0)$, $(1, -3)$, and so on.

(3) Draw a smooth curve through the points, as shown. The graph of $y = x^2 - 4x$ is a curve called a *parabola*.

● **The graph of every quadratic equation of the form $y = ax^2 + bx + c$, where a, b, and c are real numbers and $a \neq 0$, is a parabola.**

Using the following graph of the parabola $y = x^2 - 4x$, observe:

1. The parabola is symmetric with respect to a line of reflection, or an *axis of symmetry*, whose equation is $x = 2$. Just like a mirror image, every point on the parabola to the left of $x = 2$ matches a point on the parabola to the right of $x = 2$, and vice versa.

2. The parabola $y = x^2 - 4x$ *opens upward* and contains a *minimum point* $(2, -4)$ located on its axis of symmetry. This point is called the minimum because it contains the smallest value of y for the graph. Notice that as x increases from -1 to 5, y decreases until the minimum point is reached, then the graph turns, as y starts to increase. For this reason, $(2, -4)$ is also called the *turning point* of this parabola.

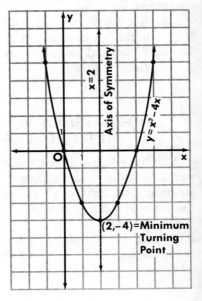

EXAMPLE 2. Graph the equation $y = -x^2 + 2x + 5$, using all integral values of x from $x = -2$ to $x = 4$ inclusive.

Solution

Develop a table of values for $-2 \le x \le 4$:

x	$-x^2 + 2x + 5$	y
-2	$-(-2)^2 + 2(-2) + 5$	-3
-1	$-(-1)^2 + 2(-1) + 5$	2
0	$-(0)^2 + 2(0) + 5$	5
1	$-(1)^2 + 2(1) + 5$	6
2	$-(2)^2 + 2(2) + 5$	5
3	$-(3)^2 + 2(3) + 5$	2
4	$-(4)^2 + 2(4) + 5$	-3

Plot the point associated with each ordered pair (x, y).

Draw the parabola through these points.

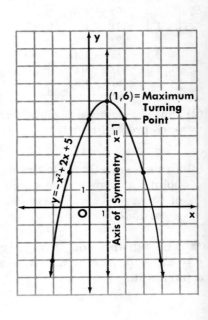

Using the graph of $y = -x^2 + 2x + 5$, observe:

1. The equation of the **axis of symmetry** is $x = 1$.

2. This parabola *opens downward* and contains a **maximum point** $(1, 6)$ located on its axis of symmetry. As x increases from -2 to 4, y increases until the maximum point is reached, then turns, and y starts to decrease. For this reason, $(1, 6)$ is also called the **turning point** of this parabola.

Rules for Graphing the Parabola

For any equation of the form $y = ax^2 + bx + c$, where a, b, and c are real numbers and $a \neq 0$, certain rules can be helpful in graphing the equation.

1. If a is *positive*, the parabola *opens upward* and contains a *minimum point*, as in the previous graph of $y = x^2 - 4x$. Here, $a = 1$, a positive number.

2. If a is *negative*, the parabola *opens downward* and contains a *maximum point*, as in the previous graph of $y = -x^2 + 2x + 5$. Here, $a = -1$, a negative number.

3. An equation of the *axis of symmetry* is $x = \dfrac{-b}{2a}$.

EXAMPLE 1.

In $y = x^2 - 4x$,
$a = 1$ and $b = -4$.

Equation of axis of symmetry:

$$x = \frac{-b}{2a}$$

$$x = \frac{-(-4)}{2(1)}, \text{ or } x = \frac{4}{2}$$

$$x = 2$$

EXAMPLE 2.

In $y = -x^2 + 2x + 5$,
$a = -1$ and $b = 2$.

Equation of axis of symmetry:

$$x = \frac{-b}{2a}$$

$$x = \frac{-(2)}{2(-1)}, \text{ or } x = \frac{-2}{-2}$$

$$x = 1$$

4. The *turning point* of the parabola is always found on the axis of symmetry. Therefore, the x-coordinate of the turning point will equal $\dfrac{-b}{2a}$, and the y-coordinate of the turning point will be found by substituting $x = \dfrac{-b}{2a}$ in the equation $y = ax^2 + bx + c$.

Since the axis of symmetry for the parabola $y = x^2 - 4x$ is given by the equation $x = 2$, the x-coordinate of the turning point is 2. Then, by substituting $x = 2$ in $y = x^2 - 4x$, we see that $y = (2)^2 - 4(2) = 4 - 8 = -4$. The turning point is $(2, -4)$, as shown on the graph.

KEEP IN MIND

For the graph of the parabola $y = ax^2 + bx + c$:

1. The axis of symmetry is a vertical line whose equation is $x = \dfrac{-b}{2a}$.

2. If a is positive, the parabola opens upward. If a is negative, the parabola opens downward.

MODEL PROBLEMS

1. Write an equation of the axis of symmetry of the graph of $y = 3x^2 + 12x - 2$.

   Solution:

   (1) The axis of symmetry for the parabola $y = 3x^2 + 12x - 2$ is a vertical line whose equation is $x = \dfrac{-b}{2a}$.

   (2) Comparing $y = 3x^2 + 12x - 2$ to $y = ax^2 + bx + c$, observe that $a = 3$ and $b = 12$.

   (3) Thus, $x = \dfrac{-b}{2a}$ becomes $x = \dfrac{-(12)}{2(3)}$, or $x = \dfrac{-12}{6}$, or $x = -2$.

   Answer: $x = -2$

2. Which is an equation of the graph shown?

   (1) $y = x^2 - 4x + 4$
   (2) $y = x^2 + 4x + 4$
   (3) $y = -x^2 - 4x + 4$
   (4) $y = -x^2 + 4x + 4$

   Solution:

   Since the parabola opens upward, the leading coefficient, a, must be positive. Therefore, we eliminate choices (3) and (4).

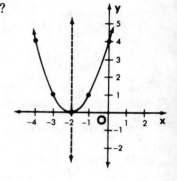

Find the equation of the axis of symmetry, $x = \dfrac{-b}{2a}$, for choices (1) and (2). In (1), $x = \dfrac{-(-4)}{2(1)}$, or $x = 2$. In (2), $x = \dfrac{-(4)}{2(1)}$, or $x = -2$. According to the given graph, choice (2) is correct.

Answer: (2)

Note. If you attempt to find the answer by substituting coordinates of points on the graph, namely, $(-4, 4)$, $(-3, 1)$, $(-2, 0)$, $(-1, 1)$, or $(0, 4)$, be careful! The point $(0, 4)$ is a solution to all four equations given as choices. If you use this method, it is recommended that you check *three or more* coordinates before claiming that the equation is correct.

EXERCISES

In 1–16, graph the quadratic equation. Use the integral values for x indicated in parentheses to prepare the necessary table of values.

1. $y = x^2$ $(-3 \le x \le 3)$ **2.** $y = 2x^2$ $(-3 \le x \le 3)$

3. $y = 3x^2$ $(-2 \le x \le 2)$ **4.** $y = -x^2$ $(-3 \le x \le 3)$

5. $y = \frac{1}{2}x^2$ $(-4 \le x \le 4)$ **6.** $y = -2x^2$ $(-3 \le x \le 3)$

7. $y = -\frac{1}{2}x^2$ $(-4 \le x \le 4)$ **8.** $y = x^2 + 1$ $(-3 \le x \le 3)$

9. $y = -x^2 + 2$ $(-3 \le x \le 3)$ **10.** $y = x^2 - 2x$ $(-2 \le x \le 4)$

11. $y = x^2 + 4x$ $(-5 \le x \le 1)$ **12.** $y = -x^2 + 6x$ $(0 \le x \le 6)$

13. $y = x^2 - 2x + 2$ $(-2 \le x \le 4)$ **14.** $y = x^2 - 8x + 7$ $(1 \le x \le 7)$

15. $y = -x^2 - 4x - 3$ $(-5 \le x \le 1)$ **16.** $y = 3x - \frac{1}{2}x^2$ $(0 \le x \le 6)$

In 17–28: **a.** Write an equation of the axis of symmetry for the given parabola. **b.** Tell whether the turning point of the parabola is a maximum point or a minimum point. **c.** Find the coordinates of the turning point.

17. $y = x^2 - 10x$ **18.** $y = x^2 + 14x - 1$

19. $y = -x^2 + 12x + 4$ **20.** $y = 2x^2 + 3$

21. $y = -2x^2 + 8x - 1$ **22.** $y = 3x^2 - 18x$

23. $y = x^2 - x$ **24.** $y = -x^2 + 8x - 6$

25. $y = -x^2 + 5x$ **26.** $y = \frac{1}{2}x^2 + 3x - \frac{1}{2}$

27. $y = \frac{1}{2}x^2 - 5x$ **28.** $y = 3 - x^2$

In 29–36, select the numeral preceding the equation or expression that best answers the question or completes the sentence.

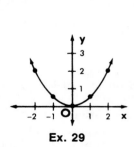

Ex. 29

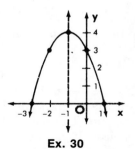

Ex. 30

29. Which is an equation of the accompanying graph?
(1) $y = 2x^2$ (2) $y = -2x^2$ (3) $y = \frac{1}{2}x^2$ (4) $y = -\frac{1}{2}x^2$

30. Which is an equation of the accompanying graph?
(1) $y = x^2 + 2x - 3$ (2) $y = -x^2 - 2x + 3$
(3) $y = -x^2 + 2x + 3$ (4) $y = x^2 - 2x + 3$

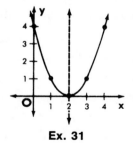

Ex. 31

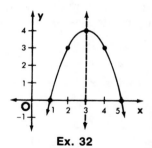

Ex. 32

31. Which is an equation of the accompanying graph?
(1) $y = x^2 - 4x + 4$ (2) $y = x^2 + 4x + 4$
(3) $y = -x^2 + 4x + 4$ (4) $y = -x^2 - 4x + 4$

32. Which is an equation of the accompanying graph?
(1) $y = x^2 - 6x + 5$ (2) $y = x^2 - 6x - 5$
(3) $y = -x^2 + 6x + 5$ (4) $y = -x^2 + 6x - 5$

33. Which is an equation of the axis of symmetry for the graph of $y = x^2 - 6x + 15$? (1) $y = 3$ (2) $x = 3$ (3) $y = -3$ (4) $x = -3$

34. Which are the coordinates of the turning point of the parabola $y = x^2 + 10x$? (1) $(-5, 25)$ (2) $(-5, -25)$ (3) $(5, 75)$ (4) $(5, -25)$

35. If $x = 2$ is an equation of the axis of symmetry of the parabola $y = ax^2 - 8x + 3$, then a equals (1) -2 (2) 2 (3) -4 (4) 4

36. If $x = -3$ is an equation of the axis of symmetry of the parabola $y = x^2 + bx - 9$, the value of b is (1) -6 (2) 6 (3) 3 (4) -3

37. a. Draw a graph of the equation $y = -x^2 + 10x - 21$, using all integral values of x from $x = 2$ to $x = 8$ inclusive.
   b. Write an equation for the axis of symmetry.
   c. Write the coordinates of the turning point.
38. For the equation $y = x^2 - 2x - 5$:
   a. Write an equation for the axis of symmetry.
   b. Write the coordinates of the turning point.
   c. Draw a graph.

10-8 GRAPHIC SOLUTIONS INVOLVING QUADRATIC EQUATIONS

In the preceding section, you learned how to graph a parabola of the form $y = ax^2 + bx + c$. You will now learn how to use graphing techniques to solve a quadratic equation.

EXAMPLE 1.   **a.** Draw the graph of the equation $y = x^2 - 2x - 3$ in the interval $-2 \leq x \leq 4$.
b. Find the roots of the quadratic equation $x^2 - 2x - 3 = 0$.

Solution

a. Develop a table of values:

x	$x^2 - 2x - 3$	y
-2	$(-2)^2 - 2(-2) - 3$	5
-1	$(-1)^2 - 2(-1) - 3$	0
0	$(0)^2 - 2(0) - 3$	-3
1	$(1)^2 - 2(1) - 3$	-4
2	$(2)^2 - 2(2) - 3$	-3
3	$(3)^2 - 2(3) - 3$	0
4	$(4)^2 - 2(4) - 3$	5

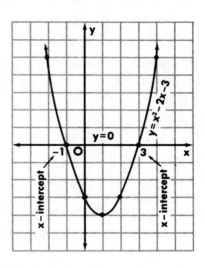

Then plot the points, and draw and label the parabola.

b. *Method 1: Factoring*

The roots of this quadratic equation can be found by factoring.

$$x^2 - 2x - 3 = 0$$
$$(x + 1)(x - 3) = 0$$
$$x + 1 = 0 \quad | \quad x - 3 = 0$$
$$x = -1 \quad | \quad x = 3$$

Method 2: Graphic Solution

Notice that the graph of the parabola intersects the *x*-axis at two points: $x = -1$ and $x = 3$. These values, -1 and 3, are called the ***x-intercepts*** of the parabola, and they are the roots of the quadratic equation $x^2 - 2x - 3 = 0$.

To understand why this is true, examine the equations involved.

The equation of the parabola is $y = x^2 - 2x - 3$.
The equation of the *x*-axis is $y = 0$.

Since the parabola intersects the *x*-axis only at points where $y = 0$, then only the values $x = -1$ and $x = 3$ will make the equation $x^2 - 2x - 3 = 0$ true.

Answer: $x = -1$ or $x = 3$ *or*   the solution set $= \{-1, 3\}$.

In this example, the parabola intersects the *x*-axis at two points. Therefore, the quadratic equation $x^2 - 2x - 3 = 0$ has *two real and unequal roots,* $x = -1$ and $x = 3$.

Recall that the discriminant of a quadratic equation describes the nature of the roots. For $x^2 - 2x - 3 = 0$, the discriminant $b^2 - 4ac = (-2)^2 - 4(1)(-3) = 16$. Since 16 is positive, the discriminant tells us that the roots are real and unequal. Since 16 is also a perfect square, the roots are rational.

EXAMPLE 2.   Using the graph of the parabola $y = x^2 - 10x + 25$, find the roots of the quadratic equation $x^2 - 10x + 25 = 0$.

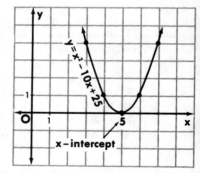

Solution:

The parabola intersects the *x*-axis at only one point. The solution of the quadratic equation $x^2 - 10x + 25 = 0$ is the single *x*-intercept, $x = 5$.

Answer: $x = 5$ *or*   the solution set $= \{5\}$.

In this example, the quadratic equation $x^2 - 10x + 25 = 0$ has *two real and equal roots.* This can be checked by factoring $x^2 - 10x + 25 = 0$.

Here, the discriminant $b^2 - 4ac = (-10)^2 - 4(1)(25) = 0$, which agrees with the finding that the roots are real and equal.

EXAMPLE 3.   Using the graph of $y = x^2 + 4$, explain why the quadratic equation $x^2 + 4 = 0$ has *no real roots*.

Solution:

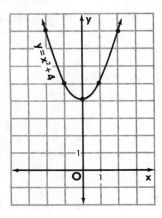

The parabola $y = x^2 + 4$ does *not* intersect the x-axis. Therefore, there is no real value of x for which $x^2 + 4 = 0$. *Ans.*

You saw earlier in this chapter why the equation $x^2 + 4 = 0$ has no real solutions: an equivalent equation is $x^2 = -4$, and there is no real number which, when squared, is -4.

Here, the discriminant is negative: $b^2 - 4ac = 0^2 - 4(1)(4) = -16$, which agrees with the finding that there are no real roots.

Let us generalize the findings of these three examples in the following three cases to show the number of points of intersection that a parabola $y = ax^2 + bx + c$ may have with the x-axis.

Case I	*Case II*	*Case III*
2 points of intersection	1 point of intersection	0 points of intersection
$ax^2 + bx + c = 0$ has *two real and unequal roots*. $b^2 - 4ac > 0$	$ax^2 + bx + c = 0$ has *two real and equal roots*. $b^2 - 4ac = 0$	$ax^2 + bx + c = 0$ has *no real roots*. $b^2 - 4ac < 0$

CASE I.   If the parabola $y = ax^2 + bx + c$ intersects the x-axis ($y = 0$) at two points, the quadratic equation $ax^2 + bx + c = 0$ has *two real and unequal roots* (the two x-intercepts). The discriminant is positive.

CASE II.   If the parabola $y = ax^2 + bx + c$ intersects the x-axis ($y = 0$) at one point, the quadratic equation $ax^2 + bx + c = 0$ has *two real and equal roots* (the single x-intercept). The discriminant is 0.

CASE III.   If the parabola $y = ax^2 + bx + c$ does not intersect the x-axis ($y = 0$), then the quadratic equation $ax^2 + bx + c = 0$ has *no real roots*. The discriminant is negative.

MODEL PROBLEMS

1. **a.** Graph the equation $y = x^2 + 2x - 1$ from $x = -3$ to $x = 1$ inclusive.
   b. Explain why the quadratic equation $x^2 + 2x - 1 = 0$ has two real and unequal roots.
   c. Locate *each* root by naming an interval of two consecutive integers such that the root lies between these integers.
   d. Find the roots of $x^2 + 2x - 1 = 0$. Express the roots in simplest radical form.

Solution:

a. Develop a table of values:

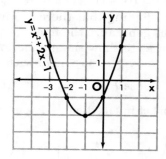

x	x² + 2x − 1	y
−3	$(-3)^2 + 2(-3) - 1$	2
−2	$(-2)^2 + 2(-2) - 1$	−1
−1	$(-1)^2 + 2(-1) - 1$	−2
0	$(0)^2 + 2(0) - 1$	−1
1	$(1)^2 + 2(1) - 1$	2

Plot the points.
Draw and label the parabola.

b. The parabola $y = x^2 + 2x - 1$ crosses the x-axis at two points. Also, $b^2 - 4ac = 2^2 - 4(1)(-1) = 8$, which is positive. Therefore, the quadratic equation $x^2 + 2x - 1 = 0$ has two real, unequal roots.

c. Since the parabola crosses the x-axis between -3 and -2, one root lies in the interval between -3 and -2, that is, $-3 < x < -2$. Also, since the parabola crosses the x-axis between 0 and 1, the second root lies in the interval between 0 and 1, that is, $0 < x < 1$.

d. Use the quadratic formula to find the roots of $x^2 + 2x - 1 = 0$.
$a = 1, b = 2, c = -1$

$$x = \frac{-b \pm \sqrt{b^2 - 4ac}}{2a}$$

$$x = \frac{-(2) \pm \sqrt{(2)^2 - 4(1)(-1)}}{2(1)}$$

$$x = \frac{-2 \pm \sqrt{4 + 4}}{2}$$

$$x = \frac{-2 \pm \sqrt{8}}{2}$$

$$x = \frac{-2 \pm 2\sqrt{2}}{2} \qquad \sqrt{8} = \sqrt{4} \cdot \sqrt{2} = 2\sqrt{2}$$

$$x = -1 \pm \sqrt{2}$$

Note that since $\sqrt{2}$ is approximately equal to 1.41, $-1 - 1.41 = -2.41$ and $-1 + 1.41 = .41$. The root -2.41 is between -3 and -2 and the root $.41$ is between 0 and 1.

Answer: **a.** See the graph.
        b. See the explanation.
        c. $-3 < x < -2$ *or* $0 < x < 1$
        d. $-1 \pm \sqrt{2}$

2. Given the equation: $y = -x^2 - 3x$

a. Graph $y = -x^2 - 3x$, using the interval $-4 \le x \le 1$ and the turning point.

b. Find the roots of the quadratic equation $-x^2 - 3x = 0$.

Solution:

a. Develop the following table of values:

x	$-x^2 - 3x$	y
-4	$-(-4)^2 - 3(-4) = -16 + 12$	-4
-3	$-(-3)^2 - 3(-3) = -9 + 9$	0
-2	$-(-2)^2 - 3(-2) = -4 + 6$	2
-1	$-(-1)^2 - 3(-1) = -1 + 3$	2
0	$-(0)^2 - 3(0) = 0 - 0$	0
1	$-(1)^2 - 3(1) = -1 - 3$	-4

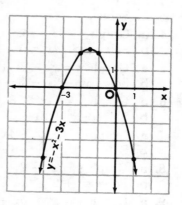

Since an equation of the axis of symmetry is $x = -\frac{3}{2}$, substitute $x = -\frac{3}{2}$ in the equation of the parabola, $y = -x^2 - 3x$, to determine the coordinates of the turning point. Thus:

$$y = -(-\tfrac{3}{2})^2 - 3(-\tfrac{3}{2}) = -(\tfrac{9}{4}) + \tfrac{9}{2} = -\tfrac{9}{4} + \tfrac{18}{4} = \tfrac{9}{4}$$

The turning point $(x, y) = (-\frac{3}{2}, \frac{9}{4})$. Plot the points from the table and the turning point. Then draw and label the parabola.

b. The parabola intersects the x-axis at two points, $x = -3$ and $x = 0$. Thus, the roots of the quadratic equation $-x^2 - 3x = 0$ are -3 and 0. (*Note.* We can check these roots by factoring, as shown at the right.)

Check

$$-x^2 - 3x = 0$$
$$-x(x + 3) = 0$$

$-x = 0 \mid x + 3 = 0$
$+x = 0 \mid x = -3$

Answer: **a.** See the graph. **b.** $x = 0$ or $x = -3$

EXERCISES

In 1–12: **a.** Graph the given equation, using the integral values of x indicated in parentheses to prepare the table.
b. From the graph drawn in part **a**, find the roots of the given quadratic equation or indicate that the equation has no real roots.
c. Where possible, check the answer to part **b** by factoring the quadratic equation given in **b**.

1. **a.** Graph $y = x^2 - 1$ $(-2 \le x \le 2)$.
   b. Solve $x^2 - 1 = 0$.
2. **a.** Graph $y = -x^2 + 4$ $(-3 \le x \le 3)$.
   b. Solve $-x^2 + 4 = 0$.
3. **a.** Graph $y = x^2 - 6x + 5$ $(0 \le x \le 6)$.
   b. Solve $x^2 - 6x + 5 = 0$.
4. **a.** Graph $y = x^2 - 4x$ $(-1 \le x \le 5)$.
   b. Solve $x^2 - 4x = 0$.
5. **a.** Graph $y = x^2 - 2x + 1$ $(-1 \le x \le 3)$.
   b. Solve $x^2 - 2x + 1 = 0$.
6. **a.** Graph $y = -x^2 + 8x - 16$ $(2 \le x \le 6)$.
   b. Solve $-x^2 + 8x - 16 = 0$.
7. **a.** Graph $y = -x^2 - 4x$ $(-5 \le x \le 1)$.
   b. Solve $-x^2 - 4x = 0$.
8. **a.** Graph $y = x^2 + 2$ $(-2 \le x \le 2)$.
   b. Solve $x^2 + 2 = 0$.
9. **a.** Graph $y = x^2 - 6x + 10$ $(0 \le x \le 6)$.
   b. Solve $x^2 - 6x + 10 = 0$.
10. **a.** Graph $y = 2x^2 + 8x + 6$ $(-4 \le x \le 0)$.
    b. Solve $2x^2 + 8x + 6 = 0$.
11. **a.** Graph $y = -2x^2 + 8x$ $(-1 \le x \le 5)$.
    b. Solve $-2x^2 + 8x = 0$.
12. **a.** Graph $y = \frac{1}{2}x^2 - 2$ $(-4 \le x \le 4)$.
    b. Solve $\frac{1}{2}x^2 - 2 = 0$.

In 13–18: **a.** Graph the given equation for the indicated interval. **b.** If $y = 0$, locate each root of the quadratic equation formed by naming an interval of two consecutive integers such that the root lies between these integers. **c.** Find the exact values in radical form of the roots located in part **b.**

13. $y = x^2 - 4x + 2$ $(-1 \le x \le 5)$.

14. $y = x^2 - 2x - 2$ $(-2 \le x \le 4)$.

15. $y = 2x^2 - 1$ $(-2 \le x \le 2)$.

16. $y = 2x^2 + 8x + 5$ $(-4 \le x \le 0)$.

17. $y = -x^2 + 6x - 7$ $(0 \le x \le 6)$.

18. $y = -\frac{1}{2}x^2 + 1$ $(-4 \le x \le 4)$.

19. Given the equation $y = x^2 - 8x + 15$.
   a. Draw a graph of the equation in the interval $1 \le x \le 7$.
   b. Write an equation of its axis of symmetry.
   c. Using the graph from part **a**, find the roots of $x^2 - 8x + 15 = 0$.

20. Given the equation $y = -x^2 + 2x + 3$.
   a. Draw the graph of the equation, using all integral values of x from $x = -2$ to $x = 4$ inclusive.
   b. Write an equation of the axis of symmetry.
   c. Write the coordinates of the turning point.
   d. What are the roots of the equation $-x^2 + 2x + 3 = 0$?

21. Given the equation $y = x^2 + 2x + 1$.
   a. Draw the graph of the equation from $x = -3$ to $x = 3$ inclusive.
   b. Write the coordinates of the turning point of this parabola.
   c. Using the graph from part **a**, find the roots of $x^2 + 2x + 1 = 0$.

22. Given the parabola $y = x^2 - 5x + 4$.
   a. Write an equation of its axis of symmetry.
   b. Write the coordinates of the turning point of the parabola.
   c. Graph $y = x^2 - 5x + 4$ from $x = 0$ to $x = 5$, including the turning point.
   d. Find the roots of the equation $x^2 - 5x + 4 = 0$.

23. a. Graph the equation $y = x^2 - 6x + 4$ from $x = 0$ to $x = 6$ inclusive.
   b. For $x^2 - 6x + 4 = 0$, it is true that
   (1) the roots are real   (2) the roots are equal
   (3) the roots are integers   (4) there are no real roots

24. Which parabola touches the x-axis at one point only?
   (1) $y = x^2 - 4$ (2) $y = x^2 + 4$
   (3) $y = x^2 - 4x + 4$ (4) $y = x^2 - 4x$

25. a. Which of the following parabolas does not touch the x-axis?
   (1) $y = x^2 - 1$ (2) $y = x^2 + 1$ (3) $y = x^2$ (4) $y = x^2 + 2x + 1$
   b. Which of the following quadratic equations has no real roots?
   (1) $x^2 - 1 = 0$ (2) $x^2 + 1 = 0$ (3) $x^2 = 0$ (4) $x^2 + 2x + 1 = 0$

10-9 GRAPHING THE EQUATION $ax^2 + by^2 = c$

You have seen that the graph of $y = ax^2 + bx + c$, a quadratic equation in which one variable is raised to the second power, is a parabola.

Now we will consider a quadratic equation in which both variables are to the second power: $ax^2 + by^2 = c$.

You will see three different graphs emerge from this equation: a *circle*, an *ellipse*, and a *hyperbola*. The nature of the graph depends on the relation of the coefficients a and b.

To obtain each graph, we will use the following procedure.

PROCEDURE. To obtain a graph of the equation $ax^2 + by^2 = c$:

1. Determine the y-intercepts and the x-intercepts.
2. Solve the equation for y in terms of x.
3. Based on the findings of steps 1 and 2, develop a table of values.
4. Plot the points and join them.

CASE 1. The Circle: $a = b$.

EXAMPLE.   Sketch the graph of $x^2 + y^2 = 9$.

Solution

(1) Determine the intercepts.
   To obtain the y-intercepts, let $x = 0$.

$$x^2 + y^2 = 9$$
$$0 + y^2 = 9$$
$$y^2 = 9$$
$$y = \pm 3$$

   To obtain the x-intercepts, let $y = 0$.

$$x^2 + y^2 = 9$$
$$x^2 + 0 = 9$$
$$x^2 = 9$$
$$x = \pm 3$$

(2) Solve the equation for y in terms of x.

$$x^2 + y^2 = 9$$
$$y^2 = 9 - x^2$$
$$y = \pm \sqrt{9 - x^2}$$

(3) Since the x-intercepts are ± 3, develop a table of values by taking $x = \pm 1$ and $x = \pm 2$.
   Note that when $x > +3$ or $x < -3$, y has no real value since the radicand is negative.

x	$\pm \sqrt{9 - x^2}$	y
0	$\pm \sqrt{9 - 0} = \pm \sqrt{9}$	± 3
± 1	$\pm \sqrt{9 - 1} = \pm \sqrt{8}$	± 2.8
± 2	$\pm \sqrt{9 - 4} = \pm \sqrt{5}$	± 2.2
± 3	$\pm \sqrt{9 - 9} = \pm \sqrt{0}$	0

(4) Plot the points. Join them with a smooth curve to obtain a *circle* whose center is at the origin and whose radius measures 3 units.

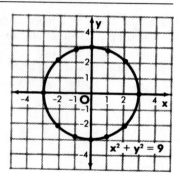

● **In general, when $a = b$ and a, b, c have the same sign, the graph of the equation $ax^2 + by^2 = c$ is a *circle*.**

When $a = b \neq 1$, the equation can be reduced. For example, $2x^2 + 2y^2 = 32$ is equivalent to $x^2 + y^2 = 16$. Following the procedure for obtaining a graph, we would find that this graph is a circle whose center is at the origin and whose radius measures 4 units. Thus, we say:

● **The graph of the equation $x^2 + y^2 = r^2$ is a circle whose center is at the origin and whose radius measures r units.**

CASE 2. The Ellipse: $a \neq b$ and they have the same sign.

EXAMPLE. Sketch the graph of $4x^2 + 9y^2 = 36$.

Solution

(1) Determine the intercepts.
To obtain the y-intercepts, let $x = 0$.

$$4x^2 + 9y^2 = 36$$
$$0 + 9y^2 = 36$$
$$y^2 = 4$$
$$y = \pm 2$$

To obtain the x-intercepts, let $y = 0$.

$$4x^2 + 9y^2 = 36$$
$$4x^2 + 0 = 36$$
$$4x^2 = 36$$
$$x^2 = 9$$
$$x = \pm 3$$

(2) Solve the equation for y in terms of x.

$$4x^2 + 9y^2 = 36$$
$$9y^2 = 36 - 4x^2$$
$$y^2 = \frac{36 - 4x^2}{9}$$
$$y = \frac{\pm \sqrt{36 - 4x^2}}{3}$$

(3) Since the x-intercepts are ± 3, develop a table of values by taking $x = \pm 1$ and $x = \pm 2$.

   Note that when $x > +3$ or $x < -3$, y has no real value.

x	$\dfrac{\pm\sqrt{36 - 4x^2}}{3}$	y
0	$\dfrac{\pm\sqrt{36 - 0}}{3} = \dfrac{\pm 6}{3}$	± 2
± 1	$\dfrac{\pm\sqrt{36 - 4}}{3} = \dfrac{\pm\sqrt{32}}{3}$	± 1.9
± 2	$\dfrac{\pm\sqrt{36 - 16}}{3} = \dfrac{\pm\sqrt{20}}{3}$	± 1.5

(4) Plot the points. Join them with a smooth curve to obtain an ellipse whose center is at the origin.

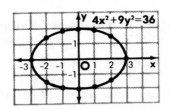

● In general, when $a \neq b$ and a, b, c have the same sign, the graph of the equation $ax^2 + by^2 = c$ is an *ellipse*.

CASE 3. The Hyberbola: a and b have different signs.

EXAMPLE 1.   Sketch the graph of $4x^2 - y^2 = 16$.

Solution

(1) Determine the intercepts.

   To obtain the y-intercepts, let $x = 0$.

$$4x^2 - y^2 = 16$$
$$0 - y^2 = 16$$
$$y^2 = -16$$

   Since the square of a real number cannot be negative, this graph does not intersect the y-axis.

   To obtain the x-intercept, let $y = 0$.

$$4x^2 - y^2 = 16$$
$$4x^2 - 0 = 16$$
$$x^2 = 4$$
$$x = \pm 2$$

(2) Solve the equation for y in terms of x.

$$4x^2 - y^2 = 16$$
$$4x^2 - 16 = y^2$$
$$\pm\sqrt{4x^2 - 16} = y$$
$$\pm 2\sqrt{x^2 - 4} = y$$

(3) The x-intercepts are ± 2.
Note that when
$-2 < x < +2$, y has no real
value.

Develop a table of values
by taking $x = \pm 3, \pm 4$.

x	$\pm\, 2\sqrt{x^2 - 4}$	y
± 2	$\pm\, 2\sqrt{4-4} = \quad 2(0)$	0
± 3	$\pm\, 2\sqrt{9-4} = \pm\, 2\sqrt{5}$	± 4.5
± 4	$\pm\, 2\sqrt{16-4} = \pm\, 2\sqrt{12}$	± 6.9

(4) Plot the points, which lie on
opposite sides of the y-axis.
Join the points that have
positive x-coordinates to
obtain one branch, and join
the points that have
negative x-coordinates to
obtain a second branch.
These two branches are the
graph of a hyperbola whose
center is at the origin.

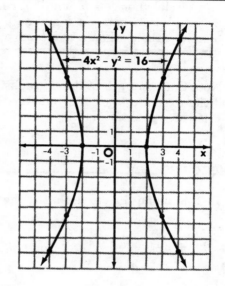

EXAMPLE 2.   Sketch the graph of $4y^2 - x^2 = 16$.

Solution

Follow the steps of the procedure.
This graph does not intersect the x-axis and the y-intercepts are ± 2.

x	$\dfrac{\pm\sqrt{16 + x^2}}{2}$	y
0	$\dfrac{\pm\sqrt{16+0}}{2} = \dfrac{\pm 4}{2}$	± 2
1	$\dfrac{\pm\sqrt{16+1}}{2} = \dfrac{\pm\sqrt{17}}{2}$	± 2.1
4	$\dfrac{\pm\sqrt{16+16}}{2} = \dfrac{\pm\sqrt{32}}{2}$	± 2.8
5	$\dfrac{\pm\sqrt{16+25}}{2} = \dfrac{\pm\sqrt{41}}{2}$	± 3.2

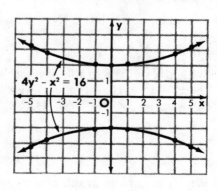

● In general, when a and b have different signs, the graph of the equation $ax^2 + by^2 = c$ is a *hyperbola*.

KEEP IN MIND

The graph of the equation $ax^2 + by^2 = c$ is:

1. a circle when $a = b$ and a, b, c have the same sign.
2. an ellipse when $a \neq b$ and a, b, c have the same sign.
3. a hyperbola when a and b have different signs.

Note that, for each of these graphs, the origin is a point of symmetry and the axes are lines of symmetry. The circle has an infinite number of lines of symmetry.

EXERCISES

In 1–9, name the curve that is the graph of the equation.

1. $x^2 + y^2 = 16$ **2.** $2x^2 + y^2 = 16$ **3.** $2x^2 - y^2 = 16$

4. $2x^2 + 2y^2 = 16$ **5.** $y^2 - 2x^2 = 16$ **6.** $x^2 + 2y^2 = 16$

7. $2y + x^2 = 16$ **8.** $2x^2 - 2y^2 = 16$ **9.** $y - 2x^2 = 16$

10. Which equation has a circle as its graph?
    (1) $3x^2 = 15 + 3y^2$ (2) $3x^2 = 15 - 3y^2$
    (3) $3x^2 = 15 - y^2$ (4) $3x^2 = 15 + y^2$

11. Which equation has an ellipse as its graph?
    (1) $9x^2 = 36 - 9y^2$ (2) $9x^2 = 9y^2 + 36$
    (3) $9x^2 = 4y^2 + 36$ (4) $9x^2 = 36 - 4y^2$

12. Which equation has a hyperbola as its graph?
    (1) $2x^2 + 3y^2 = 12$ (2) $2x^2 = 12 - 3y^2$
    (3) $2x^2 = 3y^2 + 12$ (4) $-2x^2 - 3y^2 = -12$

13. Which is not the graph of a circle?
    (1) $x^2 + y^2 = 10$ (2) $2x^2 + 2y^2 = 20$
    (3) $-3x^2 - 3y^2 = -30$ (4) $2x^2 + 3y^2 = 6$

14. Which is not the graph of an ellipse?
    (1) $3x^2 + 5y^2 = 15$ (2) $3x^2 = 15 - 5y^2$
    (3) $-3x^2 - 5y^2 = -15$ (4) $3x^2 = 5y^2 + 15$

15. Which is not the graph of a hyperbola?
    (1) $x^2 = 10 - y^2$ (2) $x^2 = 10 + y^2$
    (3) $2x^2 = 10 + y^2$ (4) $y^2 = 2x^2 + 10$

In 16–24, write the coordinates of the y-intercepts and x-intercepts. Indicate when there is no intercept on an axis.

16. $5x^2 + 5y^2 = 45$ **17.** $x^2 + y^2 = 7$ **18.** $25x^2 + 4y^2 = 100$
19. $x^2 + 9y^2 = 36$ **20.** $x^2 - y^2 = 9$ **21.** $y^2 - x^2 = 25$
22. $25x^2 - y^2 = 25$ **23.** $4x^2 - 9y^2 = 36$ **24.** $16x^2 = 64 - y^2$

In 25–30, graph the equation.

25. $x^2 + y^2 = 25$ **26.** $y^2 - x^2 = 9$ **27.** $4x^2 + y^2 = 36$
28. $3x^2 + 3y^2 = 27$ **29.** $x^2 + 4y^2 = 36$ **30.** $x^2 - y^2 = 9$

10-10   INVERSE VARIATION AND THE HYPERBOLA $xy = c$

The distance from the Hamlin Park entrance to the farthest picnic area is 8 miles. To walk that distance at 4 miles per hour takes 2 hours. Traveling that distance by bicycle at a rate of 8 miles per hour takes 1 hour. To drive 8 miles at a rate of 20 miles per hour takes $\frac{2}{5}$ of an hour. As the rate at which we travel increases, the time required to travel a constant distance decreases. We say that, for a constant distance, rate and time *vary inversely*.

Let x represent rate in miles per hour and y represent time in hours. Using the formula (rate)(time) = distance, we can write the equation $xy = 8$ to express the relationship between the rate and the time needed to travel 8 miles. This example illustrates the following principle:

● **If x and y vary inversely, then xy = a nonzero constant.**

EXAMPLE. The number of days needed to complete a job (x) varies inversely as the number of workers assigned to the job (y). If the job can be completed by 2 workers in 10 days, then the *constant of variation* is the product 2(10) or 20. To find the number of workers needed to complete the job in 5 days, let $x = 5$ and solve the equation $xy = 20$ for y.

$$xy = 20$$
$$5y = 20$$
$$y = 4$$

Therefore, 5 workers can complete the job in 4 days.

Graphing Inverse Variation

To draw the graph of $xy = 20$, we find ordered pairs that are elements of the solution set. Values of x and y can be either both positive or both negative.

x	y
1	20
2	10
4	5
5	4
10	2
20	1

x	y
−1	−20
−2	−10
−4	−5
−5	−4
−10	−2
−20	−1

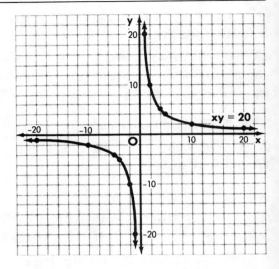

The graph, a *hyperbola*, consists of two parts. One part is in quadrant I where both x and y are positive and the other part is in quadrant III where both x and y are negative. Notice that there is no value of x for which y is 0 and no value of y for which x is 0. Therefore, the graph has no x-intercept and no y-intercept.

MODEL PROBLEMS

1. The cost of hiring a bus for a trip to Niagara Falls is $400. The cost per person (x) varies inversely as the number of persons (y) who will go on the trip.
   a. Find the cost per person if 25 persons go on the trip.
   b. Find the number of persons who are going if the cost per person is $12.50.

Solution: Since x and y vary inversely, we can write the equation $xy = 400$.

a. $xy = 400$
    $x(25) = 400$
    $x = \dfrac{400}{25}$
    $x = 16$

b. $xy = 400$
    $12.50y = 400$
    $y = \dfrac{400}{12.50}$
    $y = 32$

Answer: **a.** $16 per person.   **b.** 32 persons.

2. Draw the graph of $xy = -12$.

Solution

Since the product of x and y is negative, when x is positive, y will be negative and when x is negative, y will be positive.

x	y
1	−12
2	−6
3	−4
4	−3
6	−2
8	−1.5
12	−1

x	y
−1	12
−2	6
−3	4
−4	3
−6	2
−8	1.5
−12	1

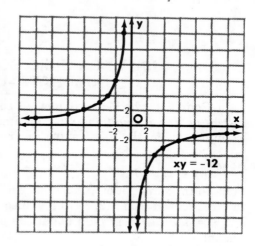

Note that the graph has both line symmetry and point symmetry. The lines $y = x$ and $y = -x$ are lines of symmetry. The origin $(0, 0)$ is a point of symmetry.

EXERCISES _____

In 1–8, draw the graph of the equation.

1. $xy = 6$ **2.** $xy = 15$ **3.** $xy = -4$ **4.** $xy = -2$

5. $y = \dfrac{10}{x}$ **6.** $y = -\dfrac{8}{x}$ **7.** $y = \dfrac{1}{x}$ **8.** $y = -\dfrac{1}{x}$

9. If 4 typists can complete the typing of a manuscript in 9 days, how long would it take 12 typists to complete the manuscript?

10. If 4 typists can complete the typing of a manuscript in 9 days, how many typists are needed to complete the typing in 6 days?

11. If a man can drive from his home to Albany in 6 hours at 45 mph, how long would it take him if he drove at 60 mph?

12. If a man can drive from his home to Albany in 6 hours at 45 mph, how fast did he drive if he made the trip in 5 hours?

13. Let S be the set of all rectangles that have an area of 600 sq. cm. The lengths of rectangles in S vary inversely as the widths.
   a. What is the length of a rectangle from the set S whose width is 20 cm?
   b. What is the width of a rectangle from the set S whose length is 100 cm?

10-11 GRAPHIC SOLUTION OF A QUADRATIC-LINEAR SYSTEM

In Course I, you learned how to solve a *system of linear equations* by graphing. For example, given the system of linear equations $\left\{\begin{array}{l} y = -\frac{1}{2}x + 4 \\ y = 2x - 1 \end{array}\right\}$, we graph the equations on the same set of axes, as shown. Since the lines intersect at (2, 3), the values $x = 2$ and $y = 3$ will satisfy both equations of this system.

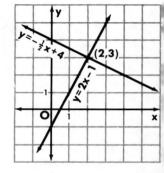

A *quadratic-linear system* consists of a quadratic equation and a linear equation. You have already studied graphs of such systems in this chapter. For example, recall that a parabola (the quadratic equation) may intersect the x-axis (the linear equation) at two, one, or no points.

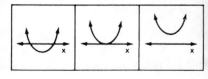

In the examples that follow, you will see quadratic-linear systems whose graphs consist of a parabola and a line, or a hyperbola and a line. Note that any line may be used, not just the x-axis.

MODEL PROBLEMS

1. a. Draw the graph of the equation $y = x^2 - 6x + 6$.
   b. On the same axes, draw the graph of the equation $y = x - 4$.
   c. Determine the coordinates of the points of intersection of the graphs in parts **a** and **b**, and check these coordinates in both equations.

Solution

a. An equation of the axis of symmetry is $x = \dfrac{-b}{2a}$.

Thus, for $y = x^2 - 6x + 6$, the axis of symmetry is $x = \dfrac{-(-6)}{2(1)}$, or $x = 3$.

Choose some values of x smaller than 3 and some values of x larger than 3 to develop the following table of values.

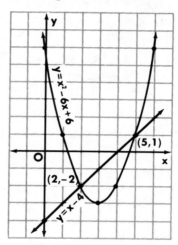

x	x² − 6x + 6	y
0	$(0)^2 - 6(0) + 6$	6
1	$(1)^2 - 6(1) + 6$	1
2	$(2)^2 - 6(2) + 6$	−2
3	$(3)^2 - 6(3) + 6$	−3
4	$(4)^2 - 6(4) + 6$	−2
5	$(5)^2 - 6(5) + 6$	1
6	$(6)^2 - 6(6) + 6$	6

Plot the points. Draw and label the parabola.

b. The linear equation $y = x - 4$ may be graphed by various methods.

Method 1: Table of Values

x	x − 4	y
0	0 − 4	−4
1	1 − 4	−3
2	2 − 4	−2

Find the coordinates of three points. Plot the points. Draw and label the straight line, extended to cross the parabola at all possible points of intersection.

Method 2: Slope-Intercept

In $y = \dfrac{1}{1}x - 4$ $\begin{cases} \text{slope} = \dfrac{\Delta y}{\Delta x} = \dfrac{1}{1} \\ y\text{-intercept} = -4 \end{cases}$

Plot the point $(0, -4)$ on the y-axis. From $(0, -4)$, use the slope to plot other points, showing that y increases by 1 as x increases by 1. Draw and label the straight line, extended to cross the parabola at two points.

c. The graphs from parts **a** and **b** intersect at two points:

$$(x, y) = (2, -2) \qquad\qquad (x, y) = (5, 1)$$

Each ordered pair must be checked in each of the two original equations. Thus, four checks are needed.

Check for x = 2 and y = -2 | *Check for x = 5 and y = 1*

$y = x^2 - 6x + 6$	$y = x - 4$	$y^2 = x^2 - 6x + 6$	$y = x - 4$
$(-2) \underset{?}{=} (2)^2 - 6(2) + 6$	$(-2) \underset{?}{=} (2) - 4$	$(1)^2 \underset{?}{=} (5)^2 - 6(5) + 6$	$(1) \underset{?}{=} (5) - 4$
$-2 \underset{?}{=} 4 - 12 + 6$	$-2 = -2$ (True)	$1 \underset{?}{=} 25 - 30 + 6$	$1 = 1$ (True)
$-2 = -2$ (True)		$1 = 1$ (True)	

Answer: **a** and **b**. See the graph.
    c. $\{(2, -2), (5, 1)\}$

2. Solve the system of equations graphically: $\begin{cases} xy = 4 \\ x - 2y = 2 \end{cases}$

Solution

(1) The graph of $xy = 4$ is a hyperbola.
  Develop a table of values:

x	y
$\frac{1}{2}$	8
1	4
2	2
4	1
8	$\frac{1}{2}$

x	y
$-\frac{1}{2}$	-8
-1	-4
-2	-2
-4	-1
-8	$-\frac{1}{2}$

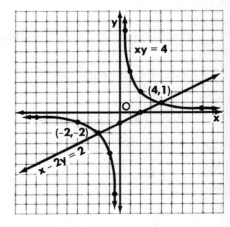

  Plot the points and sketch the curve.

(2) The graph of $x - 2y = 2$ is a line.
  Solve the equation for y:

$$x - 2y = 2$$
$$-2y = -x + 2$$
$$y = \tfrac{1}{2}x - 1$$

Select values of x and solve for y to develop a table of values:

x	$\frac{1}{2}x - 1$	y
-2	$\frac{1}{2}(-2) - 1$	-2
0	$\frac{1}{2}(0) - 1$	-1
2	$\frac{1}{2}(2) - 1$	0

Plot the points and draw the line.

(3) The graphs intersect at $(-2, -2)$ and $(4, 1)$. Each ordered pair is a solution of the system. The check is left to the student.

Answer: $\{(-2, -2), (4, 1)\}$.

EXERCISES

1. Name the maximum number of points of intersection for:
   a. two lines   **b.** a line and a parabola
   c. a line and a circle   **d.** a line and an ellipse
   e. a line and a hyperbola

2. What does it mean if the two graphs of a system do not intersect?

3. The graph of $y = -x^2 + 3$ is shown. Find the solution set for each of the following systems of equations by inspecting the graph and naming the coordinates of the points of intersection.

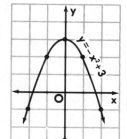

a. $\begin{array}{l} y = -x^2 + 3 \\ y = 2 \end{array}$ **b.** $\begin{array}{l} y = -x^2 + 3 \\ y = -1 \end{array}$

c. $\begin{array}{l} y = -x^2 + 3 \\ y = 3 \end{array}$ **d.** $\begin{array}{l} y = -x^2 + 3 \\ y = 5 \end{array}$

e. $\begin{array}{l} y = -x^2 + 3 \\ x = 1 \end{array}$ **f.** $\begin{array}{l} y = -x^2 + 3 \\ x = -2 \end{array}$

4. **a.** Draw the graph of $y = x^2 - 4x + 5$, using integral values for $0 \le x \le 5$.
   b. On the same set of axes, draw the graph of $y = -x + 5$.
   c. Determine the coordinates of the points of intersection of the graphs in parts **a** and **b**, and check these coordinates in both equations.

In 5–13, solve each quadratic-linear system graphically, showing the graphs of both equations on the same axes for the interval $-2 \le x \le 2$. Check the solutions in both equations.

5. $y = x^2$
$y = x + 2$

6. $y = -x^2 + 4$
$y = x + 2$

7. $y = x^2 - 2$
$y = 2x - 2$

8. $y = 2 - x^2$
$y = x + 3$

9. $y = 2x^2$
$y = -2x + 4$

10. $y = 2x^2 - 4$
$y = 2x$

11. $y = x^2 - 3$
$y = -x - 1$

12. $y = 6 - 2x^2$
$2x + y = 2$

13. $y = \frac{1}{2}x^2 + 1$
$x + y = 1$

In 14–22: **a.** Graph the given quadratic equation over an appropriate interval.
b. On the same set of axes, graph the linear equation.
c. Determine the coordinates of the points of intersection of the graphs in parts **a** and **b**, and check these coordinates in both equations.

14. $y = x^2 - 2x - 4$
$y = x$

15. $y = x^2 + 2x + 1$
$y = 2x + 5$

16. $y = 4x - x^2$
$y = x - 4$

17. $y = x^2 - 8x + 15$
$y = -x + 5$

18. $y = -x^2 + 6x - 5$
$y = 3$

19. $y = x^2 + 4x + 1$
$y = 2x + 1$

20. $y = x^2 + x - 4$
$y = 2x - 2$

21. $y = x^2 - 5x + 6$
$y = -2x + 6$

22. $y = -x^2 + 3x + 2$
$y = x - 1$

In 23–31, solve the system of equations graphically, and check.

23. $xy = 6$
$y = x + 1$

24. $xy = 8$
$x + 2y = 8$

25. $xy = -6$
$x + 3y = 3$

26. $x^2 + y^2 = 25$
$y = x - 1$

27. $x^2 + y^2 = 16$
$x - y = 4$

28. $x^2 + y^2 = 4$
$x + y = 2$

29. $x^2 + y^2 = 9$
$y = 3$

30. $x^2 + y^2 = 36$
$x = -6$

31. $2x^2 + 2y^2 = 50$
$x = 6$

10-12 ALGEBRAIC SOLUTION OF A QUADRATIC-LINEAR SYSTEM

The graphs of $y = x^2 - 4x + 3$ and $y = \frac{1}{2}x + 1$ intersect at two points. One solution to this quadratic-linear system can be read from the graph, namely, $(x, y) = (4, 3)$. However, the second solution for this system does not occur at a point where x and y are integers. Although the graph shows that x is some value between 0 and 1, and y is some value between 1 and 2, we are not able to identify the exact values of x and y graphically.

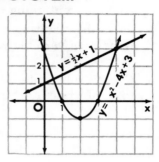

To find the exact values for x and y, we will use an algebraic technique. In Course I, you learned how to solve systems of linear equations by algebraic methods, using addition or substitution. We will now review these methods and then extend them to include quadratic-linear systems. The system shown in the above graph is solved in Model Problem 1.

EXAMPLE 1.   *Using Addition*

Solve the system of equations and check: $7x = 5 - 2y$
$$3y = 16 - 2x$$

How to Proceed	*Solution*
(1) Transform each of the given equations [A] and [B] into equivalent equations [C] and [D] in which the terms containing the variables appear on one side and the constant appears on the other side.	$7x = 5 - 2y$ [A] $3y = 16 - 2x$ [B] $7x + 2y = 5$ [C] $2x + 3y = 16$ [D]
(2) To eliminate y, multiply both members of [C] by 3; multiply both members of [D] by -2. In the resulting equivalent equations [E] and [F], the coefficients of y are additive inverses.	$21x + 6y = 15$ [E] $-4x - 6y = -32$ [F]
(3) Add the members of [F] to the corresponding members of [E] to eliminate the variable y.	$17x = -17$

(4) Solve the resulting equation for x. $\qquad$ $x = -1$

(5) Replace x by its value in any equation containing both variables.
$$3y = 16 - 2x \quad [B]$$
$$3y = 16 - 2(-1)$$

(6) Solve the resulting equation for the remaining variable y.
$$3y = 16 + 2$$
$$3y = 18$$
$$y = 6$$

(7) *Check:* Substitute -1 for x and 6 for y in each of the given equations to verify that the resulting sentences are true. This is left to the student.

Answer: Since $x = -1$ and $y = 6$, the solution is $(-1, 6)$, or the solution set is $\{(-1, 6)\}$.

EXAMPLE 2. *Using Substitution*

Solve the system of equations and check:
$$4x + 3y = 27$$
$$y = 2x - 1$$

How to Proceed	*Solution*

(1) In equation [B], both y and $2x - 1$ name the same number. Therefore, eliminate y in [A] by replacing y with $2x - 1$.
$$4x + 3y = 27 \quad [A]$$
$$y = 2x - 1 \quad [B]$$
$$4x + 3(2x - 1) = 27$$

(2) Solve the resulting equation for x.
$$4x + 6x - 3 = 27$$
$$10x - 3 = 27$$
$$10x = 30$$
$$x = 3$$

(3) Replace x with its value in any equation involving both variables.
$$y = 2x - 1 \quad [B]$$
$$y = 2(3) - 1$$

(4) Solve the resulting equation for y.
$$y = 6 - 1$$
$$y = 5$$

(5) *Check:* Substitute 3 for x and 5 for y in each of the given equations to verify that the resulting sentences are true.

$$
\begin{array}{ll}
4x + 3y = 27 & y = 2x - 1 \\
4(3) + 3(5) \stackrel{?}{=} 27 & 5 \stackrel{?}{=} 2(3) - 1 \\
12 + 15 \stackrel{?}{=} 27 & 5 \stackrel{?}{=} 6 - 1 \\
27 = 27 \text{ (True)} & 5 = 5 \text{ (True)}
\end{array}
$$

Answer: Since $x = 3$ and $y = 5$, the solution is $(3, 5)$, or the solution set is $\{(3, 5)\}$.

In a quadratic-linear system, we generally use the substitution method.

MODEL PROBLEMS

1. Solve and check: $\begin{cases} y = x^2 - 4x + 3 \\ y = \frac{1}{2}x + 1 \end{cases}$

How to Proceed	*Solution*
(1) Since y is expressed in terms of x in the linear equation, substitute the expression $\frac{1}{2}x + 1$ for y in the quadratic equation. Thus, we form one equation with one unknown.	$y = x^2 - 4x + 3$ $\frac{1}{2}x + 1 = x^2 - 4x + 3$
(2) To eliminate fractions as coefficients, multiply by the least common denominator, 2.	$2(\frac{1}{2}x + 1) = 2(x^2 - 4x + 3)$ $x + 2 = 2x^2 - 8x + 6$
(3) Transform the quadratic equation to standard form.	$0 = 2x^2 - 9x + 4$
(4) Solve the quadratic equation by any method. Here, factor to find two values for x.	$0 = (2x - 1)(x - 4)$ $2x - 1 = 0 \quad\mid\quad x - 4 = 0$ $2x = 1 \quad\quad\mid\quad x = 4$ $x = \frac{1}{2} \quad\quad\mid$

(5) Substitute each value of x in the linear equation of the system to find the corresponding value of y.

In $y = \frac{1}{2}x + 1$, substitute $\frac{1}{2}$ and 4 for x.

If $x = \frac{1}{2}$,	If $x = 4$,
$y = \frac{1}{2}(\frac{1}{2}) + 1$	$y = \frac{1}{2}(4) + 1$
$y = \frac{1}{4} + 1$	$y = 2 + 1$
$y = \frac{5}{4}$	$y = 3$

(6) Write the solution as coordinates.

$(x, y) = (\frac{1}{2}, \frac{5}{4}) \quad\mid\quad (x, y) = (4, 3)$

(7) Check each ordered pair in each original equation for a total of four checks.

Check for $x = \frac{1}{2}$ and $y = \frac{5}{4}$	*Check for $x = 4$ and $y = 3$*
$y = x^2 - 4x + 3 \qquad\qquad y = \frac{1}{2}x + 1$	$y = x^2 - 4x + 3 \qquad\qquad y = \frac{1}{2}x + 1$
$(\frac{5}{4}) \stackrel{?}{=} (\frac{1}{2})^2 - 4(\frac{1}{2}) + 3 \qquad (\frac{5}{4}) \stackrel{?}{=} \frac{1}{2}(\frac{1}{2}) + 1$	$(3) \stackrel{?}{=} (4)^2 - 4(4) + 3 \qquad (3) \stackrel{?}{=} \frac{1}{2}(4) + 1$
$\frac{5}{4} \stackrel{?}{=} \frac{1}{4} - 2 + 3 \qquad\qquad \frac{5}{4} \stackrel{?}{=} \frac{1}{4} + 1$	$3 \stackrel{?}{=} 16 - 16 + 3 \qquad\qquad 3 \stackrel{?}{=} 2 + 1$
$\frac{5}{4} \stackrel{?}{=} \frac{1}{4} + 1 \qquad\qquad \frac{5}{4} = \frac{5}{4} \text{ (True)}$	$3 = 3 \text{ (True)} \qquad\qquad 3 = 3 \text{ (True)}$
$\frac{5}{4} = \frac{5}{4} \text{ (True)}$	

Answer: $\{(\frac{1}{2}, \frac{5}{4}), (4, 3)\}$

2. Solve and check: $\begin{cases} x^2 + y^2 = 25 \\ 2x - y = 5 \end{cases}$

<table>
<tr><td align="center">How to Proceed</td><td align="center">Solution</td></tr>
</table>

(1) In the linear equation, solve for one variable in terms of the other. Here, solve for y in terms of x.

$$2x - y = 5$$
$$-y = -2x + 5$$
$$y = 2x - 5$$

(2) Substitute this expression for y in the quadratic equation.

$$x^2 + y^2 = 25$$
$$x^2 + (2x - 5)^2 = 25$$

(3) Simplify. Then transform the resulting quadratic equation to standard form.

$$x^2 + 4x^2 - 20x + 25 = 25$$
$$5x^2 - 20x + 25 = 25$$
$$5x^2 - 20x = 0$$

(4) Solve the quadratic equation. Here, factor to find two values for x.

$$5x(x - 4) = 0$$
$$5x = 0 \mid x - 4 = 0$$
$$x = 0 \mid x = 4$$

(5) Substitute each value of x in $y = 2x - 5$, a form of the linear equation of the system, to find the corresponding value of y.

In $y = 2x - 5$, substitute 0 and 4 for x.

If $x = 0$, If $x = 4$,
$y = 2(0) - 5 \mid y = 2(4) - 5$
$y = 0 - 5 \mid y = 8 - 5$
$y = -5 \mid y = 3$

(6) Write the solution as coordinates.

$(x, y) = (0, -5) \quad (x, y) = (4, 3)$

(7) Four checks are required. These are left to the student.

Answer: $\{(0, -5), (4, 3)\}$

EXERCISES

In 1–6, solve each system of equations by using an algebraic method that seems convenient. Check.

1. $y = 3x$
$ y - x = 18$

2. $3a - b = 13$
$ 2a + 3b = 16$

3. $-2c = d$
$ 6c + 5d = -12$

4. $a - \frac{2}{3}b = 4$
$ \frac{3}{5}a + b = 15$

5. $3(y - 6) = 2x$
$ 3x + 5y = 11$

6. $x + y = 300$
$ .25x + .75y = 195$

In 7–36, solve the system of equations algebraically, and check all solutions.

7. $y = x^2 - 2x$
$y = x$

8. $y = x^2 + 5$
$y = x + 5$

9. $y = x^2 - 4x + 3$
$y = x - 1$

10. $y = x^2 + 2x + 1$
$y = x + 3$

11. $x^2 + y = 9$
$y = x + 9$

12. $x^2 + y = 2$
$y = -x$

13. $x^2 + 2y = 5$
$y = x + 1$

14. $x^2 - y = 5$
$y = 3x - 1$

15. $y = x^2 - 4x + 9$
$y - 1 = 2x$

16. $x^2 - 2y = 11$
$y = x - 4$

17. $y = x^2 - x$
$x + y = 4$

18. $y = 2x^2 + 2$
$y = 5x$

19. $y = 2x^2 - 6x + 5$
$y = x + 2$

20. $y = 2x^2 + 2x + 3$
$y - x = 3$

21. $y = 3x^2 - 8x + 5$
$x + y = 3$

22. $y = x^2 + 4x$
$y = \frac{1}{2}x + 2$

23. $y = x^2 + 3x + 1$
$y = \frac{1}{3}x + 2$

24. $y = x^2 - 6x + 8$
$y = -\frac{1}{2}x + 2$

25. $y = x^2 - 4x + 4$
$3y = x$

26. $y = x^2 - 2x - 1$
$x + 2y = 0$

27. $y = x^2 + 4x + 5$
$2x + 3y = 0$

28. $xy = 6$
$y = x - 1$

29. $xy = 9$
$x = y$

30. $xy = -1$
$x + y = 0$

31. $x^2 + y^2 = 25$
$x = 2y - 5$

32. $x^2 + y^2 = 100$
$y = x + 2$

33. $x^2 + y^2 = 50$
$x = y$

34. $x^2 + y^2 = 40$
$y = 3x$

35. $x^2 + y^2 = 26$
$x = 5y$

36. $x^2 + y^2 = 2$
$y = x - 2$

37. The graphs of $y = x^2 - x$ and $y = x - 1$ are shown.
a. Name the coordinates of the point of intersection.
b. Solve the system algebraically:
$$\begin{cases} y = x^2 - x \\ y = x - 1 \end{cases}$$
c. Explain why the solution set in part **b** consists of only one ordered pair of values for x and y.

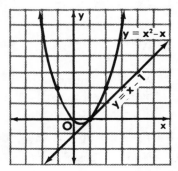

38. The graphs of $y = x^2 - x$ and $y = x - 2$ are shown.

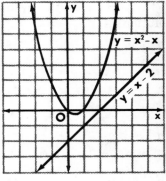

   a. Explain why the solution set for the indicated system of equations will be the empty set.

   b. Try to solve the system algebraically:
$$\begin{cases} y = x^2 - x \\ y = x - 2 \end{cases}$$

   (*Hint.* After obtaining a quadratic equation in terms of one variable only, use the quadratic formula.)
   Why are there no real roots?

In 39–47, each system of equations has a solution set that is either empty or contains at most one ordered pair. Solve the system algebraically.

39. $y = x^2 + 1$
      $y = x - 3$

40. $y = x^2 + 1$
      $y = 2x$

41. $y = -x^2 + 2x + 1$
      $y = 3$

42. $xy = 6$
      $x + y = 0$

43. $xy = -4$
      $x - y = 2$

44. $xy = -1$
      $x - y = 2$

45. $x^2 + y^2 = 2$
      $y = x + 3$

46. $x^2 + y^2 = 8$
      $y = x - 4$

47. $x^2 + y^2 = 7$
      $y = x - 4$

10-13   REVIEW EXERCISES

In 1–6, solve the equation and check.

1. $x^2 - 9x + 14 = 0$

2. $3x^2 + x = 0$

3. $2x^2 - 5x - 3 = 0$

4. $x(x + 4) = -4$

5. $\dfrac{x}{2} = \dfrac{x + 5}{x + 2}$

6. $x^2 - 6x + 7 = 0$

7. Write an equation of the form $ax^2 + bx + c = 0$ for which the solution set is $\{6, -3\}$.

8. If -2 is a root of the equation $x^2 - 3x + k = 0$, find the value of k.

9. If -2 is a root of the equation $x^2 - 3x + k = 0$, find the second root.

10. Find the positive root of $2x^2 = x + 6$.

In 11–18, select the numeral preceding the expression that best answers the question or completes the statement.

11. The solution set of $(2x + 10)(3x - 4) = 0$ is

(1) $\left\{-5, \dfrac{4}{3}\right\}$ (2) $\left\{5, \dfrac{-4}{3}\right\}$ (3) $\left\{-10, \dfrac{4}{3}\right\}$ (4) $\left\{10, \dfrac{-4}{3}\right\}$

12. An equation for the axis of symmetry of the graph of the parabola $y = 2x^2 - 8x + 10$ is   (1) $x = 2$ (2) $x = -2$ (3) $x = 4$ (4) $y = 4$.

13. Which quadratic equation has roots of -10 and 4?
(1) $x^2 - 6x - 40 = 0$ (2) $x^2 + 6x - 40 = 0$
(3) $x^2 + 6x + 40 = 0$ (4) $x^2 - 6x + 40 = 0$

14. If one root of $3x^2 - 10x + 8 = 0$ is 2, the other root is
(1) $\frac{3}{4}$ (2) $\frac{4}{3}$ (3) $\frac{8}{3}$ (4) $\frac{3}{8}$

15. The roots of $2x^2 + 3x - 7 = 0$ are

(1) $\dfrac{-3 \pm \sqrt{65}}{2}$ (2) $\dfrac{3 \pm \sqrt{65}}{2}$ (3) $\dfrac{-3 \pm \sqrt{65}}{4}$ (4) $\dfrac{3 \pm \sqrt{65}}{4}$

16. Which equation has as its solution $4 \pm \sqrt{15}$?
(1) $x^2 - 8x + 1 = 0$ (2) $x^2 + 8x + 1 = 0$
(3) $x^2 - 8x - 1 = 0$ (4) $x^2 + 8x - 1 = 0$

17. Which is an equation of the accompanying graph?
(1) $y = -x^2 + 2x + 3$ (2) $y = -x^2 - 2x + 3$
(3) $y = x^2 + 2x + 3$ (4) $y = x^2 - 2x + 3$

18. The coordinates of the turning point in the graph at the right are
(1) $(1, 4)$ (2) $(-1, 4)$
(3) $(4, -1)$ (4) $(-3, 1)$

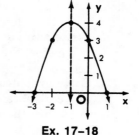

Ex. 17–18

19. a. Find in simplest radical form the roots of $x^2 - 6x + 6 = 0$.
b. Draw the graph of $y = x^2 - 6x + 6$, using all integral values of x from $x = 0$ to $x = 6$.
c. What are the coordinates of the turning point?

20. a. Draw the graph of $y = x^2 - 2x - 3$ for the interval $-2 \le x \le 4$.
b. Write an equation for the axis of symmetry of the graph.
c. What are the roots of $x^2 - 2x - 3 = 0$?

21. a. Draw a graph of $y = -x^2 + 4x - 1$ for an appropriate interval.
b. On the same set of axes, draw the graph of $x + y = 3$.
c. Determine the coordinates of the points of intersection of the graphs in parts **a** and **b**, and check.

22. Solve algebraically and check:

    a. $\begin{cases} y = x - 2 \\ 3x - y = 16 \end{cases}$ **b.** $\begin{cases} y = 3x \\ \frac{1}{3}x + \frac{1}{2}y = 11 \end{cases}$

23. Solve algebraically and check:

    a. $\begin{cases} y = 2x^2 \\ y = x + 6 \end{cases}$ **b.** $\begin{cases} x^2 + y^2 = 16 \\ y = x \end{cases}$

24. In a rectangle, the width is 4 cm and the diagonal is 6 cm.
    a. Write and solve an equation to find the length of the rectangle.
    b. Find the area of the rectangle.

25. **a.** If the length of a side of a square is represented by $x + 6$, express its area in terms of x.
    b. If the dimensions of a rectangle are represented by $3x + 2$ and $x - 2$, express its area in terms of x.
    c. If the area of the square is equal to the area of the rectangle, find the value of x and the dimensions of each quadrilateral.

26. In $\triangle ABC$, D is a point on $\overline{AC}$, E is a point on $\overline{BC}$, and $\overline{DE} \parallel \overline{AB}$. If $CE = x$, $EB = 2$, $DE = x + 4$, and $AB = 2x - 1$, find CE.

27. In right $\triangle ABC$, altitude $\overline{CD}$ is drawn to hypotenuse $\overline{AB}$. If $AD = 3$, $CD = x$, and $DB = 2x + 9$, find CD.

28. The area of a rectangle is 24 cm^2 and its perimeter is 22 cm. Let x represent the length and y represent the width of the rectangle.
    a. Write two equations, one involving the area and the other the perimeter, that can be used to find the length and width of the rectangle.
    b. Solve graphically the system of equations in part **a**.
    c. Solve algebraically the system of equations in part **a**.
    d. What are the dimensions of the rectangle?

Chapter 11

Locus
With and Without
Coordinate Geometry

11-1 THE MEANING OF LOCUS

If a point is moving so that it is always satisfying a given condition, its path is called a *locus*, which is the Latin word for *place*. The plural of *locus* is *loci* (pronounced "LOW sigh").

For example, think of a point moving in a plane so that it is always one centimeter from a given point O in the plane. If $OA = 1$ centimeter and $OB = 1$ centimeter, the point will move through positions A and B. Since $OC \neq 1$ centimeter and $OD \neq 1$ centimeter, however, the point will *not* move through positions C and D.

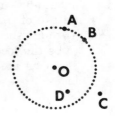

The path, or locus, is a circle whose center is O and whose radius is one centimeter in length. This circle is shown as a smooth or continuous curve, indicating that the locus consists of an infinite set of points.

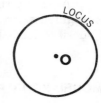

● **Definition.** A *locus* is the set of all points, and only those points, that satisfy a given condition or set of conditions.

This definition of locus contains two important phrases: "all points" and "only those points." Look at the example given above to understand what these phrases mean. These meanings are related to each other in a logical sense as follows:

1. All points ($p \rightarrow q$): If a point is on the locus, then the point satisfies the given conditions. Here, points on the circle, such as A and B, satisfy the given conditions.

485

2. Only those points ($\sim p \rightarrow \sim q$): If a point is not on the locus, then the point does not satisfy the given conditions. Here, points that are *not* on the circle, such as C and D, do *not* satisfy the given conditions.

Recall that the statement ($\sim p \rightarrow \sim q$) is the inverse of the statement ($p \rightarrow q$). Later in this chapter, when we prove that a locus is correct, it will be necessary to prove that both statements are true: the conditional and its inverse. For now, let us simply try to discover a locus.

11-2   DISCOVERING A LOCUS

PROCEDURE.   To discover a probable locus:

1. Make a diagram that contains the fixed lines or points that are given.
2. Decide what condition must be satisfied.
3. Locate a point that satisfies the given condition. Then, locate several other points that satisfy the given condition. These should be sufficiently close together to develop the shape or the nature of the locus.
4. Through these points, draw a line, or smooth curve, that appears to be the locus.
5. Describe in words the geometric figure that appears to be the locus.

Note. In this chapter, we will assume that all given points, segments, rays, lines, and circles lie in the same plane and that the desired locus lies in that plane also.

MODEL PROBLEMS ────────────────────────────────

1. What is the probable locus of points equidistant from the endpoints of a given line segment?

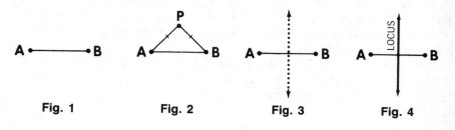

Fig. 1   Fig. 2   Fig. 3   Fig. 4

Solution:

(1) $\overline{AB}$ is the given line segment (Fig. 1).
(2) The condition to be satisfied is that P is to be equidistant from A and B, or $PA = PB$ (Fig. 2).
(3) Locate several points equidistant from A and B (Fig. 3).
(4) Through these points, draw the straight line that appears to be the locus (Fig. 4).
(5) The probable locus is a straight line that is the perpendicular bisector of the given line segment.

2. What is the probable locus of points in the interior of an angle equidistant from the rays that form the sides of the given angle?

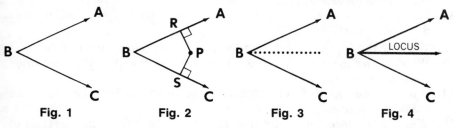

| Fig. 1 | Fig. 2 | Fig. 3 | Fig. 4 |

Solution:

(1) $\angle ABC$ is the given angle (Fig. 1).
(2) The condition to be satisfied is that P is to be equidistant from $\overrightarrow{BA}$ and $\overrightarrow{BC}$, the rays that are the sides of $\angle ABC$. Thus, for any point P, $PR = PS$ where $\overline{PR} \perp \overrightarrow{BA}$ and $\overline{PS} \perp \overrightarrow{BC}$ (Fig. 2).
(3) Locate several points equidistant from $\overrightarrow{BA}$ and $\overrightarrow{BC}$ (Fig. 3).
(4) Through these points, draw the ray that appears to be the locus (Fig. 4).
(5) The probable locus is a ray that is the bisector of $\angle ABC$.

EXERCISES

In each of the following, use the procedure illustrated in the preceding model problems to discover the probable locus.

1. What is the locus of the outer end of the hour hand of a clock during a 12-hour period?
2. What is the locus of the center of a train wheel that is moving along a straight, level track?
3. What is the locus of a car that is being driven down a street equidistant from the two opposite parallel curbs?
4. A dog is tied to a stake by a rope 6 meters long. Discover the boundary of the surface over which he may roam.

5. A boy walks through an open field that is bounded on two sides by straight intersecting roads. He walks so that he is always equidistant from the two intersecting roads. Determine his path.

6. There are two floats on a lake. A girl swims so that she is always equidistant from both floats. Determine her path.

7. A dime is rolled along a horizontal line so that the dime always touches the line. What is the locus of the center of the dime?

8. What is the locus of a point on a steering wheel of a car that makes a complete revolution? Note that the center of the wheel remains in a fixed position.

9. What is the locus of all points that are 10 cm from a given point?

10. What is the locus of all points equidistant from two points A and B that are 8 meters apart?

11. What is the locus of all points equidistant from two parallel lines 8 meters apart?

12. What is the locus of all points 4 inches away from a given line, $\overleftrightarrow{AB}$?

13. What is the locus of all points 3 in. from each of two parallel lines that are 6 in. apart?

14. What is the locus of points that are equidistant from two opposite sides of a square?

15. What is the locus of points that are equidistant from the vertices of two opposite angles of a square?

16. What is the locus of the center of a penny that is rolling around a quarter if the edges of the two coins are always touching each other?

17. What is the locus of points in the interior of a circle whose radius measures 3 inches if the points are 2 inches from the circle?

18. What is the locus of points in the exterior of a circle whose radius measures 3 inches if the points are 2 inches from the circle?

19. What is the locus of points 2 inches from a circle whose radius measures 3 inches?

20. Circle O has a radius of length r, and it is given that $r > m$.
    a. What is the locus of points in the exterior of circle O and at a distance m from the circle?
    b. What is the locus of points in the interior of circle O and at a distance m from the circle?
    c. What is the locus of points at a distance m from circle O?

21. Concentric circles have the same center. What is the locus of points equidistant from two concentric circles whose radii measure 10 cm and 18 cm?

22. A series of isosceles triangles are drawn, each of which has a fixed segment, $\overline{AB}$, as its base. What is the locus of the vertices of the vertex angles of all such isosceles triangles?

23. $\triangle ABC$ is drawn with a fixed base, $\overline{AB}$, and an altitude whose measure is 3 ft. What is the locus of points that can indicate vertex C in all such triangles?

11-3   FUNDAMENTAL LOCUS WITHOUT COORDINATES

There are five fundamental loci, each based upon a different set of conditions.

Conditions	Locus
Given A and B. Find points equidistant from these two fixed points.	The locus of points is the perpendicular bisector, $\overleftrightarrow{CD}$, of the segment, $\overline{AB}$, joining the two points.
Given $\overleftrightarrow{AB}$ intersecting $\overleftrightarrow{CD}$. Find points equidistant from these two intersecting lines.	The locus of points is a pair of lines, $\overleftrightarrow{RS}$ and $\overleftrightarrow{LM}$, which bisect the angles formed by the intersecting lines.
Given $\overleftrightarrow{AB} \parallel \overleftrightarrow{CD}$. Find points equidistant from these two parallel lines.	The locus of points is a third line, $\overleftrightarrow{EF}$, parallel to the two lines and midway between them.

Conditions	Locus
Given $\overleftrightarrow{AB}$ and a distance d. Find points that are at the distance d from the line.	The locus of points is a pair of lines, $\overleftrightarrow{CD}$ and $\overleftrightarrow{EF}$, each parallel to the given line, $\overleftrightarrow{AB}$, and at a distance d from the line.
Given point A and distance d. Find points that are at the distance d from the fixed point A.	The locus of points is a circle whose center is point A and the length of whose radius is the distance d.

Locus Theorems

Four of these five fundamental loci can be proved. There are two acceptable plans for the proof of a locus theorem.

Plan 1 for a Locus Proof: To prove a locus theorem, it is necessary to prove both the *conditional* form of the statement of the theorem and the *inverse* of the statement:

    A. *Conditional* ($p \rightarrow q$): If a point is on the locus, then the point satisfies the given conditions.

    B. *Inverse* ($\sim p \rightarrow \sim q$): If a point is *not* on the locus, then the point does *not* satisfy the given conditions.

Plan 2 for a Locus Proof: Recall that for any conditional statement ($p \rightarrow q$), its *inverse* ($\sim p \rightarrow \sim q$) and its *converse* ($q \rightarrow p$) are *logically equivalent* statements. Since $(q \to p)$ is the contrapositive form of $(\sim p \to \sim q)$, by the Law of the Contrapositive, $(q \to p)$ and $(\sim p \to \sim q)$ are equivalent. Therefore, it is also acceptable to prove a locus theorem by proving both the *conditional* form of the statement of the theorem and the *converse* of the statement:

A. *Conditional* $(p \to q)$: If a point is on the locus, then the point satisfies the given conditions.

B. *Converse* $(q \to p)$: If a point satisfies the given conditions, then
the point is on the locus.

Let us now prove the first of the fundamental locus theorems.

● **THEOREM 71. The locus of points equidistant from two fixed points (that is, the endpoints of a line segment) is the perpendicular bisector of the line segment joining the two points.**

The locus of points equidistant from the fixed points A and B is $\overleftrightarrow{CD}$, the perpendicular bisector of $\overline{AB}$. The proof follows.

Part *A* (the conditional statement, $p \to q$): If a point is on the perpendicular bisector of a line segment joining two fixed points, then the point is equidistant from the endpoints of the line segment.

Given: $\overleftrightarrow{CD}$ is the $\perp$ bisector of $\overline{AB}$.
  P is any point on $\overleftrightarrow{CD}$.

Prove: $PA = PB$.

Plan: Any point on the perpendicular bisector of a
line segment is equidistant from the endpoints of
the line segment.

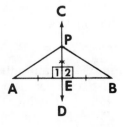

Part *B* (the converse statement, $q \to p$): If a point is equidistant from the endpoints of a line segment, the point is on the perpendicular bisector of the line segment.

Given: $PA = PB$.

Prove: P is on the $\perp$ bisector of $\overline{AB}$.

Plan: Let M be the midpoint of $\overline{AB}$. Prove that
$\overleftrightarrow{PM}$ is the perpendicular bisector of $\overline{AB}$.

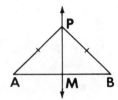

Statements	*Reasons*
1. $PA = PB$ or $\overline{PA} \cong \overline{PB}$. (s. $\cong$ s.)	1. Given.
2. Let M be the midpoint of $\overline{AB}$.	2. Every line segment has a midpoint.
3. Draw $\overleftrightarrow{PM}$.	3. Two points determine a line.
4. $\overline{AM} \cong \overline{MB}$. (s. $\cong$ s.)	4. Definition of midpoint.
5. $\overline{PM} \cong \overline{PM}$. (s. $\cong$ s.)	5. Reflexive Property of Congruence.
6. $\triangle APM \cong \triangle BPM$.	6. s.s.s. $\cong$ s.s.s.
7. $\angle PMA \cong \angle PMB$.	7. Corresponding parts of congruent triangles are congruent.
8. $\overleftrightarrow{PM} \perp \overleftrightarrow{AB}$.	8. If two intersecting lines form congruent adjacent angles, the lines are perpendicular.
9. $\overleftrightarrow{PM}$ is the $\perp$ bisector of $\overline{AB}$.	9. Definition of $\perp$ bisector.

Note. There is an alternate proof for Part *B* (the inverse statement, $\sim p \rightarrow \sim q$): If a point is not on the perpendicular bisector of a line segment, then it is not equidistant from the endpoints of the line segment.

Given: $\overleftrightarrow{CD}$ is the $\perp$ bisector of $\overline{AB}$. Point P does *not* lie on $\overleftrightarrow{CD}$.

Prove: $PA \neq PB$.

Plan: Use an indirect method of proof. Assume the negation of the conclusion, that is, assume $PA = PB$, which leads to a contradiction. Since $PA = PB$ is a false assumption, then $PA \neq PB$ must be true.

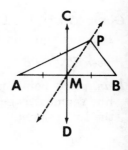

Plans for the proofs of the remaining locus theorems follow. Conditional and converse statements are proved directly, while inverse statements require an indirect proof.

KEEP IN MIND

To prove a locus theorem, either:

1. Prove the conditional ($p \rightarrow q$) and its inverse ($\sim p \rightarrow \sim q$), *or*
2. Prove the conditional ($p \rightarrow q$) and its converse ($q \rightarrow p$).

● **THEOREM 72.** **The locus of points equidistant from two inter-secting lines is the pair of lines that bisect the angles formed by the two intersecting lines.**

If $\overleftrightarrow{AB}$ and $\overleftrightarrow{CD}$ are two intersecting lines, then the locus of points equidistant from these lines is the pair of lines, $\overleftrightarrow{RS}$ and $\overleftrightarrow{LM}$, that bisect the angles formed by $\overleftrightarrow{AB}$ and $\overleftrightarrow{CD}$.

Proof: Part A (Conditional). If P is a point on a bisector of an angle formed by $\overleftrightarrow{AB}$ and $\overleftrightarrow{CD}$, then P is equidistant from $\overleftrightarrow{AB}$ and $\overleftrightarrow{CD}$.

Given: $\overrightarrow{ER}$ is the bisector of $\angle CEB$, P is any point on $\overrightarrow{ER}$, $\overline{PQ} \perp \overleftrightarrow{EB}$, and $\overline{PT} \perp \overleftrightarrow{EC}$.

Prove: $PQ = PT$.

Plan: Prove $\triangle QEP$ congruent to $\triangle TEP$ by a.a.s. $\cong$ a.a.s. Then, by corresponding parts of congruent triangles, $\overline{PQ} \cong \overline{PT}$.

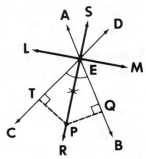

Proof: Part B (Converse). If P is a point equidistant from two inter-secting lines, $\overleftrightarrow{AB}$ and $\overleftrightarrow{CD}$, then P is a point on the bisector of an angle formed by $\overleftrightarrow{AB}$ and $\overleftrightarrow{CD}$.

Given: $\angle CEB$, $\overline{PQ} \cong \overline{PT}$, $\overline{PQ} \perp \overleftrightarrow{EB}$, and $\overline{PT} \perp \overleftrightarrow{EC}$. (See figure above.)

Prove: $\overleftrightarrow{EP}$ is the bisector of $\angle CEB$.

Plan: Prove rt. $\triangle EPQ \cong$ rt. $\triangle EPT$ by hy. leg $\cong$ hy. leg. Then, $\angle PEQ \cong \angle PET$ by corresponding parts of congruent triangles, lead-ing to $\overleftrightarrow{EP}$ as the angle bisector.

● **THEOREM 73.** **The locus of points equidistant from two parallel lines is a third line parallel to the two lines and midway between them.**

Proof: Part A (Conditional).

Given: $\overleftrightarrow{AB} \parallel \overleftrightarrow{CD} \parallel \overleftrightarrow{EF}$, $\overline{CEA} \perp \overleftrightarrow{AB}$, $\overline{CEA} \perp \overleftrightarrow{CD}$, and $EA = EC$.

Prove: $FB = FD$.

Plan: Draw $\overleftrightarrow{DFB} \perp \overleftrightarrow{AB}$. Prove that quadrilaterals $FBAE$ and $FDCE$ are parallelograms. Since $EA = FB$ and $EC = FD$, then $FB = FD$.

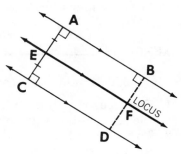

Proof: Part *B* (Converse).

Given: $\overleftrightarrow{AB} \parallel \overleftrightarrow{CD}$, $EA = EC$, $\overline{CEA} \perp \overleftrightarrow{AB}$, $\overline{CEA} \perp \overleftrightarrow{CD}$, $FB = FD$, $\overline{DFB} \perp \overleftrightarrow{AB}$, and $\overline{DFB} \perp \overleftrightarrow{CD}$.

Prove: $\overleftrightarrow{EF} \parallel \overleftrightarrow{AB}$ and $\overleftrightarrow{EF} \parallel \overleftrightarrow{CD}$.

Plan: Prove that certain quadrilaterals are parallelograms.

● **THEOREM 74.** **The locus of points at a given distance from a given line is a pair of lines, each parallel to the given line and at the given distance from it.**

Proof: Part *A* (Conditional).

Given: $\overleftrightarrow{CD} \parallel \overleftrightarrow{AB}$, $\overleftrightarrow{EF} \parallel \overleftrightarrow{AB}$, $\overline{DB} \perp \overleftrightarrow{AB}$, $\overline{CA} \perp \overleftrightarrow{AB}$, and $DB = d$.

Prove: $CA = d$.

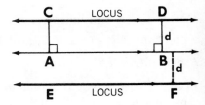

Plan: Show $\overleftrightarrow{CA} \parallel \overleftrightarrow{DB}$. Then quadrilateral *ABDC* is a parallelogram. Since $DB = CA$ and $DB = d$, $CA = d$.

Proof: Part *B* (Converse).

Given: $\overleftrightarrow{AB}$, $\overline{DB} \perp \overleftrightarrow{AB}$, $\overline{CA} \perp \overleftrightarrow{AB}$, $DB = d$, and $CA = d$.

Prove: $\overleftrightarrow{CD} \parallel \overleftrightarrow{AB}$.

Plan: Prove that quadrilateral *ABDC* is a parallelogram since it contains one pair of sides, $\overline{CA}$ and $\overline{DB}$, that are both parallel and congruent. Thus, $\overleftrightarrow{CD} \parallel \overleftrightarrow{AB}$. Similarly, it can be shown that $\overleftrightarrow{EF} \parallel \overleftrightarrow{AB}$.

The last of the five fundamental locus theorems is generally considered to be an alternate form of the definition of a circle rather than a statement to be proved. Thus:

● **Definition.** The locus of points at a given distance from a given point is a *circle* whose center is the given point and the length of whose radius is the given distance.

EXERCISES

In 1–6, determine the required locus.

1. The locus of points equidistant from the endpoints of a segment is the _____ of the segment.

2. The locus of points in the interior of an angle that are equidistant from the sides of the angle is the _____ of that angle.

3. If two lines intersect, on how many lines do points equidistant from the intersecting lines lie?
4. If two lines are parallel, on how many lines do points equidistant from the parallel lines lie?
5. The locus of the midpoints of all radii of a given circle is _____.
6. Circle O has a radius whose length is r. What is the locus of points outside circle O and at a distance k from the circle?

In 7–14, select the numeral preceding the correct answer.

7. The locus of points at a given distance from a line is (1) a circle (2) one line (3) two parallel lines (4) two intersecting lines
8. The locus of points equidistant from two fixed points is (1) one circle (2) one line (3) two circles (4) two lines
9. The locus of points equidistant from the four vertices of a given rectangle is (1) one line (2) two lines (3) one point (4) a circle
10. A series of circles with congruent radii pass through a given point. The locus of the centers of all such circles is (1) a point (2) a circle (3) a line (4) a quadrilateral
11. $ABCD$ is a quadrilateral. The locus of points equidistant from $\overleftrightarrow{AB}$ and $\overleftrightarrow{AD}$ must include point C if $ABCD$ is a (1) trapezoid (2) rectangle (3) parallelogram (4) rhombus
12. What is the locus of points in the interior of square $ABCD$ and equidistant from sides $\overline{AB}$ and $\overline{BC}$? (1) point D (2) diagonal $\overline{BD}$ (3) diagonal $\overline{AC}$ (4) sides $\overline{AD}$ and $\overline{DC}$
13. What is the locus of points on or in the interior of square $ABCD$ and equidistant from vertices B and D? (1) $\overline{AC}$ (2) $\overline{BD}$ (3) $\overline{AD}$ (4) $\overline{DC}$
14. If a side of square $ABCD$ has length 10 cm, which points are 10 cm from vertex A? (1) B, C (2) C, D (3) B, D (4) B, C, D

15. In $\triangle DEF$, points D and F are fixed with $DF = 20$ mm. *Describe* fully the locus of points E if:
   a. The area of $\triangle DEF$ is 60 mm^2.
   b. $\triangle DEF$ is isosceles with $\overline{DE} \cong \overline{EF}$. **c.** $\triangle DEF$ is equilateral.

11-4 LOCUS IN COORDINATE GEOMETRY

A locus is the set of all points, and only those points, that satisfy a given set of conditions. When the coordinates of all points on a locus determined by a given set of conditions satisfy an equation, and when all points not on the locus do not satisfy the equation, such an equation is called the ***equation of the locus***.

In the remaining sections of this chapter, you will study equations related to loci. To find these equations, we will use coordinate geometry.

EXAMPLE 1. Every point whose abscissa is 3 lies on a line parallel to the y-axis and 3 units to the right of that axis. Every point whose abscissa is *not* 3, such as $P(-1, 3)$, does *not* lie on that line. Therefore, the locus of points whose abscissas are 3 is the line whose equation is $x = 3$.

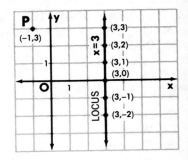

Using this example, we now generalize:

● **The locus of points whose abscissas are the constant a is the line that is parallel to the y-axis and whose equation is $x = a$.**

EXAMPLE 2. Every point whose ordinate is -2 lies on a line parallel to the x-axis and 2 units below that axis. Every point whose ordinate is *not* -2, such as $P(-2, 3)$, does *not* lie on that line. Therefore, the locus of points whose ordinates are -2 is the line whose equation is $y = -2$.

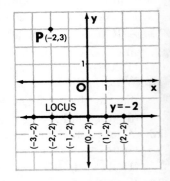

Using this example, we now generalize:

● **The locus of points whose ordinates are the constant b is the line that is parallel to the x-axis and whose equation is $y = b$.**

EXAMPLE 3. Every point on the line shown has its ordinate equal to the sum of 3 times its abscissa and -1. Every point *not* on the line, such as $P(-3, 2)$, does *not* satisfy these conditions. Therefore, the locus of points described is a line whose slope is 3 and whose y-intercept is -1. The equation of this line is $y = 3x - 1$.

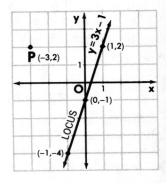

Using this example, we now generalize:

● **The locus of points in which the ordinate of each point is the sum of *m* times its abscissa and the constant *b* is a line whose slope is *m*, whose *y*-intercept is *b*, and whose equation is *y* = *mx* + *b*.**

MODEL PROBLEM

Write an equation of the locus of points in which the ordinate of each point is 3 more than 4 times the abscissa of that point.

Solution:

Replace *ordinate* by *y*, and *abscissa* by *x*.
Thus, *y* is 3 more than 4 times *x*, or $y = 4x + 3$.

Answer: $y = 4x + 3$.

EXERCISES

In 1–16: **a.** Write an equation of the locus of points that satisfy the given conditions. **b.** Graph the locus of points described.

Points for which the:

1. ordinates are 8.
2. abscissas are −5.
3. abscissas are 0.
4. ordinates are −4.
5. ordinate is equal to its abscissa.
6. ordinate is 2 times its abscissa.
7. ordinate is 2 more than its abscissa.
8. ordinate is 5 less than its abscissa.
9. ordinate is $\frac{3}{4}$ of its abscissa.
10. ordinate is 3 less than twice its abscissa.
11. ordinate is 4 more than 3 times its abscissa.
12. abscissa and ordinate have a sum of 8.
13. coordinates have a sum of −3.
14. abscissa decreased by its ordinate is 4.
15. abscissa is 4 less than one-third its ordinate.
16. ordinate is 3 more than one-half its abscissa.

17. Write an equation of the locus of all points:
   a. 2 units from the *x*-axis and above it.
   b. 5 units from the *y*-axis and to the right of it.
   c. 4 units from the *y*-axis and to the left of it.

    d. 3 units from the x-axis and below it.

    e. equidistant from the x-axis and y-axis and whose coordinates have the same sign.

    f. equidistant from the x-axis and y-axis and whose coordinates have opposite signs.

18. Write an equation of the line passing through the point (3, 4) and perpendicular to the x-axis.

19. Write an equation of the line passing through the point $(-1, 3)$ and parallel to the y-axis.

20. Write an equation of the line passing through the point (5, 2) and perpendicular to the y-axis.

21. Write an equation of the line passing through the point $(-2, -4)$ and parallel to the x-axis.

22. Determine whether the point $(8, -2)$ is on the locus whose equation is given.

    a. $x + y = 6$ **b.** $y = 10 - x$ **c.** $x = 8$

    d. $x - y = 10$ **e.** $y = \frac{1}{4}x$ **f.** $x + 4y = 0$

23. Find the value of k so that the graph of the given equation will pass through the point (2, 3).

    a. $x + y = k$ **b.** $2x - y = k$ **c.** $y = 3x + k$

    d. $y = k$ **e.** $x = 2y + k$ **f.** $3x - 2y = k$

In 24–28, select the numeral preceding the correct answer.

24. A point is on the locus whose equation is $x - y = 3$. If the ordinate of the point is 2, its abscissa is   (1) 1 (2) -1 (3) 5 (4) -5

25. A point is on the locus whose equation is $3x - y = 12$. If the abscissa of the point is 3, its ordinate is   (1) 5 (2) -3 (3) 3 (4) 4

26. An equation that represents the locus of all points 9 units to the left of the y-axis is   (1) $x = 9$ (2) $x = -9$ (3) $y = 9$ (4) $y = -9$

27. For $k > 0$, an equation that represents the locus of all points k units below the x-axis is

  (1) $x = k$ (2) $x = -k$ (3) $y = k$ (4) $y = -k$

28. The equation $y = -x$ describes the locus of points equidistant from the x-axis and the y-axis in quadrants

  (1) I and IV (2) II and III (3) I and III (4) II and IV

11-5 LOCUS, COORDINATES, FIXED POINTS, AND THE CIRCLE

In this section, we will use coordinate geometry to find the equations of loci related to fixed points.

One Fixed Point: The Circle

EXAMPLE 1. The origin $O(0, 0)$ is a fixed point. The locus of points 5 units from point O is a circle with a center at O and a radius whose length is 5. Let $P(x, y)$ be any point on the circle. Since the *distance* between the fixed point O and any point P on the circle is 5, let us apply these values to the *distance formula*.

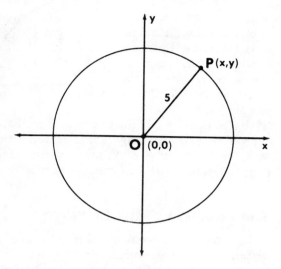

Let $P(x, y) = (x_1, y_1)$.
Let $O(0, 0) = (x_2, y_2)$.
Let distance $d = 5$.

The distance formula is:

$$\sqrt{(x_1 - x_2)^2 + (y_1 - y_2)^2} = d$$

By substitution:

$$\sqrt{(x - 0)^2 + (y - 0)^2} = 5$$

$$\sqrt{x^2 + y^2} = 5$$

Square both sides:

$$(\sqrt{x^2 + y^2})^2 = (5)^2$$

The equation of the circle is:

$$x^2 + y^2 = 25$$

The circle whose equation is $x^2 + y^2 = 25$, that is, the locus of points 5 units from the origin $O(0, 0)$, is drawn on graph paper. Note that the circle passes through the axes at $(5, 0)$, $(0, 5)$, $(-5, 0)$, and $(0, -5)$. The coordinates of each of these points, when substituted into the equation $x^2 + y^2 = 25$, will produce a true statement.

The circle also passes through the points in which one of the x- or y-coordinates is $+3$ or -3, and the remaining coordinate is $+4$

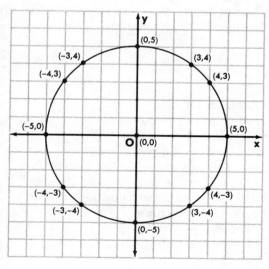

or −4. Imagine that a radius whose length is 5 is drawn from the origin to one of these points on the circle, that a perpendicular is drawn from the point to the x-axis, and that the triangle is completed. Each of these

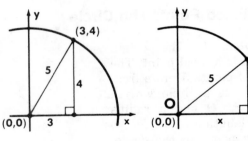

triangles is a 3-4-5 right triangle. Recall that the distance formula was derived from the Pythagorean Theorem; thus, $3^2 + 4^2 = 5^2$. In the same way, for any point $P(x, y)$ that is on the circle but not on one of the axes, a right triangle can be formed where $x^2 + y^2 = 5^2$, or $x^2 + y^2 = 25$.

The Equation of the Locus

In general, the locus of points at a given distance r from the origin (0, 0) is a circle whose center is (0, 0) and whose radius has a length of r. Thus:

● **THEOREM 75. The equation of a circle whose center is the origin (0, 0) and whose radius has a length of r is the equation $x^2 + y^2 = r^2$.**

To prove this theorem, use the distance formula with the fixed point $O(0, 0)$, the point $P(x, y)$ on the locus, and the distance r.

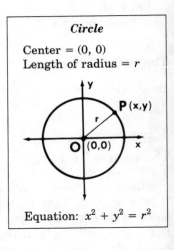

Circle

Center = (0, 0)
Length of radius = r

Equation: $x^2 + y^2 = r^2$

EXAMPLE 2. The point $A(4, 2)$ is a fixed point. The locus of points 3 units from point A is a circle with a center at A and a radius of length 3. Let $P(x, y)$ be any point on the circle. Let us again make use of the distance formula to find the equation of this circle. Here, distance $d = 3$.

Let $P(x, y) = (x_1, y_1)$.
Let $A(4, 2) = (x_2, y_2)$.

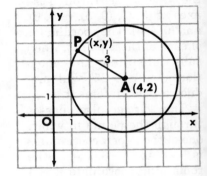

The distance formula is:	$\sqrt{(x_1 - x_2)^2 + (y_1 - y_2)^2} = d$
By substitution:	$\sqrt{(x - 4)^2 + (y - 2)^2} = 3$
Square both sides:	$[\sqrt{(x - 4)^2 + (y - 2)^2}]^2 = (3)^2$
The equation of the circle is:	$(x - 4)^2 + (y - 2)^2 = 9$

In general, the locus of points at a given distance r from any fixed point, $A(a, b)$, is a circle whose center is (a, b) and whose radius has length r. Thus:

● **THEOREM 76. The equation of a circle whose center is the fixed point (a, b) and whose radius has a length of r is the equation $(x - a)^2 + (y - b)^2 = r^2$.**

To prove this theorem, use the distance formula with the fixed point $A(a, b)$, the point $P(x, y)$ on the locus, and the distance r.

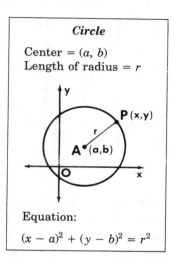

Circle

Center $= (a, b)$
Length of radius $= r$

Equation:

$(x - a)^2 + (y - b)^2 = r^2$

Two Fixed Points: The Perpendicular Bisector

PROCEDURE. To find an equation of the locus of points equidistant from two fixed points A and B:

1. Draw the segment, $\overline{AB}$, and locate its midpoint, M.

2. Through M, draw a line, $\overleftrightarrow{CD}$, perpendicular to $\overline{AB}$. The equation of $\overleftrightarrow{CD}$ (the $\perp$ bisector of $\overline{AB}$) is the equation of the locus of points equidistant from A and B.

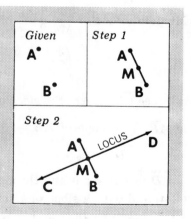

EXAMPLE 1. $A(2, 2)$ and $B(6, 2)$ are two fixed points. The midpoint of $\overline{AB}$ is $(4, 2)$. Since $\overline{AB} \parallel$ the x-axis, then $\overleftrightarrow{CD}$ (the $\perp$ bisector of $\overline{AB}$) is parallel to the y-axis, passing through $(4, 2)$. The equation of $\overleftrightarrow{CD}$ is $x = 4$.

EXAMPLE 2. $A(3, 1)$ and $B(3, -5)$ are two fixed points. The midpoint of $\overline{AB}$ is $(3, -2)$. Since $\overline{AB} \parallel$ the y-axis, then $\overleftrightarrow{CD} \parallel$ the x-axis, passing through $(3, -2)$. The equation of $\overleftrightarrow{CD}$ is $y = -2$.

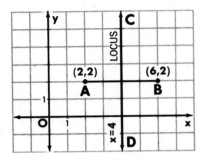

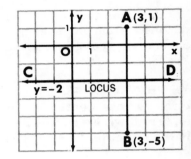

EXAMPLE 3. $A(3, 6)$ and $B(5, 2)$ are two fixed points. Since $\overline{AB}$ is not parallel to either axis, we must find the slope of $\overline{AB}$ as well as its midpoint.

Let $A(3, 6) = (x_1, y_1)$.
Let $B(5, 2) = (x_2, y_2)$.

$$\text{Midpoint of } \overline{AB} = \left(\frac{x_1 + x_2}{2}, \frac{y_1 + y_2}{2} \right)$$

$$= \left(\frac{3 + 5}{2}, \frac{6 + 2}{2} \right) = (4, 4)$$

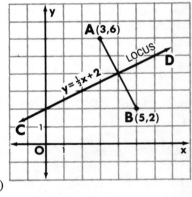

Since $\overleftrightarrow{CD} \perp \overline{AB}$, the slope of $\overleftrightarrow{CD}$ is the negative reciprocal of the slope of $\overline{AB}$. The slope of $\overline{AB} = \dfrac{y_2 - y_1}{x_2 - x_1} = \dfrac{2 - 6}{5 - 3} = \dfrac{-4}{2} = \dfrac{-2}{1}$. Therefore, the slope of $\overleftrightarrow{CD}$ is $+\frac{1}{2}$.

$\overleftrightarrow{CD}$ is a line passing through the point $(4, 4)$ and with a slope of $\frac{1}{2}$. The equation of $\overleftrightarrow{CD}$ is found by the point-slope formula.

$$(y - y_1) = m(x - x_1)$$
$$(y - 4) = \tfrac{1}{2}(x - 4)$$
$$y - 4 = \tfrac{1}{2}x - 2$$
$$y = \tfrac{1}{2}x + 2$$

Note. If $\overleftrightarrow{CD}$ is carefully drawn through (4, 4) with a slope of $\frac{1}{2}$, it is possible to observe that the line has a *y*-intercept of +2. Thus, the equation $y = \frac{1}{2}x + 2$ can be read directly from the graph.

Three Fixed Points

Let *A*, *B*, and *C* be three fixed noncollinear points. Three such points determine the vertices of a triangle. The locus of points equidistant from three fixed noncollinear points is a single point.

Line *k* is the ⊥ bisector of $\overline{AB}$. Thus, any point on line *k* is equidistant from *A* and *B*. Line *l* is the ⊥ bisector of $\overline{BC}$. Thus, any point on line *l* is equidistant from *B* and *C*. Lines *k* and *l* intersect at point *F*. This single point is therefore equidistant from *A* and *B*, and also equidistant from *B* and *C*. In other words, point *F* is equidistant from *A*, *B*, and *C*.

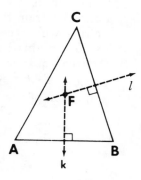

Note. Point *F* is the center of a circle that can be circumscribed about △*ABC*; that is, the circle will pass through the vertices *A*, *B*, and *C* and have point *F* as its center. Remember: *FA* = *FB* = *FC*.

   To construct a circle circumscribed about a given triangle.
See Chapter 16, Construction 14.

MODEL PROBLEMS

1. If *R* and *T* are two distinct points on a plane, describe fully the locus of points equidistant from *R* and *T*.

Answer: The locus of points equidistant from points *R* and *T* is the perpendicular bisector of $\overline{RT}$.

2. If *A* = (0, 4), describe fully the locus of points 6 units from *A*.

Answer: The locus of points 6 units from *A* is a circle whose center is *A*(0, 4) and whose radius measures 6 units.

3. a. Write an equation of the locus of points whose distance from the origin is $\sqrt{13}$.

   b. Determine whether $(-2, 3)$ is on the locus.

Solution:

a. The locus of points whose distance from the origin is r is a circle whose center is $O(0, 0)$, whose radius has length r, and whose equation is $x^2 + y^2 = r^2$. Since $r = \sqrt{13}$ in this circle, the equation of the locus is:

$$x^2 + y^2 = (\sqrt{13})^2$$
$$x^2 + y^2 = 13$$

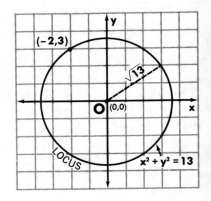

b. If the point $(-2, 3)$ is on the locus, then $x = -2$ and $y = 3$ must satisfy the equation.

$$x^2 + y^2 = 13$$
$$(-2)^2 + (3)^2 \stackrel{?}{=} 13$$
$$4 + 9 \stackrel{?}{=} 13$$
$$13 = 13 \quad \text{(True)}$$

Answer: **a.** $x^2 + y^2 = 13$

   b. The point $(-2, 3)$ is on the locus.

4. A circle has the equation: $(x - 3)^2 + (y + 7)^2 = 64$

Find the coordinates of the center of the circle and the length of the radius.

Solution

(1) Write the general form of a circle with center (a, b) and radius r.

$$(x - a)^2 + (y - b)^2 = r^2$$

(2) Rewrite the given equation in general form.

$$(x - 3)^2 + (y + 7)^2 = 64$$
$$(x - 3)^2 + (y - [-7])^2 = 8^2$$

(3) Compare the two equations.

$$a = 3, \, b = -7, \, r = 8$$

Answer: The center is at $(3, -7)$ and the radius measures 8 units.

EXERCISES

In 1–4: Find **(a)** the coordinates of the center of the circle and **(b)** the length of the radius.

1. circle O **2.** circle A **3.** circle B **4.** circle C

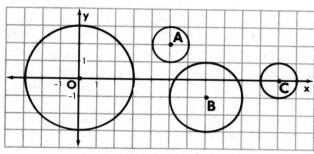

Ex. 1–4

In 5–10, describe fully the locus of points for the given equation.

5. $x^2 + y^2 = 36$ **6.** $x^2 + y^2 = 100$ **7.** $x^2 + y^2 = 5$

8. $x^2 + y^2 = 17$ **9.** $2x^2 + 2y^2 = 50$ **10.** $3x^2 + 3y^2 = 3$

11. Write an equation of the locus of points whose distance from the origin is: **a.** 2 **b.** 8 **c.** $\sqrt{3}$ **d.** $\sqrt{7}$ **e.** $\frac{1}{2}$

12. a. Write an equation of the locus of points whose distance from the origin is 13. Then, in parts **b** to **i**, tell whether or not the given point is on the locus.

    b. (0, 13)   **c.** (5, −12)   **d.** (8, 10)   **e.** (−13, 0)
    f. (7, 11)   **g.** (14, −1)   **h.** (−12, −5)   **i.** (11, $4\sqrt{3}$)

13. a. Write an equation of the locus of points whose distance from the origin is 5.
    b. Without constructing the circle, determine the coordinates of every point on the locus whose abscissa is 3.

In 14–19, for the given equation of the circle, find: **(a)** the coordinates of the center and **(b)** the length of the radius.

14. $(x - 10)^2 + (y - 7)^2 = 14^2$ **15.** $(x - 3)^2 + (y - 12)^2 = 49$

16. $(x + 6)^2 + (y - 1)^2 = 144$ **17.** $(x - 5)^2 + (y + 8)^2 = 20$

18. $(x - 2)^2 + y^2 = 25$ **19.** $x^2 + (y + 6)^2 = 1$

In 20–25, write an equation of the circle whose center and length of radius are given.

20. center (3, 4), radius = 4
22. center (0, 9), radius = 20
24. center (−2, −8), radius = 1

21. center (5, 8), radius = 15
23. center (2, −3), radius = 6
25. center (−6, 0), radius = $\sqrt{10}$

In 26–31: **a.** On graph paper, draw the locus of points equidistant from the two given points. **b.** Write the equation of the locus drawn.

26. (0, 2) and (0, 10)
28. (2, 6) and (2, 12)
30. (−3, 1) and (7, 1)

27. (3, 0) and (9, 0)
29. (9, 3) and (15, 3)
31. (−2, −4) and (−2, 8)

32. Write the coordinates of the point on the x-axis that is equidistant from the points (8, 5) and (12, 5).

33. Write the coordinates of the point on the y-axis that is equidistant from the points (4, 3) and (4, −9).

34. The equation $x = 3$ represents the locus of points equidistant from which of the following pairs of points?
   (1) (0, 2) and (0, 4)   (2) (0, 3) and (3, 0)
   (3) (10, 0) and (−4, 0)   (4) (2, 0) and (6, 0)

In 35–38:

a. On a graph, draw the locus of points equidistant from the two given points.

b. Which of the following is the equation of the locus drawn?
   (1) $y = x$ (2) $y = x + 2$ (3) $y = -x$ (4) $y = -x + 2$

35. (0, 2) and (2, 0)
37. (0, 0) and (2, 2)

36. (0, 2) and (−2, 0)
38. (0, 0) and (−2, 2)

In 39–44:

a. On graph paper, plot the given points A and B.

b. Find the coordinates of the midpoint of $\overline{AB}$.

c. Find the slope of $\overline{AB}$.

d. If $\overleftrightarrow{CD}$ is the locus of points equidistant from points A and B, what is the slope of $\overleftrightarrow{CD}$?

e. On graph paper, draw $\overleftrightarrow{CD}$.

f. Write an equation of $\overleftrightarrow{CD}$.

39. $A(1, 2)$, $B(−1, 4)$
41. $A(4, 0)$, $B(0, 4)$
43. $A(−2, 0)$, $B(4, 2)$

40. $A(−2, 1)$, $B(2, 3)$
42. $A(−3, 2)$, $B(3, −2)$
44. $A(1, 4)$, $B(3, 0)$

45. The coordinates of the vertices of $\triangle ABC$ are $A(-1, -3)$, $B(7, -3)$, and $C(2, 4)$.

   a. Find the coordinates of midpoint M of side $\overline{AB}$.

   b. Write an equation of the locus of points equidistant from A and B.

   c. Is point C equidistant from A and B? Explain why.

   d. Describe fully the locus of points 3 units from point A.

46. The coordinates of the vertices of $\triangle ABC$ are $A(1, 7)$, $B(1, -1)$, and $C(6, 3)$.

   a. Find the coordinates of midpoint M of side $\overline{AB}$.

   b. Write an equation of the locus of points equidistant from A and B.

   c. Is $\triangle ABC$ isosceles? Explain why.

   d. Write an equation of the locus of points 4 units from point B.

   e. Is M a point on the locus described in part **d**? Explain why.

47. Write an equation of the locus of points equidistant from the circles whose equations are $x^2 + y^2 = 4$ and $x^2 + y^2 = 64$.

48. Compasses and a straightedge are needed to solve this problem.

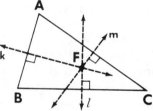

   a. Draw any triangle and label the vertices A, B, and C.

   b. Construct k, the $\perp$ bisector of $\overline{AB}$.

   c. Construct l, the $\perp$ bisector of $\overline{BC}$.

   d. Let point F be the intersection of lines k and l. Explain why F is equidistant from A and B, and also equidistant from B and C.

   e. Construct m, the $\perp$ bisector of $\overline{AC}$. Explain why F must be a point on line m.

   f. Using $FA = FB = FC$, construct a circle whose center is F so that the circle contains vertices A, B, and C of $\triangle ABC$.

11-6 LOCUS, COORDINATES, AND FIXED LINES

One Fixed Line

Given one fixed line, the locus of points at a given distance d from the line is a pair of lines, each parallel to the given line. To find an equation of the locus, it is necessary to find an equation for each of the two parallel lines.

EXAMPLE 1. Let $\overleftrightarrow{AB}$ be a fixed line whose equation is $x = 4$. The locus of points at a given distance 2 units from $\overleftrightarrow{AB}$ is a pair of lines, each parallel to $\overleftrightarrow{AB}$. By counting 2 units to the left of $\overleftrightarrow{AB}$ and 2 units to the right of $\overleftrightarrow{AB}$, we can locate the lines, $\overleftrightarrow{CD}$ and $\overleftrightarrow{EF}$.

The description of the locus is a sentence that includes an equation for each of these two parallel lines: $x = 2$ or $x = 6$. This can be written:

$$(x = 2) \lor (x = 6)$$

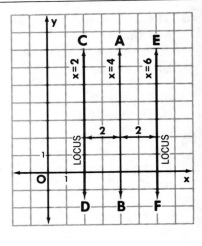

Two Fixed Parallel Lines

Given two fixed parallel lines, the locus of points equidistant from the two lines is a third line, parallel to the other two and midway between them. The equation of the locus is the equation of this third parallel line.

EXAMPLE 2. Let $\overleftrightarrow{AB}$ and $\overleftrightarrow{CD}$ be fixed parallel lines whose equations are $y = -2$ and $y = -8$, respectively. The locus of points equidistant from $\overleftrightarrow{AB}$ and $\overleftrightarrow{CD}$ is the line, $\overleftrightarrow{EF}$, which is midway between them and parallel to them. Since the distance between these two parallel lines is 6 units, count 3 units down from $\overleftrightarrow{AB}$ or 3 units up from $\overleftrightarrow{CD}$ to locate $\overleftrightarrow{EF}$, whose equation is $y = -5$.

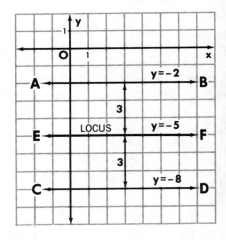

Two Fixed Intersecting Lines

Given two fixed lines that intersect, the locus of points equidistant from the two lines is a pair of lines that bisect the angles formed by the given intersecting lines. The description of this locus includes the equations of two lines.

EXAMPLE 3. Let $\overleftrightarrow{AB}$ and $\overleftrightarrow{CD}$ be fixed intersecting lines whose equations are $x = 3$ and $y = 5$, respectively. By drawing the angle bisectors through the point of intersection $(3, 5)$, we can locate the lines, $\overleftrightarrow{EF}$ and $\overleftrightarrow{GH}$. The description of the locus is a pair of equations for these two lines, read directly from the graph as:

$$y = x + 2 \quad or \quad y = -x + 8$$

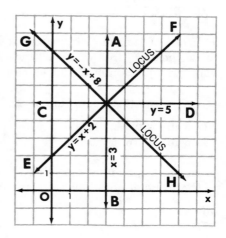

MODEL PROBLEM

Which is an equation of the locus of points equidistant from two lines whose equations are $y = \frac{1}{2}x + 6$ and $y = \frac{1}{2}x + 2$?

(1) $y = 4$ (2) $y = x + 4$ (3) $y = \frac{1}{2}x + 4$ (4) $y = \frac{1}{2}x + 8$

Solution

The lines whose equations are $y = \frac{1}{2}x + 6$ and $y = \frac{1}{2}x + 2$ are parallel lines, each with a slope of $\frac{1}{2}$. The locus of points equidistant from the two lines is a third line, midway between them and parallel to them. This line must also have a slope of $\frac{1}{2}$, eliminating choices (1) and (2).

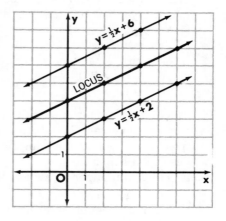

Since the locus intercepts the y-axis at 4, the equation of the locus is choice (3) $y = \frac{1}{2}x + 4$.

Answer: (3)

EXERCISES

In all of the following exercises, it is helpful to use graph paper to draw the fixed line or lines, and then draw the locus described. In this way, an equation of the locus can be read from the graph.

In 1–4, write an equation of the locus based upon the given conditions.

1. 3 units from the line $x = 5$ **2.** 2 units from the line $y = 7$
3. 5 units from the line $y = 1$ **4.** 4 units from the line $x = -4$

In 5–10, the equations of two fixed lines are given. Write an equation of the locus of points equidistant from the two fixed lines.

5. $x = 4$ and $x = 10$ **6.** $y = 3$ and $y = -8$
7. $y = -3$ and $y = -13$ **8.** $x = 2$ and $x = 9$
9. $y = x$ and $y = x + 2$ **10.** $y = -\frac{1}{2}x + 7$ and $y = -\frac{1}{2}x + 1$

In 11–14, select the numeral preceding the expression that best answers the question.

11. Which is an equation of the locus of points 5 units from the y-axis?   (1) $y = 5$ (2) $x = 5$ or $x = -5$ (3) $y = 5$ or $y = -5$
(4) $x^2 + y^2 = 25$

12. Which is an equation of the locus of points equidistant from two lines whose equations are $y = 3x + 5$ and $y = 3x - 1$?
(1) $y = 3x$ (2) $y = 3x + 2$ (3) $y = 3x + 4$ (4) $y = 3$

13. Which is an equation of the locus of points equidistant from the x-axis and the y-axis?   (1) $x = y$ (2) $x = 0$ or $y = 0$ (3) $x = y$ or $x = -y$
(4) $x^2 + y^2 = r^2$

14. Which is an equation of the locus of points equidistant from two intersecting lines whose equations are $y = x + 3$ and $y = -x + 3$?
(1) $x = 0$ or $y = 3$ (2) $x = 3$ or $y = 0$
(3) $x = 0$ or $y = 6$ (4) $x = 6$ or $y = 0$

15. a. On graph paper, draw the intersecting lines whose equations are $y = 2x$ and $y = -2x + 4$.   **b.** Draw the locus of points equidistant from these two intersecting lines.   **c.** Write an equation of the locus described in part **b**.

16. a. On graph paper, draw the intersecting lines whose equations are $y = \frac{1}{2}x + 1$ and $y = -\frac{1}{2}x + 5$.   **b.** Draw the locus of points equidistant from these intersecting lines.   **c.** Write an equation of the locus described in part **b**.

17. The vertices of $\triangle ABC$ are $A(5, 2)$, $B(10, 2)$ and $C(7, 8)$. Imagine that $\triangle ABK$ is equal in area to $\triangle ABC$, and both triangles have $\overline{AB}$ as a base. Write an equation of the locus of points that could be point K in $\triangle ABK$.

11-7   THE PARABOLA AS A LOCUS

Consider the locus of points equidistant from a fixed point and a fixed line. In order to discover this locus, let F be the fixed point and $\overleftrightarrow{AB}$ the fixed line. Locate a few of the points on the locus.

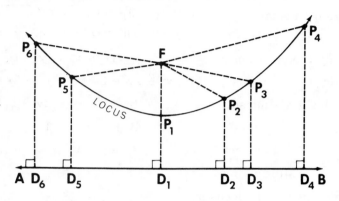

Measure the distances to verify that each point P_1, P_2, P_3, P_4, P_5, and P_6 is equidistant from F and from $\overleftrightarrow{AB}$. The locus is a curved line.

The Equation of the Locus

Given the equation of the fixed line and the coordinates of the fixed point, it is possible to find the equation of the locus of points equidistant from the fixed line and fixed point.

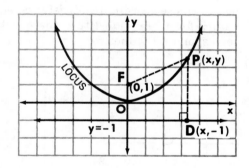

EXAMPLE.

(1) Let the fixed line be the line $y = -1$.
   Let the fixed point be the point $F(0, 1)$.
   Let any point on the locus be $P(x, y)$.

(2) $\overline{FP}$ and $\overline{PD}$ are drawn such that $\overline{PD}$ is perpendicular to the line $y = -1$. Therefore, point D has the same abscissa as point P. Point D must have an ordinate of -1 since it is a point on the line $y = -1$. Thus, the coordinates of $D = (x, -1)$.

(3) The distance from $P(x, y)$ to $D(x, -1)$ is PD. Since these points have the same abscissa,

$$PD = |y - (-1)|$$

The distance from $P(x, y)$ to $F(0, 1)$ is PF. By the distance formula,

$$PF = \sqrt{(x - 0)^2 + (y - 1)^2}$$

(4) By the given conditions of the locus, point P is equidistant from $y = -1$ and from F. In other words:

$$PD = PF$$

(5) Substitute the values:

$$|y - (-1)| = \sqrt{(x - 0)^2 + (y - 1)^2}$$

(6) Square both sides:

$$[|y - (-1)|]^2 = \left(\sqrt{(x - 0)^2 + (y - 1)^2}\right)^2$$
$$[y - (-1)]^2 = (x - 0)^2 + (y - 1)^2$$

(7) Simplify the equation:

$$(y + 1)^2 = x^2 + (y - 1)^2$$

(8) Expand the binomials:

$$y^2 + 2y + 1 = x^2 + y^2 - 2y + 1$$

(9) On both sides, subtract y^2:

$$2y + 1 = x^2 - 2y + 1$$

Add $2y$:

$$4y + 1 = x^2 + 1$$

Subtract 1:

$$4y = x^2$$

Multiply by $\frac{1}{4}$:

$$y = \tfrac{1}{4}x^2$$

(10) The equation of the locus is:

$$y = \tfrac{1}{4}x^2$$

Since the equation of the locus is of the form $y = ax^2 + bx + c$ with $a = \frac{1}{4}$, $b = 0$, and $c = 0$, the locus is a *parabola*.

Once the equation of the parabola is known, it is possible to find many points whose coordinates satisfy the equation. We can select appropriate values for x, and substitute these values into the equation to find the corresponding values for y.

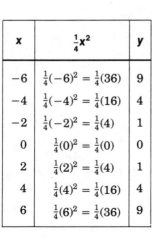

x	$\frac{1}{4}x^2$	y
-6	$\frac{1}{4}(-6)^2 = \frac{1}{4}(36)$	9
-4	$\frac{1}{4}(-4)^2 = \frac{1}{4}(16)$	4
-2	$\frac{1}{4}(-2)^2 = \frac{1}{4}(4)$	1
0	$\frac{1}{4}(0)^2 = \frac{1}{4}(0)$	0
2	$\frac{1}{4}(2)^2 = \frac{1}{4}(4)$	1
4	$\frac{1}{4}(4)^2 = \frac{1}{4}(16)$	4
6	$\frac{1}{4}(6)^2 = \frac{1}{4}(36)$	9

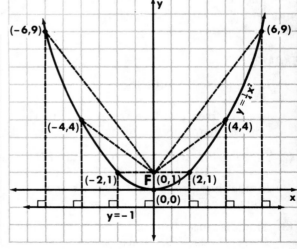

Notice how the points whose coordinates are indicated on the parabola fit the definition of the locus:

When $P = (0, 0)$: From $P(0, 0)$ to $F(0, 1)$, $PF = 1$.
From $P(0, 0)$ to $D(0, -1)$ on $y = -1$, $PD = 1$.
Therefore, $PF = PD$.

When $P = (2, 1)$: From $P(2, 1)$ to $F(0, 1)$, $PF = 2$.
From $P(2, 1)$ to $D(2, -1)$ on $y = -1$, $PD = 2$.
Therefore, $PF = PD$.

When $P = (4, 4)$: From $P(4, 4)$ to $F(0, 1)$,
$PF = \sqrt{(4 - 0)^2 + (4 - 1)^2} = \sqrt{4^2 + 3^2} = 5$.
From $P(4, 4)$ to $D(4, -1)$ on $y = -1$, $PD = 5$.
Therefore, $PF = PD$.

When $P = (6, 9)$: From $P(6, 9)$ to $F(0, 1)$,
$PF = \sqrt{(6 - 0)^2 + (9 - 1)^2} = \sqrt{6^2 + 8^2} = 10$.
From $P(6, 9)$ to $D(6, -1)$ on $y = -1$, $PD = 10$.
Therefore, $PF = PD$.

● **Definition.** The locus of points equidistant from a given point and a given line is a ***parabola***. The fixed line is the *directrix* and the fixed point is the *focus* of the parabola.

Any line can be the directrix of a parabola and any point not on the directrix can be the focus. In this book, you will study only parabolas that have a directrix that is parallel to the x-axis.

MODEL PROBLEMS

1. Given the focus $F(3, 6)$ and the directrix $y = 2$:
   a. Find the coordinates of three points equidistant from point $F(3, 6)$ and the line $y = 2$.
   b. Using the three points found in part **a**, sketch part of the parabola that is the locus of points being discussed.

Solution

(1) Plot $F(3, 6)$ and draw the directrix $y = 2$. Then draw $\overline{FD_1} \perp$ the directrix and locate the midpoint of $\overline{FD_1}$, that is, P_1. Since $FP_1 = P_1D_1$, then $P_1(3, 4)$ is a point on the parabola.

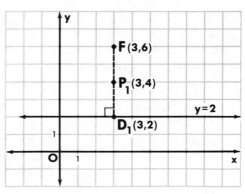

(2) The distance between the focus F and the directrix $y = 2$ is 4 units. Imagine a line parallel to the directrix passing through point F. By moving 4 units to the right of F, we can find point $P_2(7, 6)$. By moving 4 units to the left of F, we can find point $P_3(-1, 6)$. Both P_2 and P_3 are 4 units from point

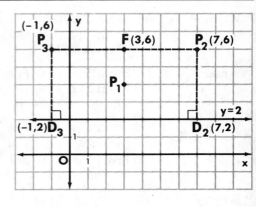

F and 4 units from the directrix $y = 2$. Therefore, P_2 and P_3 are points on the parabola.

(3) Draw a smooth curve passing through points P_3, P_1, and P_2.

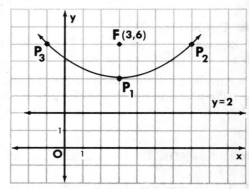

Answer: **a.** $P_1(3, 4)$, $P_2(7, 6)$, $P_3(-1, 6)$ **b.** See graph.

2. Given the focus $F(3, 6)$ and the directrix $y = 2$, find the equation of the parabola that is the locus of points equidistant from point F and the directrix.

Solution: Let $P(x, y)$ represent any point on the parabola. Let $D(x, 2)$ be a point on the directrix such that $\overline{PD} \perp$ the directrix $y = 2$.

(1) Since point P is equidistant from the directrix and the focus:

$$PD = PF$$

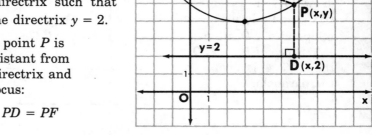

(2) By rules for distance:	$\|y - 2\| = \sqrt{(x - 3)^2 + (y - 6)^2}$
(3) Square both sides:	$(\|y - 2\|)^2 = (\sqrt{(x - 3)^2 + (y - 6)^2})^2$
	$(y - 2)^2 = (x - 3)^2 + (y - 6)^2$
(4) Expand the binomials:	$y^2 - 4y + 4 = x^2 - 6x + 9 + y^2 - 12y + 36$
(5) On both sides, subtract y^2:	$-4y + 4 = x^2 - 6x + 9 - 12y + 36$
Add $12y$:	$8y + 4 = x^2 - 6x + 9 + 36$
Subtract 4:	$8y = x^2 - 6x + 41$
Multiply by $\frac{1}{8}$:	$y = \frac{1}{8}(x^2 - 6x + 41)$
(6) The equation of the parabola is:	$y = \frac{1}{8}x^2 - \frac{6}{8}x + \frac{41}{8}$ *Ans.*

EXERCISES

Exercises 1–7 refer to the parabola shown.

1. Name the coordinates of the focus.
2. Write the equation of the directrix.

In 3–7, demonstrate that each of the given points on the parabola is equidistant from the focus and the directrix.

3. (4, 1)   4. (6, 2)   5. (2, 2)
6. (8, 5)   7. (0, 5)

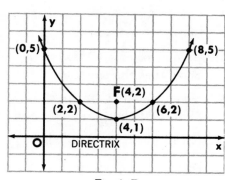

Ex. 1–7

In 8–17: **a.** Find the coordinates of three points equidistant from the given focus F and the directrix. **b.** Using the three points sketch part of the parabola that is the locus of points being discussed.

8. $F(3, 3)$, directrix $y = 1$ 9. $F(0, 4)$, directrix $y = 2$
10. $F(3, 7)$, directrix $y = 3$ 11. $F(2, 3)$, directrix $y = -3$
12. $F(-6, 0)$, directrix $y = -6$ 13. $F(-3, 1)$, directrix $y = -3$

14. $F(4, 3)$, directrix $y = 1$

15. $F(0, 1)$, directrix $y = 0$

16. $F(5, 1)$, directrix $y = 5$

17. $F(4, -2)$, directrix $y = 4$

18. For a given parabola, $F(4, 5)$ is the focus and the line $y = 1$ is the directrix. Let $P(x, y)$ be any point on the parabola, and let $D(x, 1)$ be a point on the directrix so that $\overline{PD} \perp$ the line $y = 1$.

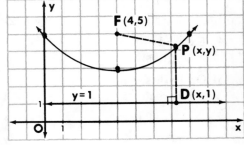

   a. Express the distance PD in terms of y.
   b. Express the distance PF in terms of x and y.
   c. By letting $PD = PF$, show that the equation for the parabola is $y = \frac{1}{8}x^2 - x + 5$.
   d. Show that points $(0, 5)$, $(4, 3)$, and $(8, 5)$ lie on the parabola.

In 19–23: Show that the locus of points equidistant from the given focus and the given directrix is the parabola whose equation is given.

19. Given: focus $(0, 7)$, directrix $y = 1$.
   Show that the equation of the parabola is $y = \frac{1}{12}x^2 + 4$.

20. Given: focus $(0, 2)$, directrix $y = 0$.
   Show that the equation of the parabola is $y = \frac{1}{4}x^2 + 1$.

21. Given: focus $(4, 6)$, directrix $y = 2$.
   Show that the equation of the parabola is $y = \frac{1}{8}x^2 - x + 6$.

22. Given: focus $(2, 0)$, directrix $y = 2$.
   Show that the equation of the parabola is $y = -\frac{1}{4}x^2 + x$.

23. Given: focus $(2, 0)$, directrix $y = -3$.
   Show that the equation of the parabola is $y = \dfrac{x^2}{6} - \dfrac{4x}{6} - \dfrac{5}{6}$.

In 24–31: Find the equation of the parabola whose points are equidistant from the given focus F and the given directrix.

24. $F(0, 4)$, directrix $y = 0$

25. $F(0, 2)$, directrix $y = -2$

26. $F(0, 0)$, directrix $y = -2$

27. $F(6, 6)$, directrix $y = 0$

28. $F(3, 4)$, directrix $y = 2$

29. $F(0, -1)$, directrix $y = 1$

30. $F(3, 6)$, directrix $y = 0$

31. $F(3, 0)$, directrix $y = 3$

11-8 INTERSECTIONS OF LOCI

Given a condition, a locus of points is determined. Given a second condition, a second locus of points is determined. The points at which the two loci intersect, and only those points, satisfy both conditions.

> **PROCEDURE.** To find points that satisfy two conditions:
>
> 1. Draw the locus of points that satisfy the first condition.
> 2. Draw the locus of points that satisfy the second condition.
> 3. Locate the points of intersection of these loci. These points must be the required points because they satisfy both conditions.

The intersection of loci may result in a single point, in two points, or in more than two points, depending upon the given conditions. In cases where the loci do not intersect, there is no point that satisfies both of the given conditions.

Since we have studied locus with and without coordinates, we make the following observations:

1. Given *general* conditions (see Model Problem 1), the loci are sketched on blank paper.
2. Given conditions involving *numbers* (see Model Problem 2), the loci can be sketched on blank paper or on graph paper.
3. Given conditions involving *coordinates* (see Model Problem 3), the loci are sketched on graph paper.

MODEL PROBLEMS

1. What is the number of points equidistant from two parallel lines and also equidistant from two points on one of the lines?

Solution

(1) Sketch two parallel lines *l* and *m*. Place two points *A* and *B* on one of the lines.

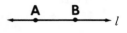

(2) The locus of points equidistant from the parallel lines l and m is a third line, k, parallel to l and m, and midway between them. Draw line k.

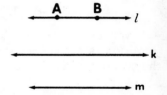

(3) The locus of points equidistant from two points A and B is $\overleftrightarrow{CD}$, which is the ⊥ bisector of $\overline{AB}$. Draw $\overleftrightarrow{CD}$. Extend the line to show all possible points of intersection. Notice that $\overleftrightarrow{CD}$ intersects line k at *only one point*, P. Thus, point P is *both* equidistant from the parallel lines l and m *and also* equidistant from the two points A and B.

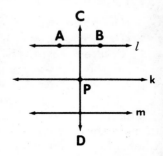

Since there is only one point in the intersection of the loci, there is only one point that satisfies both conditions.

Answer: 1 point

2. What is the number of points in a plane two units from a given line and three units from a given point on the line?

Solution

(1) Draw a line m and place one point A on the line. These represent the given conditions.

(2) The locus of points two units from the given line m is a pair of parallel lines k and t, each two units from line m. Draw the lines k and t and show that each is 2 units from line m.

(3) The locus of points 3 units from the given point A is a circle whose center is A and whose radius has length 3. Draw circle A (using compasses is best).

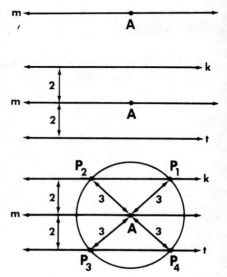

Notice that the circle intersects the locus of the first condition at four points: P_1, P_2, P_3, and P_4. Each of these four points is 3 units from point A and also 2 units from line m.

Since four points P_1, P_2, P_3, and P_4 are in the intersection of the loci, there are four points that satisfy both conditions.

Answer: 4 points

Note. If you use graph paper, you will find it easier to draw parallel lines, count given units, etc.

3. **a.** Write an equation of the locus for all points 3 units from the y-axis.
   b. Describe fully the locus of points r units from the point $A(1, 3)$.
   c. Find the number of points that simultaneously satisfy the conditions stated in parts **a** and **b** when: (1) $r = 1$ (2) $r = 4$.
   d. Write the coordinates of all points that simultaneously satisfy the conditions stated in parts **a** and **b** when $r = 2$.

Solution

a. The locus of points 3 units from the y-axis consists of two lines, each parallel to the y-axis, the lines $x = 3$ and $x = -3$.

b. The locus of points is a circle with center $A(1, 3)$ and radius r.

c. (1) When the circle has a radius of length $r = 1$, there are no points in the intersection of the loci.

(2) When the circle has a radius of length $r = 4$, there are three points (P_1, P_2, P_3) in the intersection of the loci.

Graph, part c (1): $r = 1$.

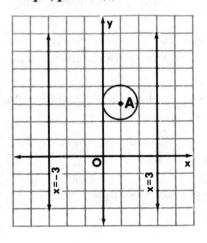

Graph, part c (2): $r = 4$.

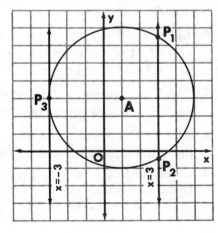

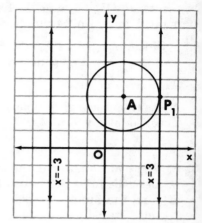

Graph, part d: $r = 2$

d. When the circle has a radius of length $r = 2$, there is one point, P_1, in the intersection of the loci. The coordinates of P_1 are (3, 3).

Answer:

a. $x = 3$ or $x = -3$, or $x = \pm 3$

b. a circle with center $A(1, 3)$ and radius r

c. (1) no points   (2) 3 points

d. (3, 3)

EXERCISES

1. What is the number of points in a plane at a given distance from a given line and also equidistant from two points on the given line?

2. How many points are there in a plane that are 4 cm from a given line and also 5 cm from a given point on that line?

3. How many points are there in a plane that are 5 cm from a given line and also 5 cm from a given point on that line?

4. Two points A and B are 6 inches apart. How many points are there that are equidistant from both A and B and also 5 inches from A?

5. How many points are there that are equidistant from two given points A and B and also 2 inches from the line passing through A and B?

6. $\overleftrightarrow{LM}$ and $\overleftrightarrow{RS}$ are two parallel lines 10 mm apart, and A is a point on $\overleftrightarrow{LM}$. How many points are there that are equidistant from $\overleftrightarrow{LM}$ and $\overleftrightarrow{RS}$ and 7 mm from A?

7. Two lines, $\overleftrightarrow{AB}$ and $\overleftrightarrow{CD}$, intersect at E. How many points are 2 units from E and also equidistant from $\overleftrightarrow{AB}$ and $\overleftrightarrow{CD}$?

8. A point P is 1 unit from a line, $\overleftrightarrow{AB}$. How many points in the plane are 2 units from $\overleftrightarrow{AB}$ and also 4 units from P?

9. Given $\angle ABC$, what is the number of points found in the interior of the angle, equidistant from the sides of the angle, and also equidistant from points A and B?

In 10–14, use the treasure map, which shows that tree *A* is 8 meters north of a house and tree *B* is 18 meters from tree *A*. Copy the map. Locate all possible points of the buried treasure based on the given conditions.

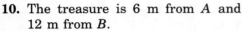

10. The treasure is 6 m from *A* and 12 m from *B*.

11. The treasure is 10 m north of the house and 3 m from *A*.

12. The treasure is 10 m from *A* and 15 m from *B*.

Ex. 10–14

13. The treasure is equidistant from *A* and the line representing the north wall of the house, and also equidistant from *A* and *B*.

14. The treasure is equidistant from *A* and *B* and also 10 m from *B*.

15. Given a line, $\overleftrightarrow{AB}$, and a point, *C*, that is 4 units from $\overleftrightarrow{AB}$.

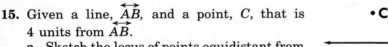

a. Sketch the locus of points equidistant from *C* and $\overleftrightarrow{AB}$.

b. Sketch the locus of points 4 units from $\overleftrightarrow{AB}$.

c. How many points simultaneously satisfy the conditions described in parts **a** and **b**?

16. Two points *A* and *B* are 7 inches apart. How many points are there that are 12 inches from *A* and also 4 inches from *B*?

In 17–26, select the numeral preceding the correct answer.

17. The number of points equidistant from two given parallel lines and at the same time equidistant from two given points on one of these lines is (1) 1 (2) 2 (3) 3 (4) 4

18. The number of points that are at a given distance from a given line and also equidistant from two given points on the line is (1) 1 (2) 2 (3) 3 (4) 4

19. The number of points in a plane 1 cm from a given line and 2 cm from a given point on the line is (1) 1 (2) 2 (3) 0 (4) 4

20. The number of points in a plane 2 cm from a given line and 1 cm from a given point on the line is (1) 1 (2) 2 (3) 0 (4) 4

21. Point *C* is 2 units from a line, $\overleftrightarrow{AB}$. How many points in $\overleftrightarrow{AB}$ are three units from point *C*? (1) 1 (2) 2 (3) 0 (4) 4

22. $\overline{AB}$ is 1 cm long. How many points in the plane are 2 cm from both A and B? (1) 1 (2) 2 (3) 0 (4) 4

23. Parallel lines k and t are 6 mm apart, and A is a point on line t. The number of points equidistant from k and t and also 3 mm from point A is (1) 1 (2) 2 (3) 0 (4) 4

24. $\overleftrightarrow{AB}$ and $\overleftrightarrow{CD}$ are parallel and are 6 inches apart. Point P is on $\overleftrightarrow{AB}$. The number of points equidistant from these two lines and also 5 inches from point P is (1) 1 (2) 2 (3) 0 (4) 4

25. Point P is 7 units from a given line. The number of points that are 3 units from the line and also 10 units from point P is (1) 1 (2) 2 (3) 3 (4) 4

26. In $\triangle ABC$, the point that is equidistant from the three vertices A, B, and C is the intersection of
    (1) the angle bisectors
    (2) the perpendicular bisectors of the sides
    (3) the medians
    (4) none of the first three choices

Locus and Coordinates

27. Write an equation of the locus of points equidistant from $(0, -3)$ and $(0, 7)$.

28. **a.** Draw the locus of points equidistant from the points $(4, 1)$ and $(4, 5)$ and write an equation for this locus.
    b. Draw the locus of points equidistant from the points $(3, 2)$ and $(9, 2)$ and write an equation for this locus.
    c. Find the number of points that satisfy both conditions stated in **a** and **b**. Give the coordinates of each point found.

29. **a.** Represent graphically the locus of points (1) 3 units from the line $x = 1$ (2) 4 units from the line $y = -2$
    b. Write the equations for the loci represented in **a**.
    c. Find the coordinates of the points of intersection of these loci.

30. **a.** Represent graphically the locus of points: (1) 8 units from the y-axis (2) 10 units from the origin
    b. Write equations for the loci represented in **a**.
    c. Find the coordinates of the points of intersection of these loci.

31. The vertices of triangle RST are $R(2, 3)$, $S(6, 3)$, and $T(3, 10)$.
    a. Draw the graph and write an equation of the locus of points equidistant from R and S.
    b. Draw a line, $\overleftrightarrow{TW}$, that passes through T and is parallel to $\overleftrightarrow{RS}$, and write an equation of $\overleftrightarrow{TW}$.
    c. Write the coordinates of the points of intersection of the lines drawn in **a** and **b**.

32. a. Draw the locus of points equidistant from the circles whose equations are $x^2 + y^2 = 4$ and $x^2 + y^2 = 36$. Write an equation of the locus.

   b. Draw the locus of points 4 units from the x-axis. Write an equation of the locus.

   c. Find the number of points that satisfy both conditions stated in **a** and **b**. Write the coordinates of each of the points found.

33. a. Using graph paper, draw the triangle whose vertices are $A(1, 2)$, $B(7, 2)$, and $C(5, 6)$.

   b. Draw the locus of points equidistant from A and B.

   c. Write an equation of the locus drawn in answer to **b**.

   d. Write an equation of the line passing through A and C.

   e. Find the coordinates of point P if P is a point on $\overleftrightarrow{AC}$ that is equidistant from points A and B.

34. The vertices of $\triangle ABC$ are $A(0, 0)$, $B(6, 0)$, and $C(0, 8)$.

   a. Write an equation of the $\perp$ bisector of $\overline{AB}$.

   b. Write an equation of the $\perp$ bisector of $\overline{AC}$.

   c. Write the coordinates of the intersection of these loci.

   d. Write the coordinates of the midpoint of $\overline{BC}$.

   e. Will the perpendicular bisectors of the sides of $\triangle ABC$ pass through the same point? That is, will they be *concurrent*?

35. a. Write an equation of the locus of points 2 units from the x-axis.

   b. Describe fully the locus of points at a distance d from $P(2, 6)$.

   c. Find the number of points that simultaneously satisfy the conditions in **a** and **b** for the following values of d:
   (1) $d = 2$ (2) $d = 4$ (3) $d = 6$ (4) $d = 8$ (5) $d = 10$

36. a. Write the equation of the locus of points 5 units from the point $(4, 0)$.

   b. Describe fully the locus of points at a distance d from the x-axis.

   c. Find the number of points that simultaneously satisfy the conditions in **a** and **b** when: (1) $d = 1$ (2) $d = 5$ (3) $d = 10$

   d. Find the coordinates for all points 5 units from the point $(4, 0)$ and also 5 units from the x-axis.

   e. Find the coordinates for all points 5 units from the point $(4, 0)$ and also 3 units from the x-axis.

37. a. Describe fully the locus of points equidistant from the x-axis and the point $(3, 2)$.

   b. Describe fully the locus of points at a distance 2 units from the point $(3, 2)$.

   c. Find the coordinates of all points that simultaneously satisfy the conditions in **a** and **b**.

38. The vertices of $\triangle RST$ are $R(1, 2)$, $S(9, 2)$, and $T(9, 8)$.
   a. Write an equation of the locus of points equidistant from R and S.
   b. Write an equation of the locus of points equidistant from S and T.
   c. Find the coordinates of all points that simultaneously satisfy the conditions in **a** and **b**.
   d. Write an equation of the locus of points 5 units from T.
   e. Find the coordinates of all points that are 5 units from T and also intersect one of the sides of $\triangle RST$.

11-9 REVIEW EXERCISES

In 1–6, describe fully the following loci. Points that are:

1. equidistant from two parallel lines.
2. equidistant from two points.
3. equidistant from two intersecting lines.
4. at a given distance d from the line $x = 0$.
5. at a given distance d from the point $(3, 1)$.
6. equidistant from a fixed point P and a fixed line $y = k$.

In 7–15, write an equation for each locus.

7. Points in which the abscissa is 3 less than the ordinate.
8. Points on a line parallel to the x-axis that passes through the point $(7, -1)$.
9. Points 8 units from the y-axis.
10. Points 8 units from the origin.
11. Points equidistant from $A(3, 2)$ and $B(3, 6)$.
12. Points equidistant from $A(3, 2)$ and $D(-9, 2)$.
13. Points equidistant from the two lines $x = 7$ and $x = 13$.
14. Points 3 units from the fixed point $(2, 6)$.
15. Points equidistant from $(0, 4)$ and the line $y = 0$.

16. For each circle whose equation is given, find (1) the coordinates of the center and (2) the length of its radius.
   a. $x^2 + y^2 = 16$ **b.** $3x^2 + 3y^2 = 108$
   c. $(x - 5)^2 + y^2 = 100$ **d.** $(x + 1)^2 + (y - 9)^2 = 10$

17. The focus of a parabola is $(5, 2)$ and its directrix is the line $y = 0$.
   a. Find the coordinates of three points on the parabola.
   b. Sketch the part of the parabola that passes through the three points found in **a**.
   c. Write an equation of the parabola.

In 18–25, select the numeral preceding the correct answer.

18. An equation that represents the locus of all points 12 units to the right of the y-axis is
   (1) $y = 12$ (2) $x = 12$ (3) $y = -12$ (4) $x = -12$

19. Which of the following points is on the circle whose equation is $x^2 + y^2 = 17^2$?
   (1) $(1, 16)$ (2) $(-8, 15)$ (3) $(10, -7)$ (4) $(12, -12)$

20. An equation of the locus of points equidistant from the points $(6, 8)$ and $(-2, 8)$ is (1) $x = 2$ (2) $x = 4$ (3) $y = 2$ (4) $y = 8$

21. The number of points equidistant from both the x-axis and the y-axis and also 3 units from the origin is (1) 1 (2) 2 (3) 3 (4) 4

22. Parallel lines p and q are 6 cm apart and point A is on line p. The number of points equidistant from p and q and also 3 cm from point A is (1) 1 (2) 2 (3) 3 (4) 4

23. How many points are 3 units from $\overleftrightarrow{AB}$ and 4 units from B?
   (1) 1 (2) 2 (3) 3 (4) 4

24. The number of points equidistant from two parallel lines and also equidistant from two points on one of the lines is
   (1) 1 (2) 2 (3) 0 (4) 4

25. If the length of $\overline{CD}$ is 20 mm, how many points are simultaneously 15 mm from C and 10 mm from D? (1) 1 (2) 2 (3) 0 (4) 4

26. Given $\triangle ABC$ with vertices $A(-1, 1)$, $B(5, 1)$, and $C(2, 3)$.
   a. Draw the locus of points equidistant from A and B.
   b. Write an equation of the locus described in **a**.
   c. Draw the locus of points 4 units from point C.
   d. Write an equation of the locus described in **c**.
   e. Write the coordinates of the points that simultaneously satisfy the loci described in **a** and **c**.

27. **a.** On graph paper, draw the locus of points 3 units from the line whose equation is $x = 1$.
   b. Write an equation of the locus described in **a**.
   c. Describe fully the locus of points at a distance d from $(2, 7)$.
   d. Write an equation of the locus described in **c**.
   e. How many points simultaneously satisfy the conditions in **a** and **b** when: (1) $d = 1$ (2) $d = 3$ (3) $d = 5$
   f. Find the coordinates of all points that are 3 units from the line $x = 1$ and also 2 units from $(2, 7)$.

28. a. Write an equation of the locus of points 13 units from the origin.
    b. Write an equation of the locus of points equidistant from $x = 0$ and $x = 10$.
    c. Solve algebraically the system of equations written in answer to parts **a** and **b** to find the coordinates of the points 13 units from the origin and equidistant from $x = 0$ and $x = 10$.

29. a. Write an equation of the locus of points 10 units from the origin.
    b. Write an equation of the locus of points whose ordinate is 2 units more than its abscissa.
    c. Solve algebraically the system of equations written in answer to parts **a** and **b** to find the coordinates of each point 10 units from the origin whose ordinate is 2 more than its abscissa.

Chapter 12

Transformation Geometry and Coordinates

12-1 LINE REFLECTIONS AND LINE SYMMETRY

What Is a Transformation?

In a classroom, the seats are arranged in four rows with five seats in each row. On the first day of school, the 20 students in the class chose seats at random as they entered the classroom. The teacher made the diagram at the left below showing where the students sat on that first day but soon assigned new seats, as shown in the diagram at the right below.

Seat				
5	Fred	Sue	Beth	Carl
4	Tim	Peg	Ann	Dave
3	Rosa	Jim	Ron	Don
2	Pat	Paul	Tony	Kay
1	Amy	Tom	Jack	Ben
	1	2	3	4
		Row		

Seat				
5	Tim	Beth	Ben	Rosa
4	Don	Peg	Jack	Jim
3	Pat	Ron	Amy	Carl
2	Paul	Dave	Kay	Fred
1	Tony	Tom	Sue	Ann
	1	2	3	4
		Row		

Amy, who was seated in row 1, seat 1, was asked to sit in row 3, seat 3. Tom, who was seated in row 2, seat 1, was asked to stay in row 2, seat 1.

The two charts that show the old and the new seating arrangements can be thought of as describing a transformation. Based on the seats to which each student moved, each seat in the classroom is associated with another seat or with itself. By extending this idea to points in a plane, we form the definition of a transformation of the plane.

● **Definition.** A *transformation of the plane* is a one-to-one correspondence between the points in a plane such that each point is associated with itself or with some other point in the plane. A transformation demonstrates a change in position or a fixed position for each point in the plane.

An infinite number of transformations can take place in a plane. In this chapter, you will study only a few special transformations, each of which follows a definite pattern or rule.

Line Reflections

In the figure, $\triangle ABC \cong \triangle A'B'C$. One triangle will "fit exactly" on top of the other by folding this page along line k, the *line of reflection*. Thus, points A and A' correspond to each other, and points B and B' correspond to each other. Point C corresponds to itself and is called a *fixed point* because C is on the line of reflection.

The term *image* is used to describe the relationship of these points, as we might think of one point as being the mirror image of its corresponding point.

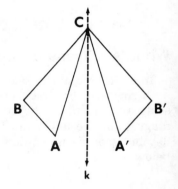

In Symbols	*In Words*
$A \to A'$, and $A' \to A$.	The image of A is A', and the image of A' is A.
$B \to B'$, and $B' \to B$.	The image of B is B', and the image of B' is B.
$C \to C$.	The image of C is C.

A reflection in the line k is indicated in symbols as r_k. Thus, to show that the images are formed under a reflection in line k, we write:

$r_k(A) = A'$. Under a reflection in line k, the image of A is A'.

$r_k(B) = B'$. Under a reflection in line k, the image of B is B'.

$r_k(C) = C$. Under a reflection in line k, the image of C is C.

$\overline{AA'}$ and $\overline{BB'}$ are drawn to connect two points and their images. Notice how line k, the line of reflection, is related to these segments:

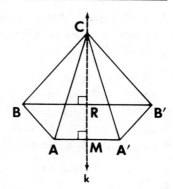

1. Line k is perpendicular to each segment, $\overline{AA'}$ and $\overline{BB'}$.

2. Line k bisects each of these segments. If M is the intersection of $\overline{AA'}$ and line k, then $AM = MA'$. Also, if R is the intersection of $\overline{BB'}$ and line k, then $BR = RB'$.

● **Definition.** A *reflection in a line k* is a transformation of the plane such that:

1. If point P is not on line k, the image of P is P', where line k is the perpendicular bisector of $\overline{PP'}$.

2. If point P is on line k, the image of P is P.

A line reflection is a transformation of the plane, since every point P of the plane has one and only one point P' of the plane that is its image; that is, there is a one-to-one correspondence of points in the plane. If the image of point P is P', then the *preimage* of point P' is P.

Under a line reflection, the image of a segment is another segment. In the preceding figure, $\overline{AB} \rightarrow \overline{A'B'}$, or $r_k(\overline{AB}) = \overline{A'B'}$. Also, the image of an angle is another angle: $\angle ABC \rightarrow \angle A'B'C$, or $r_k(\angle ABC) = \angle A'B'C$.

Line Symmetry

In nature, in art, and in industry, we find many forms that contain a line of reflection.

In each of the figures below, imagine that every point in the figure moves to its image through a reflection in the given line. The figure would appear to be unchanged. This line of reflection is called an *axis of symmetry*, and each figure is said to have *line symmetry*.

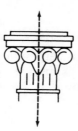
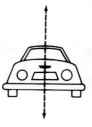

● **Definition.** *Line symmetry* occurs in a figure when the figure is its own image under a reflection in a line. Such a line is called an *axis of symmetry*.

Triangle *ABC* is an isosceles triangle with *AB* = *CB*. The axis of symmetry for △*ABC* is line *k*, drawn to contain altitude $\overline{BD}$ from vertex angle *B* to base $\overline{AC}$.

It is possible for a figure to have more than one axis of symmetry, or reflection line. Rectangle *EFGH* has two axes of symmetry, namely, line *m* and line *p*.

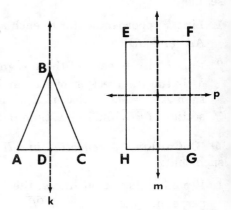

Lines of reflection, or lines of symmetry, may be found for letters and for words.

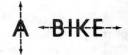

MODEL PROBLEM

On your paper, copy $\overline{AB}$ and line *m*. Then sketch as carefully as possible the image of $\overline{AB}$ under a reflection in line *m*. Let *A* → *A′*, *B* → *B′*, and label the image $\overline{A'B'}$.

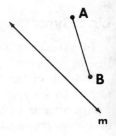

Solution:

Method 1: Using a Ruler as an Aid

Step 1. Hold the ruler perpendicular to line *m* and touching point *A*. Measure the distance from *A* to line *m*. The image *A′* is on the other side of line *m*, the same distance away from *m* as is point *A*. Mark *A′*.

Step 2. Follow a similar plan to locate B'.

Step 3. Draw $\overline{A'B'}$ by connecting A' to B'.

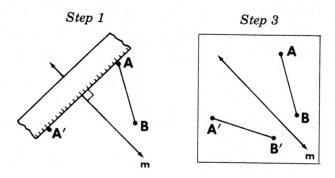

Step 1   *Step 3*

Method 2: Using Compasses and Straightedge

Step 1. With the point of the compasses on A, swing an arc passing through line m at two places. Without changing the opening of the compasses, swing two more arcs, one from each of the points on line m, to intersect on the side of line m that does not contain point A. This point of intersection is point A'. Mark A'.

Step 2. Follow a similar plan to locate B'.

Step 3. Draw $\overline{A'B'}$ by connecting A' to B'.

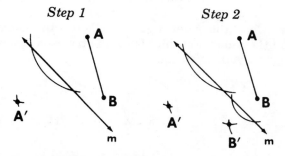

Step 1   *Step 2*

Answer: See the boxed diagram labeled *Step 3* under *Method 1*.

EXERCISES

1. On your paper, print all the capital letters of the alphabet that have line symmetry, and draw one or more lines of reflection for each of these letters.

2. Tell which of the following words have line symmetry and, if such symmetry exists, copy the word and draw the line of symmetry.

   a. DAD   **b.** MOM   **c.** HIKED   **d.** CHECK

   e. BOB   **f.** DEED   **g.** RADAR   **h.** CHOKE

   i. AVA   **j.** TOOT   **k.** AXIOM   **l.** YOUTH

3. Using the words from Exercise 2 that do *not* have line symmetry, print the letters of each word in a vertical column. Which of these words now have line symmetry?

In 4–10, the reflection of △*ABC* in line *k* is △*DEC*.

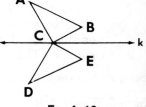

Ex. 4–10

4. What is the image of point *A* under the line reflection?
5. $r_k(B) = ?$ 6. $r_k(C) = ?$ 7. $r_k(D) = ?$
8. What is the preimage of point *B* under the line reflection?
9. $r_k(\angle ABC) = ?$ 10. $r_k(\overline{DE}) = ?$

In 11–24: **a.** Copy the given figure or sketch the geometric figure named. **b.** Tell the number of lines of symmetry each figure has, if any, and sketch them on your drawing.

Ex. 11   Ex. 12   Ex. 13   Ex. 14   Ex. 15

16. parabola	**17.** square	**18.** rectangle
19. parallelogram	**20.** rhombus	**21.** trapezoid
22. line segment	**23.** circle	**24.** equilateral triangle

In 25–32: **a.** Copy the given figure and line *m*. **b.** Sketch, as carefully as possible, the image of the given figure under a reflection in line *m*. Label image points with prime marks, as in *A* → *A'*.

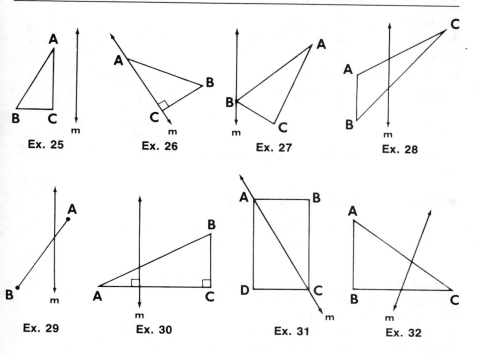

Ex. 25   Ex. 26   Ex. 27   Ex. 28

Ex. 29   Ex. 30   Ex. 31   Ex. 32

12-2 LINE REFLECTIONS IN COORDINATE GEOMETRY

Many transformations in the plane can be described by rules involving the relationship between the coordinates of the image and the pre-image. These rules are often discovered by inductive reasoning.

EXAMPLE 1. The vertices of $\triangle ABC$ are $A(1, 6)$, $B(4, 3)$, and $C(2, -1)$. These vertices are reflected in the y-axis; and their images, when connected, form $\triangle A'B'C'$. Observe:

$$A(1, 6) \rightarrow A'(-1, 6)$$
$$B(4, 3) \rightarrow B'(-4, 3)$$
$$C(2, -1) \rightarrow C'(-2, -1)$$

From these examples, we form a general rule.

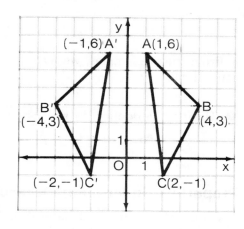

● **Under a reflection in the y-axis:**

$$P(x, y) \rightarrow P'(-x, y) \quad or \quad r_{y\text{-axis}}\,(x, y) = (-x, y)$$

EXAMPLE 2. The endpoints of $\overline{AB}$ are $A(3, 0)$ and $B(4, 3)$. These endpoints are reflected in the line whose equation is $y = x$, and $\overline{A'B'}$ is formed. Observe:

$$A(3, 0) \rightarrow A'(0, 3) \quad B(4, 3) \rightarrow B'(3, 4)$$

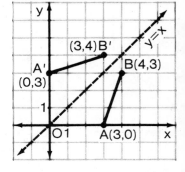

From these examples, we form a general rule.

● **Under a reflection in the line $y = x$:**

$$P(x, y) \rightarrow P'(y, x) \quad or \quad r_{y = x}(x, y) = (y, x)$$

EXAMPLE 3. The vertices of quadrilateral $ABCD$ are $A(1, 3)$, $B(2, 1)$, $C(7, 1)$, and $D(5, 5)$. These vertices are reflected in the x-axis; and their images, when connected, form quadrilateral $A'B'C'D'$. Observe:

$$A(1, 3) \rightarrow A'(1, -3)$$
$$B(2, 1) \rightarrow B'(2, -1)$$
$$C(7, 1) \rightarrow C'(7, -1)$$
$$D(5, 5) \rightarrow D'(5, -5)$$

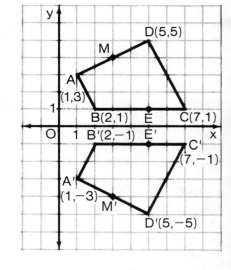

From these examples, we form a general rule.

● **Under a reflection in the x-axis:**

$$P(x, y) \rightarrow P'(x, -y) \quad or \quad r_{x\text{-axis}}(x, y) = (x, -y)$$

Properties Under a Line Reflection

Let us refer to the quadrilaterals in Example 3 to note some properties preserved under a line reflection.

1. *Distance is preserved*; that is, each segment and its image are equal in length. Here, $\overline{BC} \rightarrow \overline{B'C'}$ and $BC = B'C' = 5$. Similarly, $\overline{AB} \rightarrow \overline{A'B'}$ and $AB = A'B' = \sqrt{5}$.

2. *Angle measure is preserved*; that is, each angle and its image are equal in measure. Here, $\angle DAB \rightarrow \angle D'A'B'$. Since the slope of $\overline{DA}$ is $\frac{1}{2}$ and the slope of $\overline{AB}$ is $-\frac{2}{1}$, $\angle DAB$ is a right angle. Since the slope of $\overline{D'A'}$ is $-\frac{1}{2}$ and the slope of $\overline{A'B'}$ is $\frac{2}{1}$, $\angle D'A'B'$ is also a right angle. Thus, $m\angle DAB = m\angle D'A'B'$.

3. *Parallelism is preserved*; that is, if two lines are parallel, then their images will be parallel lines. Since the slope of $\overline{AB}$ is -2 and the slope of $\overline{DC}$ is -2, then $\overline{AB} \parallel \overline{DC}$. Examine their images: $\overline{AB} \rightarrow \overline{A'B'}$, and $\overline{DC} \rightarrow \overline{D'C'}$. Since the slope of $\overline{A'B'}$ is $+2$ and the slope of $\overline{D'C'}$ is $+2$, then $\overline{A'B'} \parallel \overline{D'C'}$.

4. *Collinearity is preserved*; that is, if three or more points lie on a straight line, their images will also lie on a straight line. Here, B, E, and C are collinear. Their images B', E', and C' are also collinear.

5. *A midpoint is preserved*; that is, given three points such that one is the midpoint of the other two, their images will be related in the same way. Here, the midpoint of $A(1, 3)$ and $D(5, 5)$ is $M(3, 4)$. Find the images A', D', and M'. Note that the midpoint of $A'(1, -3)$ and $D'(5, -5)$ is $M'(3, -4)$.

The properties observed for this specific example will be true for any figure and its image under a line reflection.

MODEL PROBLEM

Given $\triangle ABC$ whose vertices are $A(1, 3)$, $B(-2, 0)$, and $C(4, -3)$.

a. On one set of axes, draw $\triangle ABC$ and its image $\triangle A'B'C'$ under a reflection in the y-axis.

b. Find the coordinates of all points on the sides of $\triangle ABC$ that remain fixed under the given line reflection.

Solution:

a. In step 1, draw and label $\triangle ABC$. In step 2, find the images of the vertices of $\triangle ABC$ by using the rule for a reflection in the y-axis, $P(x, y) \rightarrow P'(-x, y)$.

$$A(1, 3) \rightarrow A'(-1, 3)$$
$$B(-2, 0) \rightarrow B'(2, 0)$$
$$C(4, -3) \rightarrow C'(-4, -3)$$

Draw and label $\triangle A'B'C'$.

Step 1

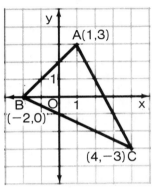

Step 2

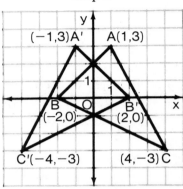

b. Under a reflection in the y-axis, points on the y-axis remain fixed. The sides of $\triangle ABC$ intersect the y-axis at $(0, 2)$ and $(0, -1)$. As seen in the graph, only these two points are common to both triangles.

Answer: **a.** See the graph labeled *Step 2*.
      b. $(0, 2)$ and $(0, -1)$

EXERCISES

1. Under a reflection in the x-axis, the image of (x, y) is _____.
2. Under a reflection in the y-axis, the image of (x, y) is _____.
3. Under a reflection in the line $y = x$, the image of (x, y) is _____.

In 4–7, find the image of the point under a reflection in the x-axis.

4. $(5, 7)$ **5.** $(6, -2)$ **6.** $(-1, -4)$ **7.** $(3, 0)$

In 8–11, find the image of the point under a reflection in the y-axis.

8. $(5, 7)$ **9.** $(-4, 10)$ **10.** $(0, 6)$ **11.** $(-1, -6)$

In 12–15, find the image of the point under a reflection in the line $y = x$.

12. $(5, 7)$ **13.** $(-3, 8)$ **14.** $(0, -2)$ **15.** $(6, 6)$

16. a. Using the rule $(x, y) \rightarrow (x, -y)$, find the images of $C(1, 4)$, $A(5, 1)$, and $T(4, 5)$, namely, C', A', and T'.

   b. On one set of axes, draw $\triangle CAT$ and $\triangle C'A'T'$.

   c. Find the lengths of $\overline{CA}$ and $\overline{C'A'}$.

   d. Is distance preserved under the given transformation?

17. a. Using the rule $(x, y) \rightarrow (-x, y)$, find the images of $D(2, 3)$, $O(0, 0)$, and $G(3, -2)$, namely, D', O', and G'.

   b. On one set of axes, draw $\triangle DOG$ and $\triangle D'O'G'$.

   c. Find the measures of $\angle DOG$ and $\angle D'O'G'$. (*Hint.* Look at the slopes.)

   d. Is angle measure preserved under the given transformation?

18. a. Using the rule $(x, y) \rightarrow (y, x)$, find the images of $B(7, 0)$, $I(7, 4)$, $R(4, 3)$, and $D(4, 1)$, namely, B', I', R', and D'.

   b. On one set of axes, draw quadrilateral $BIRD$ and quadrilateral $B'I'R'D'$.

   c. Explain why $\overline{BI} \parallel \overline{DR}$, and why $\overline{B'I'} \parallel \overline{D'R'}$.

   d. Is parallelism preserved under the given transformation?

In 19–24, the vertices of $\triangle ABC$ are given.

a. Find the coordinates of the images of the vertices, namely, A', B', and C', under the given reflection.

b. On one set of axes, draw $\triangle ABC$ and $\triangle A'B'C'$.

c. Find the coordinates of all points on the sides of $\triangle ABC$ that remain fixed under the given reflection.

In 19–21, the vertices of $\triangle ABC$ are $A(3, 0)$, $B(3, 6)$, and $C(0, 6)$. $\triangle ABC$ is reflected in:

19. the x-axis.   **20.** the y-axis.

21. the line $y = x$.

In 22–24, the vertices of $\triangle ABC$ are $A(1, 4)$, $B(3, 0)$, and $C(-3, -4)$. $\triangle ABC$ is reflected in:

22. the x-axis.   **23.** the y-axis.

24. the line $y = x$.

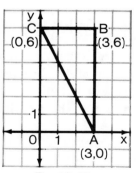

Ex. 19–21

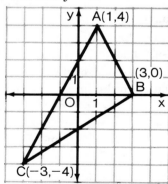

Ex. 22–24

In 25–31, the image of $\triangle ABC$ under a line reflection is $\triangle A'B'C'$.
a. Using the given coordinates, draw $\triangle ABC$ and $\triangle A'B'C'$ on one set of axes.
b. Find an equation of the line of reflection.

25. $\triangle ABC$: $A(2, 4)$, $B(2, 1)$, and $C(-1, 1)$.
   $\triangle A'B'C'$: $A'(4, 4)$, $B'(4, 1)$, and $C'(7, 1)$.

26. $\triangle ABC$: $A(1, 3)$, $B(2, 5)$, and $C(5, 3)$.
   $\triangle A'B'C'$: $A'(1, 1)$, $B'(2, -1)$, and $C'(5, 1)$.

27. $\triangle ABC$: $A(1, 4)$, $B(2, 1)$, and $C(4, 2)$.
   $\triangle A'B'C'$: $A'(-5, 4)$, $B'(-6, 1)$, and $C'(-8, 2)$.

28. $\triangle ABC$: $A(4, 2)$, $B(6, 2)$, and $C(2, -1)$.
   $\triangle A'B'C'$: $A'(2, 4)$, $B'(2, 6)$, and $C'(-1, 2)$.

29. $\triangle ABC$: $A(-1, 0)$, $B(0, 2)$, and $C(4, 1)$.
   $\triangle A'B'C'$: $A'(-1, 8)$, $B'(0, 6)$, and $C'(4, 7)$.

30. $\triangle ABC$: $A(0, 1)$, $B(3, 1)$, and $C(3, 4)$.
   $\triangle A'B'C'$: $A'(-1, 2)$, $B'(-1, 5)$, and $C'(2, 5)$.

31. $\triangle ABC$: $A(2, -1)$, $B(4, 2)$, and $C(-1, 2)$.
   $\triangle A'B'C'$: $A'(1, -2)$, $B'(-2, -4)$, and $C'(-2, 1)$.

32. Prove that the y-axis is the perpendicular bisector of the line segment joining any point $A(a, b)$ and its image $A'(-a, b)$ under a reflection in the y-axis. (*Plan:* Prove that $\overline{AA'}$ is perpendicular to the y-axis, whose equation is $x = 0$, and that the midpoint of $\overline{AA'}$ lies on the y-axis.)

33. Prove that the x-axis is the perpendicular bisector of the line segment joining any point $A(a, b)$ and its image $A'(a, -b)$ under a reflection in the x-axis. (*Plan:* Prove that $\overline{AA'}$ is perpendicular to the x-axis, whose equation is $y = 0$, and that the midpoint of $\overline{AA'}$ lies on the x-axis.)

34. Prove that the line whose equation is $y = x$ is the perpendicular bisector of the line segment joining any point $A(a, b)$ and its image $A'(b, a)$ under a reflection in $y = x$. (*Plan:* Prove that $\overline{AA'}$ is perpendicular to the line $y = x$ and that the midpoint of $\overline{AA'}$ lies on $y = x$.)

35. The vertices of $\triangle DEF$ are $D(3, 4)$, $E(4, 1)$, and $F(6, 3)$. If $\triangle DEF$ is reflected in the line whose equation is $x = 2$, find the coordinates of the images D', E', and F'.

36. The vertices of $\triangle RST$ are $R(0, 0)$, $S(1, 2)$, and $T(4, 1)$. If $\triangle RST$ is reflected in the line whose equation is $y = 3$, find the coordinates of the images R', S', and T'.

37. Under a reflection in the line whose equation is $y = 2$, the image of $\triangle ABC$ is $\triangle A'B'C'$. The vertices of $\triangle ABC$ are $A(1, 0)$, $B(4, 6)$, and $C(10, 6)$.

a. On one set of axes: Draw $\triangle ABC$, the line $y = 2$, and $\triangle A'B'C'$.

b. Name the coordinates of A', B', and C'.

c. Find the coordinates of all points on the sides of $\triangle ABC$ that remain fixed under the given reflection.

d. Using the lengths of $\overline{AB}$ and $\overline{A'B'}$, show that distance is preserved under the given reflection.

e. Using $\overline{BC}$ and $\overline{B'C'}$, illustrate that a midpoint is preserved under the reflection.

12-3 POINT REFLECTIONS AND POINT SYMMETRY

Point Reflections

Triangle ABC is reflected through point P, and its image $\triangle A'B'C'$ is formed. To find this image under a reflection through point P, the following steps are taken:

Step 1. From each vertex of $\triangle ABC$, a segment is drawn through point P to its image such that the distance from the vertex to point P is equal to the distance from point P to the image. Here, $\overline{AA'}$, $\overline{BB'}$, and $\overline{CC'}$ pass through point P so that $AP = PA'$, $BP = PB'$, and $CP = PC'$.

Step 2. The images A', B', and C' are connected to form $\triangle A'B'C'$, which is the reflection of $\triangle ABC$ through point P.

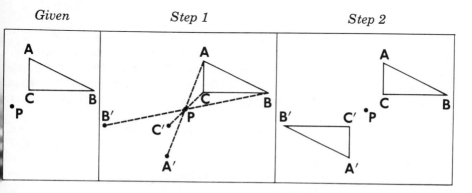

Given   *Step 1*   *Step 2*

In this point reflection, it is still correct to say that the image of A is A', and the image of A' is A by writing the symbols $A \rightarrow A'$ and $A' \rightarrow A$.

A reflection in a point P is indicated in symbols as R_P. Thus, to show specifically that the images are found under a reflection in a point P, we write:

In Symbols	*In Words*
$R_P(A) = A'$.	Under a reflection in point P, the image of A is A'.
$R_P(B) = B'$.	Under a reflection in point P, the image of B is B'.
$R_P(C) = C'$.	Under a reflection in point P, the image of C is C'.

Under the point reflection just described, point P is the midpoint of each of the segments $\overline{AA'}$, $\overline{BB'}$, and $\overline{CC'}$, leading to our definition. Notice, however, that one point remains fixed in the plane, namely, point P itself.

● **Definition.** A *reflection in a point P* is a transformation of the plane such that:

1. The image of the fixed point P is P.
2. For all other points, the image of K is K', where P is the midpoint of $\overline{KK'}$.

Point Symmetry

 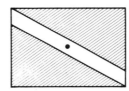  

The diagrams above include an advertising logo for a company, an ancient flag, a pinwheel, and a playing card. In each of these diagrams, imagine that every point in the figure moves to its image through a point of reflection located in the "center" of the figure. This *point of reflection* is also called a *point of symmetry*, and each design is said to have *point symmetry*.

None of the figures pictured above has line symmetry. There is no way to fold any of these pictures over a line so that all points coincide; that is, there is no way to find a "mirror image."

We can think of point symmetry, however, as "turning the picture around" or "moving the picture through a half-turn." Try it. Turn the book upside down. Do the pictures look the same? They should, if they have point symmetry.

● **Definition.** *Point symmetry* occurs in a figure when the figure is its own image under a reflection in a point.

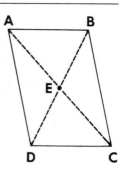

Quadrilateral *ABCD* is a parallelogram whose diagonals $\overline{AC}$ and $\overline{BD}$ intersect at point *E*. This point *E* is a point of symmetry for $\square ABCD$. Thus, $A \to C$, $B \to D$, $C \to A$, $D \to B$, and so forth. While $\square ABCD$ has point symmetry, it does *not* have line symmetry.

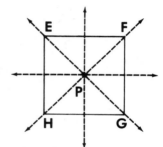

It is possible for a figure to have both line symmetry and point symmetry at the same time. Quadrilateral *EFGH* is a square containing four lines of reflection that intersect at *P*, a point of symmetry.

Points of symmetry may also be found for letters and for words.

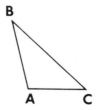

MODEL PROBLEM ————————————————————————

Copy $\triangle ABC$. Then sketch as carefully as possible the image of $\triangle ABC$ under a reflection in point *A*.

Solution:

Method 1: Using a Ruler

Step 1. Hold the ruler on side $\overline{BA}$ and measure the distance from *B* to *A*. Since *A* is the fixed point, the image *B'* is found on the line $\overleftrightarrow{BA}$ on the other side of *A*, such that $BA = AB'$. Mark *B'*.

Step 2. Follow a similar plan to locate C'.

Step 3. Connect points A, B', and C' to form $\triangle AB'C'$, the reflection of $\triangle ABC$ in point A.

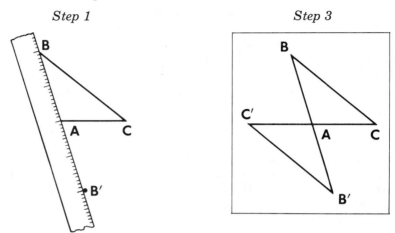

Step 1   *Step 3*

Method 2: Using Compasses and Straightedge

Step 1. Draw $\overrightarrow{BA}$ and $\overrightarrow{CA}$ so that the lines extend through point A.

Step 2. Open the compasses to measure the length AB. With the point of the compasses on A, swing this arc through $\overrightarrow{BA}$ so that $BA = AB'$. Mark B'.

Step 3. Follow a similar plan to locate C'.

Step 4. Draw $\triangle AB'C'$.

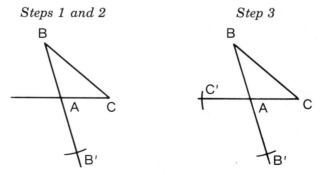

Steps 1 and 2   *Step 3*

Answer: See the boxed diagram labeled *Step 3* under *Method 1*.

Note. If the point of reflection is not a point of the given preimage, follow the procedure shown on page 539.

EXERCISES

1. On your paper, print all the capital letters of the alphabet that have point symmetry.

2. Tell which of the following words have point symmetry and, if such symmetry exists, locate the reflection point in the word.

   a. SIS   **b.** WOW   **c.** NOON   **d.** ZOO

   e. OX   **f.** SWIMS   **g.** un   **h.** pod

In 3–9, the reflection of $\triangle ABC$ through point B is $\triangle DBE$.

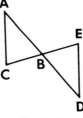

3. What is the image of A under the point reflection?
4. $R_B(C) = ?$ **5.** $R_B(D) = ?$ **6.** $R_B(B) = ?$
7. What is the preimage of C under the point reflection?
8. $R_B(\angle CAB) = ?$ **9.** $R_B(\overline{CA}) = ?$

Ex. 3–9

In 10–18: **a.** Copy the given figure, or sketch the geometric figure named. **b.** Tell whether or not the figure has a point of symmetry and, if it does, locate the point on your drawing.

10.   kite   **11.**   star   **12.** rectangle
13. parallelogram
14. rhombus
15. trapezoid
16. circle
17. line segment
18. equilateral triangle

In 19–22: **a.** Copy the given figure. **b.** Sketch as carefully as possible the image of the given figure under a reflection in point A. Label image points with prime marks, as in $B \rightarrow B'$.

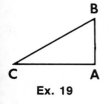
Ex. 19

Ex. 20

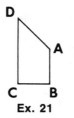
Ex. 21

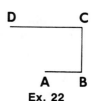
Ex. 22

In 23–27: **a.** Copy the given figure and point *P*. **b.** Sketch as carefully as possible the image of the given figure under a reflection in point *P*. Label image points with prime marks, as in *A* → *A′*.

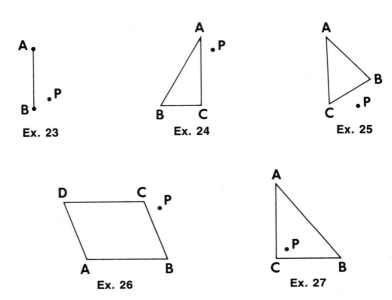

Ex. 23   Ex. 24   Ex. 25

Ex. 26   Ex. 27

28. a. Draw any triangle and label the vertices *A*, *B*, and *C*.
  b. Locate point *M*, the midpoint of $\overline{AC}$.
  c. Draw the reflection of △*ABC* through point *M*.
  d. Explain why the image of *A* is *C*, and the image of *C* is *A*.
  e. If the image of *B* is *B′*, what type of quadrilateral is *ABCB′*? Explain.

29. Crossword puzzles in the daily paper are symmetric. Cut out a crossword puzzle, study the pattern created by the black and white squares in the puzzle, and tell if the puzzle has point symmetry, line symmetry, or both.

30. a. Of the 13 cards that are hearts in a standard deck, which have point symmetry?
  b. Of the 13 cards that are diamonds in a standard deck, which have point symmetry?
  c. Of the 26 red cards in a standard deck, which have line symmetry?

12-4 POINT REFLECTIONS IN COORDINATE GEOMETRY

The most common point reflection in coordinate geometry is a reflection in the origin.

EXAMPLE 1. The vertices of $\triangle ABC$ are $A(1, 2)$, $B(5, 5)$, and $C(5, 2)$. These vertices are reflected in the origin (point O), and their images, when connected, form $\triangle A'B'C'$. Observe:

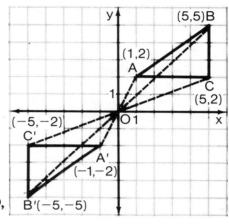

$$A(1, 2) \rightarrow A'(-1, -2)$$
$$B(5, 5) \rightarrow B'(-5, -5)$$
$$C(5, 2) \rightarrow C'(-5, -2)$$

From these examples, we form a general rule.

● **Under a reflection in point O, the origin:**

$$P(x, y) \rightarrow P'(-x, -y) \quad or \quad R_o(x, y) = (-x, -y)$$

The *properties preserved under a point reflection* include all five properties listed previously for a line reflection, namely, distance, angle measure, parallelism, collinearity, and midpoints.

Compositions of Transformations

When two transformations occur, one following another, we have a *composition of transformations*. The first transformation produces an image, and the second transformation is performed on that image.

EXAMPLE 2. Start again with $\triangle ABC$ whose vertices are $A(1, 2)$, $B(5, 5)$, and $C(5, 2)$. For the composition of transformations, we will consider two line reflections. First, by reflecting $\triangle ABC$ in the y-axis, we form $\triangle A'B'C'$, or $\triangle I$. Then, by reflecting $\triangle A'B'C'$ in the x-axis, we form $\triangle A''B''C''$, or $\triangle II$. Observe how the vertices behave:

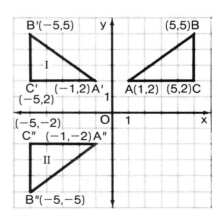

$$A(1, 2) \rightarrow A'(-1, 2) \rightarrow A''(-1, -2)$$
$$B(5, 5) \rightarrow B'(-5, 5) \rightarrow B''(-5, -5)$$
$$C(5, 2) \rightarrow C'(-5, 2) \rightarrow C''(-5, -2)$$

Now compare the original triangle, $\triangle ABC$, with its final image, $\triangle A''B''C''$. How are these two triangles related? (As a hint, look at the figure for Example 1.) Observe:

● **The composition of a line reflection in the y-axis, followed by a line reflection in the x-axis, is equivalent to a single transformation, namely, a reflection through point O, the origin.**

In Example 2, we reflected the triangle first in the y-axis and then in the x-axis. If we had reflected the triangle first in the x-axis and then in the y-axis, would this composition also be equivalent to a reflection through point O, the origin? The answer is yes. However, not all compositions will act in the same way. In general, compositions of transformations are *not* commutative.

You will see other examples of compositions later in this chapter.

MODEL PROBLEM

The vertices of parallelogram $ABCD$ are $A(1, 1)$, $B(3, 5)$, $C(9, 5)$, and $D(7, 1)$.

a. Find the coordinates of the point of symmetry for $\square ABCD$.

b. Find the image of $\overline{AB}$ under this point reflection.

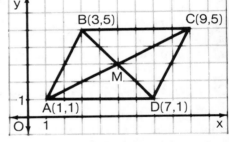

c. Find the length of $\overline{AB}$ and the length of its image to show that distance is preserved in this transformation.

Solution:

a. Since the diagonals of a parallelogram bisect each other, the point of symmetry is the intersection point of the two diagonals, or the midpoint of either diagonal.

$$M = \text{the midpoint of } \overline{AC} = \left(\frac{1+9}{2}, \frac{1+5}{2}\right) = \left(\frac{10}{2}, \frac{6}{2}\right) = (5, 3)$$

$$\text{Also, } M = \text{the midpoint of } \overline{BD} = \left(\frac{3+7}{2}, \frac{5+1}{2}\right) = \left(\frac{10}{2}, \frac{6}{2}\right) = (5, 3)$$

b. The image of $\overline{AB}$ under a reflection in point M is $\overline{CD}$, written $R_M(\overline{AB}) = \overline{CD}$.

c. The distance formula is $d = \sqrt{(x_1 - x_2)^2 + (y_1 - y_2)^2}$. Therefore:

$$AB = \sqrt{(3 - 1)^2 + (5 - 1)^2} = \sqrt{2^2 + 4^2} = \sqrt{4 + 16} = \sqrt{20}$$

$$= \sqrt{4}\,\sqrt{5} = 2\sqrt{5}$$

$$CD = \sqrt{(9 - 7)^2 + (5 - 1)^2} = \sqrt{2^2 + 4^2} = \sqrt{4 + 16} = \sqrt{20}$$

$$= \sqrt{4}\,\sqrt{5} = 2\sqrt{5}$$

Thus, $AB = CD$, illustrating that distance is preserved in a point reflection.

Answer: **a.** (5, 3) **b.** $\overline{CD}$ **c.** $AB = CD = 2\sqrt{5}$

EXERCISES

1. Under a reflection in the origin, the image of (x, y) is _____ .

In 2–5, find the image of the point under a reflection in the origin.

2. (6, −3) **3.** (−7, 1) **4.** (0, 0) **5.** (−3, 0)

6. a. Using the rule $(x, y) \rightarrow (-x, -y)$, find the images of $A(2, 1)$, $B(4, 5)$, and $C(-1, 3)$, namely, A', B', and C'.
  b. On one set of axes, draw $\triangle ABC$ and $\triangle A'B'C'$.
  c. Find the coordinates of M, the midpoint of $\overline{AB}$.
  d. Using $\overline{AB}$ and M and their images, show that a midpoint is preserved under this transformation.

7. a. Using the rule $(x, y) \rightarrow (-x, -y)$, find the images of $A(-5, -2)$, $B(-1, -2)$, $C(-1, 4)$, and $D(-3, 3)$, namely, A', B', C', and D'.
  b. On one set of axes, draw quadrilateral $ABCD$ and quadrilateral $A'B'C'D'$.
  c. Find the length of each of the sides of $ABCD$ and $A'B'C'D'$ to show that distance is preserved under the given transformation.

8. a. Draw $\triangle RST$ whose vertices are $R(-2, -1)$, $S(-2, 2)$, and $T(4, 2)$.
  b. Find the images of each of the vertices of $\triangle RST$, namely, R', S', and T', under a reflection through the origin.
  c. On the same graph used in part **a**, draw $\triangle R'S'T'$.
  d. Find the coordinates of all points on the sides of $\triangle RST$ that remain fixed under the point reflection.

9. a. On graph paper, draw the line whose equation is $y = \frac{1}{2}x + 2$.
   b. Name the coordinates of three points on this line, and call these points A, B, and C.
   c. Under a point reflection in the origin, name the coordinates of A', B', and C', the images of the three points found in **b**.
   d. On the same graph, draw the line containing A', B', and C'.
   e. What is an equation of the line drawn in **d**?

10. a. Given $A(x_1, y_1)$ and $B(x_2, y_2)$, what is the slope of $\overleftrightarrow{AB}$?
   b. Under a point reflection through the origin, find the images A' and B' of $A(x_1, y_1)$ and $B(x_2, y_2)$.
   c. What is the slope of $\overleftrightarrow{A'B'}$?
   d. Explain why $\overleftrightarrow{AB} \parallel \overleftrightarrow{A'B'}$.

In 11–18, the line whose equation is given is reflected through the origin. What is an equation of the line that is its image? (*Hint.* See procedures in Exercise 9.)

11. $x = 3$ **12.** $y = -8$ **13.** $y = x + 5$ **14.** $y = -x + 1$

15. $y = x$ **16.** $y = 2x - 3$ **17.** $y = 3x$ **18.** $y = -x$

19. The vertices of rhombus $ABCD$ are $A(0, 1)$, $B(3, 5)$, $C(8, 5)$, and $D(5, 1)$.

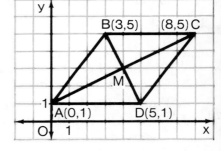

   a. Find the coordinates of M, the point of symmetry for rhombus $ABCD$.
   b. $R_M(A) = ?$ **c.** $R_M(\overline{BC}) = ?$
   d. $R_M(M) = ?$
   e. $R_M(\angle BCD) = ?$
   f. $R_M(\angle MCB) = ?$
   g. Find the length of $\overline{AB}$ and the length of its image. Is distance preserved in the given transformation?

20. The vertices of rectangle $HELP$ are $H(-2, -1)$, $E(-2, 5)$, $L(2, 5)$, and $P(2, -1)$.
   a. Find the coordinates of the point of symmetry for rectangle $HELP$.
   b. Give one example of each of the following properties of a point symmetry by selecting parts of the rectangle and their corresponding images:
   (1) Distance is preserved.
   (2) Angle measure is preserved.
   (3) A midpoint is preserved.

In 21–26, the image of △*ABC* under a point reflection is △*A'B'C'*.
a. Using the given coordinates, draw △*ABC* and △*A'B'C'* on one set of axes.
b. Find the coordinates of the point of reflection.

21. △*ABC*: *A*(2, 2), *B*(5, 2), *C*(5, 4)
△*A'B'C'*: *A'*(0, 2), *B'*(−3, 2), *C'*(−3, 0)

22. △*ABC*: *A*(2, 5), *B*(5, 6), *C*(2, 3)
△*A'B'C'*: *A'*(2, 1), *B'*(−1, 0), *C'*(2, 3)

23. △*ABC*: *A*(3, 1), *B*(5, 5), *C*(6, 3)
△*A'B'C'*: *A'*(3, 7), *B'*(1, 3), *C'*(0, 5)

24. △*ABC*: *A*(−3, 6), *B*(1, 7), *C*(2, 4)
△*A'B'C'*: *A'*(−1, 0), *B'*(−5, −1), *C'*(−6, 2)

25. △*ABC*: *A*(−1, 1), *B*(2, 5), *C*(5, 1)
△*A'B'C'*: *A'*(3, 3), *B'*(0, −1), *C'*(−3, 3)

26. △*ABC*: *A*(3, 8), *B*(0, 2), *C*(5, 4)
△*A'B'C'*: *A'*(1, 4), *B'*(4, 10), *C'*(−1, 8)

27. The vertices of △*DEF* are *D*(4, 3), *E*(8, 1), and *F*(8, 3). If △*DEF* is reflected through the point (4, 1), find the coordinates of the images, *D'*, *E'*, and *F'*.

28. The vertices of △*RST* are *R*(0, 0), *S*(4, −4), and *T*(5, −1). If △*RST* is reflected through the point (2, 1), find the coordinates of the images, *R'*, *S'*, and *T'*.

In 29 and 30, the vertices of △*ABC* are *A*(1, 3), *B*(1, 1), and *C*(5, 1).

29. a. Draw △*ABC* and its image △*A'B'C'* under a point reflection through the origin.
   b. Using the same graph, reflect △*A'B'C'* in the *x*-axis to form its image △*A"B"C"*.
   c. What single transformation is equivalent to the composition of a point reflection through the origin followed by a reflection in the *x*-axis?

30. a. Draw △*ABC* and its image △*A'B'C'* under a reflection in the line whose equation is *x* = 1.
   b. Using the same graph, reflect △*A'B'C'* through point *A* to form its image △*A"B"C"*.
   c. What single transformation is equivalent to the composition of a line reflection in *x* = 1 followed by a point reflection through point *A*?

12-5 TRANSLATIONS

If a line reflection is like a *flip*, and a point reflection is like a *half-turn*, then a **translation** is like a *slide* or a *shift*.

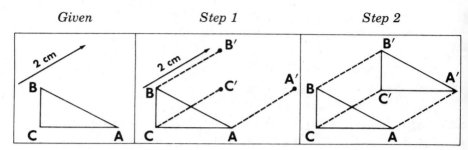

| Given | Step 1 | Step 2 |

Triangle *ABC* is moved 2 cm in the direction indicated in the diagram by the arrow, and its image $\triangle A'B'C'$ is formed.

Step 1. From each vertex of $\triangle ABC$, a segment 2 cm long is drawn parallel to the arrow that indicates the direction of this translation. Thus, $AA' = BB' = CC' = 2$ cm, and $\overline{AA'} \parallel \overline{BB'} \parallel \overline{CC'}$.

Step 2. The images A', B', and C' are connected to form $\triangle A'B'C'$.

Any transformation of the plane that slides or shifts a figure in such a fashion is called a translation, symbolized by T. Under a translation, if one point moves, then all points move and *no* point remains fixed.

● **Definition.** A **translation** is a transformation of the plane that shifts every point in the plane the same distance in the same direction to its image.

A rule for a translation is easily stated in coordinate geometry. The segment $\overline{AB}$ is translated to its image $\overline{A'B'}$ by a shift to the right and down. Notice that this translation means moving a point 3 units to the right and 2 units down. Thus, by counting these units horizontally and vertically, we form the rule for the translation:

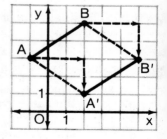

$$P(x, y) \to P'(x + 3, y - 2) \quad or \quad T_{3,-2}(x, y) = (x + 3, y - 2)$$

● **Under a translation of *a* units horizontally and *b* units vertically:**

$$P(x, y) \rightarrow P'(x + a, y + b) \quad or \quad T_{a,b}(x, y) = (x + a, y + b)$$

The *properties preserved under a translation* include all five properties listed previously for a line reflection, namely, distance, angle measure, parallelism, collinearity, and midpoints.

MODEL PROBLEM

a. Draw $\triangle ABC$ whose vertices are $A(-2, 1)$, $B(1, 4)$, and $C(2, 2)$.

b. Using the same axes, graph $\triangle A'B'C'$, the image of $\triangle ABC$ under the translation $T_{5,-1}$.

c. Using the same axes, graph $\triangle A''B''C''$, the image of $\triangle A'B'C'$ under the translation $T_{-3,5}$.

d. Name a single transformation that is equivalent to $T_{5,-1}$ followed by $T_{-3,5}$.

Solution:

a. See graph.

b. By the first translation, $T_{5,-1}(x, y) = (x + 5, y - 1)$. Thus:

$$A(-2, 1) \rightarrow A'(3, 0)$$
$$B(1, 4) \rightarrow B'(6, 3)$$
$$C(2, 2) \rightarrow C'(7, 1)$$

$\triangle A'B'C'$ is shown.

c. By the second translation, $T_{-3,5}(x, y) = (x - 3, y + 5)$. Thus:

$$A'(3, 0) \rightarrow A''(0, 5)$$
$$B'(6, 3) \rightarrow B''(3, 8)$$
$$C'(7, 1) \rightarrow C''(4, 6)$$

$\triangle A''B''C''$ is shown.

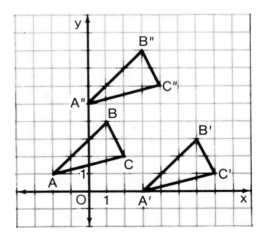

d. The translation $(T_{5,-1})$ followed by a second translation $(T_{-3,5})$ is equivalent to a single translation $(T_{5-3,-1+5})$, or simply $(T_{2,4})$. *Ans.*

EXERCISES _____

In 1–4, use the rule $(x, y) \rightarrow (x + 2, y + 3)$ to find the image of the given point.

1. $(3, -1)$ **2.** $(2, 6)$ **3.** $(0, -8)$ **4.** $(-5, -3)$

In 5–8, use the rule $(x, y) \rightarrow (x - 3, y + 12)$ to find the image of the given point.

5. $(4, 4)$ **6.** $(2, 0)$ **7.** $(-3, -15)$ **8.** $(-5, -5)$

In 9–12, find the image of the point $(2, 7)$ under the given translation.

9. $T_{1,2}$ **10.** $T_{3, -6}$ **11.** $T_{-4, 0}$ **12.** $T_{-2, -8}$

In 13–18, find the rule for the translation so the image of A is A'.

13. $A(3, 8) \rightarrow A'(4, 6)$ **14.** $A(1, 0) \rightarrow A'(0, 1)$
15. $A(2, 5) \rightarrow A'(-1, 1)$ **16.** $A(-1, 2) \rightarrow A'(-2, -3)$
17. $A(0, -3) \rightarrow A'(-7, -3)$ **18.** $A(4, -7) \rightarrow A'(4, -2)$

19. Under a given translation, the image of $(3, 3)$ is $(6, 1)$. Using the same translation, find the *preimage* of:
a. $(8, 3)$ **b.** $(3, -2)$ **c.** $(2, -5)$

In 20 and 21, the vertices of nine congruent rectangles are indicated in the accompanying diagram.

20. Under a given translation, if the image of E is B, find the image of:
a. K **b.** L **c.** $\overline{OP}$
d. $\overline{GM}$ **e.** $\overline{FP}$ **f.** $\angle FLM$

21. Under a given translation, if the image of D is M, find the image of:
a. C **b.** F **c.** $\overline{DH}$
d. $\overline{FG}$ **e.** $\overline{BD}$ **f.** $\angle BCG$

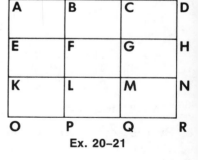

Ex. 20–21

22. a. On graph paper, draw $\triangle HOT$ whose vertices are $H(-2, 0)$, $O(0, 0)$, and $T(0, 4)$.
b. Using the same axes, graph $\triangle H'O'T'$, the image of $\triangle HOT$ under the translation $T_{2, -3}$.
c. Using the same axes, graph $\triangle H''O''T''$, the image of $\triangle H'O'T'$ under the translation $T_{1,4}$.
d. Name a single transformation that is equivalent to $T_{2, -3}$ followed by $T_{1,4}$.

23. a. On graph paper, draw quadrilateral *WARM* whose vertices are $W(-4, 3)$, $A(0, 1)$, $R(2, 5)$, and $M(0, 5)$.

b. Using the same axes, graph quadrilateral $W'A'R'M'$ where $W \rightarrow W'$ under $T_{5,-2}$.

c. Using the same axes, graph quadrilateral $W''A''R''M''$ where $W' \rightarrow W''$ under $T_{0,2}$.

d. Name a single translation that is equivalent to $T_{5,-2}$ followed by $T_{0,2}$.

24. The vertices of $\triangle ICE$ are $I(-3, 1)$, $C(-1, 0)$, and $E(-1, 4)$.

a. On graph paper, draw $\triangle ICE$ and its image $\triangle I'C'E'$ under a line reflection in the *y*-axis.

b. Using the same graph, reflect $\triangle I'C'E'$ in the line whose equation is $x = 3$ to form its image $\triangle I''C''E''$.

c. What single transformation is equivalent to a reflection in the *y*-axis followed by a reflection in the line $x = 3$?

25. The vertices of parallelogram *COLD* are $C(-1, 3)$, $O(0, 0)$, $L(2, 0)$, and $D(1, 3)$.

a. On graph paper, draw $\square COLD$ and its image, $\square C'O'L'D'$ under a reflection in the *x*-axis.

b. Using the same graph, reflect $\square C'O'L'D'$ in the line whose equation is $y = -2$ to form its image $\square C''O''L''D''$.

c. What single transformation is equivalent to a reflection in the *x*-axis followed by a reflection in the line $y = -2$?

12-6 ROTATIONS

Think of what happens to all the points on the steering wheel of a car as the wheel is turned. Except for the fixed point in the center of the wheel, every point moves through an arc so that the position of each point is changed by the same number of degrees. This transformation, which is like a turn, is called a ***rotation***.

$\triangle ABC$ is rotated 70° counterclockwise about the fixed point *P* to form its image $\triangle A'B'C'$. By drawing rays $\overrightarrow{PA}$ and $\overrightarrow{PA'}$, we see that $m\angle APA' = 70$. Notice that the distance from *P* to *A* is equal to the distance from *P* to *A'*, or $PA = PA'$. Also, $m\angle BPB' = 70$ and $PB = PB'$. In the same way, if the rays $\overrightarrow{PC}$ and $\overrightarrow{PC'}$, were drawn, we would see that $m\angle CPC' = 70$ and $PC = PC'$.

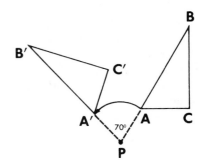

This rotation of 70° counterclockwise about point P is written in symbols as $R_{P,70°}$. Thus, $R_{P,70°}(A) = A'$ indicates that the image of A is A' under the rotation. It is understood in this symbolism that a counterclockwise direction is being taken.

Observe the following:

1. The measure of the angle of rotation is positive when the rotation is counterclockwise.

2. The measure of the angle of rotation is negative when the rotation is clockwise.

Counter-
clockwise
+70°

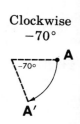

Clockwise
−70°

● **Definition.** A *rotation* is a transformation of the plane about a point P, called the *center of rotation*, and through an angle of ϕ degrees such that:

1. The image of the fixed point P is P.

2. For all other points, the image of K is K' where m∠$KPK' = \phi$ and $PK = PK'$. (The Greek letter ϕ represents the measure of the angle of rotation.)

There are two cases where the symbol for rotation is abbreviated:

1. Since a rotation of 180° about a point P is equivalent to a reflection in point P, we abbreviate $R_{P,180°}$ as R_P, the symbol for a point reflection.

2. If no point is mentioned, it is assumed that the rotation is taken about the origin. Thus, $R_{50°}$ means a 50° rotation about O, the origin.

The *properties preserved under a rotation* include all five properties listed previously for a line reflection, namely, distance, angle measure, parallelism, collinearity, and midpoints.

The geometric shapes in the figure have rotational symmetry. If the equilateral triangle is rotated 120°, it is its own image. Notice that 3(120°) = 360°. The equilateral triangle is also its own image under a rotation of 240°, which is a multiple of 120°.

If the regular pentagon is rotated 72°, it is its own image. Notice that 5(72°) = 360°. The regular pentagon is also its own image under rotations of 144°, 216°, and 288°, each of which is a multiple of 72°.

● **Definition.** *Rotational symmetry* occurs in a figure if the figure is its own image under a rotation about a fixed center point of ϕ degrees, $0° < \phi < 360°$.

The most common rotation, other than that of 180°, is a rotation of 90°, called a **quarter-turn**. We will state a rule for a quarter-turn about the origin and use this rule in the model problem to follow.

● **Under a rotation of 90° counterclockwise about the origin:**
$$P(x, y) \rightarrow P'(-y, x) \quad or \quad R_{90°}(x, y) = (-y, x)$$

MODEL PROBLEM

The vertices of $\triangle ABC$ are $A(1, 3)$, $B(5, 1)$, and $C(1, 1)$. On one set of axes, draw $\triangle ABC$ and its image $\triangle A'B'C'$ under a rotation of 90° counterclockwise about the origin.

Solution:

By the rule for a quarter-turn, $P(x, y) \rightarrow P'(-y, x)$. Thus:

$A(1, 3) \rightarrow A'(-3, 1)$
$B(5, 1) \rightarrow B'(-1, 5)$
$C(1, 1) \rightarrow C'(-1, 1)$

Connect the images A', B', and C' to form $\triangle A'B'C'$.

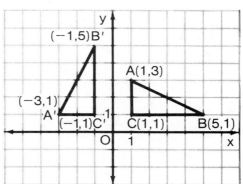

EXERCISES

1. Under a rotation of 90° counterclockwise about the origin, the image of (x, y) is _____ .
2. Under a rotation of 180° about the origin, the image of (x, y) is _____ .

In 3–9, $\triangle ABC \rightarrow \triangle DEF$ by a quarter-turn about P.

3. What is the image of A under the quarter-turn?
4. $R_{P,90°}(B) = ?$ 5. $R_{P,90°}(P) = ?$
6. $R_{P,90°}(\overline{CA}) = ?$ 7. $m\angle APD = ?$
8. What is the preimage of $\overline{FE}$ under the quarter-turn?
9. Does $m\angle BPE = m\angle CPF$? Why?

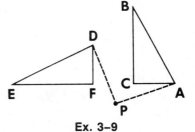

Ex. 3–9

In 10–17, $\triangle ABC$ is rotated $90°$ counterclockwise to its image $\triangle A'B'C'$.

a. Using the rule $(x, y) \rightarrow (-y, x)$ and the given coordinates, find the images of A, B, and C.

b. On one set of axes, draw $\triangle ABC$ and $\triangle A'B'C'$.

10. $A(1, 1)$, $B(1, 5)$, $C(4, 5)$ **11.** $A(1, 2)$, $B(1, 6)$, $C(3, 2)$

12. $A(4, 3)$, $B(4, -2)$, $C(1, -1)$ **13.** $A(1, 3)$, $B(3, 5)$, $C(3, 0)$

14. $A(-3, 3)$, $B(-1, 3)$, $C(-1, -1)$ **15.** $A(2, 1)$, $B(3, -1)$, $C(-2, -1)$

16. $A(-2, 2)$, $B(0, -4)$, $C(4, -4)$ **17.** $A(0, 0)$, $B(2, 1)$, $C(-2, 4)$

In 18–32, the diagram shows that each triangle is the image of another triangle under a quarter-turn about the origin. For example, $R_{90°}(\triangle ABC) = \triangle DEF$.

18. $R_{90°}(D) = ?$

19. $R_{90°}(\overline{KL}) = ?$

20. $R_{90°}(\overline{GH}) = ?$

21. $R_{90°}(\angle IHG) = ?$

22. $R_{180°}(D) = ?$

23. $R_{180°}(\overline{GH}) = ?$

24. $R_{180°}(\overline{KL}) = ?$

25. $R_{180°}(\angle DEF) = ?$ **26.** $R_{270°}(D) = ?$ **27.** $R_{270°}(\overline{DF}) = ?$

28. $R_{270°}(\angle JKL) = ?$ **29.** $R_{270°}(\angle ACB) = ?$

Ex. 18–32

30. Is the composition of two quarter-turns about the origin equivalent to a point reflection through the origin?

31. What transformation is equivalent to $R_{180°}$ followed by $R_{90°}$?

32. Explain why $R_{270°}$ is equivalent to the *clockwise* rotation, $R_{-90°}$.

In 33–48:   **a.** Tell whether or not the figure drawn or named has rotational symmetry.   **b.** Where possible, find the degree measure of the smallest angle that will rotate the figure to be its own image.

Ex. 33

Ex. 34

Ex. 35

Ex. 36

Ex. 37

Ex. 38

39. + **40.** − **41.** rectangle **42.** square

43. × **44.** ÷ **45.** parallelogram **46.** circle

47. isosceles triangle **48.** equiangular triangle

12-7 DILATIONS

When a photograph is enlarged or reduced, a change, or transformation, takes place in its size. There is a constant ratio of the distances between points in the original photograph compared to the distances between their images in the enlargement or reduction. This type of transformation is called a *dilation*.

Triangle ABC is to be dilated so that the *center of dilation* is point O and the *constant of dilation* is 2.

Step 1. From O, the center of dilation, rays are drawn to pass through each of the vertices of $\triangle ABC$. Using 2, the constant of dilation, the images (A', B', and C') are located on these rays so that $OA' = 2 \cdot OA$, $OB' = 2 \cdot OB$, and $OC' = 2 \cdot OC$.

Step 2. The images, A', B', and C', are connected to form $\triangle A'B'C'$.

Given	*Step 1*	*Step 2*
Constant of dilation = 2		

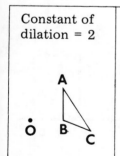
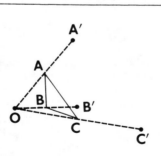
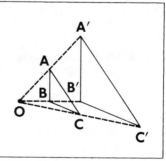

This dilation, with a constant factor of 2, is written in symbols as D_2. Thus, $D_2(A) = A'$ indicates that the image of A is A' under the dilation.

Although any point may be chosen as the center of dilation, we will limit dilations in the coordinate plane to those where point O, the origin, is the center of dilation.

● **Definition.** A *dilation* of k, where k is the *constant of dilation*, is a transformation of the plane such that:

1. The image of point O, the center of dilation, is O.
2. For all other points:
   a. When k is positive, the image of P is P', $\overrightarrow{OP}$ and $\overrightarrow{OP'}$ name the same ray, and $OP' = k \cdot OP$.
   b. When k is negative, the image of P is P', $\overrightarrow{OP}$ and $\overrightarrow{OP'}$ name opposite rays, and $OP' = |k| \cdot OP$.

A rule for a dilation is stated in coordinate geometry as follows:

● **Under a dilation of k whose center of dilation is the origin:**

$$P(x, y) \rightarrow P'(kx, ky) \quad or \quad D_k(x, y) = (kx, ky)$$

EXAMPLE 1. The image of $\triangle ABC$ is $\triangle A'B'C'$ by a dilation of $\frac{1}{2}$. The vertices of $\triangle ABC$ are $A(2, 6)$, $B(6, 4)$, and $C(4, 0)$. Under a dilation of $\frac{1}{2}$, the rule is $D_{\frac{1}{2}}(x, y) = (\frac{1}{2}x, \frac{1}{2}y)$.

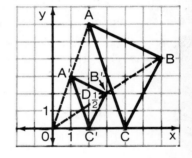

Thus: $A(2, 6) \rightarrow A'(1, 3)$
$B(6, 4) \rightarrow B'(3, 2)$
$C(4, 0) \rightarrow C'(2, 0)$

The images A', B', and C' are connected to form $\triangle A'B'C'$, marked as $D_{\frac{1}{2}}$.

EXAMPLE 2. The image of $\triangle ABC$ is $\triangle A'B'C'$ by a point reflection in the origin. Then, $\triangle A'B'C' \rightarrow \triangle A''B''C''$ by a dilation of 2. This composition of a point reflection followed by a dilation of 2 is equivalent to multiplying the x and y values in each of the coordinates by -2.

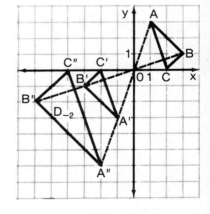

The vertices of $\triangle ABC$ are $A(1, 3)$, $B(3, 1)$, and $C(2, 0)$. Under the point reflection, $R_o(x, y) = (-x, -y)$.

Thus: $A(1, 3) \rightarrow A'(-1, -3)$
$B(3, 1) \rightarrow B'(-3, -1)$
$C(2, 0) \rightarrow C'(-2, 0)$

Under a dilation of 2, $D_2(x, y) = (2x, 2y)$. Thus:

$$A'(-1, -3) \rightarrow A''(-2, -6)$$
$$B'(-3, -1) \rightarrow B''(-6, -2)$$
$$C'(-2, 0) \rightarrow C''(-4, 0)$$

Compare each original vertex to its final image. Here:

$$A(1, 3) \rightarrow A''(-2, -6)$$
$$B(3, 1) \rightarrow B''(-6, -2)$$
$$C(2, 0) \rightarrow C''(-4, 0)$$

Since these coordinates follow the rule $(x, y) \rightarrow (-2x, -2y)$, we will symbolize this composition of transformations as D_{-2}. This example illustrates the truth of the following general statement.

● **A composition of transformations consisting of a point reflection about the origin and a dilation of k, where k is a positive number, is equivalent to the single transformation:**

$$D_{-k}(x, y) = (-kx, -ky)$$

Under a dilation there is generally only one fixed point, namely, the center of dilation. If the constant of dilation is 1, however, all points are fixed.

The *properties preserved under a dilation* include only four of the five properties listed for the other transformations studied earlier in this chapter, namely, angle measure, parallelism, collinearity, and midpoints.

● **Distance is not preserved under a dilation.**

The constant of dilation represents a constant ratio that exists between the lengths of segments and the lengths of their corresponding images under a dilation. Thus, while all previously studied transformations maintained distance so that figures and their images were congruent, we observe:

● **Under a dilation, a figure and its image are similar figures.**

EXERCISES

In 1–4, use the rule $(x, y) \rightarrow (4x, 4y)$ to find the image of the given point.

1. $(3, 5)$ **2.** $(-3, 2)$ **3.** $(7, 0)$ **4.** $(-4, 9)$

In 5–8, find the image of the given point under a dilation of 5.

5. $(2, 1)$ **6.** $(12, 20)$ **7.** $(-9, -7)$ **8.** $(0, -8)$

In 9–12, $D_{-3}(x, y) = (-3x, -3y)$ is a composition of a half-turn about the origin and a dilation of 3. Using D_{-3}, find the image of the given point.

9. $(6, -1)$ **10.** $(-4, 0)$ **11.** $(-3, -8)$ **12.** $(10, -1)$

In 13–21, write a single rule for a dilation, or a composition involving a dilation, by which the image of A is A'.

13. $A(2, 5) \rightarrow A'(4, 10)$ **14.** $A(3, -1) \rightarrow A'(21, -7)$

15. $A(10, 4) \rightarrow A'(5, 2)$ **16.** $A(-20, 8) \rightarrow A'(-5, 2)$

17. $A(4, 6) \rightarrow A'(6, 9)$ **18.** $A(4, -3) \rightarrow A'(-8, 6)$

19. $A(-2, 5) \rightarrow A'(8, -20)$ **20.** $A(-12, 9) \rightarrow A'(-8, 6)$

21. $A(0, 9) \rightarrow A'(0, -3)$

In 22–27, O is the center of dilation and $D_k(\triangle OQR) = \triangle OPS$.

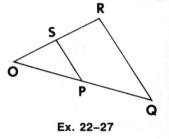

22. What is the image of R under the dilation?

23. $D_k(Q) = ?$ **24.** $D_k(\overline{OR}) = ?$

25. $D_k(O) = ?$

26. If $OP = PQ$, what is the constant of dilation k?

27. Using the value of k from Exercise 26, find the value of $RQ:SP$.

Ex. 22–27

In 28–31, copy $\triangle ABC$ and point O on your paper. Using a ruler, draw its image $\triangle A'B'C'$ under the following conditions:

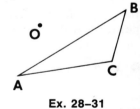

28. D_2 **29.** D_3 **30.** $D_{\frac{1}{2}}$ **31.** D_{-2}

Ex. 28–31

32. a. On graph paper, draw $\triangle ABC$ whose vertices are $A(1, 2)$, $B(2, 2)$, and $C(2, 0)$.

    b. Using the same axes, graph $\triangle A'B'C'$, the image of $\triangle ABC$ under a dilation of 3.

    c. Using $\angle ABC$ and $\angle A'B'C'$, explain why angle measure is preserved.

    d. Using $\overline{BC}$ and $\overline{B'C'}$, explain why midpoints are preserved.

33. a. Draw $\triangle HOG$ whose vertices are $H(1, 2)$, $O(0, 0)$, and $G(1, 3)$.
 b. Using the same set of axes, graph $\triangle H'OG'$ so that $D_3(\triangle HOG) = \triangle H'OG'$.
 c. Using GH and $G'H'$, show why distance is *not* preserved under the dilation.
 d. Find the value of each of the following ratios: (1) $OG:OG'$
 (2) $G'H':GH$ (3) $OH':OH$ (4) $OH:HH'$ (5) $G'G:GO$

34. The vertices of $\triangle HEN$ are $H(0, 4)$, $E(6, 4)$, and $N(4, -2)$. Under a dilation of $\frac{1}{2}$, the image of $\triangle HEN$ is $\triangle H'E'N'$.
 a. On one set of axes, graph $\triangle HEN$ and $\triangle H'E'N'$.
 b. Find the lengths of $\overline{HE}$ and $\overline{H'E'}$.
 c. Find the ratio $HE:H'E'$.
 d. Find the areas of $\triangle HEN$ and $\triangle H'E'N'$.
 e. Find the ratio of the area of $\triangle HEN$ to the area of $\triangle H'E'N'$.

35. Under a composition of transformations, $\triangle COW \rightarrow \triangle C''OW''$ when $\triangle COW \rightarrow \triangle C'OW'$ by a point reflection in the origin and $\triangle C'OW' \rightarrow \triangle C''OW''$ by a dilation of $\frac{3}{2}$. The vertices of $\triangle COW$ are $C(6, 2)$, $O(0, 0)$, and $W(2, -2)$.
 a. On one set of axes, draw $\triangle COW$, $\triangle C'OW'$, and $\triangle C''OW''$.
 b. Complete the rule by which $C \rightarrow C''$: $(x, y) \rightarrow$ _____.
 c. If $\triangle COW$ is first dilated by $\frac{3}{2}$, and then this image is reflected in the origin, will the final image be $\triangle C''OW''$?

12-8 REVIEW EXERCISES

In 1–10, for each figure drawn or named:

a. Does the figure have *line symmetry*? If yes, how many lines of symmetry does the figure have?
b. Does the figure have *point symmetry*?
c. Does the figure have *rotational symmetry*? If yes, find the degree measure of the smallest angle that will rotate the figure to be its own image.

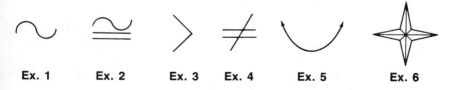

    Ex. 1   **Ex. 2**   **Ex. 3**   **Ex. 4**   **Ex. 5**   **Ex. 6**

7. parallelogram   **8.** equilateral triangle
9. line segment   **10.** regular pentagon

In 11–20, *ABCD* is a square. The midpoints of sides $\overline{AB}$, $\overline{BC}$, $\overline{CD}$, and $\overline{DA}$ are *E*, *F*, *G*, and *H*, respectively. The lines $\overleftrightarrow{AC}$, $\overleftrightarrow{BD}$, $\overleftrightarrow{EG}$, and $\overleftrightarrow{FH}$ intersect at *O*.

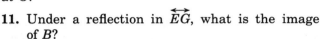

Ex. 11–20

11. Under a reflection in $\overleftrightarrow{EG}$, what is the image of *B*?

12. $r_{\overleftrightarrow{HF}}(B) = ?$ 13. $r_{\overleftrightarrow{AC}}(B) = ?$ 14. $r_{\overleftrightarrow{DB}}(B) = ?$

15. Under a reflection through point *O*, what is the image of *B*?

16. Under a rotation of 90° about *O*, what is the image of *B*?

17. $R_{0,90°}(E) = ?$ 18. $R_{0,90°}(\overline{CF}) = ?$ 19. $R_{0,90°}(\angle AOH) = ?$

20. Under a translation, $E \rightarrow D$. What is the image of *B* under this translation?

In 21–31, find the image of (5, 2) under the given transformation.

21. Reflection in the *x*-axis.
22. Reflection in the *y*-axis.
23. Reflection in the line $x = 4$.
24. Reflection in the line $y = 2$.
25. Reflection in the line $y = x$.
26. Reflection through the origin.
27. Quarter-turn about the origin.
28. The translation: $T_{3,-2}$.
29. Dilation of $1\frac{1}{2}$, center at origin.
30. D_{-3}
31. $T_{-6,0}$

In 32–37, name the single transformation that will assign a point to its image by the given rule.

32. $(x, y) \rightarrow (x, -y)$ 33. $(x, y) \rightarrow (-x, -y)$ 34. $(x, y) \rightarrow (y, x)$

35. $(x, y) \rightarrow (-x, y)$ 36. $(x, y) \rightarrow (x - 1, y)$ 37. $(x, y) \rightarrow (-y, x)$

38. What single transformation is equivalent to a composition consisting of a reflection in the *x*-axis followed by a reflection in the *y*-axis?

39. Under a reflection in the *y*-axis, the image of $\triangle YES$ is $\triangle Y'E'S'$. The vertices of $\triangle YES$ are $Y(-2, 1)$, $E(4, 4)$, and $S(1, -2)$.
   a. On the same set of axes, graph $\triangle YES$ and $\triangle Y'E'S'$.
   b. Using the lengths of $\overline{YS}$ and $\overline{Y'S'}$, show that distance is preserved in this reflection.

40. The vertices of $\triangle AYE$ are $A(2, -3)$, $Y(5, 1)$, and $E(1, -1)$. Under the transformation whose rule is $(x, y) \rightarrow (-y, x)$, $\triangle AYE \rightarrow \triangle A'Y'E'$.
   a. On the same set of axes, graph $\triangle AYE$ and $\triangle A'Y'E'$.
   b. Illustrate that angle measure is preserved under this transformation, using $\angle YEA$ and $\angle Y'E'A'$.

41. The vertices of trapezoid $UBET$ are $U(-3, 2)$, $B(0, 3)$, $E(2, 1)$, and $T(-4, -1)$. Under a reflection in the x-axis, the image of trapezoid $UBET$ is $U'B'E'T'$.

   a. On the same set of axes, graph trapezoid $UBET$ and trapezoid $U'B'E'T'$.

   b. Show that $\overline{UB} \parallel \overline{TE}$.

   c. Show that $\overline{U'B'} \parallel \overline{T'E'}$.

   d. What property is demonstrated by **b** and **c** together?

42. a. Draw $\triangle AOK$ whose vertices are $A(1, 3)$, $O(0, 0)$ and $K(4, 2)$.

   b. Using the same axes, graph $\triangle A'O'K'$, the image of $\triangle AOK$ under $T_{2,4}$.

   c. Using the same axes, graph $\triangle A''O''K''$, the image of $\triangle A'O'K'$ under $T_{1,-3}$.

   d. What single translation is equivalent to $T_{2,4}$ followed by $T_{1,-3}$?

   e. Using $\overline{OK}$ and $\overline{O''K''}$ and their midpoints, show that midpoints are preserved under this transformation.

43. $\triangle YUP \rightarrow \triangle Y'U'P'$ by a reflection in the y-axis. Then, $\triangle Y'U'P' \rightarrow \triangle Y''U''P''$ by a reflection in the line $x = 1$. The vertices of $\triangle YUP$ are $Y(-4, 2)$, $U(-2, 3)$, and $P(-3, -1)$.

   a. Using one set of axes, graph $\triangle YUP$, $\triangle Y'U'P'$, and $\triangle Y''U''P''$.

   b. Name the single transformation by which $\triangle YUP \rightarrow \triangle Y''U''P''$.

44. a. Draw $\triangle END$ whose vertices are $E(0, 2)$, $N(1, 4)$, and $D(4, 0)$.

   b. Using the same axes, graph $\triangle E'N'D'$, the image of $\triangle END$ under a point reflection in the origin.

   c. Using the same axes, graph $\triangle E''N''D''$, the image of $\triangle E'N'D'$ under a dilation of 2.

   d. Complete the statement: $\triangle END \rightarrow \triangle E''N''D''$ by the rule $(x, y) \rightarrow$ _____ .

Chapter 13

Probability

13-1 EVALUATING PROBABILITIES

In Course I, you began the study of probability by performing experiments. Using the results of these experiments, we determined **empirical probability**, the cumulative relative frequency of an event happening. For example, if a cone-shaped paper cup is tossed 1,000 times and lands on its side 753 times, we would say the probability that the cup lands on its side is $\frac{753}{1,000}$, or $P(\text{side}) = \frac{753}{1,000}$. We could simplify this fraction by saying that $P(\text{side}) = \frac{753}{1,000} \approx \frac{3}{4}$.

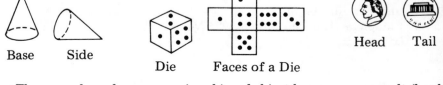

Base   Side   Die   Faces of a Die   Head   Tail

The cone-shaped paper cup is a *biased* object because one result (landing on its side) has a better chance of happening than another result (landing on its base). The die and the coin are *fair and unbiased* objects because each result has an equal chance of happening.

Theoretical Probability

Experiments can help to determine the probabilities involved in rolling a die or tossing a coin. However, you learned to define probability for fair and unbiased objects in a second way. Let us recall some terms.

1. An **outcome** is a result of some activity. In rolling a die, there are six outcomes: 1 is an outcome, 2 is an outcome, and so on.

2. A *sample space* is a set of all possible outcomes for the activity. In rolling a die, the sample space $S = \{1, 2, 3, 4, 5, 6\}$. In tossing a coin, the sample space $S = \{\text{head, tail}\}$, or simply $S = \{H, T\}$.

3. An *event* is any subset of the sample space. In rolling a die, the event of obtaining a 3 is a singleton event because it contains only one outcome, symbolized by $E = \{3\}$. The event of rolling an even number contains three outcomes, symbolized by $E = \{2, 4, 6\}$.

We can now define *theoretical probability* for fair, unbiased objects:

● **The theoretical probability of an event is the number of ways that the event can occur, divided by the total number of possible outcomes.**

In symbolic form, we write: $P(E) = \dfrac{n(E)}{n(S)}$

Here, $P(E)$ represents the probability of event E;

> $n(E)$ represents the number of elements of the event E, or the number of ways that event E can occur;

> $n(S)$ represents the number of elements or possible outcomes in sample space S.

EXAMPLE. Find the probability of rolling an even number on one toss of a die.

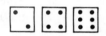

E = event of rolling an even number = $\{2, 4, 6\}$. Then $n(E) = 3$.

S = sample space of all outcomes = $\{1, 2, 3, 4, 5, 6\}$. So $n(S) = 6$.

$P(E) = \dfrac{n(E)}{n(S)} = \dfrac{\text{number of ways to roll an even number}}{\text{total number of possible outcomes}} = \dfrac{3}{6}$ or $\dfrac{1}{2}$ *Ans.*

The rule for theoretical probability applies only to fair, unbiased objects. In all such cases, the sample space is said to have *uniform probability*, or to contain equally likely outcomes.

Rules of Probability

An arrow is spun once and lands on one of five equally likely regions, numbered 1, 2, 3, 4, and 5. If the arrow lands on a line, it is not counted and the arrow is spun again. Since the sample space $S = \{1, 2, 3, 4, 5\}$, the total number of possible outcomes is five, or $n(S) = 5$.

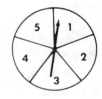

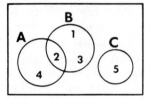

We will use this spinner to find the probability of different events, some of which are shown in the set diagram. These examples illustrate the rules of probability studied in Course I.

Event		*Probability*

Event A = spinning an even number = $\{2, 4\}$.
Since A contains two outcomes,
$n(A) = 2$.

$$P(A) = \frac{n(A)}{n(S)} = \frac{2}{5}$$

Event B = spinning a number less than 4
= $\{1, 2, 3\}$.
Since B contains three outcomes,
$n(B) = 3$.

$$P(B) = \frac{n(B)}{n(S)} = \frac{3}{5}$$

Event C = spinning a 5 = $\{5\}$.
Since C contains one outcome,
$n(C) = 1$.

$$P(C) = \frac{n(C)}{n(S)} = \frac{1}{5}$$

Event D = spinning a number less than 1 = $\{\ \}$.
Since D contains no outcomes,
$n(D) = 0$.

$$P(D) = \frac{n(D)}{n(S)} = \frac{0}{5} = 0$$

Event S = spinning a whole number
= $\{1, 2, 3, 4, 5\}$.
Since S contains five outcomes,
$n(S) = 5$.

$$P(S) = \frac{n(S)}{n(S)} = \frac{5}{5} = 1$$

Event D, spinning a number less than 1, has probability 0. When the event is the empty set, the probability is zero, or $P(\{\ \}) = 0$. Thus:

● **Rule 1. The probability of an impossible event is zero.**

Event S, spinning a whole number, has probability 1. When the event is the sample space, the probability is one, or $P(S) = 1$. Thus:

● **Rule 2. The probability of an event that is certain to occur is one.**

Each of the given events has a probability that is greater than or equal to 0 and less than or equal to 1. In symbolic form: $0 \leq P(E) \leq 1$. Thus:

● **Rule 3. The probability of an event E must be greater than or equal to zero, and less than or equal to one.**

In logic, you learned that p *and* q is true only when p is true and q is true. Thus, an outcome is in the event A *and* B only if it is in event A and also in event B. If A represents spinning an even number and B represents spinning a number less than 4, then $A = \{2, 4\}$, and $B = \{1, 2, 3\}$. Therefore, A *and* B represents spinning an even number less than 4. The sample space in $A \cap B = \{2\}$. Using these specific events, $n(A \cap B) = 1$; and $P(A$ and $B) = \dfrac{n(A \cap B)}{n(S)} = \dfrac{1}{5}$. Thus:

● **Rule 4.** $P(A$ **and** $B) = \dfrac{n(A \text{ and } B)}{n(S)}$; **or, in terms of sets,**

$$P(A \text{ and } B) = P(A \cap B) = \dfrac{n(A \cap B)}{n(S)}.$$

In logic, you learned that p *or* q is true when p is true, or when q is true, or when both p and q are true. Thus, an outcome is in the event A *or* B if the outcome is in event A, or in event B, or in both event A and event B. Using the events described above, $A = \{2, 4\}$, and $B = \{1, 2, 3\}$. Therefore, A *or* B represents spinning an even number or a number less than 4. The sample space is $A \cup B = \{1, 2, 3, 4\}$. Using these specific events, $n(A \cup B) = 4$; and $P(A$ or $B) = \dfrac{n(A \cup B)}{n(S)} = \dfrac{4}{5}$.

This same probability can be found by using rule 5, as stated below. Notice that we subtract $P(A \cap B)$ because the probability of the outcome 2 is included twice: first in $P(A)$, and then again in $P(B)$.

$$P(A \text{ or } B) = P(A \cup B) = P(A) + P(B) - P(A \cap B)$$
$$= \tfrac{2}{5} + \tfrac{3}{5} - \tfrac{1}{5} = \tfrac{4}{5}$$

Similarly, $P(A$ or $C) = P(A \cup C) = P(A) + P(C) - P(A \cap C)$
$$= \tfrac{2}{5} + \tfrac{1}{5} - 0 = \tfrac{3}{5}$$

Thus:

● **Rule 5.** $P(A$ **or** $B) = P(A) + P(B) - P(A$ **and** $B)$; **or, in terms of sets,** $P(A \cup B) = P(A) + P(B) - P(A \cap B)$.

Notice that events A and C are disjoint events and their intersection is the empty set. In such cases, the rule may be simplified to read $P(A$ or $C) = P(A \cup C) = P(A) + P(C)$.

The event *not A* consists of outcomes that are not in event A. In terms of sets, *not A* is the complement of set A, namely $\overline{A}$. Using the event described above, $A = \{2, 4\}$. Then, *not A* $= \{1, 3, 5\}$.

By the basic definition of probability, P (not $A) = \dfrac{n(\text{not } A)}{n(S)} = \dfrac{3}{5}$.

The following rule gives the same result.

● **Rule 6.** $P(\text{not } A) = 1 - P(A)$, or $P(\overline{A}) = 1 - P(A)$.

By the given rule, $P(\text{not } A) = 1 - P(A)$
$$= 1 - \tfrac{2}{5} = \tfrac{5}{5} - \tfrac{2}{5} = \tfrac{3}{5}.$$

In the spinner problem, $P(A) = \tfrac{2}{5}$. Since $A = \{2, 4\}$,
$$P(A) = P(2) + P(4) = \tfrac{1}{5} + \tfrac{1}{5} = \tfrac{2}{5}.$$

Also, $P(B) = \tfrac{3}{5}$. Since $B = \{1, 2, 3\}$,
$$P(B) = P(1) + P(2) + P(3) = \tfrac{1}{5} + \tfrac{1}{5} + \tfrac{1}{5} = \tfrac{3}{5}. \text{ Thus:}$$

● **Rule 7. The probability of any event is equal to the sum of the probabilities of the singleton outcomes in the event.**

In the spinner, $P(S) = P(1) + P(2) + P(3) + P(4) + P(5)$
$$= \tfrac{1}{5} + \tfrac{1}{5} + \tfrac{1}{5} + \tfrac{1}{5} + \tfrac{1}{5} = \tfrac{5}{5} = 1.$$

Also, in tossing a coin, $P(S) = P(H) + P(T) = \tfrac{1}{2} + \tfrac{1}{2} = \tfrac{2}{2} = 1.$ Thus:

● **Rule 8. The sum of the probabilities of all possible singleton outcomes for any sample space must always equal 1.**

General Procedure

Whether or not you recognize the rule to apply in a specific situation, there is a general procedure for finding the theoretical probability of any event:

1. Count the total number of outcomes in the sample space: $n(S)$
2. Count all the possible outcomes in event E: $n(E)$
3. Substitute these values in the formula for the probability of event E:

$$P(E) = \frac{n(E)}{n(S)}$$

MODEL PROBLEMS _____

1. A standard deck of cards contains 52 cards. There are 4 suits called hearts, diamonds, spades, and clubs. Each suit contains 13 cards: 2, 3, 4, 5, 6, 7, 8, 9, 10, jack, queen, king, and ace. The diamonds and hearts are red; the spades and clubs are black.

   In drawing a card from the deck at **random**, that is, without any special selection or without looking, find the probability that the card is **(a)** a red king, **(b)** a ten or an ace, **(c)** a jack or a club.

Solution

In all cases, the sample space S consists of 52 cards. So, $n(S) = 52$.

a. A red king must be red and a king. There are two such cards in the deck. Thus $P(\text{red king}) = \dfrac{n(\text{red king})}{n(S)} = \dfrac{2}{52}$ or $\dfrac{1}{26}$. *Ans.*

b. The word "or" is used. Here, tens and aces have no outcomes in common. So, $P(\text{ten or ace}) = P(\text{ten}) + P(\text{ace}) = \frac{4}{52} + \frac{4}{52} = \frac{8}{52}$ or $\frac{2}{13}$. *Ans.*

c. The word "or" is used. There are two methods to solve this problem.

Method 1: There are 4 jacks and 13 clubs in the deck, but 1 of these cards (the jack of clubs) is common to both events. Therefore,
$P(\text{jack or club}) = P(\text{jack}) + P(\text{club}) - P(\text{jack of clubs})$
$$= \quad \tfrac{4}{52} \quad + \quad \tfrac{13}{52} \quad - \quad \tfrac{1}{52} \quad = \tfrac{16}{52} \text{ or } \tfrac{4}{13} \quad Ans.$$

Method 2: By a counting procedure, there are 13 clubs in the deck and 3 more jacks not already counted (jack of hearts, jack of diamonds, jack of spades). Therefore, there are $13 + 3$, or 16, cards in this event. So, $P(\text{jack or club}) = \frac{16}{52}$ or $\frac{4}{13}$. *Ans.*

2. In the Sullivan family, there are 2 more girls than boys. At random, Mrs. Sullivan asks one of her children to go to the store. If she is equally likely to have asked any one of her children, and the probability that she asked a girl is $\frac{2}{3}$, how many boys and how many girls are there in the Sullivan family?

Solution:

$$\text{Let } x = \text{the number of boys.}$$
$$\text{Then, } x + 2 = \text{the number of girls.}$$
$$\text{And, } 2x + 2 = \text{the number of children.}$$

$$P(\text{girl}) = \frac{\text{number of girls}}{\text{number of children}}$$

$$\frac{2}{3} = \frac{x + 2}{2x + 2}$$
$$2(2x + 2) = 3(x + 2)$$
$$4x + 4 = 3x + 6$$
$$x = 2$$
$$x + 2 = 4$$

Answer: There are 2 boys and 4 girls.

3. A sack contains red marbles and green marbles. If one marble is drawn at random, the probability that it is red is $\frac{3}{4}$. Five red marbles are removed from the sack. Now, if one marble is drawn, the probability that it is red is $\frac{2}{3}$. How many red and how many green marbles were in the sack at the start?

Solution:

(1) Represent each unknown quantity.
  Let x = the original number of red marbles.
  Let y = the original number of green marbles.

(2) Write two equations.

$$[A] \quad \frac{x}{x + y} = \frac{3}{4}$$

$$[B] \quad \frac{x - 5}{x + y - 5} = \frac{2}{3}$$

(3) Simplify each equation.

  In [A], cross multiply and collect like terms.

$$\frac{x}{x + y} = \frac{3}{4}$$
$$3x + 3y = 4x$$
$$3y = x$$

  In [B], cross multiply and collect like terms.

$$\frac{x - 5}{x + y - 5} = \frac{2}{3}$$
$$2x + 2y - 10 = 3x - 15$$
$$2y + 5 = x$$

(4) From simplified [A], substitute $3y$ for x in simplified [B] and solve for y.

$$2y + 5 = x$$
$$2y + 5 = 3y$$
$$5 = y$$

(5) Substitute 5 for y in either simplified [A] or in simplified [B] and solve for x.

$$3y = x$$
$$3(5) = x$$
$$15 = x$$

Answer: The sack originally contained 15 red and 5 green marbles.

EXERCISES

1. A spinner is divided into 4 equal regions, numbered 1, 2, 3, 4. An arrow is spun to fall into one of the regions. For each part of this question, (1) list the outcomes for the given event and (2) state the probability of the event.

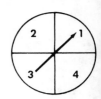

a. an odd number
c. a number less than 4
e. a number greater than 4
g. less than 4 or even
i. greater than 3 or odd

b. the number 4
d. 4 or less
f. less than 4 and even
h. not less than 2
j. greater than 1 and less than 4

2. A fair die is rolled once. The sides are numbered 1, 2, 3, 4, 5, 6. Find the probability of the event described.
   a. an odd number
   d. greater than 4
   g. odd or even
   j. less than 4 and odd
   l. less than or equal to 5
   n. greater than 5 and odd

   b. 4
   e. 4 or less
   h. 4 or 5
   k. less than 4 or odd
   m. greater than 2 and less than 5
   o. less than 6 or even

   c. less than 4
   f. not less than 2
   i. less than 1

3. From a standard deck of 52 cards, one card is drawn. Find the probability that the card will be:
   a. red
   d. five of hearts
   g. a five or a heart
   j. a club or a heart
   m. a fifteen
   o. a five or a black card
   q. not the queen of spades
   s. a club or a red card

   b. a five
   e. not a heart
   h. five of clubs
   k. a black heart
   n. a picture card (king, queen, jack)
   p. a card from the deck
   r. a red picture card
   t. an ace or a black card

   c. a heart
   f. a black five
   i. a five or a six
   l. a black club

4. An urn (jar) contains 7 marbles, all the same size; 3 are red and 4 are white. If a marble is chosen at random, find the probability that it is:
   a. red
   b. white
   c. blue
   d. not red
   e. red or white
   f. red and white

5. The English alphabet contains 26 letters; there are 5 vowels (A, E, I, O, U) and the remaining 21 letters are consonants. For each given word, find the probability that a letter chosen at random from the word is a vowel.
   a. SQUARE b. SYSTEM c. PARALLELOGRAM d. CRYPT

6. Carol McHugh has 3 quarters, 4 dimes, and 2 nickels in her purse. She takes one coin out of her purse without looking.
   a. Find the probability that Carol has taken:
      (1) a quarter (2) a dime (3) a nickel
   b. Show that the sum of the probabilities from part **a** is 1.
   c. Find the probability that the coin taken is worth:
      (1) less than 25¢ (2) less than 30¢ (3) not more than 5¢

7. Mrs. Barash, a mathematics teacher, calls students at random to the chalkboard. If the class contains 15 boys and 17 girls, find the probability that the first person called is:
   a. a boy   **b.** a girl   **c.** a student   **d.** the teacher

8. A set of polygons consists of the most general forms of a rhombus, a square, a parallelogram, a rectangle, and a trapezoid. If one of the polygons is selected 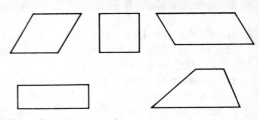 at random, find the probability that it contains:
   a. congruent diagonals
   b. diagonals that bisect each other
   c. all sides congruent
   d. one or two pairs of parallel sides
   e. all angles congruent and all sides congruent
   f. all angles congruent or all sides congruent

9. There are 300 tickets to be sold in a lottery and Andy Campbell purchases 6 of the tickets. Express as **(a)** a fraction, **(b)** a decimal, and **(c)** a percent, the probability that Andy has the winning ticket.

In 10–14, select the numeral preceding the correct answer.

10. In a standard deck of 52 cards, what is the probability of drawing a king or a spade? (1) $\frac{1}{52}$ (2) $\frac{16}{52}$ (3) $\frac{17}{52}$ (4) $\frac{28}{52}$

11. A single card is drawn at random from a 52-card deck. For which of the following events is the probability of success greater than $\frac{1}{2}$? (1) an ace or a club (2) an ace or a king (3) an ace or a red card (4) a club or a diamond

12. Exactly two sides of $\triangle ABC$ are congruent. Find the probability that the altitude from A to $\overline{BC}$ is congruent to the median from A to $\overline{BC}$. (1) 1 (2) $\frac{1}{2}$ (3) $\frac{1}{3}$ (4) $\frac{1}{6}$

13. In an isosceles triangle, what is the probability that the altitude and the median drawn from the vertex angle to the base are congruent? (1) 1 (2) $\frac{1}{2}$ (3) $\frac{1}{3}$ (4) $\frac{1}{6}$

14. If the probability that Regina reads a book every week is 0.9, what is the probability that she will not read a book next week? (1) .01 (2) 0.1 (3) .09 (4) 0.9

15. A sack contains 20 marbles. The probability of drawing a green marble is $\frac{2}{5}$. How many green marbles are in the sack?

16. There are 3 more boys than girls in the chess club. A member of the club is to be chosen at random to play in a tournament. Each member is equally likely to be chosen. If the probability that a girl is chosen is $\frac{3}{7}$, how many boys and how many girls are there?

17. A box of candy contains caramels and nut clusters. There are 6 more caramels than nut clusters. If a piece of candy is chosen at random, the probability that it is a caramel is $\frac{3}{5}$. How many caramels and how many nut clusters are in the box?

18. A bowl contains peanuts and raisins. If one item is drawn at random, the probability that it is a peanut is $\frac{4}{5}$. Twenty peanuts are removed from the bowl. Now, if one item is drawn, the probability that it is a peanut is $\frac{3}{4}$. How many peanuts and how many raisins were in the bowl at the start?

19. A sack contains yellow marbles and black marbles. If one marble is drawn at random, the probability that it is yellow is $\frac{7}{8}$. Six yellow marbles are added to the sack. Now, if one marble is drawn, the probability that it is yellow is $\frac{9}{10}$. How many yellow and how many black marbles were in the sack at the start?

20. A set of numbers contains even integers and odd integers. If one number is drawn at random, the probability that it is an even integer is $\frac{1}{6}$. Five even integers are added to the set and 10 odd integers are removed from the set. Now, if one number is drawn, the probability that it is an even integer is $\frac{8}{13}$. How many even integers and how many odd integers were in the set at the start?

13-2 THE COUNTING PRINCIPLE AND PROBABILITIES WITH TWO OR MORE ACTIVITIES

If a fair coin is tossed, it has an equal probability of landing as a head, represented by H, or as a tail, represented by T. If two coins are tossed (or a single coin is tossed two times in succession), the sample space can be represented in one of three ways:

(1) Tree diagram   (2) Set of ordered pairs   (3) Graph of ordered pairs.

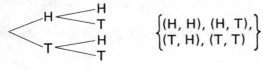

By counting, you see that there are four possible outcomes in the sample space just illustrated. A multiplication procedure that serves as a shortcut to help count the number of elements in a sample space is called the *counting principle*.

● **The Counting Principle.** If one activity can occur in any of *m* ways and, following this, a second activity can occur in any of *n* ways, then both activities can occur in the order given in *m* • *n* ways.

Thus, since one coin can fall in 2 ways, two coins can fall in 2 • 2, or 4, possible ways. By extending this multiplication process, if three coins are tossed, there are 2 • 2 • 2, or 8, outcomes in the sample space. This process is helpful in more complicated situations than that of tossing two coins. However, let us return to the original situation.

If one coin is tossed, $P(H) = \frac{1}{2}$. If a second coin is tossed, the result is completely, absolutely, and without question independent of the result obtained with the first coin. When two activities or events have nothing to do with each other, we call them ***independent events***. By extending the counting principle to include probabilities, we say:

$P(H$ on first coin$) = \frac{1}{2}$

$P(H$ on second coin$) = \frac{1}{2}$

$P(H, H) = P(H$ on both coins$) = P(H$ on first$) \cdot P(H$ on second$) = \frac{1}{2} \cdot \frac{1}{2} = \frac{1}{4}$

● **The Counting Principle With Probabilities.** If events E and F are independent events, the probability of E is m $(0 \le m \le 1)$, and the probability of F is n $(0 \le n \le 1)$, then the probability of E and F occurring jointly is the product $m \cdot n$ $(0 \le m \cdot n \le 1)$.

When an event consists of two or more separate events or activities, it is called a ***compound event***. Compound events include rolling 2 dice, tossing 3 coins, selecting 5 cards, and so on. Note that not all events are independent. Therefore, this simple product rule cannot be used to find the probability of every compound event.

MODEL PROBLEMS

1. A family has three children. Let M represent male, let F represent female, and assume that $P(M) = P(F) = \frac{1}{2}$.
   a. How many outcomes are in the sample space that indicates the sex of the three children?
   b. Find the probability that the three children are all of the same sex.

Solution

a. The sample space may be found by a tree diagram or a list of ordered triples as shown at the right.

or

Using 2 possible sexes for each child, apply the counting principle to find:

$$2 \cdot 2 \cdot 2 = 8$$

Answer: 8 outcomes

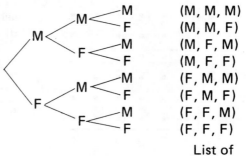

	(M, M, M)
	(M, M, F)
	(M, F, M)
	(M, F, F)
	(F, M, M)
	(F, M, F)
	(F, F, M)
	(F, F, F)
Tree diagram	List of ordered triples

b. P(all of the same sex) = P(all male or all female)

$$= P(\text{all male}) + P(\text{all female})$$

$$= \tfrac{1}{8} + \tfrac{1}{8} = \tfrac{2}{8} \text{ or } \tfrac{1}{4} \ Ans.$$

2. Two fair dice are rolled, each numbered 1 through 6. Find the probability that: **(a)** the sum of the numbers on the dice is 9; **(b)** at least one die shows a 4; **(c)** the sum of the numbers on the dice is 9 *and* at least one die shows a 4.

Solution

The sample space consists of $6 \cdot 6$, or 36, outcomes, most easily shown by a graph or ordered pairs. Thus, $n(S) = 36$.

a.   Sum of 9

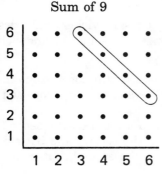

There are 4 ordered pairs, encircled in the graph to the left, where the sum of the numbers on the dice is 9: (3, 6), (4, 5), (5, 4), and (6, 3).

Call this event A. Then,

$$P(A) = \frac{n(A)}{n(S)} = \frac{4}{36} \text{ or } \frac{1}{9} \ Ans.$$

b. At least one 4

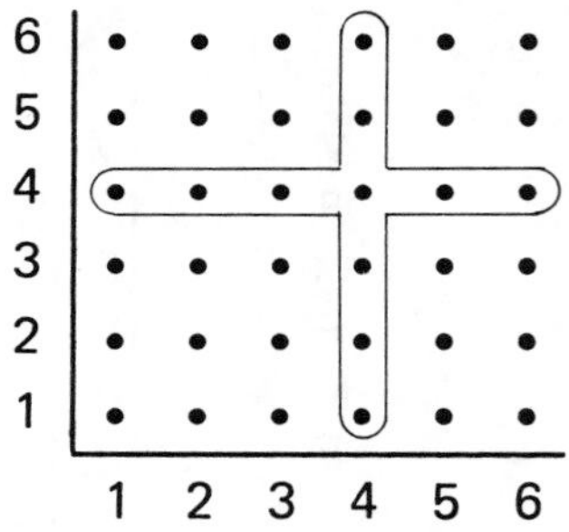

6 • • • ⦿ • •
5 • • • | • •
4 ⦅• • • | • •⦆
3 • • • | • •
2 • • • | • •
1 • • • ⦿ • •

  1 2 3 4 5 6

There are 11 ordered pairs, encircled in the graph to the left, in which at least one die shows a 4. Call this event B. Then,

$$P(B) = \frac{n(B)}{n(S)} = \frac{11}{36} \quad Ans.$$

c. Sum of 9 *and* at least one 4

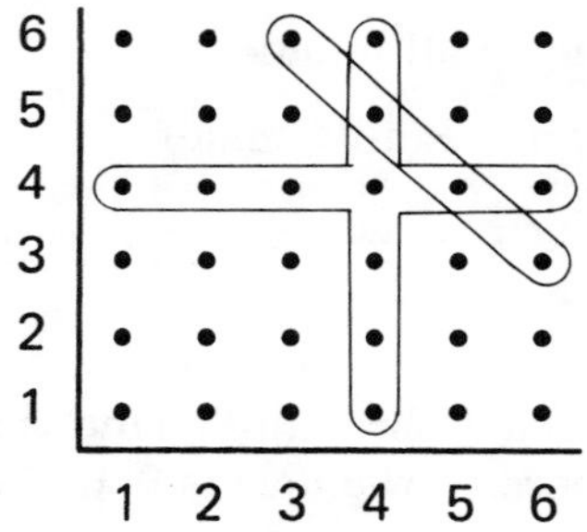

6 • • ⦿ • •
5 • • • | • •
4 ⦅• • • | • •⦆
3 • • • | • •
2 • • • | • •
1 • • • ⦿ • •

  1 2 3 4 5 6

Events A and B are both encircled in the same graph of the sample space to the left. There are 2 ordered pairs, namely (4, 5) and (5, 4), that meet the conditions for both events A and B, found in the intersection of A and B. Thus:

$$P(A \text{ and } B) = \frac{n(A \text{ and } B)}{n(S)}$$
$$= \frac{n(A \cap B)}{n(S)}$$
$$= \frac{2}{36} \text{ or } \frac{1}{18} \quad Ans.$$

EXERCISES ————————————

1. At a luncheonette, a menu lists 2 soups, 8 sandwiches, and 5 desserts. How many different meals consisting of 1 soup, 1 sandwich, and 1 dessert are possible?

2. There are 12 doors into the school and 6 staircases from the first floor to the second. How many possible ways are there for each event described?
   a. Dale goes from outside the school to a room on the second floor.
   b. Cynthia goes from the first floor to the second and back down.
   c. Walter goes from the first floor to the second, but comes back down by a different staircase.
   d. Annette goes in and out of the school, using two different doors.

3. Mr. Imre gives the class a test consisting of multiple-choice questions. Each question has 4 choices. Find the number of possible ways to answer the questions on the test if the test consists of:
   a. 1 question   **b.** 2 questions
   c. 3 questions   **d.** 4 questions

4. Bernice takes a multiple-choice test, each question having 4 choices. If Bernice has no idea of any answer and simply guesses, find the probability that she gets all questions correct if the test has:
   a. 1 question   **b.** 2 questions
   c. 3 questions   **d.** 4 questions

5. Find the probability of getting a perfect paper by guessing the answers to a test consisting of 8 true-false questions.

6. A state issues license plates consisting of letters and numbers. There are 26 letters and 10 digits, each of which may be repeated in a plate. Find the number of possible license plates a state may issue when a license consists of:
   a. three letters, followed by two numbers
   b. two letters, followed by four numbers
   c. three letters, followed by three numbers

7. Two fair coins are tossed. **a.** Find the probability of getting: (1) two heads; (2) a head and a tail; (3) two tails. **b.** Show that the sum of the probabilities in part **a** is 1.

8. In a family of three children, determine the probability that:
   a. all are male   **b.** all are female
   c. exactly two are female   **d.** the oldest is female
   e. there is at least one male
   f. the oldest and youngest are male

9. Two standard dice are rolled, each numbered 1 through 6. Find the probability of getting:
   a. a sum of 2   **b.** a sum of 11   **c.** a sum of 7
   d. a sum of 1   **e.** an even sum   **f.** an odd sum
   g. a sum that is 5 or less   **h.** a sum greater than 7
   i. a pair of even numbers   **j.** at least one die that shows a 5
   k. at least one die that shows a 5 and the sum is 7
   l. at least one die that shows a 5 or the sum is 7

10. A spinner contains 5 equally likely regions, numbered 1 through 5. If the arrow is spun twice, find the probability that: **(a)** it lands on 3 both times; **(b)** it does not land on 3 either time; **(c)** the sum of the two spins is greater than 8; **(d)** each spin results in an odd number; **(e)** the sum of the spins is odd.

11. If three fair coins are tossed, what is the probability that they will land all heads or all tails?

12. Tell the number of outcomes in the sample space when:
  a. four coins are tossed
  b. three six-sided dice are rolled
  c. a coin and a six-sided die are tossed simultaneously
  d. two coins and two six-sided dice are tossed simultaneously
  e. of 30 students, one leaves the room, then another leaves

13-3 PERMUTATIONS

A *permutation* is an arrangement of objects in some specific order. In some cases we use all the objects available to make different arrangements. In other cases we use fewer than all the objects available.

EXAMPLE 1. In Mr. Backer's class there are 4 students in the first row: Jane, Eve, Tony, and Mildred. In how many ways can Mr. Backer call on these 4 students to present one each of 4 problems at the chalkboard?

Solution: It is possible to make a tree diagram or to list ordered elements to answer this question. For example, using an initial to represent a student's name, possible arrangements include (J, E, T, M), (J, M, E, T), (E, J, M, T), (M, E, T, J), and many more.

However, the counting principle provides us with an easier method of solution. Mr. Backer has a choice of 4 students for the first problem. After this problem is assigned, he has a choice of 3 students for the second problem. Then he has a choice of 2 students for the third problem, and finally 1 student remains for the fourth problem. Therefore, there are:

$$4 \cdot 3 \cdot 2 \cdot 1 = 24 \text{ possible ways } Ans.$$

In the example just presented, we can represent the number of arrangements by the symbol $_4P_4$, read as the number of permutations of 4 things, taken 4 at a time. This is equal to 4!, read as 4 factorial or factorial 4.

Thus, $_4P_4 = 4! = 4 \cdot 3 \cdot 2 \cdot 1 = 24$.
Similarly, $_6P_6 = 6! = 6 \cdot 5 \cdot 4 \cdot 3 \cdot 2 \cdot 1 = 720$.

● **In general, for any counting number n, the number of permutations of n things, taken n at a time, can be represented as:**

$$_nP_n = n! = n(n-1)(n-2) \ldots 3 \cdot 2 \cdot 1$$

EXAMPLE 2. Miss Murray has a class of 25 students and she assigns 3 problems for homework. In how many ways can the teacher call on any 3 of the 25 students in her class to present one problem each at the board?

Solution: This is the number of permutations of 25 things, taken 3 at a time, written in symbols as $_{25}P_3$. Notice how the counting principle is again used to determine the number of arrangements, even though fewer than 25 objects are being used.

$$\begin{array}{cccccc} & \text{(Problem 1)} & \text{(Problem 2)} & \text{(Problem 3)} \\ _{25}P_3 = & 25 & \cdot & 24 & \cdot & 23 & = 13{,}800 \text{ permutations} \end{array}$$

Answer: She can call on 3 students in 13,800 different ways.

● **In general, for counting numbers n and r where $r \le n$, the number of permutations of n things, taken r at a time, is found by the formula:**

$$_{n}P_{r} = \underbrace{n(n-1)(n-2)\ldots}_{r\text{ factors}}$$

MODEL PROBLEMS

1. Evaluate $_{10}P_4$.

   Solution: This is the number of permutations of 10 things, taken 4 at a time. We begin to write the factors of 10!, but we stop upon reaching 4 factors:

   $$_{10}P_4 = \underbrace{10 \cdot 9 \cdot 8 \cdot 7}_{4\text{ factors}} = 5{,}040 \quad Ans.$$

2. A word, even if it is a "nonsense" word, is described as an arrangement of letters. If each letter is used only once in forming a word:
   a. How many 5-letter words can be formed from the word ANGLE?
   b. How many 3-letter words can be formed from the word ANGLE?

   Solution

   a. This is the number of permutations of 5 things, taken 5 at a time. Thus,

   $$_5P_5 = 5! = 5 \cdot 4 \cdot 3 \cdot 2 \cdot 1 = 120 \quad Ans.$$

   b. This is the number of permutations of 5 things, taken 3 at a time. Thus,

   $$_5P_3 = \underbrace{5 \cdot 4 \cdot 3}_{3\text{ factors}} = 60 \quad Ans.$$

3. A 3-digit numeral is formed by selecting from the digits 4, 5, 6, 7, 8, and 9, with no repetition. How many of these 3-digit numerals will be greater than 800?

Solution

(1) Think of a 3-digit numeral as 3 places to be filled in.

$\underline{}\ \underline{}\ \underline{}$

(2) To be greater than 800, the hundreds place must contain either the digit 8 or the digit 9. Thus, there are only 2 choices for the hundreds place.

$\underline{2}\ \cdot\ \underline{}\ \underline{}$

(3) Once the digit is selected for the hundreds place, we may choose any 2 of the remaining 5 digits for the other places.

$\underline{2}\ \cdot\ (_5P_2)$

(4) Substitute the value of $_5P_2$ and multiply.

$\underline{2}\ \cdot\ \underline{5}\ \cdot\ \underline{4}\ =\ 40$

Answer: 40 numerals

EXERCISES _____

In 1–12, evaluate the expression.

1. $_3P_3$ 2. $_3P_1$ 3. $_7P_7$ 4. $_7P_2$ 5. $_8P_3$ 6. $_{20}P_2$

7. $_{52}P_3$ 8. $_{12}P_4$ 9. $_8P_6$ 10. $\dfrac{8!}{6!}$ 11. $\dfrac{15!}{14!}$ 12. $\dfrac{97!}{97!}$

13. In how many different ways can 4 people line up in a row?
14. In how many different ways can 4 students take seats in a row that contains 6 chairs?
15. There are 9 players on a baseball team. In a batting order, the pitcher bats last. How many different batting orders are possible for the 8 remaining players?
16. How many 5-letter words can be formed using the letters in the word LEMON if each letter is used only once in the word?
17. How many 3-letter words can be formed from the given letters, if each letter is used only once in a word?
    a. TUG   b. SHIP   c. YACHT   d. DINGHY   e. SUBMARINE
18. A 3-digit numeral is formed using the digits 1, 2, 3, 4, and 5, with no repetition. Find the number of (a) 3-digit numerals possible; (b) 3-digit numerals less than 200; (c) 3-digit numerals greater than 300; (d) 3-digit numerals that are even. (*Hint.* Think of the units place first.)

19. How many 3-digit numerals can be formed using the digits 1, 2, 3, 4, and 5, if repetition of digits is allowed?

20. *Rule 1:* $_nP_r = \underbrace{n(n-1)(n-2)\dots}_{r \text{ factors}}$

Rule 2: $_nP_r = \dfrac{n!}{(n-r)!}$

Rule 3: $_nP_r = n(n-1)(n-2)\dots(n-r+1)$

a. Evaluate $_{10}P_2$ using (1) rule 1; (2) rule 2; (3) rule 3.
b. Evaluate $_7P_3$ using (1) rule 1; (2) rule 2; (3) rule 3.
c. Can rule 2 or rule 3 be used in place of rule 1 to find the number of permutations of n things, taken r at a time?

13-4 PERMUTATIONS WITH REPETITION

"When an infant is rocked to sleep, the parent is trying to lull or to calm the baby." Let us examine three words from this sentence: CALM, LULL, and BABY.

EXAMPLE 1. How many different 4-letter words can be formed from the letters of the word CALM?

This is the number of permutations of 4 things, taken 4 at a time. Since $_4P_4 = 4! = 4 \cdot 3 \cdot 2 \cdot 1 = 24$, there are 24 possible words. The words are:

> ACLM, ACML, ALCM, ALMC, AMCL, AMLC,
> CALM, CAML, CLAM, CLMA, CMAL, CMLA,
> LACM, LAMC, LCAM, LCMA, LMAC, LMCA,
> MACL, MALC, MCAL, MCLA, MLAC, MLCA.

Answer: 24 words

EXAMPLE 2. How many different 4-letter words can be formed from the letters of the word LULL?

This is an example of permutations with repetition because the letter L is repeated in the word. If we try to list the different words, we see that there are only four words:

> LLLU, LLUL, LULL, ULLL.

How can an answer of 4 words be obtained by a formula? If subscripts had been used to distinguish one letter L from another letter L, we could have listed 24 words as follows:

$L_1L_2L_3U$, $L_1L_3L_2U$, $L_2L_1L_3U$, $L_2L_3L_1U$, $L_3L_1L_2U$, $L_3L_2L_1U$,
$L_1L_2UL_3$, $L_1L_3UL_2$, $L_2L_1UL_3$, $L_2L_3UL_1$, $L_3L_1UL_2$, $L_3L_2UL_1$,
$L_1UL_2L_3$, $L_1UL_3L_2$, $L_2UL_1L_3$, $L_2UL_3L_1$, $L_3UL_1L_2$, $L_3UL_2L_1$,
$UL_1L_2L_3$, $UL_1L_3L_2$, $UL_2L_1L_3$, $UL_2L_3L_1$, $UL_3L_1L_2$, $UL_3L_2L_1$.

Look carefully at the first line of words with subscripted letters. There are $3! = 3 \cdot 2 \cdot 1 = 6$ ways to arrange the letters L_1, L_2, and L_3. By eliminating subscripts, every word in the first line becomes LLLU.

In a similar way, each line of six words reduces to a single word when subscripts are eliminated. The second line is reduced to LLUL; the third line to LULL; and the fourth line to ULLL.

A permutation of 4 different letters, taken 4 at a time, is 4!, or 24. Since, without subscripts, 3 of the letters are identical, we divide by 3!, or 6. By this rule:

$$\frac{4!}{3!} = \frac{4 \cdot \cancel{3} \cdot \cancel{2} \cdot \cancel{1}}{\cancel{3} \cdot \cancel{2} \cdot \cancel{1}} = 4 \text{ words} \quad Ans.$$

EXAMPLE 3. How many different 4-letter words can be formed from the word BABY?

This is the number of permutations of 4 letters, taken 4 at a time, in which 2 of the letters are identical. Here, we say:

$$\frac{4!}{2!} = \frac{4 \cdot 3 \cdot \cancel{2} \cdot \cancel{1}}{\cancel{2} \cdot \cancel{1}} = 12 \text{ words} \quad Ans.$$

Note. It is not necessary to list the words. However, as a check, the words are:

ABBY, ABYB, AYBB, BABY, BAYB, BBAY,
BBYA, BYBA, BYAB, YABB, YBAB, YBBA.

● **In general, the number of permutations of *n* things, taken *n* at a time, with *r* of these things identical, is given by $\dfrac{n!}{r!}$.**

MODEL PROBLEMS _____

1. How many different six-digit numerals can be written using all of the following six digits: 2, 2, 2, 2, 3, and 5?

Solution: This is the number of permutations of 6 things, taken 6 at a time, in which 4 of the digits (2, 2, 2, 2) are identical. Thus,

$$\frac{6!}{4!} = \frac{6 \cdot 5 \cdot \cancel{4} \cdot \cancel{3} \cdot \cancel{2} \cdot \cancel{1}}{\cancel{4} \cdot \cancel{3} \cdot \cancel{2} \cdot \cancel{1}} = 30 \text{ six-digit numerals} \quad Ans.$$

2. How many different 7-letter words can be formed from the letters in the word DIVIDED?

Solution: This is the number of permutations of 7 things, taken 7 at a time, in which certain letters repeat themselves. Since the letter D is used 3 times, we divide by 3!. Also, since the letter I is used 2 times, we divide by 2!. Thus,

$$\frac{7!}{2!\ 3!} = \frac{7 \cdot 6 \cdot 5 \cdot \overset{2}{\cancel{4}} \cdot \cancel{3} \cdot \cancel{2} \cdot \cancel{1}}{\cancel{2} \cdot 1 \quad \cancel{3} \cdot \cancel{2} \cdot \cancel{1}} = 420 \text{ words} \quad Ans.$$

EXERCISES

1. a. List the six different arrangements or permutations of the letters in the word TAR.   **b.** Write the formula that shows why six permutations are possible.

2. a. List the three different arrangements or permutations of the letters in the word TOT.   **b.** Write the formula that shows why only three permutations are possible.

3. a. List the single arrangement or permutation of the letters in the word TTT.   **b.** Write the formula that shows why only one permutation is possible.

4. How many different 5-letter permutations are there of the letters in each of the given words?
   a. APPLE   **b.** ADDED   **c.** VIVID   **d.** TESTS

5. How many different arrangements of 6 letters can be made using the letters in each of the given words?
   a. FREEZE   **b.** SIMPLE   **c.** VOODOO   **d.** SYSTEM
   e. BETTER   **f.** SEEDED   **g.** TATTOO   **h.** DEEDED

6. Find the number of distinct arrangements of the letters in:
   a. STREETS   **b.** INSISTS   **c.** ESTEEMED   **d.** DESERVED
   e. TENNESSEE   **f.** BOOKKEEPER   **g.** MISSISSIPPI

7. How many different five-digit numerals can be written using all of the five digits listed in each part?
   a. 1, 2, 3, 4, 5   **b.** 1, 2, 2, 2, 2
   c. 1, 1, 2, 2, 2   **d.** 2, 2, 2, 2, 2

8. A bookseller has 7 copies of a novel and 3 copies of a biography. In how many ways can these 10 books be arranged on a shelf?

9. In how many ways can 6 white flags and 3 blue flags be arranged one above another on a single rope on a ship?

10. When written in full length, a^2x can be *aax*, *axa*, or *xaa*. How many different arrangements of letters are possible for each of the given expressions, when written in full length?
    a. b^3y **b.** a^2x^5 **c.** abx^6 **d.** a^2by^7 **e.** a^4b^8

In 11–15, write the answers in factorial notation; do not simplify.

11. Florence has 30 blue beads, 20 white beads, and 18 green beads, all the same size. In how many different ways can she string these beads on a chain to make a necklace?

12. Frances has 8 tulip bulbs, 10 daffodil bulbs, and 28 crocus bulbs. In how many different ways can Frances plant these bulbs in a row in her garden?

13. Anna has 4 dozen Rollo bars and 1 dozen apples as treats for Halloween. In how many ways can Anna hand out one treat each to 60 children who call at her door?

14. A can of mixed nuts contains 7 dozen peanuts, 5 dozen cashews, 3 dozen filberts, and 20 almonds. In how many different ways can Jerry eat the contents of the can, one nut at a time?

15. Print your first and last names using all capital letters. How many different arrangements of letters in your full name are possible?

13-5 PROBABILITY AND PERMUTATIONS

Many problems in probability have two methods of solution: (1) a step-by-step approach learned in Course I, which uses the definition of probability and the counting principle, and (2) a solution involving permutations.

Recall the basic rule for the theoretical probability of an event E, that is, $P(E) = \dfrac{n(E)}{n(S)}$. Since we count the number of outcomes or elements in E and S to use this rule, it seems reasonable to say that $n(E)$ and $n(S)$ are sometimes found by counting permutations.

In each model problem, two methods of solution are presented.

MODEL PROBLEMS ————————————————————————

1. Two cards are drawn at random from a standard deck of 52 cards, without replacement. What is the probability that both cards drawn are fives?

Solution

Method 1: Counting Principle

(1) On the first draw, there are 4 fives in a deck of 52 cards. So, $P(\text{first } 5) = \frac{4}{52}$.

(2) Assume a five is drawn. Then, on the second draw, there are 3 fives in the deck of 51 cards remaining. So, $P(\text{second } 5) = \frac{3}{51}$.

(3) Apply the counting principle of probability.

$P(\text{both } 5) = P(\text{first } 5) \cdot P(\text{second } 5)$

$= \dfrac{4}{52} \cdot \dfrac{3}{51}$

$= \dfrac{1}{13} \cdot \dfrac{1}{17} = \dfrac{1}{221}$ *Ans.*

Method 2: Permutations

(1) For the sample space S, treat the number of ways to draw 2 cards from a deck of 52 as a permutation. Then $n(S) = {}_{52}P_2$.

(2) For event E, treat the number of ways to draw 2 cards out of 4 fives in the deck as a permutation. Then $n(E) = {}_4P_2$.

(3) Apply the rule of probability.

(4) Simplify the fraction.

If event E = both cards are 5:

$P(E) = \dfrac{n(E)}{n(S)}$

$= \dfrac{{}_4P_2}{{}_{52}P_2}$

$= \dfrac{4 \cdot 3}{52 \cdot 51}$

$= \dfrac{1}{221}$ *Ans.*

2. Two cards are drawn at random from a standard deck of 52 cards, without replacement. What is the probability of drawing a 7 and an 8 in that order?

Solution

Method 1: Counting Principle

On the first draw, there are 4 sevens in a deck of 52 cards. Then, on the second draw, there are 4 eights in the deck of 51 cards remaining. Apply the counting principle of probability.

$P(7, 8 \text{ in order}) = P(7) \cdot P(8)$

$= \dfrac{4}{52} \cdot \dfrac{4}{51}$

$= \dfrac{16}{2,652}$

$= \dfrac{4}{663}$ *Ans.*

Method 2: Permutations

(1) For the sample space S, the number of ways to draw 2 cards in order from a deck of 52 cards is $n(S) = {}_{52}P_2$.

(2) For compound event E, there are 4 ways to draw a seven, then 4 ways to draw an eight. So, $n(E) = {}_4P_1 \cdot {}_4P_1$. It is also acceptable to say that $n(E) = 4 \cdot 4 = 16$ by the counting principle.

(3) Apply the rule of probability.

(4) Simplify the fraction.

$$P(7, 8 \text{ in order}) = \frac{n(E)}{n(S)}$$

$$= \frac{{}_4P_1 \cdot {}_4P_1}{{}_{52}P_2}$$

$$= \frac{4 \cdot 4}{52 \cdot 51}$$

$$= \frac{16}{2{,}652}$$

$$= \frac{4}{663} \quad Ans.$$

Note. Suppose the question had been as follows: What is the probability of drawing a 7 and an 8 *in any order*? Since a draw of 8, then 7, has the same probability as a draw of 7, then 8, and both orders are acceptable:

$$P(7, 8 \text{ in any order}) = \tfrac{4}{663} + \tfrac{4}{663} = \tfrac{8}{663}.$$

In other words, there are 2 possible orders for drawing a 7 and an 8. Thus, the probability is double that of drawing the cards in a specific order, or $2 \cdot \tfrac{4}{663} = \tfrac{8}{663}$.

3. Eddie Dunn has homework in five subjects: English, social studies, math, science, and health. If Eddie does his homework in random order, what is the probability that he does his math assignment first?

Solution: Although this problem can be solved by using permutations, notice how the first method is far more direct and easier.

Method 1: Definition

Math is 1 of 5 subjects.

So, $P(\text{math first}) = \dfrac{1}{5} \quad Ans.$

Method 2: Permutations

(1) The number of different ways to do the 5 assignments is $n(S) = {}_5P_5$.

(2) There is only 1 way to do math first. Then, there are ${}_4P_4$ ways to do the other assignments. So, $n(E) = 1 \cdot {}_4P_4$.

(3) Apply the rule of probability; simplify the fraction.

$$P(\text{math first}) = \frac{n(E)}{n(S)}$$

$$= \frac{1 \cdot {}_4P_4}{{}_5P_5}$$

$$= \frac{1 \cdot \cancel{4} \cdot \cancel{3} \cdot \cancel{2} \cdot \cancel{1}}{5 \cdot \cancel{4} \cdot \cancel{3} \cdot \cancel{2} \cdot \cancel{1}}$$

$$= \frac{1}{5} \quad Ans.$$

EXERCISES

In this section, unless otherwise noted, use any acceptable method to solve each problem.

1. **a.** Let $n(S)$ = the number of 5-letter words that can be formed using the letters in the word RADIO. Find $n(S)$.
   b. Let $n(E)$ = the number of 5-letter words that can be formed using the letters in RADIO such that the first letter is a vowel. Find $n(E)$.
   c. If the letters in RADIO are rearranged at random, find the probability that the first letter is a vowel by using parts **a** and **b**.
   d. Find the answer to part **c** by using a more direct method.

2. If the letters in each of the given words are rearranged at random, find the probability that the first letter in the word is A.
   a. RADAR   **b.** CANVAS   **c.** AZALEA   **d.** AA   **e.** DEFINE

3. If the letters in each of the given words are rearranged at random, find the probability that the letters in the first and second positions are both vowels.
   a. RADAR   **b.** CANVAS   **c.** AZALEA   **d.** AA   **e.** DEFINE

In 4–6, there are 15 object balls in pool; solid-colored balls are numbered 1 through 8, and striped object balls are numbered 9 through 15.

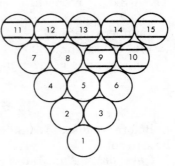

4. If Alexis pockets one of the object balls, find the probability that it is:
   a. an even number
   b. an odd number
   c. a solid color
   d. a striped ball
   e. striped and even
   f. solid and odd

Ex. 4–6

5. **a.** Starting with 15 object balls on the table, find the probability that Kevin pockets an object ball that is striped or an odd number.
   b. Assume that Kevin pocketed the 7 ball. Find the probability that the second object ball pocketed is an odd number.
   c. Find the probability that Kevin pocketed the 7 ball, followed by an odd-numbered object ball.

6. Starting with 15 object balls, 2 are pocketed, one following another. Find the probability of each event.
   a. P(both are solid colors)
   b. P(both are even numbers)
   c. P(both bear numbers that are less than 6)
   d. P(both are striped and bear odd numbers)

7. At random, a baby picks up and holds 2 blocks. Find the probability that both blocks are red if the blocks include:
   a. 2 red, 1 white, 1 green **b.** 4 white, 3 red, 2 blue
   c. 6 red, 4 orange, 5 yellow **d.** 5 white, 1 red, 6 blue

8. Two cards are drawn at random from a standard deck of 52 cards, without replacement. Find the probability of selecting:
   a. the king of hearts and queen of hearts, in that order
   b. the king of hearts and queen of hearts, in any order
   c. any king and any queen, in that order
   d. any king and any queen, in either order
   e. any two kings **f.** any two hearts
   g. any two red cards **h.** any pair

9. Three cards are drawn at random from a 52-card deck, without replacement. Find the probability of selecting:
   a. any three black cards **b.** any three clubs
   c. any three aces **d.** any three picture cards

10. If 5 cards are drawn at random from a 52-card deck, without replacement, what is the probability that all 5 cards are of the same suit? (The answer need not be simplified; leave as factors.)

11. A 3-digit numeral is formed by selecting randomly from the digits 1, 2, 3, 5, and 7, without repetition. Find the probability that the numeral formed:
    a. is less than 300 **b.** is greater than 300
    c. contains no even digits **d.** is an odd number

13-6 COMBINATIONS

Before we discuss combinations, let us start with a problem you know how to solve.

Question 1: Ann, Barbara, Carol, and Dave are the only members of a school club. In how many different ways can they elect a president and a treasurer for the club?

Any one of 4 students can be elected as president. After this happens, then any one of the 3 remaining students can be elected as treasurer. Thus, there are 4 · 3, or 12, possible arrangements. Using initials to represent the students involved, there are these 12 arrangements:

$$\begin{array}{llll}
(A, B) & (B, A) & (B, C) & (C, B) \\
(A, C) & (C, A) & (B, D) & (D, B) \\
(A, D) & (D, A) & (C, D) & (D, C)
\end{array}$$

This is the number of permutations of 4 things, taken 2 at a time. We could simply have said:

$$_4P_2 = 4 \cdot 3 = 12 \text{ arrangements } Ans.$$

Question 2: Ann, Barbara, Carol, and Dave are the only members of a school club. In how many ways can they choose two people to represent the club at student council meetings?

Look carefully at the list of 12 arrangements given in answer to the first question. While (A, B) and (B, A) are two different slates for president and treasurer, sending Ann and Barbara to the student council is exactly the same as sending Barbara and Ann. Let us match up answers that are duplicates for this problem:

$$(A, B) \leftrightarrow (B, A) \qquad (B, C) \leftrightarrow (C, B)$$
$$(A, C) \leftrightarrow (C, A) \qquad (B, D) \leftrightarrow (D, B)$$
$$(A, D) \leftrightarrow (D, A) \qquad (C, D) \leftrightarrow (D, C)$$

While order is important in listing slates of officers in the first question, there is no reason to order the elements in this second question. In fact, if we think of two representatives to the student council as a *set* of two students, we can list all possible sets of two representatives as follows:

$$\{A, B\} \qquad \{B, C\}$$
$$\{A, C\} \qquad \{B, D\}$$
$$\{A, D\} \qquad \{C, D\}$$

From this list we can find the number of *combinations* of 4 things, taken 2 at a time, written in symbols as $_4C_2$. The answer to this question is found by dividing the number of permutations of 4 things, taken 2 at a time by 2! orders. Thus:

$$_4C_2 = \frac{_4P_2}{2!} = \frac{4 \cdot 3}{2 \cdot 1} = \frac{12}{2} = 6 \text{ combinations} \quad Ans.$$

Question 3: Ann, Barbara, Carol, and Dave are the only members of a school club. In how many ways can they select a 3-person committee to work on the club's next project?

Is *order* important to this answer? If 3 officers were to be elected, such as a president, a treasurer, and a secretary, then order would be important and a permutation would be found. However, a committee is merely a set of people. In listing the elements of a set, order is not important and thus, a combination is used. Compare the permutations and combinations that follow.

Permutations							*Combinations*
(A, B, C)	(A, C, B)	(B, A, C)	(B, C, A)	(C, A, B)	(C, B, A)		{A, B, C}
(A, B, D)	(A, D, B)	(B, A, D)	(B, D, A)	(D, A, B)	(D, B, A)		{A, B, D}
(A, C, D)	(A, D, C)	(C, A, D)	(C, D, A)	(D, A, C)	(D, C, A)		{A, C, D}
(B, C, D)	(B, D, C)	(C, B, D)	(C, D, B)	(D, B, C)	(D, C, B)		{B, C, D}

While there are 24 permutations, written as ordered triples, there are only 4 combinations, written as sets. For example, in the first row of permutations, there are 3!, or $3 \cdot 2 \cdot 1$, or 6 ordered triples containing A, B, and C. However, there is only one set that contains A, B, and C, namely the set {A, B, C}.

Therefore, the number of ways to select a 3-person committee from a group of 4 people is the number of *combinations* of 4 things, taken 3 at a time, written in symbols as $_4C_3$. The answer to this question is found by dividing the number of permutations of 4 things, taken 3 at a time, by 3! orders. Thus, we write:

$$_4C_3 = \frac{_4P_3}{3!} = \frac{4 \cdot 3 \cdot 2}{3 \cdot 2 \cdot 1} = \frac{4 \cdot 3 \cdot 2}{3 \cdot 2 \cdot 1} = 4 \text{ combinations} \quad Ans.$$

● **In general, for counting numbers n and r where $r \le n$, the number of combinations of n things, taken r at a time, is found by the formula:**

$$_nC_r = \frac{_nP_r}{r!}$$

Note. The notation $\binom{n}{r}$ also represents the number of combinations of n things, taken r at a time. Thus $\binom{n}{r} = {_nC_r}$ or $\binom{n}{r} = \frac{_nP_r}{r!}$.

Some Relationships Involving Combinations

Given a group of 5 people, how many different 5-person committees can be formed? Common sense tells us that there is only 1 such committee, namely the committee consisting of all 5 people. Using combinations, we see:

$$_5C_5 = \frac{_5P_5}{5!} = \frac{5 \cdot 4 \cdot 3 \cdot 2 \cdot 1}{5 \cdot 4 \cdot 3 \cdot 2 \cdot 1} = 1$$

Also, $_3C_3 = \frac{_3P_3}{3!} = \frac{3 \cdot 2 \cdot 1}{3 \cdot 2 \cdot 1} = 1$ and $_4C_4 = \frac{_4P_4}{4!} = \frac{4 \cdot 3 \cdot 2 \cdot 1}{4 \cdot 3 \cdot 2 \cdot 1} = 1$.

Observation 1: **For any counting number n, $_nC_n = 1$.**

Given a group of 5 people, in how many different ways can we select a committee consisting of no people, or 0 people? Common sense tells us that there is only 1 way to select no one. Thus, using combinations, $_5C_0 = 1$. Let us agree to the following generalization:

Observation 2: **For any counting number n, $_nC_0 = 1$.**

In how many ways can we select a committee of 2 people from a group of 7 people? Since a committee is a combination,

$$_7C_2 = \frac{_7P_2}{2!} = \frac{7 \cdot 6}{2 \cdot 1} = \frac{7 \cdot \overset{3}{\cancel{6}}}{\cancel{2} \cdot 1} = 21$$

Now, given a group of 7 people, in how many ways can 5 people *not* be appointed to the committee? Since each set of people not appointed is a combination,

$$_7C_5 = \frac{_7P_5}{5!} = \frac{7 \cdot 6 \cdot 5 \cdot 4 \cdot 3}{5 \cdot 4 \cdot 3 \cdot 2 \cdot 1} = \frac{7 \cdot \overset{3}{\cancel{6}} \cdot \cancel{5} \cdot \cancel{4} \cdot \cancel{3}}{\cancel{5} \cdot \cancel{4} \cdot \cancel{3} \cdot \cancel{2} \cdot 1} = 21$$

Notice that $_7C_2 = {_7C_5}$. In other words, starting with a group of 7 people, the number of sets of 2 people that can be selected is equal to the number of sets of 5 people that can be *not* selected. In the same way it can be shown that $_7C_3 = {_7C_4}$, that $_7C_6 = {_7C_1}$, and that $_7C_7 = {_7C_0}$.

In general, starting with n objects, the number of ways to choose r objects for a combination is equal to the number of ways to not choose $(n - r)$ objects for the combination.

Observation 3: **For whole numbers n and r where $r \le n$,**

$$_nC_r = {_nC_{n-r}}$$

KEEP IN MIND _____

Permutations	*Combinations*
$_nP_r = \underbrace{n(n - 1)(n - 2) \ldots}_{r \text{ factors}}$	$_nC_r = \dfrac{_nP_r}{r!}$
1. *Order is important.* Think of ordered elements such as ordered pairs and ordered triples. 2. An *arrangement* indicates a permutation.	1. *Order is not important.* Think of sets. 2. A *committee*, or a *selection of a group*, indicates a combination.

MODEL PROBLEMS _____

1. Evaluate: $_{10}C_3$

Solution: This is the number of combinations of 10 things, taken 3 at a time.

$$_{10}C_3 = \frac{_{10}P_3}{3!} = \frac{10 \cdot 9 \cdot 8}{3 \cdot 2 \cdot 1} = \frac{10 \cdot \overset{3}{\cancel{9}} \cdot \overset{4}{\cancel{8}}}{\cancel{3} \cdot \cancel{2} \cdot 1} = 120 \quad Ans.$$

2. Evaluate: $\begin{pmatrix} 25 \\ 23 \end{pmatrix}$

Solution

(1) This is an alternate form for the number of combinations of 25 things, taken 23 at a time: $\begin{pmatrix} 25 \\ 23 \end{pmatrix} = {}_{25}C_{23}$

(2) Since ${}_nC_r = {}_nC_{n-r}$, observe: ${}_{25}C_{23} = {}_{25}C_2$

(3) Using ${}_{25}C_2$, perform the easier computation. Thus:

$$\begin{pmatrix} 25 \\ 23 \end{pmatrix} = {}_{25}C_{23} = {}_{25}C_2 = \frac{{}_{25}P_2}{2!} = \frac{25 \cdot \overset{12}{\cancel{24}}}{\cancel{2} \cdot 1} = 300 \quad Ans.$$

3. There are 10 teachers in the science department. How many 4-person committees can be formed in the department if Mrs. Martens and Dr. Blumenthal, two of the teachers, must be on each committee?

Solution

Since Mrs. Martens and Dr. Blumenthal are selected to be on each committee, the problem becomes one of filling 2 positions on a committee from the remaining 8 teachers.

$${}_8C_2 = \frac{{}_8P_2}{2!} = \frac{8 \cdot 7}{2 \cdot 1} = \frac{\overset{4}{\cancel{8}} \cdot 7}{\cancel{2} \cdot 1} = 28 \text{ committees} \quad Ans.$$

4. There are six points in a plane, no three of which are collinear. How many straight lines can be drawn using pairs of these six points?

Solution

Whether joining points A and B, or points B and A, only one line exists, namely $\overleftrightarrow{AB}$. Since order is not important here, this is a combination of 6 points, taken 2 at a time.

$${}_6C_2 = \frac{{}_6P_2}{2!} = \frac{6 \cdot 5}{2 \cdot 1} = \frac{\overset{3}{\cancel{6}} \cdot 5}{\cancel{2} \cdot 1} = 15 \text{ lines} \quad Ans.$$

5. In Mr. Nadolny's class there are 10 boys and 20 girls. Find the number of ways that Mr. Nadolny can select a team of 3 students from the class to work on a group project if the team consists of:
    a. any 3 students   **b.** 1 boy and 2 girls
    c. 3 girls only   **d.** at least 2 girls

Solution:

a. The class contains 10 boys and 20 girls, for a total of 30 students. Since order is not important on a team, this is a combination of 30 students, taken 3 at a time.

$$_{30}C_3 = \frac{_{30}P_3}{3!} = \frac{30 \cdot 29 \cdot 28}{3 \cdot 2 \cdot 1} = \frac{\overset{10}{\cancel{30}} \cdot 29 \cdot \overset{14}{\cancel{28}}}{\cancel{3} \cdot \cancel{2} \cdot 1} = 4{,}060 \text{ teams } \textit{Ans.}$$

b. This is a compound event. To find the number of ways to select 1 boy out of 10 boys for a team, use $_{10}C_1$. To find the number of ways to select 2 girls out of 20 for the team, use $_{20}C_2$. Then, by the counting principle, multiply the results.

$$_{10}C_1 \cdot {}_{20}C_2 = \frac{10}{1} \cdot \frac{20 \cdot 19}{2 \cdot 1} = \frac{10}{1} \cdot \frac{\overset{10}{\cancel{20}} \cdot 19}{\cancel{2} \cdot 1}$$

$$= 10 \cdot 190 = 1{,}900 \text{ teams } \textit{Ans.}$$

c. This is another compound event, in which 0 boys out of 10 boys are selected. Recall that $_{10}C_0 = 1$. Thus:

$$_{10}C_0 \cdot {}_{20}C_3 = 1 \cdot \frac{20 \cdot 19 \cdot 18}{3 \cdot 2 \cdot 1} = 1 \cdot \frac{20 \cdot 19 \cdot \overset{3}{\cancel{18}}}{\cancel{3} \cdot \cancel{2} \cdot 1}$$

$$= 1 \cdot 1{,}140 = 1{,}140 \text{ teams } \textit{Ans.}$$

d. A team of at least 2 girls can consist of exactly 2 girls (see part **b**, 1,900 teams) or 3 girls (see part **c**, 1,140 teams). Since these events are disjoint, add: $1{,}900 + 1{,}140 = 3{,}040$ teams *Ans.*

EXERCISES

In 1–12, evaluate the expression.

1. $_{15}C_2$ **2.** $_{12}C_3$ **3.** $_{10}C_4$ **4.** $_{25}C_1$ **5.** $_{13}C_0$ **6.** $_{14}C_{14}$

7. $_9C_8$ **8.** $_{20}C_{18}$ **9.** $\binom{7}{3}$ **10.** $\binom{9}{4}$ **11.** $\binom{17}{17}$ **12.** $\binom{8}{0}$

13. Find the number of combinations of 6 things, taken 3 at a time.

14. How many different committees of 3 people can be chosen from a group of 9 people?

15. How many different subsets of exactly 7 elements can be formed from the set {0, 1, 2, 3, 4, 5, 6, 7, 8, 9}?

16. For the given number of noncollinear points in a plane, how many straight lines can be drawn?
    a. 3   **b.** 4   **c.** 5   **d.** 7   **e.** 8   **f.** 10   **g.** n

17. A coach selects players for a team. If the coach pays no attention to the positions individuals will play while making this first selection, how many teams may be formed?
    a. Of 14 candidates, Coach Richko needs 5 for a basketball team.
    b. Of 16 candidates, Coach Jones needs 11 for a football team.
    c. Of 13 candidates, Coach Greves needs 9 for a baseball team.

18. A disc jockey has 25 records at hand, but has time to play only 22 on the air. How many groups of 22 records can be selected?

19. There are 14 teachers in a mathematics department. **a.** How many 4-person committees can be formed in the department? **b.** How many 4-person committees can be formed if Mr. Sforza, one of the 14, must be on the committee? **c.** How many 4-person committees can be formed if Mr. Goldstein and Mrs. Friedel, two of the 14, must be on the committee?

20. There are 12 Republicans and 10 Democrats on a senate committee. From this group, a 3-person subcommittee is to be formed. Find the number of 3-person subcommittees that consist of:
    a. any members of the senate committee   **b.** Democrats only
    c. one Republican and two Democrats   **d.** at least 2 Democrats
    e. John Clark, who is a Democrat, and any 2 Republicans

21. Sue Bartling loves to read mystery books and car-repair manuals. On a visit to the library, Sue finds 9 new mystery books and 3 car-repair manuals. She borrows 4 of these books. Find the number of different sets of 4 books Sue can borrow if:
    a. all are mystery books   **b.** exactly 2 are mystery books
    c. only 1 is a mystery book   **d.** all are car-repair manuals

22. Mr. Spartalis owns 4 suits, 8 shirts, and 10 ties. He plans to travel and packs 2 suits, 4 shirts, and 3 ties. How many different sets of clothing could Mr. Spartalis have chosen?

23. Cards are drawn at random from a 52-card deck. Find the number of different 5-card poker hands possible consisting of:
    a. any 5 cards from the deck   **b.** 3 aces and 2 kings
    c. 4 queens and any other card   **d.** 5 spades
    e. 2 aces and 3 picture cards   **f.** 5 jacks

24. Consider the formulas:

(1) $_nC_r = \dfrac{_nP_r}{r!}$ (2) $_nC_r = \dfrac{n!}{(n-r)!r!}$

(3) $_nC_r = \dfrac{n(n-1)(n-2)\ldots(n-r+1)}{r(r-1)(r-2)\ldots(1)}$

a. Evaluate $_8C_3$ using each of the 3 formulas.
b. Evaluate $_{11}C_7$ using each of the 3 formulas.
c. Can all 3 formulas be used to find the combination of n things, taken r at a time?

25. How many committees consisting of 7 people or more can be formed from a group of 10 people?

26. There are 12 roses growing in Heather's garden. How many different bunches consisting of more than 7 roses can Heather cut to bring into the house?

13-7 PROBABILITY AND COMBINATIONS

The probability of an event E is defined as $P(E) = \dfrac{n(E)}{n(S)}$. You have seen that $n(E)$ and $n(S)$ are sometimes found by counting permutations. In the model problems that follow, you will see that $n(E)$ and $n(S)$ are sometimes found by counting combinations.

Remember, if a probability question is asked in which order is not important, find $n(E)$ and $n(S)$ by using combinations.

MODEL PROBLEMS _____

1. Two cards are drawn at random from a standard deck of 52 cards, without replacement. What is the probability that both cards drawn are fives?

Solution

See Model Problem 1 on pages 584–585. This question has been answered using the counting principle and a method involving permutations. However, since order is not important in drawing 2 fives from a 52-card deck, this question can also be answered by using combinations.

Method 3: Combinations

(1) For sample space S, each set of 2 cards from a deck of 52 is a combination. Thus, $n(S) = {}_{52}C_2$.

If event E = both cards are 5,

$$P(E) = \frac{n(E)}{n(S)} = \frac{{}_4C_2}{{}_{52}C_2}$$

(2) For event E, each set of 2 cards from any of 4 fives in the deck is a combination. Thus, $n(E) = {}_4C_2$.

$$= \frac{\dfrac{4 \cdot 3}{2 \cdot 1}}{\dfrac{52 \cdot 51}{2 \cdot 1}} = \frac{\dfrac{\overset{2}{\cancel{4}} \cdot 3}{\cancel{2} \cdot 1}}{\dfrac{\overset{26}{\cancel{52}} \cdot 51}{\cancel{2} \cdot 1}}$$

(3) Apply the rule of probability.

(4) Simplify the fraction.

$$= \frac{6}{1,326} = \frac{1}{221} \quad Ans.$$

Note. Some probability questions, such as the one just asked, may be solved by using either combinations or permutations. However, this is not necessarily true for all probability questions. For example, in Model Problem 2 on pages 585–586, order is important, so elements are counted by using permutations. That question cannot be answered by using combinations.

In Model Problem 2 that follows, order is not important. As you will see, the problem is best answered by using combinations to count $n(E)$ and $n(S)$.

● **In general, use permutations where order is important, and combinations where order is not important.**

2. In a school organization, there are 4 sophomores and 5 juniors. If a committee of 4 people is to be selected from this group, what is the probability that 2 sophomores and 2 juniors are on the committee?

Solution

(1) The school organization has a total of 9 people (4 sophomores and 5 juniors). For sample space S, each 4-person committee from a group of 9 people is a combination.

$$n(S) = {}_9C_4 = \frac{9 \cdot 8 \cdot 7 \cdot 6}{4 \cdot 3 \cdot 2 \cdot 1} = \frac{9 \cdot \overset{2}{\cancel{8}} \cdot 7 \cdot \cancel{6}}{\cancel{4} \cdot \cancel{3} \cdot \cancel{2} \cdot 1} = 126$$

(2) The number of ways to choose 2 of 4 sophomores for a committee is ${}_4C_2$. The number of ways to choose 2 of 5 juniors for a committee is ${}_5C_2$. Since event E is a compound event consisting of two independent events, apply the counting principle.

$$n(E) = {}_4C_2 \cdot {}_5C_2 = \frac{4 \cdot 3}{2 \cdot 1} \cdot \frac{5 \cdot 4}{2 \cdot 1} = \frac{\overset{2}{\cancel{4}} \cdot 3}{\cancel{2} \cdot 1} \cdot \frac{5 \cdot \overset{2}{\cancel{4}}}{\cancel{2} \cdot 1} = 6 \cdot 10 = 60$$

(3) Apply the rule of probability and simplify the fraction.

$$P(E) = \frac{n(E)}{n(S)} = \frac{{}_4C_2 \cdot {}_5C_2}{{}_9C_4} = \frac{6 \cdot 10}{126} = \frac{60}{126} = \frac{10}{21} \; Ans.$$

3. An urn contains 4 white marbles and 5 blue marbles, all of equal size. If 3 marbles are drawn at random with no replacement, what is the probability that at least 2 marbles drawn are blue?

Solution

(1) For sample space S, 3 marbles are drawn from a total of 9.

$$n(S) = {}_9C_3 = \frac{\overset{3}{\cancel{9}} \cdot \overset{4}{\cancel{8}} \cdot 7}{\cancel{3} \cdot \cancel{2} \cdot 1} = 84$$

(2) For event E, at least 2 blue marbles are drawn. Therefore, either 2 are blue and 1 is white, or 3 are blue and 0 are white.
Let A = {combinations of 2 blue and 1 white marbles}
B = {combinations of 3 blue and 0 white marbles}

$$n(A) = {}_5C_2 \cdot {}_4C_1 = \frac{5 \cdot \overset{2}{\cancel{4}}}{\cancel{2} \cdot 1} \cdot \frac{4}{1} = 10 \cdot 4 = 40$$

$$n(B) = {}_5C_3 \cdot {}_4C_0 = \frac{5 \cdot \overset{2}{\cancel{4}} \cdot \cancel{3}}{\cancel{3} \cdot \cancel{2} \cdot 1} \cdot 1 = 10 \cdot 1 = 10$$

Since A and B are disjoint sets:

$$n(E) = n(A) + n(B) = 40 + 10 = 50$$

(3) Apply the rule of probability.

$$P(\text{at least 2 blue}) = \frac{n(E)}{n(S)} = \frac{50}{84} = \frac{25}{42} \; Ans.$$

EXERCISES

In 1–4, evaluate the expression.

1. $\dfrac{{}_4C_2}{{}_{11}C_2}$ **2.** $\dfrac{{}_7C_3}{{}_{12}C_3}$ **3.** $\dfrac{{}_4C_3 \cdot {}_6C_2}{{}_{10}C_5}$ **4.** $\dfrac{{}_{12}C_0 \cdot {}_5C_2}{{}_{17}C_2}$

5. a. Let $n(S)$ = the number of subsets of 2 elements that can be formed from the set $\{1, 2, 3, 4, 5\}$. Find $n(S)$.
  b. Let $n(E)$ = the number of subsets of 2 elements formed from the set $\{1, 2, 3, 4, 5\}$ where both elements are odd digits. Find $n(E)$.
  c. Using parts **a** and **b,** find the probability that a 2-element subset of $\{1, 2, 3, 4, 5\}$ contains two odd digits.

6. a. In how many ways can 2 cards be drawn from a 52-card deck?
  b. In how many ways can 2 hearts be drawn from a 52-card deck?
  c. If 2 cards are drawn from a 52-card deck, what is the probability that both cards are hearts?

7. Two cards are drawn from a 52-card deck without replacement. Find the probability that the two cards are:
  a. aces   **b.** red   **c.** spades   **d.** picture cards

8. Three cards are drawn from a 52-card deck without replacement. Find the probability that the three cards are:
  a. black   **b.** diamonds   **c.** kings   **d.** three of a kind

9. The English department consists of 5 men and 7 women.
  a. How many different 3-person committees can be chosen from the 12 teachers in the English department?
  b. Find the probability that the 3-person committee consists of:
  (1) 3 men   (2) 3 women   (3) 2 men and 1 woman
  (4) 1 man and 2 women   (5) at least 2 women

10. Find the probability that a 4-person team consists of 2 girls and 2 boys if the team is chosen at random from:
  a. 3 girls and 3 boys   **b.** 5 girls and 2 boys
  c. 2 girls and 6 boys   **d.** 3 girls and 1 boy

11. In a contest, 2 students out of 5 are to be chosen for a final playoff. All students have an equal chance of winning. The students include 4 girls (Liz, JoAnn, Claudia, Rosemary), and 1 boy (Drew).
  a. In how many ways can the 2 finalists be chosen?
  b. Find the probability that the finalists are:
  (1) 2 girls   (2) a girl and a boy
  (3) 2 boys   (4) Claudia and Drew
  c. Find the probability that one of the finalists is Liz.

12. On an examination, a student is to select any 4 questions out of 7 to answer. All questions are of equal difficulty.
  a. How many different sets of 4 questions can be selected?
  b. How many sets of 4 questions will include question 1?
  c. If a student answers any 4 questions out of 7 on a test, what is the probability that he selected question 1?

13. An urn contains 5 red marbles and 3 white marbles, all of equal size. If 3 marbles are drawn at random with no replacement, find the probability of drawing:
    a. 2 red and 1 white   b. 1 red and 2 white
    c. 3 red   d. 3 white   e. at least 2 red
    f. 3 of the same color   g. at most 1 red

14. A box of filled donuts contains 6 strawberry, 5 raspberry, and 1 grape. Renee selects 2 donuts, not knowing what the filling is. Find the probability that Renee selected:
    a. 2 strawberry   b. 2 raspberry   c. 2 grape
    d. 1 strawberry and 1 raspberry   e. 2 with the same filling

15. Baby Stephen has a box containing 4 red blocks, 3 yellow blocks, and 2 orange blocks. He picks 3 blocks at random. Find the probability that Stephen selected:
    a. 3 red blocks   b. 3 yellow blocks   c. 3 orange blocks
    d. 2 red blocks and 1 of another color
    e. at least 2 red blocks
    f. 2 yellow blocks and 1 of another color   g. no red blocks
    h. 3 blocks of the same color   i. 1 of each color

13-8 MORE PROBABILITY PROBLEMS

In this section, a variety of probability questions are presented. In some cases, permutations should be used. In other cases, combinations should be used. Keep the following in mind when answering these questions:

1. If the question asks "How many?" or "In how many ways?", the answer will be a whole number.
2. If the question asks "What is the probability?", the answer x will be a value between 0 and 1 inclusive, that is, $0 \le x \le 1$.
3. If order is important, use permutations.
4. If order is not important, use combinations.

MODEL PROBLEM _____

Mrs. Hendrix must select 4 students to represent the class in a spelling bee. Her best students include 3 girls (Helen, Maureen, and Kim) and 4 boys (Brendan, Carlos, Patrick, and Terry).

a. If Mrs. Hendrix selects 4 students out of the 7 by drawing names from a hat, how many different groups of 4 are possible?

b. What is the probability that the 4 students chosen will consist of 2 girls and 2 boys?

c. The students chosen are Helen, Kim, Carlos, and Patrick. In how many ways can these 4 students be called upon in the spelling bee?

d. What is the probability that the first two students called upon from this group are girls?

Solution

a. In choosing a group of 4 students out of 7, order is not important. Therefore, use combinations.

$$_7C_4 = \frac{_7P_4}{4!} = \frac{7 \cdot 6 \cdot 5 \cdot 4}{4 \cdot 3 \cdot 2 \cdot 1} = \frac{7 \cdot \cancel{6} \cdot 5 \cdot \cancel{4}}{\cancel{4} \cdot \cancel{3} \cdot \cancel{2} \cdot 1} = 35 \quad Ans.$$

b. The answer to part **a** indicates that 35 groups are possible, that is, $n(S) = 35$.

The number of ways to choose 2 girls out of 3 is $_3C_2$. The number of ways to choose 2 boys out of 4 is $_4C_2$. Since event E consists of choosing 2 girls and 2 boys, this is a compound event where $n(E) = {_3C_2} \cdot {_4C_2}$.

$$_3C_2 = \frac{3 \cdot \cancel{2}}{\cancel{2} \cdot 1} = 3 \qquad _4C_2 = \frac{\overset{2}{\cancel{4}} \cdot 3}{\cancel{2} \cdot 1} = 6$$

$$P(2 \text{ girls and 2 boys}) = \frac{_3C_2 \cdot {_4C_2}}{_7C_4} = \frac{3 \cdot 6}{35} = \frac{18}{35} \quad Ans.$$

c. The number of ways in which 4 students can be called upon in a spelling bee means that someone is first, someone else is second, and so on. Since order is important, use permutations.

$$_4P_4 = 4! = 4 \cdot 3 \cdot 2 \cdot 1 = 24 \text{ possible orders} \quad Ans.$$

d. This question may be answered using various methods.

Method 1: Counting Principle

There are 2 girls out of 4 students who may be called first. Once a girl is called upon, there is only 1 girl remaining out of the 3 students not yet called upon. Apply the counting principle of probability.

$P(\text{first 2 are girls}) = P(\text{girl first}) \cdot P(\text{girl second})$

$$= \frac{2}{4} \cdot \frac{1}{3} = \frac{2}{12} = \frac{1}{6} \quad Ans.$$

Method 2: Permutations

Let $n(S)$ equal the number of ways to call 2 of the 4 students in order, and let $n(E)$ equal the number of ways to call 2 of the 2 girls in order.

$$P(\text{first 2 are girls}) = \frac{n(E)}{n(S)} = \frac{{}_2P_2}{{}_4P_2} = \frac{2 \cdot 1}{4 \cdot 3} = \frac{2}{12} = \frac{1}{6} \quad Ans.$$

EXERCISES

1. The art club consists of 4 girls (Jennifer, Joanna, Gloria, Teresa) and 2 boys (Joe and Arthur).
   a. In how many ways can the club elect a president and a treasurer?
   b. Find the probability that the 2 officers elected are both girls.
   c. How many 2-person teams can be selected to work on a project?
   d. Find the probability that a 2-person team consists of:
      (1) 2 girls   (2) 2 boys   (3) 1 girl and 1 boy
      (4) 2 people, each having J as a first initial

2. A committee of 4 is to be chosen from 4 men and 3 women.
   a. How many different 4-member committees are possible?
   b. How many 4-member committees contain 3 men and 1 woman?
   c. What is the probability that a 4-member committee will contain exactly 1 woman?
   d. What is the probability that a man will be on the committee?

3. A committee of 6 people is to be chosen from 9 available people.
   a. How many 6-person committees can be chosen?
   b. The committee, when chosen, has 4 students and 2 teachers. Find the probability that a 3-person subcommittee from this group contains: (1) students only   (2) exactly 1 teacher
   (3) at least 2 students

4. A box of chocolate-covered candies contains 7 caramels and 3 creams, all exactly the same in appearance. Jim selects 4 pieces of candy.
   a. Find the number of selections possible of 4 pieces of candy that include:
      (1) 4 caramels   (2) 1 caramel and 3 creams
      (3) 2 caramels and 2 creams   (4) any 4 pieces
   b. Find the probability that Jim's selection included:
      (1) 4 caramels   (2) 1 caramel and 3 creams
      (3) 2 caramels and 2 creams   (4) no caramels

5. Two cards are drawn at random from a 52-card deck without replacement. Find the probability of drawing:
   a. the ace of clubs and jack of clubs in any order
   b. an ace and a jack in that order   c. two jacks
   d. an ace and a jack in any order   e. two clubs
   f. a red ace and a black jack in either order

6. Mrs. Pegrum has 4 quarters and 3 nickels in her purse. If she takes 3 coins out of her purse without looking at them, find the probability that the 3 coins are worth:
   a. exactly 75 cents   b. exactly 15 cents
   c. exactly 35 cents   d. exactly 55 cents
   e. more than 10 cents   f. less than 40 cents

7. A 3-digit numeral is formed by selecting digits at random from {2, 4, 6, 7} without repetition. Find the probability that the number formed:
   a. is less than 700   b. is greater than 600
   c. contains only even digits d. is an even number

8. a. There are 10 runners on the track team. If 4 runners are needed for a relay race, how many different relay teams are possible?
   b. Once the relay team is chosen, in how many different orders can the four runners run the race?
   c. If Nicolette is on the relay team, what is the probability that she will lead off the race?

9. Lou Grant is an editor at a newspaper employing 10 reporters and 3 photographers.
   a. If Lou selects 2 reporters and 1 photographer to cover a story, from how many possible 3-person teams can he choose?
   b. If Lou hands out one assignment per reporter, in how many ways can he assign the first 3 stories to his 10 reporters?
   c. If Lou plans to give the first story to Rossi, a reporter, in how many ways can he now assign the first 3 stories?
   d. If 3 out of 10 reporters are chosen at random to cover a story, what is the probability that Rossi is on this team?

10. Chris, Willie, Tim, Matt, Juan, Bob, and Steffen audition for roles in the school play.
    a. If two male roles in the play are those of the hero and the clown, in how many ways can the director select 2 of the 7 boys for these roles?
    b. Chris and Willie got the two leading male roles.
       (1) In how many ways can the director select a group of 3 of the remaining 5 boys to work in a crowd scene?
       (2) How many of these groups of 3 will include Tim?
       (3) Find the probability that Tim is in the crowd scene.

11. There are 8 candidates running for 3 seats in the student government. The candidates include 3 boys (Alberto, Peter, Thomas) and 5 girls (Elizabeth, Maria, Joanna, Rosa, Danielle). If all candidates have an equal chance of winning, find the probability that the winners include:
    a. 3 boys   **b.** 3 girls   **c.** 1 boy and 2 girls
    d. at least 2 girls   **e.** Maria, Peter, and anyone else
    f. Danielle and any other two candidates

12. A gumball machine contains 6 lemon, 4 lime, 3 cherry, and 2 orange-flavored gumballs. Five coins are put into the machine and 5 gumballs are obtained.
    a. How many different sets of 5 gumballs are possible?
    b. How many of these will contain 2 lemon and 3 lime gumballs?
    c. Find the probability that the 5 gumballs dispensed by the machine include:
    (1) 2 lemon and 3 lime   (4) lemon only
    (2) 3 cherry and 2 orange   (5) lime only
    (3) 2 lemon, 2 lime, and 1 orange   (6) no lemon

13. The letters in the word HOLIDAY are rearranged at random.
    a. How many 7-letters words can be formed?
    b. Find the probability that the first 2 letters are vowels.
    c. Find the probability of no vowels in the first 3 letters.

14. At a bus stop, 5 people enter a bus that has only 3 empty seats.
    a. In how many different ways can 3 of the 5 people occupy these empty seats?
    b. If Mrs. Costa is one of the 5 people, what is the probability that she will not get a seat?
    c. If Ann and Bill are two of the 5 people, what is the probability that they both get seats?

13-9 REVIEW EXERCISES

In 1–5, evaluate the expression.

1. $_5P_5$ **2.** $_{12}P_2$ **3.** $_5C_5$ **4.** $_{12}C_3$ **5.** $_{40}C_{38}$

6. From a list of 10 books, Gwen selects 4 to read over the summer. In how many ways can Gwen make a selection of 4 books?

7. Mrs. Moskowitz, the librarian, checks out the 4 books Gwen has given her. In how many different orders can the librarian stamp these 4 books?

8. A coach must choose a team of 5 from 8 candidates. How many different teams can be chosen?

9. Find how many 3-letter words can be formed from the letters in QUESTION, if each letter is used only once in a word.

10. A SYZYGY is a nearly straight-line configuration of three celestial bodies such as the earth, moon, and sun during an eclipse.
    a. How many different 6-letter arrangements can be made using the letters in the word SYZYGY?
    b. Find the probability that the first letter in an arrangement of SYZYGY is: (1) G (2) Y (3) a vowel

11. Two fair dice are tossed, each numbered 1 through 6. Find the probability that: (a) at least one die shows a 2; (b) the sum of the numbers on the dice is 8; (c) at least one die shows a 2 and the sum of the numbers on the dice is 8.

12. a. How many 3-digit numerals can be formed using the digits 2, 3, 4, 5, 6, 7, and 8 if repetition is not allowed?
    b. What is the probability that such a 3-digit numeral is greater than 400?

13. a. If a 4-member committee is formed from 3 girls and 6 boys in a club, how many committees can be formed?
    b. Find the probability that the 4-member committee includes:
       (1) 2 girls and 2 boys (2) 1 girl and 3 boys (3) 4 boys
    c. What is the probability that a boy is on the committee?

14. From a 52-card deck, two cards are drawn at random without replacement. Find the probability of selecting:
    a. a ten and a king, in that order   b. two tens
    c. a ten and a king, in either order   d. two spades

15. If a card is drawn at random from a 52-card deck, find the probability that the card is:
    a. an 8 or a queen   b. an 8 or a club   c. red or an 8

16. From an urn, three marbles are drawn at random with no replacement. Find the probability that the 3 marbles are the same color if the urn contains the given marbles:
    a. 3 red and 2 white   b. 2 red and 2 blue
    c. 3 red and 4 blue   d. 4 white and 5 blue
    e. 10 blue   f. 2 red, 1 white, 3 blue

17. A committee of 5 is to be chosen from 4 men and 3 women.
    a. How many different 5-person committees are possible?
    b. Find the probability that the committee consists of:
       (1) 2 men and 3 women   (2) 3 men and 2 women
       (2) at least 2 women   (4) all women
    c. In how many ways can this 5-person committee select a chairman and a secretary?
    d. If Hilda and Joan are on the committee, what is the probability that one is selected as chairman and the other as secretary?

Chapter 14

Mathematical Systems

14-1 THE NATURE OF A MATHEMATICAL SYSTEM

In geometry, you learned that a *postulational system* is one in which definitions and postulates are used to prove theorems, and definitions, postulates, and proven theorems are used to deduce other theorems. This type of deductive reasoning is not limited to a system of geometry.

In other *mathematical systems* as well, we make use of a new set of definitions and postulates to prove theorems and then use definitions, postulates, and proven theorems to deduce other theorems. This chapter may appear to be very different from geometry because most of the examples studied are numerical or algebraic in nature. Try to keep in mind, however, that you are studying another example of a deductive system of reasoning.

Most of this chapter is devoted to understanding the workings and definitions of a mathematical system, so that theorems are proved only at the end of the chapter. For now, let us note the components of a mathematical system.

● A *mathematical system* consists of:

1. **A known set of elements.**

2. **One or more operations defined on this set of elements.**

3. **Definitions and postulates concerning operations on the set of elements.**

4. **Theorems that can be deduced from the given definitions and postulates.**

14-2 CLOCK SYSTEMS

In Course I, you learned that an *operation* is a procedure or a rule that relates elements in a set. Notice that it is important to know the *set* with which we are working as well as the *operation* defined on that set.

In general, if S represents a set of elements and $*$ represents an operation on the elements of that set, we can identify this system by the symbols $(S, *)$.

EXAMPLE 1. The set of *whole numbers* is symbolized by W, and the operation of *addition* is symbolized by $+$. Thus, the following statements are true for the system $(W, +)$:

$$5 + 3 = 8$$
$$10 + 4 = 14$$
$$7 + 12 = 19$$

EXAMPLE 2. However, if we use a different set of numbers and the operation of addition is defined in a different way, it can be shown that the following statements are true for another system:

$$5 + 3 = 8$$
$$10 + 4 = 2$$
$$7 + 12 = 7$$

The problems in Example 1 make sense to us. But what set of numbers is being used in Example 2? How can $10 + 4 = 2$ or $7 + 12 = 7$? It's simple. Think of the set of numbers found on a clock. This set consists of only twelve numbers. The set is called *clock 12*, and can be written as follows:

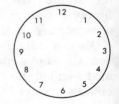

Clock 12 = $\{1, 2, 3, 4, 5, 6, 7, 8, 9, 10, 11, 12\}$

Clock Addition

Study the examples that follow to see how addition works on the set of clock 12 numbers. In every case, notice that:

a. The first number is the starting point on the clock.
b. The second number is *added* by counting or moving a given number of units in a *clockwise* direction.
c. The answer, called the sum, is the point arrived at on the clock.

  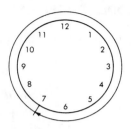

Start at 5 o'clock. *Add* 3 hours (count 3 units in a *clockwise* direction). The time is 8 o'clock. Thus, in (Clock 12, +):	Start at 10 o'clock. *Add* 4 hours (count 4 units in a *clockwise* direction). The time is 2 o'clock. Thus, in (Clock 12, +):	Start at 7 o'clock. *Add* 12 hours (count 12 units in a *clockwise* direction). The time is again 7 o'clock. Thus, in (Clock 12, +):
5 + 3 = 8	10 + 4 = 2	7 + 12 = 7

A table is a convenient form in which to show all the possible sums of two numbers in a clock 12 system. List the twelve elements of the set in the left-hand column and along the top row to create the table. Indicate that the entries in the table are the sums of these numbers by writing + in the upper left-hand corner of the table.

+	1	2	3	4	5	6	7	8	9	10	11	12
1	2	3	4	5	6	7	8	9	10	11	12	1
2	3	4	5	6	7	8	9	10	11	12	1	2
3	4	5	6	7	8	9	10	11	12	1	2	3
4	5	6	7	8	9	10	11	12	1	2	3	4
5	6	7	8	9	10	11	12	1	2	3	4	5
6	7	8	9	10	11	12	1	2	3	4	5	6
7	8	9	10	11	12	1	2	3	4	5	6	7
8	9	10	11	12	1	2	3	4	5	6	7	8
9	10	11	12	1	2	3	4	5	6	7	8	9
10	11	12	1	2	3	4	5	6	7	8	9	10
11	12	1	2	3	4	5	6	7	8	9	10	11
12	1	2	3	4	5	6	7	8	9	10	11	12

(Clock 12, +)

You can now use this table to find sums and to solve equations.

MODEL PROBLEMS ————————————————————

1. In (Clock 12, +), find the sum 8 + 5.

Solution

Method 1

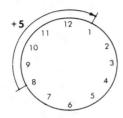

Start at 8 on the clock. *Add* 5 by counting 5 units in a *clockwise* direction to arrive at the sum of 1.

Answer: 1

Method 2

Use the (Clock 12, +) table on page 607.

Find the 8 in the left-hand column. Move along its row to the entry in the column below the 5.

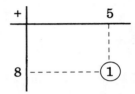

2. In (Clock 12, +), find the sum 7 + (9 + 6).

Solution

Whether numbers in (Clock 12, +) are added on the clock or in its table, it is necessary first to obtain the sum within the parentheses. Thus, 7 + (9 + 6) = 7 + (3) = 10.

Answer: 10

———————————————————————————————

Our clock, consisting of twelve elements that repeat themselves, is only one example of a cyclic system, or clock system. There are many other clock systems, each consisting of a finite number of elements.

The Days of the Week: Clock 7

If today is Thursday, what day will it be four days from now? To answer this question, think of a clock with seven equally spaced elements to show the days of the week.

Sunday is day 1, Monday is day 2, and so on. Since Thursday is day 5, add 4 days to Thursday by counting *clockwise* around the circle.

Thus $5 + 4 = 2$, or four days from Thursday will be Monday.

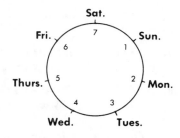

Let us make an agreement at this point. In (Clock 12, +), the identity element is 12 because, for any clock 12 number x, it is true that $x + 12 = x$ and $12 + x = x$. In (W, +), the identity element is 0 because, for any whole number x, it is true that $x + 0 = x$ and $0 + x = x$. In (Clock 7, +), the identity element will be 7. However, to eliminate the burden of remembering a new identity element in each new clock system, let us agree to *include the 0 element with each new clock system.* As you shall soon see, 0 will be the identity element for any set of clock numbers under the operation of addition.

Since a clock 7 system can contain *only* seven elements and since we now include 0, we redesign the clock to include the following elements:

$$\text{Clock } 7 = \{0, 1, 2, 3, 4, 5, 6\}$$

In any clock system, *addition* is accomplished by counting or moving a given number of units in a *clockwise* direction.

Clock 7

The table shown can be used to find sums and to solve equations in (Clock 7, +).

+	0	1	2	3	4	5	6
0	0	1	2	3	4	5	6
1	1	2	3	4	5	6	0
2	2	3	4	5	6	0	1
3	3	4	5	6	0	1	2
4	4	5	6	0	1	2	3
5	5	6	0	1	2	3	4
6	6	0	1	2	3	4	5

(Clock 7, +)

Still More Clock Systems

A clock system consists of a finite set of elements that repeat themselves in a cyclic manner. There are many examples of such systems in our real world.

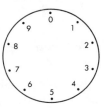

A dial on an electric range is numbered from 0, for "off," through 9, for "highest temperature." The dial can be turned continuously in a clockwise direction, illustrating a (Clock 10, +) system.

Dial on an
Electric Range

In general, for any (Clock *n*, +) system where *n* is a counting number:

1. **The set consists of *n* elements, namely {0, 1, 2, . . . , *n* − 1}, which repeat themselves in a cyclic pattern.**

2. **Addition is defined as counting or moving a given number of units in a clockwise direction.**

A *clock system* is sometimes called a ***modulo system*** or a ***mod system***. For example, *clock 4* is also called *modulo 4* or *mod 4*.

MODEL PROBLEM

Given (*Z*, +) where *Z* = {0, 1, 2, 3, 4} and + is addition mod 5.

a. Construct an addition table for *Z* as defined.

b. Use the table in part **a** to calculate (4 + 2) + 3.

c. Use the table in part **a** to find *x*, if *x* + 4 = 2.

Solution

a. (1) Addition mod 5 indicates the (Clock 5, +) system. Write the given elements in both the left-hand column and the top row; write + in the upper left-hand corner to show addition.

+	0 1 2 3 4
0	
1	
2	
3	
4	

(2) By drawing clock 5 and counting on the clock, construct the table.

For example, in the third row: 2 + 0 = 2, 2 + 1 = 3, 2 + 2 = 4, 2 + 3 = 0, and 2 + 4 = 1.

The table, which is the answer to part **a**, appears at the right.

+	0	1	2	3	4
0	0	1	2	3	4
1	1	2	3	4	0
2	2	3	4	0	1
3	3	4	0	1	2
4	4	0	1	2	3

(Mod 5, +)

b. To calculate $(4 + 2) + 3$, operate within parentheses first.

(1) Add $4 + 2$.   (2) To the sum of 1, add 3.

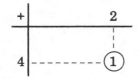   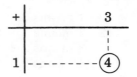

Thus, $(4 + 2) + 3 = (1) + 3 = 4$.

Answer: 4

c. Find x, given $x + 4 = 2$.

(1) Locate the second number 4 in the top row of the table. Look down the column containing 4 to find the sum 2.

(2) From the sum 2, look to the left in that row to find that $x = 3$, the number in the left-hand column.

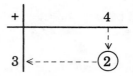

Thus, if $x + 4 = 2$, then $x = 3$. (*Check:* $3 + 4 = 2$, or $2 = 2$.)

Answer: $x = 3$

Multiplication

Compare the two problems that follow, each showing an operation with the set of whole numbers:

EXAMPLE 1. $19 + 19 + 19 + 19 + 19 + 19 + 19 + 19 + 19 + 19 = 190$

EXAMPLE 2. $19 \times 10 = 190$

How are these problems related? In Example 1, we added ten numbers, each of which is 19, to obtain a sum of 190. In Example 2, we multiplied 19 by 10 to obtain a product of 190. The following statement is true for all systems:

● **Multiplication is a shortcut for repeated addition.**

To apply this concept to a clock system, consider clock 5 = {0, 1, 2, 3, 4}. We will take 2 · 0 to mean no sets of 2. Thus, 2 · 0 = 0. In other cases, we will treat multiplication as repeated addition:

$$2 \cdot 1 \text{ means } 2.$$
$$2 \cdot 2 \text{ means } 2 + 2.$$
$$2 \cdot 3 \text{ means } 2 + 2 + 2.$$
$$2 \cdot 4 \text{ means } 2 + 2 + 2 + 2.$$

The figures below, based upon repeated addition, show how multiplication is developed with the set of clock 5 numbers.

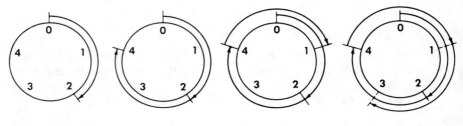

In (Clock 5, ·):   In (Clock 5, ·):   In (Clock 5, ·):   In (Clock 5, ·):
$2 \cdot 1 = 2$ $2 \cdot 2 = 4$ $2 \cdot 3 = 1$ $2 \cdot 4 = 3$

As a table for (Clock 5, ·) is constructed, the five products we have just obtained are entered in the row containing 2 in the left-hand column. This row may be thought of as the "2-times" table for clock 5 multiplication.

Other rows in the (Clock 5, ·) table are found in a similar way. For example, the "3-times" table for clock 5 is found by "repeatedly adding 3." Try it yourself. Using clock 5, count by threes to get the following products:

·	0	1	2	3	4
0					
1					
2	0	2	4	1	3
3					
4					

$$3 \cdot 0 = 0 \qquad 3 \cdot 1 = 3 \qquad 3 \cdot 2 = 1 \qquad 3 \cdot 3 = 4 \qquad 3 \cdot 4 = 2$$

From the completed table for multiplication with the set of clock 5 numbers, observe:

1. Multiplication is a *binary operation* on the set of clock 5 numbers.
2. The set of clock 5 numbers is *closed* under multiplication.

·	0	1	2	3	4
0	0	0	0	0	0
1	0	1	2	3	4
2	0	2	4	1	3
3	0	3	1	4	2
4	0	4	3	2	1

(Clock 5, ·)

The table for (Clock 5, ·) can be used to solve equations that involve multiplication.

EXAMPLE 1. Solve for x in (Clock 5, •): $3x = 2$

Remember: $3x$ means $3 • x$. Using the table, examine the row starting with 3 in the left-hand column to see that $3 • 4 = 2$. Thus, if $3x = 2$, then $x = 4$.

EXAMPLE 2. Solve for x in (Clock 5, •): $x^2 = 4$

Remember: x^2 means $x • x$. Replacing x with the various elements of clock 5, we find that $2 • 2 = 4$, and $3 • 3 = 4$. Other replacements, when squared, do not equal 4. A second method is shown in the figure. By looking along the diagonal of the table, we can again find the two solutions: $x = 2$, or $x = 3$.
Thus, if $x^2 = 4$, the solution set is $\{2, 3\}$.

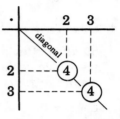

Note that since the set of elements of the system is finite, trying all values is a possible method of solution.

MODEL PROBLEMS

In 1–4, use the accompanying tables, which represent addition and multiplication in clock 4.

+	0 1 2 3
0	0 1 2 3
1	1 2 3 0
2	2 3 0 1
3	3 0 1 2

(Clock 4, +)

•	0 1 2 3
0	0 0 0 0
1	0 1 2 3
2	0 2 0 2
3	0 3 2 1

(Clock 4, •)

1. In clock 4, is the statement true or false?

If $a • b = 0$, then $a = 0$ or $b = 0$.

Solution: In (Clock 4, •), one product is $2 • 2 = 0$. Here, the product is zero, but neither a nor b is equal to zero. In clock 4, the statement is false.

Answer: False

2. Solve for x: $2x = 2$

Solution: The equation $2x = 2$ means $2 • x = 2$. Using the table for (Clock 4, •), look at the row containing 2 in the left-hand column. There are two ways to obtain the product of 2: $2 • 1 = 2$ and $2 • 3 = 2$. Thus, $x = 1$ or $x = 3$. The solution set is written $\{1, 3\}$.

Answer: $x = 1$ or $x = 3$ *or* the solution set $= \{1, 3\}$.

3. Evaluate: $2 + 3(2 \cdot 2 + 1)$

Solution: Use the standard order of operations learned in arithmetic, operating within parentheses first.
(1) Within parentheses, multiply: $2 + 3(2 \cdot 2 + 1) = 2 + 3(0 + 1)$
(2) Within parentheses, add: $= 2 + 3(1)$
(3) Multiply: $= 2 + 3$
(4) Add: $= 1$ *Ans.*

4. Solve for x in clock 4: $x^2 + x = 0$

Solution: Replace the variable x with each of the clock 4 numbers to see which replacements make the sentence true. Remember that x^2 means $x \cdot x$.

Let $x = 0$:	Let $x = 1$:	Let $x = 2$:	Let $x = 3$:
$x^2 + x = 0$	$x^2 + x = 0$	$x^2 + x = 0$	$x^2 + x = 0$
$0^2 + 0 \stackrel{?}{=} 0$	$1^2 + 1 \stackrel{?}{=} 0$	$2^2 + 2 \stackrel{?}{=} 0$	$3^2 + 3 \stackrel{?}{=} 0$
$0 \cdot 0 + 0 \stackrel{?}{=} 0$	$1 \cdot 1 + 1 \stackrel{?}{=} 0$	$2 \cdot 2 + 2 \stackrel{?}{=} 0$	$3 \cdot 3 + 3 \stackrel{?}{=} 0$
$0 + 0 \stackrel{?}{=} 0$	$1 + 1 \stackrel{?}{=} 0$	$0 + 2 \stackrel{?}{=} 0$	$1 + 3 \stackrel{?}{=} 0$
$0 = 0$	$2 \neq 0$	$2 \neq 0$	$0 = 0$
(True)			(True)

There are two solutions, $x = 0$ or $x = 3$.

Answer: $x = 0$ or $x = 3$ *or* the solution set $= \{0, 3\}$.

EXERCISES

In 1–5, find the sum in $(W, +)$, where W represents the set of whole numbers.

1. $3 + 5$ **2.** $8 + 4$ **3.** $5 + 9$ **4.** $8 + 6$ **5.** $12 + 4$

In 6–15, find the sum in (Clock 12, +)

6. $3 + 5$ **7.** $8 + 4$ **8.** $5 + 9$ **9.** $8 + 6$ **10.** $12 + 4$
11. $9 + 11$ **12.** $3 + 12$ **13.** $10 + 7$ **14.** $2 + 11$ **15.** $7 + 8$

16. a. The expression "6 hours after 10 o'clock" can be shown as $10 + 6$. Find the sum.
   b. The expression "10 hours after 6 o'clock" can be shown as $6 + 10$. Find the sum.
   c. Is $10 + 6 = 6 + 10$?
   d. Using pairs of numbers for x and y from the set of clock 12 numbers, list three examples showing that the statement $x + y = y + x$ is true for (Clock 12, +).

In 17–41, use the table for (Clock 7, +) on page 609.

In 17–26, find the sum in (Clock 7, +).

17. $4 + 2$ **18.** $3 + 1$ **19.** $2 + 5$ **20.** $6 + 0$ **21.** $5 + 4$

22. $4 + 3$ **23.** $6 + 4$ **24.** $4 + 5$ **25.** $5 + 5$ **26.** $3 + 6$

In 27–29, compute the sums in **a** and **b** using (Clock 7, +) before answering part **c**.

27. a. $(5 + 2) + 4$ **b.** $5 + (2 + 4)$ **c.** Is $(5 + 2) + 4 = 5 + (2 + 4)$?
28. a. $(1 + 3) + 4$ **b.** $1 + (3 + 4)$ **c.** Is $(1 + 3) + 4 = 1 + (3 + 4)$?
29. a. $(5 + 6) + 3$ **b.** $5 + (6 + 3)$ **c.** Is $(5 + 6) + 3 = 5 + (6 + 3)$?

In 30–37, solve for x in (Clock 7, +).

30. $x + 2 = 6$ **31.** $x + 1 = 3$ **32.** $5 + x = 5$ **33.** $5 + x = 3$
34. $x + 6 = 2$ **35.** $x + 3 = 1$ **36.** $x + x = 2$ **37.** $x + x = 3$

38. If today is Tuesday, name the day of the week it will be:
(a) 7 days from now, (b) 14 days from now, (c) 21 days from now, and (d) 70 days from now.

39. If today is Friday, name the day of the week it will be:
(a) 3 days from now, (b) 10 days from now, (c) 17 days from now, and (d) 73 days from now.

40. A salesman returns home on a regular schedule every five days. If the salesman is home on Monday, name in order the next three days of the week when he will return home. (*Hint.* See the clock for days of the week on page 609.)

41. This year, Cathy's birthday falls on Saturday. Using 365 days in a year, name the day of the week on which Cathy's birthday will fall next year.

In 42–58, use the table for (Mod 5, +) on page 610.

In 42–49, find the sum in (Mod 5, +).

42. $3 + 1$ **43.** $4 + 0$ **44.** $(1 + 4) + 2$ **45.** $1 + (4 + 2)$
46. $4 + 3$ **47.** $3 + 3$ **48.** $(4 + 4) + 2$ **49.** $4 + (4 + 2)$

In 50–57, solve for x in (Mod 5, +).

50. $x + 1 = 4$ **51.** $x + 2 = 3$ **52.** $4 + x = 4$ **53.** $3 + x = 0$
54. $x + 4 = 1$ **55.** $x + 3 = 2$ **56.** $x + x = 3$ **57.** $x + x = 4$

58. Classes are taught five days each week: Monday, Tuesday, Wednesday, Thursday, and Friday. Mr. Fontana gives a math quiz every four school days. If the last quiz was given on Monday and there are no holidays, name in order the next three days of the week when Mr. Fontana will give the class a quiz.

In 59–79, use the tables for clock 4 operations on page 613.

In 59–71, find the value of the given expression in clock 4.

59. $1 + 2$ **60.** $3 + 1$ **61.** $0 + 3$ **62.** $2 \cdot 0$ **63.** $2 \cdot 3$

64. $(2 \cdot 1) + 1$ **65.** $2 \cdot (1 + 1)$ **66.** $2 + (1 + 1)$ **67.** $(2 + 1) \cdot 2$

68. $(3 + 2) + 1$ **69.** $3 + (2 + 1)$ **70.** $3(2 + 1)$ **71.** $2(1 + 2)$

In 72–79, solve for x in clock 4.

72. $3x = 1$ **73.** $2x = 0$ **74.** $2x = 3$ **75.** $x + 2 = 1$

76. $x + 3 = 1$ **77.** $3x + 1 = 3$ **78.** $2x + 1 = 3$ **79.** $2x + 3x = x$

Exercises 80–98 refer to clock 6 operations. For calculations, refer to tables or answer the questions without the use of tables.

Clock 6

80. Construct a multiplication table for clock 6 = $\{0, 1, 2, 3, 4, 5\}$.

81. True or false: In clock 6, if $a \cdot b = 0$, then $a = 0$ or $b = 0$. Why?

In 82–90, find the values in clock 6.

82. $4 + 2$ **83.** $5 + 4$ **84.** $5 \cdot 3$ **85.** $2 \cdot 3$ **86.** $2 \cdot 2 \cdot 2$

87. $3(5 + 2)$ **88.** $(3 \cdot 5) + 2$ **89.** $(3 + 5) \cdot 2$ **90.** $4(1 + 2 \cdot 3)$

In 91–98, solve for x in clock 6.

91. $x + 3 = 2$ **92.** $x + 4 = 3$ **93.** $2x = 4$ **94.** $3x = 5$

95. $x^2 = 1$ **96.** $4x + 1 = 5$ **97.** $2x + 1 = 4$ **98.** $x^2 = x$

Exercises 99–116 refer to clock 7 operations. For calculations, refer to tables or answer the questions without the use of tables.

Clock 7

99. Construct a multiplication table for clock 7 = $\{0, 1, 2, 3, 4, 5, 6\}$.

100. True or false: "In clock 7, if $a \cdot b = 0$, then $a = 0$ or $b = 0$." Why?

In 101–108, evaluate in clock 7.

101. $6 + 1$ **102.** $5 + 4$ **103.** $3 \cdot 4$ **104.** $2 \cdot 5$

105. $2 \cdot 2 \cdot 2$ **106.** $2(4 + 1)$ **107.** $2 \cdot 4 + 1$ **108.** $3(1 + 5)$

In 109–116, solve for x in clock 7.

109. $x + 1 = 4$ **110.** $x + 5 = 2$ **111.** $6x = 2$ **112.** $5x = 3$

113. $x^2 = 2$ **114.** $2x + 1 = 5$ **115.** $3x + 2 = 6$ **116.** $x^2 = x$

14-3 PROPERTIES OF A MATHEMATICAL SYSTEM

In this section, we will investigate properties of mathematical systems. You have seen most of these properties in earlier studies of mathematics.

Binary Operations

When we operate on two elements from a set and if the result is in the set, we are performing a *binary* operation. Binary operations include addition, subtraction, multiplication, and division. Of course we sometimes add columns consisting of more than two numbers, but remember that we add *only two* numbers at any one time.

Consider the operation of subtraction and the set of integers, that is, $\{\ldots, -3, -2, -1, 0, 1, 2, 3, \ldots\}$. Here, $7 - 2 = 5$ and $2 - 7 = -5$. These examples help show why the order of the elements must be clearly defined before we apply the operation.

● **Definition.** A *binary operation* $*$ in a set S is a way of assigning to every ordered pair of elements, a and b, from the set a unique response called c, where c is also from the set S.

In symbolic form, we write:

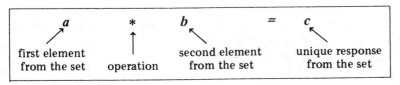

Examples of binary operations exist in almost every branch of mathematics.

Closure

Once it is known that an operation is defined on a set, it can also be said that the set is *closed* under the operation. This property is called *closure of the set under the operation*, or simply **closure**. For example, when we add two numbers in clock 3, the sum is always a clock 3 number. Thus:

1. Addition is a binary operation on the set of clock 3 numbers.

2. The set of clock 3 numbers is *closed* under addition.

● **Definition.** The set S is **closed** under the binary operation $*$ if and only if, for all elements a and b of set S, $a * b = c$ where c is an element of set S.

Tables help us to see almost immediately whether or not a finite set is closed under a given operation. Remember that the elements of the set are read from the left-hand column and the top row of the table.

EXAMPLE 1. Set $S = \{0, 1\}$ and the operation is multiplication. Within the table, all possible answers under multiplication are elements of the set S, that is, the answers are 0 or 1. Thus:

$\cdot$	0	1
0	0	0
1	0	1

Set S is closed under multiplication, or $(S, \cdot)$ is closed.

EXAMPLE 2. Set $S = \{0, 1\}$ and the operation is addition. Within the table, $1 + 1 = 2$. Since 2 is not an element of set S:

$+$	0	1
0	0	1
1	1	2

Set S is *not* closed under addition, or $(S, +)$ is *not* closed.

Note that set S is not the same as clock 2. In (Clock 2, $+$), $1 + 1 = 0$.

MODEL PROBLEMS ─────────────

1. If the operation $*$ is defined on the set of whole numbers as $a * b = a + 2b$, find the value of $3 * 5$.

Solution

The operation is defined as: $a * b = a + 2b$
Substitute the given values: $3 * 5 = 3 + 2(5)$
Compute: $= 3 + 10 = 13$ *Ans.*

2. The *average* (avg) of two numbers is defined as $a \text{ avg } b = \dfrac{a + b}{2}$.

   a. Evaluate 6 avg 16.   **b.** Evaluate 70 avg 91.

   c. Is the set of whole numbers closed under the operation of average?

Solution

a. By the definition: $6 \text{ avg } 16 = \dfrac{6 + 16}{2} = \dfrac{22}{2} = 11$ *Ans.*

b. By the definition: $70 \text{ avg } 91 = \dfrac{70 + 91}{2} = \dfrac{161}{2} = 80.5$ *Ans.*

c. In part **b,** the average of two whole numbers, 70 and 91, is 80.5, which is not a whole number. Therefore, the set of whole numbers is not closed under the operation of *average.* (*Note. Average* is a binary operation on the set of rational numbers, and the set of rational numbers is closed under this operation.)
Answer: No

Associativity

● **Definition.** The operation $*$ is *associative* on the set S if and only if, for all elements a, b, and c of set S, $(a * b) * c = a * (b * c)$.

EXAMPLE 1. The associative property of addition.

When adding three numbers, we may group the numbers in different ways without changing the sum. In general, we say:

$$(a + b) + c = a + (b + c)$$

For $(W, +)$:	For (Clock 12, +):
$(5 + 8) + 6 = 5 + (8 + 6)$	$(5 + 8) + 6 = 5 + (8 + 6)$
$13 + 6 = 5 + 14$	$1 + 6 = 5 + 2$
$19 = 19$	$7 = 7$

EXAMPLE 2. The associative property of multiplication.

When multiplying three numbers, we may group the numbers in different ways without changing the product. In general, we say:

$$(a \cdot b) \cdot c = a \cdot (b \cdot c)$$

For $(W, \cdot)$:	For (Clock 5, $\cdot$):
$(3 \cdot 4) \cdot 2 = 3 \cdot (4 \cdot 2)$	$(3 \cdot 4) \cdot 2 = 3 \cdot (4 \cdot 2)$
$12 \cdot 2 = 3 \cdot 8$	$2 \cdot 2 = 3 \cdot 3$
$24 = 24$	$4 = 4$

In general, addition and multiplication are associative operations. To prove that any operation is associative, however, we should test all possible cases. To test $(a \cdot b) \cdot c = a \cdot (b \cdot c)$ for the set of clock 12 numbers, a can be any of 12 numbers, b can be any of 12 numbers, and c can be any of 12 numbers. By the *counting principle* learned in probability, we would have to test $12 \cdot 12 \cdot 12$, or 1,728 cases. Let us agree that in clock arithmetic, addition and multiplication are associative.

For the set of whole numbers or any other infinite set, we would have to test infinitely many cases. Let us follow this plan:

1. *If an operation is associative:* Test one or two cases and, where possible, offer a reason to explain why the operation is associative.

To test the operation of *maximum* on the set of whole numbers, we cite one case:

Let a max b be the larger of the numbers a and b.
$(a \text{ max } b) \text{ max } c = a \text{ max } (b \text{ max } c)$
$(5 \text{ max } 9) \text{ max } 20 = 5 \text{ max } (9 \text{ max } 20)$
$9 \text{ max } 20 = 5 \text{ max } 20$
$20 = 20$

Knowing that the maximum number must always emerge from any grouping of the same numbers, we claim that the operation is associative.

2. *If an operation is **not** associative:* We need to find only one case where $(a * b) * c$ and $a * (b * c)$ produce different answers to say that the operation $*$ does not satisfy the associative property.

Subtraction of whole numbers is *not* associative because:	Division of whole numbers is *not* associative because:
$(12 - 7) - 3 \neq 12 - (7 - 3)$	$(20 \div 10) \div 2 \neq 20 \div (10 \div 2)$
$5 - 3 \neq 12 - 4$	$2 \div 2 \neq 20 \div 5$
$2 \neq 8$	$1 \neq 4$

Commutativity

● **Definition.** The operation $*$ is **commutative** on the set S if and only if, for all elements a and b of set S, $a * b = b * a$.

EXAMPLE 1. The commutative property of addition.

The order in which two numbers are added does not affect their sum. In general, we say:

$$a + b = b + a$$

For $(W, +)$: $3 + 2 = 2 + 3$ For (Clock 4, +): $3 + 2 = 2 + 3$
$5 = 5$ $1 = 1$

EXAMPLE 2. The commutative property of multiplication.

The order in which two numbers are multiplied does not affect their product. In general, we say:

$$a \cdot b = b \cdot a$$

For $(W, \cdot)$: $3 \cdot 2 = 2 \cdot 3$
$$6 = 6$$

For (Clock 4, $\cdot$): $3 \cdot 2 = 2 \cdot 3$
$$2 = 2$$

A Quick Test of Commutativity Using Tables

Imagine folding the table along its diagonal as shown by the dotted line in the figure. Once the table is folded, if the elements from one side of the diagonal are equal to the elements upon which they fall, then the operation is commutative.

Here, addition is commutative on the set of clock 4 numbers.

+	0	1	2	3
0	0	1	2	3
1	1	2	3	0
2	2	3	0	1
3	3	0	1	2

(Clock 4, +)

Notice: $3 + 2 = \boxed{1}$, and $2 + 3 = \boxed{1}$. Thus, $3 + 2 = 2 + 3$.

$2 + 0 = (2)$, and $0 + 2 = (2)$. Thus, $2 + 0 = 0 + 2$.

If *all* such pairs match, then we know $a + b = b + a$.

If an operation is *not* commutative, we need to find only one case where $a * b$ and $b * a$ produce different results. For example, in the set of real numbers, subtraction is not commutative because $10 - 4 \neq 4 - 10$, or $6 \neq -6$.

Another example of an operation that is not commutative is subtraction in a clock 4 system, as shown in the table at the right. Notice that $1 - 0 = 1$, and $0 - 1 = 3$. Since these numbers that fold onto each other are not equal, we know $1 - 0 \neq 0 - 1$. Thus, $a - b \neq b - a$ for all a and b.

−	0	1	2	3
0	0	3	2	1
1	1	0	3	2
2	2	1	0	3
3	3	2	1	0

(Clock 4, −)

The Identity Element

● **Definition.** For set S and operation $*$, there exists an **identity element** e in set S if and only if, for all elements x in set S, $x * e = x$ and $e * x = x$.

EXAMPLE 1.   The identity element for addition.

In the set of real numbers, 0 is the identity element for addition (also called the additive identity) because, for all numbers x:

$$x + 0 = x \quad and \quad 0 + x = x$$

By including the element 0 in clock systems, we can also claim that 0 is the additive identity for clock systems.

EXAMPLE 2.   The identity element for multiplication.

In the set of real numbers, 1 is the identity element for multiplication (also called the multiplicative identity) because, for all numbers x:

$$x \cdot 1 = x \quad and \quad 1 \cdot x = x$$

As you shall soon see, 1 is also the multiplicative identity in clock systems.

A Quick Test for Finding the Identity Element Using Tables

In the (Clock 3, +) table, notice that the column headed by 0 matches the left-hand column of the table, and the row starting with 0 matches the top row of the table. Thus, for (Clock 3, +), 0 is

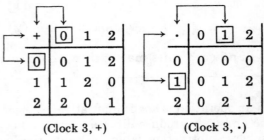

(Clock 3, +)   (Clock 3, ·)

the identity element because $x + 0 = x$ and $0 + x = x$.

In the (Clock 3, ·) table, the column headed by 1 matches the left-hand column and the row starting with 1 matches the top row of the table. Thus, for (Clock 3, ·), 1 is the identity element because $x \cdot 1 = x$, and $1 \cdot x = x$.

In clock arithmetic, subtraction is equivalent to moving counterclockwise.

The table at the right defines subtraction in a clock 3 system. The column headed by 0 matches the left-hand column in the (Clock 3, −) table. Thus, $x - 0 = x$. However, the row starting with 0 does not match the top row of the table. Thus, $0 - x \neq x$. Since one of the conditions is *not* met, we say there is *no identity element* under subtraction for the set of clock 3 numbers.

−	0	1	2
0	0	2	1
1	1	0	2
2	2	1	0

(Clock 3, −)

Inverse Elements

● **Definition.** For set S and operation $*$, there exists an *inverse element* a^{-1} in set S for the element a in set S if and only if, where e is the identity element in set S, $a * a^{-1} = e$ and $a^{-1} * a = e$.

EXAMPLE 1. Inverse elements under addition.

In the set of real numbers, the identity element under addition is 0. Therefore, we think of the additive inverse of a as $-a$ because:

$$a + (-a) = 0 \quad and \quad (-a) + a = 0$$

For example, the additive inverse of 3 is -3 because $3 + (-3) = 0$ and $(-3) + 3 = 0$. Also, the additive inverse of -6 is 6 because $(-6) + 6 = 0$ and $6 + (-6) = 0$.

EXAMPLE 2. Inverse elements under multiplication.

In the set of real numbers, the identity element under multiplication is 1. Therefore, we think of the multiplicative inverse of a as $\frac{1}{a}$ because:

$$a \cdot \left(\frac{1}{a}\right) = 1 \quad and \quad \left(\frac{1}{a}\right) \cdot a = 1$$

For example, the multiplicative inverse of 3 is $\frac{1}{3}$ because $3 \cdot \frac{1}{3} = 1$ and $\frac{1}{3} \cdot 3 = 1$. Also, the multiplicative inverse of $\frac{-6}{5}$ is $\frac{-5}{6}$ because $\left(\frac{-6}{5}\right)\left(\frac{-5}{6}\right) = 1$ and $\left(\frac{-5}{6}\right)\left(\frac{-6}{5}\right) = 1$.

Note. Zero has no multiplicative inverse. No inverse, a^{-1}, exists such that $0 \cdot (a^{-1}) = 1$ and $(a^{-1}) \cdot 0 = 1$.

A Quick Test for Finding Inverse Elements Using Tables

Find the pairs that produce the identity for the system.

The identity for (Clock 3, +) is 0. Thus, the inverse of 0 is 0, the inverse of 1 is 2, and the inverse of 2 is 1 in the (Clock 3, +) system.

+	0	1	2
0	0	1	2
1	1	2	0
2	2	0	1

Identity = 0
(Clock 3, +)

·	0	1	2
0	0	0	0
1	0	1	2
2	0	2	1

Identity = 1
(Clock 3, ·)

The identity for (Clock 3, ·) is 1. Since $1 \cdot 1 = 1$ and $2 \cdot 2 = 1$, the inverse of 1 is 1 and the inverse of 2 is 2 in (Clock 3, ·). Notice that there is *no* inverse for 0 under multiplication.

If a system does not have an identity element, then inverses do not exist in the system. In both $(W, -)$ and (Clock 3, $-$), there is no identity element. Since we cannot name the identity element needed for the definition of inverses, inverses do not exist under subtraction for the set of whole numbers and for the set of clock 3 numbers.

MODEL PROBLEM

The accompanying table represents the operation $*$ for the set $\{p, q, r, t\}$.

a. What is the identity element of the system?
b. What is the inverse of t?
c. Is the operation $*$ commutative?
d. Is $(p * q) * q = p * (q * q)$?
e. Solve for X: $t * X = r * p$.
f. If the element k appeared somewhere within the table, but not in the left-hand column and top row, what property of systems would *not* be satisfied?

$*$	p	q	r	t
p	q	t	p	r
q	t	r	q	p
r	p	q	r	t
t	r	p	t	q

Solution

a.
Method 1

$p * r = p$ and $r * p = p$
$q * r = q$ $\quad$ $r * q = q$
$r * r = r$ $\quad$ $r * r = r$
$t * r = t$ $\quad$ $r * t = t$

Therefore, the identity element $= r$.

Method 2

The left-hand column and the top row of the table are reproduced when operated upon by r. Thus, the identity element $= r$.

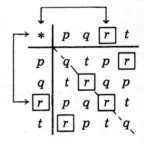

Answer: r

Note that in a finite system, a general statement can be proved by showing that it is true in all possible cases.

b. The elements t and p operate upon each other to produce the identity r. Since $t * p = r$ and $p * t = r$, the inverse of t is p.

Answer: p

c. If the table were folded along the dotted line, which is the diagonal, the elements that fall upon each other are equal. Thus, $a * b = b * a$ and the operation $*$ is commutative.

Answer: Yes

d. Write the given sentence: $(p * q) * q \overset{?}{=} p * (q * q)$
Operate within parentheses first: $t * q \overset{?}{=} p * r$
The results are equal: $p = p$
(This example demonstrates the associative property of $*$ for one case. All cases would have to be examined and found to be true before we could say that the operation $*$ was associative.)

Answer: Yes

e. Write the given equation: $t * X = r * p$
Perform the operation on the right: $t * X = p$
From the table, it is known that: $t * q = p$
By replacement, it is known that: $X = q$

Answer: $X = q$

f. Since k is not an element of the set $\{p, q, r, t\}$, the property of closure would not be satisfied.

Answer: closure

EXERCISES

1. The *union* of two sets is a binary operation, defined as the set of elements contained in one or the other or both sets. For example, $\{1, 2\} \cup \{2, 3\} = \{1, 2, 3\}$. Using the subsets of $\{1, 2, 3, 4\}$, evaluate the expressions **a–e**.
  a. $\{1\} \cup \{4\}$ **b.** $\{1, 3\} \cup \{3, 4\}$ **c.** $\{1, 2, 3\} \cup \{4\}$
  d. $\{1, 2\} \cup \{1\}$ **e.** $\{2\} \cup \{\ \}$
  f. Is union a binary operation on the set of subsets of $\{1, 2, 3, 4\}$?
  g. Is the set of subsets of $\{1, 2, 3, 4\}$ closed under the operation union?

2. The *minimum* (min) of two numbers is defined as the smaller of the two numbers. If two numbers are equal, the minimum is that number, as in 9 min 9 = 9. In **a–e**, find the value of the given expression.
  a. -8 min 5   **b.** -2 min -2 **c.** 0 min -6
  d. -8 min -10 **e.** -18 min -11
  f. Is the set of integers closed under the operation min?

3. Using clock 8 = $\{0, 1, 2, 3, 4, 5, 6, 7\}$ and clock addition, calculate the sums in parts **a–g**.
  a. $4 + 3$ **b.** $5 + 3$ **c.** $6 + 5$ **d.** $2 + 7$
  e. $6 + 6$ **f.** $(5 + 7) + 4$ **g.** $5 + (7 + 4)$
  h. Explain why (Clock 8, $+$) is closed.

In 4–8, the rule defines a binary operation. In parts **a–e**, evaluate the given expression. In part **f**, tell whether or not the set of whole numbers is closed under the given operation.

4. Operation: $a * b = 3a + b$
   a. $4 * 1$ b. $1 * 4$ c. $8 * 10$
   d. $0 * 57$ e. $50 * 3$ f. Is $(W, *)$ closed?

5. Operation: $a \triangle b = a^2 b$
   a. $3 \triangle 2$ b. $2 \triangle 3$ c. $2 \triangle 10$
   d. $0 \triangle 150$ e. $150 \triangle 0$ f. Is $(W, \triangle)$ closed?

6. Operation: $a \# b = ab - 1$
   a. $5 \# 3$ b. $9 \# 11$ c. $95 \# 0$
   d. $1 \# 1$ e. $0 \# 18$ f. Is $(W, \#)$ closed?

7. Operation: $a \phi b = 2a \div b$
   a. $4 \phi 8$ b. $3 \phi 2$ c. $0 \phi 5$
   d. $1 \phi 3$ e. $3 \phi 0$ f. Is (W, ϕ) closed?

8. Operation: $a \Omega b = 3b - a$
   a. $2 \Omega 4$ b. $4 \Omega 2$ c. $3 \Omega 1$
   d. $0 \Omega 10$ e. $10 \Omega 0$ f. Is (W, Ω) closed?

9. a. Add $3x^2$ and $5x^2$.
   b. Add $2ab$ and ab.
   c. Add $a^2 y$ and ay^2.
   d. Is the set of monomial terms closed under addition? Why?
   e. Is the set of polynomial terms closed under addition? Why?

10. The operation $*$ is defined on the set $S = \{a, b, c\}$, as shown in the table at the right.

$*$	a	b	c
a	a	b	c
b	b	c	a
c	c	a	b

    a. Evaluate $c * a$.
    b. Evaluate $c * b$.
    c. Evaluate $(b * b) * c$.
    d. Evaluate $b * (b * c)$.
    e. Explain why set S is closed under the operation $*$.

11. a. In the real number system, what is the identity under addition?
    b. Write the additive inverses of 5, -14, 0, $\frac{1}{3}$, and $-\frac{2}{5}$.
    c. In the real number system, what is the identity under multiplication?
    d. Write the multiplicative inverses of 5, -14, $\frac{1}{3}$, and $-\frac{2}{5}$.

Exercises 12–20 refer to clock 7 operations. The table for (Clock 7, +) is found on page 609. The table for (Clock 7, ·) appears below.

12. What is the identity element under addition for clock 7 numbers?

13. Write the additive inverse for each clock 7 number, or explain why no inverse exists for: **a.** 1   **b.** 2   **c.** 3   **d.** 4   **e.** 5   **f.** 6   **g.** 0

14. What is the identity element under multiplication for clock 7 numbers?

15. Write the multiplicative inverse for each clock 7 number, or explain why no inverse exists for: **a.** 1   **b.** 2   **c.** 3   **d.** 4   **e.** 5   **f.** 6   **g.** 0

·	0	1	2	3	4	5	6
0	0	0	0	0	0	0	0
1	0	1	2	3	4	5	6
2	0	2	4	6	1	3	5
3	0	3	6	2	5	1	4
4	0	4	1	5	2	6	3
5	0	5	3	1	6	4	2
6	0	6	5	4	3	2	1

(Clock 7, ·)

In 16–19, compute parts **a** and **b** in clock 7; then answer part **c**.

16. a. $5 + 4$ **b.** $4 + 5$ **c.** Is $5 + 4 = 4 + 5$?

17. a. $(6 + 2) + 5$ **b.** $6 + (2 + 5)$ **c.** Is $(6 + 2) + 5 = 6 + (2 + 5)$?

18. a. $3 \cdot 4$ **b.** $4 \cdot 3$ **c.** Is $3 \cdot 4 = 4 \cdot 3$?

19. a. $(5 \cdot 4) \cdot 4$ **b.** $5 \cdot (4 \cdot 4)$ **c.** Is $(5 \cdot 4) \cdot 4 = 5 \cdot (4 \cdot 4)$?

20. Using any numbers from clock 7, write an example that demonstrates:
   a. addition is associative
   b. multiplication is commutative
   c. subtraction is not associative
   d. subtraction is not commutative

Exercises 21–33 refer to *digital multiplication* with the set {2, 4, 6, 8}.

21. In digital multiplication, answers are single digits. Such answers are obtained by writing only the last digit, or the units digit, from a product in standard multiplication. Compare the given examples.

⊙	2	4	6	8
2			8	6
4			6	2
6				
8				

Standard:
   $2 \cdot 4 = 8$ $4 \cdot 4 = 16$ $4 \cdot 8 = 32$
Digital:
   $2 \odot 4 = 8$ $4 \odot 4 = 6$ $4 \odot 8 = 2$

Copy and complete the above table for digital multiplication with the set {2, 4, 6, 8}.

22. What is the identity element for ({2, 4, 6, 8}, ⊙)?

23. Name the inverse under digital multiplication for:
   a. 2   **b.** 4   **c.** 6   **d.** 8

24. Is digital multiplication commutative on the set {2, 4, 6, 8}?

25. a. Compute 4 ⊙ (8 ⊙ 2).   **b.** Compute (4 ⊙ 8) ⊙ 2.
   c. Is 4 ⊙ (8 ⊙ 2) = (4 ⊙ 8) ⊙ 2?
   d. Is digital multiplication associative? Explain why.

In 26–33, solve for x within the set {2, 4, 6, 8}.

26. 4 ⊙ x = 8   **27.** 8 ⊙ x = 4   **28.** x ⊙ 2 = 6 ⊙ 4
29. x ⊙ 4 = 8 ⊙ 8   **30.** x ⊙ x = 4   **31.** x ⊙ x = 2
32. x ⊙ x = x **33.** 6 ⊙ x = x

34. For the set of whole numbers and the operation of *average*, symbolized by *avg*, evaluate the expressions in parts **a** through **f**.
   a. 3 avg 33   **b.** 33 avg 3   **c.** (12 avg 4) avg 8
   d. 12 avg (4 avg 8) **e.** 81 avg 81   **f.** 70 avg 73
   g. Is the set closed under avg?
   h. Is the operation commutative?
   i. Is the operation associative?

35. a. Using the set = {1, 2, 3} and the operation of *maximum*, symbolized by *max*, copy and complete the table.
   b. Is the set {1, 2, 3} closed under max?
   c. Name the identity element.
   d. For each element having an inverse, name the element and its inverse.
   e. Is the operation commutative?
   f. Is the operation associative?
   g. For the set {5, 6, 7} and the operation of *maximum*, what is the identity element?

max	1 2 3
1	
2	
3	

36. Let the set = positive numbers. Let the operation = P, which produces the perimeter of a rectangle when the numbers given are its length l and its width w. Thus, $l \, P \, w = 2l + 2w$, as in $10P4 = 2 \cdot 10 + 2 \cdot 4 = 20 + 8 = 28$. Find the values of the expressions in **a** through **d**.
   a. 25P7   **b.** 7P25   **c.** (2P3)P1   **d.** 2P(3P1)
   e. Is the set of positive numbers closed under the operation P?
   f. Is the operation commutative?
   g. Is the operation associative?
   h. Solve for x: 2Px = 30
   i. Solve for x: xP8 = 28
   j. Explain why there is no identity, using the equation 10Px = 10.

In 37–39, answer the following questions for the given table:

a. Is the set closed under the given operation?
b. Is the operation commutative?
c. Is the operation associative?
d. Name the identity element, or explain why none exists.
e. For each element having an inverse, name the element and its inverse.

ϕ	J	O	A	N
J	A	N	J	O
O	N	A	O	J
A	J	O	A	N
N	O	J	N	A

Ex. 37

@	S	A	L
S	S	S	S
A	S	A	L
L	S	L	A

Ex. 38

■	M	A	R	Y
M	Y	M	A	R
A	R	A	Y	M
R	A	R	M	Y
Y	M	Y	R	A

Ex. 39

40. The set $\{g, e, a, r\}$ is shown in a partially completed table under the operation $*$.

a. What is the inverse of a?
b. If the operation is known to be commutative, what is the value of $a * r$?

$*$	g	e	a	r
g	g	e	a	r
e	e	a	g	
a	a	g	r	
r	r	r	e	

14-4 GROUPS WITH FINITE SETS

Now that we have studied properties with mathematical systems, we are able to identify an important structure in mathematics called a *group*.

● **Definition.** A *group* is a mathematical system consisting of a set G and an operation $*$ that satisfies four properties:

1. The set G is *closed* under the operation $*$.
2. The operation $*$ is *associative* on the set G.
3. There is an *identity element* e under the operation $*$ where e is in set G.
4. Every element a in set G has an *inverse* a^{-1} from set G under the operation $*$.

Groups were first introduced in the eighteenth century. Examples of groups can be found in algebra, geometry, art, and nature. The properties of groups play an important role in science. For example, the symmetries of crystals of minerals form groups, and the symmetries of particles and of fields of force form groups.

In this section, you will study some finite systems, and test to see whether each system is or is not a group.

EXAMPLE 1.   (Clock 5, •)

1. *Closure:* Every pair of numbers from clock 5 has a product of 0, 1, 2, 3, or 4, as seen in the table. Therefore, (Clock 5, •) is closed.
2. *Associativity:* Earlier in this chapter, we agreed that multiplication of clock numbers is associative.
3. *Identity:* The identity is 1 because, for all clock 5 numbers x, $x \cdot 1 = x$ and $1 \cdot x = x$.
4. *Inverses:* This condition fails!

•	0 1 2 3 4
0	0 0 0 0 0
1	0 1 2 3 4
2	0 2 4 1 3
3	0 3 1 4 2
4	0 4 3 2 1

(Clock 5, •)

The inverse of 1 is 1 (written $1^{-1} = 1$) because $1 \cdot 1 = 1$ and $1 \cdot 1 = 1$.
The inverse of 2 is 3 (written $2^{-1} = 3$) because $2 \cdot 3 = 1$ and $3 \cdot 2 = 1$.
The inverse of 3 is 2 (written $3^{-1} = 2$) because $3 \cdot 2 = 1$ and $2 \cdot 3 = 1$.
The inverse of 4 is 4 (written $4^{-1} = 4$) because $4 \cdot 4 = 1$ and $4 \cdot 4 = 1$.
However, *there is no inverse for zero.*

Because one of the four properties fails: *(Clock 5, •) is **not** a group.*

EXAMPLE 2.   (Clock 5/{0}, •).

(Clock 5, •) is not a group because 0 does not have an inverse. Let us study this system after eliminating 0 from the set. To indicate the set of clock 5 numbers without 0, namely {1, 2, 3, 4}, we write clock 5/{0}. To develop the table for (Clock 5/{0}, •):

1. Start with the table for (Clock 5, •).

2. Cross out the row and column showing multiplication by 0.

•	0 1 2 3 4
0	0 0 0 0 0
1	0 1 2 3 4
2	0 2 4 1 3
3	0 3 1 4 2
4	0 4 3 2 1

(Clock 5, •)

•	1 2 3 4
1	1 2 3 4
2	2 4 1 3
3	3 1 4 2
4	4 3 2 1

(Clock 5/{0}, •

The part of the table that remains is called (Clock 5/{0}, •). Notice that this is *not* a clock 4 system. Multiplication is shown for clock 5 numbers, leaving out the "0 row" and "0 column."

1. *Closure:* The set of clock 5/{0} numbers = {1, 2, 3, 4}. The table shows that every pair of numbers from this set has a product of 1, 2, 3, or 4. Thus, (Clock 5/{0}, •) is closed.

2. *Associativity:* Multiplication of clock numbers is associative.
3. *Identity:* The identity is 1, as it was in (Clock 5, •).
4. *Inverses:* Every element has an inverse: $1^{-1} = 1$, $2^{-1} = 3$, $3^{-1} = 2$, $4^{-1} = 4$. Since all four properties have been satisfied: *(Clock 5/{0}, •) is a group.*

Commutative Group

Commutativity is not required for a mathematical system to be a group. However, many groups have operations that are commutative. When this occurs, we have a special group called a *commutative group,* or an *Abelian group.*

● **Definition.** $(G, *)$ is a *commutative group* if and only if five properties are satisfied:

1. $(G, *)$ is a group, satisfying the four properties of closure, associativity, the existence of an identity, and the existence of inverses.
2. The operation $*$ is commutative on the set G.

For example, (Clock 5/{0}, •) is a commutative group because it is a group in which $ab = ba$ for all elements of clock 5/{0}.

KEEP IN MIND ⎯⎯⎯⎯⎯⎯⎯⎯⎯⎯⎯⎯⎯⎯

$(G, *)$ is a *group* if and only if four properties are satisfied: closure, associativity, the existence of an identity, and the existence of inverses.

MODEL PROBLEMS ⎯⎯⎯⎯⎯⎯⎯⎯⎯⎯⎯⎯⎯⎯

1. Is (Clock 5, +) a group?

Solution:

(1) *Closure:* Every pair of numbers from clock 5 has a sum of 0, 1, 2, 3, or 4, as seen in the table. Therefore, (Clock 5, +) is closed.
(2) *Associativity:* Earlier in this chapter, we agreed that addition of clock numbers is associative.
(3) *Identity:* The identity is 0 because, for all clock 5 numbers x, $x + 0 = x$ and $0 + x = x$. This is seen in the table by having the left-hand column and top row reproduced by the element 0.

+	0	1	2	3	4
0	0	1	2	3	4
1	1	2	3	4	0
2	2	3	4	0	1
3	3	4	0	1	2
4	4	0	1	2	3

(Clock 5, +)

(4) *Inverses:* Find the pairs in the table that have a sum of 0, which is the identity.

> The inverse of 0 is 0 because $0 + 0 = 0$ and $0 + 0 = 0$.
> The inverse of 1 is 4 because $1 + 4 = 0$ and $4 + 1 = 0$.
> The inverse of 2 is 3 because $2 + 3 = 0$ and $3 + 2 = 0$.
> The inverse of 3 is 2 because $3 + 2 = 0$ and $2 + 3 = 0$.
> The inverse of 4 is 1 because $4 + 1 = 0$ and $1 + 4 = 0$.

Answer: (Clock 5, +) is a group.

2. The accompanying table shows multiplication for the set of clock 4 numbers without 0. Give two reasons why (Clock 4/{0}, •) is *not* a group.

•	0	1	2	3
0	0	0	0	0
1	0	1	2	3
2	0	2	0	2
3	0	3	2	1

(Clock 4, •)

•	1	2	3
1	1	2	3
2	2	0	2
3	3	2	1

(Clock 4/{0}, •)

Solution:

(1) In (Clock 4/{0}, •), $2 \cdot 2 = 0$. However, 0 is not an element of the set {1, 2, 3}. Therefore, the property of closure is not satisfied.

(2) The identity for (Clock 4/{0}, •) is 1. There is no inverse for 2 because there is no number a^{-1} such that $2 \cdot a^{-1} = 1$ and $a^{-1} \cdot 2 = 1$.

Answer: (Clock 4/{0}, •) is not a group because: (1) the set is not closed, and (2) there is no inverse element for 2.

EXERCISES

In 1–10, answer the following questions for the set and operation shown in the accompanying table.

a. Is the set closed under the given operation?
b. Is the operation associative on the given set?
c. Name the identity element for the system.
d. For every element having an inverse, name the element and its inverse.
e. Is the system a group?

·	pos	neg
pos	pos	neg
neg	neg	pos

Ex. 1

·	−1	0	1
−1	1	0	−1
0	0	0	0
1	−1	0	1

Ex. 2

·	0	1	2
0	0	0	0
1	0	1	2
2	0	2	1

Ex. 3

·	1	2
1	1	2
2	2	1

Ex. 4

1. Set $S = \{$pos, neg$\}$, to represent positive and negative integers. The operation is multiplication.
2. Set $S = \{-1, 0, 1\}$. The operation is multiplication.
3. Set $S = $ clock $3 = \{0, 1, 2\}$. The operation is multiplication.
4. Set $S = $ clock $3/\{0\} = \{1, 2\}$. The operation is multiplication.

·	odd	even
odd	odd	even
even	even	even

Ex. 5

min	1	2	3
1	1	1	1
2	1	2	2
3	1	2	3

Ex. 6

∗	a	b	c	d
a	c	d	a	b
b	d	a	b	c
c	a	b	c	d
d	b	c	d	a

Ex. 7

5. Set $S = \{$odd, even$\}$, to represent odd and even integers. The operation is multiplication.
6. Set $S = \{1, 2, 3\}$. The operation is min, finding the minimum, or smaller, of two numbers.
7. Set $S = \{a, b, c, d\}$. The operation ∗ is defined by the table.

#	w	x	y	z
w	x	w	z	y
x	w	x	y	z
y	z	y	x	w
z	y	z	w	x

Ex. 8

@	e	f	g
e	e	f	g
f	f	e	g
g	g	f	g

Ex. 9

·	1	2	3	4	5	6	7
1	1	2	3	4	5	6	7
2	2	4	6	0	2	4	6
3	3	6	1	4	7	2	5
4	4	0	4	0	4	0	4
5	5	2	7	4	1	6	3
6	6	4	2	0	6	4	2
7	7	6	5	4	3	2	1

Ex. 10

8. Set $S = \{w, x, y, z\}$. The operation # is defined by the table.
9. Set $S = \{e, f, g\}$. The operation @ is defined by the table.
10. Set $S = $ clock $8/\{0\} = \{1, 2, 3, 4, 5, 6, 7\}$. The operation is multiplication.

11. a. Construct the table for (Clock 6, +).
   b. Is (Clock 6, +) a group?

12. a. Construct the table for (Clock 6, ·).
   b. Is (Clock 6, ·) a group?

13. a. Construct the table for (Clock 6/{0}, ·).
   b. Is (Clock 6/{0}, ·) a group?

14. True or false: For any counting number n, (Clock n, +) is a group.

15. True or false: For any counting number n, (Clock n/{0}, ·) is a group.

16. True or false: For any *prime* number n, (Clock n/{0}, ·) is a group.

17. a. If $S = \{0\}$, is $(S, +)$ a group?
   b. If $S = \{1\}$, is $(S, ·)$ a group?
   c. If S contains a single element x, and $x * x = x$, is $(S, *)$ a group?

+	0		·	1		*	x
0	0		1	1		x	x

  a.   **b.**   **c.**

Exercises 18–30 refer to *digital multiplication* with the set $\{1, 3, 5, 7, 9\}$.

18. In digital multiplication, answers are single digits, obtained by writing only the units digit from a product in standard multiplication. Compare the given examples.

⊙	1	3	5	7	9
1					
3			5	1	7
5					
7					
9					

Standard:
  $3 · 5 = 15$ $3 · 7 = 21$ $3 · 9 = 27$
Digital:
  $3 ⊙ 5 = 5$ $3 ⊙ 7 = 1$ $3 ⊙ 9 = 7$

Copy and complete the table given here for digital multiplication with the set $\{1, 3, 5, 7, 9\}$.

19. a. Compute $(3 ⊙ 9) ⊙ 7$.
   b. Compute $3 ⊙ (9 ⊙ 7)$.
   c. Is $(3 ⊙ 9) ⊙ 7 = 3 ⊙ (9 ⊙ 7)$?
   d. Is digital multiplication associative? Explain why.

20. a. Name the identity element for $(\{1, 3, 5, 7, 9\}, ⊙)$.
   b. For every element having an inverse, name the element and its inverse.

21. Is the set closed under the operation of digital multiplication?

22. Is the set $\{1, 3, 5, 7, 9\}$ under digital multiplication a group? Why?

In 23–30, solve for x within the set $\{1, 3, 5, 7, 9\}$.

23. $3 ⊙ x = 9$ **24.** $3 ⊙ x = 7$ **25.** $9 ⊙ x = 7 ⊙ 3$

26. $x ⊙ 7 = 3 ⊙ 5$ **27.** $x ⊙ x = 9$ **28.** $x ⊙ x = 3$

29. $x ⊙ x = x$ **30.** $x ⊙ 5 = 5$

31. a. Construct a table for the set {1, 3, 7, 9} under digital multiplication.

 b. Is the set {1, 3, 7, 9} under digital multiplication a group? Why?

 c. How does the table for part **a** compare to the table constructed in Exercise 18?

32. a. Using set $S = \{0, 2, 4\}$ and the operation of *average*, symbolized by *avg*, copy and complete the table shown at the right.

 b. Given three reasons why this system is *not* a group.

avg	0 2 4
0	
2	
4	

14-5 GROUPS WITH INFINITE SETS

If a system contains a finite set of elements, we can construct a table to examine the system for group properties. However, some sets are infinite. In cases like this, we cannot construct tables. Rather, we must rely on common sense and sound arguments to show whether or not these systems are groups.

In Course I, you studied many infinite sets of numbers. Let us now recall some of these infinite sets, each of which is a subset of the real numbers.

1. **Counting numbers, or natural numbers:** $N = \{1, 2, 3, 4, \ldots\}$.

2. **Whole numbers:** $W = \{0, 1, 2, 3, \ldots\}$.

3. **Integers:** $\{\ldots, -3, -2, -1, 0, 1, 2, 3, \ldots\}$.

4. **Rational numbers:** numbers that can be expressed in the form $\dfrac{a}{b}$ where a and b are integers and $b \neq 0$. Since $2 = \frac{2}{1}$, $0 = \frac{0}{1}$, and $-3 = \dfrac{-3}{1}$, the integers are included in the set of rational numbers. Recall that every rational number can be expressed as a repeating decimal. For example:

$$\tfrac{3}{4} = .75 = .750000\ldots = .75\overline{0} \quad and \quad 6\tfrac{1}{3} = 6.3333\ldots = 6.\overline{3}$$

5. **Irrational numbers:** numbers that are nonrepeating decimals. Thus, irrational numbers can*not* be expressed in the form $\dfrac{a}{b}$ where a and b are integers and $b \neq 0$. Examples of irrational numbers include $\sqrt{2}$, $3\sqrt{3}$, and π.

6. *Real numbers:* R = the union of the set of rational numbers and the set of irrational numbers. Every real number corresponds to a point on the real number line. Some of the real numbers and the points to which they correspond are shown below.

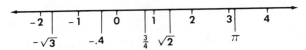

The first five infinite sets listed above are subsets of the real numbers. Many other infinite sets can be constructed. Here we list only a few.

1. *Positive odd integers:* $\{1, 3, 5, 7, \ldots\}$.

2. *Positive even integers:* $\{2, 4, 6, 8, \ldots\}$.

3. *Odd integers:* $\{\ldots, -5, -3, -1, 1, 3, 5, \ldots\}$.

4. *Even integers:* $\{\ldots, -4, -2, 0, 2, 4, 6, \ldots\}$.

5. *Multiples of a number:*
   (a) *Positive multiples of 5:* $\{5, 10, 15, 20, \ldots\}$.
   (b) *Nonnegative multiples of 5:* $\{0, 5, 10, 15, 20, \ldots\}$.

   Since $5 \times 0 = 0$, and 0 is not a negative number, it is included in the second set.

6. *Powers of a number:*
   (a) *Powers of 3 with whole-number exponents:*
   $\{3^0, 3^1, 3^2, 3^3, \ldots\} = \{1, 3, 9, 27, \ldots\}$.

   (b) *Powers of 3 with integral exponents:*
   $\{\ldots, 3^{-2}, 3^{-1}, 3^0, 3^1, 3^2, \ldots\} = \{\ldots, \frac{1}{9}, \frac{1}{3}, 1, 3, 9, \ldots\}$.

   In the second set, recall that $x^{-a} = \dfrac{1}{x^a}$. Thus, $3^{-2} = \dfrac{1}{3^2} = \dfrac{1}{9}$.

7. *Positive numbers:*
   all positive real numbers, sometimes written as R^+.

8. *Negative numbers:*
   all negative real numbers, sometimes written as R^-.

Group Properties

To study group properties with infinite sets, consider these hints:

1. *Associativity.* Addition and multiplication are associative on the set of real numbers. Therefore, these operations will also be associative on any subset of the real numbers.

2. *Identity.* In the set of real numbers, the identity under addition is 0, and the identity under multiplication is 1. Therefore, given any set under addition, we should look for 0 in the set. Also, given any set under multiplication, we should look for 1 in the set.

3. *Inverses.* In the set of real numbers, the additive inverse of a is $-a$, and the multiplicative inverse of a is $\dfrac{1}{a}$. Again, given any subset of the real numbers, we should look for these elements in the set. Note that 0 is the only real number that lacks a multiplicative inverse.

4. *Closure.* This property demands careful investigation. We should try many examples, either to convince ourselves that the set is closed under the given operation or to find one counterexample that shows that the set is not closed.

Let us make an agreement at this point:

● **If an operation is discussed but no specific set is mentioned, the set is assumed to be that of the real numbers.**

MODEL PROBLEMS _____

1. Which of the following systems is a group?
   (1) $(W, +)$ (2) $(W, \cdot)$ (3) $(R, +)$ (4) $(R, \cdot)$

Solution

In three of the four systems, find a group property that *fails*.

$(W, +)$. The identity element, 0, is in the set. With the exception of 0, however, no other elements have inverses.
For example, $2 + (-2) = 0$, but $-2 \notin W$.

$(W, \cdot)$. The identity element, 1, is in the set. With the exception of 1, however, no other elements have inverses.
For example, $2 \cdot (\frac{1}{2}) = 1$, but $\frac{1}{2} \notin W$.

$(R, \cdot)$. Recall that 0 has no multiplicative inverse. Since $0 \in R$, and the operation is multiplication, the inverse property is not met for 0.

$(R, +)$. Having eliminated the other three choices, we should find that $(R, +)$ is a group. By applying the properties of a group, we are assured that the system is closed, is associative, has an identity of 0, and that every element a has an inverse $(-a)$.

Answer: (3)

2. Which set is closed under subtraction?   (1) whole numbers
(2) natural numbers   (3) odd integers   (4) even integers

Solution

Select one or more pairs of numbers from each set and subtract.

whole numbers: 3 and 8. Since $3 - 8 = -5$, and $-5 \notin W$, the set is *not* closed under subtraction.

natural numbers: 4 and 4. Since $4 - 4 = 0$, and $0 \notin N$, the set is *not* closed under subtraction.

odd integers: 7 and 5. Since $7 - 5 = 2$, and $2 \notin$ odd integers, the set is *not* closed under subtraction.

even integers: 10 and 6. Here, $10 - 6 = 4$, and $6 - 10 = -4$.

These examples indicate that the difference of two even integers is an even integer. Thus, (Even integers, $-$) is closed.

Answer: (4)

EXERCISES

In 1–16, tell whether or not the given set is closed under the indicated operation.

1. $(W, +)$ **2.** $(W, -)$ **3.** $(W, \cdot)$ **4.** $(W, \div)$ **5.** $(N, +)$
6. $(N, \cdot)$ **7.** $(R, +)$ **8.** $(R, -)$ **9.** $(R, \cdot)$ **10.** $(R, \div)$
11. (Integers, $+$)   **12.** (Integers, $-$)   **13.** (Integers, $\cdot$)
14. (Integers, $\div$)   **15.** (Rationals, $\cdot$)   **16.** (Irrationals, $\cdot$)

In 17–28: **a.** Is the system a group? **b.** If the answer to part **a** is No, tell which of the four group properties are not satisfied.

17. $(W, +)$ **18.** $(W, \cdot)$ **19.** (Integers, $+$)   **20.** (Integers, $-$)
21. $(N, \cdot)$ **22.** $(N, \div)$ **23.** (Integers, $\cdot$)   **24.** (Rationals, $+$)
25. $(R, +)$ **26.** $(R, \cdot)$ **27.** $(R/\{0\}, \cdot)$ **28.** (Rationals/$\{0\}$, $\cdot$)

In 29–40, select the numeral preceding the word or expression that best answers the question or completes the statement.

29. Under which operation is the set of odd integers closed?
(1) addition   (2) subtraction   (3) multiplication   (4) division
30. Under which operation is the set $\{1, 3, 9, 27, 81, \ldots\}$ closed?
(1) addition   (2) subtraction   (3) multiplication   (4) division
31. Under which operation is the set of even integers *not* closed?
(1) addition   (2) subtraction   (3) multiplication   (4) division
32. Under which operation is the set of rational numbers *not* closed?
(1) addition   (2) subtraction   (3) multiplication   (4) division

33. Under which operation is the set of positive numbers *not* closed?
(1) addition　　(2) subtraction　　(3) multiplication　　(4) division

34. Which set is closed under addition?
(1) integers　　　　　　　　　(2) odd integers
(3) $\{1, 3, 9, 27, \ldots\}$　　　　　(4) $\{1, 2, 4, 8, 16, \ldots\}$

35. Which set is closed under subtraction?
(1) positive rational numbers　　(2) negative rational numbers
(3) rational numbers　　　　　(4) $\{1, 2, 4, 8, 16, \ldots\}$

36. Which set is closed under division?
(1) integers　　　　　　　　　(2) even integers
(3) real numbers　　　　　　　(4) positive real numbers

37. Which set is *not* closed under multiplication?
(1) even integers　　　　　　　(2) odd integers
(3) irrational numbers　　　　　(4) rational numbers

38. The set of counting numbers fails to form a group under addition
because the system　　(1) is not closed　　(2) is not associative
(3) does not have an identity element　　(4) is not commutative

39. A set contains the element b. If $b * x = x$ and $x * b = x$ for every
element x in the set, it can be concluded that
(1) b is the inverse of x　　(2) b is the identity under $*$
(3) the set is closed under $*$　　(4) x is the identity under $*$

40. In $(S, \#)$, the identity element is i. If a and b are elements of set S
so that $a \# b = i$ and $b \# a = i$, it can be concluded that
(1) b is the inverse of i　　(2) the set is closed under $\#$
(3) b is the inverse of a　　(4) b is the identity under $\#$

41. True or false: Subtraction is associative on the set of rational numbers.

42. True or false: Division is associative on the set of rational numbers.

43. The binary operation $*$ is defined as $a * b = a^2 + b^2$. Evaluate parts
a–d; then answer parts **e–g**.
a. $2 * 3$　　**b.** $8 * 0$　　**c.** $(1 * 3) * 4$　　**d.** $1 * (3 * 4)$
e. Is $(W, *)$ closed?　**f.** Is $(W, *)$ associative?　**g.** Is $(W, *)$ a group?

44. On a computer, $B \uparrow C$ is a binary operation defined as B raised to
the C power. In parts **a** through **i**, find the values of the given statements. Then answer parts **j–m**.
a. $3 \uparrow 4$　　**b.** $4 \uparrow 3$　　**c.** $7 \uparrow 1$　　**d.** $1 \uparrow 7$　　**e.** $14 \uparrow 0$
f. $0 \uparrow 14$　　**g.** $10 \uparrow 6$　　**h.** $(2 \uparrow 3) \uparrow 2$　　**i.** $2 \uparrow (3 \uparrow 2)$
j. Is $(W, \uparrow)$ closed?　　**k.** Is $(W, \uparrow)$ commutative?
l. Is $(W, \uparrow)$ associative?　　**m.** Is $(W, \uparrow)$ a group?

45. Which property is *not* necessary for a system to be a group?
(1) an identity element　　　　(2) existence of an inverse
(3) commutative property　　　(4) associative property

14-6 GROUP THEOREMS

In geometry, definitions and postulates are used to prove theorems. This type of deductive reasoning is not limited to geometry. In this section, we will see that a *postulational* system can be applied to a *group.* Let us establish the definitions and postulates we will use to prove theorems.

Definitions:

1. Within every group, we accept the definition of a *binary operation.*

2. Within every group, four properties must hold true: *closure, associativity, the existence of an identity element,* and *the existence of inverses.*

Postulates:

1. *Reflexive Property of Equality* ($a = a$): Every quantity is equal to itself.

2. *Substitution Property of Equality:* A quantity may be substituted for its equal in any expression.

Theorems:

Many theorems can be proved for groups from this short list of definitions and postulates. Here, we list only a few of these theorems.

● **GROUP THEOREM 1 (Right-Hand Operation).**
In group (G, $*$), for all a, b, $c \in G$:

$$\text{If } a = b, \text{ then } a * c = b * c.$$

Statements	*Reasons*
1. $a = b$.	1. Given.
2. $a * c = a * c$.	2. Reflexive property of equality.
3. $a * c = b * c$.	3. Substitution property of equality.

● **GROUP THEOREM 2 (Left-Hand Operation).**
In group (G, $*$), for all a, b, $c \in G$:

$$\text{If } a = b, \text{ then } c * a = c * b.$$

The proof of this theorem is similar to the proof of Group Theorem 1.

● **GROUP THEOREM 3 (The Right-Hand Cancellation Law).**
In group (G, $*$), for all a, b, $c \in G$:

$$\text{If } a * c = b * c, \text{ then } a = b.$$

Statements	*Reasons*
1. $a * c = b * c$.	1. Given.
2. $c^{-1} \in G$.	2. Every element in a group has an inverse.
3. $(a * c) * c^{-1} = (b * c) * c^{-1}$.	3. Right-hand operation.
4. $a * (c * c^{-1}) = b * (c * c^{-1})$.	4. Associative property of $*$.
5. $\quad\quad a * e = b * e$	5. Definition of inverse elements.
6. $\quad\quad\quad a = b$	6. Definition of identity element.

Why are these theorems important? Consider how we solve equations in algebra.

	EXAMPLE 1.	**EXAMPLE 2.**
Given the equation:	$x + 7 = 18$	$x \cdot \frac{1}{3} = 5$
Apply the inverse under a right-hand operation:	$(x + 7) + (-7) = 18 + (-7)$	$(x \cdot \frac{1}{3}) \cdot 3 = 5 \cdot 3$
The associative, inverse, and identity properties are applied:	$x + [7 + (-7)] = 18 + (-7)$ $x + 0 = 18 + (-7)$ $x = 18 + (-7)$	$x \cdot (\frac{1}{3} \cdot 3) = 5 \cdot 3$ $x \cdot 1 = 5 \cdot 3$ $x = 5 \cdot 3$
The solution is found:	$x = 11$	$x = 15$

Of course, we have come to use shortcuts in solving equations, but the reasoning that allows us to simplify an equation, and thus find its solution, is based on the fact that a group exists. To solve $x + 7 = 18$, we use the group $(R, +)$ and the additive inverse -7. To solve $x \cdot \frac{1}{3} = 5$, we use the group $(R/\{0\}, \cdot)$ and the multiplicative inverse 3.

● **GROUP THEOREM 4 (The Left-Hand Cancellation Law).**
In group $(G, *)$, for all $a, b, c \in G$:

$$\text{If } c * a = c * b, \text{ then } a = b.$$

The proof of this theorem is similar to the proof of Group Theorem 3.

Note. Recall that *commutativity is not a group property*. For this reason, we must operate or apply cancellation laws either on the right-hand side of two sets of equal terms, or on the left-hand side. Knowing only than an equation is true for a group, we can*not* commute terms within the equation. Of course we do this in our number system because the real numbers are commutative under addition and multiplication. But remember, these theorems apply to *all* groups, and commutativity is *not* a group property.

● **GROUP THEOREM 5** In group $(G, *)$, for all $a, b, x \in G$:

$$\text{If } a * x = b, \text{ then } x = a^{-1} * b.$$

Statements	*Reasons*
1. $a * x = b$.	1. Given.
2. $a^{-1} \in G$.	2. Every element in a group has an inverse.
3. $a^{-1} * (a * x) = a^{-1} * b$.	3. Left-hand operation.
4. $(a^{-1} * a) * x = a^{-1} * b$.	4. Associative property of $*$.
5. $\qquad e * x = a^{-1} * b$.	5. Definition of inverse elements.
6. $\qquad x = a^{-1} * b$.	6. Definition of identity element.

Note. We have proved that the equation, $a * x = b$, has a solution, $x = a^{-1} * b$. It would be incorrect to say here that $x = b * a^{-1}$ because this would require the use of commutativity, a property that a group does not necessarily have.

● **GROUP THEOREM 6** In group $(G, *)$, for all $a, b, x \in G$:

$$\text{If } x * a = b, \text{ then } x = b * a^{-1}.$$

The proof of this theorem is similar to the proof of Group Theorem 5.

MODEL PROBLEMS ─────────────────────────────

1. True or false: If $0 \cdot x = 0 \cdot y$, then $x = y$.

Solution

Substitute values for x and y. Let $x = 3$ and $y = 5$. The conditional statement "If $0 \cdot 3 = 0 \cdot 5$, then $3 = 5$" has a true hypothesis and a false conclusion. Therefore, the statement is false. (Note that a cancellation law depends upon an inverse, and there is no inverse for 0 under multiplication.)

Answer: False.

2. The statement "If $2x = 2y$, then $x = y$" is *false* for which set?

(1) rational numbers   (2) real numbers   (3) clock 3   (4) clock 4

Solution

The cancellation law is true when inverses exist under the given operation. The cancellation law may or may not be true when inverses do not exist. Under multiplication, the inverse of 2 is $\frac{1}{2}$ for both rational and real numbers. In clock 3, the inverse of 2 is 2 because $2 \cdot 2 = 1$.

In clock 4, however, there is *no inverse* for 2. In the table shown for (Clock 4, •) on page 613, $2 \cdot 0 = 0$ and $2 \cdot 2 = 0$. Thus, it is true that $2 \cdot 0 = 2 \cdot 2$, but it is false that $0 = 2$. The cancellation law does not hold in (Clock 4, •) or in (Clock 4/{0}, •), systems that are not groups.

Answer: (4)

EXERCISES

In 1–10, tell whether the given statement is true or false for the set of real numbers under the given operation.

1. If $5 \cdot x = 5 \cdot y$, then $x = y$.   **2.** If $3 + x = 3 + k$, then $x = k$.
3. If $x - 4 = 10 - 4$, then $x = 10$.   **4.** If $x - 18 = 12$, then $x = 30$.
5. If $5 \max x = 5 \max y$, then $x = y$.
6. If $12 \text{ avg } x = 12 \text{ avg } y$, then $x = y$.
7. If $x \div 2 = y \div 2$, then $x = y$.
8. If $x \div x = y \div y$, then $x = y$.
9. If $0 \div x = 0 \div y$, then $x = y$.
10. If $x - x = y - y$, then $x = y$.

In 11–20, cancellation laws have been applied. Tell whether the statement is true or false for the given system.

11. For whole numbers: If $0 \max x = 0 \max y$, then $x = y$.
12. For rational numbers: If $\frac{2}{5}x = \frac{2}{5}y$, then $x = y$.
13. For rational numbers: If $0 \cdot x = 0 \cdot y$, then $x = y$.
14. For the set $\{1, 2, 3\}$: If $3 \max x = 3 \max y$, then $x = y$.
15. For the set $\{1, 2, 3\}$: If $1 \max x = 1 \max y$, then $x = y$.
16. For clock 5: If $2x = 2y$, then $x = y$.
17. For clock 6: If $2x = 2y$, then $x = y$.
18. For clock 7: If $2 + x = 2 + y$, then $x = y$.
19. For clock 8: If $4x = 4y$, then $x = y$.
20. For clock 9: If $x + 4 = y + 4$, then $x = y$.

21. Write, in statement-reason format, the proof of Group Theorem 2:
In group $(G, *)$, for all $a, b, c \in G$: If $a = b$, then $c * a = c * b$.

22. Write, in statement-reason format, the proof of Group Theorem 4:
In group $(G, *)$, for all $a, b, c \in G$: If $c * a = c * b$, then $a = b$.

23. The statements for Group Theorems 2 and 4 are related in that:
(1) one is the inverse of the other
(2) one is the converse of the other
(3) one is the contrapositive of the other
(4) they are the same statement

24. Write, in statement-reason format, the proof of Group Theorem 6:
In group $(G, *)$, for all $a, b, x \in G$: If $x * a = b$, then $x = b * a^{-1}$.

25. The following group theorem states that the inverse of the inverse of an element is the element itself. Copy the following proof and fill in the missing reasons.

● **GROUP THEOREM 7** **In group $(G, *)$, for all $a \in G$:**

$$(a^{-1})^{-1} = a.$$

Statements	*Reasons*
1. $a^{-1} * a = e$.	1. _____
2. $a^{-1} * (a^{-1})^{-1} = e$.	2. _____
3. $a^{-1} * (a^{-1})^{-1} = a^{-1} * a$.	3. _____
4. $(a^{-1})^{-1} = a$.	4. Left-hand cancellation law.

26. Copy the proof of the following group theorem and fill in all missing reasons.

● **GROUP THEOREM 8** **In group $(G, *)$, for all $a, b \in G$:**

$$\text{If } a = b, \text{ then } a^{-1} = b^{-1}.$$

Statements	*Reasons*
1. $a = b$.	1. _____
2. $a * a^{-1} = e$.	2. _____
3. $b * b^{-1} = e$.	3. _____
4. $a * a^{-1} = b * b^{-1}$.	4. _____
5. $a * a^{-1} = a * b^{-1}$.	5. _____
6. $a^{-1} = b^{-1}$.	6. _____

27. Write a proof of the statement: In group $(G, *)$, for all $a, b, c \in G$:
If $a * b = c$, then $a = c * b^{-1}$.

28. Write a proof of the statement: In group $(G, *)$, for all $a, b, x \in G$:
If $x = (a * b) * b^{-1}$, then $x = a$.

14-7 FIELDS

The Distributive Property

You have already studied an important property called the ***distributive property of multiplication over addition,*** written in symbolic form as:

$$a(b + c) = ab + ac \quad \text{and} \quad ab + ac = a(b + c)$$

The importance of the distributive property is that it links together *two* operations. Here, the operations are addition and multiplication. You used the distributive law throughout your study of algebra. Recall how you learned to add like monomial terms: $5x + 4x = (5 + 4)x = 9x$.

The distributive property is *not* limited to multiplication over addition. Care must be taken however, to test the distributive property for any two given operations. Sometimes the property is true, and sometimes it is false.

EXAMPLE 1. Is addition distributive over multiplication?

In the example at the right, this property fails. Thus:

$$a + (b \cdot c) \neq (a + b) \cdot (a + c)$$

$$a + (b \cdot c) \overset{?}{=} (a + b) \cdot (a + c)$$
$$3 + (2 \cdot 7) \overset{?}{=} (3 + 2) \cdot (3 + 7)$$
$$3 + 14 \overset{?}{=} 5 \cdot 10$$
$$17 \neq 50$$

EXAMPLE 2. Is multiplication distributive over *average*?

We can test the property with a specific example, as follows:

$$a \cdot (b \text{ avg } c) \overset{?}{=} a \cdot b \text{ avg } a \cdot c$$
$$4 \cdot (3 \text{ avg } 9) \overset{?}{=} 4 \cdot 3 \text{ avg } 4 \cdot 9$$
$$4 \cdot 6 \overset{?}{=} 12 \text{ avg } 36$$
$$24 = 24$$

However, one correct application of the property does not mean that the property will always be true.

In more general terms, apply the definition of average:

$$a(b \text{ avg } c) \overset{?}{=} ab \text{ avg } ac$$
$$a \left(\frac{b + c}{2} \right) \overset{?}{=} \frac{ab + ac}{2}$$

On the left, use the distributive property of multiplication over addition to obtain:

$$\frac{ab + ac}{2} = \frac{ab + ac}{2}$$

Thus, the property is always true:

$$a(b \text{ avg } c) = ab \text{ avg } ac$$

Although it is possible to write a more general definition of the distributive property of one operation $*$ over another operation $\#$, as in $a * (b \# c) = (a * b) \# (a * c)$, we will limit our definition to the more familiar operations.

● **Definition.** In set S, multiplication is **distributive** over addition if and only if for all a, b, and c in S,

$$a(b + c) = ab + ac \quad \text{and} \quad ab + ac = a(b + c)$$

A Field

Just as the distributive property links together two operations, there is a mathematical system called a *field* that contains two operations. Since most fields consist of the operations of addition and multiplication, we will use these operations in our definition.

● **Definition.** A *field* is a mathematical system consisting of a set F and two operations, normally addition and multiplication, which satisfies eleven properties:

1. The set F is a commutative group under the operation of addition, satisfying five properties: closure, associativity, the existence of an identity for addition (usually 0), the existence of inverses under addition, and commutativity.
2. The set F without the additive identity (usually $F/\{0\}$) is a commutative group under the operation of multiplication, satisfying five properties: closure, associativity, the existence of an identity for multiplication (usually 1), the existence of inverses under multiplication, and commutativity.
3. The second operation, multiplication, is distributive over the first operation, addition.

Thus, if we know the properties of a group, it becomes relatively easy to remember the definition of a field. The definition is now rewritten in symbolic form. Notice that *two* operations are included with the set F by writing $(F, +, \cdot)$.

● **Definition.** $(F, +, \cdot)$ is a *field* if and only if

1. $(F, +)$ is a commutative group.
2. $(F/\{0\}, \cdot)$ is a commutative group.
3. Multiplication distributes over addition.

Equations such as $x + 5 = 20$ and $x \cdot \frac{1}{4} = 2$ were solved by using group properties. How do we solve an equation like $3x + 7 = 19$? This equation involves the operations of addition and multiplication. Since we simplify the equation, and thus find its solution, by using the additive inverse -7 and the multiplicative inverse $\frac{1}{3}$, it appears as if we are using the properties of a field. This is indeed true because the set of real numbers under addition and multiplication forms a field. The properties of this field are listed in Example 1.

EXAMPLE 1. (Real numbers, $+$, $\cdot$) is a field.

1. $(R, +)$ is closed.
2. $(R, +)$ is associative: $(a + b) + c = a + (b + c)$.
3. In $(R, +)$, the identity is 0.
4. In $(R, +)$, the inverse of a is $-a$.
5. $(R, +)$ is commutative: $a + b = b + a$.

$(R, +)$ is a commutative group.

6. $(R/\{0\}, \cdot)$ is closed.
7. $(R/\{0\}, \cdot)$ is associative: $(ab)c = a(bc)$.
8. In $(R/\{0\}, \cdot)$, the identity is 1.
9. In $(R/\{0\}, \cdot)$, the inverse of a is $\dfrac{1}{a}$.
10. $(R/\{0\}, \cdot)$ is commutative: $ab = ba$.

$(R/\{0\}, \cdot)$ is a commutative group.

11. In $(R, +, \cdot)$, $a(b + c) = ab + ac$.

Multiplication distributes over addition.

Thus, in the real number system, these field properties are true. We use these properties to solve equations and to perform computations.

Now let us consider a finite system.

EXAMPLE 2. (Clock 3, $+$, $\cdot$) is a field.

1. (Clock 3, $+$) is closed.
2. (Clock 3, $+$) is associative.
3. In (Clock 3, $+$), the identity is 0.
4. In (Clock 3, $+$):
   The additive inverse of 0 is 0.
   The additive inverse of 1 is 2.
   The additive inverse of 2 is 1.
5. (Clock 3, $+$) is commutative.

(Clock 3, $+$) is a commutative group.

$+$	0	1	2
0	0	1	2
1	1	2	0
2	2	0	1

(Clock 3, $+$)

6. (Clock 3/$\{0\}$, $\cdot$) is closed.
7. (Clock 3/$\{0\}$, $\cdot$) is associative.
8. In (Clock 3/$\{0\}$, $\cdot$), the identity is 1.
9. In (Clock 3/$\{0\}$, $\cdot$):
   The multiplicative inverse of 1 is 1.
   The multiplicative inverse of 2 is 2.
10. (Clock 3/$\{0\}$, $\cdot$) is commutative.

(Clock 3/$\{0\}$, $\cdot$) is a commutative group.

$\cdot$	1	2
1	1	2
2	2	1

(Clock 3/$\{0\}$, $\cdot$)

11. In (Clock 3, $+$, $\cdot$),
    $a(b + c) = ab + ac$.

Multiplication distributes over addition.

Let us list some examples of the distributive property that can be shown in (Clock 3, +, ·).

$1(0 + 2) \stackrel{?}{=} 1 \cdot 0 + 1 \cdot 2$	$2(2 + 1) \stackrel{?}{=} 2 \cdot 2 + 2 \cdot 1$	$2(1 + 1) \stackrel{?}{=} 2 \cdot 1 + 2 \cdot 1$
$1 \cdot 2 \stackrel{?}{=} 0 + 2$	$2 \cdot 0 \stackrel{?}{=} 1 + 2$	$2 \cdot 2 \stackrel{?}{=} 2 + 2$
$2 = 2$	$0 = 0$	$1 = 1$

It can be shown that all possible arrangements of clock 3 numbers in the rule $a(b + c) = ab + ac$ will result in true statements.

Of course, we can also identify mathematical systems that are *not* fields. In such cases, it is necessary to list only one field property that fails in order to show that the system is not a field.

EXAMPLE 3. (Integers, +, ·) is *not* a field.

Of the eleven field properties, one fails to be satisfied. With the exception of 1 and −1, integers do *not* have *multiplicative inverses*.

EXAMPLE 4. (Clock 4, +, ·) is *not* a field.

Of the eleven field properties, two fail to be satisfied. Clock 4/{0} is *not closed* under multiplication since $2 \cdot 2 = 0$, which is not in the set. Also, there is *no multiplicative inverse* for the element 2.

KEEP IN MIND
(Real numbers, +, ·) is a field.
(Rational numbers, +, ·) is a field.

Field Theorems

Within every field, there are two groups. Therefore, the definitions and postulates used to prove group theorems can be used to prove field theorems. It is also possible to use the commutative properties and the distributive property to prove field theorems because these properties are, by definition, present in fields.

The field theorems presented here are important to the study of algebra.

● **FIELD THEOREM 1 (The Multiplication Property of Zero).** In field $(F, +, \cdot)$, for all $a \in F$:

$$a \cdot 0 = 0 \quad and \quad 0 \cdot a = 0$$

Statements	*Reasons*
1. $a \cdot 0 + a \cdot 0 = a(0 + 0)$.	1. Distributive property of multiplication over addition.
2. $a \cdot 0 + a \cdot 0 = a \cdot 0$.	2. Definition of identity under addition $(0 + 0 = 0)$.
3. $a \cdot 0 + a \cdot 0 = 0 + a \cdot 0$.	3. Definition of identity under addition $(a \cdot 0 = 0 + a \cdot 0)$.
4. $a \cdot 0 = 0$.	4. Right-hand cancellation law.
5. $0 \cdot a = 0$.	5. Commutative property of multiplication.

Let us look at another theorem. Is the following statement true or false?

If $a \cdot b = 0$, then $a = 0$ or $b = 0$.

In clock 4, the statement is false because $2 \cdot 2 = 0$. In clock 6, the statement is false because $2 \cdot 3 = 0$ and $3 \cdot 4 = 0$. But (Clock 4, +, ·) and (Clock 6, +, ·) are *not* fields. In every field, such as (Clock 5, +, ·) and (Real numbers, +, ·), the statement can be proved to be true.

In the logical sense, $a = 0$ or $b = 0$ means $a = 0$, or $b = 0$, or both a and b equal 0. In the theorem to follow, it must be proved that one or the other quantity equals 0. However, it is not necessary to prove the case where both equal 0.

● **FIELD THEOREM 2.** **In field $(F, +, \cdot)$, for all $a, b \in F$:**

If $a \cdot b = 0$, then $a = 0$ or $b = 0$.

Proof of Part 1 (If $a \neq 0$, then $b = 0$.)

Statements	*Reasons*
1. $a \cdot b = 0$.	1. Given.
2. Let $a \neq 0$.	2. Assumption.
3. $\frac{1}{a} \in F$.	3. Every element of $F/\{0\}$ has a multiplicative inverse.
4. $\frac{1}{a} \cdot (a \cdot b) = \frac{1}{a} \cdot 0$.	4. Left-hand operation.
5. $\left(\frac{1}{a} \cdot a\right) \cdot b = \frac{1}{a} \cdot 0$.	5. Associative property of multiplication.

6. $1 \cdot b = \dfrac{1}{a} \cdot 0.$

      6. Definition of inverses under multiplication.

7. $b = \dfrac{1}{a} \cdot 0.$

      7. Definition of the identity under multiplication.

8. $b = 0.$

      8. Field Theorem 1: The multiplication property of zero.

[The proof of part 2 (if $b \neq 0$, then $a = 0$) is similar to the proof of part 1.]

The importance of this theorem is seen in the solution of quadratic equations that are factorable. For example:

Given a quadratic equation:	$x^2 - 8x + 15 = 0$
The trinomial is factored:	$(x - 3)(x - 5) = 0$
By the field theorem just proved, one factor or the other must equal zero:	$x - 3 = 0 \mid x - 5 = 0$
The equations are solved:	$x = 3 \mid x = 5$

As we end this chapter, note two key ideas:

1. The definitions, postulates, theorems, and use of deductive reasoning in this chapter show that a mathematical system is as much a postulational system as the one studied earlier in geometry.

2. The properties and theorems of groups and fields are important tools that allow us to perform computations and to solve equations in our number system, the field of (Real numbers, $+$, $\cdot$).

MODEL PROBLEM

Given the clock 5 field $(F, +, \cdot)$ where $F = \{0, 1, 2, 3, 4\}$ and the operations $+$ and $\cdot$ are defined by the tables:

+	0 1 2 3 4
0	0 1 2 3 4
1	1 2 3 4 0
2	2 3 4 0 1
3	3 4 0 1 2
4	4 0 1 2 3

$\cdot$	0 1 2 3 4
0	0 0 0 0 0
1	0 1 2 3 4
2	0 2 4 1 3
3	0 3 1 4 2
4	0 4 3 2 1

a. Find the value of $3(4 + 3)$.
b. Find the value of $3 \cdot 4 + 3 \cdot 3$.
c. Is $3(4 + 3) = 3 \cdot 4 + 3 \cdot 3$? If yes, name the property demonstrated by the statement.
d. Find x, if $3x + 4 = 1$.

Solution

a. Operate within parentheses first:
$$3(4 + 3) = 3(2) = 1$$

b. Multiply before performing the addition:
$$3 \cdot 4 + 3 \cdot 3 = 2 + 4 = 1$$

c. From **a** and **b**, $3(4 + 3) = 3 \cdot 4 + 3 \cdot 3$, or $1 = 1$. This demonstrates the distributive property of multiplication over addition.

d. In the equation $3x + 4 = 1$, replace the variable x with each of the clock 5 numbers.

$$3x + 4 = 1$$
Let $x = 0$: $3 \cdot 0 + 4 = 1$ becomes $0 + 4 = 1$, or $4 = 1$. (false)
Let $x = 1$: $3 \cdot 1 + 4 = 1$ becomes $3 + 4 = 1$, or $2 = 1$. (false)
Let $x = 2$: $3 \cdot 2 + 4 = 1$ becomes $1 + 4 = 1$, or $0 = 1$. (false)
Let $x = 3$: $3 \cdot 3 + 4 = 1$ becomes $4 + 4 = 1$, or $3 = 1$. (false)
Let $x = 4$: $3 \cdot 4 + 4 = 1$ becomes $2 + 4 = 1$, or $1 = 1$. (true)

Since $x = 4$ is the only replacement that makes $3x + 4 = 1$ a true statement, the solution set is $\{4\}$.

Answer: **a.** 1. **b.** 1. **c.** Yes, the distributive property of multiplication over addition. **d.** $x = 4$.

EXERCISES

In 1–9: **a.** Is the system a field? **b.** If the answer to part **a** is "No," name a field property that is not satisfied.

1. $(W, +, \cdot)$ **2.** (Rational numbers, $+, \cdot$)
3. (Real numbers, $+, \cdot$)   **4.** (Integers, $+, \cdot$)
5. (Positive numbers, $+, \cdot$)   **6.** (Even integers, $+, \cdot$)
7. (Clock 3, $+, \cdot$)   **8.** (Clock 4, $+, \cdot$)   **9.** (Clock 5, $+, \cdot$)

10. Give a reason why $(R, +)$ is not a field.
11. If set $S = \{0\}$, give a reason why $(S, +, \cdot)$ is not a field.

Exercises 12–32 refer to the field (Clock 5, $+, \cdot$). The tables for these operations are found on page 650.

12. What element does not have an inverse under multiplication?
13. What element is its own inverse under multiplication?
14. What is the additive inverse of 4?
15. Evaluate $3 + 3 + 3$.   **16.** Evaluate $3 \cdot 3 \cdot 3$.

In 17–19, evaluate parts **a** and **b**; then answer part **c**.

17. **a.** $4(2 + 4)$ **b.** $4 \cdot 2 + 4 \cdot 4$ **c.** Is $4(2 + 4) = 4 \cdot 2 + 4 \cdot 4$?
18. **a.** $2(3 + 2)$ **b.** $2(3) + 2(2)$ **c.** Is $2(3 + 2) = 2(3) + 2(2)$?
19. **a.** $3 \cdot 4 + 3 \cdot 2$ **b.** $3(4 + 2)$ **c.** Is $3 \cdot 4 + 3 \cdot 2 = 3(4 + 2)$?

20. What is the name of the field property being tested in Exercise 19?

In 21–32, solve for x in (Clock 5, +, •).

21. $x^2 = 4$
22. $x - 2 = 4$
23. $4x = 2$
24. $2 - x = 4$
25. $2x + 1 = 4$
26. $3x + 2 = 3$
27. $1 + 2x = 2$
28. $2x - 3 = 2$
29. $2 - x = 1 + 3$
30. $x^2 = x$
31. $x^2 = 3x + 1$
32. $x + x = 2x$

Exercises 33–58 refer to the set $S = \{0, 2, 4, 6, 8\}$ under the operations of digital addition and digital multiplication, shown in the tables that follow.

33. Is $(S, \oplus)$:
  a. closed?
  b. associative?
  c. commutative?

34. Name the identity for $(S, \oplus)$.

35. For every element in $(S, \oplus)$ having an inverse, name the element and its inverse.

$\oplus$	0 2 4 6 8
0	0 2 4 6 8
2	2 4 6 8 0
4	4 6 8 0 2
6	6 8 0 2 4
8	8 0 2 4 6

$\odot$	0 2 4 6 8
0	0 0 0 0 0
2	0 4 8 2 6
4	0 8 6 4 2
6	0 2 4 6 8
8	0 6 2 8 4

36. Is $(S, \oplus)$ a commutative group?

37. Is $(S/\{0\}, \odot)$: **a.** closed? **b.** associative? **c.** commutative?

38. Name the identity for $(S/\{0\}, \odot)$.

39. For every element in $(S/\{0\}, \odot)$ having an inverse, name the element and its inverse.

40. Is $(S/\{0\}, \odot)$ a commutative group?

41. a. Is $4 \odot (2 \oplus 6) = (4 \odot 2) \oplus (4 \odot 6)$?
  b. Is $8 \odot (2 \oplus 4) = (8 \odot 2) \oplus (8 \odot 4)$?
  c. Does the operation $\odot$ distribute over the operation $\oplus$?

42. Is $(S, \oplus, \odot)$ a field?

In 43–50, evaluate the given expression in $(S, \oplus, \odot)$, using the standard order of operations.

43. $8 \oplus 8 \oplus 8$
44. $8 \odot 8 \odot 8$
45. $2 \oplus 4 \odot 4$
46. $8 \odot (4 \oplus 8)$
47. $8 \odot 4 \oplus 8 \odot 8$
48. $(2 \oplus 6) \odot 2$
49. $2 \odot 2 \oplus 6 \odot 2$
50. $2 \oplus 6 \odot 2$

In 51–58, solve for x in $(S, \oplus, \odot)$.

51. $x \oplus 8 = 6$
52. $x \odot 8 = 6$
53. $x \odot x = 4$
54. $x \oplus x = 2$
55. $2 \odot x \oplus 4 = 6$
56. $2 \odot (x \oplus 4) = 6$
57. $8 \odot x \oplus 6 = 4$
58. $2 \oplus 4 \odot x = 8$

Exercises 59–63 refer to the set $S = \{a, b, c\}$ under the operations of Δ and $*$, as shown in the tables that follow.

Δ	a	b	c
a	b	c	a
b	c	a	b
c	a	b	c

$*$	a	b	c
a	b	a	c
b	a	b	c
c	c	c	c

59. In (S, Δ), the operation Δ is associative and the identity element $= c$. Is (S, Δ) a commutative group?

60. In $(S, *)$, which element does not have an inverse?

61. By removing c (the identity element under Δ) from the set S, the set $S/\{c\}$ is formed. Is $(S/\{c\}, *)$ a commutative group?

62. One of the operations distributes over the other operation.
  a. Is $b \Delta (a * c) = (b \Delta a) * (b \Delta c)$?
  b. Is $b * (a \Delta c) = (b * a) \Delta (b * c)$?
  c. Which operation is distributive over the other?

63. Is $(S, \Delta, *)$ a field?

In 64–68, select the numeral preceding the word or expression that answers the question or completes the statement.

64. Which system does *not* have an identity under addition?
  (1) $(W, +, \cdot)$ (2) (Odd integers, $+, \cdot$)
  (3) (Even integers, $+, \cdot$)   (4) $(R, +, \cdot)$

65. Which system does *not* have an identity under multiplication?
  (1) $(W, +, \cdot)$ (2) (Odd integers, $+, \cdot$)
  (3) (Even integers, $+, \cdot$)   (4) $(R, +, \cdot)$

66. Not every element has an additive inverse in which system?
  (1) $(W, +, \cdot)$ (2) (Integers, $+, \cdot$)
  (3) (Even integers, $+, \cdot$)   (4) $(R, +, \cdot)$

67. Not every element has a multiplicative inverse in which system?
  (1) $(R, +, \cdot)$ (2) (Integers, $+, \cdot$)
  (3) (Rational numbers, $+, \cdot$)   (4) (Positive real numbers, $+, \cdot$)

68. (Clock n, $+, \cdot$) will be a field when n is   (1) a counting number
  (2) a positive odd integer   (3) a prime number   (4) a real number

14-8 REVIEW EXERCISES

Exercises 1–19 refer to addition and multiplication in clock 6, as shown in the accompanying tables.

In 1–6, find the value of the given expression.

+	0	1	2	3	4	5
0	0	1	2	3	4	5
1	1	2	3	4	5	0
2	2	3	4	5	0	1
3	3	4	5	0	1	2
4	4	5	0	1	2	3
5	5	0	1	2	3	4

$\cdot$	0	1	2	3	4	5
0	0	0	0	0	0	0
1	0	1	2	3	4	5
2	0	2	4	0	2	4
3	0	3	0	3	0	3
4	0	4	2	0	4	2
5	0	5	4	3	2	1

1. $4 + 3$ **2.** $5 + 5 + 5$
3. $4 \cdot 3$ **4.** $2 \cdot 2 \cdot 2$
5. $3 \cdot 5 + 1$ **6.** $3(5 + 1)$

7. What is the identity element under multiplication?

8. What is the inverse of 5 under multiplication?

9. Name the elements of clock 6 that do *not* have multiplicative inverses.

10. Is addition commutative on the set of clock 6 numbers?

11. In each part, tell if the given sentence is true or false.
  a. (Clock 6, +) is a group   **b.** (Clock 6, ·) is a group.
  c. (Clock 6/{0}, ·) is a group.   **d.** (Clock 6, +, ·) is a field.

In 12–19, solve for x in the set of clock 6 numbers.

12. $x + 4 = 1$ **13.** $x \cdot 4 = 4$ **14.** $x + x = 4$ **15.** $x \cdot x = 4$

16. $2x + 1 = 5$ **17.** $3x - 2 = 3$ **18.** $5x + 4 = 2$ **19.** $x^2 + x = 0$

Exercises 20–33 refer to the table for operation @ defined on the set $\{D, A, V, E\}$.

20. Is the set closed under the operation @?

21. What is the identity element?

22. For each element having an inverse, name the element and its inverse.

23. Is the operation commutative?

24. What is the value of $A @ V @ A$?

@	D	A	V	E
D	A	E	D	V
A	E	D	A	D
V	D	A	V	E
E	V	D	E	A

25. a. Evaluate $(D @ D) @ D$.
  b. Evaluate $D @ (D @ D)$.
  c. Is the operation associative (based on parts **a** and **b**)?

In 26–33, solve for x in the given system.

26. $D @ x = V$ **27.** $A @ x = D$ **28.** $A @ x = V$ **29.** $x @ D = E$

30. $x @ E = E$ **31.** $x @ V = x$ **32.** $x @ x = V$ **33.** $x @ x = E$

In 34–43, select the numeral preceding the word or expression that answers the question.

34. If $a * b$ is a binary operation defined as $\dfrac{a + b}{b}$, evaluate $4 * 2$.
  (1) $\frac{6}{4}$ (2) 2   (3) 3   (4) 4

35. If the binary operation $a \square b = 2a + b$, what is the value of x when $3 \square x = 7$?
  (1) 1   (2) 2   (3) 3   (4) 4

36. Which set is closed under subtraction?
  (1) positive integers   (2) negative integers
  (3) even integers   (4) odd integers

37. Under which operation is the set of positive real numbers not closed?
(1) addition   (2) subtraction   (3) multiplication   (4) division

38. Which property is not necessary for a system to be a group?
(1) associativity   (2) commutativity
(3) closure   (4) existence of inverses

39. In (Clock 5, ·), which statement is illustrated by the sentence $2 \cdot 3 = 1$?
(1) Multiplication is commutative.
(2) The identity is 3.
(3) 2 and 3 are inverses.
(4) The set is closed under multiplication.

40. Which of the following systems is a group?
(1) (Clock 8, +)   (2) (Clock 8, ·)
(3) (Clock 8/{0}, ·)   (4) (Clock 4, ·)

41. Which of the following systems is a group?
(1) $(W, +)$ (2) $(W, \cdot)$ (3) (Integers, +)   (4) (Integers, ·)

42. Which of the following systems is a field?
(1) (Integers, +, ·)   (2) (Rational numbers, +, ·)
(3) (Clock 6, +, ·)   (4) (Clock 9, +, ·)

43. Which system does not have an identity under addition?
(1) $(W, +, \cdot)$ (2) (Odd integers, +, ·)
(3) (Even integers, +, ·)   (4) $(R, +, \cdot)$

44. Prove *Part 2* of *Field Theorem 2:* **In field $(F, +, \cdot)$, for all $a, b \in F$: If $a \cdot b = 0$, then $a = 0$ or $b = 0$.**

Part 2: (If $b \neq 0$, then $a = 0$.)

(*Hint.* An inverse $\dfrac{1}{b}$ should be used in a right-hand operation.)

45. Copy the proof of the following field theorem, and fill in the missing reasons.

Field Theorem: **In field $(F, +, \cdot)$, for all $x \in F$: $0 \cdot x = 0$.**

Statements	Reasons
1. $0 \cdot x + 0 \cdot x = (0 + 0)x.$	1. _____
2. $0 \cdot x + 0 \cdot x = 0 \cdot x.$	2. _____
3. $0 \cdot x + 0 \cdot x = 0 \cdot x + 0.$	3. _____
4. $\qquad\quad 0 \cdot x = 0.$	4. _____

Chapter 15

Operations With Fractions

15-1 THE MEANING OF A FRACTION

A fraction is a symbol that indicates the quotient of any number divided by any nonzero number. For example, the arithmetic fraction $\frac{3}{4}$ indicates the quotient $3 \div 4$.

The definition of division in terms of multiplication gives another way of thinking about a fraction.

● **Definition.** $a \div b = x$ if and only if $bx = a$. We use the multiplicative inverse of b to solve for x.

$$bx = a$$

$$\frac{1}{b}(bx) = \frac{1}{b}(a)$$

$$\left(\frac{1}{b} \cdot b\right)x = \frac{1}{b}(a)$$

$$1 \cdot x = \frac{1}{b}(a)$$

$$x = \frac{1}{b}(a)$$

Therefore, any fraction $\frac{a}{b}$ may be defined as the product of a times the multiplicative inverse of b.

$$\frac{a}{b} = \frac{1}{b} \cdot a = a \cdot \frac{1}{b}$$

There are two important results of this relationship.

(1) $a \div b$ is undefined when $b = 0$ because 0 has no multiplicative inverse.

(2) $b \div b = b \cdot \dfrac{1}{b} = 1$ when $b \neq 0$ because the product of any number and its multiplicative inverse is the identity 1.

An algebraic fraction is the quotient of polynomials. An algebraic fraction is defined or has meaning only for those values of the variable for which the denominator is not zero.

MODEL PROBLEMS ————————————————————

1. For what value(s) of x is $\dfrac{x - 3}{x^2 - 9}$ undefined?

Solution: $\dfrac{x - 3}{x^2 - 9}$ is undefined when $x^2 - 9 = 0$.

$$x^2 - 9 = 0$$
$$(x + 3)(x - 3) = 0$$
$$x + 3 = 0 \quad | \quad x - 3 = 0$$
$$x = -3 \quad | \quad x = 3$$

Answer: ± 3

2. For what value(s) of x does $\dfrac{x - 3}{x^2 - 9} = 1$?

Solution: $\dfrac{x - 3}{x^2 - 9} = 1$ when $x - 3 = x^2 - 9$.

$$x - 3 = x^2 - 9$$
$$-x^2 + x + 6 = 0$$
$$x^2 - x - 6 = 0$$
$$(x - 3)(x + 2) = 0$$
$$x - 3 = 0 \quad | \quad x + 2 = 0$$
$$x = 3 \quad | \quad x = -2$$

For $x = 3$ the fraction is undefined. Thus, the value of the fraction is 1 only for $x = -2$.

Answer: -2

Check: Let $x = -2$

$$\frac{x - 3}{x^2 - 9} \overset{?}{=} 1$$

$$\frac{-2 - 3}{(-2)^2 - 9} \overset{?}{=} 1$$

$$\frac{-5}{4 - 9} \overset{?}{=} 1$$

$$\frac{-5}{-5} \overset{?}{=} 1$$

$$1 = 1 \quad \text{(True)}$$

EXERCISES ────────────────────────────────

In 1–10, find the value(s) of the variable for which the fraction is not defined.

1. $\dfrac{3}{2x}$ **2.** $\dfrac{x}{x+1}$ **3.** $\dfrac{x+1}{x^2-1}$ **4.** $\dfrac{2y}{y^2-25}$

5. $\dfrac{a}{a^2+4a-5}$ **6.** $\dfrac{3}{b^2-2b+1}$ **7.** $\dfrac{8c}{c^2+7c+10}$ **8.** $\dfrac{4}{x^2-x-12}$

9. $\dfrac{x}{x-5}$ **10.** $\dfrac{x}{x^2-5}$

In 11–15, find the value(s) of the variable for which the fraction equals 1.

11. $\dfrac{x+5}{2x+1}$ **12.** $\dfrac{3a+2}{a-3}$ **13.** $\dfrac{2x}{x^2+1}$ **14.** $\dfrac{b+2}{b^2}$ **15.** $\dfrac{x^2+4}{6x}$

16. Which expression is defined for all values of x?

    (1) $\dfrac{x}{x+2}$ (2) $\dfrac{x}{x-2}$ (3) $\dfrac{x}{x^2-2}$ (4) $\dfrac{x}{x^2+2}$

17. Which expression is defined for all values of x except 3?

    (1) $\dfrac{1}{x^2-3}$ (2) $\dfrac{1}{x-3}$ (3) $\dfrac{1}{x^2+9}$ (4) $\dfrac{1}{x+3}$

18. If M is the midpoint of $\overline{AB}$ and $AB = x - 1$, express AM in terms of x.

19. If the perimeter of equilateral triangle PQR is $5a - 7$, express PQ in terms of a.

20. If the area of a rectangle is represented by $x^2 - 12$ and the width by $2x$, represent the length in terms of x.

15-2 REDUCING FRACTIONS TO LOWEST TERMS

A fraction is in lowest terms when its numerator and denominator have no common factor other than 1 or -1. A fraction can be reduced to lowest terms by using the common factor in the numerator and denominator to form a factor equal to 1.

$$\frac{15x^2}{35x^4} = \frac{5x^2 \cdot 3}{5x^2 \cdot 7x^2} = \frac{5x^2}{5x^2} \cdot \frac{3}{7x^2} = 1 \cdot \frac{3}{7x^2} = \frac{3}{7x^2}$$

This process of reducing a fraction to lowest terms can be written more simply by using cancellation, an alternate form of showing that a fraction whose numerator and denominator are equal can be replaced by the multiplicative identity 1.

$$\frac{15x^2}{35x^4} = \frac{\overset{1}{\cancel{5x^2}} \cdot 3}{\cancel{5x^2} \cdot 7x^2} = \frac{3}{7x^2}$$

Note that cancellation of polynomials can be used only after the numerator and denominator have been factored.

EXAMPLE. Express $\dfrac{2x^2 - 8}{2x^2 - 5x + 2}$ in lowest terms.

Solution:

Factor the numerator.

(1) Find the greatest common monomial factor.

$$2x^2 - 8 = 2(x^2 - 4)$$

(2) Factor the difference of two squares.

$$= 2(x - 2)(x + 2)$$

Factor the denominator.

(3) Factor a trinomial into two binomials.

$$2x^2 - 5x + 2 = (2x \quad)(x \quad)$$

    a. Factor the first term $2x^2$.

$$(2x - 1)(x - 2)$$

    b. Factor the last term $+2$.

$$-1x$$

    c. Arrange the factors of $+2$ so that the inner and the outer products have a sum equal to the middle term $-5x$.

$$(2x - 1)(x - 2)$$

$$-4x$$

$$-1x + (-4x) = -5x$$

Express the fraction in factored form and cancel common factors.

$$\frac{2x^2 - 8}{2x^2 - 5x + 2} = \frac{2(\cancel{x - 2})(x + 2)}{(2x - 1)(\cancel{x - 2})} = \frac{2(x + 2)}{2x - 1} \quad Ans.$$

From the previous example, observe that:

(1) The fraction is undefined when $x = \frac{1}{2}$ and when $x = 2$, the values that make the denominator equal to 0.

(2) For any value of x other than $\frac{1}{2}$ and 2, the given fraction is equal to the reduced fraction. For example, when $x = 4$:

$$\frac{2x^2 - 8}{2x^2 - 5x + 2} = \frac{2(4)^2 - 8}{2(4)^2 - 5(4) + 2} = \frac{32 - 8}{32 - 20 + 2} = \frac{24}{14}$$

$$\frac{2(x + 2)}{2x - 1} = \frac{2(4 + 2)}{2(4) - 1} = \frac{2(6)}{8 - 1} = \frac{12}{7}$$

Observe that the value of the given fraction $\frac{24}{14}$ is equal to the value of the reduced fraction $\frac{12}{7}$. Note that the values of the numerators and the values of the denominators of these two fractions, $\frac{24}{14}$ and $\frac{12}{7}$, differ by the factor 2, which is the value of the cancelled factor $x - 2$ when $x = 4$.

MODEL PROBLEM

Reduce to lowest terms: $\dfrac{3y^3 - 3y^2 - 18y}{9y^2 - 36}$

Solution:

(1) Factor the numerator.

$$\begin{aligned} 3y^3 &- 3y^2 - 18y \\ &= 3y(y^2 - y - 6) \\ &= 3y(y + 2)(y - 3) \end{aligned}$$

(2) Factor the denominator.

$$\begin{aligned} 9y^2 &- 36 \\ &= 9(y^2 - 4) \\ &= 9(y + 2)(y - 2) \end{aligned}$$

(3) Express the fraction in factored form and cancel common factors.

$$\frac{3y^3 - 3y^2 - 18y}{9y^2 - 36} = \frac{\overset{1}{3}y\overset{1}{(y + 2)}(y - 3)}{\underset{3}{9}(y + 2)(y - 2)} = \frac{y(y - 3)}{3(y - 2)} \quad \text{when } y \neq \pm 2 \quad Ans.$$

EXERCISES

In 1–20, reduce the fraction to lowest terms.

1. $\dfrac{3x^2}{6x}$ 2. $\dfrac{5a^2b}{7ab}$ 3. $\dfrac{-4c}{-2cd}$ 4. $\dfrac{4y}{8y^2}$

5. $\dfrac{2x - 4}{3x - 6}$ 6. $\dfrac{5y - 20}{4y - 16}$ 7. $\dfrac{2a + 4}{2a - 6}$ 8. $\dfrac{3y^2 - 9}{3y^3}$

9. $\dfrac{a^2 - 4}{2a - 4}$

10. $\dfrac{b^2 - 25}{3b + 15}$

11. $\dfrac{3x^2 - 27}{3x - 9}$

12. $\dfrac{5y + 20}{y^2 - 16}$

13. $\dfrac{c^2 - 1}{c^2 + 4c + 3}$

14. $\dfrac{2a + 8}{a^2 + 8a + 16}$

15. $\dfrac{5y - 15}{y^2 - 6y + 9}$

16. $\dfrac{6x^2 - 6}{3x^2 - 6x + 3}$

17. $\dfrac{2a^2 + 8}{4a^2 + 16}$

18. $\dfrac{3b^2 + 3}{6b + 6}$

19. $\dfrac{x^2 - 25}{x^2 + 10x + 25}$

20. $\dfrac{x^2 + x - 6}{x^2 - 3x + 2}$

21. Which of the following is in lowest terms?

   (1) $\dfrac{x - 1}{x^2 - 1}$ (2) $\dfrac{x + 1}{x^2 - 1}$ (3) $\dfrac{x - 1}{x^2 + 1}$ (4) $\dfrac{x}{x^2 + x}$

22. Which of the following is not equal to $\frac{1}{2}$?

   (1) $\dfrac{2x - 1}{2x - 2}$ (2) $\dfrac{2x - 2}{4x - 4}$ (3) $\dfrac{x^2 - 1}{2x^2 - 2}$ (4) $\dfrac{3x^3}{6x^3}$

15-3 MULTIPLYING FRACTIONS

The product of two fractions is a fraction whose numerator is the product of the given numerators and whose denominator is the product of the given denominators.

$$\frac{a}{b} \cdot \frac{x}{y} = \frac{ax}{by} \text{ when } b \neq 0 \text{ and } y \neq 0$$

In the following example, we use two procedures. In Method 1, we multiply the fractions and then reduce the product to lowest terms. In Method 2, we cancel each pair of common factors in the numerators and denominators before finding the product.

      Method 1   *Method 2*

$$\frac{3}{5} \cdot \frac{10}{9} = \frac{30}{45} = \frac{15}{15} \cdot \frac{2}{3} = 1 \cdot \frac{2}{3} = \frac{2}{3} \quad \bigg| \quad \frac{3}{5} \cdot \frac{10}{9} = \frac{\overset{1}{\cancel{3}}}{\cancel{5}} \cdot \frac{2 \cdot \overset{1}{\cancel{5}}}{3 \cdot \cancel{3}} = \frac{2}{3}$$

When the numerators and denominators of the fractions involve variables, the same procedures may be used.

                                      Method 1

$$\frac{2a^2}{5b} \cdot \frac{15b^3}{4a^2} = \frac{30a^2b^3}{20a^2b} = \frac{10a^2b}{10a^2b} \cdot \frac{3b^2}{2} = 1 \cdot \frac{3b^2}{2} = \frac{3b^2}{2}$$

Method 2

$$\frac{2a^2}{5b} \cdot \frac{15b^3}{4a^2} = \frac{\overset{1}{\cancel{2}} \cdot \overset{1}{\cancel{a}} \cdot \overset{1}{\cancel{a}}}{\cancel{5} \cdot \cancel{b}} \cdot \frac{3 \cdot \overset{1}{\cancel{5}} \cdot \overset{1}{\cancel{b}} \cdot b \cdot b}{2 \cdot \cancel{2} \cdot \cancel{a} \cdot \cancel{a}} = \frac{3b^2}{2}$$

The model problem shows Method 2 applied to fractions with polynomial numerators and denominators.

MODEL PROBLEM

Express in simplest form the product: $\dfrac{x^2 - x}{3x} \cdot \dfrac{x^2 - x - 2}{x^2 - 1}$

How to Proceed	*Solution*
	$\dfrac{x^2 - x}{3x} \cdot \dfrac{x^2 - x - 2}{x^2 - 1}$
(1) Factor all numerators and denominators.	$= \dfrac{x(x - 1)}{3x} \cdot \dfrac{(x - 2)(x + 1)}{(x - 1)(x + 1)}$
(2) Cancel common factors in the numerators and denominators.	$= \dfrac{\overset{1}{\cancel{x}}(\overset{1}{\cancel{x - 1}})}{3\cancel{x}} \cdot \dfrac{(x - 2)(\overset{1}{\cancel{x + 1}})}{(\cancel{x - 1})(\cancel{x + 1})}$
(3) Multiply the remaining factors in the numerators; multiply the remaining factors in the denominators.	$= \dfrac{x - 2}{3}$ when $x \neq 0, \pm 1$ *Ans.*

EXERCISES

In 1–18, multiply, and express each product in simplest form.

1. $\dfrac{3x}{8y} \cdot \dfrac{12y^2}{9}$

2. $\dfrac{4a^2}{5b^3} \cdot \dfrac{10b}{6a^3}$

3. $\dfrac{5xy}{14} \cdot \dfrac{21}{10x^2}$

4. $\dfrac{2x + 8}{3} \cdot \dfrac{6x^2}{4x + 16}$

5. $\dfrac{3y - 3}{7} \cdot \dfrac{35y}{5y - 5}$

6. $\dfrac{2a}{2a - 2} \cdot \dfrac{3a - 3}{3a}$

7. $\dfrac{x^2 - 1}{5x^2 + 5x} \cdot \dfrac{15x^2}{3x - 3}$

8. $\dfrac{12}{b^2 - 25} \cdot \dfrac{5b^2 - 25b}{20}$

9. $\dfrac{6s - 18}{30} \cdot \dfrac{5s + 15}{s^2 - 9}$

10. $\dfrac{r^2 - 4}{10} \cdot \dfrac{2}{2r^2 + r - 10}$

11. $\dfrac{3a}{2a^2 + a - 3} \cdot \dfrac{4a + 6}{3a - 6}$

12. $\dfrac{x^3 - x^2}{3x} \cdot \dfrac{x^2 + 2x + 1}{x^2 - 1}$

13. $\dfrac{x^2 + 5x + 4}{7x + 7} \cdot \dfrac{28}{x^2 - 16}$

14. $\dfrac{2b^2 + b - 1}{2b^2} \cdot \dfrac{5b}{b^2 - 1}$

15. $\dfrac{x^2 + 1}{3x^2} \cdot \dfrac{3x + 3}{x^2 + 2x + 1}$

16. $\dfrac{a^2 - 64}{8a^2 - 64a} \cdot \dfrac{8a}{9a + 72}$

17. $\dfrac{x^2 + 16x + 64}{x^2 + 64} \cdot \dfrac{x^3 + 64x}{x^2 + 8x}$

18. $\dfrac{2c^2 - c - 6}{4c - 8} \cdot \dfrac{12}{6c + 9}$

19. The product $\dfrac{x + 3}{x - 1} \cdot \dfrac{x^2 + x - 2}{x^2 - 9} = \dfrac{x + 2}{x - 3}$ for all values of x except

(1) 3   (2) ± 3 and 1   (3) ± 3 (4) 3 and -2

20. If the area of a rectangle is $2x^2 - 8$ and the length of the rectangle is $2x - 4$, then the width of the rectangle is

(1) $x + 2$ (2) $x - 2$ (3) $2(x - 2)$ (4) $2(x + 2)$

15-4   DIVIDING FRACTIONS

Division was defined in terms of multiplication.

$$a \div b = a \cdot \frac{1}{b}$$

Since this definition is true for any numbers, it can be used to write a rule for dividing fractions. To use it, we must be able to write the reciprocal of a fraction.

Two numbers are reciprocals or multiplicative inverses if and only if their product is 1, the identity for multiplication.

$\dfrac{2}{3} \cdot \dfrac{3}{2} = 1$. Therefore, $\dfrac{2}{3}$ and $\dfrac{3}{2}$ are reciprocals.

$\dfrac{5y}{2} \cdot \dfrac{2}{5y} = 1$ when $y \neq 0$. Therefore, $\dfrac{5y}{2}$ and $\dfrac{2}{5y}$ are reciprocals.

$\dfrac{x}{x^2 - 1} \cdot \dfrac{x^2 - 1}{x} = 1$ when $x \neq 0, \pm 1$. Therefore, $\dfrac{x}{x^2 - 1}$ and $\dfrac{x^2 - 1}{x}$ are reciprocals.

In general $\dfrac{c}{d} \cdot \dfrac{d}{c} = \dfrac{cd}{cd} = 1$. Therefore $\dfrac{c}{d}$ and $\dfrac{d}{c}$ are reciprocals. A fraction $\dfrac{c}{d}$ and its reciprocal $\dfrac{d}{c}$ are defined if $c \neq 0$ and $d \neq 0$.

Now we can apply the rule $a \div b = a \cdot \dfrac{1}{b}$ to fractions. To divide two fractions, multiply the dividend by the reciprocal of the divisor.

MODEL PROBLEM

Express in simplest form the quotient: $\dfrac{x^2 - 5x + 4}{3x^2} \div \dfrac{x^2 - 16}{12x}$

Solution:

$$\dfrac{x^2 - 5x + 4}{3x^2} \div \dfrac{x^2 - 16}{12x} = \dfrac{x^2 - 5x + 4}{3x^2} \cdot \dfrac{12x}{x^2 - 16}$$

$$= \dfrac{\overset{1}{\cancel{(x - 4)}}(x - 1)}{\underset{x}{\cancel{3}} \cdot \cancel{x} \cdot x} \cdot \dfrac{\overset{1}{\cancel{3}} \cdot 4 \cdot \overset{1}{\cancel{x}}}{(x + 4)\cancel{(x - 4)}}$$

$$= \dfrac{4(x - 1)}{x(x + 4)} \text{ when } x \neq 0 \text{ and } x \neq \pm 4 \quad Ans.$$

EXERCISES

In 1–18, divide, and express the quotient in lowest terms.

1. $\dfrac{3}{4} \div \dfrac{9}{10}$

2. $\dfrac{7}{8} \div \dfrac{1}{4}$

3. $\dfrac{15}{a^3} \div \dfrac{5}{a}$

4. $\dfrac{x}{y^2} \div \dfrac{x}{y}$

5. $\dfrac{2x + 4}{12} \div \dfrac{x + 2}{3}$

6. $\dfrac{10b + 5}{9} \div \dfrac{2b + 1}{3}$

7. $\dfrac{12a^4}{a - 3} \div \dfrac{2a}{3a - 9}$

8. $\dfrac{b^2 - b}{4a^2} \div \dfrac{b}{2a}$

9. $\dfrac{2d - 6}{d^4} \div \dfrac{3d - 9}{3d^2}$

10. $\dfrac{2x^2 - 4x}{x^3} \div 2x$

11. $\dfrac{x^2 - 1}{x} \div (x + 1)$

12. $\dfrac{a^2 - 9}{4a} \div \dfrac{a - 3}{12}$

13. $\dfrac{3b + 6}{b^2 + 4b + 4} \div \dfrac{3}{b + 2}$

14. $\dfrac{x^2 - 10x + 25}{x - 5} \div \dfrac{x^2 - 25}{5x + 25}$

15. $\dfrac{c^2 - 2c - 24}{c^2 + 4c} \div \dfrac{c^2 - 36}{c + 6}$

16. $\dfrac{a^4 - 16}{a + 2} \div (a^2 + 4)$

17. $\dfrac{2x^3 + 10x^2 + 8x}{x^2 + 2x - 8} \div \dfrac{2x}{x^2 - 1}$

18. $\dfrac{2x^2 - x - 6}{2x^2} \div (4x^2 - 9)$

19. Express in lowest terms the length of a rectangle whose area is represented by $\dfrac{3x^2 + 4x - 4}{x}$ and whose width is represented by $3x^2 - 2x$.

20. Express in lowest terms the height of a right prism whose volume is represented by $\dfrac{16y^2 + 8y + 1}{y + 1}$ and the area of whose base is represented by $4y + 1$.

15-5 ADDING OR SUBTRACTING FRACTIONS THAT HAVE THE SAME DENOMINATOR

The distributive property of multiplication over addition or subtraction provides the basis for a method of adding or subtracting fractions that have the same denominator.

EXAMPLES. $\dfrac{4}{9} + \dfrac{7}{9} = 4 \cdot \dfrac{1}{9} + 7 \cdot \dfrac{1}{9} = (4 + 7) \cdot \dfrac{1}{9} = 11 \cdot \dfrac{1}{9} = \dfrac{11}{9}$

$\dfrac{7}{3} - \dfrac{5}{3} = 7 \cdot \dfrac{1}{3} - 5 \cdot \dfrac{1}{3} = (7 - 5) \cdot \dfrac{1}{3} = 2 \cdot \dfrac{1}{3} = \dfrac{2}{3}$

$\dfrac{a}{c} + \dfrac{b}{c} = a \cdot \dfrac{1}{c} + b \cdot \dfrac{1}{c} = (a + b) \cdot \dfrac{1}{c} = \dfrac{a + b}{c}$ when $c \neq 0$

Once you understand the mathematical principle involved, the computation may be written more simply.

$$\dfrac{4}{9} + \dfrac{7}{9} = \dfrac{11}{9} \qquad \dfrac{7}{3} - \dfrac{5}{3} = \dfrac{2}{3} \qquad \dfrac{a}{c} + \dfrac{b}{c} = \dfrac{a + b}{c} \text{ when } c \neq 0$$

This principle applies to any algebraic fraction. Often the sum or difference can be simplified.

$$\dfrac{4a}{3b} + \dfrac{7a}{3b} - \dfrac{2a}{3b} = \dfrac{(4a + 7a - 2a)}{3b} = \dfrac{9a}{3b} = \dfrac{3a}{b} \text{ when } b \neq 0.$$

MODEL PROBLEMS

Perform the indicated operation and reduce the answer to lowest terms.

1. $\dfrac{3x - 1}{x - 1} + \dfrac{x^2 - 3x}{x - 1} = \dfrac{x^2 - 1}{x - 1} = \dfrac{(\overset{1}{\cancel{x - 1}})(x + 1)}{\cancel{x - 1}}$

$$= x + 1 \text{ when } x \neq 1 \quad Ans.$$

2. $\dfrac{a^2 + 3a}{2a - 10} - \dfrac{7a + 5}{2a - 10} = \dfrac{(a^2 + 3a) - (7a + 5)}{2a - 10} = \dfrac{a^2 + 3a - 7a - 5}{2a - 10}$

$$= \dfrac{a^2 - 4a - 5}{2a - 10} = \dfrac{(a + 1)(\overset{1}{\cancel{a - 5}})}{2(\cancel{a - 5})}$$

$$= \dfrac{a + 1}{2} \text{ when } a \neq 5 \quad Ans.$$

EXERCISES

In 1–16, perform the indicated operation and express the result in lowest terms.

1. $\dfrac{3}{2a} + \dfrac{5}{2a}$

2. $\dfrac{3x}{5} - \dfrac{2x}{5}$

3. $\dfrac{y^2}{8} + \dfrac{y^2}{8}$

4. $\dfrac{5a}{12} - \dfrac{a}{12}$

5. $\dfrac{x + 3}{2} + \dfrac{3x - 1}{2}$

6. $\dfrac{a + 2}{4} - \dfrac{a - 6}{4}$

7. $\dfrac{9b + 1}{2b} + \dfrac{b - 1}{2b}$

8. $\dfrac{4d + 2}{3d} + \dfrac{2d + 1}{3d}$

9. $\dfrac{2x^2 - 7}{x - 2} - \dfrac{x^2 - 3}{x - 2}$

10. $\dfrac{4a^2 + 2a}{a + 1} - \dfrac{4 + 2a}{a + 1}$

11. $\dfrac{b^2 + 4b}{3b + 6} + \dfrac{2 - b}{3b + 6}$

12. $\dfrac{5c + 1}{c + 1} - \dfrac{3c - c^2}{c + 1}$

13. $\dfrac{d^2 - 5d}{5d} - \dfrac{d^2 - 15}{5d}$

14. $\dfrac{x^2 + x}{4x + 10} + \dfrac{x^2 - 10}{4x + 10}$

15. $\dfrac{a^3}{a - 1} - \dfrac{a^2}{a - 1}$

16. $\dfrac{x^2 + x}{x^2 - 25} - \dfrac{x^2 - 5}{x^2 - 25}$

17. The sum of $\dfrac{x}{x^2 - 1} + \dfrac{1}{x^2 - 1}$ is $\dfrac{1}{x - 1}$ when

(1) $x \neq \pm 1$ (2) $x \neq 1$ (3) $x \neq -1$ (4) x is any real number

18. The difference $\dfrac{x^2 + 2x}{x - 1} - \dfrac{2x - 1}{x - 1}$ is equal to

(1) $x + 1$ when $x \neq 1$ (2) $x + 1$ for all x

(3) $\dfrac{x^2 + 1}{x - 1}$ when $x \neq 1$ (4) $\dfrac{x^2 + 1}{x - 1}$ for all x

15-6 ADDING OR SUBTRACTING FRACTIONS THAT HAVE DIFFERENT DENOMINATORS

In order to add or subtract fractions, it is necessary that the fractions have the same denominator. Using the multiplicative identity in the form of a fraction whose numerator is equal to its denominator, it is possible to change fractions into equivalent fractions that have the same denominator.

EXAMPLE 1.   Add: $\frac{3}{5} + \frac{1}{2}$

It is possible to change each fraction into an equivalent fraction whose denominator is the product of the given denominators, that is 5(2) or 10.

$$\frac{3}{5} = \frac{3}{5} \cdot \frac{2}{2} = \frac{6}{10}$$

$$\frac{1}{2} = \frac{1}{2} \cdot \frac{5}{5} = \frac{5}{10}$$

$$\frac{3}{5} + \frac{1}{2} = \frac{6}{10} + \frac{5}{10} = \frac{11}{10}$$

Although the product of the denominators of the given fractions is always a possible common denominator, that product is not always the smallest or *lowest common denominator*. The lowest common denominator (L.C.D.) is the product of the highest power of each prime factor of the given denominators.

EXAMPLE 2.   Add: $\frac{1}{12} + \frac{5}{18}$

(1) Find the L.C.D.

$$12 = 2^2 \cdot 3$$
$$18 = 2 \cdot 3^2$$
$$\text{L.C.D.} = 2^2 \cdot 3^2 = 36$$

(2) Write each fraction as an equivalent fraction with the L.C.D. as its denominator.

$$\frac{1}{12} = \frac{1}{12} \cdot \frac{3}{3} = \frac{3}{36}$$

$$\frac{5}{18} = \frac{5}{18} \cdot \frac{2}{2} = \frac{10}{36}$$

(3) Use the equivalent fractions with common denominators to find the sum or difference.

$$\frac{1}{12} + \frac{5}{18} = \frac{3}{36} + \frac{10}{36} = \frac{13}{36}$$

We apply this procedure to algebraic fractions.

EXAMPLE 3. Add: $\dfrac{1}{x^2 + x} + \dfrac{-1}{2x + 2}$

(1) Find the L.C.D.
$$x^2 + x = x(x + 1)$$
$$2x + 2 = 2 (x + 1)$$
$$\text{L.C.D.} = 2x(x + 1) = 2x^2 + 2x$$

(2) Write each fraction as an equivalent fraction with the L.C.D. as its denominator.

$$\frac{1}{x^2 + x} = \frac{1}{x^2 + x} \cdot \frac{2}{2} = \frac{2}{2x^2 + 2x}$$

$$\frac{-1}{2x + 2} = \frac{-1}{2x + 2} \cdot \frac{x}{x} = \frac{-x}{2x^2 + 2x}$$

(3) Use the equivalent fractions with common denominators to find the sum or difference.

$$\frac{1}{x^2 + x} + \frac{-1}{2x + 2} = \frac{2}{2x^2 + 2x} + \frac{-x}{2x^2 + 2x}$$

$$= \frac{2 - x}{2x^2 + 2x} = \frac{2 - x}{2x(x + 1)} \text{ when } x \neq 0, -1$$

Mixed Expressions

A mixed number is the sum of an integer and a fraction. For example, $2\frac{3}{4}$ is the sum of 2 and $\frac{3}{4}$. A mixed number may be written as a fraction by writing the integer as an equivalent fraction having the same denominator as the fraction.

$$2\frac{3}{4} = 2 + \frac{3}{4} = 2 \cdot \frac{4}{4} + \frac{3}{4} = \frac{8}{4} + \frac{3}{4} = \frac{11}{4}$$

This same procedure can be used with the sum of algebraic expressions.

$$2 + \frac{1}{x - 1} = 2 \cdot \frac{x - 1}{x - 1} + \frac{1}{x - 1} = \frac{2x - 2}{x - 1} + \frac{1}{x - 1}$$

$$= \frac{2x - 1}{x - 1} \text{ when } x \neq 1$$

MODEL PROBLEM

Add, and express the sum in lowest terms: $\dfrac{x-4}{x^2-4} + \dfrac{1}{x^2-2x}$

Solution

(1) Find the L.C.D.
$$x^2 - 4 = (x-2)(x+2)$$
$$x^2 - 2x = x(x-2)$$
$$\text{L.C.D.} = x(x-2)(x+2)$$

(2) Express each fraction as an equivalent fraction with the denominator $x(x-2)(x+2)$.

$$\frac{x-4}{x^2-4} = \frac{x-4}{(x-2)(x+2)} \cdot \frac{x}{x} = \frac{x^2-4x}{x(x-2)(x+2)}$$

$$\frac{1}{x^2-2x} = \frac{1}{x(x-2)} \cdot \frac{x+2}{x+2} = \frac{x+2}{x(x-2)(x+2)}$$

(3) Add the equivalent fractions and reduce the sum to lowest terms.

$$\frac{x-4}{x^2-4} + \frac{1}{x^2-2x} = \frac{x^2-4x}{x(x-2)(x+2)} + \frac{x+2}{x(x-2)(x+2)}$$

$$= \frac{x^2-3x+2}{x(x-2)(x+2)} = \frac{\overset{1}{\cancel{(x-2)}}(x-1)}{x\cancel{(x-2)}(x+2)}$$

$$= \frac{x-1}{x(x+2)} \text{ when } x \neq 0, \pm 2$$

EXERCISES

In 1–29, perform the indicated operation and express the result in lowest terms.

1. $\dfrac{1}{7} + \dfrac{1}{5}$ **2.** $\dfrac{a}{3} - \dfrac{a}{4}$ **3.** $\dfrac{b}{8} + \dfrac{2b}{6}$ **4.** $\dfrac{c}{2} + \dfrac{3c}{4}$

5. $\dfrac{1}{a} + \dfrac{1}{b}$ **6.** $\dfrac{3}{x} - \dfrac{2}{y}$ **7.** $\dfrac{1}{a} + \dfrac{1}{a^2}$ **8.** $\dfrac{3}{2d} - \dfrac{5}{4d}$

9. $\dfrac{3}{8a} + \dfrac{5}{a^2}$ **10.** $\dfrac{9}{4c} - \dfrac{5}{2c^2}$ **11.** $\dfrac{2a}{b^2} - \dfrac{3a}{b^3}$ **12.** $\dfrac{x}{5y^3} + \dfrac{2x}{3y^2}$

13. $\dfrac{5}{2x-2} + \dfrac{3}{6x-6}$ **14.** $\dfrac{1}{2b+4} - \dfrac{1}{3b+6}$ **15.** $\dfrac{2}{a^2-a} + \dfrac{3}{2a-2}$

16. $\dfrac{4}{a-3} - \dfrac{4a}{5a-15}$ **17.** $\dfrac{1}{x+2} + \dfrac{x}{2x+4}$

18. $\dfrac{2x+1}{x^2+x} - \dfrac{1}{x}$ **19.** $\dfrac{2}{c^2-1} + \dfrac{1}{c+1}$

20. $\dfrac{2a+5}{a^2+5a+6} - \dfrac{1}{a+3}$ **21.** $\dfrac{2b-1}{b^2-b-12} - \dfrac{1}{b-4}$

22. $\left(\dfrac{1}{x+2} \cdot \dfrac{x^2-4}{x}\right) + \dfrac{x+2}{3x}$ **23.** $\left(\dfrac{3}{a^2-1} \div \dfrac{9}{a+1}\right) + a + 1$

24. $2 - \dfrac{x^2-1}{x^2} \cdot \dfrac{x}{x+1}$ **25.** $\dfrac{c^2+2c-15}{3c} \div (c+5) + \dfrac{1}{c}$

26. $(x+1) \div \left(1 + \dfrac{1}{x}\right)$ **27.** $\dfrac{2a}{a+1} \div \left(2 - \dfrac{2}{a+1}\right)$

28. $(d-1) \div \left(d - \dfrac{1}{d}\right) + \dfrac{1}{d+1}$ **29.** $\left(1 - \dfrac{1}{b^2}\right)\left(1 - \dfrac{1}{b}\right)$

30. Express as a single fraction in lowest terms the sum of the reciprocals of $3x + 3$ and $6x + 6$.

15-7 SOLVING FRACTIONAL EQUATIONS

An equation is called a *fractional equation* when a variable appears in the *denominator* of one, or more than one, of its terms. For example, $\dfrac{1}{3} + \dfrac{1}{x} = \dfrac{1}{2}$ and $\dfrac{2}{3d} + \dfrac{1}{3} = \dfrac{11}{6d} - \dfrac{1}{4}$ are called fractional equations. To solve such an equation, we can clear the equation of fractions by multiplying both of its members by the lowest common denominator (L.C.D.) for the denominators of the fractions present in the equation.

As with all algebraic fractions, a fractional equation has meaning only for those values of the variable that do not lead to a denominator of 0.

MODEL PROBLEMS

1. Solve and check: $\dfrac{1}{3} + \dfrac{1}{x} = \dfrac{1}{2}$

Solution: Multiply both members of the equation by the L.C.D., $6x$.

$$\frac{1}{3} + \frac{1}{x} = \frac{1}{2}$$

$$6x\left(\frac{1}{3} + \frac{1}{x}\right) = 6x\left(\frac{1}{2}\right)$$

$$6x\left(\frac{1}{3}\right) + 6x\left(\frac{1}{x}\right) = 6x\left(\frac{1}{2}\right)$$

$$2x + 6 = 3x$$

$$6 = x$$

Answer: $x = 6$

Check

$$\frac{1}{3} + \frac{1}{x} = \frac{1}{2}$$

$$\frac{1}{3} + \frac{1}{6} \overset{?}{=} \frac{1}{2}$$

$$\frac{2}{6} + \frac{1}{6} \overset{?}{=} \frac{1}{2}$$

$$\frac{3}{6} \overset{?}{=} \frac{1}{2}$$

$$\frac{1}{2} = \frac{1}{2} \quad \text{(True)}$$

2. Solve and check: $\dfrac{5x + 10}{x + 2} = 7$

Solution: Multiply both members of the equation by the L.C.D., $x + 2$.

$$(x + 2)\left(\frac{5x + 10}{x + 2}\right) = (x + 2)(7)$$

$$5x + 10 = 7x + 14$$

$$10 = 2x + 14$$

$$-4 = 2x$$

$$-2 = x$$

Check

$$\frac{5x + 10}{x + 2} = 7$$

$$\frac{5(-2) + 10}{-2 + 2} \overset{?}{=} 7$$

$$\frac{-10 + 10}{-2 + 2} \overset{?}{=} 7$$

$$\frac{0}{0} = 7 \quad \text{(False)}$$

Since the only possible value of x is a value for which the equation has no meaning because it leads to a denominator of 0, there is no solution for this equation.

Answer: The solution set is $\varnothing$.

KEEP IN MIND ────────────────────────────────

When both members of an equation are multiplied by a variable expression that may represent zero, the resulting equation may not be equivalent to the given equation. Each solution, therefore, must be checked in the given equation.

EXERCISES ─────────────────────────────────

In 1–17, solve and check.

1. $\dfrac{10}{x} = 5$

2. $\dfrac{15}{y} = 3$

3. $\dfrac{6}{x} = 12$

4. $\dfrac{8}{b} = -2$

5. $\dfrac{3}{2x} = \dfrac{1}{2}$

6. $\dfrac{15}{4x} = \dfrac{1}{8}$

7. $\dfrac{7}{3y} = -\dfrac{1}{3}$

8. $\dfrac{4}{5y} = -\dfrac{1}{10}$

9. $\dfrac{10}{x} + \dfrac{8}{x} = 9$

10. $\dfrac{15}{y} - \dfrac{3}{y} = 4$

11. $\dfrac{7}{c} + \dfrac{1}{c} = 16$

12. $\dfrac{9}{2x} = \dfrac{7}{2x} + 2$

13. $\dfrac{30}{x} = 7 + \dfrac{18}{2x}$

14. $\dfrac{y-2}{2y} = \dfrac{3}{8}$

15. $\dfrac{5}{c} + 6 = \dfrac{17}{c}$

16. $\dfrac{y+9}{2y} + 3 = \dfrac{15}{y}$

17. $\dfrac{5+x}{2x} - 1 = \dfrac{x+1}{x}$

In 18–20, explain why each fractional equation has no solution.

18. $\dfrac{6x}{x} = 3$

19. $\dfrac{4a+4}{a+1} = 5$

20. $\dfrac{2}{x} = 4 + \dfrac{2}{x}$

In 21–31, solve and check.

21. $\dfrac{6}{3x-1} = \dfrac{3}{4}$

22. $\dfrac{2}{3x-4} = \dfrac{1}{4}$

23. $\dfrac{5x}{x+1} = 4$

24. $\dfrac{3}{5-3a} = \dfrac{1}{2}$

25. $\dfrac{4z}{7+5z} = \dfrac{1}{3}$

26. $\dfrac{1-r}{1+r} = \dfrac{2}{3}$

27. $\dfrac{3}{y} = \dfrac{2}{5 - y}$ **28.** $\dfrac{5}{a} = \dfrac{7}{a - 4}$ **29.** $\dfrac{2}{m} = \dfrac{5}{3m - 1}$

30. $\dfrac{y}{y + 1} - \dfrac{1}{y} = 1$ **31.** $\dfrac{x}{x^2 - 9} = \dfrac{1}{x + 3}$

32. If 24 is divided by a number, the result is 6. Find the number.

33. If 10 is divided by a number, the result is 30. Find the number.

34. The sum of 20 divided by a number, and 7 divided by the same number, is 9. Find the number.

35. If 3 times a number is increased by one-third of that number, the result is 280. Find the number.

36. When the reciprocal of a number is decreased by 2, the result is 5. Find the number.

37. The numerator of a fraction is 8 less than the denominator of the fraction. The value of the fraction is $\frac{3}{5}$. Find the fraction.

38. If one-half of a number is 8 more than one-third of the number, find the number.

15-8   REVIEW EXERCISES

1. a. For what value(s) of x is $\dfrac{2x^2 - x - 1}{x^2 - 3x + 2}$ undefined?

    b. For what value(s) of x is $\dfrac{2x^2 - x - 1}{x^2 - 3x + 2}$ the identity for multiplication?

In 2–20, perform the indicated operations and express the result in simplest form.

2. $\dfrac{x - 5}{5x} + \dfrac{x + 2}{2x}$ **3.** $x - 2 + \dfrac{1}{x - 3}$ **4.** $\dfrac{3a}{a - 8} \cdot \dfrac{a^2 - 64}{6a^2}$

5. $\dfrac{3}{x} + \dfrac{x - 9}{3x}$ **6.** $\dfrac{5}{r} \div \dfrac{15}{r^3}$ **7.** $\dfrac{2d^2}{d + 2} \cdot \dfrac{d^2 - 4}{d^2 - 2d}$

8. $\dfrac{r^2 - 9}{4r - 12} \cdot \dfrac{8}{r^2 - r - 12}$ **9.** $\dfrac{b^2 - 2b - 24}{3} \div \dfrac{b + 4}{9}$

10. $\dfrac{2x}{x + 2} - \dfrac{x - 2}{x + 2}$ **11.** $\dfrac{s^2 - s}{5s} \div (s^2 - 1)$

12. $\dfrac{3a + 1}{2a + 2} - \dfrac{a}{a + 1}$ **13.** $\dfrac{x - 7}{5x} + \dfrac{1}{x^2}$ **14.** $\dfrac{a^2 - 7a + 12}{a - 4} \cdot \dfrac{1}{2a - 6}$

15. $\dfrac{2x^2 - x - 6}{4x^2 - 9} \div \dfrac{4x - 8}{6x - 9}$ **16.** $\dfrac{x}{3} + \dfrac{x - 2}{x - 3}$

17. $\left(\dfrac{1}{x} - \dfrac{1}{x + 1} \right)(x + 1)$ **18.** $\dfrac{1}{x} - \dfrac{1}{x + 1}(x + 1)$

19. $\dfrac{3b}{4} + \dfrac{b}{b - 1} \div \dfrac{3}{3b - 3}$ **20.** $(2c - 6) \div \left(c - \dfrac{9}{c} \right)$

21. Express in terms of x the width of a rectangle whose area is represented by $3x^2 - 2x - 8$ and whose length is represented by $\dfrac{3x + 4}{2}$.

22. Which of the following is in lowest terms?

(1) $\dfrac{a}{a^2 - a}$ (2) $\dfrac{a - 2}{a^2 - 4a + 4}$ (3) $\dfrac{a - 2}{a^2 + 4}$ (4) $\dfrac{a - 2}{a^2 - 4}$

23. Which of the following is defined for all values of x?

(1) $\dfrac{x}{x^2 - 1}$ (2) $\dfrac{x}{x^2 + 1}$ (3) $\dfrac{x}{x^2 + x}$ (4) $\dfrac{x}{x^2 - x}$

24. A farmer can plow a field in d days. It takes his son 4 fewer days to plow the field.
   a. Express in terms of d the part of the field that the farmer can plow in a day.
   b. Express in terms of d the part of the field that the son can plow in a day.
   c. Express as a fraction in lowest terms the part of the field that the farmer and his son can plow in a day working together.

In 25–30, solve and check.

25. $\dfrac{b}{20} = \dfrac{3}{4}$ **26.** $\dfrac{a - 3}{10} = \dfrac{4}{5}$ **27.** $\dfrac{x}{2} - \dfrac{x}{6} = 4$

28. $\dfrac{6}{q} = \dfrac{20}{q} - 2$ **29.** $\dfrac{2t}{5} - \dfrac{t - 2}{10} = 2$ **30.** $\dfrac{3}{y} + 4 = \dfrac{3}{y}$

31. If 3 is added to the reciprocal of a number, the result is $\frac{11}{3}$ decreased by the reciprocal of the given number. Find the number.

$$Chapter\ \mathbf{16}$$

Constructions

When draftspersons draw scale drawings for blueprints, they may use rulers to measure lengths, protractors to measure angles, and parallel rulers to draw parallel lines. In your work in geometry, when you *draw* a figure, you may also use these instruments. However, when you **construct** a figure in geometry, you may use only the two tools of geometry: the straightedge, which is an unmarked ruler, and the compasses. The straightedge is used to draw a line, and a pair of compasses is used to locate points at any given distance from a fixed point.

This chapter presents important constructions, the methods of performing these constructions, and plans for proving that the constructions are valid.

16-1　BASIC CONSTRUCTIONS

The first six constructions presented here are the basic procedures. In all of the constructions, a pair of compasses is used. The point of the compasses is fixed as the center of a circle, while the pencil point draws an arc, a part of a circle. If the distance between the points of the pair of compasses is not changed, all arcs drawn are arcs of congruent circles and all line segments from a center to a point on an arc are radii of congruent circles. To prove that a construction has accomplished what was required, we use the following postulate.

● **POSTULATE 52.　Radii of congruent circles are congruent.**

Construction 1

To construct a line segment congruent (equal in length) to a given line segment.

Given:　$\overline{AB}$.

Required: To construct a line segment, $\overline{XY}$, congruent to $\overline{AB}$.

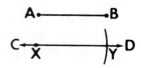

Construction:

1. With a straightedge, draw any line, $\overleftrightarrow{CD}$, and mark a point X on it.

2. On $\overline{AB}$, place the compasses so that the point is at A and the pencil point is at B.

3. Keeping the setting on your compasses, place the point at X and draw an arc intersecting $\overleftrightarrow{CD}$ at Y.

Conclusion: $\overline{XY} \cong \overline{AB}$.

Plan for Proof: The construction makes $\overline{XY} \cong \overline{AB}$ because $\overline{XY}$ and $\overline{AB}$ are radii of congruent circles.

Construction 2

To bisect a given line segment.

[To construct the perpendicular bisector of a given line segment.]

Given: $\overline{AB}$.

Required: To bisect $\overline{AB}$.

Construction:

1. Open the compasses so that the distance between the point and the pencil point (this distance will be called the radius) is more than half the length of $\overline{AB}$.

2. Using point A as a center, draw one arc above $\overline{AB}$ and one arc below $\overline{AB}$.

3. Using the same radius and point B as a center, draw another pair of arcs, one above $\overline{AB}$ and the other below $\overline{AB}$, which intersect the first pair of arcs at points C and D.

4. Use a straightedge to draw $\overleftrightarrow{CD}$ intersecting $\overline{AB}$ at E.

Conclusion: The construction makes $\overleftrightarrow{CD}$ the perpendicular bisector of $\overline{AB}$. Therefore, $\overline{AE} \cong \overline{EB}$.

Plan for Proof: If $\overline{CA}$, $\overline{CB}$, $\overline{DA}$, and $\overline{DB}$ are drawn, the construction makes $\overline{CA} \cong \overline{CB}$ and $\overline{DA} \cong \overline{DB}$ (radii of congruent circles are congruent). Therefore, $\overleftrightarrow{CD}$ is the perpendicular bisector of $\overline{AB}$ because two points, each equidistant from the endpoints of a line segment, determine the perpendicular bisector of the line segment.

Construction 3

To construct an angle congruent to a given angle.

Given: ∠ABC and point D.

Required: To construct at D an angle congruent to ∠ABC.

Construction:

1. Through point D, draw any line, $\overleftrightarrow{RS}$.

2. With B as a center and any convenient radius, draw an arc that intersects $\overrightarrow{BC}$ at E and $\overrightarrow{BA}$ at F.

3. With D as a center and using the same radius as in step 2, draw an arc that intersects $\overrightarrow{DS}$ at G. Label this arc $\overparen{GJ}$.

4. With the compasses, measure the distance EF. With G as a center and a radius whose length is EF, draw an arc that intersects $\overparen{GJ}$ at H.

5. Draw $\overrightarrow{DH}$.

Conclusion: ∠HDS ≅ ∠ABC.

Plan for Proof: If $\overline{GH}$ is drawn, the construction makes $\overline{DH} \cong \overline{BF}$, $\overline{DG} \cong \overline{BE}$, $\overline{GH} \cong \overline{EF}$. Therefore, △DHG ≅ △BFE by s.s.s. ≅ s.s.s. Hence, ∠HDS ≅ ∠ABC.

Construction 4

To bisect a given angle.

[To construct the bisector of a given angle.]

Given: ∠ABC.

Required: To bisect ∠ABC.

Construction:

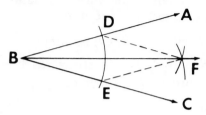

1. With B as a center and any convenient radius, draw an arc that intersects $\overrightarrow{BA}$ at D and $\overrightarrow{BC}$ at E.

2. With D and E as centers and with equal radii of sufficient length, draw arcs that intersect at F.

3. Draw $\overrightarrow{BF}$.

Conclusion: Since $\angle ABF \cong \angle CBF$, then $\overrightarrow{BF}$ bisects $\angle ABC$.

Plan for Proof: If $\overline{FD}$ and $\overline{FE}$ are drawn, then the construction makes $\overline{BD} \cong \overline{BE}$ and $\overline{DF} \cong \overline{EF}$. Also, $\overline{BF} \cong \overline{BF}$. Thus $\triangle BDF \cong \triangle BEF$ by s.s.s. $\cong$ s.s.s. Hence, $\angle ABF \cong \angle CBF$.

Construction 5

To construct a line perpendicular to a given line through a given point on the line.

Given: Point P is on $\overleftrightarrow{AB}$.

Required: To construct a line through P perpendicular to $\overleftrightarrow{AB}$.

Construction:

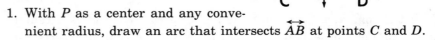

1. With P as a center and any convenient radius, draw an arc that intersects $\overleftrightarrow{AB}$ at points C and D.

2. With C and D as centers and with a radius greater in length than the one used before, draw arcs that intersect at E.

3. Draw $\overleftrightarrow{EP}$.

Conclusion: $\overleftrightarrow{EP}$ is perpendicular to $\overleftrightarrow{AB}$ at P.

Plan for Proof: The construction bisects straight angle APB. Angle APE and angle BPE are right angles. Therefore, $\overleftrightarrow{EP}$ is perpendicular to $\overleftrightarrow{AB}$ because two lines that intersect at right angles are perpendicular to each other.

Construction 6

To construct a line perpendicular to a given line through a given point outside the line.

Given: Point P is outside $\overleftrightarrow{AB}$.

Required: To construct a line through P perpendicular to $\overleftrightarrow{AB}$.

Construction:

1. With P as a center and any convenient radius, draw an arc that intersects $\overleftrightarrow{AB}$ at C and D.

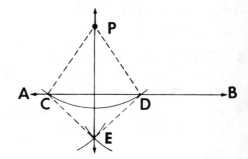

2. With C and D as centers and with a radius greater in length than $\frac{1}{2}CD$, draw arcs that intersect at E.

3. Draw $\overleftrightarrow{EP}$.

Conclusion: $\overleftrightarrow{EP}$ is perpendicular to $\overleftrightarrow{AB}$.

Plan for Proof: If $\overline{PC}, \overline{PD}, \overline{EC}$, and $\overline{ED}$ are drawn, the construction makes $\overline{PC} \cong \overline{PD}$ and $\overline{EC} \cong \overline{ED}$. Therefore, $\overleftrightarrow{PE}$ is the perpendicular bisector of $\overline{CD}$ because two points each equidistant from the endpoints of a line segment determine the perpendicular bisector of the line segment. Hence, $\overleftrightarrow{PE}$ is perpendicular to $\overleftrightarrow{AB}$.

EXERCISES

In 1–6, draw the given figures and do the required constructions. (Where needed, enlarge the given figures for your convenience.)

1. *Given:* Line segment AB.

   Required:
   a. Copy $\overline{AB}$.
   b. Construct a line segment whose measure is twice AB.
   c. Construct the perpendicular bisector of $\overline{AB}$.
   d. Construct a line segment whose measure is $2\frac{1}{2}(AB)$.

2. *Given:* Acute $\angle A$.

   Required:
   a. Copy $\angle A$.
   b. Construct an angle whose measure is $2(m\angle A)$.
   c. Construct the bisector of $\angle A$.
   d. Construct an angle whose measure is $1\frac{1}{2}(m\angle A)$.

3. *Given:* Line segments a and b.

   Required:
   a. Construct an isosceles triangle with base a and leg b.
   b. Construct an equilateral triangle with side a.
   c. Construct a line segment whose measure is $a + b$.
   d. Construct a line segment whose measure is $a - b$.

4. *Given:* Point *P*.   •**P**

Required:
a. Construct an angle whose measure is 60° and whose vertex is *P*.
b. Construct an angle whose measure is 30° and whose vertex is *P*.
c. Construct an angle whose measure is 15° and whose vertex is *P*.
d. Construct an angle whose measure is 75° and whose vertex is *P*.

5. *Given:* Point *P* not on line ℓ.   •**P**

Required: ℓ
a. Construct a line through *P*
that is perpendicular to ℓ.
b. Construct an angle whose measure is 45°.
c. Construct an angle whose measure is 135°.

6. *Given:* Acute △*ABC*.

Required:
a. Construct by s.s.s. a triangle
that is congruent to △*ABC*.
b. Construct by s.a.s. a triangle that is congruent to △*ABC*.
c. Construct by a.s.a. a triangle that is congruent to △*ABC*.

7. Draw any two points *A* and *P*. Construct *A'*, the image of *A* under a reflection in *P*.

8. Draw any line, $\overleftrightarrow{PQ}$, and any point, *A*, that is not on $\overleftrightarrow{PQ}$. Construct *A'*, the image of *A* under a reflection in $\overleftrightarrow{PQ}$.

9. Draw any two points *A* and *P*.
a. Construct *A'*, the image of *A* under a rotation of 90° about *P* in the counterclockwise direction.
b. Construct *A''*, the image of *A* under a rotation of 45° about *P* in the clockwise direction.

10. Prove Construction 1.   **11.** Prove Construction 2.
12. Prove Construction 3.   **13.** Prove Construction 4.
14. Prove Construction 5.   **15.** Prove Construction 6.

16-2   USING THE BASIC CONSTRUCTIONS

Each of the constructions that follows uses one or more of the basic constructions. In each case, some definition or previously proved theorem is used to develop the method of the construction.

Construction 7

To construct an altitude of a given triangle.

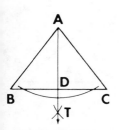

Acute Triangle

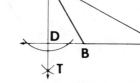

Obtuse Triangle

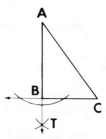

Right Triangle

Given: △ABC.

Required: To construct an altitude from vertex A to side $\overline{CB}$.

Construction:

Through point A, construct $\overrightarrow{AT}$, a ray perpendicular to $\overline{CB}$. Extend $\overleftrightarrow{CB}$ through an endpoint of $\overline{CB}$ if necessary.

Conclusion:

In acute triangle ABC, $\overrightarrow{AT}$ intersects $\overline{CB}$ at D. $\overline{AD}$ is the altitude from vertex A to side $\overline{CB}$.

In obtuse triangle ABC, $\overrightarrow{AT}$ intersects $\overleftrightarrow{CB}$, the line containing $\overline{CB}$, at D. $\overline{AD}$ is the altitude from vertex A to side $\overline{CB}$.

In right triangle ABC, $\overrightarrow{AT}$ intersects $\overline{CB}$ at B. $\overline{AB}$ is the altitude from vertex A to side $\overline{CB}$.

Plan for Proof: For each type of triangle ABC, $\overrightarrow{AT}$ is perpendicular to $\overline{CB}$. Therefore, $\overline{AD}$ is the altitude from vertex A to side $\overline{CB}$ because an altitude of a triangle is the line segment from a vertex perpendicular to the opposite side (or the line containing that side).

Note. If the three altitudes of a triangle are constructed, they will all intersect in the same point. In the case of the acute triangle, the three altitudes will intersect in the interior of the triangle; in the case of the obtuse triangle, in the exterior of the triangle; and in the case of the right triangle, at the vertex of the right angle. Hence, the three altitudes of a triangle are *concurrent*.

Construction 8

To construct a median of a given triangle.

Given: △ABC.

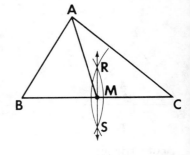

Required: To construct a median from vertex A to side $\overline{BC}$.

Construction:

1. Construct $\overleftrightarrow{RS}$, the perpendicular bisector of $\overline{BC}$.

2. $\overleftrightarrow{RS}$ intersects $\overline{BC}$ at M.

3. Draw $\overline{AM}$.

Conclusion: $\overline{AM}$ is the median from vertex A to side $\overline{BC}$.

Plan for Proof: Since $\overleftrightarrow{RS}$ is the perpendicular bisector of $\overline{BC}$, point M is the midpoint of $\overline{BC}$. Therefore, $\overline{AM}$ is the median from vertex A to side $\overline{BC}$ because a median of a triangle is the line segment that joins a vertex and the midpoint of the opposite side.

Note. If the three medians of a triangle are constructed, they will all intersect in the same point in the interior of the triangle. Hence, the three medians of a triangle are *concurrent*.

Construction 9

To construct the bisector of an angle of a given triangle.

Given: △ABC.

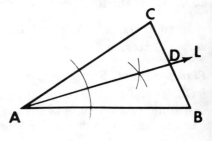

Required: To construct the bisector of ∠A.

Construction:

1. Construct $\overrightarrow{AL}$, the bisector of ∠A.

2. Label as D the point where $\overrightarrow{AL}$ intersects $\overline{BC}$, the side opposite ∠A.

Conclusion: $\overline{AD}$ is the bisector of ∠A in △ABC.

Plan for Proof: Since $\overrightarrow{AL}$ bisects ∠A, $\overline{AD}$ is the bisector of ∠A in △ABC because a bisector of an angle of a triangle is the line segment, drawn from a vertex, that bisects that angle and that terminates in the opposite side.

Note. If the bisectors of the three angles of a triangle are constructed, they will all intersect in the same point in the interior of the triangle. Hence, the three angle bisectors of a triangle are *concurrent*.

Construction 10

To construct a line parallel to a given line through a given external point.

Given: $\overleftrightarrow{AB}$ and external point P.

Required: Through P, to construct a line parallel to $\overleftrightarrow{AB}$.

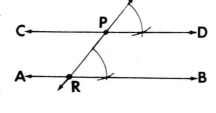

Construction:

1. Through P, draw any line, intersecting $\overleftrightarrow{AB}$ at R. Let S be any point on the ray opposite $\overrightarrow{PR}$.

2. At P, construct $\angle SPD \cong \angle PRB$, to make a pair of congruent corresponding angles.

Conclusion: $\overleftrightarrow{PD}$ passes through P and is parallel to $\overleftrightarrow{AB}$.

Plan for Proof: The construction makes $\angle SPD \cong \angle PRB$. Therefore, $\overleftrightarrow{AB} \parallel \overleftrightarrow{PD}$ because if two lines are cut by a transversal making a pair of corresponding angles congruent, the lines are parallel.

Construction 11

To construct an angle of 60° with a given point as vertex, or to construct an equilateral triangle.

Given: Point A.

Required: To construct an angle containing 60° whose vertex is A.

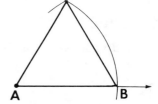

Construction:

1. Draw a ray with endpoint A, and any point B.

2. Using A as the center and a radius whose length is equal to AB, draw an arc.

3. Using B as the center and a radius whose length is equal to AB, draw another arc that intersects the first arc at C.

4. Draw $\overline{CA}$ and $\overline{CB}$, forming equilateral triangle ABC.

Conclusion: ∠ *CAB* contains 60°.

Plan for Proof: The construction makes △ *ABC* an equilateral triangle. Since an equilateral triangle is equiangular, m∠ *CAB* = $\frac{1}{3}$ of 180, or m∠ *CAB* = 60.

Construction 12

To construct a triangle similar to a given triangle on a given line segment as a base.

Given: △ *ABC* and $\overline{RS}$.

Required: On $\overline{RS}$, corresponding to side $\overline{AB}$ of △ *ABC*, to construct a triangle similar to △ *ABC*.

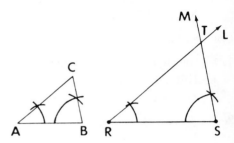

Construction:

1. At *R*, construct ∠ *SRL* congruent to ∠ *BAC*.

2. With $\overrightarrow{SR}$ as one ray, construct ∠ *RSM* congruent to ∠ *ABC*.

3. Represent by *T* the point of intersection of $\overrightarrow{RL}$ and $\overrightarrow{SM}$.

Conclusion: The required triangle is △ *RST*.

Plan for Proof: The construction makes ∠ *R* ≅ ∠ *A* and ∠ *S* ≅ ∠ *B*. Therefore, △ *RST* ~ △ *ABC* because two triangles are similar if two angles of one triangle are congruent respectively to two angles of the other triangle.

Construction 13

To divide a given line segment into any number of congruent parts.

Given: $\overline{AB}$.

Required: To divide $\overline{AB}$ into any number of congruent parts (for example, three congruent parts).

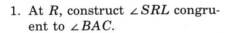

Construction:

1. Draw $\overrightarrow{AR}$, making any convenient angle *BAR*.

2. On $\overrightarrow{AR}$, start at *A* and lay off any convenient length, *AC*, the required number of times, so that *AC* = *CD* = *DE*. Draw $\overline{EB}$.

3. Through *D*, construct $\overrightarrow{DG} \parallel \overline{EB}$. Through *C*, construct $\overrightarrow{CF} \parallel \overline{EB}$.

Conclusion: $\overline{AF}$, $\overline{FG}$, and $\overline{GB}$ are the three congruent parts of $\overline{AB}$.

   Note: This construction also determines proportional segments. For example, *AF*:*FB* = 1:2.

Plan for Proof: The construction makes $\overline{AC} \cong \overline{CD} \cong \overline{DE}$ and also makes $\overrightarrow{CF} \parallel \overrightarrow{DG} \parallel \overline{EB}$. Therefore, $\overline{AF} \cong \overline{FG} \cong \overline{GB}$ because if three or more parallel lines cut off segments of equal length on one transversal, they cut off segments of equal length on any transversal.

Construction 14

To construct a circle circumscribed about a given triangle.

Given: △ *ABC*.

Required: To circumscribe a circle about △ *ABC*.

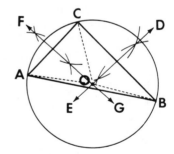

Construction:

1. Construct $\overleftrightarrow{DE}$ and $\overleftrightarrow{FG}$, the perpendicular bisectors of $\overline{BC}$ and $\overline{AC}$.

2. Using as the center point *O*, the point of intersection of the perpendicular bisectors, construct a circle with radius of length *OA*.

Conclusion: Circle *O* is the required circle.

Plan for Proof: Draw $\overline{OA}$, $\overline{OC}$, and $\overline{OB}$. Since $\overleftrightarrow{FG}$ is the perpendicular bisector of $\overline{AC}$, *OA* = *OC* because any point on the perpendicular bisector of a line segment is equidistant from the endpoints of the segment. Similarly, since $\overleftrightarrow{DE}$ is the perpendicular bisector of $\overline{BC}$, *OC* = *OB*. Hence, *OA* = *OB* = *OC*. Therefore, a circle with *O* as its center and a radius whose length is *OA* passes through *A*, *B*, and *C*. That is, circle *O* circumscribes △ *ABC*.

EXERCISES ──────────────────────────────────

In 1–6, draw the given figures and do the required constructions. (Where needed, draw separate figures for parts **a**, **b**, etc., and enlarge the given figures for your convenience.)

1. *Given:* Obtuse $\triangle ABC$.

   Required:
   a. Construct the median to $\overline{AC}$.
   b. Construct the bisector of $\angle A$.
   c. Construct the altitude to $\overline{AC}$.
   d. Construct the altitude to $\overline{BC}$.
   e. Construct the perpendicular bisector of $\overline{BC}$.

2. *Given:* Parallel lines ℓ and m.

   Required:
   a. Construct a line that is parallel to ℓ and to m, and is above ℓ.
   b. Construct a line that is parallel to ℓ and to m, and is below m.
   c. Construct a line that is parallel to ℓ and to m, and is anywhere between ℓ and m.
   d. Construct a line that is parallel to ℓ and to m, and is exactly midway between ℓ and m.

   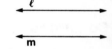

3. *Given:* Line segments a and b, and $\angle A$.

   Required:
   a. Construct a rectangle with base a and altitude b.
   b. Construct a square with side a.
   c. Construct a parallelogram with consecutive sides a and b and an angle congruent to $\angle A$.
   d. Construct a rhombus with side a and an angle congruent to $\angle A$.

4. *Given:* $\triangle ABC$ and $\overline{PQ}$.

   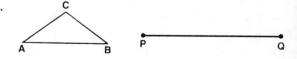

   Required: Construct $\triangle PQR$ so that $\dfrac{AB}{PQ} = \dfrac{BC}{QR} = \dfrac{CA}{RP}$.

5. *Given:* $\overline{AB}$.

Required:

a. Divide $\overline{AB}$ into four congruent parts, using Construction 13.

b. Divide $\overline{AB}$ into four congruent parts, using the construction of a perpendicular bisector.

c. Explain when the method used in part **a** *must* be used to divide a given line segment into any number of congruent parts and when the method involving the perpendicular bisector can be used.

6. *Given:* Right $\triangle ABC$.

Required:

a. Circumscribe a circle about $\triangle ABC$.

b. Describe the position of hypotenuse $\overline{AB}$ with respect to the circumscribed circle.

7. Draw $\triangle ABC$ and point A'. Construct $\triangle A'B'C'$, the image of $\triangle ABC$ under a translation.

8. Draw $\triangle ABC$ and point P. **a.** Construct $\triangle A'B'C'$, the image of $\triangle ABC$ under a dilation with center at P and constant of dilation 2. **b.** Construct $\triangle A''B''C''$, the image of $\triangle ABC$ under a dilation with center at P and constant of dilation $\frac{1}{2}$.

16-3 REVIEW EXERCISES

In 1–6, draw the given figures and do the required constructions. (Where needed, enlarge the given figures for convenience.)

1. *Given:* $\overline{AB}$.

Required:

a. Construct a 30°–60° right triangle with hypotenuse $\overline{AB}$.

b. Construct an isosceles right triangle with hypotenuse $\overline{AB}$.

c. Construct an isosceles right triangle with leg $\overline{AB}$.

2. *Given:* $\overline{AB}$.

Required:

a. Construct $\overline{A'B'}$ so that $AB:A'B' = 1:4$.

b. Construct $\overline{A'B'}$ so that $AB:A'B' = 2:5$.

c. Construct $\overline{A'B'}$ so that $AB:A'B' = 3:4$.

d. Construct P on $\overline{AB}$ so that $AP:PB = 1:3$.

e. Construct P on $\overline{AB}$ so that $AP:PB = 1:4$.

f. Construct P on $\overline{AB}$ so that $AP:PB = 2:3$.

3. *Given:* $\overline{PR}$ and $\overline{PS}$.

P •———————• R P •———————————————• S

Required:

a. Construct a right triangle with legs $\overline{PR}$ and $\overline{PS}$.

b. Construct a right triangle with leg $\overline{PR}$ and hypotenuse $\overline{PS}$.

4. *Given:* $\overline{AB}$ and $\overline{CD}$.

A •——• B C •————————————————• D

Required:

a. Construct an isosceles triangle with base $\overline{AB}$ and the sum of the measures of the legs equal to CD.

b. Construct an isosceles triangle with the measure of the altitude equal to AB and the sum of the measures of the legs equal to CD.

c. Construct an equilateral triangle with the perimeter equal to CD.

d. Construct an isosceles triangle with perimeter equal to CD and the measure of the base equal to one-half the measure of a leg.

5. *Given:* $\overline{AB}$ and $\overline{AC}$.

A •————————• B A •————————————————• C

Required:

a. Construct a parallelogram with adjacent sides $\overline{AB}$ and $\overline{AC}$ and $m\angle A = 60$.

b. Construct a parallelogram with adjacent sides $\overline{AB}$ and $\overline{AC}$ and $m\angle A = 30$.

c. Construct a parallelogram with adjacent sides $\overline{AB}$ and $\overline{AC}$ and $m\angle A = 120$.

6. *Given:* $\overline{PQ}$ and $\angle P$.

Required:

a. Construct a rhombus with side $\overline{PQ}$ and one angle congruent to $\angle P$.

P •————————• Q

b. Construct a rhombus with side $\overline{PQ}$ and one angle equal in measure to one-half $m\angle P$.

Summary of Formulas and Numerical Relationships

1 ANGLE RELATIONSHIPS

1. The sum of the measures of supplementary angles is 180. If the measure of an angle is represented by x, then the measure of its supplement is represented by $(180 - x)$.
2. The sum of the measures of complementary angles is 90. If the measure of an acute angle is represented by x, then the measure of its complement is represented by $(90 - x)$.
3. In any $\triangle ABC$, $m\angle A + m\angle B + m\angle C = 180$.
4. Corresponding angles of congruent polygons are equal in measure.
5. Vertical angles are equal in measure.
6. Base angles of an isosceles triangle are equal in measure.
7. The sum of the measures of the acute angles of a right triangle is 90.
8. The measure of an exterior angle of a triangle is equal to the sum of the measures of the two nonadjacent interior angles.
9. If two parallel lines are cut by a transversal, then:
   a. alternate interior angles are equal in measure.
   b. alternate exterior angles are equal in measure.
   c. corresponding angles are equal in measure.
   d. the sum of the measures of two interior angles on the same side of the transversal is 180.
10. In any quadrilateral $ABCD$, $m\angle A + m\angle B + m\angle C + m\angle D = 360$.
11. The opposite angles of a parallelogram are equal in measure.
12. The sum of the measures of two consecutive angles of a parallelogram is 180.
13. The measure of an angle formed by intersecting lines that are perpendicular is 90.
14. The diagonals of a rhombus meet at right angles.
15. For any polygon of n sides:
    a. the sum of the measures of its interior angles is equal to $180(n - 2)$.
    b. the sum of the measures of its exterior angles is 360.
16. For a regular polygon of n sides (all sides are congruent and all angles are congruent):
    a. the measure of one interior angle is $\dfrac{180(n - 2)}{n}$.
    b. the measure of one exterior angle is $\dfrac{360}{n}$.

2   LENGTH OF SEGMENTS

1. Corresponding sides of congruent polygons are equal in length.
2. The legs of an isosceles triangle are equal in length.
3. The legs of an isosceles trapezoid are equal in length.
4. Opposite sides of a parallelogram are equal in length.
5. The diagonals of a parallelogram bisect each other. Thus, each diagonal is separated into two segments that are equal in length.
6. The diagonals of a rectangle (and square) are equal in length.
7. The sides of a rhombus (and square) are equal in length.
8. The length of a line segment that joins the midpoints of two sides of a triangle is equal to one-half the length of the third side.

3   PROPORTION AND PRODUCT RELATIONSHIPS

1. In a proportion, the product of the means is equal to the product of the extremes. That is, if $a:b = c:d$ or if $\dfrac{a}{b} = \dfrac{c}{d}$, then $bc = ad$.
2. A line parallel to one side of a triangle divides the other two sides of the triangle proportionally.
3. Corresponding sides of similar polygons are in proportion.
4. In similar polygons, perimeters p and p' have the same ratio as the lengths of any two corresponding sides s and s'. That is, $p:p' = s:s'$.
5. If the altitude is drawn to the hypotenuse of a right triangle:
   a. the length of the altitude is the mean proportional between the lengths of the segments of the hypotenuse.
   b. the length of each leg is the mean proportional between the length of the whole hypotenuse and the length of the projection of that leg on the hypotenuse.

4   RIGHT TRIANGLE RELATIONSHIPS

1. In a right triangle, when a and b are the lengths of the legs and c is the length of the hypotenuse (the longest side of the triangle), then $a^2 + b^2 = c^2$.
2. In a 30-60-degree right triangle, if the length of the side opposite the 30° angle is represented by x, then:
   a. the length of the hypotenuse (opposite the 90° angle) is equal to $2x$.
   b. the length of the side opposite the 60° angle is equal to $x\sqrt{3}$.

3. In an equilateral triangle whose side has a length of s, the length of an altitude is $\frac{1}{2}s\sqrt{3}$.

4. In a 45-45-degree right triangle, if the length of a side opposite a 45° angle is represented by x, then the length of the hypotenuse (opposite the 90° angle) is equal to $x\sqrt{2}$.

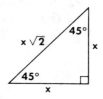

5. In a square whose side has a length of s, the length of a diagonal is $s\sqrt{2}$.

6. In a square whose diagonal has a length of d, the length of a side of the square is $\frac{1}{2}d\sqrt{2}$.

5   TRIGONOMETRIC RELATIONSHIPS

In right $\triangle ABC$:

$$\sin A = \frac{\text{length of leg opposite } \angle A}{\text{length of hypotenuse}} = \frac{a}{c}.$$

$$\cos A = \frac{\text{length of leg adjacent to } \angle A}{\text{length of hypotenuse}} = \frac{b}{c}.$$

$$\tan A = \frac{\text{length of leg opposite to } \angle A}{\text{length of leg adjacent to } \angle A} = \frac{a}{b}.$$

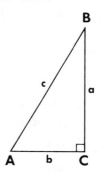

6   AREA RELATIONSHIPS

1. Area of rectangle $= bh$, where b is the length of the base and h is the length of the altitude. Also, area of a rectangle $= lw$, where l and w are the measures of the length and width of the rectangle.

2. Area of a square $= s^2$, where s is the length of a side of the square.

3. Area of a parallelogram $= bh$, where b is the length of a base and h is the length of an altitude drawn to the base.

4. Area of a triangle $= \frac{1}{2}bh$, where b is the length of a side (base) of the triangle and h is the length of an altitude drawn to that side.

5. Area of a trapezoid $= \frac{1}{2}(b_1 + b_2)h$, where b_1 and b_2 are the lengths of the bases and h is the length of the altitude.

6. Area of a rhombus $= \frac{1}{2}d_1 d_2$, where d_1 and d_2 are the lengths of the diagonals of the rhombus.

7. In similar polygons, areas A and A' have the same ratio as the squares of the lengths of any two corresponding sides s and s'. That is, $A:A' = (s)^2:(s')^2$.

7   INEQUALITY RELATIONSHIPS

1. A whole is greater than any of its parts.
2. The sum of the lengths of two sides of a triangle is greater than the length of the third side.
3. The measure of an exterior angle of a triangle is greater than the measure of either nonadjacent interior angle.
4. If two sides of a triangle are unequal, the angles opposite these sides are unequal and the greater angle lies opposite the greater side.
5. If two angles of a triangle are unequal, the sides opposite these angles are unequal and the greater side lies opposite the greater angle.

8   COORDINATE GEOMETRY

1. The distance d between two points (x_1, y_1) and (x_2, y_2) is given by the formula $d = \sqrt{(x_2 - x_1)^2 + (y_2 - y_1)^2}$.

2. If a line segment joins the endpoints (x_1, y_1) and (x_2, y_2), the coordinates of the midpoint of the segment are $\left(\dfrac{x_1 + x_2}{2}, \dfrac{y_1 + y_2}{2}\right)$.

3. If a line passes through the points (x_1, y_1) and (x_2, y_2), where $x_1 \neq x_2$, the slope of the line $= m = \dfrac{\triangle y}{\triangle x} = \dfrac{y_2 - y_1}{x_2 - x_1}$.

4. A vertical line has no slope, and all vertical lines are parallel.
5. The slope of a horizontal line is 0.
6. If two nonvertical lines are parallel, then their slopes are equal. That is, if m_1 is the slope of one line and m_2 is the slope of a second line and the lines are parallel, then $m_1 = m_2$.
7. If two nonvertical lines are perpendicular, then the slope of one line is the negative reciprocal of the slope of the other line. That is, $m_1 = -\dfrac{1}{m_2}$, or $m_2 = -\dfrac{1}{m_1}$, or $m_1 m_2 = -1$.

8. A horizontal line (slope of zero) and a vertical line (no slope) are perpendicular.
9. An equation of a line parallel to the y-axis is $x = a$, where a is the abscissa of every point on the line.
10. An equation of a line parallel to the x-axis is $y = b$, where b is the ordinate of every point on the line.
11. An equation of the line passing through the point (x_1, y_1) and having the slope m is $y - y_1 = m(x - x_1)$.
12. An equation of the line whose slope is m and whose y-intercept is b is $y = mx + b$.
13. The equation of a circle whose center is the origin $(0, 0)$ and whose radius has a length of r is $x^2 + y^2 = r^2$.
14. The equation of a circle whose center is the point (a, b) and whose radius has a length of r is $(x - a)^2 + (y - b)^2 = r^2$.

9   QUADRATIC EQUATIONS

1. The graph of every equation of the form $y = ax^2 + bx + c$, where a, b, and c are real numbers and $a \neq 0$, is a parabola.
2. For the parabola $y = ax^2 + bx + c$, the equation of its axis of symmetry is $x = \dfrac{-b}{2a}$.
3. In $y = ax^2 + bx + c$, the leading coefficient is a. If a is positive, the parabola opens upward and contains a minimum point. If a is negative, the parabola opens downward and contains a maximum point.
4. The x-intercepts formed when the graph of the parabola $y = ax^2 + bx + c$ crosses the x-axis are the real roots of the quadratic equation $ax^2 + bx + c = 0$.
5. The two roots of the equation $ax^2 + bx + c = 0$, where $a \neq 0$, are found by the quadratic formula: $x = \dfrac{-b \pm \sqrt{b^2 - 4ac}}{2a}$.

10   PROBABILITY FORMULAS

1. For fair, unbiased objects, $P(E) = \dfrac{n(E)}{n(S)}$, where:

   $P(E)$ represents the probability of event E.

   $n(E)$ represents the number of elements of event E or the number of ways that event E can occur.

   $n(S)$ represents the number of elements or possible outcomes in sample space S.

2. The probability of an impossible event is zero, or $P(\{\ \}) = 0$.
3. The probability of an event that is certain to occur is 1.
4. For any event E: $0 \leq P(E) \leq 1$.
5. $P(A$ and $B) = P(A \cap B) = \dfrac{n(A \cap B)}{n(S)}$.
6. $P(A$ or $B) = P(A) + P(B) - P(A$ and $B)$; or, in terms of sets, $P(A \cup B) = P(A) + P(B) - P(A \cap B)$.
7. $P(\text{not } A) = 1 - P(A)$; or $P(\overline{A}) = 1 - P(A)$.
8. The probability of any event is equal to the sum of the probabilities of the singleton outcomes in the event.
9. The Counting Principle: If one activity can occur in m ways and, following this, a second activity can occur in n ways, then both activities can occur in the order given in $m \cdot n$ ways.
10. The Counting Principle with probabilities: If events E and F are independent events, $P(E) = m$ and $P(F) = n$, then the probability of E and F occurring jointly is the product mn.

11. In permutations (or arrangements), order is important.
    a. "The permutation of n things, taken n at a time" is given by
    $$_nP_n = n! = n(n-1)(n-2)\ldots 3 \cdot 2 \cdot 1$$
    b. "The permutation of n things, taken r at a time" where $r \leq n$ is found by:
    $$_nP_r = \underbrace{n(n-1)(n-2)\ldots}_{r \text{ factors}}$$

12. The number of permutations of n things, taken n at a time, with r of these things identical, is given by $\dfrac{n!}{r!}$.

13. In combinations (or sets), order is not important.
    a. "The combination of n things, taken r at a time" where $r \leq n$ is found by:
    $$_nC_r = \frac{_nP_r}{r!}$$
    b. $_nC_n = 1$.
    c. $_nC_0 = 1$.
    d. For whole numbers n and r where $r \leq n$: $_nC_r = {_nC_{n-r}}$.

Squares and Square Roots

No.	Square	Square Root	No.	Square	Square Root	No.	Square	Square Root
1	1	1.000	51	2,601	7.141	101	10,201	10.050
2	4	1.414	52	2,704	7.211	102	10,404	10.100
3	9	1.732	53	2,809	7.280	103	10,609	10.149
4	16	2.000	54	2,916	7.348	104	10,816	10.198
5	25	2.236	55	3,025	7.416	105	11,025	10.247
6	36	2.449	56	3,136	7.483	106	11,236	10.296
7	49	2.646	57	3,249	7.550	107	11,449	10.344
8	64	2.828	58	3,364	7.616	108	11,664	10.392
9	81	3.000	59	3,481	7.681	109	11,881	10.440
10	100	3.162	60	3,600	7.746	110	12,100	10.488
11	121	3.317	61	3,721	7.810	111	12,321	10.536
12	144	3.464	62	3,844	7.874	112	12,544	10.583
13	169	3.606	63	3,969	7.937	113	12,769	10.630
14	196	3.742	64	4,096	8.000	114	12,996	10.677
15	225	3.873	65	4,225	8.062	115	13,225	10.724
16	256	4.000	66	4,356	8.124	116	13,456	10.770
17	289	4.123	67	4,489	8.185	117	13,689	10.817
18	324	4.243	68	4,624	8.246	118	13,924	10.863
19	361	4.359	69	4,761	8.307	119	14,161	10.909
20	400	4.472	70	4,900	8.367	120	14,400	10.954
21	441	4.583	71	5,041	8.426	121	14,641	11.000
22	484	4.690	72	5,184	8.485	122	14,884	11.045
23	529	4.796	73	5,329	8.544	123	15,129	11.091
24	576	4.899	74	5,476	8.602	124	15,376	11.136
25	625	5.000	75	5,625	8.660	125	15,625	11.180
26	676	5.099	76	5,776	8.718	126	15,876	11.225
27	729	5.196	77	5,929	8.775	127	16,129	11.269
28	784	5.292	78	6,084	8.832	128	16,384	11.314
29	841	5.385	79	6,241	8.888	129	16,641	11.358
30	900	5.477	80	6,400	8.944	130	16,900	11.402
31	961	5.568	81	6,561	9.000	131	17,161	11.446
32	1,024	5.657	82	6,724	9.055	132	17,424	11.489
33	1,089	5.745	83	6,889	9.110	133	17,689	11.533
34	1,156	5.831	84	7,056	9.165	134	17,956	11.576
35	1,225	5.916	85	7,225	9.220	135	18,225	11.619
36	1,296	6.000	86	7,396	9.274	136	18,496	11.662
37	1,369	6.083	87	7,569	9.327	137	18,769	11.705
38	1,444	6.164	88	7,744	9.381	138	19,044	11.747
39	1,521	6.245	89	7,921	9.434	139	19,321	11.790
40	1,600	6.325	90	8,100	9.487	140	19,600	11.832
41	1,681	6.403	91	8,281	9.539	141	19,881	11.874
42	1,764	6.481	92	8,464	9.592	142	20,164	11.916
43	1,849	6.557	93	8,649	9.644	143	20,449	11.958
44	1,936	6.633	94	8,836	9.695	144	20,736	12.000
45	2,025	6.708	95	9,025	9.747	145	21,025	12.042
46	2,116	6.782	96	9,216	9.798	146	21,316	12.083
47	2,209	6.856	97	9,409	9.849	147	21,609	12.124
48	2,304	6.928	98	9,604	9.899	148	21,904	12.166
49	2,401	7.000	99	9,801	9.950	149	22,201	12.207
50	2,500	7.071	100	10,000	10.000	150	22,500	12.247

Values of the Trigonometric Functions

Angle	Sine	Cosine	Tangent	Angle	Sine	Cosine	Tangent
1°	.0175	.9998	.0175	46°	.7193	.6947	1.0355
2°	.0349	.9994	.0349	47°	.7314	.6820	1.0724
3°	.0523	.9986	.0524	48°	.7431	.6691	1.1106
4°	.0698	.9976	.0699	49°	.7547	.6561	1.1504
5°	.0872	.9962	.0875	50°	.7660	.6428	1.1918
6°	.1045	.9945	.1051	51°	.7771	.6293	1.2349
7°	.1219	.9925	.1228	52°	.7880	.6157	1.2799
8°	.1392	.9903	.1405	53°	.7986	.6018	1.3270
9°	.1564	.9877	.1584	54°	.8090	.5878	1.3764
10°	.1736	.9848	.1763	55°	.8192	.5736	1.4281
11°	.1908	.9816	.1944	56°	.8290	.5592	1.4826
12°	.2079	.9781	.2126	57°	.8387	.5446	1.5399
13°	.2250	.9744	.2309	58°	.8480	.5299	1.6003
14°	.2419	.9703	.2493	59°	.8572	.5150	1.6643
15°	.2588	.9659	.2679	60°	.8660	.5000	1.7321
16°	.2756	.9613	.2867	61°	.8746	.4848	1.8040
17°	.2924	.9563	.3057	62°	.8829	.4695	1.8807
18°	.3090	.9511	.3249	63°	.8910	.4540	1.9626
19°	.3256	.9455	.3443	64°	.8988	.4384	2.0503
20°	.3420	.9397	.3640	65°	.9063	.4226	2.1445
21°	.3584	.9336	.3839	66°	.9135	.4067	2.2460
22°	.3746	.9272	.4040	67°	.9205	.3907	2.3559
23°	.3907	.9205	.4245	68°	.9272	.3746	2.4751
24°	.4067	.9135	.4452	69°	.9336	.3584	2.6051
25°	.4226	.9063	.4663	70°	.9397	.3420	2.7475
26°	.4384	.8988	.4877	71°	.9455	.3256	2.9042
27°	.4540	.8910	.5095	72°	.9511	.3090	3.0777
28°	.4695	.8829	.5317	73°	.9563	.2924	3.2709
29°	.4848	.8746	.5543	74°	.9613	.2756	3.4874
30°	.5000	.8660	.5774	75°	.9659	.2588	3.7321
31°	.5150	.8572	.6009	76°	.9703	.2419	4.0108
32°	.5299	.8480	.6249	77°	.9744	.2250	4.3315
33°	.5446	.8387	.6494	78°	.9781	.2079	4.7046
34°	.5592	.8290	.6745	79°	.9816	.1908	5.1446
35°	.5736	.8192	.7002	80°	.9848	.1736	5.6713
36°	.5878	.8090	.7265	81°	.9877	.1564	6.3138
37°	.6018	.7986	.7536	82°	.9903	.1392	7.1154
38°	.6157	.7880	.7813	83°	.9925	.1219	8.1443
39°	.6293	.7771	.8098	84°	.9945	.1045	9.5144
40°	.6428	.7660	.8391	85°	.9962	.0872	11.4301
41°	.6561	.7547	.8693	86°	.9976	.0698	14.3007
42°	.6691	.7431	.9004	87°	.9986	.0523	19.0811
43°	.6820	.7314	.9325	88°	.9994	.0349	28.6363
44°	.6947	.7193	.9657	89°	.9998	.0175	57.2900
45°	.7071	.7071	1.0000	90°	1.0000	.0000	

Index